MW00852290

A COMMENTARY ON
JUDGES AND RUTH

KREGEL EXEGETICAL LIBRARY

A Commentary on Exodus
Duane A. Garrett

A Commentary on Judges and Ruth
Robert B. Chisolm, Jr.

A Commentary on 1 & 2 Chronicles
Eugene H. Merrill

A Commentary on the Psalms, vol. 1 (1–41)
A Commentary on the Psalms, vol. 2 (42–89)
A Commentary on the Psalms, vol. 3 (90–150)
Allen P. Ross

A Commentary on the Book of the Twelve,
The Minor Prophets
Michael Shepherd

A Commentary on Romans
John D. Harvey

A Commentary on James
Aída Besançon Spencer

KREGEL EXEGETICAL LIBRARY

A COMMENTARY ON
JUDGES AND RUTH

Robert B. Chisholm Jr.

KREGEL
ACADEMIC

A Commentary on Judges and Ruth

© 2013 by Robert B. Chisholm Jr.

Published by Kregel Publications, a division of Kregel Inc., 2450 Oak Industrial Dr. NE, Grand Rapids, MI 49505.

The English translations of the original Hebrew texts of the Bible are the author's own, adapted from his translation in the NET Bible. Used by permission. NET Bible, copyright © 1996-2005 by Biblical Studies Press, LLC. All rights reserved.

ISBN 978-0-8254-2556-1

Printed in the United States of America
21 22 23 24 25 26 27 / 6 5 4 3 2

To my children—

Doug,
who has always enjoyed
rousing stories of heroism,

Stephanie,
who, like Acsah of old, has always known
how to charm her daddy,

Jenny,
who, since joining our family's story,
has brightened our lives,

and Chip,
who, like Othniel of old, is an able son-in-law
who values his wife

CONTENTS

ABBREVIATIONS

AB	Anchor Bible
AnBib	Analecta biblica
AOAT	Alter Orient und Altes Testament
ASOR	American Schools of Oriental Research
AUSS	*Andrews University Seminary Studies*
AYBC	Anchor Yale Bible Commentary
BA	*Biblical Archaeologist*
BAR	*Biblical Archaeology Review*
BASOR	*Bulletin of the American Schools of Oriental Research*
BBR	*Bulletin for Biblical Research*
BDB	Brown, F., S. R. Driver, and C. A. Briggs. A Hebrew and English Lexicon of the Old Testament. Oxford, 1907.
BHS	*Biblia Hebraica Stuttgartensia*
Bib	*Biblica*
BibInt	*Biblical Interpretation*
BJS	Brown Judaic Studies
BkBC	Blackwell Bible Commentaries
BN	*Biblische Notizen*
BNEAS	*Bulletin of the Near East Archaeological Society*
BO	Berit Olam commentary series
BRev	*Bible Review*

ABBREVIATIONS

BSac	*Bibliotheca sacra*
BST	The Bible Speaks Today
BT	*The Bible Translator*
BTB	*Biblical Theology Bulletin*
CBQ	*Catholic Biblical Quarterly*
CC	Concordia Commentary
ConJ	*Concordia Journal*
COS	*The Context of Scripture.* Edited by W. W. Hallo and K. L. Younger Jr. 3 vols. Leiden: Brill, 1997-2000.
CTJ	*Calvin Theological Journal*
CurBS	*Currents in Biblical Research*
DNWSI	*Dictionary of the North-West Semitic Inscriptions*
Dtr	Deuteronomist
EQ	*Evangelical Quarterly*
ErIsr	*Eretz-Israel*
ExpTim	*Expository Times*
FCB	Feminist Companion to the Bible
FCBSS	Feminist Companion to the Bible: Second Series
GCAJS	*Gratz College Annual of Jewish Studies*
GKC	Gesenius' Hebrew Grammar. Edited by E. Kautzsch, translated by A. E. Cowley. 2nd ed. Oxford, 1910.
HALOT	*The Hebrew and Aramaic Lexicon of the Old Testament.* L. Koehler, W. Baumgartner, and J. J. Stamm. Translated and edited under the supervision of M. E. J. Richardson. 4 vols. Leiden: Brill, 1994-1999.
HAR	*Hebrew Annual Review*
HBT	*Horizons in Biblical Theology*
Heb.	Hebrew
HS	*Hebrew Studies*
HSM	Harvard Semitic Monographs
HSS	Harvard Semitic Studies
HTR	*Harvard Theological Review*
HUCA	*Hebrew Union College Annual*
IBHS	*Introduction to Biblical Hebrew Syntax.* B. K. Waltke and M. O'Connor. Winona Lake: Eisenbrauns, 1990.
ICC	International Critical Commentary
Int	*Interpretation*
JAAR	*Journal of the American Academy of Religion*
JANES	*Journal of the Ancient Near Eastern Society*
JAOS	*Journal of the American Oriental Society*
JBL	*Journal of Biblical Literature*
JBQ	*Jewish Bible Quarterly*

ABBREVIATIONS

JETS	*Journal of the Evangelical Theological Society*
JJS	*Journal of Jewish Studies*
JNES	*Journal of Near Eastern Studies*
JNSL	*Journal of Northwest Semitic Languages*
JOTT	*Journal of Translation and Textlinguistics*
JPSBC	JPS Bible Commentary
JSem	*Journal for Semitics*
JSNTSup	Journal for the Study of the New Testament: Supplement Series
JSOT	*Journal for the Study of the Old Testament*
JSOTSup	Journal for the Study of the Old Testament: Supplement Series
JSPSup	Journal for the Study of the Pseudepigrapha: Supplement Series
JSS	*Journal of Semitic Studies*
JTS	*Journal of Theological Studies*
KJV	King James Version
LBH	late biblical Hebrew
LHBOTS	Library of Hebrew Bible/Old Testament Studies
LXX	Septuagint
MT	Masoretic Text
NAC	New American Commentary
NASB	New American Standard Bible
NCBC	New Cambridge Bible Commentary
NET	New English Translation
NIB	*New Interpreter's Bible*
NICOT	New International Commentary on the Old Testament
NIDOTTE	*New International Dictionary of Old Testament Theology and Exegesis.* Edited by W. VanGemeren. 5 vols. Grand Rapids: Zondervan, 1997.
NIV	New International Version
NIVAC	NIV Application Commentary
NLT	New Living Translation
NRSV	New Revised Standard Version
Or	*Orientalia*
OTE	*Old Testament Essays*
OTL	Old Testament Library
OTWSA	*Ou Testamentiese Werkgemeenskap van Suid-Afrika*
PEGLMBS	Proceedings of the Eastern Great Lakes and Midwest Biblical Societies
PEQ	*Palestine Exploration Quarterly*
PIBA	Proceedings of the Irish Biblical Association

ABBREVIATIONS

Proof	*Prooftexts: A Journal of Jewish Literary History*
PRSt	*Perspectives in Religious Studies*
ResQ	*Restoration Quarterly*
RevQ	*Revue de Qumran*
RTR	*Reformed Theological Review*
SBH	standard biblical Hebrew
SBLDS	Society of Biblical Literature Dissertation Series
SHBC	Smyth & Helwys Bible Commentary
SJOT	*Scandinavian Journal of the Old Testament*
SJT	*Scottish Journal of Theology*
TBT	*The Bible Today*
TDOT	*Theological Dictionary of the Old Testament*
TynBul	*Tyndale Bulletin*
TZ	*Theologische Zeitschrift*
USQR	*Union Seminary Quarterly Review*
VE	*Vox evangelica*
VT	*Vetus Testamentum*
VTSup	Vetus Testamentum: Supplement Series
WBC	Word Biblical Commentary
WTJ	*Westminster Theological Journal*
ZAW	*Zeitschrift für die alttestamentliche Wissenschaft*

PREFACE

Some readers of the Bible shy away from the book of Judges. After all, it's filled with violence and doesn't seem very spiritually uplifting. If Hollywood were to do a movie of the book, it would probably get an X rating for its scenes of mutilation, child sacrifice, and gang rape, not to mention the bloodshed that appears on almost every page. But the book is in the Bible for a good reason. It illustrates how corrupt human nature really is and how far a society can fall when it turns its back on God and his moral standards. On a more positive note, in the midst of the moral chaos depicted in the book, we see a God who is patient and compassionate as he disciplines and preserves his covenant people.

As we move from the book of Judges to the book of Ruth, a bright light suddenly shines against the dark backdrop of a morally corrupt time period. Indeed, the book of Ruth is a fresh breath of air after reading Judges. Its story of God's concern for two widows and of Ruth's devotion to her mother-in-law and first husband is inspiring and foreshadows the sacrificial love of the Savior. It is probably one of the most "preachable" books in the entire Old Testament.

Preaching is important to me and I have designed this commentary with pastors and teachers in mind. Accurate, relevant exposition of the Bible needs to answer three important questions: (1) What did the text mean in its ancient Israelite context? (2) What theological principles emerge from or are illustrated by a thematic analysis of the text? (3) How is the message of the text relevant to the church? In this commentary I attempt to answer these questions through a three-step process: (1) I begin with a close exegetical-literary reading of the text that surfaces the thematic emphases of each major literary unit. Such analysis yields an exegetical idea for each unit that succinctly captures the message of that unit in its cultural-historical context. (2) In step two I move outside the boundaries of the specific text being studied and develop a theological idea for each literary unit. These theological ideas express the enduring principles or truths that are rooted in the text and are relevant for a modern audience. (3) In the third step I develop homiletical trajectories from the theological idea of the passage. These trajectories begin from thematic vantage points that reflect the overall message of the book of Judges. Following the trajectories enables us to produce one or more preaching ideas for each literary unit. If this process is done with skill and savvy, the audience will be able to see how the ancient text yields the principles and how they, the audience, both individually and corporately, should and can appropriate the principles in their own experience and in the life of the church.

The commentary includes my own translation of the books. The translation is a slightly revised version of the one I prepared for the NET Bible. I wish to thank Bible.org and its Executive Director Michael Garrett for granting me permission to use my work for the NET Bible. In the commentary I have arranged the translation in a format that may seem strange to readers. Yet I think that the arrangement is helpful because it reflects the clausal structure of the original Hebrew text and allows us to see the text's contours as envisioned by the author. I distinguish between the three main elements of a narrative: (1) mainline clauses, (2) offline clauses (highlighted in bold), and (3) quotations (or discourse). All mainline and offline clauses in the narrative framework are classified. Clauses within quotations are not analyzed; quotations are simply set apart by italics. I explain the method of categorization in more detail in the introductions to both Judges and Ruth.

For the most part, the commentary is based on the traditional Hebrew text. With some notable exceptions, I do not interact with the various versions or provide extensive text-critical analysis. For this type of analysis, I would point readers to more technical works, such as Trent Butler's WBC commentary on Judges and Frederic Bush's WBC commentary on Ruth

I have chosen to use a literary-theological method that is sensitive to the author's literary strategies and techniques and seeks to identify the text's theological message. I have chosen not to use speculative diachronic methods that seek to isolate alleged sources and to reconstruct the supposed evolution of the text. Since we are not in a position to trace the book's literary evolution with any degree of confidence, I prefer to focus on the book's canonical form and to understand its various parts within this literary framework. I believe that the book, when examined in its canonical form, is a unified work. Such an approach is preferable to diachronic methods because it deals with the text as we have it and consequently is not as susceptible to the kind of speculative fancy that litters the history of biblical higher criticism. The individual stories may have functioned within specific geographical and temporal frameworks at one time, but we are not in a position to resurrect those contexts. The stories are now part of a larger entity. The book has an anthological appearance, but it is not purely anthological. The presence of the formulaic framework in the central section creates at least the semblance of a macroplot. Furthermore, as synchronic critics have shown, the placement of the stories is strategic and certain themes emerge and develop, linking them together. While the stories are juxtaposed, they are integrated thematically. Like paintings on a theme in a wing of an art gallery, they illustrate themes and contribute to the book's overall purposes and message.

In presenting my interpretive conclusions I interact with other commentaries that a pastor or teacher may be consulting. In fact, in the introductions to both Judges and Ruth, I include a list and brief assessment of the most helpful commentaries. Knowing that busy pastors do not always have ready access to periodical literature, I have also interacted with many specialized studies on Judges and Ruth. However, I concluded my research, for the most part, in 2010, when I sent the commentary to the publisher. Consequently, those who keep abreast of research on Judges-Ruth will notice that I do not interact with the very latest material. Perhaps the most notable omission is Barry Webb's fine commentary on Judges in the NICOT series. Fortunately, I was able to interact with and benefit from Webb's earlier work on Judges.

I want to thank several individuals for their assistance and encouragement. Over the past thirty years I have taught Judges and Ruth at Dallas Theological Seminary and benefited greatly from the insights offered by dozens of students. Special thanks go to my very first research assistant, Brian Leicht, who did bibliographical research for me on Judges, and to my former student Greg Wong, who has gone on to publish extensively on Judges. Over the past several years Greg and I have enjoyed an ongoing dialogue about the interpretation of the book. I also want to express my gratitude to David Howard, who edited the commentary. David's constructive criticism, penetrating questions, and valuable insights have improved the quality of my work. I also appreciate my friend Jim Weaver, formerly of Kregel Academic, for his encouragement over the years and his commitment to making this commentary beneficial to pastors. Thanks also to Dennis Hillman and Paul Hillman at Kregel Academic, who believed in the project and have seen it through to publication. Special thanks to my wife Deb, my son Doug, and my daughter Stephanie for their moral support and for the joy they have given me. Each has shown me the kind of unconditional, sacrificial love that would make Ruth and our Savior smile. Finally, all praise is due to the one who has delivered us from the bondage of sin through his sacrificial love and atoning work.

Robert Chisholm
September 2013

INTRODUCTION
TO JUDGES

The book of Judges is part of a history that begins in Deuteronomy with a vision of a unified covenant community obedient to the God who delivered his people from bondage and oppression. As this history unfolds, Israel succeeded in defeating their enemies and establishing a foothold in the promised land. But the challenge of actually occupying the land remained as Joshua passed from the scene. Judges picks up the story at this point. It tells how the covenant community disintegrated morally and socially as it assimilated Canaanite culture and beliefs. God both punished and delivered wayward Israel, but the downward spiral continued. The need for competent, godly leadership becomes apparent, paving the way for the next part of the story, recorded in Samuel–Kings.

LITERARY STRUCTURE AND THEMES
The book of Judges exhibits three main literary units: a prologue (1:1–3:6), a central section containing several accounts of individual judges (3:7–16:31), and an epilogue (17:1–21:25).

The prologue contains two parallel, complementary subunits. The first (1:1–2:5) describes what happened following the death of Joshua

17

(1:1; cf. Josh. 24:29).[1] Chapter one is primarily descriptive, reflecting for the most part an observer's perspective of what transpired.[2] The narrator does give a theological perspective at points (vv. 19a, 22), but this seems to be for rhetorical purposes, since he allows the people's perspective to dominate (v. 19b; see the commentary below). The matter-of-fact description of Israel's failure to carry out God's commission prompts the reader to ask: Why did the people fail?[3] The account of the incident at Bokim (2:1–5) provides at least a partial answer by making it clear that Israel's failure was not really due to Canaanite military power and persistence (the impression given by 1:19, 27, 35), but was the result of assimilation to Canaanite culture and idolatry. Through his messenger, the Lord reminded Israel of his warning that he would not drive out the nations if the people engaged in idolatry.

The second subunit in the prologue (2:6–3:6) begins with a flashback to the time when Joshua was still alive. The opening verses (2:6–10) reiterate Joshua 24:28–31 and continue the story from that point. When compared to 1:1–2:5, this account is more theological and evaluative in its orientation, reflecting God's perspective on what took place.[4] Picking up on the theme of 2:1–5, the narrator identifies idolatry as Israel's fundamental problem (2:11–13). He gives an overview of the period, which displays a cyclical pattern. During this period Israel would sin, prompting the Lord to hand them over to enemies for disciplinary purposes (vv. 14–15). When the people cried out in their pain (v. 18b), the Lord provided deliverers ("judges") to rescue them (vv. 16, 18a).[5] These judges, who also performed a prophetic function, brought some stability for a time, but the people persisted in their ways (vv.

---

1. Despite the chronological notation, some consider Judges 1 to be an account of the invasion of Canaan that parallels the book of Joshua. See, for example, Moore 1895, 7–10; and Burney 1970, 2–3. Soggin treats verse 1 as an interpolation (1981, 20). *BHS* even suggests that we replace "Joshua" with "Moses." However, as it stands chapter one relates what happened after Joshua's death.
2. Polzin points out that 1:1–2:5 "is narrated from a psychological point of view *external* to the characters of the story." He adds: "What we are told is what any onlooker could have experienced, known, or surmised were he present at the events described" (1980, 149).
3. On the narrator's strategy in chapter one, see Eslinger 1989, 56–61, especially p. 61.
4. See Polzin 1980, 150.
5. This cyclical pattern of disobedience-punishment-contrition-deliverance is attested as early as the second half of the second millennium B.C. See Kitchen, who cites parallels from Egypt (2003, 217–18).

17, 19). Israel's persistence in sin prompted the Lord to announce that he would no longer drive out the nations, but would use them to test Israel's loyalty (2:20–3:4).

A summary of the period appears in 3:5–6. Verse five reflects the descriptive style of chapter one and reiterates its main theme (Israel lived among the native peoples). Like chapter two, verse six is more theological and evaluative in tone, identifying Israel's underlying problem as its assimilation to Canaanite culture, including its idolatry.

The central section of the book utilizes a structural framework based on the statement in 2:11a: וַיַּעֲשׂוּ בְנֵי־יִשְׂרָאֵל אֶת־הָרַע בְּעֵינֵי יְהוָה, "Then the Israelites did evil in the eyes of the Lord." Each subunit within the central section begins with this same statement (see 3:7; 6:1) or a slightly altered form of it (וַיֹּסִפוּ בְנֵי־יִשְׂרָאֵל לַעֲשׂוֹת הָרַע בְּעֵינֵי יְהוָה, "the Israelites again did evil [or "continued to do evil"] in the eyes of the Lord," see 3:12; 4:1; 10:6; 13:1). Following this introductory statement, each of the accounts describes how the Lord, in response to Israel's sin, handed Israel over to an oppressive enemy. When Israel cried out, a deliverer appeared. An account of how the deliverer rescued Israel then follows. Each story has a formal conclusion, though these conclusions differ in content (see below). Other literary forms, such as a song of celebration (chapter 5) and reports of so-called minor judges (10:1–5; 12:7–15), are integrated into this basic framework. The following chart outlines the structure of the central portion of the book:[6]

(1) The Account of Othniel (3:7–11)
    Israel did evil (v. 7)
    The Lord handed Israel over to an enemy (v. 8)
    Israel cried out to the Lord (v. 9a)

---

6. Building on a proposal that originated in the nineteenth century, Wong attempts to show that the central section includes representative judges for all twelve tribes arranged in a roughly south to north pattern (2006a, 239–46). To make this theory work, he must make the following arguments, at least some of which appear to be tenuous: (1) The Gileadites Jair and Jephthah represent the Transjordanian tribes, despite the fact that their tribal designations are not specified. (2) Ibzan is from Bethlehem of Zebulun (cf. Josh. 19:15), not Judah, and serves as a "surrogate Asherite" (239). (3) The omission of a Simeonite judge is explained by Simeon's close association with Judah (cf. Judg. 1:3). (4) The apparent transposition of Barak of Naphtali and Abdon of Ephraim can be attributed to a complex and subtle rhetorical purpose. (5) Samson of Dan is placed last (even though he lived in the south) because the tribe of Dan "eventually ended up being the northernmost tribe" (246).

The Lord provided a deliverer (v. 9b)
Account of deliverer's deeds (v. 10)
The land had rest (v. 11a)
Summary of deliverer's death (v. 11b)

(2) The Account of Ehud (3:12–31)
Israel did evil (v. 12a)
The Lord handed Israel over to an enemy (vv. 12b–14)
Israel cried out to the Lord (v. 15a)
The Lord provided a deliverer (v. 15b)
Account of deliverer's deeds (vv. 16–29)
Summary of Israel's victory (v. 30a)
The land had rest (v. 30b)
Appendix: Shamgar (v. 31)

(3) The Account of Deborah and Barak (4:1–5:31)
Israel did evil (4:1)
The Lord handed Israel over to an enemy (4:2)
Israel cried out to the Lord (4:3)
Introduction of deliverer (4:4–7)
Account of deliverer's deeds (4:8–22)
Summary of Israel's victory (4:23)
Song of celebration (5:1–31a)
The land had rest (5:31b)

(4) The Account of Gideon (6:1–10:5)
Israel did evil (6:1a)
The Lord handed Israel over to an enemy (6:1b–6a)
Israel cried out to the Lord (6:6b)
The Lord confronted his people concerning their sin (6:7–10)
Introduction of deliverer (6:11)
Account of deliverer's deeds (6:12–8:27)
Summary of Israel's victory (8:28a)
The land had rest (8:28b)
Summary of deliverer's career, death, and burial (8:29–32)
Sequel: The story of Abimelech (8:33–9:57)
Reports of minor judges (10:1–5)

(5) The Account of Jephthah (10:6–12:15)
Israel did evil (10:6)
The Lord handed Israel over to an enemy (10:7–9)
Israel cried out to the Lord (10:10)

The Lord refused to deliver (10:11–14)
Israel appealed to the Lord again (10:15)
The Lord softened his stance (10:16)
Israel chose a deliverer (10:17–11:11)
Account of deliverer's deeds (11:12–12:6)
Summary of deliverer's career, death, and burial (12:7)
Reports of minor judges (12:8–15)

(6) The Account of Samson (13:1–16:31)
Israel did evil (13:1a)
The Lord handed Israel over to an enemy (13:1b)
Account of deliverer's birth (13:2–25)
Account of deliverer's deeds (14:1–15:19)
Summary of deliverer's career (15:20)
Account of deliverer's death (16:1–30)
Summary of deliverer's burial and career (16:31)

Though these stories illustrate the basic pattern outlined in chapter two (sin—punishment—painful cry—deliverance), they are not structurally identical. Significant variations appear within this template, especially in the stories of Jephthah and Samson:[7]

(1) The precise terminology used to describe divine punishment differs in the stories: note, וַיִּחַר "(The Lord) moved," in 3:12; וַיִּתְּנֵם, "(the LORD) handed them over," in 6:1 and 13:1; and וַיִּמְכְּרֵם, "(The Lord) turned them over," in 3:8, 4:2, and 10:7. In 3:8 and 10:7 a reference to the Lord's anger precedes (Greenspahn 1986, 87).

(2) In contrast to the account of Othniel (3:9) and the story of Ehud (3:15), there is no formal statement of the Lord providing a deliverer in the stories that follow. In the story of Deborah and Barak, the narrator simply introduces Deborah, who on God's behalf commissions the warrior Barak to fight the oppressor. The story of Gideon omits a formal statement about the Lord providing a deliverer, though it does include a commissioning account in which the Lord commands Gideon to deliver Israel (6:14). There is no indication that the Lord raised up Jephthah or even commissioned him for battle, though he did energize him for war (11:29). Finally, though no formal statement about the Lord raising up Samson appears, the Lord made it clear to his mother

---

7. In this regard see Gunn 1987, 105, as well as Greenspahn 1986, 387–88, and Olson 1998, 763–64.

that he was to deliver Israel (13:5) and the Lord later empowered him toward that end.

(3) The introduction to Jephthah's story differs from earlier accounts in that the Lord initially refused to respond to Israel's cry (Mullen 1982, 197–98). While the Lord seemed to soften when Israel persisted in seeking his aid (10:16), the text stops short of attributing Jephthah's rise to leadership to divine action or commissioning.

(4) In the Samson story there is no reference to Israel crying out to the Lord. Despite the people's apathy (see 15:11–12) and Samson's subsequent failure to understand his role, the Lord was determined to deliver them anyway.

Other structural variations occur within the book's central section. In the Othniel, Ehud, Deborah-Barak, and Gideon accounts there is no summarizing reference to a leader "judging" Israel for a specified number of years. The land simply has "rest" for a period of time (see 3:11, 30; 5:31; 8:28). This changes with the minor judges listed in chapter 10. From this point on summary statements appear for each leader, telling us that he "judged" Israel for a specified time period (see 10:2–3; 12:7, 9, 11, 14; 15:20; 16:31) (Mullen 1982, 194–95). After Gideon there are no more references to the land having rest. Following the account of the civil turmoil introduced by Abimelech and perpetuated by Jephthah, the narrator decides not to depict the land as experiencing genuine peace. This alarming change prepares us for the epilogue, where civil discord is the order of the day.[8]

The central portion of the book illustrates the dominant themes of the prologue—Israel's propensity to sin, the Lord's disciplinary judgment, and the Lord's willingness to deliver his people from their oppressors. The prologue pictures God reminding his people that idolatry would jeopardize the conquest of the land (2:1–5). He then announced that the conquest would be put on hold until he had tested Israel's

---

8. This does not mean that the sequence is chronological. The Gideon, Jephthah, and Samson accounts may actually overlap chronologically with earlier accounts (see the discussion of the book's chronological framework below, as well as Chisholm 2009a and Chisholm 2010d). Furthermore, the epilogue appears to record events that occurred at the very beginning of the Judges period (see below). It appears that the transition from the land having rest to the absence of rest and then to the chaos described in the epilogue has a rhetorical function.

loyalty (2:20–3:4). The book's central section gives specific evidence for why this decision was necessary, as it depicts persistent or recurring idolatry and an increasing alienation between God and his people.

The stories also clarify the prologue's simple prayer-divine response model by showing that God cannot be manipulated like some good luck charm and that he often operates outside the expected norms. In the Gideon story he confronts his people with their sin before commissioning a deliverer; in the Jephthah story he wearies of intervening, even when they persist in crying out to him and seemingly repent of their idolatry. But in the Samson story he decides to deliver even though no one asks for his help. The prologue depicts God delivering his people through his chosen instruments; the stories show that deliverance often comes in unexpected ways, even through flawed instruments.

While the stories illustrate the prologue's thematic concerns, they are not restricted to this literary role. Several themes surface in the stories that do not appear in the prologue:

(1) The prologue describes the judges in fairly positive terms as instruments of God who attempted to give the people moral guidance (see 2:17).[9] The stories depict them as victorious warriors energized by God, but portray their flaws as well. In fact, one can trace a pattern of declining quality in the judges, culminating in Samson.[10] The prologue indirectly contributes to this thematic development by providing paradigms of competent, godly leadership in Joshua and Caleb, who become foils for the failed leaders presented in the stories. But the prologue does not speak of the judges in negative terms. This theme of failed leadership, rather than emerging from the prologue, arises in the stories and paves the way for the epilogue, which specifically laments the

---

9. Regarding the portrayal of the judges in the prologue, Gillmayr-Bucher (2009, 690) observes: "The personality of the judges does not come into focus, nor does their faith or their loyalty to YHWH, or their individual contributions. The focus lies yet again on God. God raises the judge and is with him; thus, it is God who saves. Furthermore, the cause for this change in God's behavior lies only within God himself; he acts because he is moved by pity."

10. This pattern of declining leadership runs concurrently with the subtheme of changing female roles. See Chisholm 1994b, 34–46. For a summary of how these themes interrelate see the section below, entitled "What Role Do the Female Characters Play?"

moral condition that overtook the land because of the leadership void (see 17:6; 21:25; as well as 18:1 and 19:1).

(2) The stories also portray escalating civil conflict, a theme that is not present in the prologue, at least in a direct way. Deborah's and Barak's victory song criticizes some tribes for not contributing to the common cause (5:15b–17), while Gideon faced opposition from his own countrymen in the aftermath of his victory over the Midianites (7:24–8:17).[11] Gideon's son Abimelech instigated a civil war (chapter 9) and Jephthah massacred the Ephraimites in the aftermath of his victory over the Ammonites (12:1–6). In Samson's story, the men of Judah hand Samson the Danite over to the Philistines. All of this paves the way for the epilogue, where civil conflict is the order of the day.

This comparison of the stories with the prologue reveals that the latter is not an all-encompassing overview of the book, but rather an extension of the book of Joshua (esp. chapter 24), which emphasizes the need for Israel to maintain its covenantal distinctiveness and loyalty to God as prerequisites to the complete conquest of the land. The prologue facilitates the transition from Joshua's era to the Judges period and provides a structural pattern for the frame of the stories that integrates them with Joshua thematically. But the stories surface other themes as well and facilitate a transition to the book's epilogue and its thematic focus.

The epilogue (chapters 17–21) contains two stories. The first of these (17:1–19:1a) tells of Micah's homemade shrine and how the Danites confiscated his cultic equipment and his priest and set up their own private tribal cult in the distant north, far from the land they had been allotted. The second story (19:1b—21:25) is a sordid account of

---

11. I use the term "tribe(s)" here and later as a traditional label that reflects usage in Joshua. However, Judges does not use this designation often or in a consistent manner. The term מַטֶּה, "tribe," does not appear in Judges, but שֵׁבֶט, "tribe" is used in the singular of Dan (18:1, 19, 30), Benjamin (21:3, 6, 17), and each Israelite tribe (21:24), and in the plural of the Israelite tribes (18:1; 20:2, 10, 12; 21:5, 8, 15), as well as the "tribes" (= subtribal groups?) within Benjamin (20:12; cf. 1 Sam. 9:21). מִשְׁפָּחָה, "clan," is used of Dan (13:2; 18:2, 11) and Judah (17:7). It appears to refer to a clan within a larger tribal group in 9:1; 18:19; and 21:24. For a survey of the use of these terms in Judges, see Auld, 1998a, 72–73. Of course, the concept that early Israel was a tribal confederation is not problematic in theory, as Kitchen has demonstrated from ancient Near Eastern parallels dating to the second millennium B.C. (2003, 220–21).

rape and murder in Gibeah that precipitated a civil war in Israel. The war nearly wiped out the tribe of Benjamin and resulted in further atrocities against Israelite women.[12]

The events recorded in the epilogue appear to have occurred early in the Judges period. Judges 18:30 identifies the Levite who set up the Danite cult as "Jonathan son of Gershom son of Moses" (literal translation). He may have been a grandson of Moses, in which case the events described in chapters 17–18 occurred within two generations of Moses. However, it is possible that בֵּן, "son," indicates he was a descendant of Gershom, not his son *per se*.[13] In this case there may have been several generations between Gershom and Jonathan, making it possible that the events of chapters 17–18 occurred later in the period. We can be more certain concerning the dating of the events recorded in chapters 19–21. Judges 20:28 indicates that Phinehas son of Eleazar son of Aaron was the priest at Bethel at this time. Phinehas was a contemporary of Moses and Joshua (see Exod. 6:25; Num. 25:7, 11; 31:6; Josh. 22:13, 30–32; 24:33; 1 Chron. 6:4, 50; 9:20; Ezra 7:5), so the Benjaminite civil war must have occurred very early in the period.

If the events of chapters 17–21 did indeed occur relatively early in the period, this means that the narrator of Judges has not followed a strictly chronological sequence. Instead he has arranged his material thematically. After an overview of the period in the prologue, he gives accounts of various individual judges and then concludes in the epilogue with stories that epitomize the period.

The theme of the epilogue appears in 17:6 and 21:25 (see as well the abridged version of this in 18:1 and 19:1). The epilogue's two accounts illustrate what happened in Israelite society when there was an absence of competent, godly leadership and show why Israel needed an ideal king (see Deut. 17:14–20). The epilogue describes the violation of all Ten Commandments (Olson 1998, 864–65). The ideal king depicted in Deuteronomy 17 was to promote God's law and guide the covenantal community down the right moral and ethical path. The epilogue brings the leadership theme of the stories to its alarming conclusion and thus paves the way for 1 Samuel, which describes how the Lord restored godly, Joshua/Caleb-like leadership to Israel.

Wong argues that the epilogue contains several subtle allusions to the stories of the central section. As such, it provides additional support

---

12. Levites play a prominent role in both stories. On the parallels between the two stories, see Olson 1998, 863–64.
13. 1 Chronicles 23:16, though mentioning the "*sons* of Gershom," lists only one son, Shebuel (cf. 1 Chron. 26:24).

for viewing the judges in a negative light. Wong explains, "through the allusions, the bizarre episodes in the epilogue are shown to be not quite as unprecedented as one might initially think. But in creating them, the author of the epilogue has actually managed in one brilliant stroke to redirect the focus of the reader back to the lives of the major judges" (2006a, 138). He adds: "Certainly, by showing that the bizarre acts in the epilogue have all found precedents in the lives of the judges, the author has managed to cast the judges in a very uncomplimentary light. For by showing them to have engaged in the same sort of un-principled behaviour that characterises (sic) the various protagonists in the epilogue, the judges are essentially portrayed as being no better than characters that are consistently derided in the epilogue" (139).[14]

Some scholars have proposed that the book of Judges exhibits a chiastic or concentric structure. For example, Gooding sees the two-part introduction corresponding to the two-part epilogue and arranges the central narratives in chiastic fashion with the Gideon narrative occupying the center position:[15]

A Introduction, Part I (1:1–2:5)
  B Introduction, Part II (2:6–3:6)
    C Othniel (3:7–11)
      D Ehud (3:12–31)
        E Deborah, Barak, Jael (4:1–5:31)
          F Gideon (6:1–8:32)
        E' Abimelech (8:33–10:5)
      D' Jephthah (10:6–12:15)
    C' Samson (13:1–16:31)
  B' Epilogue, Part I (17:1–18:31)
A' Epilogue, Part II (19:1–21:25)

---

14. When Wong speaks of the events of the epilogue having "precedents in the lives of the judges," we must understand these as *literary* precedents, for, as noted above, the events of the prologue (at least those recorded in chapters 19–21) occurred early in the period, prior to most, if not all, of the events recorded in the central section.

15. Gooding 1982, 70*–79*. Globe's proposed chiastic outline is identical to Gooding's, except that he isolates 3:31 and the minor judges sections (10:1–5; 12:8–15) as corresponding E/E' sections (with 4:1–5:31 corresponding to 8:33–9:57 as F/F' sections and the Gideon story being the central G unit). See Globe 1990, 246. Combining the minor judges sections is problematic since it breaks the proposed concentric pattern. Furthermore, one could argue they form a bracket around the Jephthah story.

Gooding sees a chiastic arrangement within the central Gideon unit (1982, 74*):

A Gideon stands against idolatry (6:1–32)
  B Gideon fights the enemy (6:33–7:25)
  B' Gideon fights against his own nationals (8:1–21)
A' Gideon lapses into idolatry (8:22–32)

Dorsey agrees with Gooding's analysis of the book's macrostructure and the Gideon narrative.[16] He even proposes a chiastic structure for each major section of the book.[17] Tanner also follows Gooding's proposal for the book's macrostructure, but he arranges the Gideon narrative a bit differently:[18]

A 6:1–10
  B 6:11–32
    C 6:33–7:18
  B' 7:19–8:21
A' 8:22–32

While the book of Judges does contain thematic correspondences, one wonders if these writers have imposed these chiastic structures on the text.[19] There is at least a loose structural and thematic

---

16. Dorsey 1999, 114, 119. He detects a concurrent chiastic structure within the Gideon narrative (110):
  A Beginning of oppression (6:1–10)
    B Gideon's divine call; his destruction of idolatry at Ophrah (6:11–40)
      C Troops gather for the battle (7:1–14, or 7:1–8)
        D Turning Point: The Lord gives victory (7:15–22, or 7:9–22)
      C' Troops disperse after battle (7:23–8:21)
    B' Gideon's call by Israelites and his lapse into idolatry at Ophrah (8:22–27)
  A' End of oppression (8:28–32)
17. Ibid, 106–18.
18. Tanner 1992, 151–52. Tanner also sees the pivotal subunit (6:33–7:18) as chiastic, though there are corresponding central passages, rather than a pivot (p. 157): A (6:33–35) B (6:36–40) C (7:1–8) C' (7:9–11) B' (7:12–14) A' (7:15–18).
19. See the critique of Gooding's work in Brettler 2002, 105–06, and in Frolov 2009, 39–40.

correspondence between the double introduction and the double conclusion.[20] However, why should the Gideon narrative be regarded as pivotal in the central section? The Jephthah narrative is just as likely a candidate for this role since it is framed by the lists of minor judges.[21] In fact there are structural patterns that indicate Jephthah's story is a "literary focal point" (Smith 2005, 289). Why is the Abimelech narrative separated from the Gideon narrative in the outline? While it is the sequel to the Gideon narrative and can be treated as a distinct story (see the commentary below), it belongs with 6:1–8:32 in the book's macrostructure, for the formulaic introduction and structural marker for this central section of the book ("the Israelites [again] did evil in the eyes of the Lord") appears in 6:1 and 10:6, but not in 8:33. The proposed link between Othniel and Samson is suspect because the length of the narratives is so disproportionate (Brettler 2002, 106). Furthermore the alleged thematic connections, which are developed in contrastive terms, are inaccurate, contrived, or too general to be convincing.[22] Advocates of a chiasmus link Ehud and Jephthah because both had dealings with Ephraim (cf. 3:27 and 12:1–6) and captured the fords of the Jordan. But Gideon also captured the fords and had an encounter with Ephraim (7:24–8:3). Since this theme is not restricted

---

20. See Younger 2002, 30–33, as well as Gooding 1982, 75*–76*, and Wong 2006a, 29–46, who discusses five thematic links.
21. Tanner responds to this view in his dissertation (1990, 222–28).
22. For example, Dorsey (1999, 115) states that Othniel's wife convinced him to acquire a good thing (1:14–15), while Samson's unauthorized "pagan wives" enticed him to betray secrets (14:15–17; 16:15–17). But it is unlikely that Othniel is even referred to in 1:14–15 (see the commentary below), Samson's attraction to the Timnite woman was God's doing (14:4), and the text does not support Dorsey's assumption that Samson was married to Delilah. Dorsey also points out that Othniel delivered Israel from enemies, whereas Samson was humiliated by enemies. However, one of the remarkable features of the Samson narrative is that the Lord did begin to deliver Israel through Samson (cf. 13:5 with 16:30). Dorsey also states that Israel was "united under Othniel's leadership, but fragmented under Samson." But this contrast could be made between Othniel and several of the judges. Fragmentation is a feature of each of the major stories after the Ehud narrative, not just the Samson story. Dorsey also observes: "Othniel appears to be a good judge; Samson is a bad judge and a sinner." The statement about Othniel being a "good judge" is too general to be helpful in establishing chiastic links. As a paradigmatic figure (see the commentary below), Othniel serves as a foil for all of the major figures after Ehud, not just Samson.

to the proposed D/D' units, it cannot be used to establish a concentric structure.

THE BOOK'S PAN-ISRAELITE PERSPECTIVE

The book's prologue portrays Israel as a unity. While chapter one focuses on the individual efforts of the various tribes, the encounter at Bokim is presented as encompassing the entire nation (2:4). The theological interpretation of the period in 2:6–3:6 consistently takes a national perspective. It is Israel that sins, suffers, cries out in pain, and experiences the Lord's deliverance. This perspective also marks the Othniel account at the beginning of the book's central section (3:7–11). Othniel's tribal affiliation is not mentioned; he is simply Israel's deliverer. From the book's prologue we know Othniel lived in the south, yet he rescued Israel from a northern invader. This phenomenon is only explicable if we assume a pan-Israelite perspective.[23] The pan-Israelite perspective also appears in the framework of the central section that reflects the overview of chapter two. It is also present in the epilogue, where we see the tribes congregating at Mizpah and Bethel to handle the problems raised by Gibeah's treatment of the Levite's concubine (see chapters 20–21).

This pan-Israelite perspective does not appear to be consistent with the stories of the central section, where the narrated events were restricted to specific locations.[24] The Canaanite oppression under Jabin and Sisera included only the northern tribes. Zebulun and Naphtali were specifically summoned for battle (4:6, 10; cf. 5:18), though the victory song mentions the involvement, as well as the nonparticipation, of others (5:14–17). Judah is conspicuous by its absence.[25] Gideon's forces

---

23. Unless one assumes this perspective, the geographical problem presented by the account is insurmountable. As Brettler (2002, 4) states, "this account is like saying that Mexico fought the United States, and the army from North Dakota defended it!"

24. Sellin and Fohrer state with respect to the judges: "Within the framework of the presentation, they all appear to exercise their judgeship over the entire nation as regents of Israel and forerunners of the kings. The narratives themselves still show the inaccuracy of this interpretation. As in the Hexateuch, figures that appeared and events that took place in a small portion of Israel have been made to refer to the entire nation" (1968, 207). See as well Lindars 1979, 95–112.

25. De Moor proposes a textual reconstruction of verses 13–14 that includes references to Judah and Levi (1993, 483–94). Ahlström, reflecting an evolutionary view of Israel's origins, concludes that the song "was composed at a time when Judah was not a part of Israel or had not yet come into closer contacts with the peoples of central and northern Canaan" (1977, 288).

came from the northern and central regions (6:35), not the south, and Abimelech, though called a ruler over Israel (9:22), seems to have operated only in the Shechem area. Jephthah operated primarily in the central and southern regions (10:8–9), while Samson's activities were localized in the south. Despite the statement that he ruled Israel for twenty years, he was opposed, at least initially, by the people of Judah (15:12–13).

The localized traditions of the book's central section may very well have originated independently and functioned initially within tribal or regional circles. But to speculate on their *Sitz im Leben* and prior oral or literary life is ultimately futile, though it may yield some creative, scholarly conjecture. The reality is that these stories now have a *Sitz im Buch*. They have been integrated with the prologue thematically and given a pan-Israelite framework.

This may look artificial and anachronistic, for the united Israel depicted in Joshua reemerges only after the Judges period and then only for a relatively brief time. But it is best to give the editor(s) the benefit of the doubt. By viewing regional developments as national in scope, the present structure of the book keeps before its readers the ideal of a unified Israel portrayed in Joshua.[26] It also forces readers to consider the broader, theological ramifications of tribal incidents. For the editor(s), when one region suffered invasion, all Israel suffered invasion. Divine discipline may have impacted only some of the tribes directly, but it expressed God's displeasure with the entire sinful nation.[27] When peace was restored to one region, all Israel was made intact and the whole land experienced rest.[28] Portraying regional judges as having national authority reflects the ideal of national solidarity under a suitable leader (Deut. 17:14–20; cf. Judg. 17:6; 21:25). In short, the editorial frame militantly counters the spirit of national disunity and disintegration portrayed in the stories, keeps

---

26. This pan-Israelite perspective is especially apparent in Joshua in the accounts pertaining to the Transjordanian tribes. These tribes were required to assist the other tribes militarily before settling in their own territory (Josh. 1:12–15; 22:1–9), and they were to maintain solidarity of worship with the western tribes (22:10–34). In the Achan account one also sees this corporate dimension. Even though one man, from the tribe of Judah, sinned, the Lord declared that "Israel" had sinned (Josh. 7:11–13) and "all Israel" executed Achan (Josh. 7:25).
27. In this regard note how Amos 4:7 speaks of divine selectivity in judgment (one city received rain, another did not) in the context of national discipline. Both affected and unaffected cities were to heed the warning and turn back to God.
28. On the book's pan-Israelite perspective, see Goldingay 2003, 530–34.

alive the ideal presented in Joshua, and paves the way for the realization of the ideal under the monarchy. True, for the most part Israel was not united during the period of the judges and the events described did not impact all of the tribes directly. But this does not mean that it is inappropriate to view the period from an idealized perspective.[29]

However, even if it is legitimate for the narrator to utilize a pan-Israelite perspective for rhetorical purposes, certain historical realities must be recognized. As noted above, the incidents in the central section are localized, so one may not assume that foreign rule extended over the entire land. This means that "the land" or "Israel" in any given case actually refers to only the region of the particular judge who is in view, not the entire nation. If, in any given case, it is a particular tribe or group of tribes that experiences conquest and oppression, then the deliverance and subsequent rest pertains in actuality to that localized tribe or tribal group.

As for the expression "the land," the term refers to the entire land in 1:32–33; 2:1–2, 6; 11:21; 18:2, 17. However, in several cases "the land" actually refers to a smaller region within the larger geographical area: 1:2 (Judah's territory is called "the land"); 6:4 ("the land" refers specifically to the region invaded by the Midianites); 9:37 ("the land" is the area of Shechem); 18:9–10 ("the land" refers to the northern region targeted by the Danites), 18:30 ("the land" may refer here to the northern kingdom). The evidence shows that "the land," like "Israel," can be used rhetorically (in a whole for part style). This may very well be the case in 3:11, 30; 5:31; 8:28, where we read that the land had rest, or was "undisturbed."

---

29. Of course, to speak of "Israel" in this early period is hardly anachronistic in light of the Egyptian Merneptah Stela, which dates to the late thirteenth century B.C. In this inscription the Pharaoh boasts: "The (foreign) chieftains lie prostrate, saying 'Peace.' Not one lifts his head among the Nine Bows. Libya is captured, while Hatti is pacified. Canaan is plundered, Ashkelon is carried off, and Gezer is captured. Yenoam is made into nonexistence; Israel is wasted, its seed is not; and Hurru is become a widow because of Egypt. All lands united themselves in peace. Those who went about are subdued by the king of Upper and Lower Egypt . . . Merneptah" (*COS* 2:41). Hoffmeier observes that the name Israel is accompanied by "the determinative (semantic indicator) for an ethnic group, and not for a geographic region or city." He adds: "This scenario is in complete agreement with the picture portrayed in the books of Joshua and Judges, viz. the Israelites had no clearly defined political capital city, but were distributed over a region" (*COS* 2:41). See as well Kitchen 2003, 220; and Sparks 2005, 389–90. For a translation of the full inscription see Lichtheim 1976, 73–77.

Surely we would not want to claim that Israel, in its entirety, experienced absolute peace during the periods of rest. In such a troubled period of Israelite history, invasions would have occurred periodically, if not regularly. Even if one wants to push the pan-Israelite language to its limits and take "the land had rest" statements as referring to the entire land, one must make allowances for hyperbole and generalization.

One can see this from an examination of similar language in 1–2 Samuel. According to 1 Samuel 7:13, following Samuel's victory over the Philistines at Ebenezer, "the Philistines were subdued and did not invade Israelite territory again. Throughout Samuel's lifetime, the hand of the Lord was against the Philistines." The expression "the hand was against" does not refer simply to opposition, but implies domination (Deut. 2:15; Judg. 2:15; 1 Sam. 5:9; 12:15). However, not long after this, well within Samuel's lifetime, we read how the Philistines were again oppressing Israel to such an extent that the Lord decided to raise up a king to deliver his people (1 Sam. 9:16; 10:5; 13:19). 1 Samuel 7:13, if read in isolation, might be misinterpreted to mean that Israel had no more trouble with the Philistines and exercised complete control over their enemies, rather than being viewed correctly as a generalized, hyperbolic characterization of the time of Samuel. We find a similar kind of generalized, hyperbolic statement in 2 Samuel 7:1, where the narrator states that the Lord "had given him [David] rest from all his enemies around him." Yet the following chapters describe David's wars against the surrounding nations, while 1 Kings 5:3–4 suggests that David never enjoyed peace. Furthermore, in the Lord's response to David (2 Sam. 7:11) he promised to give David rest from all his enemies, as if this had not yet been achieved.

Regarding this issue, one final point is in order. If the narrator had wanted to suggest that the land had rest from all military conflict, he could have stated this more clearly. When the narrator of the Former Prophets wants to convey this idea elsewhere, the idiom of choice appears to be the *hiphil* of נוּחַ collocated with מִסָּבִיב and/or an all-inclusive reference to enemies (Josh. 21:44; 23:1; 2 Sam. 7:1, 11; 1 Kings 5:4 [18 in Hebrew]), or שָׁקַט collocated with "from battle/war" (Josh. 11:23; 14:15).

Regarding the use of "Israel" in Judges, Satterthwaite observes that the book's references to "'Israel' and even 'the Israelites' are not the same as 'all Israel.'" He adds, "Most likely, Judges aims to represent Israel as a political or covenantal unity, so that what happens to a part affects the whole: the frequent references to 'Israel' and 'the Israelites' are not meant to imply that all Israel was directly involved in all the events narrated but rather to emphasize that these tribes are part of a larger but increasingly fragmented whole" (Satterthwaite 2005, 583).

Statistical evidence bears this out. The phrase כָּל־יִשְׂרָאֵל, "all Israel," is used only twice in Judges (8:27; 20:34), in contrast to its frequent appearance in Deuteronomy (fourteen times) and Joshua (seventeen times):

Book	Total uses of "Israel"	Uses of "all Israel"
Deuteronomy	72	14 (19.4 % of total uses)
Joshua	160	17 (10.6% of total uses)
Judges	184	2 (1.1% of total uses)

It should be pointed out that Judges does use the phrase כָּל־בְּנֵי יִשְׂרָאֵל, literally, "all the sons of Israel," four times (2:4; 10:8; 20:1, 26).[30] This expression does not appear in Deuteronomy and occurs only three times in Joshua. (It is used fifteen times in Exodus–Numbers.) Judges also uses the expression, כָּל־שִׁבְטֵי יִשְׂרָאֵל "all the tribes of Israel," three times (20:2, 10; 21:5), as opposed to once each in Deuteronomy and Joshua. So if we combine passages using these phrases with those using the phrase "all Israel" the totals and percentages are as follows:

Book	Total uses of "Israel"	Uses of "all" collocated with "Israel"
Deuteronomy	72	15 (20.8 % of total uses)
Joshua	160	21 (13.1 % of total uses)
Judges	184	9 (4.9 % of total uses)

In either case, it is clear that Deuteronomy and Joshua describe Israel in its entirety (that is, as "all Israel" or "all the sons/tribes of Israel") much more frequently than does Judges. The ratios between uses of Israel not collocated with "all" to those where "all" is collocated with "Israel" or "sons/tribes of Israel" are as follows:

---

30. We have retained Judges 10:8 in the list, even though it does not refer to the entire nation. It is qualified by the clause "living east of the Jordan in Amorite country in Gilead."

Deuteronomy	3.8 to 1
Joshua	6.6 to 1
Judges	19.4 to 1

It is also noteworthy that six of the nine cases where Judges uses "all Israel" or "all the sons/tribes of Israel," appear in chapters 20–21, where Israel unites to fight a civil war against the tribe of Benjamin. So, ironically, even when the narrator depicts Israel as a national unity, the surrounding context indicates that the perceived unity is fragile.

To summarize, Judges does insist on viewing Israel as a unity, but it also reflects the disintegration that marred this period in the nation's history. The linguistic evidence shows that the pan-Israelite perspective, though idealized to some degree and characterized by hyperbole, is balanced by a realism about the nature of the period.

CHRONOLOGICAL FRAMEWORK

The tension between the pan-Israelite and localized tribal perspectives is apparent in the way scholars deal with the chronological framework provided in the book's central section. The following chronological notations appear:

3:8	Cushan-Rishathaim oppresses Israel	8 years
3:11	Land rests after deliverance	40 years
3:14	Moab oppresses Israel	18 years
3:30	Land rests after deliverance	80 years
4:3	Sisera oppresses Israel	20 years
5:31	Land rests after deliverance	40 years
6:1	Midian oppresses Israel	7 years
8:28	Land rests after deliverance	40 years
9:22	Abimelech rules after Jotham's curse	3 years
10:2	Tola leads Israel	23 years
10:3	Jair leads Israel	22 years
10:7–8	Philistines and Ammon oppress Israel	18 years
12:7	Jephthah leads Israel	6 years
12:9	Ibzan leads Israel	7 years
12:11	Elon leads Israel	10 years

12:14	Abdon leads Israel	8 years
13:1	Philistines oppress Israel	40 years
15:20	Samson leads Israel	20 years
Total years		410 years

The Problem

Since 1 Kings 6:1 states that the period between the Exodus from Egypt and Solomon's fourth regnal year (966 B.C.) lasted 480 years, the chronological scheme presented by Judges is problematic. In addition to the 410 years of Judges, we must also take into account the wilderness wanderings, the conquest, the remaining years of Joshua and his contemporaries prior to the oppression of Cushan-Rishathaim, the judgeships of Eli and Samuel, the career of Saul, and the reign of David. When all the figures are tallied up, the total number of years, which probably exceeds six hundred, is beyond what 1 Kings 6:1 allows.[31] There may even be additional gaps in the chronological scheme. It is not clear if the periods of apostasy were concurrent with the periods of peace. If they were not, then we must make room for them between the periods of peace and subsequent periods of oppression (Washburn 1990, 416).

Some Proposed Solutions

To alleviate the tension, some argue that the periods in Judges are not necessarily in chronological sequence and that some of the judgeships may have overlapped.[32] For example, Washburn argues that the

---

31. See the helpful charts provided by Block 1999, 59–61. Block gives the total number of years as 593, but does not incorporate the period between the end of the conquest and the beginning of the Judges chronology. The text indicates that the falling away described in Judges 3:7, which initiates the book's chronological scheme, occurred after Joshua and his contemporaries had passed off the scene (Judg. 2:7, 11). This would have taken place some time after the conquest (cf. Josh. 23:1); Merrill suggests a date of 1366 B.C. for Joshua's death, 33 years after the conquest (1987, 147). Combining the biblical data with estimates regarding Saul's reign, Samuel's tenure as leader, and the period between the conquest and the death of Joshua and the elders, Hoffmeier computes the total number of years to be 633 (2007, 227–28). Kitchen gives the "minimal" figure as 591/596 years (2003, 203).
32. See, for example, Washburn 1990, 414–25. For a survey of how scholars down through the centuries have tried to solve the problem, see Yuan 2006, 29–40.

recurring statement "Once again the Israelites did evil in the eyes of the Lord" (וַיֹּסִפוּ בְּנֵי־יִשְׂרָאֵל לַעֲשׂוֹת הָרַע בְּעֵינֵי יְהוָה; see 3:12; 4:1; 10:6; 13:1), is an "episode-initial clause" that "does not generally designate consecutive events" (1990, 417). Consequently, he is able to make Gideon, Jephthah, and Samson contemporaries. He takes "after him" in 10:3 to refer to Abimelech (not Tola), allowing Tola and Jair to be contemporaries. Furthermore he takes "after him" in 12:8, 11, 13 to refer to Jephthah, making Ibzan, Elon, and Abdon contemporaries. In this scheme all of the "minor" judges follow Gideon/Jephthah/Samson. By this ingenious proposal he is able to compress the Judges period into the framework suggested by 1 Kings 6:1.

The linguistic evidence militates against Washburn's proposal. Elsewhere, when used in narrative texts, the *hiphil wayyiqtol* of יסף almost always describes an action that repeats another action reported in the preceding context (though not necessarily the preceding sentence). Often the adverb עוֹד, "again," follows the construction, but even when it does not the construction indicates sequence.[33] In Genesis 25:1 the episode-initial statement may involve a flashback in the overall chronology of the story, but it still describes an action subsequent to the marriages mentioned previously. In 1 Kings 16:33 and 2 Chronicles 28:22 the construction indicates intensification of action, rather than repetition. In Judges 3:12; 4:1; 10:6; 13:1, the formula is best understood as describing a sinful action that in essence repeats/is subsequent to the previously mentioned sinful action. So 3:12 must be understood in relation to 3:7; 4:1 in relation to 3:12; 10:6 in relation to 6:1 (where יסף is not used in the formula); and 13:1 in relation to 10:6.

As for Washburn's interpretation of אַחֲרָיו, "after him," in the "minor" judges lists, in each case the most natural place to seek the referent of the pronoun is in the immediately preceding pericope, not in a pericope two or three places removed. In both 10:1–5 and 12:8–15, the phrase "after him" follows a notation of the preceding judge's death and burial, suggesting *chronological* succession. Furthermore, in 2 Samuel 23:9–11 אַחֲרָיו appears in a list of David's warriors and in each case the pronominal suffix refers to the nearer antecedent. In verse 9a (which begins a pericope about Eleazar) the suffix refers to Josheb-Basshebeth (v. 8), the subject of the preceding pericope. In verse 11a (which begins a pericope about Shammah) the suffix most naturally refers to Eleazar

---

33. See Genesis 4:2; 8:10; 25:1; Exodus 9:34; Numbers 22:25–26; Judges 20:22; 1 Samuel 3:8, 21; 9:8; 18:29; 19:8, 21; 20:17; 2 Samuel 3:34; 24:1 (cf. vv. 1–14); 1 Chronicles 14:13; Esther 8:3; Job 27:1; 29:1; 42:10; Isaiah 7:10; 8:5.

(vv. 9–10), not Josheb-Basshebeth. This same pattern is apparent in Nehemiah 3:16–31.

One senses this line of approach eliminates chronological problems at the expense of the book's rhetorical strategy. The pan-Israelite flavor of the chronological notations, as well as the cyclical literary structure they reinforce, strongly suggest that the notations are intended to be taken as indicating successive periods.

It is conceivable that the Philistine oppression (see 13:1), if localized, overlapped with one or more of these minor judges. O'Connell suggests the Philistine oppression described in chapters 13–16 is to be equated with the one mentioned in 10:7.[34] Like O'Connell, Steinmann proposes that the eighteen-year Ammonite oppression (10:8) overlapped with the forty-year Philistine oppression (13:1; cf. 10:7) (2005, 491–500). In this view 10:6–7 and 13:1 are parallel and refer to the same apostasy and divine response. He places the judgeships of Jephthah and his three successors (31 years total) within this period of oppression, while "Samson's judgeship happened sometime during the forty years of the Philistine oppression." He adds: "This means that his judgeship may have overlapped with any of the judges in the fifth cycle, but at the very least must have overlapped with the judgeships of Elon and Abdon" (496).[35] In this way he is able to reduce the length of the judges period from 410 years to 330. By overlapping Eli's judgeship with earlier judges, he is able to fit the judges period into the chronological scheme reflected in 1 Kings 6:1.

This proposal is attractive in some respects, but encounters at least three problems: (1) It seems unlikely that the Ammonite oppression continued after Jephthah's great victory over them (cf. 11:32–33). If the six years of leadership mentioned in 12:7 were concurrent with the oppression, then they have to be placed at the end of the period of oppression, not at the beginning as Steinmann suggests.[36] However,

---

34. O'Connell 1996, 318–19. Though advocating a redactional model of the text's evolution, Moore offers a similar explanation. He suggests that the final editor of Judges 10:7 may have inserted the reference to the Philistines "for the purpose of extending the scope of the introduction to include ch. 13–16" (1895, 277).

35. However, table 4 (499) does not seem to reflect this assertion, for the table shows the dates of the judges as follows: Jephthah (1088–1083), Ibzan (1083–1077), Elon (1077–1068), Abdon (1068–1061), and Samson (with a question mark after the name) (1049–1030). The table also speaks of an oppression of the Midianites (dated 1088–1071) as concurrent with the Philistine oppression, but surely the Ammonites are meant (see table 3 on p. 497).

36. See his table 4 (p. 499), where he dates the Midianite (*sic!*) oppression to 1088–1071 and Jephthah's reign to 1088–1083.

it seems just as likely that the six years of Jephthah's judgeship followed his victory over the Ammonites.[37] (2) Samson's twenty years of leadership (15:20; 16:31) may have overlapped with the forty years of Philistine oppression mentioned in 13:1 (see note 56 below), but this need not be the case. His twenty-year period of leadership may have followed (cf. 15:20). It came to a tragic end after the Delilah affair (cf. 16:31). In other words, twenty years or so passed between the events recorded in chapter 15 and those recounted in chapter 16. We are told in 15:20 that Samson led Israel for twenty years "during the days of the Philistines." However, this need not refer to the period of oppression *per se*. The Philistines remained a constant threat to Israel until the time of David and "the days of the Philistines" may refer more generally to the rather extended time period in which the Philistines were a major player in the life of Israel. (3) Finally, and most importantly, the formulaic statement "the Israelites again did evil" (cf. 13:1), when used elsewhere in Judges, marks the beginning of an era that chronologically follows what immediately precedes (see 3:12; 4:1; 10:6). Steinmann's view requires that 13:1 be parallel to 10:6–7 (with both then being chronologically subsequent to 10:5).

Nöldeke attempted to harmonize the figures in Judges with 1 Kings 6:1 by proposing that the 480 years mentioned in the latter is an artificial figure that excludes the periods of oppression and the three years of the usurper Abimelech's reign.[38] According to Moore, in this system "the beginning of each judge's rule" is "reckoned, not from the victory which brought him into power, but from the death of his predecessor" (Moore 1895, xli). This scheme works as follows:

---

37. The Lord gave Jephthah a great victory over the Ammonites that broke the back of their oppressive rule over Israel. The use of כָּנַע in verse 33 recalls earlier victories that ended oppression (cf. 3:30; 4:23; 8:28). Jephthah devastated (literally, "struck down [with] a very great striking down") twenty Ammonite towns (v. 33). The only time this emphatic construction is used in the Former Prophets prior to this is in Joshua 10:20 (see also v. 10, though מְאֹד is omitted there) to describe Israel's annihilation of the Canaanite coalition at Gibeon. The narrator may allude to this event to emphasize the extent of Jephthah's victory and to depict Jephthah as being a new Joshua of sorts, at least militarily. The text also states that the Lord gave the Ammonites into Jephthah's hand (11:32; cf. 12:3), an expression that is used earlier of victories that brought deliverance from oppression (3:10; 4:7, 14; 7:7, 14–15).

38. Nöldeke's view is summarized in Moore 1895, xli, and in Burney 1970, lii.

Moses	40
Joshua	x
Othniel	40
Ehud	80
Barak	40
Gideon	40
Minor Judges	76
Samson	20
Eli	40
Samuel	20
Saul	y
David	40
Solomon's four years	4
Total	440 + x + y
If one assumes that x + y equals a total of forty, then the resulting figure is 480.	

Moore prefers to shorten Eli's judgeship to twenty years and eliminate Saul's illegitimate reign from the chronology. This allows him to assign forty years each to Joshua and Samuel (1895, xli-xlii).

Both of these schemes are ingenious, but problematic. If the judgeships are viewed as successive with no gaps, then the periods of oppression must be subsumed under the periods of peace (cf. 3:11 with 3:14; 3:30 with 4:3; 5:31 with 6:1; 8:28 and 10:2–3 with 10:8).[39] Yet one gets the impression that these periods of peace are chronologically distinct from the periods of oppression and that they began with the deliverance from oppression.

Galil suggests that the reference to 480 years in 1 Kings 6:1 reflects the chronology of the Deuteronomistic History and that the chronological notations related to the minor judges were not originally part of this chronological scheme. By overlapping Eli's judgeship and the period of the ark's exile with the events recorded in Judges 9–16, he is able to compress the Judges period to 314 years. He then assigns Moses, Joshua, Samuel, and David each forty years, Saul two years (admittedly artificial, but the figure that the Deuteronomist found in his sources; cf. 1 Sam. 13:1), and Solomon four years. This scheme yields a period of 480 years, corresponding to the figure given in 1 Kings 6:1 (2004, 713–21). Galil's proposal is creative, but dependent

---

39. In his attempt to solve the chronological problem, Faiman also subsumes the periods of oppression under the periods of peace (1993, 31–40).

upon rather arbitrary assumptions regarding the development of the Deuteronomistic History and the chronological relationship between events described in Judges and 1 Samuel.

Three Alternative Proposals

In this section we offer three alternative proposals for the chronology of Judges. The first two assume a date for the Exodus in the fifteenth century B.C. The third assumes a date for the Exodus in the thirteenth century B.C.

Proposal One. This first proposal assumes an early date for the Exodus with no overlapping of the judges. It views the rounded numbers forty and eighty in Judges as stylized and compresses the figures. It also understands the careers of Eli and Samuel as overlapping with the end of the Judges period.

The fourfold appearance of the number forty in the chronological notations, as well as the use of eighty (a multiple of forty), indicates these numbers may be stylized.[40] However, there are also seemingly precise numbers (non-multiples of ten) in the notations, suggesting the figures are meant to be taken as literal, rather than stylized or rounded. Block points out that the formulas in which the numbers appear differ. The precise numbers appear in references to lengths of judgeships and periods of oppression, while forty and eighty occur in the "land had rest" formula (with the exception of 13:1). Block states: "The differences in the types of numbers employed in the book probably derive from the sources used by the author, who was not concerned to synchronize them with external chronological data or make them conform to a predetermined quota" (1999, 63). If this is the case, then the numbers forty (with the possible exception of 13:1) and eighty may indeed be idiomatic, referring to the time of one generation's prominence, or perhaps even hyperbolic, exaggerating the length of the periods of rest for rhetorical effect. If so, the actual number of years involved could be significantly less than the literal aggregate total of two hundred years for the periods of rest.

Compressing the figures in this way, in and of itself, still does not reduce the total number of years enough to harmonize the Judges chronology with 1 Kings 6:1. Nevertheless, if one places the era of Eli and

---

40. For a brief discussion of the use of forty as a stylized figure in the Bible, see Ryken, Wilhoit, & Longman 1998, 305–6. "Forty" may also be used in a stylized manner in the Mesha (Moabite) inscription. For a translation of this inscription, see *COS*, 2:137–38. For a discussion of the use of the numeral forty in this text, see Parker 1997, 48–49.

Samuel within the Judges period, harmonization is possible. Eli served as a judge for forty years (1 Sam. 4:18), but it is possible that this period was concurrent with one (Samson) or more of the final judges. Earlier we argued against overlapping periods for the judges because the expressions "again did evil" and "after him" most naturally indicate chronological succession. However, the notation about the length of Eli's tenure is not part of this chronological scheme.[41] Furthermore, our earlier argument pertained to the *literary* structure of Judges. It does not preclude the *historical* possibility that more than one individual served in a leadership capacity at any given time. The leaders named in Judges, while presented in chronological order, may well constitute a selective list. If this is the case, then it is possible that Eli and Samuel served within the period covered by Judges. Assuming this was the case, we offer the following chronological scheme for the Judges period:

3:8	Cushan-Rishathaim oppresses Israel	1360–1352[42]
3:11	Land rests after deliverance	1352–1332[43]
3:14	Moab oppresses Israel	1332–1314

---

41. In the overall structure of the history, 1 Samuel follows the epilogue of Judges (chapters 17–21), which is not in chronological sequence with the central section of the book (see our comments on Judg. 18:30 and 20:28 in the commentary below). So, it is possible the incidents recorded in the early chapters of 1 Samuel, like those recorded in Judges 17–21, occurred during the judges period. 1 Samuel begins with an introductory formula that is similar to the introductory formula in Judges 17:1, suggesting they are linked at the macrostructural or discourse level:
    - Judges 17:1   וַיְהִי־אִישׁ מֵהַר־אֶפְרַיִם וּשְׁמוֹ מִיכָיְהוּ
    (literally) "Now there was a man from the hill country of Ephraim whose name was Micaiah"
    - 1 Samuel 1:1   וַיְהִי אִישׁ אֶחָד מִן־הָרָמָתַיִם . . . וּשְׁמוֹ אֶלְקָנָה
    (literally) "Now there was a certain man from Ramathaim whose name was Elkanah"
    - The introductory formula in Judges 19:1c is similar:
    וַיְהִי אִישׁ לֵוִי גָּר בְּיַרְכְּתֵי הַר־אֶפְרַיִם,
    "there was a Levite living temporarily in the remote region of the Ephraimite hill country."
42. If we date Joshua's death around 1366 B.C. (cf. Merrill 1987, 147), then Othniel's judgeship probably began shortly after.
43. This assumes that the "forty" years mentioned in the "land had rest" formula is stylized, indicating a generation, or hyperbolic. Somewhat arbitrarily, we have cut the figure in half. We do the same with the figure "forty" in 5:31 and 8:28, and with the number "eighty" in 3:30.

3:30	Land rests after deliverance	1314–1274
4:3	Sisera oppresses Israel	1274–1254
5:31	Land rests after deliverance	1254–1234
6:1	Midian oppresses Israel	1234–1227
8:28	Land rests after deliverance	1227–1207
9:22	Abimelech rules after Jotham's curse	1207–1204
10:2	Tola leads Israel	1204–1181
10:3	Jair leads Israel	1181–1159
10:7–8	Philistines and Ammon oppress Israel	1159–1141
12:7	Jephthah leads Israel	1141–1135
12:9	Ibzan leads Israel	1135–1128
12:11	Elon leads Israel	1128–1118
12:14	Abdon leads Israel	1118–1110
13:1	Philistines oppress Israel	1110–1070[44]
15:20	Samson leads Israel	[20-year period between 1110–1070][45]

---

44. The number forty is taken literally here because (1) it refers to a period of oppression (not rest, as in 3:11, 30; 5:31; 8:28), and (2) the other numbers associated with periods of oppression appear to be precise and are best taken as literal.

45. Though there are problems with the proposal (see above), it is possible that Samson's twenty-year tenure as judge occurred within the forty-year period of Philistine oppression. While the linguistic structure of 13:1 suggests it is in chronological sequence with 10:6, this does not demand that Samson's twenty-year period of leadership followed the Philistine oppression. In fact, the introductory formula in 13:2 has the same pattern we find in Judges 17:1 and 1 Samuel 1:1:

Judges 13:2   וַיְהִי אִישׁ אֶחָד מִצָּרְעָה . . . וּשְׁמוֹ מָנוֹחַ
(literally) "Now there was a certain man from Zorah . . . whose name was Manoah"

Judges 17:1   וַיְהִי־אִישׁ מֵהַר־אֶפְרָיִם וּשְׁמוֹ מִיכָיְהוּ
(literally) "Now there was a man from the hill country of Ephraim whose name was Micaiah"

1 Samuel 1:1   וַיְהִי אִישׁ אֶחָד מִן־הָרָמָתַיִם . . . וּשְׁמוֹ אֶלְקָנָה
(literally) "Now there was a certain man from Ramathaim whose name was Elkanah"

Just as the epilogue is not in chronological succession with the central section of Judges, perhaps the Samson story is not in strict chronological succession to the statement in 13:1. In this case we are able to position Samson's time of leadership within the forty-year period of oppression.

As for Eli and Samuel, we suggest the following dates:

Eli's forty years of leadership (1 Sam. 4:18)	1130–1090
Philistines capture ark (1 Sam. 4:11)	1090
Ark at Kiriath-Jearim (1 Sam. 7:2)	1090–1070[46]
Samuel's victory over the Philistines (1 Sam. 7:3–12)	1070
Israel enjoys relief from Philistine oppression (1 Sam. 7:13–14)	1070–1050
Samuel anoints Saul (1 Samuel 10)	1050

In this scheme Samuel's victory over the Philistines (1 Samuel 7) terminated the period of Philistine oppression mentioned in Judges 13:1. In this regard, it is important to recall that Samson, while winning impressive victories over the Philistines, only "began" the deliverance of Israel (Judg. 13:5). While one could argue that his victory at Lehi ended the Philistine oppression (see above), the text does not necessarily indicate this was the case. Samuel may have finished what Samson only started.

Another factor that impacts the discussion of the chronology of the Judges period is Jephthah's statement that Israel had occupied the Transjordanian region for three hundred years (Judg. 11:26). If one understands the chronological notations in Judges as successive and takes all the numbers literally, then roughly 319 years had elapsed between the onset of Cushan-Rishathaim's oppression and Jephthah's speech. As noted earlier, one must also make room for the conquest of Canaan and the remaining years of Joshua and his contemporaries, for the text indicates that the falling away described in Judges 3:7 occurred after they had passed off the scene (Judg. 2:7, 11). If one adds another forty years to the total, then the conquest of Transjordan would have taken place about 359 years before Jephthah's speech. It is possible that Jephthah used a rounded, approximate figure. Though he may have had a generally accurate idea of the length of Israel's occupation of the region, he was hardly a historian conversant with such details. An approximate figure would have sufficed for his purposes. If we treat forty and eighty as stylized, inflated figures in Judges and harmonize the chronology of Judges with the chronological notation in 1 Kings 6:1

---

46. The ark was in Philistine territory for seven months (1 Sam. 6:1). According to 1 Samuel 7:2, it was in Kiriath-Jearim for twenty years, but this cannot refer to the entire time period between its arrival in Kiriath-Jearim and David's retrieving it, for this period, which included Saul's reign and the early part of David's, was longer than twenty years. The chronological notation in 1 Samuel 7:2 refers to the time that elapsed between the ark's arrival in Kiriath-Jearim and the incident recorded in 1 Samuel 7.

in the manner outlined above, then the period of time between the conquest and Jephthah's speech would be approximately 265 years, less than the figure given by Jephthah. In this case Jephthah was rounding the figure up to the nearest hundred and/or slightly exaggerating.

Proposal Two. This second proposal, like the first, assumes an early date for the Exodus. However, unlike the first view, it sees chronological overlap in Judges. Taking a cue from the text itself, it proposes that there are two overlapping panels. Unlike the first view, it places the careers of Eli and Samuel after the judges.[47]

The first main literary unit of the book's central section is introduced with the statement, "the Israelites did evil before the Lord" (3:7). In the introduction to the next two units this statement is repeated, but the verb, וַיֹּסִפוּ literally, "and they added" appears as well, indicating that the earlier pattern of sin has been repeated (cf. 3:12; 4:1). However, in 6:1, the introduction to the Gideon story, the statement used in 3:7 is repeated almost verbatim and the verb יסף omitted. However, 10:6 and 13:1 include יסף. The pattern is as follows:

A 3:7	וַיַּעֲשׂוּ בְנֵי־יִשְׂרָאֵל אֶת־הָרַע בְּעֵינֵי יְהוָה
B 3:12	וַיֹּסִפוּ בְנֵי־יִשְׂרָאֵל לַעֲשׂוֹת הָרַע בְּעֵינֵי יְהוָה
B 4:1	וַיֹּסִפוּ בְנֵי־יִשְׂרָאֵל לַעֲשׂוֹת הָרַע בְּעֵינֵי יְהוָה
A 6:1	וַיַּעֲשׂוּ בְנֵי־יִשְׂרָאֵל הָרַע בְּעֵינֵי יְהוָה
B 10:6	וַיֹּסִפוּ בְנֵי־יִשְׂרָאֵל לַעֲשׂוֹת הָרַע בְּעֵינֵי יְהוָה
B 13:1	וַיֹּסִפוּ בְנֵי־יִשְׂרָאֵל לַעֲשׂוֹת הָרַע בְּעֵינֵי יְהוָה

Given the absence of יסף, it is possible that Judges 6:1 is not to be understood as chronologically successive to 4:1. Perhaps the stories of the central section are arranged in two panels that are chronologically concurrent. The Othniel (3:7) and Gideon (6:1) stories are parallel, with Ehud (3:12) and Deborah (4:1) following Othniel in succession, and Jephthah (10:6) and Samson (13:1) following Gideon-Abimelech in succession.[48] Furthermore, the minor judges can be placed in

---

47. The author has defended this proposal, which is his personal preference, and presented what follows in Chisholm 2009a, 247–55. For a critique of this view, see Steinmann 2010. A reply to Steinmann's critique appears in Chisholm 2010d.

48. There may be further support for this view from the linguistic evidence. First, when one examines the verbs used to describe the Lord's response to Israel's sin, the following pattern emerges:

chronological sequence after both Gideon-Abimelech (10:1–5) and Jephthah (12:7–15). If so, then the following chronological scheme emerges:

Panel One

3:8	Cushan-Rishathaim oppresses Israel	1336–1328
3:11	Land rests after deliverance	1328–1288
3:14	Moab oppresses Israel	1288–1270
3:30	Land rests after deliverance	1270–1190
4:3	Sisera oppresses Israel	1190–1170[49]

Panel One

3:8   וַיִּמְכְּרֵם, literally, "he *sold* them," from the root מכר
3:13   וַיְחַזֵּק, literally, "and he *strengthened*," from the root חזק
4:2   וַיִּמְכְּרֵם, literally, "he *sold* them," from the root מכר

Panel Two

6:1   וַיִּתְּנֵם, literally, "and he *gave* them," from the root נתן
10:7   וַיִּמְכְּרֵם, literally, "he *sold* them," from the root מכר
13:1   וַיִּתְּנֵם, literally, "and he *gave* them," from the root נתן

One notes the alternating appearance of מכר (in the first, third, and fifth accounts), but there is another structure evident if we think in terms of parallel panels. Panel one uses מכר in the first and third accounts and a different verb (חזק) in between. This creates a bookend pattern (sold-strengthened-sold). Panel two uses נתן around a different verb (מכר) to create a similar bookend pattern (gave-sold-gave) as in panel one.

Second, when one examines the length of the periods of the oppressions, there is an increase in panel one from eight (3:8) to eighteen (3:14) to twenty (4:3) years. But then the length of oppression drops back down to seven years in 6:1, before escalating to eighteen (10:7–8) and then forty (13:1) years. The reduction in 6:1 appears to be an aberration, but if we view the numbers in terms of parallel panels, there is symmetry in that the numbers increase in both panels. The numbers for the first oppression in each panel are almost identical, the number for the second oppression in each is the same, and the third number doubles in the second panel:

	Panel One	**Panel Two**
First oppression	Eight years (3:8)	Seven years (6:1)
Second oppression	Eighteen years (3:14)	Eighteen years (10:7–8)
Third oppression	Twenty years (4:3)	Forty years (13:1)

49. Dating Jabin's oppression in 1190–1170 B.C. may seem problematic since Hazor was destroyed sometime during the fourteenth–thirteenth centuries and remained unsettled until the time of Solomon. (Yadin's date of 1230 for its destruction cannot be proven.) See Ben-Tor 1998, 462–65. Kitchen, who dates the Jabin of Judges 4 to 1180, acknowledges the chronological problem, but provides a plausible explanation (2003, 213). Based on the

5:31	Land rests after deliverance	1170–1130

Panel Two

6:1	Midian oppresses Israel	1334–1327
8:28	Land rests after deliverance	1327–1287
9:22	Abimelech rules after Jotham's curse	1287–1284
10:2	Tola leads Israel	1284–1261
10:3	Jair leads Israel	1261–1239
10:7–8	Philistines and Ammon oppress Israel	1239–1221
12:7	Jephthah leads Israel	1221–1215[50]
12:9	Ibzan leads Israel	1215–1208
12:11	Elon leads Israel	1208–1198
12:14	Abdon leads Israel	1198–1190

---

description of Jabin as "king of Canaan," Kitchen proposes that he was a regional ruler who retained the traditional title "king of Hazor." He offers ancient Near Eastern parallels as support. (For a response to Kitchen, see Wood 2005, 487–88.) Hoffmeier (2007, 244) makes the important point that Judges 4–5 does not say or imply that Hazor was destroyed: "A close reading of the text indicates that God gave Israel victory over her oppressors in a major battle 25 miles away from Hazor, but the text is absolutely silent regarding any military action against Hazor itself. Furthermore, the terminology used in 4:23–24 is not found in Joshua or Judges to indicate attacks on cities. Consequently, there is no basis to believe that the destruction of the final LB IIB (late thirteenth century) city was caused by Deborah and Barak's triumph over Jabin and Sisera." (For a response to Hoffmeier, see Wood 2007, 255–56.) It is important to note that the archaeological evidence does not allow us to identify the conqueror. According to Ben-Tor, "candidates" include "the Sea Peoples; a Canaanite rival city or coalition; the Egyptians; or the Israelites." There are good reasons for ruling out the first three options, but "all of this is, of course, circumstantial evidence" (1998, 465). By appealing to Kitchen and Hoffmeier for support, I am not endorsing their date for the Exodus. However, both have shown that the events recorded in Judges 4 could have occurred in the early twelfth century. The fact of the matter is that the material evidence from Hazor does not tell us precisely when the city fell, nor does it indicate who was responsible. Some associate the destruction with Joshua, others with Barak and Deborah. But we cannot be sure the Israelites were the conquerors. Given the current state of our information (or lack thereof), it is best to leave Hazor out of the discussion of the chronology of Judges.

50. In this case Jephthah delivered his speech to the Ammonite king (1221) approximately 185 years after the conquest of Transjordan (1406), making his reference to three hundred years (Judg. 11:26) either hyperbolic or simply inaccurate. For further discussion, see below.

13:1	Philistines oppress Israel	1190–1150
15:20	Samson leads Israel	1150–1130[51]

Eli's forty years of leadership (1 Sam. 4:18)	1130–1090
Philistines capture ark (1 Sam. 4:11)	1090
Ark at Kiriath-Jearim (1 Sam. 7:2)	1090–1070
Samuel's victory over the Philistines (1 Sam. 7:3–12)	1070
Israel enjoys relief from Philistine oppression (1 Sam. 7:13–14)	1070–1050
Samuel anoints Saul (1 Samuel 10)	1050

This scheme allows for a period of 63 years between the completion of the conquest (1399) and the first oppression (1336) and satisfies nicely the demands of Joshua 23:1, which indicates that "many days" passed between the end of the conquest and Joshua's death, and of Judges 2:7, which suggests there was a period of peace following Joshua's death.

This proposal preserves the pan-Israelite rhetorical strategy of the chronological notations, as well as the cyclical literary structure they reinforce, by allowing one to understand the notations (namely, "Once again the Israelites did evil," in the narrative framework and the phrase "after him" in the minor judges lists) as indicating successive periods. The lone exception to this is the statement in 6:1, but, as noted above, the absence of יָסַף sets this text apart from the others.

This scheme assumes that references to "the land" and to Israel, though reflecting a pan-Israelite rhetorical strategy, actually refer in any given case to the geographical region in which the particular judge lived (see above). So panel one focuses on the south for the period 1336–1190 (Othniel and Ehud), and on the north for the period 1190–1130 (Deborah and Barak). Panel two focuses, for the most part, on the north for the period 1334–1190 (Gideon and Jephthah), and on the south for the period 1190–1130 (Samson). The so-called minor judges mentioned in panel two operated north of Shiloh, with the exception of Ibzan of Bethlehem (12:8–9), whose seven year career as a leader (1215–1208) fits nicely into the 80-year period of peace in the

---

51. If we place Samson's career within the period of oppression (see our earlier discussion of this possibility), then all of the dates in panel two would be reduced by twenty years (for example, the Midianite oppression would date to 1314–1307, Jephthah's career to 1201–1195, etc.). In this case Jephthah's speech would occur 205 years after the conquest of Transjordan.

south (1270–1190) mentioned in 3:30.[52] The initial period of peace in the south (1328–1288) corresponds to the initial period of peace in the north (1327–1287). While the south experienced a lengthy period of peace from 1270–1190, there was some turmoil in the north during this period (1239–1221). The Canaanite oppression in the north and subsequent peace (1190–1130) coincided with the Philistine oppression and Samson's career.

If this scheme is correct, then it is reasonable to assume that it may have important implications for understanding the book's rhetorical design. We noted earlier that there are references to the land having rest after each of the first four accounts in the book's central section (3:11, 30; 5:31; 8:28), but these disappear in the Jephthah and Samson accounts. Put another way, the pattern of the first panel is disrupted in the second. At the end of the Gideon account, we read again (as in the first panel) that the land had rest (8:28), but then subsequently no such statement appears. Perhaps this signals a key thematic difference between the panels. Panel one characterizes the period as one where conflict was followed by rest. But panel two breaks that pattern and refuses, after the Gideon account, and especially its sequel involving Abimelech, to characterize the period as one where there was rest. In other words, rhetoric and differing perspectives are at work: Panel one presents a more optimistic perspective of the period as one where there was rest, but panel two qualifies this with a more pessimistic view. There may have been rest, albeit localized and temporary, but it was not worth mentioning. This less optimistic view paves the way for the epilogue, which describes events chronologically prior to the central section and characterizes the period as one of moral chaos and civil strife.

If this proposal concerning the rhetorical design of the panels is correct, it would explain another variation that occurs within the second panel. The first panel speaks of Israel subduing (or overpowering, in the case of Othniel) an oppressor, followed by rest for the land (3:10–11, 30; 4:23/5:31). The second panel continues this pattern initially (8:28), but then, as noted above, drops the rest formula, while retaining the reference to subduing an enemy (11:32). But then it omits both in the Samson account, which is no surprise given the messenger's statement to his mother in 13:5. This gradual, step-by-step removal of key elements from the first panel contributes powerfully to the alternative portrait of the period that the second panel seeks to paint.

---

52. For a helpful map showing the geographical distribution of the various judges, see Aharoni & Avi-Yonah 1977, 57 (map 82).

Of course, any view of the chronology of Judges must address Jephthah's statement that Israel had occupied the Transjordanian region for 300 years (Judg. 11:26). In the chronological scheme proposed above, Jephthah would have delivered his speech to the Ammonite king in 1221, 185 years after the conquest of Transjordan (1406), or 115 years shy of the number he gives in his speech.

Jephthah was a brigand (cf. Judg. 11:3), not a historian. Nevertheless, his speech does exhibit an impressive degree of historical awareness and subtlety of argument. His argument may be summarized as follows: (1) Since the Lord transferred the region in question from Sihon the Amorite to Israel, the Ammonites had no right to claim it. They should have been content with ancient divine decisions about national boundaries. (2) The Ammonite king should follow the example of Balak of Moab, who, when thwarted in his attempt to bring a curse on Israel, refused to attack Israel and returned to his home (see Numbers 22–24). He claimed no right to the conquered territory. (3) Israel had been occupying the region in question for 300 years, but the Ammonites had not tried to take it. This was odd, especially if Israel had stolen it from them in the first place. Their failure to invade the region for so long a period suggested they had never viewed it as originally theirs prior to this king's bogus claim.

However, there is at least one major inaccuracy in Jephthah's speech. In verse 24 he identifies the Ammonite king's god as Chemosh. Other texts, as well as the extrabiblical Mesha inscription, associate Chemosh with Moab (Num. 21:29; 1 Kings 11:7, 33; 2 Kings 23:13; Jer. 48:7, 13, 46), while Milkom is identified as the god of the Ammonites (1 Kings 11:5, 7, 33; 2 Kings 23:13).[53]

It is possible, as Boling suggests, that Ammon had subdued Moab and that the Ammonite king now regarded himself as heir of all lands formerly held by Moab (1975, 203–4). Originally Moab, not Sihon or Ammon, had owned the disputed territory, meaning that Chemosh could have been viewed as the god of the region.[54] It would make sense to refer to Chemosh as the Ammonite king's god if the latter now ruled Moab under Chemosh's authority. However, the text gives no indication that Ammon had conquered Moab, so Boling's proposal remains speculative and unsubstantiated.

---

53. Aufrecht (1999, 159) argues that El was actually the chief god of the Ammonites, though he acknowledges that Milkom was popular. For a critique of this view, see Hess 2007, 272, note 116.
54. According to Numbers 21:26–29, Sihon took the region in question from Moab.

Rather than proposing a historical-cultural explanation for linking the king of Ammon with Moab's god, it may be better to view Jephthah's statement as purely rhetorical. The Ammonite king was claiming land that his people had never controlled, as Jephthah's history lesson makes clear. Moab and then Sihon had controlled it before Israel conquered it. By speaking to the Ammonite king as if he were a Moabite king, Jephthah sarcastically reminds him that he could claim the land only if he were Moabite. But even if this were the case, he could only claim what Chemosh granted and the Moabite god had surrendered this area long ago. If Jephthah could make such a seemingly inaccurate statement in service of his rhetorical strategy, then it is possible that he could hyperbolically inflate a number for rhetorical effect. In this regard, Block observes: "Since this is a political speech, Jephthah crafts his comments deliberately for propaganda purposes rather than factual reconstruction." After drawing a parallel to the Moabite Mesha Inscription, he adds: "Surely Jephthah knew that the Israelites had lived in this area for generations. A figure like three hundred years was intended to make an impression on the Ammonites" (1999, 363). One can readily detect the dynamics of the hyperbole—he rounds the number up (185 to 200), and then adds one hundred for good effect.

There is, of course, a simpler solution to this problem. Younger argues that Jephthah was ignorant of the facts and mistakenly thought Chemosh was the Ammonite deity (2002, 256–57). It may seem unlikely that one who had lived in Transjordan in proximity to Ammon and Moab would not know such a basic fact, but he may have indeed been confused on this matter. If he was wrong on such a basic and simple point as this, it is certainly possible that his chronological comment in verse 24 is inaccurate as well. Commenting on Jephthah's reference to 300 years, Block states, "Since Jephthah is either incorrectly or purposefully mistaken in other details (Chemosh for Milkom), one should perhaps not make this speech the final word on the point" (1999, 363).

Proposal Three. Of course, some will insist on a thirteenth century date for the Exodus on the basis of archaeological and biblical (cf. Exod. 1:11) evidence. Can the numbers in Judges be harmonized with this view? This third proposal offers such a harmonization, adapting the chronological scheme of Kitchen (see below). Like proposal one above, it (1) treats the numbers forty and eighty as stylized and compresses them, and (2) overlaps the careers of Eli and Samuel with the end of the Judges period. Like proposal two above, it understands two overlapping panels in the chronological scheme, but with some variations in details.

Kitchen, who argues for a thirteenth century date for the Exodus, appeals to alleged ancient Near Eastern parallels from "intermediate periods" to support his proposal that the judges fit into the period 1210/1200–1042 B.C. He divides the judges into seven geographical regions and, like others, argues that they overlap chronologically (2003, 204–10). He states, "only a limited number of 'after him' phrases link successive judges, leaving open the option that some may have served as contemporaries in different districts of Canaan" (202). Kitchen correctly treats "after him" as a sequential continuity marker in the minor judges lists (207).[55] However, he does not identify the recurring statement "again did evil" as a sequential continuity marker and dates concurrently the oppressions of Cushan-Rishathaim (1200–1192) and of Eglon (1200–1182), as well as those of Ammon (1091–1073) and of the Philistines (1100–1060).

To make his theory work, Kitchen must dismiss Jephthah's statement in 11:26 as "the report of a brave but ignorant man's bold bluster in favor of his people, not a mathematically precise chronological datum." It "can offer us no practical help" (209). It is true that Jephthah was not a professional historian and it is possible that he was speaking hyperbolically, but to inflate a period of approximately 130 years (1200–1070 in Kitchen's proposed scheme) to three hundred years seems excessive. For those preferring a thirteenth century date for the Exodus, it would be simpler to understand Jephthah's statement as inaccurate (see the discussion above in relation to the second proposal).

For proponents of a thirteenth century date for the Exodus, we propose an alternative to Kitchen's scheme. This proposal, like Kitchen's, understands references to "the land" and to "Israel" (whatever their rhetorical function may be in the book's pan-Israelite perspective) as referring in actuality only to the region of the particular judge in view, not to the entire land. In this alternative scheme both the phrase "after him" in the minor judges lists and the statement "again did evil" in the framework of the central section are treated as sequential continuity markers at the discourse level.

Furthermore, as noted above, the central section is viewed as containing two parallel panels that are roughly chronologically concurrent: (1) Othniel-Ehud-Barak // (2) Gideon-Jephthah-Samson. The

---

55. In the chart on p. 207 he lists Tola's dates as 1136–1113 and Jair's as 1113–1091. However, in the chart on p. 210 he dates Tola to "ca. 1025" and Jair to "ca. 1100." Based on the more precise dates given on p. 207, I am assuming that Tola's date on p. 210 is a typographical error and should be corrected to ca. 1125.

Ehud and Barak accounts are taken as chronologically subsequent to the Othniel account, and the Jephthah and Samson narratives follow the Gideon story chronologically. However, this proposal makes two significant alterations to the paneled scheme outlined earlier. Rather than dating Jabin's oppression after the period of peace that followed Ehud's victory, we overlap it with that period. The introduction to the Barak narrative states that Jabin's oppression occurred after Ehud's death (4:1), which likely took place sometime during the period of peace. Furthermore, this proposal also understands the Philistine-Ammonite oppression mentioned in 10:7 as concurrent with the Philistine oppression described in 13:1.[56] Using these principles, we propose the following dates:

Exodus	1260
Invasion of Canaan	1220
Completion of conquest	1213

Panel One

3:8	Cushan-Rishathaim oppresses Israel (Judah)	1190–1182
3:11	Land (Judah) rests after deliverance	1182–1157[57]
3:14	Moab oppresses Israel (Benjamin-Ephraim)	1157–1139
3:30	Land (Benjamin-Ephraim) rests after deliverance	1139–1089
4:3	Sisera oppresses Israel (northern tribes)	1114–1094[58]
5:31	Land (north) rests after deliverance	1094–1069

Panel Two

6:1	Midian oppresses Israel (north central region)	1190–1183
8:28	Land (north central region) rests after deliverance	1183–1158

---

56. In this case the statement "again did evil" in both 10:6 and in 13:1 is in relation to 6:1. In other words 13:1 is chronologically sequential to 6:1, not to 10:6.

57. This assumes that the "forty" years mentioned in the "land had rest" formula is stylized, indicating a generation. If we assume a thirteenth century date for the Exodus (ca. 1260), then the 480 years of 1 Kings 6:1 would have to be taken as indicating twelve traditional generations of forty years in length. In actuality these periods are approximately twenty-five years in length. (If the Exodus occurred in 1260, then the period of time between it and Solomon's fourth year [966] was 294 years, or twelve periods of approximately twenty-five years.) We reduce the figure "forty" in 5:31 and 8:28 to twenty-five, and the number "eighty" in 3:30 to fifty.

58. We place Ehud's death, somewhat arbitrarily, in the middle of the period of peace.

9:22	Abimelech rules Shechem after Jotham's curse	1158–1155
10:2	Tola leads Israel (northern Ephraim)	1155–1133
10:3	Jair leads Israel (Gilead)	1133–1110
10:7–8	Philistines and Ammon oppress Israel (Gilead)	1110–1092
12:7	Jephthah leads Israel (Gilead)	1092–1086[59]
12:9	Ibzan leads Israel (Judah)	1086–1079[60]
12:11	Elon leads Israel (Zebulun)	1079–1069[61]
12:14	Abdon leads Israel (Ephraim)	1069–1061
13:1	Philistines oppress Israel (south)	1110–1070
15:20	Samson leads Israel	[20-year period between 1110–1070][62]

Eli's forty years of leadership at Shiloh (1 Sam. 4:18)	1130–1090
Philistines capture ark (1 Sam. 4:11)	1090
Ark at Kiriath-Jearim (1 Sam. 7:2)	1090–1070
Samuel's victory over the Philistines (1 Sam. 7:3–12)	1070
Israel enjoys relief from Philistine oppression (1 Sam. 7:13–14)	1070–1050
Samuel anoints Saul (1 Samuel 10)	1050

WHEN WAS JUDGES WRITTEN?

Six times the authorial/editorial comment "to this day" appears in the book's narrative framework (1:21, 26; 6:24; 10:4; 15:19; 18:12). It is not certain if these all come from the same source.[63] Only one gives any clue for dating. The reference in 1:21 to the Jebusites still living

---

59. In this case Jephthah delivered his speech to the Ammonite king (1092) approximately 128 years after the conquest of Transjordan (1220), making his reference to three hundred years (Judg. 11:26) hyperbolic. As suggested above in our critique of Kitchen's proposal, Jephthah's use of three hundred years is problematic for any dating scheme that assumes a thirteenth century date for the Exodus.

60. Ibzan is depicted as a leader, but not a deliverer (12:8–10), so he could have led Judah during the time of the Philistine oppression of 1110–1070 (cf. 13:1).

61. Elon's career in Zebulun would have fallen within the period of northern peace (1094–1069) mentioned in 5:31.

62. See our earlier discussion of this issue.

63. In his study of the expression in the Deuteronomistic History, Childs concluded that the formula appears in a diversity of sources and reflects the work of various redactors (1963, 279–92, especially 290–92). Geoghegan argues that diversity of sources does not necessarily indicate that various redactors were involved. His study of the formula in the Deuteronomistic History leads him to conclude that the expression derives from Dtr, who employed a variety of traditions (2003, 201–227, especially 203, 225–27).

in Jerusalem predates David's conquest of the city (2 Sam. 5:6–8). However, this cannot be a guide to the date of the book as a whole, for 18:30 refers to "the exile of the land" and must postdate the exile of the northern kingdom, an event that occurred between 734–721 B.C.[64] The most we can safely say is that these comments reflect sources or editorial activity deriving from different time periods. The comment in 1:21 may indicate an early date for the prologue, but it could simply be part of an early source that was incorporated into the prologue without the temporal notation being edited out.[65] The statement in 18:30 is probably a later gloss, for verse 31 seems to focus on the early period (see the commentary on these verses below). The epilogue's references to the absence of a king point to a date (at least for the editorial comments) after the rise of the monarchy. The narrator appears to be living in a time period distinct from "those days" in which the narrated events occurred (the judges period or at least the early part of the period). The book's anti-Benjaminite elements point to a time of compilation after the Saulide-Davidic conflict had arisen, while the anti-Ephraimite

---

64. Since the statement is made with regard to the history of the Danite cult, the exile of the northern kingdom is the likely referent here. In 734–732 B.C., Tiglath-pileser III of Assyria annexed much of Israel's territory and reduced Samaria to a puppet state, governed by a ruler handpicked by the Assyrians. Danite territory would have been annexed to Assyria at this time. For more detailed accounts of the Assyrian invasion of the west in 734–732 B.C., see Pitard 1987, 186–89, and Otzen 1979, 251–61. On the textual issue in 18:30 (some propose that we read "ark" instead of "land"), see the commentary below.

65. The statement in 1:29, which says that the Canaanites continued to live among the Ephraimites in Gezer, may be explained in a similar way. According to 1 Kings 9:16, Pharaoh captured Gezer, killed the Canaanite population living there, and gave the city to Solomon. Thus, it is argued, Judges 1:29 must date to a time prior to Solomon's reign. See Young 1964, 169. This may well be true for the *source* or even the first part of the prologue, but the reference is not necessarily a guide to the date of the book *as a whole*. Some (e.g., Young 1964, 169) also contend that the reference in 3:3 to Sidon (rather than Tyre) as the "chief Phoenician city" (see also 1:31) points to a date of authorship prior to the twelfth century. While this could be a clue to an early date, at least for the statement itself or the source employed, Guillaume argues that Judges 1 derives from the period 709–677 B.C., when "Tyre had lost all its continental possessions to Sidon" (2001, 131–37, and 2004, 96–103). The statement in 3:3 could be explained in the same manner.

flavor suggests a time of compilation after the division of the kingdom.[66] (See below under the heading "Does Judges Have a Political Agenda?")

Scholars have expended a great deal of energy trying to reconstruct the literary evolution and redactional history of Judges.[67] Since Martin Noth's proposal of a Deuteronomistic History, most critical scholarship on Judges has interacted with, challenged, revised, and/or refined Noth's conclusions.[68] But one gets the distinct impression that the energy being expended is bringing diminishing returns and that the debate is moving in a circle.[69] The various proposals testify to their authors' creativity and attention to detail, but one is struck by the subjectivity and arbitrary nature of the hypotheses, which have yielded no consensus. The simple fact of the matter is that we are not in a position to reconstruct the history of the text's literary evolution with any degree of confidence.[70] At a very basic level most scholars conclude that the book is comprised of different sources—because of the stylistic and thematic variation that seems evident.[71] But even this position has been challenged because, as Guest argues, "there is no concrete

---

66. In this regard see Dillard and Longman 1994, 121.
67. It is beyond the scope of this work to trace the history of critical scholarship on this issue. See the standard introductions and commentaries, as well as the surveys in O'Connell 1996, 347–66; Wong 2006a, 1–22; and Butler 2009, xlv–li.
68. For recent surveys of these efforts see O'Brien 1994, 235–59; and Römer and de Pury 2000, 116–23. See as well Campbell and O'Brien 2000, 165–214.
69. Commenting on Becker's response to Richter's revision of Noth's proposal concerning the pre-Deuteronomistic stage of Judges, Römer and de Pury state: "We seem to have come full circle, but the questions raised by Richter and others remain" (2000, 118).
70. See Sternberg 1987, 64. He observes: "The sad truth is that we know practically nothing about biblical writers—even less than about the processes of writing and transmission—and it looks as though we never will." For a recent example of such a speculative attempt to reconstruct the evolution of Judges, see Guillaume 2004.
71. A Qumran fragment (4QJudg^a) provides some objective support for the redactional model. It omits Judges 6:7–10, the account of a prophet's confrontation with Israel in response to Israel's cry of distress. In the past some scholars, without the aid of the Qumran evidence, were suspicious of this passage being a secondary addition, a theory that may now be validated by the evidence. See, for example, Burney 1970, xli-xlii. For discussion of the issue see O'Connell 1996, 467; Block 1999, 254; Trebolle Barrera 1989, 236, 245; Mobley 2005, 124–26; Brettler 2002, 41–42; Wong 2006a, 183, note 118; Niditch 2008, 87; Hess 1997, 124–27; and Butler 2009, 185.

evidence for any of the conjectured sources." She adds, "Apart from the book of Judges in its present form, nothing is available" (1998, 58).

To summarize, there is no scholarly consensus on when the book was written. There is internal evidence that may point to a relatively early pre-Davidic date, at least for the source material used, but there is other evidence suggesting a date of origin, at least for various editorial comments, during the period of the divided monarchy.

HOW SHOULD WE APPROACH THE BOOK?

Because we are not in a position to trace the book's literary evolution with any degree of confidence, some scholars prefer to focus on the book's canonical form and to understand its various parts within this literary framework.[72] Proponents of this approach, while not necessarily denying that the book has a redactional history, assert that the book, when examined in its present form, emerges as a unified work. Advocates of this newer synchronic approach do not always agree on details and their methods and conclusions have hardly won the day.[73] However, a synchronic approach, as long as it remains rooted in history and recognizes the contextualized nature of the ancient text, is preferable to more traditional diachronic methods because it deals with the text as we have it and consequently is not as susceptible to the kind of speculative fancy (often presented with cocksure arrogance) that litters the history of biblical higher criticism and has produced such a bewildering assortment of scholarly fiction.[74]

---

72. See, for example, the major book-length studies by Klein 1988, O'Connell 1996, Polzin 1980, Webb 1987, and Wong 2006a.
73. See, for example, the strong and detailed critique by Andersson 2001. For a critique of Andersson's work, see Wong 2006a, 16–22, and 2006c, 216–30. For a reply, see Andersson 2007.
74. Of course, some synchronic approaches, such as reader-response criticism, disengage interpretation from the text's historical context. At a fundamental level, reader-response critics are hermeneutical hypocrites. They construct their interpretive studies in a well-reasoned fashion with the intent to convince readers that their proposals and ideas are correct. They give every indication that they expect their readers to understand what they write in accordance with their intention and as if they have authority over their own work. One suspects that if one were to "make meaning" of their essays and/or deconstruct their work, they would protest, probably vehemently so. Yet they do not accord the text of Scripture and its narrator the same respect they expect to receive. In the final analysis their work lacks any authority beyond themselves and can be dismissed as a guide to the meaning of the text. All a reader-response critic can legitimately

A synchronic approach takes seriously the text as it stands. It assumes the material within Judges reflects larger purposes, which are revealed in the book itself. The individual stories may have functioned within specific geographical and temporal frameworks at one time, but we are not in a position to resurrect those contexts. The stories are now part of a larger entity. The book has an anthological appearance, but it is not purely anthological. The presence of the formulaic framework in the central section creates at least the semblance of a macroplot. Furthermore, as synchronic critics have shown, the placement of the stories is strategic and certain themes emerge and develop, linking them together. While the stories are juxtaposed, they are integrated thematically. Like paintings on a theme in a wing of an art gallery, they illustrate themes and contribute to the book's overall purposes and message.

A synchronic study also looks beyond the boundaries of the book. Judges must not be isolated; it is part of a larger history encompassing Joshua–Kings (the Former Prophets) in the Hebrew Bible.[75] This history begins with the conquest and ends with the exile. As a synchronic study isolates and develops the book's themes, it must integrate these with the surrounding literary context, as well as with the final exilic historical setting and theological mind-set. When one seeks to do this,

---

claim is that the text means this to *him or her*. But since the reader of the critic's work is not "him or her," the critic's subjective interpretation has no authority beyond the confines of his or her own mind. Why then even publish one's notions?

75. In this regard see Frolov 2009. He argues that synchronic analysis of Judges indicates that it is not a "literary entity" in and of itself. On the contrary, he says it is a "combination of three major components: the conquest account in 1:1–26, which belongs with what we know as the Book of Joshua; the sequence of apostasy-oppression-repentance-deliverance cycles in Judg 3:7–21:25, which extends at least through 1 Samuel 7; and the introduction to the latter in Judg 1:27–3:6" (40). While we disagree with Frolov's understanding of the structure of 1:1–3:6 and argue for the literary integrity of Judges as a book (see above), his essential point is important—Judges is part of a larger literary entity. The second subunit in the prologue links with and picks up where Joshua leaves off (cf. Judg. 2:6–9 with Josh. 24:28–30), and the Samson story and the epilogue are linked structurally with 1 Samuel. The formula "now there was a (certain) man from (geographical name) . . . whose name was (personal name)" appears only in Judges 13:2; 17:1; 1 Samuel 1:1; 9:1. This suggests it is a linking device at the macrostructural or larger discourse level (for further discussion see below).

the purposes of the book come into even clearer focus. This brings us to the next pertinent question.

WHAT IS THE POINT OF JUDGES?

As one reads Judges and reflects on its themes (see our earlier discussion), it becomes apparent that the book has a distinct agenda, which includes at least three major purposes:

The thematic emphases of the prologue indicate that Judges is in part a defense of the Lord's reputation, which was jeopardized by Israel's failure.[76] The prologue explains why Israel failed and makes it clear that the Lord warned the people about this possibility from the very beginning (Laato 2003, 193–96). The rest of the book justifies the Lord's decision to test his people by allowing the enemy to remain in the land. Israel's defeats were punitive, rather than being due to some alleged weakness in the Lord or to the strength of foreigners and their gods.

This kind of theological agenda is not unique to the Bible and reflects the cultural context in which Judges originated and developed. In the Moabite Stone, King Mesha attributes Israel's victory over Moab to the anger of his god Chemosh.[77] He then tells how Chemosh restored his divine favor and enabled him to defeat Israel once and for all (*COS* 2:137–39).[78]

Another element in the book's defense of the Lord's honor is the prologue's affirmation of his commitment to his people. Despite their failure and his harsh divine discipline, the Lord showed compassion and continued to deliver them from oppression. The stories within the

---

76. Eslinger (1989, 55–80) would disagree with this perspective. In his analysis of Judges 1–2, he attempts to show that the Lord bears some culpability for what happened during the Judges period. Yet he concludes that the narrator maintains a degree of objectivity and refuses to lay the blame for Israel's failure on either God or Israel. He concludes that Judges 1–2 is descriptive, not analytical; it "offers theology, not theodicy" (80).

77. See Philippe Guillaume 2004, 22–23. He also compares the theology of the framework in the Judges stories to that of the Mesha inscription.

78. On Mesha's theology see Albrektson 1967, 100–01; and Parker 1997, 47. Parker observes: "For the narrator, the only reason why Omri was able to oppress Moab was Chemosh's displeasure with his country, which left it at the mercy of its neighbor. This also establishes that, while Moab may have lost its sovereignty, Chemosh had not lost his." If one substitutes "Yahweh" for "Chemosh," "Israel" for "Moab," and "the enemy" for "Omri," this quotation would be a fair summary of what Judges says about the Lord's punishment of Israel.

book's central section support this affirmation as they tell how the Lord responded to the people's pain and intervened to save them.[79] As Fretheim states: "We are surprised by a God who finds ways of working in, with, and under very compromising situations in which people have placed themselves in order to bring about good. In the midst of unfaithfulness, the faithfulness of God is revealed, a God who never breaks covenant" (1983, 98; see also McCann 2002, 138–39).

A third feature of the book's Yahwistic defense is its polemical dimension. On a very general level, the book demonstrates that Israel's obsession with idols did not bring success. On the contrary, idolatry consistently brought defeat and humiliation. The book is particularly concerned to denounce Israel's devotion to the Canaanite deity Baal (2:13; 6:25–32; 8:33; 10:6). It gives ample reason why Israel should have chosen Yahweh over Baal. The Song of Deborah depicts Yahweh as the lord of the storm who defeats the Canaanite armies (5:4–5). The Gideon account, along with its sequel about Abimelech, also contains a strong anti-Baal polemic, as Baal is unable to avenge fully Gideon's (Jerubbaal's) attack on his altar and ends up having his Shechemite temple burned to the ground (Bluedorn 2001). The polemical dimension takes a different turn in the Samson story, where Samson burns the grain supposedly provided by the Philistine grain-god Dagon (15:4–5). Though Dagon seems to prevail initially (16:23–24), Samson ends up bringing Dagon's temple to the ground (16:30). The polemic against both of these gods continues in 1 Samuel. Hannah celebrates the Lord's ability to give fertility (1 Sam. 2:1–10), the ark of the Lord humiliates Dagon in the latter's very own temple (1 Samuel 5), and the Lord thunders against and defeats the Philistines following Israel's rejection of Baal-worship (1 Samuel 7) (see Chisholm 2007b).

Isolating this purpose does not allow us to pinpoint the date of the book or its sources (cf. Bluedorn 2001, 291). This Yahwistic defense, especially the polemical dimension, would have been relevant in the pre-exilic period, when the people were so tempted to worship other gods. It also would have been relevant in the exilic and postexilic periods when Israel's history had seemingly culminated in failure and many were probably wondering about the implications of this failure for Yahwistic faith. Recent events mirrored the nation's early history and were actually the inevitable consequence of its early failure. Israel's moral

---

79. Once again there is a parallel to this in the Moabite Stone, where Mesha affirms that Chemosh "saved" him "from all the kings." The verb translated "saved" is the causative (H) stem form of the root יׁשע, which is the same form used of the Lord's saving acts in Judges 2:16.

decline and exile were rooted in the assimilation to Canaanite culture and religion that had begun after the death of Joshua and his generation. As in the period of the judges, the Lord had once more allowed his people to experience defeat, but this did not mean he had abandoned them. Judges demonstrates that even in the darkest of times, God is always there, working out his salvific purposes for his people.

(2) The book of Judges also warned Israel of the dangers of assimilation to their environment.[80] As the prologue to the book makes clear, Israel failed to complete the conquest of the land. They intermarried with the Canaanites and embraced Canaanite gods.[81] Their persistent idolatry brought defeat and oppression in its wake. In fact, God decided to put on hold his original plan to give his people the land. The nations would remain to test Israel's loyalty. The stories in the book's central section support this theme. Each account revolves around a divinely enabled deliverer who rescues Israel from oppression brought on by judgment due to idolatry. Though God was sensitive to Israel's self-induced suffering, the vicious cycle continued as long as Israel "did evil in the eyes of the Lord."

As Israel became more like the Canaanites, their national identity as God's covenant community began to dissolve. The unified nation of Joshua's time began to disintegrate, making it more vulnerable to invasion, as the stories illustrate. Tribal conflict threatened the nation's stability; tribal loyalty at the expense of justice eventually precipitated a civil war.[82] Wong proposes that the dominant theme in Judges is "progressive deterioration," which is portrayed through both the book's structure and content (2006a, 249–52).

This theme of deterioration through assimilation to paganism and loss of national unity would have been relevant throughout Israel's history. The preexilic generations perpetuated the sins of the Judges period. They failed the test of loyalty by refusing to separate from the pagan influences around them. The nation, now split in two, was moving inexorably on a path leading to the disaster of exile. From the exilic and postexilic perspective, Judges exposed the root of the exiles'

---

80. Guest demonstrates the importance of this theme in Judges. She probes its social, political, and religious dimensions (1997, 241–69).

81. Block argues that "the Canaanization of Israel" is "the unifying theme" of Judges (1990, 337–41).

82. Wong shows that there is "decreasing participation of the tribes" in the "successive military campaigns" described in the book's central section. This attests to a growing disintegration of the nation during this period (2006a, 176–78).

problem and the ultimate reason why they were in such dire straits. The prophets held out the hope of a restored nation, but there must be genuine covenant renewal to avoid the old cycle of sin and judgment being repeated in the future. The people must take seriously their calling to be distinct from the nations around them and embrace a renewed vision of a united covenant community.[83]

(3) The book of Judges also demonstrated Israel's need for competent, godly leadership. The prologue speaks of the judges in positive terms, probably because it is seeking to demonstrate the Lord's provision for his people. When the people cried out to the Lord, he provided leaders to deliver them. The stories, in harmony with the prologue, tell how God accomplished great deeds through human leaders. However, the stories also introduce another perspective. They illustrate how lack of faith and wisdom marred Israel's leaders and kept them from realizing their potential.[84]

The epilogue looks at Israel's leadership from the more critical perspective of the stories, rather than the positive perspective of the prologue. Israel needed a leader who, in accordance with the Deuteronomic ideal (Deut. 17:14–20), would point the nation back to God and his covenant demands and lay the foundation for spiritual renewal.[85] More specifically, Israel needed a king to ensure social order and cultic purity. Without such a leader, the nation rejected God's authority and each person followed his or her own code of conduct. Only when Israel again acknowledged God as their ultimate King would the original vision, which had seemingly died with Joshua, be realized.[86]

---

83. McCann concludes that Judges "is ultimately a call to covenant loyalty as it witnesses to the amazing reality that 'explains' God's incredible perseverance—an unfailing love that is inevitably manifest as grace" (2002, 139). Pressler observes: "The Deuteronomists are clear: Sin does have consequences; God cannot and will not allow human rebellion against God to continue. Nonetheless, these theologians also insist that judgment is not the final word. Divine mercy reaches beyond righteous wrath" (2002, 4).

84. See the section below entitled, "What Role Do the Female Characters Play?"

85. Deuteronomy 17:14–20 depicts the ideal king as follows: (1) He must be chosen by the Lord. (2) He must be an Israelite, not a foreigner. (3) He must not accumulate horses (probably for the purposes of developing a chariot force), wives, or money. (4) He must study God's covenantal Law so that he may obey and implement it. (5) He must not view himself as superior to his fellow Israelites.

86. Wong argues that the "root" of Israel's deterioration was spiritual, not political (2006a, 252). More specifically, "the central problem is Israel's

This theme would have been relevant at any point in Israel's history. In the preexilic period Judges would have provided justification for the monarchy, and the Davidic dynasty in particular, but Gideon's words to the people (8:23) were a reminder that human kings must be subservient to the ultimate King.[87] As the epilogue makes clear, an effective king points people toward God's authority so that each person is not a law to him- or herself. Rather than giving kingship a blanket endorsement, Judges should have reminded Israel of the royal ideal and served as a rebuke to the rebellious kings of the preexilic period. For the exilic and postexilic community Judges complemented the message of the prophets. The Israel of the future needed a king—the right kind of king—to avoid the errors of the past.

DOES JUDGES HAVE A POLITICAL AGENDA?

Because of the pro-monarchical sentiment in the epilogue, some argue that Judges promoted an agenda that was pro-Judah/David and anti-Benjamin/Ephraim. For example, O'Connell concludes: "The strategy of Judges, which entails an anti-Benjaminite but pro-Judahite rhetoric of entrapment, implicitly spurns the monarchy of Saul but idealizes the monarchy of David" (1996, 342). Brettler affirms that a "strongly pro-Davidic redactor" has left his fingerprints on the book.[88] Sweeney

---

refusal to recognize YHWH's ultimate kingly authority. The implied solution, therefore, is that the nation must return to YHWH and begin honouring His kingly authority before the deterioration can be halted and reversed." He also contends that Israel's leaders were responsible for this problem. He explains: "This seems clear from the way most of the non-YHWH-honouring behaviour associated with the general populace in the epilogue actually echoes similar types of behaviour witnessed among Israel's leaders in the central section" (253). When one correlates the refrain of the epilogue with the content of its stories, it becomes apparent that Israel desperately needed "godly leaders" to "set proper examples so as to lead the nation back to a YHWH-honouring path" (254).

87. By referring to God as Israel's "ultimate King," we do not mean to imply that human kingship should be viewed in a negative light. Indeed our argument is that an ideal king, as envisioned by Deuteronomy 17:14–20, was to remind the people of God's authority and Law.

88. See Brettler 1989b, 416, and 2002, 88–89, 97–102, 111–16. Brettler detects a "polemic against northern kingship" in 8:1–3 and 12:1–6 (1989b, 408). He sees in chapters 17–18 "a polemic against the religio-political institutions of the north," and in chapters 19–21 "a polemic against the kingship of the Saulide dynasty" (415). See as well van Midden 2001, 77–85. He argues that Judges is a preface to Kings and foreshadows the history of

argues that Judges juxtaposes a polemic against Ephraim/Bethel with an idealized view of Judah, which "emerges as the tribe best able to achieve the Deuteronomic ideal for Israel" (Sweeney 1997, 528). Amit detects a "hidden polemic" against Bethel (a major cult site of the northern kingdom) in chapters 17–18 and against Saul in chapters 19–21 (see Amit 1990, 4–20, and 1994, 28–40). Tollington speaks of a "pro-Judah, anti-Israel bias" in the book's epilogue (Tollington 1998, 194), while Amit sees the book teaching that defeat and oppression could have been avoided if all the tribes had followed Judah's example (Amit 1999, 381). Butler, though acknowledging that the book "does not picture Judah as a perfect example of faithfulness," states that "Judah is the least of the evils among the tribes and the one twice designated as God's chosen leader." He then affirms that this positive portrayal of Judah, albeit qualified, "stands in contrast to the image of Benjamin, Ephraim, and Dan" (2009, lxxviii).

Not everyone accepts the theory of a pro-Judah agenda. For example, Webb states: "Judges begins by presenting Judah in a favourable light, and ends by presenting it in an unfavorable light" (Webb 1987, 201). Niditch points out that even the prologue is not entirely favorable, for Judah fails to take all of its allotted territory (1:19) (Niditch 1999, 200). Van der Toorn observes that the Levite in chapters 17–18 comes from Judah (cf. 17:7; 18:12) and that the text's concern to locate Bethlehem and Kiriath-Jearim in Judah betrays a "northern provenance" and "Ephraimite origin" (van der Toorn 1996, 248). Wong mounts a particularly strong challenge to the view that Judges reflects a pro-Judah polemic (Wong 2005, 84–110). He shows that the allegedly pro-Judah passages in chapter one are more ambiguous than many acknowledge and rightly points out that Judah failed to carry out, at least fully, the Lord's will (see especially 1:19). Appealing to the inclusio between chapter 1 and chapters 20–21, he draws out the implications of Judah's role as leader in both the prologue (1:1–2) and epilogue (20:18). He suggests that the events recorded in these chapters are "practically two sides of the same coin." He adds, "While one records Israel's failure to do what is right, the other records Israel's success in doing what is

---

the monarchy. He associates Othniel with David, Ehud with Saul, Gideon with Solomon, Abimelech with Jeroboam, Jephthah with the Omrides, and Samson with Zedekiah. He concludes that the "real issue" of the author of Judges "is the question of the throne of David and its re-establishment." Judges is designed to bring one to the conclusion that "only an other [sic] David can rescue Judah" (85).

wrong, and both resulted in diminishing national fortune that justifiably deserved to be wept over and mourned" (105).[89]

What can we say about the book's presentation of these various tribes? Benjamin does indeed appear in a negative light in 1:21, especially in contrast to Judah (cf. 1:8). The notation in 1:21, which observes that Benjamin could not dislodge the Jebusites from Jerusalem, looks especially tendentious when compared to Joshua 15:63, where it is Judah, not Benjamin, that fails in this regard (Mullen 1993, 127–28). When we come to chapters 19–21, Gibeah of Benjamin is virtually another Sodom, populated by thugs capable of the vilest crimes. This city, the hometown of Saul (1 Sam. 11:4; 15:34; 2 Sam. 21:6; Isa. 10:29), is mentioned twenty-two times in these chapters. Later readers would certainly not miss the connection (see Amit 1994, 31–32, and Unterman 1980, 164–65). The tribe of Benjamin was unwilling to stand up for justice but more than willing to fight against their fellow Israelites in defense of tribal honor. One is left asking, "Can any good thing come out of Benjamin?" This negative portrayal of Benjamin, and of Gibeah in particular, prepares the way literarily for the story of Saul, whose failed kingship comes as no surprise given his tribal roots and connection with Gibeah.

However, one must not overlook the positive portrayal of Ehud the Benjaminite in 3:12–30.[90] Yet this positive presentation hardly offsets the negative portrayal of the tribe in the prologue and epilogue. It is likely that Ehud functions as a foil. Schneider states: "The book presents a decent judge from the tribe of Benjamin early in the narrative to highlight the extent of the downward spiral, especially by the tribe of Benjamin, exhibited in the book's final stories" (Schneider 2000, 47). Ehud may also serve as a foil for Shimei, a member of Saul's clan who was, like Ehud, a Benjaminite "son of Gera" (see Judg. 3:15; 2 Sam. 16:5). Ehud rallied Israel against a foreign king, but Shimei opposed God's chosen Israelite king, though eventually he was forced by circumstances to admit he had done wrong (2 Sam. 16:5; 19:16–19; 1 Kings 2:8).

The tribe of Ephraim also appears in a negative light in the book of Judges.[91] Ephraim failed to drive the Canaanites from Gezer (1:29).

---

89. For a critique of Wong's argument, see Frolov 2007.
90. Some view Ehud's behavior and tactics in a very negative light, while others consider his exploits as exemplary. See the discussion in the commentary below, where I attempt to defend the latter view.
91. See Butler 2009, 472. He writes: "Judges also exercises a strong polemic against Ephraim as the troublesome tribe constantly demanding leadership roles and being the home of unheroic heroes."

They rallied in support of Ehud's revolt (3:27), but later were not as cooperative with their fellow Israelites. The Ephraimites confronted Gideon after his victory; only Gideon's diplomacy averted a civil conflict (7:24–8:3). This propensity to defend their tribal honor surfaces again after Jephthah's victory, when the Ephraimites threatened to burn Jephthah's house down. Jephthah was not as diplomatic as Gideon had been; a civil war broke out and a multitude of Ephraimites ended up dead (12:1–6). As Janzen observes, the narrator depicts "the Ephraimites as foreigners unmasked by foreign accents who, like the Ammonites, do not belong in the land that God has not given to them" (Janzen 2005, 353). The initial support of the Ephraimite city of Shechem made Abimelech's murderous regime possible.[92] Nelson points out that none of the so-called minor judges comes from Ephraim and suggests this may hint at an anti-Ephraimite viewpoint (Nelson 2007, 358–61). The negative portrayal of Ephraim continues in chapters 17–18, where an Ephraimite named Micah, who had his own private cult center, ended up, albeit against his will, providing the priest and paraphernalia for the Danites' renegade cult. So the book of Judges depicts Ephraimites contributing to both civil war and religious apostasy. This portrait foreshadows the rebellion and apostasy of the northern tribes (the most prominent of which was Ephraim) under the leadership of the Ephraimite Jeroboam I (1 Kings 11:26).[93]

After giving an overview of the book's negative portrayal of both Benjamin and Ephraim, Butler states that the tribe of Dan "receives similar treatment" (2009, lxxx). He explains: "Not only could they not conquer the towns in their inheritance, but the Amorite armies pressed them back to the hill country, not allowing them to enter the valley (Judg 1:34)." Furthermore, they seem to be depicted negatively in 5:17

---

92. Though Joshua 17:7 seems to locate Shechem in Manasseh's territory, the city is later associated with Ephraim (Josh. 20:7; 21:21). See Globe 1990, 239.

93. Na'aman draws several parallels between Micah and Jeroboam I and concludes that Micah is "a disguised figure" of Jeroboam (2005, 48–50). In the canonical shape of the history the Micah episode foreshadows Jeroboam's sins, but Na'aman, who regards Judges 17–18 as postexilic, concludes "the author of Judges xvii-xviii had before him the text of 1 Kings xi-xiii in its late form." He adds: "Certain outlines of the satirical-polemical work were shaped in line with the history of Jeroboam as it appears in the Book of Kings, the figure of Micah being a twisted and distorted reworking of the figure of Jeroboam" (51). One wonders what really is "twisted and distorted"—the narrator's characterization of Micah or Na'aman's tortuous, speculative diachronic reconstruction.

and the "only judge from Dan" was a failed leader. Eventually the tribe had to move to the north, committing atrocities on the way and once they arrived at their new home.

Butler offers a convincing reason why these three tribes are depicted so negatively: "Ephraim and Bethel became the center of northern Israelite worship and political power. Dan and Bethel became the center of northern Israel's cult. And Benjamin was the home of Saul, the first king of Israel. The authors who collected the materials of Judges into a final 'book' apparently wanted Judah to go first ahead of the shameful trio of Benjamin, Ephraim, and Dan" (2009, lxxx).

The book of Judges portrays Judah in a more favorable light. Twice the Lord commissioned Judah to lead the Israelites into battle (1:2; 20:18). Their relative success in capturing their allotted territory (1:2–20) stands in contrast to the failure of most of the northern tribes (cf. 1:27–36). However, as some have observed, the portrait is tainted. Despite the Lord's presence with them, Judah did not execute Adoni-Bezek (1:6–7), and they failed to defeat the people of the plains because of their iron chariots (1:19).[94] They did not support Samson in his conflict with the Philistines. Instead they were seemingly content to be Philistine subjects and handed Samson over to the enemy (15:10–11).[95] Finally, though not singled out for criticism, they were part of the fiasco that perpetuated Gibeah's crime on a larger scale (see chapters 20–21).

To summarize, the book of Judges has an anti-Benjamin/anti-Ephraim agenda that paves the way for the less than positive portrayal of these tribes in the history to follow in Samuel–Kings. Judah is presented in a better light, but some have overstated the book's so-called pro-Judah dimension. The Lord gave Judah a leadership role,

---

94. Note also the textual ambiguity in 1:18, where the Hebrew text states that Judah conquered the three cities, but the Septuagint says they did not. See the commentary below for a fuller discussion.

95. Wong aptly comments: "For by marching down three thousand strong to apprehend Samson so as to turn him over to the Philistines (15, 11–13), the men of Judah are portrayed not only as cowardly, but also as the only Israelites in the book so content with serving their foreign overlords that they actually sided with them and turned against their own deliverer. In this respect, one can say that Judah is portrayed more negatively than any other tribe in the book! Considering how a most favourable portrayal of Judah at the beginning of the central section is almost completely reversed by the time the section comes to an end, one can justifiably question whether a pro-Judah polemic was ever present in the first place" (2005, 106). For a more sympathetic and positive view of Judah's actions in this instance, see Butler 2009, 342.

suggesting the king who was so desperately needed might arise from that tribe. But this endorsement of Judah (and indirectly, of David and his dynasty) is not unqualified. One could argue that the book presents Judah as a tragic failure whose potential and initial success quickly turned to fear and failure. What Israel needed was not just a leader from Judah, but an effective leader who upheld God's standards and values. The book contributes to the overall endorsement of the Davidic dynasty in Samuel–Kings, but like Samuel–Kings, it also challenges that dynasty to live up to God's ideal by promoting religious and cultic purity, demonstrating faith and wisdom, creating national unity, and ensuring social justice.[96]

WHAT WAS THE ROLE OF THE "JUDGES"?

The traditional translation of the book's title, "Judges," suggests that the leaders depicted in the book carried out a legal function in Israel. However, this does not seem to be case, when one examines the book's use of the verb שׁפט, traditionally translated "to judge."

---

96. See Satterthwaite 1993, 87–88. He argues that Judges 17–21 demonstrates the need for a strong, righteous king. However, it hardly endorses what later kings did. He observes: "Judges 17–21, so far from being unqualifiedly pro-monarchic, is intended to lead one towards a highly critical evaluation of much of what the kings described in Samuel and Kings actually do" (88). Mayes, in his treatment of Judges 17–21, makes a distinction between the narrator-narratee and implied author-implied reader. He writes: "It is the narratee who is being led to endorse the Judahite king and to reject the Benjaminite; it is the narratee's understanding which is being shaped in anticipation of the rivalry between David and Saul, and its outcome, to be developed in the Books of Samuel." However, this is not "the definitive theology." Mayes explains: "The narrator here is not a wholly reliable narrator, and the implied reader is going to be expected to distance himself from the narratee's expectations. For it is precisely the Davidic dynasty which from its foundation proved itself incapable of securing Israel's freedom from the atrocities which Judges 17–21 identified as arising from the lack of a Judahite king." He adds: "The implied author and implied reader know well how the story turns out in the end, thus offering a critical perspective on the narrator's and narratee's confident expectations relating to the Judahite monarchy" (Mayes 2001, 249–50). As far as Mayes is concerned, "at the level of implied author the story is in fact referring to an ideal king" (257, note 48). For Mayes "it was not possible to identify the historical Judean king of the Davidic line as the dependable guarantor of Israel's welfare independent of the law" (257). Mayes' proposal, while certainly creative and worthy of consideration, seems overly complex and a bit strained.

In the broader context of Deuteronomy and the Former Prophets, the legal function of judges (שֹׁפְטִים), including kings (see 2 Sam. 15:4 in this regard), is well-attested (see especially Deut. 16:18; 17:9, 12; 19:17–18; 21:2; 25:1–2; 1 Sam. 7:15–17; 2 Sam. 15:4; 1 Kings 3:9, 28). When Samuel appointed his sons as judges, their role was clearly legal, as the reference to their accepting bribes and perverting justice indicates (1 Sam. 8:1–5). In Judges this legal nuance appears to be present in 4:4, where Deborah adjudicates for Israel when they come to her for judgment (לַמִּשְׁפָּט).[97] Deborah is not actually called a judge here (the participle is used predicatively, not substantivally); rather she is called a prophetess. In 11:27 Jephthah casts the Lord in the role of Judge as he appeals to him to adjudicate his dispute with the Ammonite king.

However, elsewhere in Judges the verb שׁפט does not carry a legal nuance. Apart from Judges 11:27, the substantival participle appears only in the prologue (2:16–19), where it describes the leaders' function as being primarily military and secondarily didactic. The Lord raised up these "judges" to deliver his people from oppression (vv. 16, 18) and apparently to instruct the people in obedience (v. 17), though we do not see the "judges" actually carrying out this secondary function in the central section of the book. When Judges uses the finite form of the verb שׁפט of human leaders, it is not evident that a legal function is in view.[98] In several cases the leader's role appears to be strictly military (see 3:10 [Othniel, cf. v. 9]; 10:2 [Tola, cf. v. 1]; 12:7 [Jephthah]; 15:20 [Samson]; 16:31 [Samson]). It is not certain in what sense the term is being used of the other so-called minor judges (10:3; 12:8, 9, 11, 13, 14), because so little information is given about their careers. However, it is possible that a military role is implied, based on the use of the verb with reference to Tola, who heads the twofold list in 10:1–5, and Jephthah, who heads the list in 12:7–15. It would seem, then, that Block is correct when he argues that the so-called judges are more aptly viewed as "deliverers" in the book of Judges and that the verb שׁפט is better translated "lead, govern" (2002, 23–24).[99]

---

97. Block has challenged this view (1994, 229–53; 2002, 195–97). For a full discussion of the issue and defense of the traditional view of Deborah's role, see the commentary below.

98. In addition to a substantival participle, a finite form of the verb is used in Judges 11:27 of the Lord as the Divine Judge.

99. As noted above, we understand the verb to have a legal connotation in Judges 4:4 (contrary to Block) and 11:27. Outside Judges, one finds diversity of usage with the verb. For example, the more general meaning occurs

WHAT ROLE DO THE FEMALE CHARACTERS PLAY?[100]

Declining Male Leadership and Changing Female Roles

The book of Judges demonstrates, albeit in a negative manner, the importance of competent, godly leadership to the people of God. After a notice of the great leader Joshua's death (1:1; cf. 2:8), the book tells how God raised up judges to deliver certain Israelite tribal groups from their enemies. Though these leaders often accomplished great military victories through God's power, many failed miserably in other respects. Despite their military successes, the spiritual climate in Israel grew bitterly cold as violence and anarchy swept through society. The book's final chapters include a sordid account of idolatry, gang rape, civil war, and kidnapping. The book concludes with the somber words, "In those days Israel had no king; each man did what he considered to be right" (21:25; cf. 17:6; 18:1; 19:1), setting the stage for the rise of Samuel and David, through whom God restored some semblance of covenantal loyalty and societal order.

One cannot read through the book of Judges without noticing that women appear at several strategic points in the narrative. They assume a variety of roles, including heroine, seductress, and innocent victim, among others.[101] Their changing roles vis-à-vis the male characters contribute powerfully to the book's portrayal of the disintegration of Israelite society.[102] This portrait culminates in 1 Samuel 1 with the oppressed figure of Hannah, through whom the Lord reverses the downward spiral detailed in Judges and brings to realization the leadership ideal presented at the beginning of the book. An examination of the interrelationship between the male and female characters in Judges helps us understand the book's overall evaluation of Israel's male leadership during this time period.

Othniel, Acsah, and Caleb. In chapter three the narrator relates the exploits of Othniel, Ehud, and Shamgar, three judges who delivered Israel from foreign oppressors. Though the accounts are relatively brief, the narrator paints a picture of militarily effective men who displayed daring and courage. He presents Othniel as a divinely

---

in 1 Samuel 4:18; 7:6; 2 Kings 15:5; 23:22. A legal connotation applies in Exodus 18:13, 22, 26; Deut. 18:16; 1 Sam. 7:15–17; 1 Kings 3:9.

100. This section is an abridged and revised version of Chisholm 1994b, 34–46.

101. For general surveys of the role of women in Judges, see O'Connor 1986, 277–93, and Klein 1993a.

102. Williams comments on the changing roles of certain key women characters and asks if "this juxtaposition of roles is purely a matter of happenstance." However, he fails to develop this observation. See Williams 1991, 82.

empowered warrior who demonstrated military efficiency in an almost matter-of-fact way. Ehud, who seemed to have "ice in his veins," exhibited unhesitating courage and remarkable cunning in assassinating Eglon and subduing the Moabites. Shamgar, though mentioned in only one verse, displayed extraordinary military prowess.

Othniel in particular is a model of the ideal warrior. He also appears in chapter one in a positive light. In response to Caleb's challenge, he followed Joshua's directive, bravely defeated the enemy, and aggressively took the land God had given to his people.

Othniel's wife, Acsah, the daughter of Caleb, is the first woman to appear in Judges (1:12–15). Caleb promised the conqueror of Debir his daughter's hand in marriage (v. 12), thereby guaranteeing that she would have a worthy husband and that Caleb would have a capable son-in-law who shared his faith and bravery. Othniel, Caleb's nephew (or younger brother), responded to the challenge, took the city, and won the promised bride (v. 13). To complement her land holdings in the Negev, Acsah asked her father for "springs of water," a request with which he readily complied (vv. 14–15).

Acsah's role as the maiden won by bravery in battle contrasts sharply with that of the women described later in the book. Rather than inspiring great military acts, subsequent female characters are forced to assume the typically male role of warrior because of character flaws in certain male leaders, and, by the end of the book, Israelite women are brutally abused by their own countrymen.

Caleb's gift to his daughter provides more than a pleasant, heart-warming touch to the story. Like his acquisition of a worthy husband for his daughter, Caleb's gift illustrates the protective concern which Israelite men should display toward their wives and daughters. However, as the story unfolds, women become the victims of male oppression rather than the beneficiaries of male protection. The life-giving springs, which symbolize fertility and are actually called a "blessing" (בְּרָכָה), stand in sharp contrast to the death and infertility that another Israelite daughter would experience as a result of her father's misguided zeal and lack of foresight (11:34–40).

To summarize, the early chapters, while not entirely positive in their assessment of Israel's early history, paint a somewhat ideal picture of heroic warriors and of an Israelite woman who inspires great deeds and receives a blessing from her father.

Deborah, Barak, and Jael. Unfortunately, this ideal becomes somewhat tarnished in chapter four, the opening verses of which state that King Jabin of the Canaanites had been oppressing the Israelites for twenty years (4:2–3). A woman, Deborah, was exercising leadership in Israel at the time. Her duties included prophesying and judging the people's legal disputes (vv. 4–5). She summoned Barak, of the tribe of Naphtali, and commissioned him to lead Israel into battle against the oppressor. Barak's reaction was less than enthusiastic. He said to Deborah: "If you go with me, I will go; but if you do not go with me, I will not go" (v. 8). Deborah's response suggests that Barak's attitude was inappropriate. She told Barak he had forfeited the honor that could have been his; the Lord would hand the enemy general over to a woman.

With a little more prodding from Deborah (v. 14), hesitant Barak led the Israelite forces to a decisive victory (vv. 15–16). However, the Canaanite general Sisera escaped Barak's clutches and fled from the battle. Exhausted and thirsty, he came to the tent of a woman named Jael, the wife of Heber, a Kenite ally of Sisera. Despite her husband's allegiance to Sisera, Jael's loyalties proved to be with Israel. She invited Sisera into her tent, gave him some milk, tucked him into bed, and then, while he lay sleeping at her feet, drove a tent peg through his head. Barak arrived on the scene a little too late and discovered, in fulfillment of Deborah's words, that the honor of slaying the Canaanite general belonged to a woman (vv. 17–22). In Judges 5, which records Deborah's and Barak's song of celebration, Barak receives honorable mention in passing (vv. 12, 15), while Deborah and especially Jael are the focus of attention. Verses 7 and 12 speak of Deborah's role in the victory, while verses 24–27 rehearse at length Jael's courageous, though devious, exploits.

Judges 5:28–30 introduce another woman, Sisera's mother, who peered out her window in anticipation of her son's return. At first she was concerned about the delay, but then she realized that the warriors were probably plundering the enemy. She assumed that each warrior was grabbing "a girl or two" to satisfy his lust (v. 30). The text is dripping with sarcasm at this point. Rather than brutally raping "a girl or two," the unfortunate Sisera met his violent demise at the feet of a courageous woman.[103] Furthermore the language of sexual submission that permeates the description of Sisera's death adds to the irony of his mother's words (Alter 1985, 43–49; Niditch 1989, 47–51). However, not only do these verses lend dramatic irony to the present context, but they also set up a tragic contrast with the book's final chapters.

Though Barak enjoyed great success, he failed to display the courage of his predecessors. On the contrary, when God challenged, indeed commanded, him to lead Israel's armies into battle, he hesitated.

---

103. See Bal 1988, 134; Brenner 1990, 133; and Cohen-Kiener 1991, 208.

Unlike Othniel, who charged into battle to win Acsah's hand in marriage, Barak demanded the military support of a woman, Deborah, before agreeing to go into battle. He thereby forfeited to Jael, another woman, the blessing that could have been his.

Ironically the warrior-ideal established in Judges 3 was carried on by a woman, rather than by Barak. As Brenner notes, Jael "goes about her task in a true 'male' manner" (Brenner 1990, 132). Webb observes that Jael's actions mirrored the exploits of Ehud, another "lone assassin" who used deception to slay a foreign oppressor behind closed doors. Webb also notes parallels between Jael and Shamgar: "Like Shamgar she is a makeshift fighter who uses an improvised weapon. And if Shamgar was *probably* not an Israelite, Jael is *certainly* not; she is a member of a Kenite splinter group which is at peace with Jabin, Israel's arch enemy" (Webb 1987, 137, emphasis his).

By the end of the story one senses that Israel had taken a step backward. Fortunately two courageous women rose to the occasion and compensated for Barak's weakness. However, the necessity of women playing a militaristic role, rather than inspiring the hero, was symptomatic of a decline in the quality of male leadership.

Gideon, Abimelech, and the Woman on the Wall. Gideon, despite being famous for his great victory over the Midianites with a force of only three hundred men, was less than an ideal ruler.[104] Like Barak, he was initially hesitant when called to action by the Lord (6:12–22, 36–40) and responded to the divine challenge with the word אִם, "if." When Barak heard the Lord's promise of victory, he told Deborah, "*If* you go with me, I will go; but *if* you do not go with me, I will not go" (4:8). Similarly Gideon, in response to the Lord's promises of his presence and military success, said, "*If* you really are pleased with me, then give me a sign as proof that it is really you speaking with me" (6:17). Later he proposed, "*If* you really intend to use me to deliver Israel, as you promised, then give me a sign as proof . . . *If* there is dew on just the fleece, and the ground around it is dry, then I will be sure you will use me to deliver Israel, as you promised" (vv. 36–37). No wonder the Lord later declared, "But *if* you are afraid to attack, go down to the camp with Purah your servant and listen to what they are saying. Then you will be brave and attack the camp" (7:10–11).

Though ridding the land of a foreign oppressor, Gideon also contributed to the religious decline and political disintegration of Israel

---

104. For a list of his numerous faults, see Tanner 1992, 154, as well as Gooding 1982, 74*–75*; Block 1997, 353–66; and Wenham 2004, 119–27.

by failing to exercise the spiritual sensitivity and wisdom needed by a truly competent, godly leader. He made a golden ephod that became a stumbling block for the nation and for his family (8:23–27). He also took many wives (who gave him seventy sons), and kept a concubine at Shechem, who gave him a son named Abimelech (vv 30–31). The power struggle inherent in this less-than-ideal family situation eventually became reality. Power-hungry Abimelech (whose name means, "my father is king") convinced the people of Shechem to hand over his seventy half-brothers, whom he murdered, with the exception of Jotham. Conflict broke out between Abimelech and the Shechemites, which ended with Shechem being burned, in fulfillment of Jotham's curse. Abimelech met his demise at Thebez when an unidentified woman, perched in a tower, dropped an upper millstone on his head (9:53). The text emphasizes her singularity (אַחַת) and states that she "threw" (וַתַּשְׁלֵךְ) the stone on him, a verb that suggests a heroic act of strength and tends to cast the woman in the role of a warrior (Janzen 1987, 35, 37, note 6).

A comparison of this account with the narrative of Sisera's death is instructive. In the earlier account a woman (Jael) delivered Israel from a *foreign* oppressor. In the account of Abimelech's death a woman delivered Israel again (once more, ironically, by a fatal blow to the head with an unconventional weapon; cf. 5:26 with 9:53), only this time from an oppressive *Israelite*.[105] The quality of Israelite leadership had steadily regressed as the brave warrior Othniel was replaced by hesitant Barak and unwise and timid Gideon, who in turn gave way to the "anti-judge" Abimelech, a power-hungry and bloodthirsty initiator of civil discord. The changing roles of the women are symptomatic of this decline. Unlike Acsah, who inspired worthy and brave deeds, women were forced to assume the role of warrior, first to deliver the nation from a foreign oppressor (Sisera) and then from a power-hungry countryman (Abimelech).

---

105. Gooding also notes this parallel and comments on its implications: "Things have seriously deteriorated when the bondage from which Israel has to be delivered in this fashion is no longer a bondage to some foreign power but a bondage to one of Israel's own number who, instead of being a deliverer of Israel, has installed himself as a tyrant, and is maintaining his tyranny by ruthless destruction" (1982, 74*). O'Connor also notes the similarity between Jael and Abimelech's slayer, calling the latter "a sister to Jael" who "acts in a woman's sphere, i. e., from the inside, in killing an oppressing male" (1986, 286).

Jephthah and His Daughter. Jephthah, identified as a "brave warrior" and the son of a prostitute (11:1), was cut from the same mold as Barak and Gideon. Though he won military victories, he also demonstrated uncertainty before charging into battle. Despite being divinely empowered for battle (11:29), he bargained with God by making a vow (11:30). Like Barak and Gideon (4:8; 6:17, 36–37), his use of אם, "if," before the battle testifies to his uncertainty about its outcome. The precise wording of his vow also attests to his sense of desperation and his lack of confidence. The description of the promised offering (11:31) suggests that Jephthah intended to offer a human being, not an animal, perhaps thinking that such a radical (but pagan!) bribe would guarantee divine support.

Of course, the vow proved to be a rash and foolish one, for as Jephthah returned victoriously from the battle he was shocked to see that his daughter, his only child, was the first to come out of the house to meet him. True to his word and at the insistence of his daughter (v. 36), he sacrificed her as a burnt offering to the Lord (v. 39). But in accordance with her request he first allowed her two months to mourn the fact that she would never have the opportunity to be a wife and mother. Ironically Jephthah, who should have been a great hero because of his military success, ended up being one of the most tragic figures on the pages of Scripture because of his lack of faith and foresight. His "allegiance" to God (if one dare call it that) took the grotesque form of human sacrifice and brought a curse, rather than a blessing, on his daughter.

Once again the crisis in Israelite leadership at this period is evident. The radically changing role of the story's major female character draws attention to this. In the earlier stories women heroically delivered the nation from oppressors; now an Israelite woman became an innocent victim of her own father's lack of wisdom. In contrast to Acsah, who received a blessing and a source of agricultural fertility from her father Caleb, Jephthah's daughter was doomed to a brief life of infertility culminating in a cruel and unnecessary death. To make matters worse, Jephthah's slaughter of his own flesh and blood foreshadowed the battle between the Gileadites and Ephraimites (cf. 12:1–7) and the bloody civil war described in the final chapters of the book, in which many Israelite women, like Jephthah's daughter, became victims of a misplaced oath and male brutality.[106]

---

106. See Exum 1990, 423, 430. Gooding explains that Jephthah's actions contrast with those of Ehud's: "Ehud with the Ephraimites takes the fords of Jordan against the Gentile enemy and slaughters them. Jephthah adopts

Samson and Delilah. On the surface Israel's most famous judge, Samson, seemed to have the qualities necessary for a great leader. His supernatural conception seemingly placed him in line with the great patriarchs Isaac, Jacob, and Joseph. Like Othniel, he was divinely empowered and did not hesitate to attack the Lord's enemies. His apparent delight in riddles suggests a capacity for cunning, much like Ehud possessed. Like Shamgar, he was able to slaughter hundreds, even with an unconventional weapon.

However, one does not have to read far before noticing chinks in Samson's armor. His rash behavior and lack of foresight, as in the case of Jephthah, led to the violent death of an innocent young woman (14:1–15:6; both Jephthah's daughter and Samson's Timnite bride died by fire; 11:31, 39 and 15:6). Regardless of how one evaluates Samson's marriage to the Timnite woman, his later involvement with a Philistine prostitute (16:1–3) was proof of his moral weakness, and his disastrous affair with Delilah (16:4–22) revealed an embarrassing lack of wisdom on a par with Eglon.

Samson, following the pattern established by Barak, Gideon, and Jephthah, made several statements beginning with the word אִם, "if," the last of which led to his downfall. At his wedding feast, he challenged the Philistines with a riddle (cf. 14:14) and proposed the following wager: "*If* you really can solve it during the seven days the party lasts, I will give you thirty linen robes and thirty sets of clothes. But *if* you cannot solve it, you will give me thirty linen robes and thirty sets of clothes" (14:12–13a). The Philistines forced Samson's wife to persuade him to reveal the answer to the riddle. When Samson realized what they had done, he killed thirty men of Ashkelon, took their clothes to pay the debt, abandoned his Timnite wife, and went home to his parents.

Samson's inability to anticipate the Philistines' ingenuity and his willingness to capitulate to his wife's pleas foreshadow his fateful encounter with Delilah, recorded in chapter 16. Once again the cunning Philistines used a woman to coax important information from Samson. Delilah asked about the secret of Samson's success. Three times he

---

precisely the same tactics with equal success. Alas, he uses them not against the Gentile enemy but against his fellow nationals, the Ephraimites" (1982, 74*). Of course, Jephthah's battle with the Ephraimites foreshadows the civil war of chapters 20–21 only in a literary sense, for the events of chapters 20–21 chronologically precede Jephthah's career. See the discussion of the chronological background of the epilogue in the introduction to the commentary.

toyed with her before yielding (in each case he prefaced his lie with the word "if"—16:7, 11, 13). Exasperated by Delilah's constant nagging, he finally revealed the true secret of his strength: "*If* my head were shaved, my strength would leave me. I would become weak, and be just like all other men" (16:17). Samson's lack of foresight brought about his personal downfall. Once his hair was cut, the Lord departed from him, enabling the Philistines to subdue him. The Philistines then blinded him, forced him to grind grain, and publicly taunted him.

At this point the story has come full circle from the account of Jael and Sisera. On that earlier occasion Israel's ally Jael lured a *foreign* general to his death; now the Philistines' ally Delilah had lured the greatest of *Israel's* warriors to his demise. Samson was now in the role of Sisera, and Delilah in the role of Jael.[107] Ironically, the great warrior Samson had been reduced to the position of a woman. He was forced to perform the typically female task of grinding grain (Niditch 1990, 616–17), and, as in the case of Sisera, the suggestive language of sexual submission is used to describe his humiliation (Niditch 1990, 617; Bal 1988a, 26).

Samson's story does not end on an entirely sour note, however. God's sovereign power, revealed in response to Samson's desperate suicidal plea for revenge, brought destruction to the taunting Philistines. Their confidence in their god Dagon, coupled with their failure to notice Samson's returning hair, contributed to their defeat. Despite this divine victory, Samson's death in the rubble of the Philistine temple makes the decline in Israel's leadership complete. Deficient faith has given way to lack of wisdom. No more individual leaders will appear in the book, the final chapters of which describe a period of anarchy that surpasses the turmoil produced by the anti-judge Abimelech.

Suffering Women. Devoid of effective spiritual leadership, it is little wonder that the people of Israel, with their propensity to rebel, fell away from the Lord. Chapters 17–21 of Judges illustrate the depths of Israel's moral decline, describing the rise of an idolatrous cult and the

---

107. Both Webb (1987, 164) and Klein (1988, 137) note thematic and verbal links between the Jael-Sisera and Delilah-Samson accounts. Also see O'Connor 1986, 289. In addition to the more obvious parallels, the Philistine assembly that gathers to celebrate the captivity of Samson may correspond to Deborah and Barak in the earlier account. Just as Deborah and Barak celebrated Israel's victory over Sisera in song; so the Philistine lords and ladies praised Dagon for giving Samson into their hands (16:23–24).

outbreak of civil war. In chapters 19–21 Israelite women play a prominent role, tragically, like Jephthah's daughter, as innocent victims. In chapter 19 one reads of a Levite who was traveling with his concubine. He decided it would be safer to spend the night in Israelite territory than in the land of the foreign Jebusites. One of the men of Gibeah invited them in for a meal and lodging. However, a group of local thugs surrounded the house and demanded that the Levite be sent out so they could have sexual relations with him. (The parallel to the Sodom-Gomorrah account is obvious.) The Levite and his host sent the concubine out instead and the thugs raped her all night and left her to die.

Once news of this crime reached the rest of the tribes, they demanded that the Benjaminites hand over the perpetrators. When the Benjaminites refused, a civil war erupted and the tribe of Benjamin was almost wiped out. Its cities were destroyed; its women, children, and soldiers killed. Only six hundred men escaped to the hills. The other tribes took an oath that they would not allow any of their daughters to marry the Benjaminite survivors. Unfortunately this oath, like Jephthah's, brought suffering in its wake (Exum 1990, 430). Not wanting the tribe of Benjamin to disappear entirely, the Israelites devised a two-part plan to supply the remaining Benjaminites with wives. Because the town of Jabesh Gilead failed to send a contingent to the war, it was wiped out, with the exception of four hundred virgins who were given to the Benjaminite men. Two hundred more women were needed, so the remaining wifeless Benjaminites were told to go to Shiloh, hide in the trees, and kidnap some of the young women who came out to dance in the vineyard in celebration of the harvest. As Exum observes, the Israelites, though initially appalled by the treatment of the Levite's concubine, "repeat on a mass scale the crimes they found so abhorrent in the men of Gibeah."[108]

By the end of the book Israel's moral decline is complete. Women, who at the beginning of the book inspired Israelite men to great deeds and then played the role of national deliverers, were then raped, slaughtered (21:16), and kidnapped by their countrymen. Ironically the brutalization of Israelite women anticipated by Sisera's mother (5:28–30) is realized, not through a ruthless foreign conqueror, but through Israelite men.

Summary. The early chapters of Judges present an ideal of male leadership, especially through the portrait of Othniel. Unfortunately, later leaders, who were plagued by deficient faith (Barak, Gideon, Jephthah)

---

108. Exum 1990, 430–31. See also Lasine 1984, 49; and Trible 1984, 83–84.

and/or lack of wisdom (Gideon, Jephthah, Samson), failed to live up to this ideal.[109] By the end of Samson's story, Israel's greatest warrior was reduced to a helpless and vulnerable female role, much like the Canaanite general Sisera earlier in the book. By the end of the book, there are no leaders present. Instead, Israelite men war with each other and cause untold suffering for Israelite women.

The changing roles of the women vis-à-vis the male leaders contribute to this account of Israel's societal decline. In contrast to Acsah, who inspired mighty deeds, women were soon forced into other roles. Due to Barak's weak faith and Gideon's lack of wisdom, Deborah, Jael, and the unnamed woman in Thebez assume the role of warriors, demonstrating the same courage, cunning, and prowess as the earlier heroes Othniel, Ehud, and Shamgar. As the male leaders continued to lose effectiveness and then disappeared altogether, the highly valued and heroic women of the early chapters step aside for the brutalized victims of the later chapters. In contrast to Acsah, who received her father's rich blessing, Jephthah's daughter had to swallow the bitter pill of infertility and death served up by her father. Her painful experience foreshadowed the widespread oppression and bloodshed that stain the pages of the book's final chapters.

Anyone familiar with Hebrews 11 might be tempted to object that our appraisal of the judges is overly negative. After all, in Hebrews 11:32 the leaders Gideon, Barak, Samson, and Jephthah are listed, along with Samuel, David, and the prophets, as examples of those who accomplished great deeds through faith (see as well 1 Sam. 12:11). In the case of the judges, the narrator probably has in mind conquering kingdoms (cf. v. 33) and defeating foreign armies through mighty exploits in battle (cf. v. 34). Of course, each of the leaders listed did win significant victories over foreign enemies and each exhibited a degree of faith in doing so. The point of Hebrews 11 seems to be that God can accomplish great things through human instruments when faith is present, as illustrated by the experience of the judges and others. The narrator's use of the Old Testament text in this regard is neither strained nor improper.

---

109. Wong argues that one can detect a weakness of faith in Samson, as well (cf. 15:18). In fact, Samson's weakness comes *after* a God-given victory, in contrast to earlier judges, who expressed weakness of faith *prior* to victory (2006a, 163–65). Wong also proposes that one can detect an "increasing prominence" in "self-interest as motivation" for action as one moves from Gideon to Jephthah to Samson (165–76). This contributes to the theme of deteriorating leadership in the book's central section.

However, when one examines the book of Judges as a thematic whole, one finds that these leaders, though possessing a measure of faith that the omnipotent God used for his purpose, did not possess the degree of faith necessary to lead Israel competently and successfully. The leadership theme is not the point of Hebrews 11, but must be addressed when one views the careers of the judges in light of the assessment given by the narrator of Judges in the book's epilogue. So, when we evaluate these four judges as poor leaders who lacked the faith and wisdom necessary to lead Israel effectively, we do not intend to contradict what Hebrews 11:32–34 states. The difference between the negative assessment given in Judges and the positive one presented in Hebrews 11 is due to different perspectives and emphases. One will recall that this tension is present even within the book of Judges, where the prologue assesses the judges positively (cf. 2:16–18; 1 Sam. 12:11), in contrast to the stories in the book's central section and epilogue. (See our earlier remarks in this regard in the section "Literary Structure and Themes.")

Paving the Way for Hannah

The downward spiral of Judges reaches its lowest point in 1 Samuel 1. Barren Hannah was oppressed, not by a man, but by another woman. Though loved by her husband, she had to endure the taunts of a rival wife. Yet Hannah became a pivotal figure in Israel's story. God enabled her to give birth to a son who revived Israel's prophetic movement and paved the way for the arrival of God's chosen kings.

In addition to tracing a pattern of oppression that culminates in Hannah, the book of Judges sets the stage for her appearance in another important way. The anonymous mothers of Samson (Judges 13) and Micah (Judges 17) serve as foils for Hannah (1 Samuel 1). In fact there are structural links between the Samson story, the account of Micah and the Danites, and the birth of Samuel. In contrast to Samson's mother, whose miraculously conceived Nazirite son failed to understand his true role as the Lord's deliverer and never rose to the level of an effective leader, Hannah supernaturally gave birth to a son through whom the Lord restored effective leadership to Israel. While Samson began the deliverance of Israel (Judg. 13:5), Samuel and David, whom Samuel anointed as king, achieved a more complete and lasting victory over the enemies of Israel (1 Sam. 7:14; 17:1–58; 2 Sam. 5:17–25; 8:1). In contrast to Micah's mother, whose misguided actions and obsession with idols contributed to the Danites' unauthorized cult, Hannah's commitment to the Lord was the catalyst for the revival of genuine Yahweh worship through the spiritual leadership of her son Samuel.

As noted earlier, the three accounts even begin the same way:

Judges 13:2   וַיְהִי אִישׁ אֶחָד מִצָּרְעָה . . . וּשְׁמוֹ מָנוֹחַ
(literally) "Now there was a certain man from Zorah . . .
whose name was Manoah"

Judges 17:1   וַיְהִי־אִישׁ מֵהַר־אֶפְרָיִם וּשְׁמוֹ מִיכָיְהוּ
(literally) "Now there was a man from the hill country
of Ephraim whose name was Micaiah"

1 Samuel 1:1   וַיְהִי אִישׁ אֶחָד מִן־הָרָמָתַיִם . . . וּשְׁמוֹ אֶלְקָנָה
(literally) "Now there was a certain man from
Ramathaim whose name was Elkanah"

The formula "now there was a (certain) man from (geographical
name) . . . whose name was (personal name)" seems to be a stylized way
of introducing a new story. However, in Judges–1 Samuel this formula
appears only in these three passages and in 1 Samuel 9:1, where Saul's
family background is introduced.[110] This suggests that the introductory
formula is a linking device at the macrostructural or larger discourse
level.

Epilogue: Another Othniel Arrives
The birth of Samuel marked a significant turning point in Israel's history. Though the tragic death of Phinehas's wife (1 Sam. 4:19–20) carries on the theme of female suffering and oppression so characteristic
of Judges, the supernatural reversal of Hannah's situation signals
the dawning of a new era. Quality male leadership was about to be
restored. After the notice of Phinehas's wife's death, the next women
characters to appear in the story (omitting the young women [נְעָרוֹת]
who give Saul directions; 9:11–13) are the singers and dancers who celebrated the victories of Saul and David (18:6–7).[111] Shortly thereafter

---

110. On the parallels between Samson and Saul, see Brooks 1996, 19–25, as
well as Dragga 1987, 42–43, and Exum 1992, 16–44.
111. There may be an intentional contrast with Jephthah's daughter (Judg.
11:34) and the young women of Shiloh (21:21, 23), whose dancing was
quickly transformed into brutality. Trible discusses parallels and contrasts
between Judges 11:34 and Exodus 15:19–21/1 Samuel 18:6–7 (1984, 100–
1). She notes that Jephthah's daughter, unlike Miriam and the women of
1 Samuel 18:6–7, "comes alone and no words of a song appear on her lips."
She adds: "The difference accents the terrible irony of an otherwise typical
and joyful occasion." In addition to Trible's observations, one should also
note that, in contrast to Miriam and the women of 1 Samuel 18:5–6, other
women only join Jephthah's daughter in her lamentation (Judg. 11:38–40).

Saul's daughters Merab and Michal, like Acsah of old, were offered (in their respective turns; 18:17–21) to a conquering hero as a reward for bravery in battle (17:25). In David, the conqueror of Goliath, another Othniel had arrived—at least for a time.

NARRATIVE STRUCTURE OF JUDGES

In the commentary to follow I combine my translation of Judges with an analysis of the text's narrative structure. The outline distinguishes between the three main elements of a narrative: (1) mainline (*wayy-iqtol*) clauses, (2) offline clauses, and (3) quotations. Offline clauses can vary in form, including (a) disjunctive clauses (*waw* + non-verb, usually the subject + predicate, whether stated or implied); (b) *weqatal* clauses; (c) negated perfects; and (d) asyndetic perfects. All mainline and offline clauses in the narrative framework are classified. Clauses within quotations are not analyzed; quotations are simply set apart by italics.

In analyzing the clausal structure of the text, I utilize the following categories:

Mainline (wayyiqtol) Clauses

(1) Sequential / Consequential
Most mainline (*wayyiqtol*) clauses indicate sequential or consequential action. The latter involves logical as well as chronological sequence.

(2) Introductory
Often a *wayyiqtol* clause (especially one consisting of וַיְהִי and a temporal word or phrase) introduces an episode or scene by providing background for the story to follow.[112] Examples include: 1:1a, 14a; 6:25c; 7:9a; 8:33a; 9:42a; 11:4a, 39a; 15:1a; 16:4a; 17:1a, 7a; 19:1a; 19:1b; 21:4a. In 13:2a no temporal word appears but the indefinite וַיְהִי, "and there was," introduces the story proper.

(3) Initiatory
Frequently a *wayyiqtol* clause sets an episode or scene in motion. Sometimes such a clause follows an introductory וַיְהִי or disjunctive clause (1:1b; 6:25b, 33b; 7:9b; 8:33b; 9:42b, 51b; 11:39b; 13:3a; 15:1b; 16:4b; 17:2a, 8a; 18:2b, 27b; 19:1c, 11c; 21:4b), but this need not be the case (1:22a; 2:1a, 11a; 3:7, 12a; 4:1a; 6:1a, 11a, 22a; 7:1a; 8:13a, 18a;

---

112. On the introductory function of וַיְהִי temporal clauses, see Heller 2004, 433–34.

9:1a, 7a, 22a, 26a, 50a; 10:1a, 3a, 6a, 17a; 11:12a, 29a, 34a; 12:1a, 8, 11, 13; 13:1a; 14:1a, 5a, 7a, 10a; 16:1a; 20:1a, 18a). On occasion an initiatory *wayyiqtol* clause involves a chronological flashback (2:6a; 8:4a, 29a; 11:4b; 12:1a).

(4) Flashback
Sometimes the narrator interrupts the chronological sequence of events and uses a *wayyiqtol* clause to refer to a prior action that now becomes relevant. The flashback can initiate an episode or scene (2:6a; 8:4a; 11:4b; 12:1a), refer back to an action that preceded the episode or scene chronologically (cf. 2:23a; 3:16a; 11:1c; 17:5b?), or, more often than not, recall an event that occurred within the timeframe of the story being related (5:1a; 7:21a?; 8:29a; 9:42c; 11:30a?; 16:3a; 20:36b; 21:6a, 24a).

(5) Transitional
The collocation of וַיְהִי with a temporal clause can signal a transition within an episode or scene (cf. 16:16a). Sometimes the action described is sequential to what precedes but not as important as the action that follows (cf. 11:35a; 14:11a). As the temporal construction makes a transition, it can also give a circumstance of what follows (19:5a) or reiterate what has been described earlier (2:4a; 3:18a, 27a; 6:7; 7:15a; 11:5a). Occasionally וַיְהִי is followed by a mere temporal phrase that facilitates a transition (14:15a, 17b).

(6) Focusing
A *wayyiqtol* often has a focusing or specifying function. It can focus on a particular individual involved in the event just described, give a more detailed account of the event or an aspect of the event, or provide a specific example of a preceding statement. Examples include: 1:5a, 10c, 20a, 35a; 2:11b, 12c; 3:7b, 10ac; 6:2a, 5c, 38b, 40b; 7:13c, 20a, 20c, 21c; 8:33c; 9:25a, 28a; 10:6b; 11:6a, 30b; 12:9d; 13:20ab; 16:2e; 17:12a; 19:4c; 20:15, 35b, 36b; 21:10b, 12a, 23b.

(7) Resumptive
A *wayyiqtol* can serve a resumptive function. When used in this manner it follows a supplementary, focusing, or flashback statement (1:11a, 12a, 17a, 24a; 3:16c, 28a; 4:3a, 12a, 21h; 6:6b, 19e, 28a; 7:2a, 13a, 19c; 8:27a, 32a; 9:6a; 10:5a; 13:10a; 16:5a, 12f, 28a; 18:8a, 13a, 28c, 30a; 19:3c, 17a; 20:3b, 28a, 35a, 39a; 21:9a); such examples are labeled resumptive-(con)sequential. On a few occasions the resumptive *wayyiqtol* repeats a statement made prior to the embedded comment or

scene that interrupted the narrative (11:4b, 32a; 17:4a). These clauses are labeled resumptive-reiterative.

(8) Reiterative
In this case the *wayyiqtol* clause repeats a preceding or earlier statement, usually to emphasize or complement the preceding statement (2:12b, 13a, 13b, 14d; 16:16b; 21:24b), but sometimes to focus in more detail on an aspect of a situation or event (7:22a; 12:9d, 14b; 20:20b).

(9) Complementary
A *wayyiqtol* clause sometimes complements the preceding statement by giving the other side of the same coin or by describing an action that naturally or typically accompanies what precedes (2:10b, 12a, 12b; 3:7c; 4:5b, 21b; 6:34c; 7:20b, 21d; 8:17b; 9:27g, 27h; 10:6c, 16b, 17c; 11:1c, 2a; 17:12c; 19:4d, 25e; 20:21a, 25a, 26c–e, 30a, 31a, 35b; 21:24a).

(10) Supplemental
On occasion a *wayyiqtol* clause provides supplemental information of a consequential (1:17d; 11:39), qualifying (1:28a, 30c, 35b; 6:27c; 9:5c; 20:3c), explanatory (4:21g; 14:19f), or descriptive nature with וַיְהִי in 8:26a 10:4a; 12:9a, 14a; 16:30e.

(11) Summarizing or Concluding
A *wayyiqtol* clause occasionally makes a summarizing statement, often in relation to the preceding narrative (1:19a, 34a; 3:4, 30a, 31b; 4:23; 8:28a; 9:56; 11:33b; 12:6f; 20:44, 46), and/or can be used to conclude a narrative or scene, sometimes with a formulaic comment (3:11a, 30b; 5:31b; 8:27d; 8:28c; 9:57b; 15:20; 20:36a).

Disjunctive Clauses

(1) Introductory
Disjunctive clauses sometimes mark the beginning of a new scene or episode; they typically provide background information for the story that follows (1:9a; 4:4, 5a; 6:19a, 33a; 7:24a, 25e; 8:10a; 9:51a; 16:23a; 17:7b, 7c; 18:1b, 27a; 19:1c, 11a, 11b, 22a; 21:1a, 15a.) In at least one instance a disjunctive clause introduces a more focused or detailed account of what has just been described (9:44a).[113]

---

113. Heller, in his discourse analysis of Genesis 37–47, 2 Samuel 9–20, and 1 Kings 1–2 discovered that introductory independent non-*wayyiqtol* clauses use *qatal* as predicate (2004, 434–35.) Most of the examples in Judges also

(2) Supplemental
Disjunctive clauses very frequently give supplemental or parenthetical information that is embedded within a story (1:10b, 11b, 16a, 23b, 26d, 33c, 36; 3:1–3, 16b, 17b, 31a; 4:2b, 2c, 11a; 6:2b, 5a, 19c; 7:1a, 1c, 12a, 19b; 8:10b, 26b, 30a, 31a; 10:1b, 4b, 4c; 11:1a, 1b, 34c, 40; 12:9b, 9c; 13:2b, 2c, 9d; 14:4a, 4b, 6d, 9f; 15:19e; 16:4c, 12e, 20f, 27a; 17:1b, 5a; 18:7d, 7e, 12c, 12d, 28a, 28b, 29b, 30b; 19:3b, 10d, 10e, 16b–d; 20:16a, 16b, 17b, 27b, 28a, 34c, 38).[114]

(3) Circumstantial
Disjunctive clauses sometimes describe the circumstances attending to an action, such as time or manner (1:22b; 3:26b; 4:1b, 14d, 21f, 22h; 6:11c; 8:11c; 13:9c, 20c; 14:6c; 16:9a; 18:18a; 19:27e; 20:42c).[115]

(4) Synchronic
On a few occasions disjunctive clauses are juxtaposed to indicate synchronic actions (3:20ab, 24ab; 13:19cd; 15:14ab; 18:3ab, 22ab; 20:33a, 33c).[116]

(5) Complementary or Specifying
At times a disjunctive clause makes a statement that complements what precedes by giving the other side of the coin, as it were, or by looking at an action or situation from a related, but different angle (2:17b; 3:6b; 6:19d, 28c, 28d; 7:20d, 25c; 8:10c, 17a; 9:44c, 45c, 57a; 11:34d; 12:9c; 17:6b; 18:27d; 21:25b). Occasionally the disjunctive clause gives more specific information that has an emphatic function (6:5b; 7:12b; 16:27b, 27c).

---

follow this pattern, though there appear to be a few exceptions where the clause has a participial predicate (4:4a) or is verbless (8:10a).

114. Heller classifies "comment clauses" as "inner-paragraph" and "extra-paragraph" (2004, 441–56). Such clauses have a variety of specific forms, most of which are attested in Judges. For a study of "parenthetical clauses" in biblical Hebrew, see as well Zewi 2007, 31–101.

115. Heller classifes this type of clause as an "inner-paragraph" comment (see the previous note). This is certainly an appropriate way to analyze it structurally. Our classifications "supplemental" and "circumstantial" seek to make a more subtle functional distinction within the general inner-paragraph offline category.

116. Note that in 20:33b a *wayyiqtol* clause (sequential to v. 33a) appears between the disjunctive clauses.

(6) Contrastive
Sometimes a disjunctive clause describes an action that contrasts with
what precedes or qualifies it in some way (1:21a, 25c, 28c; 2:17a; 3:19a;
6:40c; 7:3c, 6b, 8b; 20:42b).

(7) Dramatic
A disjunctive clause, especially when introduced by וְהִנֵּה, can have a
dramatic function, inviting the audience to enter into the story as a
participant or eyewitness observer. This device can signal a shift in
focus, sometimes involving a flashback (cf. 20:39–48). For examples
of the dramatic use of the disjunctive clause without וְהִנֵּה see 3:26a;
4:16a, 17a; 6:34a; 9:45a; 20:37a, 39b, 40a, 41a, 48a. Examples with וְהִנֵּה
include 3:24d, 25b, 25e; 4:22a, 22g; 6:28b; 7:13b; 9:43e; 11:34b; 14:5c,
8c; 19:16a, 22b, 27d; 20:40c; 21:8c, 9b.

(8) Summarizing
Disjunctive clauses sometimes provide a summary statement (1:29a,
30a, 31, 33a; 2:15a; 3:5; 7:8c; 8:12d).

(9) Concluding
Disjunctive clauses can be used to signal closure for an episode or scene
(1:8d; 2:10a; 6:21e, 24c, 40c; 7:8d; 8:3b, 12d; 11:28, 29d, 39d; 16:31d;
17:6a; 18:1a; 19:15d; 20:17a, 48c; 21:25a).[117]

Negated sentences
Negated sentences, typically with the structure וְלֹא followed by the perfect, sometimes interrupt the narrative mainline. Such clauses have a
variety of functions:
   (1) Contrastive/qualifying (1:19c; 8:20c; 11:28; 15:1e; 19:10a, 25a;
20:13b; 21:14c)
   (2) Complementary/reiterative (2:14e, 17c, 23b; 3:28e, 29b; 4:16c;
6:4c; 8:28b, 34; 10:6d; 12:6c; 13:2d)
   (3) Summarizing (1:27a; 2:19c; 8:35; 16:9e)
   (4) Supplemental (13:21a; 14:6d, 9f)

Weqatal Clauses
Within the narrative framework one sometimes finds a *weqatal* (*waw*
+ perfect) clause where one might expect a *wayyiqtol*. These clauses

---

117. According to Heller's research, terminal markers can take a variety of
     forms (2004, 435–39.) Most of the examples in Judges have a *qatal* verbal
     form as predicate.

are usually characterizing (or customary-procedural) (2:18a, 18b, 19a, 19b; 6:3a, 3b; 12:5b; 19:30a, 30b), but the pattern appears to describe a complementary action in 3:23c.

Asyndetic (i.e., no conjunction) Perfect
The asyndetic perfect is used in the narrative frame to highlight an action and lend rhetorical vividness and excitement to the telling of the story (18:17b, 17c; 20:31b, 43a–c). The style is quasi-poetic (cf. 5:26–27).

MODERN PROCLAMATION OF JUDGES

Building a Bridge: Overview of a Proposed Method
Can an ancient book like Judges have any relevance for a modern audience? For those of us who believe the Scriptures are the inspired word of God, Paul's statement to Timothy provides the answer to this question: "Every scripture is inspired by God and useful for teaching, for reproof, for correction, and for training in righteousness" (2 Tim. 3:16, NET). However, affirming the relevance of Scripture is easy to do; showing how Scripture is relevant is a more challenging task. An imposing temporal, geographical, and cultural chasm separates Judges from our modern world. Before we can discuss the book's relevance for us, we must first build a bridge across the chasm.

Homileticians attempt to build this bridge in various ways. Some simply use the stories of the Old Testament for illustrative purposes or reduce them to moralizing lessons. While these approaches may have their place, they fail to deal with Judges as a literary-theological entity that exhibits specific themes and expresses an overall purpose. As such, they fail to apply Judges in the form in which God has given the book to us. Instead they merely use Judges to illustrate truths and principles taught elsewhere in the Bible.

To determine how Judges, as a book, is relevant for us, we must take a different approach, one that does justice to the book's own agenda. This approach involves three steps: (1) thematic analysis, (2) theological analysis, and (3) contemporary application.

Step one involves moving back into the world of the text and attempting to answer the question: What did this text mean in its ancient Israelite context? This begins with a close exegetical-literary reading of the text that surfaces the thematic emphases of each major literary unit. Such analysis will yield an exegetical idea for each unit that succinctly captures the message of that unit in its cultural-historical context.

In step two we move outside the boundaries of the specific text being studied and attempt to answer the following questions: What theological principles emerge from, or are illustrated by, a thematic analysis of the text? How, if at all, are these principles nuanced in their larger canonical context? Answers to these questions will enable us to develop a theological idea for each literary unit. These theological ideas express the enduring principles or truths that are rooted in the text and are relevant for a modern audience.

The third step is to return to our modern world, where we develop homiletical trajectories from the theological idea of the passage. These trajectories begin from homiletical vantage points that reflect the overall message of the book of Judges (see a fuller discussion below). Following the trajectories enables us to produce one or more preaching ideas for each literary unit.

If this process is done with skill and savvy, the audience will be able to see how the ancient text yields the principles and how they, the audience, both individually and corporately, should and can appropriate the principles in their own experience and in the life of the Church.

Homiletical Vantage Points: Wedding the Book's Purpose with Modern Application

To be faithful to the message of the book, a homiletical approach should be sensitive to each of the book's major themes as they emerge and are developed. As noted and discussed earlier, the book of Judges has at least three major purposes:

(1) The book is in part a defense of God's character. Israel's defeats were due to sin, not some deficiency on God's part. Yet despite Israel's disobedience and unfaithfulness, the Lord remained faithful to them. He disciplined them, but then provided leaders to deliver them and to restore peace and stability to the land. Though Israel was intent upon worshiping foreign gods, the Lord proved his superiority to all rivals, demonstrating that he alone was worthy of his people's devotion.

(2) The book also demonstrates how Israel's assimilation to Canaanite religion and culture through syncretism and intermarriage threatened the nation's very identity. This in turn fostered a tribal mentality that threatened national unity and resulted in internal conflict and civil war.

(3) The book also shows how this Canaanized culture produced deficient leaders, who failed to live up to the ideal established by Joshua,

Caleb, Othniel and Ehud. Their lack of adequate faith and/or wisdom made them unable to lead Israel out of its steady descent into chaos. The epilogue highlights this leadership void by illustrating how Israel followed its own moral code during this period. By reminding us there was no king, it keeps before us the Deuteronomic kingship ideal and prepares us for the realization of that ideal in 1 Samuel.

These themes provide us with homiletical angles or vantage points from which we can consider the text's relevance for us. They allow us to build a bridge from the theological idea to the preaching idea and to root the sermon in the intention of the original author. In the commentary to follow, after our exegetical and theological analyses of each major literary unit, we will consider what the text teaches and illustrates about (1) God's relationship to his covenant community, (2) the effects of disobedience and compromise upon God's covenant community, and (3) the need for competent, godly leadership in the covenant community. Starting from these vantage points, we can develop homiletical trajectories that begin at the theological idea and lead to one or more preaching ideas for each literary unit.

Preaching Judges

In the commentary to follow, we apply the method outlined above to each of the major literary units in Judges. This includes a summary of the literary unit's thematic emphases accompanied by an exegetical idea, as well as an examination of the text's theological principles accompanied by a theological idea that connects the principles to the text's broader canonical setting. Next we develop homiletical trajectories—various homiletical paths one may take in the exposition of the book—leading to one or more preaching ideas. When preaching any given section of the book, one may integrate the homiletical trajectories into one all-encompassing preaching idea or focus on just one trajectory in any given sermon. Assuming that all three homiletical angles are represented in any given passage (this is not always the case, however) one may preach as many as three sermons on that text, following a different trajectory in each one. However, for those wishing to preach just one sermon on each literary unit, we have included a preaching idea for each section that attempts to capture the main point of that unit. Obviously, with longer literary units, such as the Gideon story, it is more difficult to formulate a succinct preaching idea for the unit.

For the convenience of the would-be expositor, we include here a proposed preaching series on the book of Judges that provides an overview of the homiletical process discussed in more detail in the commentary to follow. In each case we provide an exegetical idea, a theological idea, a discussion of homiletical trajectories in light of the book's major themes, and a primary preaching idea. We include here only the primary preaching idea, but within the commentary, several other preaching strategies for each major literary unit are included.

Sermon One: Settling Down with the Enemy (Judges 1:1–2:5)

Exegetical idea: *Despite their faithful God's powerful presence, Israel failed to take the promised land because they disobeyed God's command to exterminate the Canaanites and embraced Canaanite culture and religion.*

Theological idea: *God's promises are reliable, but they may be only partially realized and placed in jeopardy when his people disobey his commands and compromise their special position.*[118]

Homiletical Trajectories

(1) The exposition of this passage should highlight God's faithfulness. Because of his character, he is reliable (Heb. 11:11; 1 John 1:9). His people can depend on him to fulfill his promises. At the homiletical-applicational level one must remind a modern audience of God's specific promises to those within his new covenant community.

(2) The exposition of this passage should also emphasize human responsibility before God. God has made promises and is faithful to his people. But his people must do their part as well. The text illustrates the dangers of disobedience and compromise. The Hebrews passages cited above are relevant in this regard. It is beyond the scope of our discussion to enter into the debate over the interpretation of the Hebrews warning passages. Suffice it to say that one's theological framework (Reformed, Arminian, or somewhere in between) will determine how one nuances this principle for one's modern audience.

The leadership theme is present in this passage, but it is not as prominent as the other major themes developed above. Judah takes a leadership role, but their success is compromised (see 1:19). Caleb

---

118. The main idea of the passage is perhaps most clearly illustrated in (1) Judges 1:19, where Judah fails to conquer the enemy, despite God's presence with them, and (2) Judges 2:3, where God reminds the people that their disobedience will jeopardize his plan for them.

and Othniel emerge as paradigmatic figures, but they function more as foils for the failed leadership that subsequently appears. There is not enough material in the first part of the prologue to develop this homiletical trajectory yet.

Primary preaching idea: *As the new covenant community of our faithful God and as recipients of his reliable promises, we must be obedient and preserve our identity as his people in order to experience the full realization of his promises.*

Sermon Two: Worshiping the Enemy's Gods (Judges 2:6–3:6)

Exegetical idea: *God severely disciplined his idolatrous people and then compassionately confronted them, challenging them to demonstrate their loyalty to him.*

Theological idea: *When God's people are unfaithful, his anger is aroused, prompting him to discipline them and to take drastic measures to bring reconciliation. Yet God is patient and shows compassion to his sinful people, responding to their cries and even giving them an opportunity to demonstrate renewed allegiance to him.*

Homiletical Trajectories

(1) Once again (cf. 1:1–2:5) the exposition of this passage should highlight God's faithfulness to his covenant community. Because God is committed to his people, their sin angers him and prompts him to confront and discipline them (cf. Heb. 12:4–11). God refuses to have a dysfunctional relationship with his people and will do what is necessary to heal the rift. At the same time God is patient and compassionate (see Judg. 2:18). He responds to his people's sin-inflicted suffering and even gives them an opportunity to renew and prove their allegiance to him when they do not deserve a "second chance."

(2) The passage also reminds us that God tolerates no rivals; he expects our full devotion and loyalty. He views unfaithfulness as spiritual adultery (cf. Judg. 2:17). If we violate the relationship, God's anger is aroused and his discipline can bring humiliating defeat that robs us of the security and blessings that could be ours.

In developing this theme for a contemporary audience, one must address the issue of what constitutes idolatry. Most of those in a modern audience, at least in the context of the western church, will not be involved in idolatry as described in Judges 2. However, the New Testament, while denouncing literal idolatry, also gives the concept an ethical dimension. Paul calls greed "idolatry" (Col. 3:5).[119] According to James 4:4, "friendship with the world" constitutes spiritual adultery (a metaphor for idolatry in the Hebrew Bible). In this context, James associates friendship with the world with greed and the pride, envy, and hostility it invariably produces (see vv. 1–3, 5–6).

(3) The leadership theme is present in this passage (see Judg. 2:16), but, as in the first part of the prologue, it is not as prominent as the other major themes developed above. Preparing us for the accounts of the individual judges, the text simply makes the point that God provided leaders as his instruments of deliverance. There is not enough material here to develop this homiletical trajectory at this point.

Preaching idea: *We must remain loyal to our faithful God, realizing that he tolerates no rivals. When we fail and experience his discipline, we should respond positively to his compassionate discipline with the confidence that renewed loyalty will bring restoration.*

Sermon Three: Setting a Standard for Leadership (Judges 3:7–31)

Exegetical idea: *God disciplined his sinful people, but, when they cried for help, he rescued them by raising up effective deliverers—empowering one with his spirit, rewarding another's courageous faith, and providentially using the exploits of an unlikely foreigner.*

Theological idea: *The Lord disciplines his rebellious people, but he is predisposed to save them when they cry for help. God sometimes accomplishes deliverance through human instruments, intervening in a variety of ways and demonstrating that he is superior to his enemies and deserving of his people's devotion.*

Homiletical Trajectories

(1) The accounts in chapter three, like each of the stories in the book's central section, support the theme of God's faithfulness, highlighted in the prologue (see our discussion of the homiletical trajectories for 2:6–3:6). They also demonstrate God's absolute superiority to the enemies

---

119. For a brief, but insightful, treatment of how greed constitutes idolatry, see Younger 2002, 95–96.

of his people. Whether he intervenes directly through his spirit or operates providentially, he can defeat his enemies. He often accomplishes his purposes through human instruments, sometimes in surprising and unexpected ways.

(2) Like the prologue, these accounts also remind us that God expects his people's full devotion. Unfaithfulness arouses God's anger. As objects of divine anger and discipline, his people lose the security and blessing that could be theirs. The Ehud story is particularly instructive in this regard. As one reads the story, the Moabites come across as overfed, brutish dolts who are easily victimized by Ehud's cunning and daring. Yet to read the story strictly as nationalistic humor misses the point. After all, the Moabites subjugated Israel for eighteen long years. How could that be? The text's answer is sobering. God's people can experience such humiliation when they are unfaithful to him. The enemy is merely an instrument of divine discipline, easily vanquished by God's power. Israel should never have had to suffer such humiliation. Their sin, not Moab, was the real enemy. When God's people sin, they forfeit divine blessing and become vulnerable to the enemy.

(3) As we move into the accounts of the individual judges, the leadership theme becomes more prominent, allowing us to develop the third of our homiletical trajectories. Set in their larger canonical context, these stories make an important contribution to Israel's understanding of leadership. Joshua and Caleb were models of the ideal Israelite leader; they trusted God to fulfill his promises. They provide a paradigm of leadership and illustrate what great things God can accomplish for his people through leaders who rely on him. Othniel is a paradigmatic character who, like Joshua and Caleb, becomes a foil for the failed leaders described in subsequent chapters. Ehud's story is particularly instructive, for it shows that God need not directly intervene to win the victory. Armed with a dagger, a plan, and his faith, Ehud seized the moment afforded him by divine providence. The task was not without its obstacles; some might even call his plan foolhardy. But Ehud exhibited foresight (his plan took into account contingencies) and daring, for he was undoubtedly conscious of God's ability to give him success (see 3:28).

Primary preaching ideas: *(1) Though God may allow us to suffer the humiliating consequences of our sin, he is willing to deliver us and is able to do so in ways that demonstrate his power and his right to our loyalty and worship. (2) Confident that our faithful God seeks what is* *best for his covenant community and is superior to all opposition, we should exhibit courageous faith as we seek to advance the cause of God's kingdom.*

Sermon Four: A Hesitant General and a Heroic Woman (Judges 4–5)

Exegetical idea: *Responding to his sinful people's pain, the Lord commissioned Barak to deliver his people from the Canaanite oppression he had brought upon them as discipline for their sin. Despite Barak's hesitant response, the Lord gave Israel a great victory, using the forces of nature and an unlikely human instrument to demonstrate his royal power and superiority to the Canaanites and their god Baal.*

Theological idea: *When humans are weak and hesitant, God can still accomplish his purposes, even through unlikely instruments, for he alone is the mighty king who is compassionate toward his people and worthy of their devotion.*

Homiletical Trajectories

(1) God is the compassionate, incomparable king (cf. 1 Tim. 1:17; 6:15) who intervenes on behalf of his people and defeats their enemies. In winning victories he may intervene in power (as he did in the storm) or use unlikely instruments (such as a woman armed only with a tent peg and hammer). Because he alone is the king, God's people must look to him as their sole source of security. Of course, in the context of the New Testament, God does not guarantee physical protection in the here-and-now, but he does promise that nothing, not even physical death, can separate us from his love in Christ Jesus (Rom. 8:31–39).

(2) As in the story of Ehud, Israel's sin brings humiliation and makes the covenant community vulnerable. A related theme emerges in chapter 5. Israel is no longer united; some tribes fail to rally to the aid of their brothers in their time of need.[120] Apparently Israel's assimilation to Canaanite culture eroded the tribes' sense of uniqueness. In the same way, if the Church becomes like the world, its sense of uniqueness will be weakened, as will the bond that unites Christians together.

---

120. Wong (2007b) argues that the poem is primarily "a polemic against Israelite non-participation in military campaigns against external enemies" (p. 20), not a victory song.

(3) The leadership ideal established in the earlier stories becomes tainted in this account. God wins the victory through Barak, but Barak's hesitancy is disturbing and is a portent of things to come. Ineffective leaders lack adequate faith and need crutches. They forfeit the full success that could be theirs. Yet God is not limited by such failure; he accomplishes his purposes through unlikely, seemingly powerless instruments, who act with what assets they have, however limited they may seem.

Primary preaching idea: *We need not hesitate to carry out God's purposes, for he is the great king who is capable of defeating his enemies, through even the most unlikely of instruments, and is worthy of our full devotion.*

Sermon Five: The Lord Wins Another Victory through a Hesitant Hero (Judges 6:1–8:32)

Exegetical idea: *Israel's persistence in sin created a climate of spiritual blindness and insensitivity, but God once more showed compassion to his people and accomplished a great victory through hesitant Gideon. The Lord patiently developed Gideon's faith. However, God's purposes were compromised when Gideon lost focus of his mission, made naïve and unwise leadership decisions, and allowed his lifestyle to contradict a theologically correct message.*

Theological idea: *Persistence in sin creates a climate of spiritual blindness and insensitivity, but during such times God continues to show compassion to his people and can accomplish great things through unlikely instruments. In such dark times the Lord can patiently develop hesitant people into heroes of faith. However, God's purposes can be compromised when his chosen instruments lose focus of their mission, make naïve and unwise leadership decisions, and allow their lifestyle to contradict a theologically correct message.*

Homiletical Trajectories

(1) God is the compassionate king. Even when his people continue to drift from him, he remains active in their experience and seeks to win back their allegiance. He shows up their false gods for what they really are and demonstrates his ability to protect his people. He is superior to all other so-called gods and is deserving of his people's undivided loyalty and worship.

(2) When the covenant community becomes assimilated to the surrounding pagan culture, it can develop an irrational attachment to false gods and fail to see God's hand at work. When God acts in the world, the covenant community is apt to bestow honor on God's human instruments rather than the One who is truly worthy of their praise. As the community becomes more pagan in its outlook, it loses its sense of unity and common purpose. Petty self-interest and pride can threaten to tear the community apart.

(3) Even in less than ideal conditions God chooses to accomplish his purposes through human instruments. Potential leaders raised in a pagan environment are susceptible to cynicism and likely to possess deficient faith. Yet God is willing to work with such people and mold them into effective instruments through whom he accomplishes great things. However, such individuals may be prone to put personal honor first and to make unwise decisions that foster paganism and threaten the community's unity (see the sequel to Gideon's story in 8:33–10:5).

Primary preaching idea: *Even in times of spiritual darkness, we should realize that God is accomplishing his purposes, often through hesitant, weak people. We should be willing to carry out God's purposes, trusting him to develop our faith in the process. When we achieve God-given success, however, we must be careful not to undermine God's work by losing focus, making unwise decisions, or acting inconsistently with our profession of faith.*

Sermon Six: Seeds of Discord Bring a Harvest of Chaos (Judges 8:33–10:5)

Exegetical idea: *When unwise and inconsistent Gideon planted the seeds of discord, chaos resulted as his son, the power-hungry megalomaniac Abimelech, tried to become Israel's king. He and the people who supported him brought conflict and violence to the covenant community, but God punished the perpetrators and restored a semblance of order to the land. Unfortunately, Gideon's bad example of acting in a kinglike manner was perpetuated by Jair.*

Theological idea: *When unwise and inconsistent leaders plant the seeds of discord, chaos can be the result as power-hungry megalomaniacs move into the leadership void. Such leaders and the people who find them attractive can bring misery to God's people, but God is just and will punish those who abuse others and spread strife through the* *covenant community. Even so, the negative example of an unwise leader often lives on in his successors.*

Homiletical Trajectories
The Abimelech story is actually part of one large literary unit (6:1–10:5); it is the sequel to Gideon's story. Since it describes events that occurred after Gideon's death, it may be treated separately for homiletical purposes. Nevertheless, one should recognize its relationship to what precedes. The story of Abimelech, as well as the brief notice about Jair, illustrate how unwise leadership decisions can have destructive long-range consequences for the covenant community.

(1) The Lord is the ultimate King of his people and will not allow power-hungry imposters or false gods to usurp his position. He faithfully fulfills his royal responsibility of dispensing justice. Acting both directly and providentially, he brings down those who commit murderous deeds and threaten to destroy the covenant community.

(2) When the covenant community becomes paganized, it looks to the wrong kind of people to lead it and ends up being torn by dissension.

(3) Power-hungry opportunists threaten to destroy the covenant community. They inevitably elevate themselves, rather than God. But God opposes such individuals and those who follow them (cf. 3 John 9–11).

Primary preaching idea: *When we embrace the attitude of the pagan culture in which we live, power-hungry opportunists sometimes seize leadership and spread conflict, but God opposes such people and will hold them accountable for their abusive, self-serving behavior.*

Sermon Seven: Triumph Turns to Tragedy (Judges 10:6–12:15)

Exegetical idea: *Persistent ingratitude alienated God from his people. God was predisposed to show compassion to his people, but he brought them relief only when they radically repudiated their sin. Even when God intervened, the contaminating effects of paganism were still evident in the community and in Jephthah. Jephthah's deficient faith diluted his victory and Ephraim's pride, coupled with Jephthah's offended honor, led to civil war.*

Theological idea: *Persistent ingratitude can alienate God from his people. God is predisposed to show compassion to his people, but* *sometimes he will bring them relief only when they radically repudiate their sin. Even when God intervenes, the contaminating effects of paganism are sometimes still evident in the community and its leaders. Deficient leaders can dilute God's blessing and pride can lead to conflict within the covenant community.*

Homiletical Trajectories

(1) This story, like those that precede it, illustrates God's commitment to his people. As usual, he confronts their sin by implementing disciplinary measures. He is willing to show compassion, but we should not assume that relief comes if we simply push the right buttons and say we are sorry for our misdeeds. Persistent sin must be confronted in a genuine, sometimes even radical, manner. This involves recognizing that the Lord alone is the source of salvation. Genuine repentance in turn opens the door to God's compassion, which prompts him to intervene.

(2) Like earlier stories, this account also illustrates how assimilation to the surrounding pagan culture results in the covenant community losing its sense of unity and common purpose. Petty self-interest and pride can tear the community apart.

(3) As the covenant community becomes more like the pagan world around it, the leaders who emerge in the community may display some frightening pagan traits. God can use such flawed leaders to accomplish his purposes, but their deficient faith may turn triumph into tragedy and their deficient wisdom may prove inadequate to promote and sustain unity within the community.

Primary preaching idea: *Persistent ingratitude can so alienate us from God that he will bring relief only when we radically repudiate our sin. Even then, the contaminating effects of our pagan culture are sometimes still evident in our community and its leaders. Deficient leaders can dilute God's blessing and pride can lead to conflict within the community.*

Sermon Eight: Lion Killer with a Sweet Tooth (Judges 13–16)

Exegetical idea: *God was at work among his people, even when they were insensitive to his presence. He accomplished his purpose through unwise Samson, though Samson failed to understand his role as God's deliverer and was motivated by personal gratification and vengeance,* *not some sense of a higher calling. His failure to understand his role in God's plan led to tragic personal failure and pain, and kept him from enjoying the benefits of God's mighty deeds.*

Theological idea: *God is always at work among his people, even when they are insensitive to his presence. He can even accomplish his purposes through unwise instruments who fail to understand their role as his servants and are primarily motivated by personal gratification. However, a failure to understand one's role in God's plan can lead to tragic personal failure and pain, and keep one from enjoying the benefits of God's mighty deeds.*

Homiletical Trajectories

(1) God is always at work accomplishing his purposes, even when his people are apathetic and clueless. In so doing, he demonstrates his sovereignty, bringing triumph out of tragedy. When the story of Samson is viewed from this perspective, it may be entitled, "A Sovereign God Can Win with His Hands Tied Behind His Back."

(2) Persistence in sin and assimilation to the surrounding pagan culture can make God's people insensitive to his purposes for them. Unfortunately, a clueless community fails to experience, appreciate, and enjoy the benefits of God's work in their midst. Subsequent generations, who inherit the story, are the primary beneficiaries.

(3) Even when a leader is used mightily by God, his life can end up in personal tragedy if he makes personal gratification his priority and never understands his role in God's plan. Samson's miraculous conception seemed to foreshadow a great career, but his failure to understand his divinely ordained destiny seriously handicapped him from the start. When we are ignorant of God's larger purposes, we can miss the significance of his work in our lives and give priority to personal gratification. A preoccupation with satisfying our physical appetites, especially when coupled with an unclear vision of our spiritual destiny, can jeopardize our status as God's servants and lead to tragic failure and humiliation.

Primary preaching idea: *We should be encouraged to know that God is always at work among his people and can accomplish his purposes in far less than ideal circumstances. Yet when we fail to understand our role in God's plan, we can experience personal failure and pain and miss enjoying the benefits of God's mighty deeds.*

Sermon Nine: Renegade Religion (Judges 17–18)

Exegetical idea: *As Israel persisted in paganism and quality spiritual leadership was absent, spiritual confusion and chaos overtook the covenant community as a corrupt and superficial form of religion replaced genuine worship.*

Theological idea: *When God's people persist in paganism and quality spiritual leadership is absent, spiritual confusion and chaos can overtake the covenant community as a corrupt and superficial form of religion replaces genuine worship.*

Homiletical Trajectories

(1) God is present in this story in name only. His absence from the narrative *per se* is striking. Though we know from the book's prologue and stories that God was active throughout the Judges period, his absence here reminds us that his rebellious people forfeit the blessing of God's presence in their experience.

(2) This story illustrates how corrupt the covenant community can become when they embrace a pagan worldview. Selfishness, greed, intimidation, and violence become the order of the day. A renegade, pagan form of religion emerged in Israel at this time. Renegade, paganized religion is characterized by:
  (a) a view of God that is pagan to the core (17:1–6). (Micah's mother devalued ethics, the core of genuine worship of the Lord, and tried to manipulate God for her own benefit.)
  (b) a greedy spirit that tries to manipulate God for material benefits (17:7–18:1a). (Micah and the Levite are greed personified. They used their religion for financial gain.)
  (c) a self-centered attitude that uses power to further its own interests (18:1b–31). (The Danites, while desiring God's stamp of approval on their self-serving efforts, rejected God's purposes and ethical standards, and resorted to violent methods that had no place for the rights of others.)

(3) The story also reminds us of the importance of godly leadership for the covenant community. The narrator's comment in 17:6 (cf. also 18:1; 19:1) informs us that the paganism evident in the story could have been curtailed or prevented if there had been a leader who promoted covenant fidelity by word and example.

Primary preaching idea: *When we persist in the paganism of our culture and quality spiritual leadership is absent, a renegade form of religion can replace genuine worship, bring spiritual confusion and chaos with it, and prevent us from experiencing the blessing of God's presence.*

Sermon Ten: Anarchy Engulfs a Nation (Judges 19–21)

Exegetical idea: *As God's people persisted in paganism and had no competent, godly leaders to confront them with God's standards, a moral cancer invaded the covenant community, making it capable of the vilest sins. Uncontrollable lust and cruel disregard for the vulnerable and helpless characterized a community contaminated by moral pluralism, where individuals and communities lived by their own self-serving "standards" of right and wrong, rather than by God's covenant principles. God's people desperately needed godly leadership.*

Theological idea: *When God's people persist in paganism and have no competent, godly leaders to confront them with God's standards, a moral cancer can invade the covenant community, making it capable of the vilest sins. Uncontrollable lust and cruel disregard for the vulnerable and helpless are signs of a community contaminated by moral pluralism, where individuals and communities live by their own self-serving "standards" of right and wrong, rather than by God's covenant principles. God's people desperately need godly leadership.*

Homiletical Trajectories

(1) As the just king of Israel, God works to preserve order in the midst of chaos. He punishes evildoers and those who support them. Yet ideally he purposes to create a community that promotes justice modeled by an ideal leader. (See point three below.)

(2) When the covenant community becomes like the surrounding pagan world, it can sink to unprecedented moral depths. People become lustful and cruel, and will give personal "honor" and pride higher priority than morality and ethics. The community becomes prone to strife that inflicts pain and suffering on innocent and helpless people throughout the community.

(3) The covenant community needs godly leadership because sinful people are prone to rebel. It is here that Judges yields a christotelic theme that should be the capstone of the exposition of the book. The

epilogue to Judges anticipates the rise of the Davidic monarchy, but the historical kings ultimately failed. God's ideal leader is Jesus the Messiah, who will establish his kingdom on earth. He is currently ruling over his Church, whose leaders and members are to model the character of their Lord and King.[121]

Primary preaching idea: *We must reject the paganism of the surrounding culture and seek competent, godly leaders to confront us with God's standards. Otherwise lust and cruelty can contaminate the new covenant community as people live by their own self-serving "standards" of right and wrong, rather than by God's covenant principles.*

MAJOR CONTEMPORARY COMMENTARIES ON JUDGES
This section offers a brief evaluation of several contemporary commentaries on Judges, dividing them into two categories: (1) technical, semitechnical and (2) expositional.

Technical, Semitechnical

Highly Recommended:
Block, Daniel. 1999. *Judges, Ruth*. NAC. Nashville: Broadman & Holman. 765 pp. (The Judges portion is 566 pages.)
   Approach: The author's approach is exegetical, literary, and theological. The NAC series is aimed at "the minister or Bible student who wants to understand and expound the Scriptures."
   Format: Each major literary unit includes the NIV translation, brief introductory remarks, exegetical comments arranged in verse-by-verse format, and concluding observations on "theological and practical implications." More technical issues are discussed in the footnotes. Hebrew is confined to the footnotes; transliteration is used in the body of the text.
   Usability: The commentary's format is user-friendly and its exegetical and theological insights, presented from an evangelical perspective, are helpful in sermon preparation. Its thorough, verse-by-verse treatment of the text makes it a significant exegetical reference work.

Butler, Trent. 2009. *Judges*. WBC. Nashville: Thomas Nelson. 537 pp.
   Approach: The author's approach is primarily exegetical. The

---

121. I intend this statement to be understood within the framework of so-called progressive dispensationalism, which promotes an "already-not yet" hermeneutic with regard to God's kingdom.

WBC series is aimed at a broad spectrum of readers, including "the fledgling student, the working minister, and colleagues in the guild of professional scholars and teachers." Depending on the extent of their language training, some may find the exegetical comments overly technical in places.

Format: Each major literary unit includes the author's translation accompanied by technical notes, a discussion of "form/structure/ setting," detailed exegetical comments arranged in a verse-by-verse manner, and a concluding section entitled "explanation" that offers a synthetic overview of the unit from a literary perspective. Hebrew is used liberally throughout the notes and comments.

Usability: The clearly organized format facilitates use of the commentary. The strengths of this commentary are its exhaustive bibliographical lists, detailed technical notes (most of which deal with text-critical issues), and thorough presentations of various scholarly viewpoints. This commentary is more a convenient compendium of scholarly opinion than Butler's own interpretation of the text, though he does offer critique and often expresses his preferences. Those interested in the exposition of Judges should find this commentary to be a valuable exegetical research tool.

Recommended

Boling, Robert. 1975. *Judges.* AB. New York: Doubleday. Now available in paperback in the AYBC series (Yale University Press, 2005). 360 pp.

Approach: Boling's approach is historical-critical and exegetical. The commentary is aimed at "layman and scholar alike," but it definitely tilts toward the scholarly side.

Format: In the commentary proper, each section includes the author's translation, extensive technical notes (many of which deal with archaeological and geographical background issues) and relatively brief exegetical comments. Transliteration, rather than Hebrew script, is used throughout.

Usability: Most should find the commentary useful as an exegetical reference work, but it will provide little help with literary synthesis and biblical theology.

Matthews, Victor. 2004. *Judges and Ruth.* NCBC. Cambridge: Cambridge University Press. 292 pp.

Approach: Matthews takes a sociological and literary approach. The somewhat vague aim of the NCBC series is "to elucidate the Hebrew and Christian Scriptures for a wide range of intellectually curious individuals."

Format: The commentary provides an overview of the text's structure and message, but its primary focus is backgrounds, especially social customs and laws. Interspersed through the commentary are a few sections entitled "Bridging the Horizons" in which the author addresses especially important interpretive issues and attempts to show how the message of Judges may be contemporized. The relatively few references to Hebrew use transliteration.

Usability: The commentary's main strength is its stress on sociological backgrounds. As such, it serves as a supplement to more technical works, not as a primary exegetical reference work. Both laypersons and scholars should find the commentary readable and informative.

Niditch, Susan. 2008. *Judges.* OTL. Louisville: Westminster John Knox. 336 pp.

Approach: Niditch's approach is historical-critical and exegetical. The commentary appears to be intended primarily for the professional scholar.

Format: In the commentary proper, each section includes the author's translation of the text (accompanied by extensive technical notes focusing primarily on text-critical issues) and relatively brief exegetical comments on paragraphs within the text (the format is not verse-by-verse). References to Hebrew use transliteration. A "literal translation" of Judges appears in an appendix (pp. 213–81), making the volume appear more substantial than it really is.

Usability: Some may find it useful as an exegetical reference, but they will receive little help here with literary synthesis and biblical theology.

Expositional

Highly Recommended

Davis, Dale Ralph. 1990. *Such a Great Salvation: Expositions of the Book of Judges.* Expositor's Guide to the Historical Books. Grand Rapids: Baker. Also available in an updated version, entitled *Judges: Such a Great Salvation* (CF4K, 2007). 240 pp.

Approach: Davis' approach is literary and theological. The book is written by a pastor for pastors.

Format: Davis weaves the book's theological theme(s), developed with a theocentric focus, into readable and insightful expositions of the book's major literary units that include illustrative material as well.

Usability: While the volume is based on sound exegetical method, it is not an exegetical reference work *per se* and will not substitute for one. But it should prove helpful as one seeks to build the bridge from text to sermon.

Recommended

McCann, J. Clinton. 2002. *Judges*. Interpretation. Louisville: John Knox. 146 pp.

Approach: McCann takes a literary and theological approach. Like other volumes in the *Interpretation* series, it is aimed at "those who teach, preach, and study the Bible in the community of faith." It falls somewhere between a "historical critical commentary" and "homiletical aids to preaching." It seeks "to provide a third kind of resource, a commentary which presents the integrated result of historical and theological work with the biblical text."

Format: The commentary does not proceed in verse-by-verse fashion, but instead divides the book up into its major literary units. For each of these the author focuses on key themes and exegetical issues.

Usability: McCann's comments reflect interaction with the scholarly literature and with the Hebrew text, yet the style is readable and nontechnical. This volume is useful for its literary insights. However, there is no apparent hermeneutical method or strategy evident; it is not clear how McCann derives his suggested homiletical trajectories.

Wilcock, Michael. 1992. *The Message of Judges*. BST. Downers Grove: InterVarsity. 175 pp.

Approach: Wilcock's approach is literary and theological. The BST series has a "threefold ideal: to expound the biblical text with accuracy, to relate it to contemporary life, and to be readable." The editors specifically say that the volumes in the series are neither commentaries (which they view as primarily works of reference) nor sermons (which, in their view, may not take Scripture seriously enough), but rather expositions.

Format: The author divides the book up into its major literary units and focuses on key literary themes.

Usablility: As the editors suggest, the volume should not be used as a substitute for an exegetical commentary. This work should be helpful for literary synthesis and building a bridge from text to sermon.

Younger, K. Lawson Jr. 2002. *Judges and Ruth*. NIVAC. Grand Rapids: Zondervan. 512 pp. (The Judges portion is 367 pages.)

Approach: Like other commentaries in this category, the approach is literary and theological. The NIVAC series is designed to bring "an ancient message into a modern context" by helping the reader "think through the *process* of moving from the original meaning of a passage to its contemporary significance." According to the series editors, these volumes are "commentaries" and "works of reference," not "popular expositions" or "devotional literature."

Format: Each major literary unit includes the NIV translation and a discussion of the text's "original meaning" focusing on its paragraphs (the format is not verse-by-verse), followed by sections entitled "bridging contexts" and "contemporary significance." In these last two sections the author brings the text's theological themes to the surface and builds a bridge from text to sermon.

Usability: The well-organized format makes the commentary user-friendly. Its exegetical insights are helpful, especially as regards the text's literary features and cultural background. In fact, this volume could be listed in the technical/semi-technical section above. The sections on bridging contexts and contemporary significance provide useful insights and homiletical trajectories. However, despite the editors' concern to guide the reader through the process of moving from text to sermon, the third section does not reflect a clear-cut, well-defined homiletical philosophy or method.

PART ONE

Prologue to Chaos

JUDGES 1:1–2:5
Settling Down with the Enemy

TRANSLATION AND NARRATIVE STRUCTURE[1]

1a   After Joshua died, (*introductory-temporal backgrounding*)

1b   the Israelites asked the LORD, (*initiatory*)

1c   *"Who should lead the invasion against the Canaanites and launch the attack?"*

2a   The LORD said, (*sequential*)

2b   *"The men of Judah should take the lead. Be sure of this! I am handing the land over to them."*

3a   The men of Judah said to their brothers, the men of Simeon, (*sequential*)

3b   *"Invade our allotted land with us and help us attack the Canaanites. Then we will go with you into your allotted land."*

3c   So the men of Simeon went with them. (*consequential*)

4a   The men of Judah attacked, (*sequential*)

4b   and the LORD handed the Canaanites and Perizzites over to them. (*sequential*)

---

1. The translation of Judges appearing in this commentary is the author's. It is a slightly revised version of a translation the author originally prepared for the NET Bible.

4c They killed ten thousand men at Bezek. (*sequential*)[2]
5a They met Adoni-Bezek at Bezek (*focusing*)[3]
5b and fought him. (*sequential*)
5c They defeated the Canaanites and Perizzites. (*sequential*)

---

2. For lack of a better alternative, we have followed the traditional reading, which states that Judah struck down ten thousand enemy soldiers. It is doubtful that such large numbers can be taken at face value in light of demographic analysis of ancient Palestine by modern archaeologists. See the population estimates for Palestine in the 13th–11th centuries B.C. given in Dever 2003, 97–98, and 2004, 77 (cf. Hess 2007, 232). In the thirteenth century B.C. there were roughly fifty thousand people living in Canaan, a figure that tripled by the eleventh century. Population estimates for Israel are fifty thousand for the twelfth century B.C. and seventy-five thousand for the eleventh century. One possibility is that the Hebrew term אֶלֶף, traditionally understood as a numeral (a "thousand"), actually refers to a contingent of troops (numbering much less than a thousand), at least in military contexts. Boling, taking this approach, translates עֲשֶׂרֶת אֲלָפִים, traditionally "ten thousand," as "ten contingents" in verse 4 (1975, 54–55). Another option is that such large numbers are hyperbolic. See Fouts 1997, 377–88, and 2003, 283–99. 1 Kings 20:30 demonstrates beyond a shadow of a doubt that numbers were either sometimes inflated in military accounts or have been misunderstood by later interpreters. According to that passage, after Israel had killed one hundred thousand Arameans in battle (v. 29), the rest of the Aramean army fled to Aphek, where the town wall collapsed and killed twenty-seven thousand of them, a preposterous claim if the figure is taken literally.

   Boling's view is appealing, but problematic in some respects. In 20:10 (a military context) it appears that אֶלֶף is a numeral, "a thousand," for one-tenth of אֶלֶף is מֵאָה, "a hundred," and one-tenth of מֵאָה is עֲשָׂרָה, "ten." Boling translates the terms as numerals and simply remarks that "the total of the army activated was much smaller" (1975, 280, 284). The figure in 20:35 (twenty-five thousand and one hundred) is also problematic for Boling's view. He translates "twenty-five contingents (one hundred men)," as if there were only four men per contingent (1975, 282). But he explains, "Here the indication is that 'twenty-five' of those contingents [i.e., of Benjamin's twenty-six contingents, cf. v. 15] were engaged, leaving only one unit in reserve and that from these units 'one hundred men' were lost." He estimates that the total Benjaminite force was probably seven hundred men, so their losses amounted to approximately fourteen percent (1975, 287). Furthermore, in 9:49 and 16:27 Boling retains the traditional translation for אֶלֶף, apparently because the term does not refer to military troops in these passages (1975, 169, 247).

3. Verse 4 gives an overview of Judah's success, while verse 5 begins a more detailed report of the victory, focusing on the enemy leader Adoni-Bezek.

6a   When Adoni-Bezek ran away, (*sequential*)
6b   they chased him (*sequential*)
6c   and captured him. (*sequential*)
6d   Then they cut off his thumbs and big toes. (*sequential*)
7a   Adoni-Bezek said, (*sequential*)
7b   *"Seventy kings, with thumbs and big toes cut off, used to lick up food scraps under my table. God has repaid me for what I did to them."*
7c   They brought him to Jerusalem, (*sequential*)
7d   where he died. (*sequential*)
8a   The men of Judah attacked Jerusalem (*sequential*)
8b   and captured it. (*sequential*)
8c   They put the sword to it (*sequential*)
8d   **and set the city on fire.** (*concluding*)[4]

9   **Later the men of Judah went down to attack the Canaanites living in the hill country,** the Negev, and the lowlands. (*introductory*)[5]
10a The men of Judah attacked the Canaanites living in Hebron. (*sequential*)
10b **(Hebron used to be called Kiriath Arba.)** (*supplemental*)
10c They killed Sheshai, Ahiman, and Talmai. (*focusing*)
11a From there they attacked the people of Debir. (*resumptive-sequential*)
11b **(Debir used to be called Kiriath Sepher.)** (*supplemental*)
12a Caleb said, (*resumptive-sequential*)
12b *"To the man who attacks and captures Kiriath Sepher I will give my daughter Acsah as a wife."*
13a Othniel son of Kenaz, Caleb's younger brother, captured it, (*sequential*)
13b so Caleb gave him his daughter Acsah as a wife. (*consequential*)

14a One time Acsah came (*introductory: new scene embedded within larger story*)[6]

---

4. The disjunctive clause in verse 8d signals closure for the account of the first campaign.
5. The disjunctive clause in verse 9 formally signals a new scene and introduces the next campaign. The temporal adverb אַחַר, "later," indicates that this scene follows the previous one chronologically.
6. Before continuing the account of the military campaign, the narrator includes a brief episode about Caleb, whose role in the campaign has just

14b   and charmed her father so she could ask him for some land.
     (*sequential*)
14c   When she got down from her donkey, (*sequential*)
14d   Caleb said to her, (*sequential*)
14e   *"What would you like?"*
15a   She answered, (*sequential*)
15b   *"Please give me a special present. Since you have given me land
     in the Negev, now give me springs of water."*
15c   So Caleb gave her both upper and lower springs. (*consequential*)

16a   **Now the descendants of the Kenite, Moses' father-in-law,
     went up with the people of Judah from the City of Date-
     Palm Trees to Arad in the Desert of Judah, located in the
     Negev.** (*supplemental*)
16b   They went (*sequential*)
16c   and lived with the people of Judah. (*sequential*)

17a   The men of Judah went with the men of Simeon, their brothers,
     (*resumptive-sequential*)[7]
17b   and defeated the Canaanites living in Zephath. (*sequential*)
17c   They wiped out Zephath. (*sequential*)
17d   So people now call the city Hormah.
     (*supplemental-consequential*)[8]

---

been described (vv. 12–13), and his daughter (vv. 14–15, note the introductory וַיְהִי). This in turn prompts a supplemental note about the Kenites
(introduced with a disjunctive clause, v. 16a). See the commentary below
on the function of verse 16. The *wayyiqtol* clauses in verse 16bc are sequential in relation to verse 16a, but do not resume the main line of the
narrative.

7. The account of the military campaign (cf. vv. 9–13) resumes in verse 17a,
though the resumptive nature of the statement is unmarked (there is no
repetitive link with vv. 9–13).

8. The text reads literally, "and one calls the name of the city Hormah." The
subject of the singular verb is indefinite; one could translate with the passive, making the grammatical object in Hebrew the subject in English:
"and the name of the city was/is called Hormah." (For other examples of
this verb with an indefinite subject followed by the object "name," see Genesis 25:26; 35:8; 38:29–30; Num. 11:3; 21:3; Josh. 5:9.) Our translation
assumes the *wayyiqtol* clause in verse 17d is etiological. It describes a
consequence of the previous action (the annihilation of Zephath), but is
supplemental in that it does not describe an event that was part of the
campaign *per se*. In other words, it refers to what people later called the

18   The men of Judah captured Gaza, Ashkelon, Ekron, and the territory surrounding each city. (*resumptive-sequential*)

19a   The LORD was with the men of Judah; (*summarizing*)[9]
19b   they conquered the hill country, (*consequential*)
19c   **but they could not conquer the people living in the coastal plain because they had chariots with iron-rimmed wheels.** (*contrastive*)[10]
20a   Caleb received Hebron, just as Moses had promised. (*focusing*)[11]
20b   He drove out the three Anakites. (*sequential*)
21a   **The men of Benjamin did not conquer the Jebusites living in Jerusalem.** (*contrastive*)[12]
21b   The Jebusites live with the people of Benjamin in Jerusalem to this very day. (*consequential*)

22a   The men of Joseph attacked Bethel (*initiatory*)
22b   **accompanied by the Lord.** (*circumstantial*)[13]
23a   When the men of Joseph spied out Bethel (*sequential*)
23b   (**it used to be called Luz**), (*supplemental*)
24a   the spies spotted a man leaving the city. (*resumptive-sequential*)
24b   They said to him, (*sequential*)
24c   *"If you show us a secret entrance into the city, we will reward you."*

---

city in light of what happened there. However, if one were to follow the LXX and read the plural here ("and then they named it Hormah"), one could understand this as describing the culminating event of the campaign against Zephath and treat it simply as sequential. In other words, in conjunction with their victory over the city, the Israelites then named it Hormah.

9. The statement in verse 19a begins a summary of the campaign.
10. The negated perfect in verse 19c (which follows an adversative use of כִּי, translated "but") contrasts sharply with the preceding comment about Judah's success in the hill country.
11. Verse 20 has a focusing function in relation to verse 19b, but also in relation to verse 10, which tells how the men of Judah defeated Hebron and the Anakites who lived there. We now discover it was Caleb who accomplished this.
12. Verse 21a (which has a disjunctive structure, as well as a negated verb) contrasts the success of Judah and especially Caleb with Benjamin's inability to conquer Jerusalem.
13. The disjunctive clause in verse 22b gives an important circumstance attendant to the main action.

25a He showed them a secret entrance into the city, (*consequential*)

25b and they put the city to the sword. (*sequential*)

25c **But they let the man and his extended family leave safely.** (*contrastive*)[14]

26a He moved to Hittite country (*sequential*)

26b and built a city. (*sequential*)

26c He called its name Luz, (*sequential*)

26d **It has kept that name to this very day.** (*supplemental*)[15]

27a **Manasseh did not conquer Beth Shan, Taanach, or their surrounding towns. Nor did they conquer the people living in Dor, Ibleam, Megiddo or their surrounding towns.** (*summarizing*)[16]

27b The Canaanites managed to remain in those areas. (*consequential*)

28a Whenever Israel was strong militarily, (*supplemental-qualifying*)

28b they forced the Canaanites to do hard labor, (*consequential*)

28c **but they never totally conquered them.** (*contrastive*)

29a **Ephraim did not conquer the Canaanites living in Gezer.** (*summarizing*)

29b The Canaanites lived among them in Gezer. (*consequential*)

---

14. The disjunctive clause in verse 25c draws attention to the contrasting treatment received by the individual who told the spies about the secret entrance to the city. Note the fronted compound object, which is juxtaposed with "the city" in the previous clause.

15. The disjunctive clause in verse 26d is asyndetic (i.e., it is not introduced by a conjunction, but simply by the pronominal subject of the clause).

16. Verses 27–36 are more of a report than a mini-story (such as we find in vv. 22–26). Each part of the report begins with a summary statement pertaining to one of the tribes. The summary is given with a negated sentence in verse 27a, while disjunctive clauses are utilized in verses 29a, 30a, 31, and 33 (all but the first are asyndetic). The summary report concerning Dan begins with a *wayyiqtol* clause (v. 34).

    In verses 27–33 each introductory summary is followed by a *wayyiqtol* clause giving the consequence of tribal failure. In three of five cases additional material appears. The Manasseh report has a supplementary section introduced by וַיְהִי + temporal כִּי, translated "whenever" (v. 28a); it ends with a contrastive or qualifying observation (cf. v. 28c with v. 27a). The Zebulun report concludes with a brief qualifier (v. 30c; *wayyiqtol* clause), while the Naphtali report uses a disjunctive clause for the same purpose (v. 33c).

30a **Zebulun did not conquer the people living in Kitron and Nahalol**. (*summarizing*)
30b The Canaanites lived among them (*consequential*)
30c and did hard labor. (*supplemental-qualifying*)

31 **Asher did not conquer the people living in Acco or Sidon. Nor did they conquer Ahlab, Aczib, Helbah, Aphek, or Rehob**. (*summarizing*)
32 The people of Asher live among the Canaanites residing in the land because they did not conquer them. (*consequential*)

33a **Naphtali did not conquer the people living in Beth Shemesh or Beth Anath**. (*summarizing*)
33b They live among the Canaanites residing in the land. (*consequential*)
33c **The Canaanites living in Beth Shemesh and Beth Anath did hard labor for them**. (*supplemental-qualifying*)

34 The Amorites forced the people of Dan to live in the hill country, for they did not allow them to live in the coastal plain. (*summarizing*)
35a The Amorites managed to remain in Har Heres, Aijalon, and Shaalbim. (*focusing*)[17]
35b Whenever the tribe of Joseph was strong militarily, (*supplemental-qualifying*)
35c the Amorites were forced to do hard labor. (*consequential*)
36 **The border of Amorite territory ran from the Pass of the Scorpions to Sela and on up**. (*supplemental*)

2:1a The Lord's messenger went up from Gilgal to Bokim. (*initiatory*)[18]
1b He said, (*sequential*)
1c *"I brought you up from Egypt and led you into the land I had solemnly promised to give to your ancestors. I said, 'I will never break my agreement with you,*

---

17. Verse 35 (which contains three clauses, all of which begin with a *wayyiqtol* form) lists some of the specific towns occupied by the Amorites and provides a supplemental-qualifying note that is similar in content to statements made in preceding reports (cf. v. 35bc with vv. 28ab, 30c, 33c).
18. The first statement in verse 1, while sequential to what has preceded, also initiates a new episode.

2   *but you must not make a treaty with the people who live in this*
    land. You should tear down the altars where they worship.' But
    you have disobeyed me. Why would you do such a thing?

3   *At that time I also warned you, 'If you disobey, I will not drive*
    out the Canaanites from before you. They will ensnare you and
    their gods will lure you away.'"

4a   When the Lord's messenger spoke these words to all the
    Israelites, *(transitional)*[19]

4b   the people wept loudly. *(sequential)*

5a   They named that place Bokim *(consequential)*

5b   and offered sacrifices to the Lord there. *(sequential)*

OUTLINE

A Good But Tainted Start (1:1–21)
  Judah takes the lead (1:1–8)
    An assuring word 1:1–3
    God's instrument of judgment 1:4–8
  More successes (1:9–18)
    Hebron falls 1:9–11
    Caleb: wise and kind father (1:12–15)
    A promise fulfilled (1:16)
    Genocide implemented (1:17)
    Invading the coastal plain (1:18)
  A hint of trouble (1:19–21)
    Good news: The Lord energizes Judah (1:19a)
    Bad news: Judah is run off by iron chariots (1:19b)
    Good news: The Lord keeps a promise to Caleb (1:20)
    Bad news: Benjamin coexists with Jebusites (1:21)
A Litany of Failure (1:22–36)
  Joseph cuts a deal with a Canaanite (1:22–26)
  A dismal report card (1:27–36)
    Manasseh can't do the job (1:27–28)
    Ephraim coexists with the Canaanites (1:29)
    Zebulun coexists with the Canaanites[20] (1:30)

---

19. The statement in verse 4a marks a transition within the scene from the message to the people's response (note the use of וַיְהִי + temporal preposition -כְּ [translated "when"] + infinitive construct). It describes an action that is sequential to what precedes, but not as important as the statement that follows. See 11:35a.

20. Issachar's absence between Zebulun and Asher is puzzling (see Josh. 19:17–23). See the commentary below for discussion.

Asher lives among the Canaanites (1:31–32)
Naphtali lives among the Canaanites (1:33)
Dan gets pushed around by the Amorites (1:34–36)
A Tearful Encounter at Bokim (2:1–5)
The root of the problem (2:1–3)
Altars remain visible through tears and smoke (2:4–5)

LITERARY STRUCTURE

This section has three major literary units: (1) an account of Judah's and Simeon's conquests (1:1–21), (2) a report of Joseph's and the other tribes' successes and failures (1:22–36), and (3) an account of the incident at Bokim (2:1–5). The repetition of the verb עלה, "go up," is used as a structural device (O'Connell 1996, 60). The introductory *wayyiqtol* forms וַיַּעֲלוּ ("attacked") in 1:22 and וַיַּעַל ("went up") in 2:1, correspond to וַיַּעַל ("attacked") in 1:4. In response to the Lord's commission (1:2) Judah went up against the Canaanites (1:4), followed by Joseph (1:22). When the tribes eventually failed, the Lord's messenger went up to confront them (2:1).

The first of these units (1:1–21) contains two main subsections (vv. 1–8, 9–18), followed by an appendix/conclusion (vv. 19–21). Closure for the first subsection is signaled by the disjunctive clause in verse 8b (וְאֶת־הָעִיר, "and the city"), while the next subsection begins with the disjunctive clause וְאַחַר יָרְדוּ בְּנֵי יְהוּדָה ("Later the men of Judah went down," v. 9). The verb ירד, "go down," nicely complements עלה, "go up" (v. 4).

Within the second subsection, verses 14–15 (note introductory וַיְהִי) present a brief scene describing Caleb's dealings with his daughter and verse 16 (note the disjunctive clause וּבְנֵי קֵינִי, "Now the descendants of the Kenite,") contains a parenthetical note that is thematically related to its context by its references to Moses and the Negev. Verses 17–18 resume the main conquest theme of verses 9–13, but the reference to Judah helping Simeon (v. 17) links the passage with verse 3, where Judah enlists Simeon's support in its campaign, and signals closure for the unit.

The appendix (vv. 19–21), introduced with וַיְהִי (cf. v. 1), has both concluding and transitional functions: (1) Verse 19a summarizes Judah's successes and rounds off the section by referring to the Lord's enablement (cf. v. 2). (2) Verse 19b, with its negative qualifying remark, makes a transition to the next major section (vv. 22–36) and paves the way for the concluding section (2:1–5) by raising the audience's curiosity. (3) Verse 20 parallels the positive comment of verse 19a and summarizes the focal point of verses 10–18. (4) Verse 21 (which links thematically with vv. 7–8) shares the negative tone of verse 19b and also has a transitional, preparatory role.

The second main unit (1:22–36) consists of three subsections: (1) an account of Joseph's conquest of Bethel (vv. 22–26), (2) a report of the northern tribes' failure to drive out the Canaanites (vv. 27–33), and (3) a concluding note concerning Amorite resistance (vv. 34–36).

The structure of the report (vv. 27–33) deserves special consideration. It may be outlined as follows:

Manasseh's failure (v. 27a, note "Manasseh did not conquer")
Canaanite determination to remain in the land (v. 27b)
Canaanites reduced to forced labor (v. 28a)
Manasseh's failure (v. 28b, note "never totally conquered them," which forms an inclusio with v. 27a)
Ephraim's failure (v. 29a, note "Ephraim did not conquer")
Canaanites dwell among Ephraim (v. 29b, note וַיֵּשֶׁב, literally, "and he lived")
Zebulun's failure (v. 30a, note "Zebulun did not conquer")
Canaanites dwell among Zebulun (v. 30b, note וַיֵּשֶׁב)
Canaanites reduced to forced labor (v. 30b)
Asher's failure (v. 31, note "Asher did not conquer")
Asher dwells among Canaanites (v. 32a, note וַיֵּשֶׁב)
Asher's failure (v. 32b, note לֹא הוֹרִישׁוֹ "they did not conquer," at the end of v. 32)
Naphtali's failure (v. 33a, note "Naphtali did not conquer")
Naphtali dwells among Canaanites (v. 33b, note וַיֵּשֶׁב)
Canaanites reduced to forced labor (v. 33b)

The concluding report of Amorite resistance (vv. 34–36) pertains to the tribe of Dan. It is marked out as a separate unit by its introductory verb (לחץ, "force") and subject (the Amorites), which contrast with the pattern of the preceding verses (Israelite tribe as subject + negated הוֹרִישׁ, "conquer"), and by the switch in focus from the Canaanites to the Amorites. This introductory statement about the Amorites' domination of Dan is followed by a reference to their determination to remain in the land (v. 35a, cf. v. 27b), a qualifying statement (v. 35b, cf. vv. 28, 30, 33), and a concluding disjunctive clause emphasizing how entrenched the Amorites remained (v. 36).

The third main unit (2:1–5) contains two subsections: (1) the messenger's encounter with the people at Bokim (vv. 1–3), (2) the people's response (vv. 4–5, note introductory וַיְהִי). The messenger's speech takes the form of a lawsuit: (a) reminder of God's gracious deeds and loyalty

(v. 1b), (b) reminder of God's covenant demands (v. 2a), (c) accusation and demand for an explanation (v. 2b), (d) reminder of threatened penalty for disobedience (v. 3).

EXPOSITION

Joshua's death marked the end of an era. The very formula that begins the book of Judges ("After Joshua died") signals an important transition in the life of Israel. An important era had ended; a new challenge awaited the people.[21] Under the leadership of this able warrior, Israel broke the back of Canaanite resistance and established a foothold in the promised land. Joshua assigned land to the individual tribes and promised them that the Lord would enable each one to occupy its territory. He reminded them that God had fought for them and had kept his promises by leading them into the land and giving them victory over enemy armies. The land belonged to Israel, by title deed if not in fact. Their continued military success depended on the miraculous power of God.

Joshua also warned the Israelites not to worship the gods of the land or to form alliances with the pagan peoples remaining there. Failure in this regard would deprive the Israelites of the Lord's enablement and prevent the total conquest of Canaan. The Canaanites would then ensnare them spiritually and oppress them until Israel, rather than the Canaanites, disappeared from the land. God's plan for Israel would be ruined. He intended for Israel to be a model society, a showcase of justice that would attract the surrounding nations to the Lord. Ideally Israel would become a "kingdom of priests," a mediator of God's revelation and blessings to the pagan world and his instrument in reclaiming the nations.

Following the death of Joshua, the Israelites faced the challenge of bringing the conquest to its completion, ridding the land of the Canaanites and their corrupt religion, and establishing a great theocratic empire that would become the talk of the ancient world.

A Good But Tainted Start (1:1–21)

Judah takes the lead (1:1–8). At first the Israelites were eager to accept Joshua's challenge and complete the conquest. Recognizing the importance of divine guidance in this task, they asked the Lord who should

---

21. Niditch (1999, 199) cites other examples of "the death of leader formula" (see, e.g., Josh. 1:1) and observes that its appearance signals "that what follows is a significant phase in the life of the people."

take the lead in this renewed campaign against the Canaanites.[22] The question (v. 1, literally, "Who will be the first to go up and fight for us?") does not mean the tribes were trying to shirk their collective responsibility. The inclusion of בַּתְּחִלָּה, "first," indicates they simply wanted to know who was to initiate the campaign. In fact, the inclusion of לָנוּ, "for us," expresses "the concept of a united Israel" (Webb 1987, 82). Boling argues that the question posed in verse 1 was the wrong one. Instead the people should have asked: "Shall we again resume the march to battle?" (Boling 1975, 53–54). However, this question would have suggested hesitancy. Joshua had already urged the people to complete the conquest (Josh. 23:4–5). Here the people express their willingness to obey this command and acknowledge the Lord's leadership in the campaign (Block 1999, 86).

The Lord designated Judah to take the lead and promised a successful mission. In his statement (v. 2, literally, "I have given the land into their hands"), the Lord employs a perfect verbal form (נָתַתִּי) in a rhetorical manner, describing what is still future as if it had already taken place.[23] The Lord's choice of Judah should come as no surprise, for Judah's leadership was well-established in Israel's ancient traditions. In his blessing of his sons prior to his death, Jacob portrayed Judah as a powerful warrior and a leader among his brothers (Gen. 49:8–12). Judah also occupied a prime position in the arrangement of the tribal encampment in the wilderness (Numbers 2) and was the first tribe to whom Joshua allotted land west of the Jordan (Joshua 14–15).

Judah enlisted the support of the tribe of Simeon in its campaign against the Canaanites. Judah was ready for battle and not hesitant in any way. As Webb points out, the statement "help us attack" (literally, "and let us fight," וְנִלָּחֲמָה) is emphasized by its central position in the quotation (Webb 1987, 83). Klein sees Judah's request for help in a negative light. She writes: "Yahweh tells Israel (here Judah) specifically what to do, but Israel only partially heeds Yahweh's command:

---

22. The expression שָׁאַל בְּ–, "ask, inquire of," refers in verse 1 to seeking an oracle from the Lord. See Judges 18:5; 20:18, 23, 27; 1 Samuel 10:22; 14:37; 22:10, 13, 15; 23:2, 4, 5; 28:6; 30:8; 2 Samuel 2:1; 5:19, 23; 16:23. Though the precise means of inquiry is not given here, 1 Samuel 28:6 mentions dreams, the Urim (cf. Num. 27:21, as well as the LXX of 1 Sam. 14:41), and prophets as the usual means whereby one received a word from God.

23. Another option is that the verb refers here to the fact that God had already given them the land in the sense that it had been assigned to them and they possessed, as it were, the title deed to it. In this case, the perfect form may be understood as simple past or present perfect.

Judah immediately establishes a battle pact with his brother Simeon. Thus, from the outset, Israel exerts self-determination, evidencing automatic trust in *human* perception" (Klein 1988, 23, emphasis Klein; cf. Younger 2002, 64–65). Marais follows Klein's lead in this regard. He sees Judah's seemingly harmless alliance with Simeon as foreshadowing the harmful alliances made by Israel later in the book (Marais 1998, 73–74; cf. Hess 1999, 143). However, the text makes it clear that the alliance was a natural one (note "their brothers, the men of Simeon"). Joshua had allotted land to the Simeonites within the borders of Judah's territory (Josh. 19:1–9). By inviting Simeon to participate in the campaign, Judah begins to exercise its God-given leadership role. Literary foreshadowing may indeed be present, but it need not mean or imply that Judah's alliance with Simeon should be viewed in a negative light. It may function as a foil in that this legitimate alliance between brothers for the purpose of accomplishing God's will contrasts with the illegitimate alliances described later in the chapter and the book.

Judah won an overwhelming victory over the Canaanites and Perizzites at Bezek.[24] Just as he had done in the days of Joshua (Josh. 6:2; 8:1, 7; 10:8, 19, 30; 21:44) and in fulfillment of his promise (cf. v. 2), the Lord gave the enemy into Israel's hands, demonstrating that he was still fully capable of winning victories on their behalf and giving them the promised land.

The men of Judah also captured the ruler of Bezek and cut off his thumbs and big toes. From a purely pragmatic point of view this form of punishment humiliated the victim, eliminated any possibility of his taking up arms in the future, and symbolized the cessation of his rule as a warrior-king. This might at first seem to be cruel and unusual punishment, but we quickly discover that this king was getting what he deserved, for he had mutilated seventy other kings in this same way.[25] In fact he had gone one step further and forced his victims to crawl like dogs for scraps of food under his dinner table. Adoni-Bezek himself acknowledged that God (note his use of אֱלֹהִים, "Elohim, God" the generic name for deity) was justly repaying him for his cruelty.[26]

---

24. This site should not be confused with the Bezek mentioned in 1 Samuel 11:8, which was far to the north of Jerusalem. See McCarter 1980, 204.
25. As a multiple of the symbolic number seven, the number seventy is probably hyperbolic, indicating an indefinite, but large figure. Note its use in Judges 9:2, 5 and 2 Kings 10:6–7.
26. The use of the verb שָׁלַם with God as its subject shows that the king's fate is not viewed as the mere natural consequence of his actions. It "indicates

Why was this gory account included in the story? Was its inclusion a form of ancient Israelite taunting designed to appeal to Israelite prejudice or to some primitive sense of vengeance characteristic of a precivilized society? Probably not. The account of Adoni-Bezek should not be viewed in isolation. Rather he likely represents the entire Canaanite population, which had sinned greatly against the Lord, had polluted the land, and deserved God's severe judgment (Gen. 15:16; Lev. 18:24–28). God's just punishment of this cruel Canaanite king was an object lesson of what he intended to do to this entire decadent society and a reminder that he executes justice according to the eye-for-an-eye, tooth-for-a-tooth principle (Exod. 21:24; Lev. 24:20; Deut. 19:21).[27] Those who violate his standards receive an appropriate punishment. In the macrostructure of the book Adoni-Bezek serves as a foil for Abimelech (cf. 9:5), who exhibits similar cruelty by killing his seventy half-brothers and, like Adoni-Bezek, receives God's just penalty for his sins (9:56).[28]

Despite the emphasis on the justice of the king's punishment, it is possible that this episode gives a hint of trouble. Block argues that the text portrays Israel as adopting "a Canaanite ethic."[29] Rather than executing the king on the spot, they allowed him to live and resorted to a Canaanite method of treating captives, one that Adoni-Bezek, by his own acknowledgement, had practiced on several occasions. Later Saul is severely reprimanded for failing to destroy an Amalekite ruler who had been devoted to destruction (cf. 1 Samuel 15).

The last part of verse seven informs us that Adoni-Bezek was taken to Jerusalem, where he died. We are not told specifically who took him there, but since he was a captive it is reasonable to assume that the Judahite army did. Support for this comes from the immediate context. Collective Judah is the subject of the plural verbs prior to this (see vv. 5b–6) and verse 8 tells how the "men of Judah" attacked

---

rather that God has freely decided to pay back Adoni-bezeq for his deeds to others." See Miller 1982, 94.

27. It is beyond the scope of this commentary to address the philosophical problem posed by the divinely authorized genocide inherent in the Israelite conquest of Canaan. For a presentation of four different views on the subject and a lively debate between their proponents, see Gundry 2003. See as well Howard 1998, 180–87.

28. On the thematic connection between Adoni-Bezek and Abimelech, see Wong 2006a, 204–06. Gunn and Fewell see in Adoni-Bezek's words a foreshadowing of the nation's destiny. The Davidic king Jehoiachin would someday end up eating at the table of a captor (1993, 162–63).

29. Block 1999, 90–91. Schneider concurs with Block's viewpoint (2000, 7).

Jerusalem. However, we are not told for what purpose they took the king to Jerusalem or how he happened to die.

The men of Judah next turned their attention to Jerusalem, which they sacked and burned. The terse, matter-of-fact style of the report reflects the apparent ease with which Judah made quick work of the city. The language is reminiscent of Joshua's campaigns (see Josh. 6:24; 8:19, 24; 10:28–37; 11:10–14), again serving as a reminder of the living God's presence with his people as they tried to complete what Joshua had started.[30]

More successes (1:9–18). Having succeeded at Bezek and Jerusalem, Judah turned its attention southward and westward. They moved against Hebron and defeated Sheshai, Ahiman, and Talmai, three of the gigantic sons of Anak (Num. 13:22, 33; Josh. 15:14, as well as Deut. 2:10; 9:2). Verse 20 suggests that it was actually Caleb who accomplished this feat.[31] These same Anakites had terrified the Israelite

---

30. Webb notes the verbal parallels with the Joshua account (1987, 85). Olson states that "the story elevates Judah's accomplishments to the same level as Joshua and pushes them even a notch higher. In capturing the city of Jerusalem, Judah does what Joshua could not" (1998, 736–37).

31. According to Joshua 15:13, Joshua gave Hebron to Caleb in accordance with the Lord's promise (see Josh. 14:6–15). Caleb's request (Josh. 14:12), in which he anticipates defeating the Anakites, appears to postdate the initial conquest. Joshua 15:14 gives the impression that Caleb conquered Hebron during Joshua's lifetime, but Judges 1 suggests that Caleb did not actually take the city until after Joshua died. Harmonizing Numbers 13:22, 33/Joshua 14:12; 15:14/Judges 1:20 with Joshua 10:36–37/11:21–22 is difficult. The former set of texts seems to indicate that the three Anakites lived in Hebron from the time of Moses until Caleb finally dislodged them in conjunction with the Judahite invasion of Hebron, presumably after the initial conquest of the land (Josh. 14:12) and Joshua's death (Judg. 1:9–10). However, Joshua 10:36–37/11:21–22 state that Joshua and his army wiped out the inhabitants of Hebron, including the Anakites, during the initial invasion of the land. Perhaps Joshua 10:36–37/11:21–22 are telescoped and proleptic, attributing Caleb's and Othniel's later deeds to Joshua because they were an extension of the great leader's exploits. Another option is that Judges 1:9–11 flashes back to the time of Joshua's campaign against this region. See Merrill, who also sees a flashback in verse 8 (1987, 144). In this case one may make a distinction between Joshua's initial attack on Hebron and Debir (Josh. 10:36–39) and Joshua's/Caleb's later victory over the Anakites at these cities (Josh. 11:21–22; 15:14–15). Caleb's request in Joshua 14:11–12, as well as the narratival accounts in 14:13–15 and 15:13–15, would have to be flashbacks to that campaign,

spies during their surveillance of the land (see Num. 13:22, 33). At
that time Caleb remained unafraid and advised Moses to invade the
land (Num. 13:30). Because of his unwavering faith, the Lord rewarded
Caleb and promised him the portion of land occupied by the Anakites
(Num. 14:24; Josh. 14:6–15). When the time came for action, Caleb
aggressively and fearlessly seized what the Lord had guaranteed him,
demonstrating that his earlier call to faith in the wilderness had been
no empty boast (see Num. 13:30; 14:6–9). The reminder that Hebron
was once named Kiriath Arba ("city of Arba"), after the greatest of the
Anakites (cf. Josh. 14:15; 15:13), highlights the fact that the Lord had
displaced the Canaanites and given the land to faithful men like Caleb.

Caleb promised the conqueror of Debir his daughter Acsah's hand in
marriage, guaranteeing that she would have a worthy husband and that
he would have a capable son-in-law who shared his faith and courage.
The marriage of this conquering Israelite to an Israelite woman also
served as a model of the covenantal purity that should be maintained in
all Israelite families in accordance with Moses' and Joshua's instructions
(Exod. 34:16; Deut. 7:3–4; Josh. 23:12; contrast the situation described
in Judg. 3:6) (Webb 1987, 87; Olson 1998, 738). It also serves as a contrastive foil for the marriages by abduction described in the book's final
chapter (Wong 2006a, 42–46). Caleb's nephew Othniel responded to the
challenge, took the city, and won the promised bride.[32] As in the case of
Hebron, the comment that Debir was once named Kiriath-Sepher reminds the reader that Israel had displaced the Canaanites in the land.

To complement her land holdings Acsah asked her father for
"springs of water," a request with which he readily complied.[33] The

---

even though the text of Joshua gives the impression that both the request
and Caleb's taking of the cities occurred during the occupational phase
after the campaigns of chapters 10–11.

32. In verse 13 the Hebrew text reads "Othniel, son of Kenaz, the younger
brother of Caleb." It is not clear if "brother" qualifies Kenaz (in which
case Caleb and Kenaz were brothers and Othniel was Caleb's nephew) or
Othniel (in which case Othniel was Caleb's younger brother and both were
sons of Kenaz). Since Caleb's father is identified as Jephunneh in several
texts, it might seem more likely that Caleb and Kenaz were brothers and
that Othniel was Caleb's nephew. However, three texts describe Caleb as
"son of Jephunneh the Kenizzite" (Num. 32:12; Josh. 14:6, 14), indicating
that Kenaz (perhaps the ancestor of the Kenizzites) might have been a
more distant ancestor of both Othniel and Caleb.

33. The Hebrew term translated "springs" is used elsewhere of a bowl or the
bowl-shaped top of a pillar. Here it probably refers to spring-fed pools. On
the location of these pools, see Hallo 2004, 331.

Hebrew text of verse 14 reads literally, "And it came to pass, when she came she urged him to ask from her father the field, and she got off the donkey and Caleb said to her, 'What would you like?'" Some (see NIV) understand Othniel as the object of the verb סוּת, translated "urged" in NIV. In this case Acsah urges Othniel to request the field from her father. Oddly enough, however, the subsequent narrative presents no such scene. Indeed it is Acsah who does the asking (v. 15).[34] The Septuagint solves this problem by making Othniel the subject of the verb "urged" (though in Hebrew the verb is feminine) and Acsah the object (though in Hebrew the pronoun is masculine).[35] In this case Othniel urges Acsah to request land from her father. However, there is a better solution to this problem. It is preferable to take Caleb, not Othniel, as the object of the verb סוּת. (Note that Caleb, not Othniel, is the subject of the verb "gave" in v. 13b.) If one then takes סוּת in the sense of "beguile, charm," one can translate, "When she came, she charmed him (i.e., her father Caleb) so that she could ask her father for the field."[36] In this case the text notes that she "buttered" her father up (as daughters are apt to do!) to set the stage for her request and make him more receptive to it.[37] It is not entirely clear how she did

---

34. In verse 15 Acsah asks her father specifically for "springs of water" rather than "land" (v. 14). Apparently "land" (literally, "field") is metonymic; the springs were in a field. The use of the article with "land" (הַשָּׂדֶה, "the field") suggests that she had a specific field in mind. However, the synoptic parallel in Joshua 15:18 has simply שָׂדֶה, "a field." It is possible that the article (*he*) in Judges 1:14 is dittographic. Note that the preceding word (אָבִיהָ, "her father") ends with the letter *he*.

35. For a thorough discussion of the Greek textual evidence, see O'Connell 1996, 438–40.

36. The verb סוּת is used elsewhere of riches enticing a man (Job 36:18), of one individual persuading or inciting another to follow a certain course of action (1 Kings 21:25; 2 Kings 18:32 = Isa. 36:18; 2 Chron. 18:2; 32:11, 15; Jer. 38:22; 43:3), of a prophet enticing people to worship idols (Deut 13:6), and of "the Adversary" inciting God to test Job (Job 2:3). With God as subject the word is used of God drawing an enemy away from Jehoshaphat (2 Chron. 18:31) and of God attempting to lure people from destruction to blessing (Job 36:16). The word also appears in 2 Samuel 24:1, where God's anger causes him to entice David to sin, and in the parallel text in 1 Chronicles 21:1, where an adversary of Israel does the enticing. Viewed in a general way, the word refers to behavior designed to lure or entice someone into following a course of action desired by the subject.

37. For a discussion of this verse that essentially interprets the syntax as I have done, see Mosca 1984, 18–22. Mosca, however, understands the infinitive (לִשְׁאוֹל, "to ask") as a gerundive, "by asking." Apart from these

this, though verse 14b may give a clue. When she came to her father, she "got down" (צָנַח) from her donkey, perhaps in a manner that emphasized her respect for her father.[38] In this regard Klein states: "The Hebrew is so concentrated that it almost sounds like Achash [*sic*] falls off her donkey before her father. That she gets down from her donkey is unimportant; what matters is that she shows her father utmost respect, 'dropping down' before him" (Klein 1988, 25–26).[39]

Caleb's gift to his daughter provides more than a pleasant, heart-warming touch to the story. Its function is not entirely appreciated until one reads on. This scene contrasts sharply with later accounts in the book. Like his acquisition of a worthy husband for his daughter, Caleb's gift illustrates the protective concern that Israelite men should display toward their wives and daughters. However, as the book of Judges unfolds, women become victims of male oppression, rather than the beneficiaries of male protection. Caleb's gift of life-giving springs, which symbolize fertility and are actually called a blessing (בְּרָכָה, v. 15), stands in sharp contrast to the death and infertility which another Israelite daughter would experience as a result of her father's misguided zeal and lack of foresight (see Judg. 11:34–30) and to the mistreatment of women described in chapters 19–21 (see the commentary below).[40]

---

parallel texts, the verb סוּת is collocated with the preposition -לְ and infinitive construct in seven other texts. The infinitive is gerundive in 2 Samuel 24:1 (literally, "he incited David . . . by saying") and in 2 Kings 18:32 (literally, "when he entices you by saying," cf. Isa. 36:18 as well); indicates purpose in Job 2:3 (literally, "you incited me against him in order to ruin him") and in 2 Chronicles 32:11 (literally, "he is misleading you to let you die"). It indicates an objective complement in 1 Chronicles 21:1 (literally, "he incited David to number Israel") and in 2 Chronicles 18:2 (literally, "and urged him to attack"). Klein regards Mosca's interpretation as "strained and unconvincing" (1999, 23).

38. The meaning of this rare verb is debated. For a discussion of the various proposals see Lindars 1995, 29–31. The verb appears only here and in Judges 4:21, where it describes how the tent peg, having been driven through Sisera's head, penetrated into the ground. Thus, it seems to carry the meaning "descend, go down."

39. Niditch understands the language of the text differently. She speaks of Acsah "leaping from her donkey and offering an angry complaint to her father" (2008, 41). If our understanding of סוּת is correct, this cannot be the case. Rather, Acsah uses a more subtle approach.

40. Gunn and Fewell see Acsah's aggressive quest for land and blessing as contrasting with Judah's alleged hesitancy to take the land allotted to them (cf. Judg. 1:19) (1993, 161–62).

The descendants of Moses' father-in-law accompanied the tribe of Judah and settled in the Negev.[41] This information is probably included to inform us that God (through Judah) fulfilled Moses' promise

---

41. Several textual and interpretive problems in verse 16 require our attention (though this is not an exhaustive list of difficulties): (1) The form קֵינִי, "Kenite(s)," is problematic; one expects the article when the term refers to an individual, as the appositional "Moses' father-in-law" indicates it does. Some prefer to emend "sons of" to "Hobab" (cf. Judg. 4:11) and read: "Hobab the Kenite, the father-in-law of Moses." This necessitates emending the plural verb עָלוּ, "(they) went up" to עָלָה, "(he) went up," but it accommodates nicely the singular verbs in verse 16b. See Moore 1895, 31–33. However, it is more likely that קֵינִי, "Kenite(s)," is a corruption of an original קַיִן, "Kain," the eponymous ancestor of the Kenites mentioned in Judges 4:11 (and perhaps also in Num. 24:22). (Proposing such a corruption would explain the absence of the article.) Once the far more common קֵינִי was accidentally read, the referent was naturally understood to be Moses' father-in-law (see 4:11). Some Greek witnesses add the name Jethro here, while others read Hobab (see 4:11). To summarize, we propose that the original text read: "The sons of Kain went up." (2) The "City of Palms" elsewhere refers to Jericho (see Deut. 34:3, 2 Chron. 28:15, and probably also Judg. 3:13). If that is the case here, then the text implies the Kenites had crossed into the land with the Israelites. The Kenites then embarked from the Jericho area with the Judahites when the latter began their campaign. See Moore 1895, 31. (3) If one retains the reading "sons" in verse 16a, then the singular verb forms in verse 16b are problematic, especially in light of the plural verb in verse 16a. Lindars understands them as collective, with the subject being the "sons" mentioned earlier in the verse (1995, 35). However, as the text stands, it appears more likely that their subject is "the father-in-law of Moses." If, as proposed above, "Kain" was the original reading, verse 16b is likely a later addition. (4) At the end of verse 16 the Hebrew text reads: "and he went and he lived with the people." The reference to "the people" is vague; as it stands it seems to refer to the "sons of Judah" mentioned earlier in the verse, though Block sees the referent as the Canaanites (1999, 98). Another option is that the *wayyiqtol* clauses are supplemental, rather than sequential, referring to the fact that Moses' father-in-law had joined Israel. The Old Latin reads "Amalek" instead of "people" while some Greek witnesses add "Amalek" after "people." The Hebrew text could be the result of haplography (note the sequence in vv. 16b–17a, וַיֵּלֶךְ [הָעֲמָלֵקִי] הָעָם), but it is more likely that an intentional change has occurred. On the one hand, the omission in MT may be an attempt to soften the "potentially more offensive" reference to Amalek (see O'Connell 1996, 444–45). On the other hand, the addition of Amalek may reflect a harmonization to 1 Samuel 15:6, which indicates that by the time of Saul the Kenites lived with the Amalekites.

to his wife's family, which was a reward for the assistance they had given Israel (Num. 10:29–32) (Webb 1987, 88). This brief note fits well in this context, which highlights God's reward to Caleb, also promised through Moses and recorded in Numbers.

Verse 17 describes further military successes by Simeon and Judah. Their naming the defeated Canaanite city Hormah is significant for two reasons. The name (חָרְמָה) is a play on the verb translated "wiped out" (וַיַּחֲרִימוּ) earlier in the verse and thus serves as a constant reminder that the city was acquired through divinely ordained warfare. The shift in name (from Canaanite Zephath), as in the case of Hebron and Debir, emphasizes that Israel had displaced the Canaanites in the land.[42]

The term translated "wiped out" probably means in this context "put under a ban, devote to destruction," as a religious act of war. As Israel prepared for the conquest of the promised land, Moses instructed them to exterminate the native population of the land (Deut. 7:2; 20:17), just as they had annihilated the Amorites living on the eastern side of the Jordan (Deut. 2:34; 3:6; Josh. 2:10). The Lord placed Jericho under the "ban" (חֵרֶם), meaning that the Israelites were to kill all living things and place the articles of gold, silver, bronze and iron in the Lord's treasury (Josh. 6:17–21). When Achan violated this command, Israel was placed under the ban until the offender, whose deeds had made him liable to destruction, was executed and the community purged of its sin (Josh. 7:1, 11–13).[43]

According to verse 18, Judah conquered Gaza, Ashkelon, and Ekron, cities Joshua had allotted to Judah (Josh. 15:45–47). Joshua 13:3 indicates these cities remained unconquered toward the end of Joshua's life, but Judges 1:18 informs us that Judah took them after Joshua's death. Judges 3:3 mentions the "five lords of the Philistines" as having been left unconquered by Joshua. In itself this is not problematic, but just prior to this the Lord announced that these cities would remain unconquered so that the Lord might test his people (2:21a).

---

42. Numbers 21:1–3 appears to give an alternate tradition about the conquest and naming of Hormah. According to this account, the Israelites under Moses conquered the cities in the region of Arad and named the place Hormah. Merrill sees Numbers 21:1–3 and Judges 1:17 as referring to separate events (1987, 144, note 6). He suggests that Zephath (= Hormah; Judg. 1:17) was "a city rebuilt" from the ruins left by the conquest described in Numbers 21:1–3.

43. For a detailed study of the concept of the ban in the context of Israel's holy wars, see Niditch 1993, 28–77.

Furthermore Judges 1:19 tells how the Judahites did not conquer the plains, which would have included the cities mentioned in verse 18 (Moore 1895, 37; Lindars 1995, 43). Perhaps this tension motivated the Septuagint to translate here, "Judah did not inherit."[44] This variant in the Greek tradition allows one to harmonize verse 18 with verse 19 and with 2:21. However, if one opts for the Hebrew text here, the tension with verse 19 and with 2:21 remains unresolved. O'Connell theorizes that Judah conquered the cities (v. 18), but subsequently lost them (v. 19) (O'Connell 1996, 446). However, Lindars points out that if verses 18–19 had intended "to record capture and loss," they "would have been worded very differently" (Lindars 1995, 43; cf. Moore 1895, 37).

A hint of trouble (1:19–21). By way of summary the narrator affirms that the Lord was "with the men of Judah" as they conquered the hill country, but then he surprises us by noting that they were unable to conquer the plains because the people living there had iron chariots.[45] Since when have chariots been able to thwart God's purposes and power? The Lord destroyed the Egyptian chariots in the Red Sea (Exod. 14:23–28; 15:4). He promised to give the Canaanite chariots into Israel's hands and instructed Joshua to burn them (Josh. 11:4–6), orders which Joshua carefully obeyed (Josh. 11:9). Later Joshua assured the men of Joseph that the Canaanite iron chariots would not prevent them from conquering the plains (Josh. 17:16–18).[46] But here we read

---

44. See, for example, O'Connell 1996, 445–46. He points out that the Hebrew text has the harder reading and that the Greek reading may be imported from 1:27.

45. The Hebrew text has simply, "though not to conquer the residents of the plain." It is likely that the verb יָכְלוּ has been accidentally omitted after the negative particle. The original text may have read כִּי לֹא יָכְלוּ לְהוֹרִישׁ, "though they were not able to conquer . . ." or כִּי לֹא יָכֹל לְהוֹרִישׁ, "though he [Judah] was not able to conquer . . ." The use of the collective singular in verses 18–19a favors the latter. For discussion of the textual issues, see Lindars 1995, 45, and O'Connell 1996, 447.

46. In what sense the chariots were iron is not clear. They were not made entirely of iron. Perhaps they had iron rimmed wheels or iron axles. See Block 1999, 99–100; King and Stager 2001, 189; and Hess 1999, 145. Sawyer argues that references to iron in this early period cannot be literal, for the archaeological evidence does not support such widespread use of iron at this time. He suggests that references to iron are literary, having connotations of ugliness and barbarism (1983, 129–34). See also Drews 1989, 15–23; and McNutt 1990, 224. McNutt argues: "Iron technology was not adopted in Israel until at least the time of the establishment of the

that the Judahites were unable to overcome the iron chariots, even though the Lord was with them! We soon discover that there is more here than meets the eye. A few verses later the narrator explains that the people's failure was not due to iron chariots (as many of them had thought), but was because of spiritual compromise and idolatry (Judg. 2:1–5). Thus Judges 1:19 reflects the limited and erroneous perspective of the people, not the narrator's own interpretation. The narrator is at his rhetorical best here. He raises our curiosity, gives a signal that something is wrong, and prepares the way for the real explanation for Israel's partial success.[47]

---

monarchy in the tenth century BCE." She concludes that the references to iron chariots in Joshua-Judges "retroject into the past the knowledge of iron technology that developed sometime during the monarchic period." She suggests that once iron's "superior qualities were recognized, it was used symbolically to speak of the superior military and technological strength of the external powers that continually posed threats to Israel's well-being." She cites numerous texts in the Hebrew Bible where iron symbolizes oppression (225–26).

47. See Webb 1987, 90; Gunn and Fewell 1993, 159; and Chisholm 2002, 407. Eslinger observes that verse 19b "raises a critical theological question by answering a trivial, logistic one." Eslinger points out that "the reader can only draw one conclusion from Judg 1:19; Yahweh did not support the campaign." He adds that "the narrator leaves the question—why has God done so?—unanswered" until chapter two (1989, 58–59). Failing to detect the literary irony and obviously troubled by the apparent implications of the statement, the Targum reads here, "because they sinned, they were not able to drive out." See O'Connell 1996, 447. Marais does not recognize the rhetorical role of perspective in this passage. He contends that Judges reflects various fields of reference. In the frame of reference exhibited in Judges 1:19 "Yahweh is not expected to overcome every stumbling block." He suggests that this text may represent "a human perspective on Yahweh and his influence on history, or it may be a perspective born from the human experience that Yahweh's presence does not guarantee an ideal history." He adds, "Whichever way one looks at it, it is clear that the premise of this text is not the logic of an almighty deity" (1998, 80). Olson exonerates Judah and attributes their lack of success to the mystery of divine providence. He writes: "The underlying lesson is that it may take time and other circumstances for God to accomplish God's will against certain powers and enemies . . . God may not always act immediately or in the way we would like, but God does remain true to God's ultimate promises. Such apparent delays or alternate routes in God's work to overcome evil and oppression are not necessarily caused by the sinfulness of the person or community involved. Judah is obedient and faithful, and God is

Verse 21 informs us of Benjamin's failure to dislodge the Jebusites from Jerusalem. This brief notice raises at least two difficult questions when compared with earlier statements. If Judah was able to seize and burn Jerusalem (v. 8), why could Benjamin not remove the Jebusites from the city? Which tribe, Benjamin or Judah, was supposed to take the city? Joshua 15:63 is virtually identical to Judges 1:21, except that Judah is substituted for Benjamin. It appears that different traditions are represented in these various texts.[48] Of course, harmonizations of the disparate traditions are always possible, though they are subject to the criticism of being contrived. One such harmonization may be constructed as follows: Judah's sack of the city was partial or led only to temporary and/or partial occupation. The Jebusites remained entrenched in their stronghold throughout the attack and/or eventually retook the city (cf. 2 Sam. 5:6). Joshua had allotted the city to Benjamin (Josh. 18:28), but it was also located on Judah's northern border (Josh. 15:8). It is understandable that both tribes would try to subdue it. Despite Judah's initial success, both tribes subsequently failed to dislodge the Jebusite element living at the site.[49] Another harmonization sees 1:8 as a flashback to the time of Joshua, when Israel defeated the king of Jerusalem in battle (Josh. 10:22–27) and presumably burned the city. Though the Israelites captured the city, they did not conquer the Jebusites, who shortly thereafter reoccupied the city and successfully resisted subsequent efforts to drive them out (Josh. 15:63; Judg. 1:21) (Merrill 1987, 144).

While the historical facts may be unclear, the inclusion of this notice of Benjamin's failure does appear to have a literary function in the chapter, the book, and Israel's unfolding history. Benjamin's dwelling with the Jebusites foreshadows the dominant theme of the chapter's

---

with Judah; nevertheless, Judah encounters some enemies that cannot be overcome in the present moment" (1998, 739).

48. Amit argues that Judges 1 depicts Judah in a generally favorable light, in contrast to the other tribes (1999, 145–48). In her view the editor of Judges 1 has purposely presented his material in such a way as to promote his pro-Judah agenda. In some cases this results in a different historical scenario than the one presented in Joshua. See as well Brettler 2002, 97–101; and Weinfeld 1993, 388–400.

49. See Boling 1975, 56; O'Connell 1996, 446; and Kitchen 2003, 214–15. Younger emphasizes that one must carefully distinguish between "initial victory and subjugation" when dealing with the conquest accounts in Joshua and Judges. He cites an example from the Assyrian royal annals of Ashurnasirpal II in which a city is conquered twice. See Younger 1994, 227.

final verses (27–36). Benjamin's failure also stands in stark contrast to Caleb's success (v. 20), perhaps suggesting that Benjamin does not have the same caliber of faith as the elderly hero. This suspicion is eventually justified (see the horrifying account in Judges 19–21 and the tragic story of the Benjaminite Saul in 1 Samuel), though Ehud proves to be an exception (3:15).[50] Finally, when compared with the earlier notice of Judah's victory (v. 8), verse 21 gives the reader the impression that Benjamin was unable to finish what Judah started. Indeed in the course of time David of Judah (not Saul of Benjamin) took the city from the Jebusites and established it as the Lord's dwelling-place (2 Sam. 5:6–7).

A Litany of Failure (1:22–36)

Joseph cuts a deal with a Canaanite (1:22–26). Bethel was an important city to the Israelites because of its prominence in the patriarchal traditions. Abram camped near the site after arriving in the promised land (Gen. 12:8) and after returning from Egypt (Gen. 13:3). Jacob actually gave the place its name "Bethel" (meaning "house of God") after his vision there in which the Lord promised to give him and his descendants the very land upon which he was lying (Gen. 28:10–22). When the Lord later appeared in a dream to Jacob and told him to return to the land of promise, he introduced himself as the "God of Bethel" (Gen. 31:13). After Jacob returned to the land, God instructed him to return to Bethel, where he reiterated his earlier promise to make Jacob fruitful and give his descendants the land (Gen. 35:1–15). To summarize, Israel regarded Bethel as especially significant because God appeared there to Jacob and promised to make his descendants into a great nation and to give them the land of Canaan. As Israel moved into the land, God's promise to Jacob was materializing before their very eyes. The taking of Bethel promised success in occupying the entire land, for it was a reminder that the same God who promised was actively with them, just as he had been with Jacob (cf. v. 22b with Gen. 28:15).

Israel's tactics in conquering Bethel remind one of the conquest of Jericho.[51] In both accounts a native Canaanite cooperates with Israelite

---

50. Wong suggests that this brief reference to the Benjaminites' failure to dislodge the Jebusites provides "the crucial setting needed to understand the subsequent narrative in Judges 19." It is one of several thematic links between the book's prologue and epilogue (2006a, 31).

51. Wong discusses the allusion to the conquest of Jericho in Judges 1:22–26 (2006a, 51–55).

spies, who promised the individual that she/he would be spared when the Israelites conquered the city. However, the resemblances end here. Jericho was miraculously destroyed by God's power, while Bethel's fall came through the instrumentality of a pagan.[52] In contrast to Rahab the harlot, who risked her life, testified to the Lord's greatness, and subsequently lived among Israel, this unnamed resident of Bethel moved to a foreign land, built a city, and called it Luz (the earlier Canaanite name for Bethel). His actions were motivated purely by self-interest and Israel's conquest of the city made no significant impact on him. After all, as far as he was concerned, Israel might not have been successful without his help! Canaanite Luz had not been totally conquered; it had merely been moved to another location (Webb 1987, 96). Joseph's compromise with this Canaanite foreshadowed a more serious form of compromise described in the following context.[53]

The promise made by the spies to the man is especially ironic (v. 24). They assured him that in exchange for his help, they would treat him well. The Hebrew reads literally, "we will deal with you fairly." The Hebrew word חֶסֶד, frequently means "loyalty, devotion, commitment." Elsewhere when the noun appears in the idiom used here (עשׂה, "do" + עִם, "with," + object + חֶסֶד), it refers to fair and/or benevolent treatment as a reward for good deeds rendered as an act of allegiance.[54] Israelite spies made this same promise to Rahab in exchange for her aid (Josh. 2:12, 14). But, as noted above, Rahab's help was self-initiated and she allied herself with Israel from that day forward. By way of contrast, the spies solicited the help of the unnamed man of Bethel, who subsequently went his own separate way.[55]

A dismal report card (1:27–36). These verses continue the account of how the men of Joseph tried to take their inheritance. The sub-tribal group of Manasseh (which also possessed land east of the Jordan) did not occupy several commercially and militarily strategic cities, some of

---

52. The Israelites apparently invaded the city through a rear gate or tunnel. See Yadin 1963, 254.
53. For a more detailed argument along these lines, see Webb 1987, 96–97. Webb also contrasts the tactics of the men of Joseph with the tribe of Judah's aggressive and uncompromising treatment of Adoni-Bezek recorded earlier in the chapter (94–95).
54. See Joshua 2:12, 14; Ruth 1:8; 2 Samuel 2:5–6; 9:1, 3, 7; 10:2.
55. For helpful discussions of the contrast between this event and the conquest of Jericho, see Gunn and Fewell 1993, 160, and Wong 2006a, 53–55.

which Joshua had defeated (cf. Josh. 12:21, 23).[56] They were hesitant to attack these cities as far back as Joshua's day because the Canaanites living in this region had iron chariots (cf. Josh. 17:11–18). The *wayy-iqtol* verb form in verse 27b (וַיּוֹאֶל, "managed") is best understood as consequential in relation to what precedes. In other words, Manasseh's failure to drive out the native people resulted in the Canaanites becoming even more obstinate in their determination to stay in the land.[57] The statement highlights the fact that as time passed and Israel failed to follow up on the victories of Joshua, the impact of those victories upon the Canaanites diminished as terror (Exod. 15:15) turned into resistance.

Only united Israel, not Manasseh, had any success in subduing these Canaanites (v. 28). Even this note is not entirely positive, for its reference to making the native population forced laborers recalls the Gibeonite compromise (Joshua 9), one of the few blots on the conquest account in Joshua.

Like their brother Manasseh, the Ephraimites also experienced only partial success, as the city of Gezer, also an earlier loser against Joshua (Josh. 10:33; 12:12), resisted their efforts. Here the alarming statement "the Canaanites lived *among them*" appears, a distressing shift from the more general "live in that land" (literal translation) of verse 27.

The litany of failure continues in verses 30–36. The recurring

---

56. See Boling 1975, 60. Olson points out that Judges 1:27, 29 states simply that Manasseh and Ephraim "did not drive out" the Canaanites, while the parallel text in Joshua 17:12 says that Manasseh was "*could not* drive out" the Canaanites (1998, 744). Judges 1:27, 29 omits וְלֹא יָכֹל, "and they were unable." Olson writes: "The change is subtle but telling. The Joshua account makes the failure to drive out the Canaanites a matter of power and ability; they wanted to but were not able. The failure is somewhat excusable. The Judges 1 account, however, suggests less excusable reasons for the failure: The failure of Manasseh and Ephraim to drive out the Canaanites may have involved less a lack of ability and more a lack of desire. They *could* have driven the Canaanites out, but they did not *want* to do so." In favor of Olson's proposal is the fact that Joshua 17:18 refers to the Canaanite iron chariots, while Judges 1:27–29 makes no mention of them.

57. *NIV* ("for the Canaanites were determined to live in the land") assumes that the *wayyiqtol* form in verse 27b is explanatory. In this case the statement would reflect the people's, not the narrator's, perspective, for Canaanite obstinance should not have been able to thwart the conquest. See our comments on 1:19.

statement "X (Israelite tribal group) did not conquer Y (Canaanite people group)" dominates verses 30–33, creating a less-than-positive mood about Israel's success and raising once again the lingering question of why this was so (cf. vv. 19, 21). If the Lord had promised the land to the Israelites, why were they only partially successful in their efforts? The omission in these verses of any note concerning the Lord's enabling presence (cf. vv. 19a, 22b) is a signal that something is wrong, but our question will not be answered completely until the next section.

The omission in verses 30–36 of any reference to the tribe of Issachar is peculiar. For the most part the arrangement corresponds to Joshua 19:10–48, with the notable absence of Issachar:

Zebulun	Josh. 19:10–16	Judg. 1:30
Issachar	Josh. 19:17–23	—
Asher	Josh. 19:24–31	Judg. 1:31–32
Naphtali	Josh. 19:32–39	Judg. 1:33
Dan[58]	Josh. 19:40–48	Judg. 1:34–36

In Joshua the tribes of Benjamin (18:11–28) and Simeon (19:1–9) are listed before the northern tribes, while Joshua himself appears at the end (19:49–51). The sevenfold (plus one!) list has an aura of completeness about it.[59] In Judges 1:27–36 Manasseh and Ephraim appear with the northern tribes, reflecting their geographical proximity in Joshua's allotment.[60] The omission of Issachar reduces the list to

---

58. The list of tribes in both Joshua 14–19 and Judges 1 reflects a south to north orientation, though in Joshua 14–19 Joseph appears before Benjamin and Simeon. Dan's placement as the last tribe in both lists reflects Dan's subsequent partial migration to the distant north (see Josh. 19:47; Judges 18). This is somewhat artificial, since Joshua 19:40–46 describes Dan's southern allotment and Judges 1:34–36 focuses on Dan's failure to take this allotted area. See Kallai 1997, 41. Kallai detects this same phenomenon in the Song of Deborah, which groups Dan with the northern tribes, but describes Dan in light of its southern allotment near the maritime plain (40).

59. Judah and Joseph (Ephraim and Manasseh) appear in the preceding section (Joshua 14–17), which is separated from the second list by the narrative in 18:1–10. Judah's and Joseph's textual prominence in Joshua reflects their importance and size. (See Numbers 1–2.) The order of the Joseph tribes (Ephraim first, cf. Joshua 16–17) reflects the reversal that occurred during Jacob's blessing recorded in Genesis 48.

60. Judah, Simeon, and Benjamin appear together earlier in Judges 1, for Joshua's allotment made it clear that they would live closely together in the south.

six, suggesting incompleteness and signaling that reality has fallen short of the ideal.[61]

Other signs of trouble appear in these verses. In verse 26 the survivor of the conquest of Bethel takes up residence outside the land, and in verses 27–30 the Canaanites live among the Israelite tribes. However in verses 31–33 the Israelites (Asher and Naphtali) live among the Canaanites, as if the latter are now the more dominant group, and in verse 34 the Amorites even force the Danites to the hill country.[62] The placement of Dan, who was allotted territory in the south, at the end of a list oriented from south to north hints at the tribe's eventual migration, recorded in the book's epilogue.[63]

Some of the unoccupied towns mentioned here were located on tribal boundaries, namely, Gezer (cf. Josh. 16:3), Aczib (Josh. 19:29), Rehob (Josh. 19:28, 30), and Beth Shemesh (Josh. 15:10; 19:22). By not securing these sites, the tribes left themselves vulnerable in strategic places. Of the fourteen towns named in verses 30–35 as resisting Israel's efforts, only Aphek is mentioned as being defeated in earlier conquest accounts (Josh. 12:18). This is not surprising, for if the men of Joseph were unable to take previously defeated cities (see vv. 27–29), why should one expect the other tribes to be able to subdue areas which escaped Joshua's victories? References to the survival of Beth Shemesh (meaning "house of the sun") and Beth Anat (meaning "house of Anat") are disconcerting, for both call to mind the Canaanite deities after whom they are named and suggest that Canaanite culture and religion were still alive and well. The reference to Amorites holding out in Aijalon is sadly ironic, for it was here that the Lord, not too long before, had miraculously given the Israelites a victory over an Amorite coalition (cf. Josh. 10:12).[64] In contrast to several Israelite tribes, the Amorites had apparently secured their borders. The location of the

---

61. Most interpreters attempt to explain the omission of Issachar on historical, not literary, grounds. See, for example, Amit 1999, 149; Lindars 1995, 63; and the works cited in Younger 1995, 84, note 28.

62. Webb develops this progression nicely (1987, 99). See also Younger 1995, 83, 88–89, and Amit 2003, 24–26. On the manner in which the language and placement of verses 34–35 seek to present Dan as dishonored, see Bartusch 2003, 114–18. He argues that Dan is contrasted with Judah: "Dan represents everything antithetical to Judah" (p. 118).

63. For a more detailed analysis of Dan's placement at the end of the list, see Wong 2006a, 151–53.

64. Several texts in Joshua distinguish Amorites and Canaanites: 3:10; 5:1; 9:1; 11:3; 12:8; 13:4; 24:11 (cf. Judg. 3:5). For a discussion of these two peoples see Schoville 1994, 157–82.

Amorite boundary ("from the Pass of the Scorpions to Sela [which literally means "crag, cliff"] and on up") suggests they had become a dangerous foe (cf. Deut. 8:15; Ezek. 2:6), strongly entrenched in the land and incapable of being dislodged.[65]

The recurring theme of the tribes reducing the Canaanites to forced labor even has a negative effect, for, as noted above, it reminds one of the Gibeonite compromise, and suggests that the efforts of the northern tribes parallel the dark side of the original conquest account more than they do Joshua's victories. Two of the four references to the Canaanites being reduced to forced labor actually highlight the impotence of individual tribes. Manasseh could not defeat the five Canaanite cities listed in verse 27; only a concerted effort by all Israel was able to subjugate these Canaanites, and then only to a limited degree (v. 28a). Dan was pushed back by the Amorites; only Joseph's strength was able to subdue them, again only in a limited way (v. 35b).

A Tearful Encounter at Bokim (2:1–5)

Israel's failure to conquer the land completely was not really due to the Canaanites' iron chariots or obstinance (cf. 1:19, 27). Instead their partial success could be attributed to their willingness to compromise with the native population and tolerate their pagan religion.

Israel's failure prompted God to confront his people. The angel of the Lord, who had accompanied Israel when they left Egypt and when they entered the land (Exod. 14:19; 23:20), possessed full authority as God's special messenger and could therefore speak on God's behalf (Exod. 23:21).[66] The angel came from Gilgal, Israel's main campsite

---

65. Some ancient textual witnesses read "Edomite(s)" instead of "Amorite(s)" in verse 36. For a defense of the traditional reading of the Hebrew text, see O'Connell 1996, 449–52, and Block 1999, 107–08.

66. It is unclear from the immediate context if this divine spokesman (literally, "messenger") is a prophet or an angel, but later descriptions of "the angel of the Lord" suggest that a superhuman being is in view (see Judg. 6:11–22; 13:3–21). Ausloos argues that the messenger is angelic, not human, based on "strong similarities" between Judges 2:1–5 and Exodus 23:20–33, where the messenger is supernatural (cf. especially v. 21) (2008, 9–10). See also Martin 2009, 334. It is not clear if the title refers to a particular angel. The phrase (construct noun + proper name) is definite, but it may simply refer to a definite angel in any given context without implying the same angel is always the referent. (See the use of the phrase "the servant of the Lord," which refers to a servant who is definite in a given context but not the same servant in every passage.) Several texts equate this angel with God/Yahweh. The angel seems to speak as God at times

after they crossed the Jordan River and during the conquest period (Josh. 4:19; 10:15, 43). Gilgal was especially important because its heap of twelve stones was a symbolic reminder of the nation's unity and of God's miraculous power and ability to fulfill his promises to his people (Josh. 4:20–24). At Gilgal a new generation of Israelites renewed the nation's covenantal commitment to the Lord through circumcision, observed the Passover, and tasted the fruit of the promised land for the first time (Josh. 5:2–12). The angel's coming from Gilgal, rather than Shiloh or Shechem (cf. Josh. 18:1; 24:1), may be ominous, for it suggests that the God who sent him was still residing in or had retreated to Joshua's campsite at the entry point of the land. This in turn reinforces the point that the conquest was far from complete and suggests that Israel's hold on the land was still quite tenuous.[67]

The Lord's message consists of an accusation sandwiched between two reminders of his deeds and words.[68] The brief message draws on earlier traditions, especially those found in Exodus 34 and Joshua 23. The Lord recalled how he had delivered Israel from Egypt, brought them into the promised land, and promised never to break his cove-

---

(Gen. 31:11–13; Exod. 3:2, 4; Judg. 2:1–3), while humans who encounter the angel sometimes react as if they have seen God himself (Gen. 16:13; Judg. 6:22; 13:22; cf. also Gen. 32:28–30 in light of Hos. 12:3–4). On the other hand, the angel sometimes speaks as if he is distinct from God (Gen. 21:17; 22:11–12, 15–17; Zech. 1:12). In certain texts a close reading reveals that the angel and God are distinct entities (see Exod. 3:2–4; Judg. 6:11–23). The angel who accompanied Israel out of Egypt (called the "angel of God" in Exod. 14:19) is distinct from God (cf. Num. 20:16), yet he is called the "angel of his [God's] presence" (Isa. 63:9) and possesses God's "name" (full authority) in his inner being (Exod. 23:21). A survey of usage suggests that the angel should be equated with God in a representative, not an essential or personal sense. (The passages that distinguish the angel from God in essence must be determinative.) The angel comes with full divine authority and can therefore speak on God's behalf (sometimes in the first person!). Those who encounter the angel realize his authoritative representative status and therefore act appropriately. As Ross states, "It would seem that the question of the messenger's authority could be answered simply: it is that of the one who sends him. Thus a messenger is to be treated as if he were his master" (1987, 114). For studies of the role of messengers in the ancient Near East, see Meier 1988, and Greene 1989.

67. Martin (2009, 339) notes that the reference to Gilgal "recalls the victories of Joshua as they stand in sharp contrast to the defeats just recounted in Judges Chapter 1."

68. On the central position of verse 2b in the structure of verses 1–5, see Spronk 2001a, 89.

nantal agreement with them.[69] He also reminded them of two important commands: (1) they were not to form a covenant with the native population of the land and (2) they were to destroy the pagan altars, for these were symbols of the false worship system of the land's inhabitants and, if allowed to remain, would tempt Israel to turn away from the Lord to other gods (cf. Exod. 23:24, 32–33; 34:12–14; Deut. 7:1–6, 16).[70]

Israel, rather than showing gratitude for God's gracious deeds, had disobeyed him, prompting a brief but powerful accusation and a probing question as to their motive in doing so. This precise question ("Why would you do such a thing?"), when used elsewhere, comes in response to an action that is viewed as foolhardy or even malicious and deceitful.[71]

The Lord concluded his message with an allusion to an earlier warning delivered through Joshua (Josh. 23:13).[72] Joshua warned that

---

69. It is not clear which covenant is in view here. Moore argues that the covenant is the one made between God and Israel in Exodus 34:10–28, to which allusion is made in Judges 2:2–3 (cf. Judg. 2:2 with Exod. 34:12–13, and Judg. 2:3 with Exod. 34:11) (1895, 58). In this case "my agreement" refers specifically to God's provisional promise to drive out the inhabitants of the land before the Israelites (see Exod. 34:11). However, the statement "I will never break my agreement with you" does not appear in Exodus 34. Webb maintains that the covenant in view is God's unconditional promise to the patriarchs that their descendants would inherit the land (Gen. 24:7; 26:3; Exod. 13:5, 11; 32:13; 33:1; Deut. 6:10, 18, etc.) (1987, 104). A reference to this oath immediately precedes the statement in Judges 2:1. Leviticus 26:44 lends support to this interpretation. Using terminology parallel to Judges 2:1b, God says that he will not break his covenant, which refers here to his promise to give the patriarchs' descendants the land (see vv. 42, 45). Block takes a mediating position, arguing that the promise to the patriarchs "is fully integrated into the Sinai covenant" in the covenant curses of Leviticus 26, as verses 42–44 demonstrate (1999, 113). Note as well Jeremiah 11:4–5, which makes the realization of God's oath to the patriarchs conditional upon the nation's obedience to God's commandments.
70. Oddly enough, no mention is made of the warning against intermarriage that is prominent in Exodus 34:16, Deuteronomy 7:3–4, and Joshua 23:12. This theme has not been forgotten, however, and will make its appearance in due time (see Judg. 3:6).
71. Note its use in Genesis 12:18; 26:10; 29:25; 42:28; Exodus 14:11; Judges 15:11; Jonah 1:10. Apart from Judges 2:2, God asks the question only in Genesis 3:13, where he questions the woman as to why she encouraged the man to be disobedient.
72. The Hebrew perfect verbal form אָמַרְתִּי, literally, "I said," is most naturally taken as a simple past (see NASB), in which case the Lord recalls an

---

if Israel formed alliances with the people of the land, the Lord would abort the conquest and allow the nations to entrap his people and bring about their destruction. The messenger's words, while faithful to the overall thrust of Joshua's statement, are a paraphrase of the earlier warning and include adaptations from other passages as well as other modifications:

(1) In Judges the messenger speaks for God in the first person (Joshua referred to God in the third person), emphasizing that Joshua's warning was the very word of God.

(2) The messenger uses a different word for "drive out" (Heb. אֲגָרֵשׁ) than the one appearing in Joshua 23:13 (cf. לְהוֹרִישׁ). He is probably alluding to Exodus 34:11, where this same verb is used in God's promise that he would drive out the inhabitants of the land if Israel obeyed his covenant and maintained their loyalty to him (see also Exod. 23:28–31; 33:2). By alluding again to Exodus 34, a text that also provides background for the messenger's words in verses 1–2 (see above), the messenger links Joshua's warning with the divine promise through Moses and makes it clear that the ancient promise to drive out the nations is in jeopardy (for the very reasons Moses warned about, cf. Judg. 2:2 with Exod. 34:12–13).

(3) The statement in the middle of verse 3b differs from Joshua 23:13. The statement in Judges should probably be emended from וְהָיוּ לָכֶם בְּצִדִּים, "and they will become for you . . ." to either (1) וְהָיוּ לָכֶם לְצִנִּנִים בְּצִדֵּים, "and they will become thorns in your sides,"[73] or (2) וְהָיוּ לָכֶם לְצָרִים, "and they will become your adversaries."[74] Some prefer to retain MT and understand צִדִּים as an otherwise unattested derivative from the verb צוּד, "to hunt," meaning "snares, traps." In support of this view, one can point to the following statement, which also mentions snares (Block 1999, 116).

The people named the site of this solemn encounter Bokim, meaning

---

earlier warning. NIV interprets the form as a simple present ("I tell you"). See also Hess, "Judges 1–5," 146. In this case the Lord formally announces his judgment on the people. However, the presence of וְגַם, "and also," at the beginning of verse 3 favors understanding the following verb in a past tense. The form is parallel to וָאֹמַר, "and I said," in verse 1b. גַּם is needed to indicate a resumption of God's former words following the accusation of verse 2b. See Moore 1895, 59, and van der Kooij 1995, 297–98.

73. See Numbers 33:55 and Joshua 23:13 for similar readings. In this case a scribe, having written the לצ sequence in לצנינים, may have jumped ahead to the צ of בצדים, leaving out the letters (נינים בצ) that intervene.

74. Note the statement in Numbers 33:55, וְצָרֲרוּ אֶתְכֶם, "and they will be hostile to you." In this case the reading צדים in MT is the product of *dalet-resh* confusion.

"Weeping Ones."[75] This is the second reference in the book to Israel naming a city or place. The contrast with 1:17, where the conquering armies of Judah and Simeon annihilate the Canaanite city of Zephath and rename it Hormah, is striking. The name Hormah symbolized Israel's God-given success as a result of their willingness to obey God's orders concerning the native population. Bokim, on the other hand, was a reminder of the sorrow that results when God's commands are compromised and neglected. Perhaps the naming of Bokim also signals that a period of failure and sorrow has replaced an era of conquest and glory.

MESSAGE AND APPLICATION

Thematic Emphases
Like the book of Joshua, this account highlights God's faithfulness and his enabling presence. In fulfillment of his promise to the fathers (cf. 2:1), the Lord announced that he had given the land into the hands of his people (1:2). He was present with Israel as they attempted to occupy the land (1:19, 22) and, at least in some cases, delivered the enemy over to Israel's army (1:4). Faithful men like Caleb received their divinely promised inheritance (1:12–15, 20).

However, complete success was not automatic. Israel was responsible to remain loyal to God, avoid alliances with the native population, and destroy their system of worship (2:2). Compromise would jeopardize the entire conquest (2:3). The sinful Canaanites were under God's decree of judgment (cf. 1:7); Israel was to have nothing to do with them.

As chapter one makes painfully clear, Israel did not completely succeed in occupying the land. Though Israel may have thought their partial success was due to the Canaanites' military strength (cf. 1:19), the real reason for their failure was their disobedience and assimilation to Canaanite religion and culture (2:1–5). Perhaps they thought God's command to exterminate the Canaanites was unrealistic or unnecessary. They were satisfied with partial obedience and partial blessing. But their partial obedience robbed them of more than full blessing; it also jeopardized the partial blessing they did experience.

---

75. Amit, following the lead of the Septuagint (see 2:1), argues that a "hidden polemic" is at work here and that Bokim is a concealed reference to Bethel. She points out that weeping is associated with Bethel in Judges 20:26 and 21:2–4 (2000, 121–31). For a detailed discussion of the textual evidence, see O'Connell 1996, 452–53.

Exegetical idea: *Despite their faithful God's powerful presence, Israel failed to take the promised land because they disobeyed God's command to exterminate the Canaanites and embraced Canaanite culture and religion.*

Theological Principles

God is faithful to his promises. The background for Judges 1 is God's promise to give the land to Abraham's descendants. God had given Joshua success in breaking the back of Canaanite resistance and in establishing a foothold in the land. As the book begins, Israel stands poised to take God's gift to them. The ensuing history tells how Israel possessed the land, lost possession of it in the exile, and returned to live in it again after the exile, albeit under the authority of the Persians.

God's promise to Abraham continues to be an important theme as we move from the historical setting of ancient Israel into the New Testament. God's promise to Abraham is extended to the new covenant community of faith, the spiritual offspring of Abraham (Rom. 4:13–17, Gal. 3:29, Eph. 2:12–13). The new covenant community does not anticipate a land and nationhood, but rather receives the gift of the Spirit (Gal. 3:14; Eph. 1:13) and the promise that God will preserve his people until the second coming of Jesus (1 Cor. 1:9).

However, as in Israel's case, God's relationship to his people is not one-sided. They are not simply passive recipients of his promises and blessings. God's people are responsible to obey him. If they fail to do so, they forfeit the blessings afforded by the promise (Heb. 4:1; 6:11–12; 10:23, 36–39; James 1:12). When allegiance to God is the goal, going halfway is not good enough. The good news is that the gift of the Spirit enables the new covenant community to succeed where the old covenant community failed (Jer. 31:31–34; Ezek. 36:27).

Theological idea: *God's promises are reliable, but they may be only partially realized and placed in jeopardy when his people disobey his commands and compromise their special position.*[76]

Homiletical Trajectories

(1) The exposition of this passage should highlight God's faithfulness. Because of his character, he is reliable (Heb. 11:11; 1 John 1:9). His people can depend on him to fulfill his promises. At the

---

76. The main idea of the passage is perhaps most clearly illustrated in (1) Judges 1:19, where Judah fails to conquer the enemy, despite God's presence with them, and (2) Judges 2:3, where God reminds the people that their disobedience will jeopardize his plan for them.

homiletical-applicational level one must remind a modern audience of God's specific promises to those within his new covenant community.

(2) The exposition of this passage should also emphasize human responsibility before God. God has made promises and is faithful to his people. But his people must do their part as well. The text illustrates the dangers of disobedience and compromise. The Hebrews passages cited above are relevant in this regard. It is beyond the scope of our discussion to enter into the debate over the interpretation of the Hebrews warning passages. Suffice it to say that one's theological framework (Reformed, Arminian, or somewhere in between) will determine how one nuances this principle for one's modern audience.

(3) The leadership theme is present in this passage, but it is not as prominent as the other major themes developed above. Judah takes a leadership role, but their success is compromised (see 1:19). Caleb and Othniel emerge as paradigmatic figures, but they function more as foils for the failed leadership that subsequently appears. There is not enough material in the first part of the prologue to develop this homiletical trajectory yet.

Preaching idea: *As the new covenant community of our faithful God and as recipients of his reliable promises, we must be obedient and preserve our identity as his people in order to experience the full realization of his promises.*

In the process outlined above we have focused on the first part of the prologue as a unified whole. However, before or after preaching the passage as a whole, one might want to look at the major parts and themes of the text in more detail. For example, one might preach a message on 1:1–18 that develops the first homiletical trajectory and is theocentric in focus. A *preaching idea* for such a sermon might be: *We should be eager to carry out God's purposes, for God keeps his promises to us and empowers us.*

A second sermon would focus on 1:19–2:5 and develop the second, more anthropocentric, homiletical trajectory. A *preaching idea* for this sermon might be: *We must not compromise our position as God's people, for doing so may jeopardize the full realization of God's promises to us.*

A comparison of 1:19 with 2:1–5 yields another, related, *preaching idea*: *When we compromise our position as God's people and embrace the gods of our culture, we may misinterpret the reason for our ineffectiveness and failure as being the power of the enemy, rather than our own sinfulness.*

PART TWO

Prologue to Chaos

JUDGES 2:6–3:6

Worshiping the Enemy's Gods

TRANSLATION AND NARRATIVE STRUCTURE

6a   When Joshua dismissed the people, (*initiatory-flashback / resumptive*)[1]

6b   the Israelites went to their allotted portions of property, intending to take possession of the land. (*sequential*)

7   The people worshiped the LORD throughout Joshua's lifetime and as long as the elderly men who outlived him remained alive. These men had witnessed all the great things the LORD had done for Israel. (*sequential*)[2]

8   Joshua son of Nun, the LORD's servant, died at the age of 110. (*sequential*)

9   The people buried him in his allotted land in Timnath Heres in the hill country of Ephraim, north of Mount Gaash. (*sequential*)

---

1. The *wayyiqtol* form at the beginning of verse 6 initiates a new literary unit within the prologue. The form flashes back beyond Joshua's death (see 1:1) and resumes the story with wording almost identical to Joshua 24:28.

2. In the Hebrew text there is only one main clause in this verse. The translation simplifies matters by dividing the complex Hebrew sentence into two parts.

10a **That entire generation passed away**; (*concluding*)
10b a new generation came along that had not personally
experienced the LORD's presence or seen what he had done for
Israel. (*complementary*)

11a The Israelites did evil before the LORD. (*initiatory*)[3]
11b They served the Baals. (*focusing*)
12a They abandoned the LORD, the God of their ancestors who
brought them out of the land of Egypt. (*complementary*)
12b They followed other gods—the gods of the nations who lived
around them. (*complementary-reiterative*)
12c They worshiped them (*focusing*)
12d and made the LORD angry. (*consequential*)
13a They abandoned the LORD (*reiterative*)
13b and served Baal and the Ashtar idols. (*reiterative*)
14a The LORD was furious with Israel (*consequential*)
14b and handed them over to robbers (*consequential*)
14c who plundered them. (*consequential*)
14d He turned them over to their enemies who lived around them.
(*reiterative*)
14e **They could not withstand their enemies' attacks**.
(*complementary*)
15a **Whenever they went out to fight, the Lord did them harm,
just as he had warned and solemnly vowed he would do**.
(*summarizing*)
15b They suffered greatly. (*consequential*)
16a The LORD raised up leaders (*consequential*)
16b who delivered them from these robbers. (*sequential*)

---

3. The use of the *wayyiqtol* forms in 2:11–14 demands special attention. Longacre observes that the *wayyiqtol* forms used here are "only weakly sequential." Instead they tend to be reiterative, complementary, or focusing/specifying. Longacre suggests, "this departure from the usual narrative norm coincides, however, with the broader function of the passage in marking the whole book's *inciting incident*." He explains that such "inciting incidents" use "synonyms and repetitions as if successive actions were being portrayed" (1994, 64). Verse 12b reiterates verse 11b, but complements verse 12a. Verse 13a reiterates verse 12a, while verse 13b reiterates verse 11b. For a discussion of the overall structure of verses 11–13, see the commentary below.

17a **However, they did not obey their leaders, but prostituted themselves to other gods and worshiped them.** (*contrastive*)[4]

17b **They quickly turned aside from the path their ancestors walked when they obeyed the Lord's commands;** (*complementary*)

17c **they did not follow in their footsteps.** (*complementary*)

18a **When the Lord raised up leaders for them, the Lord was with each leader** (*characterizing*)[5]

18b **and delivered the people from their enemies while the leader remained alive, for the Lord felt sorry for them when they cried out in agony because of what their harsh oppressors did to them.** (*characterizing-sequential*)

19a **After a leader died, the next generation would persist in rebellion** (*transitional-characterizing*)

19b **and act more wickedly than the previous one by following other gods, serving them and bowing down to them.** (*characterizing-sequential*)

19c **They did not give up their practices or their stubborn ways.** (*summarizing*)

20a The LORD was furious with Israel. (*consequential*)

20b He said, (*sequential*)

20c *"This nation has violated the terms of the agreement I made with their ancestors by disobeying me.*

21 *So I will no longer remove from before them any of the nations that Joshua left unconquered when he died.*

---

4. The *wayyiqtol* clause translated "and worshiped them" is not part of the main line; it has a specifying function in relation to the preceding clause ("but prostituted themselves to other gods"), which is subordinated to the main clause by כִּי.

5. The Hebrew style utilized in verses 18–19 makes it clear that the narrator is characterizing the period and describing a pattern that time and again repeated itself. Following the construction כִּי, "when," + perfect verbal form (הֵקִים, "raised up") in verse 18a (technically a subordinate clause), two *weqatal* forms appear in verse 18 where one might have expected *wayyiqtol* forms. In verse 19, after a transitional וְהָיָה, literally, "and it was," with temporal clause, a customary imperfect appears (יָשֻׁבוּ, "would persist"), followed by a *weqatal* form. Longacre explains the use of the *weqatal* in these verses as indicating "a how-it-was-done" procedural discourse that expresses "a customary, script-predictable routine" (1994, 56, 64–65).

22 *They will remain to test Israel so I can see whether or not the people will carefully walk in the path marked out by the* LORD, *as their ancestors were careful to do."*

23a The LORD permitted these nations to remain and did not conquer them immediately; (*flashback*)[6]

23b **he did not hand them over to Joshua.** (*complementary*)

3:1 **These were the nations which the Lord permitted to remain so he could use them to test Israel, especially all those who had not experienced battle against the Canaanites—** (*supplemental*)

2 **He left those nations simply because he wanted to teach the subsequent generations of Israelites, who had not experienced the earlier battles, how to conduct war—** (*supplemental*)

3 **They included the five lords of the Philistines, all the Canaanites, the Sidonians, and the Hivites living in Mount Lebanon, from Mount Baal Hermon to Lebo-Hamath.** (*supplemental, cf. v. 1*)

4 They were left to test Israel, so the LORD would know if his people would obey the commands he gave their ancestors through Moses. (*summarizing*)[7]

5 **The Israelites lived among the Canaanites, Hittites, Amorites, Perizzites, Hivites, and Jebusites.** (*summarizing*)[8]

6a They took the Canaanites' daughters as wives (*sequential*)

---

6. The reference to Joshua having left some nations unconquered (2:22) prompts a review of that earlier period in 2:23–3:3. This supplemental section is introduced by a *wayyiqtol* form that flashes back to Joshua's time (v. 23a). The disjunctive clause at the beginning of 3:1 introduces a list of the nations, but before the list is actually given (v. 3), the narrator mentions the general reason why Joshua left these nations in the land (v. 1b) and then elaborates on this (v. 2).

7. How one interprets this entire section determines the function of verse 4 (see the commentary for the two main options). If one accepts Webb's interpretation, then verse 4 reiterates what precedes. However, our analysis assumes the traditional view. In this case verse 4 returns to the main story line and summarizes God's decision to leave the nations as a moral test for disobedient Israel (cf. 2:20–22).

8. Verse 5 begins the summary for the entire prologue and reflects the main theme of chapter one.

6b   **and gave their daughters to the Canaanites**;
     (*complementary*)
6c   they served their gods as well. (*consequential or complementary*)

OUTLINE

The End of an Era (2:6–10)
  A faithful generation (2:6–7)
  The great leader passes away (2:8–9)
  A new generation emerges (2:10)

A Monotonous Downward Cycle (2:11–3:4)
  Israel chases other gods (2:11–13)
  The Lord carries out a threat (2:14–15)
  Israel spurns the Lord's mercy (2:16–19)
  The nations stay (2:20–3:4)

A Sad Summary (3:5–6)
  Settling down with the enemy (3:5–6a)
  Worshiping the enemy's gods (3:6b)

LITERARY STRUCTURE

This section of the book parallels 1:1–2:5 in that it outlines in broad terms Israel's spiritual decline following Joshua's death. Both sections begin with references to Joshua (1:1 and 2:6–9), outline Israel's spiritual failures, and conclude with an account of divine disfavor (2:1–3 and 2:20–3:4).[9] The final verses (3:5–6) summarize the major themes

---

9. The *wayyiqtol* verb form at the beginning of verse 6 could be read sequentially to verses 1–5, in which case the incident at Bokim occurred during Joshua's lifetime. See Sweeney 1997, 521–22; and Frolov 2008, 316–17. The traditional chapter division and the reference to Joshua dismissing the people in verse 6a might support this. It is possible that 2:1 marks a flashback after the review of Judges 1, which clearly postdates Joshua's death (see 1:1), but verse 1, like verse 6, begins with a *wayyiqtol* form as well. It is more likely that the flashback occurs at 2:6, which begins an account that parallels 1:1–2:5. The statement "when Joshua dismissed the people" at the beginning of 2:6 is identical to Joshua 24:28a and introduces a paragraph that essentially repeats Joshua 24:28–31. Through this resumptive technique the narrator links this new narrative (Judg. 2:10–3:4) with Joshua 24. Judges 2:6 provides an example of what Buth calls "unmarked temporal overlay." As he explains, when such overlay occurs "some lexical redundancy or reference specifically points back to a previous event" (1994, 147).

of the first two chapters. The reference to Israel dwelling among the Canaanites (3:5) recalls 1:32–33, while the statement about Israel serving other gods (3:6b) recalls 2:11, 13. At the same time this section serves as a formal introduction to the central portion of the book (3:7–16:31). Its formulaic report ("The Israelites did evil before the Lord," 2:11) becomes the structural key for this main section of the book (see 3:7, 12; 4:1; 6:1; 10:6; 13:1).

This section contains two main units: (1) an introduction (2:6–10),

---

Frolov rejects this approach. He acknowledges that a flashback must occur somewhere between 1:1 (which refers to Joshua's death) and 2:6 (where Joshua dismisses the people) (2008, 318). He argues that this flashback occurs at 1:27 (which is introduced by a negated perfect). In his scheme Judges 1:27–2:9 is parallel to Joshua chapters 14–24 chronologically (318–19). Judges 1:1–26 postdates these parallel accounts, and Judges 2:10–23 follows Judges 1:1–26 chronologically (321–23). Frolov sees Judges 1:1–26 as a "largely upbeat account of Israel's quest for its own land" that contrasts with "the sorry tale that explains how the land was lost" (321). However, his proposal downplays the negative elements of verses 1–26 (see vv. 19, 21, and 25–26) and overlooks the downward spiral that is evident when one views the tribal structural arrangement of chapter one as a literary unity.

Frolov's main objection (following Sweeney) to seeing a flashback in 2:6 is the fact that the verse begins with a *wayyiqtol* form. Admittedly, *wayyiqtol* forms usually describe events in sequential order, but this is not always the case. As noted earlier (see the section "Narrative Structure of Judges" in the introduction to the commentary), the narrator at times uses *wayyiqtol* forms where the context clearly indicates the action described is chronologically prior, not subsequent, to what precedes. See Judges 8:4a; 11:4b; 12:1a for episode or scene initial examples. In the case of 8:4a and 11:4b, the text refers back to a statement made earlier in the narrative (see 7:25e and 10:9a, respectively). Other examples of nonsequential *wayyiqtol* forms describing chronologically prior actions occur in 2:23a; 3:16a; 5:1a; 8:29a; 9:42c; 16:3a; 20:36b; 21:6a, 24a, and possibly in 7:21a; 11:30a; and 17:5b.

Frolov seems to think that the negated *qatal* form at the beginning of 1:27 more readily marks a flashback, but this seems unlikely. When negated sentences with the structure וְלֹא followed by the perfect interrupt the narrative mainline elsewhere in Judges, they are (1) contrastive or qualifying (8:20c; 11:28; 15:1e; 19:10a, 25a; 20:13b; 21:14c), (2) complementary or reiterative (2:14e, 23b; 3:28e, 29b; 6:4c; 8:28b, 34; 10:6d; 12:6c; 13:2d), (3) summarizing (8:35; 16:9e), or (4) supplemental (13:21a; 14:6d, 9f). In no case does this clausal structure indicate a chronological flashback.

and (2) an account of Israel's subsequent idolatry and God's angry response (2:11–3:4). As noted above, the conclusion (3:5–6, note the disjunctive clause structure in v. 5a), functions as a summary for the entire prologue.

The introduction reports the faithfulness of Joshua's contemporaries (2:6–7), the death and burial of Israel's great leader (vv. 8–9), the passing away of Joshua's contemporaries (v. 10a), and the rise of a new generation that had not experienced God's mighty deeds (v. 10b).

With this transition from one generation to another accomplished, the second unit reports the spiritual decline of subsequent generations of Israelites. The statement in verse 11 becomes a formulaic structural marker in the subsequent chapters (see above). Verses 11–13 comprise a self-contained subsection in that the main verbs of verse 13 ("abandoned" and "served") repeat those of verses 11b and 12a.[10]

Eight *wayyiqtol* verb forms are used in verses 11–13 to describe Israel's sin. The first statement ("The Israelites did evil . . .") summarizes Israel's rebellion, while the following seven elaborate on it. The use of eight (seven + one) *wayyiqtol* verbs suggests completeness, depicting Israel's rebellion as more than thorough.[11] The section displays the following structure:[12]

Summary (v. 11a):
"The Israelites *did evil* before the Lord."

Couplet A (vv. 11b–12a):
"They *served* the Baals.
They *abandoned* the Lord, the God of their ancestors who brought them out of the land of Egypt."

Central Triplet (v. 12b):

---

10. See Webb's helpful diagram of the structure (1987, 108) and our detailed outline of the verses in the text below.
11. Compare Amos 2:14–16, which contains seven descriptive statements of Israel's military defeat, emphasizing that its demise would be thorough and complete. In Amos 1–2 the prophet lists seven oracles of judgment capped off by an eighth directed against Israel, the primary target of his denunciation. Ugaritic myth speaks of Baal's "seven lightning bolts" and "eight magazines of thunder," emphasizing that he has a full arsenal of lightning and thunder at his disposal. See Day 1985, 58–59.
12. For a helpful diagram and discussion of the structure of verses 11–13 see Younger 2002, 88.

"They *followed* other gods—the gods of the nations who lived around them.
They *worshiped* them
and *made* the Lord *angry*,"

Couplet B (v. 13):
"They *abandoned* the Lord,
and *served* Baal and the Ashtar idols."

Couplets A and B, each of which contains the verbs "serve" and "abandon" and refers to Baal, form a ring around the central unit and mark out verses 11–13 as a distinct subunit. In couplet A the order of the verbs is "serve"—"abandon." This order is reversed in couplet B, creating a chiastic pattern for the frame (Fretheim 1983, 91–92). The central triplet speaks more generally of Israel's pagan worship and ends with a reference to the impact of their rebellion upon the Lord. This reference to provoking the Lord's anger is developed further in verses 14–15.

Verse 14, with its shift to a new subject (the Lord), introduces a new subsection that reports the Lord's angry reaction to the sins described in verses 11–13. Verses 15–19 elaborate on verse 14 and outline the pattern that characterized the era: judgment—deliverance—renewed sin. Within this subsection verses 18–19 are parallel to and elaborate on verses 16–17 (note the verbs "raised up" and "delivered" in vv. 16a and 18a, the contrast with the fathers in vv. 17 and 19, and the description of idolatry in vv. 17 and 19). Verse 20, with its reference to the Lord's anger, is parallel to verse 14 and begins a new subsection which reports the Lord's decision not to drive out the nations whom Joshua had left (vv. 20–22). Verse 23 elaborates on and clarifies the meaning of verses 21b–22. The references to Joshua in verses 21 and 23 round out the section (cf. 2:6–8) and signal closure. Verses 3:1–4 (introduced by the disjunctive וְאֵלֶּה, "and these") expand upon 2:23 by identifying the nations in question and by reviewing the reasons why the Lord allowed these nations to escape Joshua's conquest.

EXPOSITION

The End of an Era (2:6–10)

Verses 6–9 essentially repeat Joshua 24:28–31, but there are several differences: (1) the order of the verses is different,[13] (2) Judges 2:6 con-

---

13. The LXX of Joshua 24:28–31 has the same order as Judges 2:6–9.

tains the additional words "they went . . . to take possession of the land" (cf. Josh. 24:28), (3) the introductory words of Joshua 24:29 ("After all this") are omitted in Judges 2:8, (4) the name of Joshua's burial place differs, (5) Judges 2:7 has "the people," rather than "Israel" (cf. Josh. 24:31), (6) Judges 2:7 uses the verb "witnessed" (cf. Deut. 11:7), rather than "experienced" (literally, "knew," cf. Josh. 24:31), and (7) Judges 2:7 describes the Lord's work as "great" (see Deut. 11:7), unlike Joshua 24:31.[14]

Some of these differences are noteworthy. The order of the material in Judges 2 is clearly thematic, the idea of faithful service (vv. 6–7) being followed by the theme of death (vv. 8–9, cf. also v. 10a). This in turn raises the question of whether death will bring an end to faithfulness. The addition of the words "to take possession of the land" emphasizes the task before the people. The verb "witnessed" and the adjective "great" draw attention to the perspective of Joshua's contemporaries and explain the motivation for their service. They had seen the greatness of their God with their very own eyes and this experience had generated within them a commitment to God.[15]

Why does the narrator include the details of Joshua's death and burial? The reference to Joshua being buried in his promised inheritance, coupled with the reminder that he was the Lord's servant, highlights the theological theme that God rewards the faithful. In the midst of a great crisis, Caleb and Joshua had remained faithful. They had marched into the land and courageously followed the Lord's instructions. Both received the land God had promised them. Joshua's burial in the land of his inheritance demonstrated that it belonged to him and his descendants as their God-given heritage (cf. Gen. 49:29–32; 50:24–25; Josh. 24:32–33). Joshua's epitaph reminds us that faithful service to God is rewarded by God's rich blessing (often in the form of long life, cf. Gen. 50:22).[16]

---

14. For discussions of the differences between the two texts, see Amit 1999, 136–41; Block 1999, 120–21; Klein 1988, 32; Lindars 1995, 95–96; and Moore 1895, 65–66.

15. Deuteronomy 11:7 uses the same expression (literally, "all the great work of the Lord which he did") as Judges 2:7, though it omits the final phrase ("for Israel"). In Deuteronomy 11:7 the mighty deeds of the Lord are specifically described as the crossing of the Red Sea, God's provision for the people during the wilderness wandering, and his judgment of Dathan and Abiram.

16. It is also noteworthy that Joshua is here (and in Josh. 24:29) called "the Lord's servant," a title consistently used of Moses prior to this.

At the same time the notation of Joshua's death has a foreboding quality about it. The finality of death and burial highlights the fact that an era was quickly coming to an end for Israel. Would the next generation rise to the challenge and complete what Joshua and his contemporaries had started?

Verse 10 suggests that this question will receive a negative answer. The next generation, in contrast to Joshua and his contemporaries, was not acquainted with the Lord or his deeds in a personal way. The absence of the verb "witnessed" and the adjective "great" (cf. v. 7) reflects this new generation's perspective. They had not "witnessed" God act and consequently were experientially unaware of his greatness.[17] This remoteness became the seedbed for spiritual rebellion and adultery.[18]

A Monotonous Downward Cycle (2:11–3:4)

Israel chases other gods (2:11–13). If verse 10 signals a storm on the

---

17. According to verse 10, the new generation "had not personally experienced the Lord's presence" (literally, "did not know [לֹא־יָדְעוּ] the Lord"). This obviously does not mean that they were unaware of him intellectually. The following statement ("or seen what he had done for Israel") suggests that firsthand experience of the Lord is in view, as does the contrasting statement in verse 7, which characterizes the earlier generation as one "who had witnessed [רָאוּ] all the great things the Lord had done." (Note the parallel statement in Josh. 24:31, which refers to the earlier generation as one "who had experienced firsthand [יָדְעוּ] everything the Lord had done.") The construction "know the Lord" appears to be used in this same manner in 1 Samuel 3:7, which says that the youthful, inexperienced Samuel "did not yet know the Lord." The verb יָדַע often has the semantic nuance "know by experience" (see *HALOT*, 391; BDB, 393–94). Another option is that the expression "know the Lord" in Judges 2:10 carries the nuance "acknowledge, recognize," understood within a covenantal framework. Usage of the construction "know the Lord" elsewhere supports this. With the exception of the aforementioned 1 Samuel 3:7, the expression means, "recognize the Lord's authority" in its other uses (cf. Exod. 5:2; 1 Sam. 2:12; Isa. 19:21; Jer. 31:34; Hos. 2:20 [Heb. v 22]; 6:3). Boling (1975, 72), Olson (1998, 752), and Pressler (2002, 137) prefer this latter nuance in Judges 2:10.

18. Following the lead of earlier writers, Eslinger highlights the linguistic parallels between Judges 2:8, 10 and Exodus 1:6, 8, which describes how Joseph and his generation died off and a new Pharaoh arose who did not know Joseph (1989, 70–71). He suggests that the narrator uses allusion here to cast the post-Joshua generation of Israelites in the role of the new Pharaoh of ancient times. The proposal is more creative than convincing; the verbal parallels may be purely coincidental.

horizon, then these verses describe how it swept through Israel with full, destructive force. As predicted by Moses, Israel "did evil before the Lord." The expression refers to idolatry (see Deut. 4:25; 9:18; 17:2–3; 31:29; Judg. 3:7; 10:6).[19] In contrast to Joshua's contemporaries, who had served the Lord (v. 7), Israel now served the Canaanite storm-fertility god Baal and the war/love goddess Astarte in their various local forms (hence the plurals "Baals" in v. 11 and "Ashtar idols" [literally, "Ashtoreths"] in v. 13).[20] These deities were especially attractive to Israel, for they promised their worshipers agricultural prosperity, abundant offspring, and national security. By rejecting the God of their ancestors who had delivered them from Egypt and by worshiping instead the pagan gods of the surrounding people, Israel provoked the Lord's jealous anger.[21]

The Lord carries out a threat (2:14–15). In his anger God took away the prosperity and security Israel hoped their pagan gods would provide. He delivered his people into the hand of plundering invaders and the hostile nations around them. When the armies of Israel went out to fight, the Lord actively opposed them and brought about their defeat, just as he had threatened to do (see Lev. 26:17; Deut. 28:25). The reference to the Lord's "hand" being "against them" (cf. v. 15, where we translate the idiomatic expression "the Lord did them harm") is tragically ironic, for it casts this new generation in the same role as the generation that perished in the wilderness and forfeited God's richest blessings (see Deut. 2:15). The punishment was appropriate. Israel had

---

19. The wording of Judges 2:12 appears to reflect Deuteronomy 6:12–15. See Latvus 1998, 38.
20. The plural forms "Baals" in verse 11 and "Ashtar idols" in verse 13 most likely refer to various local manifestations of the deities Baal and Astarte, respectively, though the pairing of the two could be a way of referring to Canaanite male and female deities in general. See Day 2000, 68–69, 131. Hebrew עַשְׁתָּרוֹת, "Ashtaroth" (NIV "Ashtoreths") is the plural of the singular form עַשְׁתֹּרֶת, "Ashtoreth." The latter is a deliberate distortion of Astarte's name which vocalizes the last two syllables of the name to reflect the Hebrew word בֹּשֶׁת, "shame." See Day 2000, 128.
21. For this nuance of the verb כָּעַס, "to anger," see Deuteronomy 32:16, 21, where it parallels קָנָא "to make jealous." When used of Israel's provoking the Lord's anger, this verb consistently refers to idolatry. See Deuteronomy 4:25; 9:18; 31:29; 32:16, 21; 1 Kings 14:9, 15; 15:30; 16:13, 26, 33; 22:53; 2 Kings 17:11, 17; 21:6, 15, 17; 23:19, 26; etc.

done "evil" (עָרַע, v. 11); the hostile hand of the Lord brought calamity (רָעָה, v. 15) upon them.[22]

Israel spurns the Lord's mercy (2:16–19). The Lord's anger did not cause him to abandon Israel. When they groaned under the oppressive hand of their conquerors, the Lord took pity on them.[23] The absence of any reference to repentance highlights God's mercy and also suggests Israel's spiritual poverty.[24] The description of Israel's affliction is reminiscent of the Exodus account, which tells how the oppressive Egyptians (Exod. 3:9) caused the Israelites to groan (Exod. 2:24; 6:5).

God's pity moved him to deliver his people through divinely appointed military leaders ("judges") who were also responsible for giving the people moral guidance (v. 17a). However, God's goodness and direction had no lasting influence on the nation. In contrast to Joshua's contemporaries (see v. 7) they quickly turned from the path of obedience, like an earlier generation had done (see Exod. 32:8; Deut. 9:12, 16), and prostituted themselves to pagan gods (see Exod. 34:15–16; Deut. 31:16). Each new generation reached new depths of corruption and became more stubbornly entrenched in its idolatry (Webb 1987, 112). The first part of verse 19b reads literally, "They acted corruptly, more than

---

22. Webb notes this wordplay and observes, "the punishment fits the crime" (1987, 110).

23. The *niphal* form of the verb נחם (v. 18b) is translated in a variety of ways (including "be grieved, be comforted, regret, relent, change one's mind"). The various uses of the word can actually be placed under two categories: (1) "be grieved" and (2) "be consoled, comforted." The former category can be divided into three subcategories: (a) "regret," that is, "be grieved to the point that one seeks to reverse the effects of a past course of action," (b) "relent, experience a change of heart or mind," that is, "be grieved to the point that one deviates from or reverses a present or anticipated course of action," and (c) "be moved to pity," that is, "be grieved to the point where one extends help and thereby seeks to reverse a present condition." See Chisholm 1995, 388, as well as Parunak 1975, 512–32. Here in Judges 2:18 the verb appears to carry this third shade of meaning ("be moved to pity"). Note that the action described by the verb is the basis (note כִּי, "for," prior to the verb) for God's salvific intervention (v. 18a) and that the action is prompted by oppressed Israel's suffering (note the causal use of מִן, "from, on account of," with "their agony"). The verb has this same nuance in Judges 21:6, 15.

24. In Judges 3:9 and elsewhere we discover that Israel did "cry out" (זָעַק) to the Lord, but the verb used does not necessarily imply repentance. See our discussion of the term in our comments on 3:9.

their fathers." The "fathers" mentioned here are the successive generations that followed Joshua's generation, not Joshua's contemporaries,
referred to in verse 17. (Our translation attempts to reflect this: "the
next generation would persist in rebellion and act more wickedly than
the previous one.")

The nations stay (2:20–3:4). This recurring cycle of disobedience (divine
anger—punishment—relief) could not continue forever. Israel's persistence in sin so angered God that he decided to take more drastic measures. In fulfillment of Joshua's earlier warning (see Josh. 23:13), the
Lord declared that he would not drive out the nations that had escaped
Joshua's conquests.

Verse 22 may be interpreted in one of two ways. The verse reads literally, "in order to test by them, Israel, (as to) whether they will/would
keep the way of the Lord to walk in them as their fathers did, or not."
The standard interpretation (reflected in *NIV*) subordinates "to test" to
the preceding declaration "I will no longer drive out" (see v. 21). In this
case the Lord announces that he will suspend the conquest of the land
for a time and use the remaining nations to test the loyalty of present
and future generations of Israelites. In this view 2:23–3:3 go on to explain that the Lord had allowed these nations to escape Joshua's conquest for the sole purpose of teaching new generations of Israelites the
art of warfare, a skill they would need in a hostile world.[25] However,
now these nations would be used to test Israel's loyalty to God (3:4).[26]

A second view understands the phrase "to test" as modifying
"Joshua left" (v. 21) (Weinfeld 1967, 100). In this case the Lord recalls
that he initially left the nations to test Israel's loyalty. Israel flunked
the exam, so the Lord now announces his intention to let the nations
remain as a punishment. Webb, a proponent of this view, summarizes
it as follows, "The nations which were originally left as a test are now

---

25. In this regard see Fretheim 1983, 97. If one follows this line of interpretation, then "test" in 3:1 must mean something akin to "teach" (cf. v. 2) or
"train." This nuance of the verb נסה is not clearly attested elsewhere in the
Hebrew Bible, though it may be present in Exodus 20:20.
26. Verse four specifically indicates that the purpose of the test was "to know"
(i.e., acquire information). Other texts mentioning a divine test include
Genesis 22:1, 12 (the test reveals that Abraham does indeed fear God);
Deuteronomy 8:2 (the test is designed to reveal Israel's true character);
13:3 (the test will determine if Israel really is loyal to the Lord); and 2
Chronicles 32:31 (the test will reveal Hezekiah's inner thoughts). For a
discussion of these texts, particularly Genesis 22:1, 12, as they relate to
the doctrine of divine omniscience, see Chisholm 2007a, 3–20.

to be left as a punishment."[27] If one follows this line of interpretation, must one assume that Israel was doomed from this point on? The announcement is indeed an ominous development and suggests that Israel's future is in grave jeopardy. But it is important to observe that the other aspects of Joshua's warning (see Josh. 23:13) are not mentioned, including any reference to Israel's exile. The declaration is not formalized, meaning that it may be implicitly conditional. Israel was on the road to doom, but a reversal of direction was still possible.

The following verses (2:23–3:3) are problematic for Webb's view. They indicate that God left the nations in order to teach the next generation of Israelites (the children of those who had participated in the conquest under Joshua) the art of warfare. The presence of "only" (Hebrew רַק) at the beginning of 3:2 suggests that God's sole purpose in leaving the nations was to train Israel militarily.[28] If one understands 2:22 (and 3:4) as indicating the purpose for *Joshua* leaving the nations (Webb's view), then 2:22 seemingly contradicts 3:2. Webb attempts to harmonize the texts by equating the two stated purposes. He argues that the warfare in view in 3:2 was holy war and that the next generation's willingness to learn warfare and complete the conquest would be proof of its loyalty to the Lord (Webb 1987, 114–15; cf. Olson 1998, 759). In this case "teach" in 3:2 means "give an opportunity to develop skill at holy war as proof of their loyalty to God."[29] As Judges 1 reports, subsequent generations failed to conduct divinely sanctioned war and consequently failed the test of loyalty.

Verse 3 lists the nations referred to generally in the preceding verses (and in Josh. 23:12–13). The list appears to be a condensed version of the one given in Joshua 13:2–5. Judges 3:3 mentions the five kings of

---

27. Webb 1987, 115. A grammatical parallel to the proposed syntax of verses 21–22 can be found in 2 Chronicles 32:31, where the infinitive of נָסָה, "test," indicating purpose is subordinated to the perfect of עָזַב, "leave alone." See also Hosea 4:10, where the infinitive of שָׁמַר, literally, "guard," indicating manner is subordinated to the perfect of עָזַב. However, the appearance of the *wayyiqtol* וַיָּמֹת, literally, "and he died," in Judges 2:21, between עָזַב, "[Joshua] left" (v. 21), and לְמַעַן, literally, "in order to, so that" (v. 22), is problematic for this view.

28. This statement is in tension with Exodus 23:27–33 and Deuteronomy 7:22, which indicate that the conquest was gradual by divine design so that wild animals would not overrun the land before the Israelites could occupy it. See Amit 1999, 156.

29. This is very similar to the view of Young, who argued that "to learn war" means "to learn to depend upon the Lord for help in fighting against Canaan" (1964, 172).

the Philistines (cf. Josh. 13:3), Canaanites, and Sidonians (Josh. 13:4), and it specifies the Hivites as the inhabitants of the Lebanon region (cf. Josh. 13:5).

One's interpretation of the preceding verses determines how verse 4 is to be understood. According to the standard view, verse 4 summarizes the announcement made by God in 2:20–22. According to Webb's view, it is parallel to 2:22–23 and summarizes why the Lord allowed the nations to remain in Joshua's day.

The following chart outlines and summarizes the two views discussed above:

STANDARD VIEW	WEBB'S VIEW
Announcement (2:20–22)	Announcement (2:20–22)
The Lord will not drive out the remaining nations; they will be left to test Israel's loyalty.	The Lord will not drive out the nations which Joshua left to test Israel's loyalty.
Reflection on past (2:23–3:3) The Lord had allowed these nations to remain in order to teach Israel how to fight	Reflection on past (2:23–3:4) The Lord had allowed these nations to remain to test Israel's loyalty, which would be demonstrated by their willingness to fight.[30]
Conclusion (3:4) But now, as announced in 2:20–22, the Lord would let these nations remain to test Israel's loyalty.	
Summary: The nations that were left by Joshua to teach Israel to fight are now left to test Israel.	Summary: The nations that were left by Joshua to teach war/test Israel are now left to punish those who failed the test.

---

30. According to Webb (1987, 114), 2:23–3:4 displays a chiastic structure: (A) Recapitulation (2:23), (B) Identification of the remaining nations (3:1a), (C) Parenthesis on the test (3:1b–2), (B') Identification of the remaining nations (3:3, the list anticipated in 3:1a is now given), (A') Recapitulation (3:4).

The precise chronological relationship between the announcement of 2:20–22 and the one made at Bokim (2:1–3) is unclear. In 2:3 God reminds Israel that he had threatened not to remove the nations; in 2:21 he announces that he will not in fact remove them. (Different terminology is employed—לֹא אֲגָרֵשׁ in 2:3; לֹא אוֹסִיף לְהוֹרִישׁ in 2:21.) Since 2:21 is more emphatic, it may be that the confrontation recorded in 2:20–22 came later than the encounter at Bokim.

A Sad Summary (3:5–6)
As noted above, these verses summarize the major themes of the first two chapters. Israel settled down among the Canaanites and served foreign gods. An additional observation concerning Israel's apostasy is included. Israel intermarried with the native population of the land, in direct violation of earlier warnings (Exod. 34:16; Deut. 7:3–4; Josh. 23:12). This particular sin, though prominent in Moses' and Joshua's warnings, has not been mentioned prior to this in Judges, not even in the messenger's indictment at Bokim. It is the missing piece in the puzzle that explains how the compromises of 1:1–2:5 led to the outright paganism of 2:6–3:6. Israel had settled down in the midst of the Canaanites and allowed the pagan altars to stand. Rather than conducting divinely sanctioned war and wiping out the remaining nations, Israel rejected the Lord's plan and prostituted themselves to the gods of the nations. A key factor in this decline, as feared by Moses and Joshua, was Israel's willingness to intermarry with the native population, for close alliances of this type pollute the covenant community and inevitably lead to compromise and sin.

MESSAGE AND APPLICATION

Thematic Emphases:
This section of the book highlights God's patience and compassion. His people persisted in spiritual adultery by worshiping Baal and the pagan gods. This aroused God's jealous anger and prompted him to discipline his wayward people, but he did not destroy them. When they cried out for mercy, he provided leaders to deliver them.

However, God could not allow this cycle to go on indefinitely. As each new generation repeated its fathers' sins and became even more corrupt (2:19), the Lord eventually announced that Israel would now have to live with the continual reality of a hostile presence within and upon its borders (2:20–3:4). A decisive test of the nation's loyalty was necessary. This test was like a two-edged sword. If Israel persisted in sin and failed the test, these foreigners would inevitably swallow up the nation. The announcement that God would not defeat these nations was a potential death sentence for Israel, which needed divine enablement to become secure in their land. Yet even here we see God's compassion (Davis 1990, 40–41). Because Israel had already failed so miserably, some might conclude that such a test was undeserved and doomed to fail. Cynics might argue that God's decision to test his people was simply postponing the inevitable. From the cold, calculating perspective of justice alone, all of this is probably true, but God's seemingly irrational decision to give his people another opportunity to meet his spiritual demands testifies to his heart's desire that his people return to him and reciprocate his great love for them.

The anatomy of Israel's sin comes into sharper focus in this section. Israel's compromise with the Canaanites was not merely political; it went much deeper. Israel intermarried with the native population, contaminating its family structure (3:6). This in turn contributed to religious apostasy as Israel turned its back on the Lord and worshiped the pagan fertility gods (2:11–13, 17). Somehow the vision of God's greatness and the reality of his presence did not reach the later generations who had not personally seen God's great miracles (2:10).[31]

Exegetical idea: *God severely disciplined his idolatrous people and then compassionately confronted them, challenging them to demonstrate their loyalty to him.*

Theological Principles:

As noted earlier, God's relationship to his people is not one-sided. They are responsible to obey him and remain faithful to him. If they fail to do so and give other so-called gods their allegiance, God's anger is aroused, prompting him to discipline them, sometimes severely, in an effort to get their attention and motivate them to return to him. The theological background for Judges 2 is the Decalogue, where God demands his people's total devotion and prohibits them from worshiping idols (Exod. 20:2–5; Deut. 5:7–9).

God is committed to the relationship he establishes with his covenant people. He cares enough about the relationship to confront disobedience when it occurs and to discipline his people. Yet when they

---

31. For a brief but insightful discussion of this subtheme, see Olson 1998, 753–54.

cry out in pain, he is predisposed to show compassion and mercy.[32] The picture presented in Judges 2 (note especially v. 18) is consistent with what we see elsewhere in the Hebrew Bible. Because of his compassionate nature, God typically relents from judgment (Joel 2:13; Jonah 4:2). The New Testament likewise affirms that God's capacity to show compassionate mercy is one of his fundamental character qualities (2 Cor. 1:3; James 5:11). God's decision to test his people, while attributed to his anger (Judg. 2:20), also testifies to his great patience, which is an expression of his compassion and, more fundamentally, of his yearning desire for a relationship with his people characterized by reciprocal love (cf. Hos. 1–2; Matt. 23:37).[33] Even when God expresses his anger, one detects his mercy![34]

Theological idea: *When God's people are unfaithful, his anger is aroused, prompting him to discipline them and to take drastic measures to bring reconciliation. Yet God is patient and shows compassion to his sinful people, responding to their cries and even giving them an opportunity to demonstrate renewed allegiance to him.*

Homiletical Trajectories:

(1) Once again (cf. 1:1–2:5) the exposition of this passage should highlight God's faithfulness to his covenant community. Because God is committed to his people, their sin angers him and prompts him to confront and discipline them (cf. Heb. 12:4–11). God refuses to have a dysfunctional relationship with his people and will do what is necessary to heal the rift. At the same time God is patient and compassionate (see Judg. 2:18). He responds to his people's sin-inflicted suffering and even gives them an opportunity to renew and prove their allegiance to him when they do not deserve a "second chance."

---

32. For helpful remarks in this regard, see Fretheim 1983, 94–95. McCann observes, "God cannot help but be gracious to a people who apparently cannot help but be unfaithful" (2002, 37).
33. As Fretheim (1983, 96–97) points out, "God seeks to bring good out of evil, as always."
34. As noted earlier in the commentary section, the approach I have taken here assumes the traditional view of the test (contrary to Webb's position). If one takes Webb's view, then the test has been taken and failed and one's theological analysis and homiletical treatment of this passage will differ from what I have proposed. Given Webb's view, the passage would teach that God's compassion and mercy have their limits.

(2) The passage also reminds us that God tolerates no rivals; he expects our full devotion and loyalty. He views unfaithfulness as spiritual adultery (cf. Judg. 2:17). If we violate the relationship, God's anger is aroused and his discipline can bring humiliating defeat that robs us of the security and blessings that could be ours.

In developing this theme for a contemporary audience, one must address the issue of what constitutes idolatry. Most of those in a modern audience, at least in the context of the western church, will not be involved in idolatry as described in Judges 2. However, the New Testament, while denouncing literal idolatry, also gives the concept an ethical dimension. Paul calls greed "idolatry" (Col. 3:5).[35] According to James 4:4, "friendship with the world" constitutes spiritual adultery (a metaphor for idolatry in the Hebrew Bible). In this context, James associates friendship with the world with greed and the pride, envy, and hostility it invariably produces (see vv. 1–3, 5–6).

(3) The leadership theme is present in this passage (see Judg. 2:16), but, as in the first part of the prologue, it is not as prominent as the other major themes developed above. Preparing us for the accounts of the individual judges, the text simply makes the point that God provided leaders as his instruments of deliverance. There is not enough material here to develop this homiletical trajectory at this point.

Preaching idea: *We must remain loyal to our faithful God, realizing that he tolerates no rivals. When we fail and experience his discipline, we should respond positively to his compassionate discipline with the confidence that renewed loyalty will bring restoration.*

This preaching idea focuses on part two of the prologue as an entire literary unit. However, as we suggested with part one of the prologue, before or after preaching the passage as a whole, one might want to develop in more detail the homiletical trajectories. Some *preaching ideas* might include:

(1) *God will confront us when we anger him by setting our affections on the gods of our culture and robbing him of the full loyalty he deserves from us.*

---

35. For a brief, but insightful, treatment of how greed constitutes idolatry, see Younger 2002, 95–96.

(2) *God's anger is tempered by compassion, prompting him to discipline us with "tough love" and to give us new opportunities to demonstrate renewed loyalty.*

(3) *When we persist in sin, God will sometimes test us to reveal if we really are loyal.*

JUDGES 3:7–11

Othniel Sets the Standard

TRANSLATION AND NARRATIVE STRUCTURE

7a   The Israelites did evil before the LORD. (*initiatory*)

7b   They forgot the LORD their God (*focusing*)

7c   and worshiped the Baals and the Asherahs. (*complementary*)

8a   The LORD was furious with Israel (*consequential*)

8b   and turned them over to Cushan-Rishathaim, king of Aram-Naharaim. (*consequential*)

8c   They were Cushan-Rishathaim's subjects for eight years. (*sequential*)

9a   So the Israelites cried out to the LORD, (*consequential*)

9b   and he raised up a deliverer for the Israelites (*consequential*)

9c   who rescued them. His name was Othniel son of Kenaz, Caleb's younger brother. (*consequential*)[1]

---

1. In the Hebrew text verse 9bc reads literally, "and the Lord raised up a deliverer for the sons of Israel and he rescued them—Othniel son of Kenaz, Caleb's younger brother." "Othniel . . ." is appositional to "deliverer" in the preceding clause.

10a The LORD's spirit empowered him, (*focusing*)[2]
10b and he led Israel. (*consequential*)
10c When he went to do battle, (*focusing*)[3]
10d the LORD handed over to him Cushan-Rishathaim, king of Aram, (*sequential*)
10e and he overpowered him. (*consequential*)
11a The land was undisturbed for forty years; (*concluding*)
11b then Othniel son of Kenaz died. (*sequential*)

OUTLINE

Israel sins (3:7)
The Lord punishes (3:8)
The Lord responds to Israel's cry (3:9)
The Lord energizes Othniel (3:10)
Peace is restored/Othniel dies (3:11)

LITERARY STRUCTURE

The report of Othniel's deliverance of Israel is the first of six sections that provide specific examples of the general pattern outlined in 2:11–19. This brief section unfolds as follows: (1) Israel's apostasy (v. 7), (2) the Lord's discipline through a foreign oppressor (v. 8), (3) Israel's cry (v. 9), (4) the Lord's deliverance (vv. 9–10), (5) conclusion (v. 11). Within verses 9–10 the narrator uses a summary statement-elaboration technique. Verse 9 reads literally: "When the Israelites cried out to the Lord, he raised up a deliverer for the Israelites and he (the deliverer) saved them—Othniel son of Kenaz, Caleb's younger brother." Verse 9b identifies more specifically the "deliverer" mentioned in 9a, while verse 10 elaborates on how this deliverer "rescued" Israel.

EXPOSITION

Not long after Joshua's death, Israel rebelled against the Lord by forgetting him and serving the Canaanite deities Baal and Asherah.[4] To

---

2. Verse 10a gives additional information related to the preceding statement. It tells how Othniel was able to rescue Israel.
3. Verse 10c begins a more detailed, focused account of the deliverance mentioned in verse 9c and shows one of the primary ways in which spirit-empowered Othniel led Israel (cf. v. 10ab).
4. The plural forms probably refer to local manifestations of the two deities. Elsewhere the term Asherah usually refers to a cultic symbol, but on a few occasions, as here, the word is a proper name of a deity. See Day 2000, 42–46. Two medieval Hebrew manuscripts, as well as the Syriac and Vulgate

forget the Lord involves neglect of his covenant demands, ingratitude for his blessings, and a self-sufficient attitude. This in turn opens the door to idolatry. (See Deut. 6:10–12; 8:10–20; 32:15–18.)

The Lord resents being forgotten and will not tolerate being replaced by other gods. As Moses warned would happen, his jealous anger was stirred (cf. Deut. 6:15) and he delivered his covenant people over to the oppressor Cushan-Rishathaim from Aram-Naharaim in upper Mesopotamia.[5] This king's cruelty is suggested by his name, which by popular etymology could be taken to mean "Cushan the Doubly Wicked."[6] The reference to Aram-Naharaim is both ironic and menacing, for this region was Abraham's native land (Gen. 24:10, cf. v. 4) and it was from here that Balak of Moab brought Balaam to curse Israel (Deut. 23:4; cf. Num. 23:5). With another note of irony the text tells us that those who willingly "worshiped (literally, "served") the Baals and Asherahs" (v. 7) were forced to be subjects of (literally, "serve") a foreign king (Webb 1987, 128). ("They were subjects" translates Hebrew עָבַד, translated "worshiped" in v. 7.)

Overwhelmed by their oppressors, the people "cried out" to the Lord. The verb translated "cried out" (זָעַק) carries the basic idea of a cry of distress or terror as a response to suffering or impending doom (see especially Exod. 2:23; Judg. 6:6–7; 1 Sam. 5:10; 8:18; 12:8; 2 Sam. 13:19; 19:4; 1 Kings 22:32; 2 Chron. 20:9; Isa. 14:31; 26:17; Jer. 30:15; 47:2; 48:20; Jon. 1:5). The verbal content of the cry can vary; it can include a confession of sin (Judg. 10:10; 1 Sam. 12:10; see also Neh. 9:4 and Joel 1:14), a complaint/lament (1 Sam. 4:13; 15:11; 28:12; 2

---

versions, read "Ashtaroth" here, rather than "Asheroth," but this reading is probably a harmonization to Judges 2:13; 10:6; 1 Samuel 7:3–4; 12:10 (Day 2000, 45). Asherah (Athirat in Ugaritic) was a fertility goddess, associated in the Ugaritic texts with the patriarchal god El, not the storm god Baal. For a detailed summary of recent scholarly opinion on Asherah, see Day 2000, 42–67. Recent studies of Asherah include Hadley 2000; Binger 1997; Wiggins 1993; and Pettey 1990. On the reference to Asherah in the Kuntillet Ajrud texts, where there appears to be a reference to "Yahweh and his Asherah," see Hess 2007, 283–89.

5. For a summary of proposals as to the identity of this ruler, see Younger 2002, 106–07.

6. See Boling 1975, 80. Kitchen suggests that Rishathaim as it stands is a "pejorative epithet" (like Ishbosheth for Ishbaal) of an original Resh 'Athaim, "chief of 'Athaim." This individual was probably "an Aramean adventurer who based himself on some town ('Athaim) in the west bend [of the Euphrates] area not yet known to us and bedecked himself with the pompous title of king of Aram-Naharaim" (Kitchen 2003, 212).

Sam. 19:4; Esth. 4:1; Isa. 15:4–5, 8; 65:19; Jer. 20:8, 16; 25:34; 48:31; Ezek. 9:8; 11:13; 21:12; 27:30; Hos. 7:14; Hab. 1:2), a request for help (Judg. 10:14; 12:2; 1 Sam. 7:8–9; 2 Sam. 19:28; Isa. 57:13; Jer. 11:11–12; Lam. 3:8; Mic. 3:4; Pss. 22:5; 107:13, 19), or even a declaration of confidence accompanying a request for aid (Ps. 142:5–6; see also Hos. 8:2). While such an outcry does on occasion include a confession of sin (Judg. 10:10; 1 Sam. 12:10), this word does not seem to be a technical term for repentance. Usage suggests it is fundamentally a cry of pain (see especially 2 Sam. 13:19; 19:4), often accompanied by a lament over one's condition and/or by a request for divine help. If the context does not specifically indicate that the cry was accompanied by a confession of sin, we should not assume that repentance took place. Consequently, with respect to its usage here in Judges 3:9, all we can say for certain is that oppressed Israel cried out in their pain to the Lord.

Understanding the verb in this more limited way, Greenspahn argues that Israel never did turn from their idolatry (Greenspahn 1986, 391–95).[7] Consequently, he reasons, the statement in the introductory framework (3:12; 4:1; 10:6; 13:1) should be translated "they continued to" do evil, not "they again" did evil (Greenspahn 1986, 394).[8] In this view, the people persisted in idolatry, rather than oscillating back and forth between faithfulness and idolatry. God did not respond to a repentant people, but rather mercifully intervened to relieve the suffering of his disobedient people (Greenspahn 1986, 394–96). The Gideon account appears to support this interpretation, for after the people cried out (6:7) they remained involved in Baal worship (6:25–32).

---

7. Judges 13:1 would seem to be an exception to this, since the preceding account does picture the people abandoning their idols (cf. 10:16). Judges 8:33 seems to indicate that the Israelites returned to their idolatry after the death of Gideon, implying that they had repudiated idols for a time. The text collocates a *wayyiqtol* form of שׁוּב, "return," with a *wayyiqtol* form of זנה, "commit adultery." This precise construction occurs only here, but adverbial שׁוּב often indicates renewed action when collocated with a following *wayyiqtol* form. See, for example, Genesis 26:18; Numbers 11:4; Judges 19:7; 1 Kings 19:6; 2 Kings 1:11, 13; 19:9; 21:3; Zechariah 5:1; 6:1. On occasion, however, adverbial שׁוּב seems to refer to continuing (see 1 Kings 13:33) or regularly repeated (Ps. 78:41) action, so the syntax is not decisive.

8. Outside of Judges, the collocation of adverbial יָסַף, literally, "add," with עשׂה, "do," occurs only in Deuteronomy 13:12 (English v. 11) and 19:20; it is not clear if renewed or continuous action is in view. In 1 Kings 16:33 the collocation וַיּוֹסֶף . . . לַעֲשׂוֹת, "and he did more," precedes another infinitive and seems to indicate intensification of action.

However, Samuel's survey of the Judges period in 1 Samuel 12:9–11 seems to imply that the people confessed their sin on each occasion when they cried out to the Lord for deliverance from oppression. The language of 1 Samuel 12:10 is reminiscent of Judges 10:10, 15, the only passage in Judges where a confession of sin is included as the content of the cry. But Samuel gives the impression that such confession of sin was typical of the period, for in verse 9 he refers to several oppressions as prompting the confession and in verse 11 he lists a series of salvific events as following the confession. This gives the distinct impression that the confession occurred in all of these cases and served as the catalyst for the divine intervention that reversed the effects of judgment. Furthermore, the fact that the Israelites cried out *to Yahweh*, rather than to Baal or some other deity, implies at least some recognition of Yahweh's authority and may suggest some degree of repentance.[9]

As he had done when Israel was suffering in Egypt (cf. Exod. 2:23), the Lord responded to his people's cry and provided a deliverer, Caleb's son-in-law Othniel. As a heroic conqueror of the Canaanites who married within the covenant community (cf. 1:12–13), Othniel stood in stark contrast to those in the nation who had settled down among and intermarried with the native population (cf. 3:5–6). As a link to Joshua and Caleb, he is a model of the ideal Israelite leader whose faith produces courage and obedience. It comes as no surprise that he is the first divinely appointed judge, who sets the standard for all who follow.[10]

As in 1:13, the matter-of-fact tone of verses 9–10 highlights the Lord's power as well as Othniel's effectiveness as a divinely enabled warrior.[11] With a rapid, "just the facts" style, the narrator tells us that the Lord raised up Othniel who in turn delivered Israel. Elaborating ever so briefly on this, he then informs us that the Lord's spirit empowered Othniel for military leadership and that the Lord gave the enemy into his hand (cf. 1:4). In each case God's action is primary, assuring Othniel's success:

(1) "he raised up a deliverer for the Israelites . . . who (note the *wayyiqtol* form) rescued them" (v. 9bc)

(2) "the Lord's spirit empowered him, and he led (*wayyiqtol* again) Israel" (v. 10ab)

---

9. I owe this observation to my former student, Dr. John Harman.
10. On Othniel's paradigmatic function, see Gunn 1987, 113; Klein 1988, 33–34; Boling 1975, 82–83; and Brettler 1989b, 405–6, and 2002, 25–28.
11. Gunn points out that the brevity and positive focus are consistent with Othniel's paradigmatic role (1987, 113).

(3) "the Lord handed over to him. . . and he overpowered" (*wayy-iqtol* again) (v. 10de)

The conclusion to this brief section, with its notice that the land experienced peace for forty years, indicates that equilibrium had been restored to the covenant community. Israel had returned to the place it occupied at the conclusion of Joshua's military campaigns (cf. Josh. 11:23b; 14:15b). The land lay before the people, ready to be taken in fulfillment of the Lord's promise. Would Israel prove equal to the challenge?

MESSAGE AND APPLICATION

Thematic Emphases:

Israel's worship of foreign gods prompted God to subject them to an oppressive foreign invader, but in response to Israel's suffering, God provided a deliverer, Caleb's son-in-law Othniel. Othniel is a model leader, a man of faith who inherited the Joshua-Caleb legacy and unhesitatingly took hold of God's promised blessings, even when the challenge was great (cf. 1:13). It is not surprising that he appears as Israel's first deliverer in the Judges period. When God's spirit empowered him, he acted decisively, without laying down any conditions, seeking any special assurances, or foolishly partying with the enemy.

(Judges 3:7–11 and 3:12–31 are distinct literary units in the book's structure, but they may be combined in exposition because both pericopes present a leadership ideal that provides a foil for the failed leaders whose stories follow. For a discussion of the theological principles that emerge from 3:7–11 and a proposal regarding its homiletical use, see the sections entitled "Theological Principles" and "Homiletical Trajectories" following the commentary on 3:12–31.)

JUDGES 3:12–31

Man on a Mission

TRANSLATION AND NARRATIVE STRUCTURE

12a The Israelites again did evil before the LORD. (*initiatory*)[1]

12b The LORD moved Eglon, king of Moab, against Israel because they did evil before the LORD. (*consequential*)

13a Eglon allied with the Ammonites and Amalek. (*sequential*)

13b He came (*sequential*)

13c and defeated Israel (*sequential*)

13d and they seized the City of Date Palm Trees. (*sequential*)

14a The Israelites were subject to Eglon, king of Moab, for eighteen years. (*sequential*)

15a So the Israelites cried out to the LORD (*consequential*)

15b and the LORD raised up a deliverer for them—Ehud son of Gera the Benjaminite, a left-handed man. (*consequential*)

---

1. A *wayyiqtol* form initiates the narrative and the story line then develops in a reportorial, matter-of-fact style that uses thirteen *wayyiqtol* forms. The *wayyiqtol* form at the beginning of verse 12 initiates the action, but it can also be viewed as sequential at the macrostructural level. It introduces a historical account that follows the story of Othniel recorded in verses 7–11.

15c The Israelites sent him to Eglon, king of Moab, with their tribute payment. (*sequential*)

16a Ehud had made himself a sword. (*flashback*)[2]

16b **It had two edges and was eighteen inches long**. (*supplemental*)[3]

---

2. The initial clause in verse 16 (introduced with a *wayyiqtol* form) involves a flashback. At the end of verse 15 we are told that the Israelites sent their tribute to Eglon by the hand of Ehud. Verse 17a informs us that Ehud then brought the tribute to the king. However, verse 16a flashes back to a time when Ehud made the sword, presumably before he was actually sent off with the tribute. The chronological order of events was probably as follows: (1) Ehud made his sword (v. 16a), (2) the Israelites sent Ehud to the king (v. 15c), (3) Ehud strapped on his sword (v. 16c), (4) Ehud brought the tribute to the king (v. 17a). The text presents the first two actions in reverse order, perhaps for literary effect. The references to making and strapping on the sword naturally complement each other and, when combined, facilitate the presentation of Ehud as a man who is on a different mission (assassinating the king) than the one he appears to be on (delivering tribute to the king). By reversing the verb order, the narrator creates a structure in which the secret mission is embedded within the ostensible mission: (A) Israel sends Ehud to deliver tribute, (B) Ehud makes a murder weapon, (B') Ehud straps on the murder weapon, (A') Ehud arrives with the tribute.

   For another example of successive *wayyiqtol* forms where the chronological order of events may very well be rearranged for literary effect, see Genesis 22:3. One would think that Abraham would have split the wood before saddling the donkey and taking the servants and Isaac. Assuming that the actions are listed in chronological order, interpreters propose that Abraham was not thinking straight, that he was trying to keep everyone in the dark about the purpose of the trip, or that he was putting off the inevitable as long as possible. But the order may be literary. The narrator includes the routine actions first (saddling the donkey, summoning the servants), setting the stage for the scene to follow and signaling that Abraham will obey. Then he mentions Isaac and puts the most ominous action (chopping the wood) last in the list of preparatory actions for dramatic effect. When he saddles the donkey, one thinks: Hmmm! It looks like he's going to do it. When he splits the wood, one thinks: Wow, he really is going to do it!

3. The disjunctive clauses in verses 16b and 17b give supplemental information that will become more important as the story unfolds. The two statements are related conceptually, for Ehud will drive, or perhaps bury, his sword into the king's well-fed belly. The translation "eighteen inches" assumes that the term גֹּמֶד, which occurs only here in the Old Testament, is a unit of measure, namely, a "cubit." This is reasonable given the fact

16c He strapped it under his coat on his right thigh.
(*resumptive-sequential*)

17a He brought the tribute payment to Eglon, king of Moab.
(*sequential*)

17b **Now Eglon was a very well-fed[4] man.** (*supplemental*)

18a After Ehud brought the tribute payment, (*transitional*)[5]

---

that אָרְכָּה, "its [the sword's] length," follows. But Stone (2009, 660–62), appealing to etymological, contextual, and archaeological data, suggests that גֹּמֶד is not a unit of measure, but refers instead to the sword being "rigid or stiff over its entire length" (661). He explains that this sword (labeled by archaeologists as the Naue Type II), in contrast to what was typical of the period in Canaan, had its hilt and blade cast in one piece to facilitate thrusting and slashing. It arrived in Canaan with the Sea Peoples. If גֹּמֶד is not a unit of measure, then the text does not inform us how long the sword was. Stone explains that "the whole inventory of eastern Mediterranean Naue Type II swords ranges from 19.5 inches to just over 33 inches, with 24 inches being typical" (662). He suggests that "Ehud's sword could represent a slightly shorter version of this weapon," presumably to facilitate keeping it hidden under his garment.

4. The term בָּרִיא is typically translated "fat" here. Elsewhere the word usually refers to animals that are well-fed and physically healthy, often in contrast to those who are under-nourished and thin (cf. Gen. 41:2, 4–5, 7, 20; 1 Kings 4:23; Ezek. 34:3, 20; Zech. 11:16). The term is used of people in only two other texts. In Psalm 73:4 it describes the well-nourished rich, and in Daniel 1:15 it is used of Daniel and his friends who, despite their restricted diet, looked healthy and well-fed after the ten-day experiment. In Habakkuk 1:16 the word describes abundant food. Considered by itself, the use of בָּרִיא does not necessarily suggest that Eglon was fat or obese. See Stone 2009, 650–51. Nevertheless, the interpretive consensus that Eglon was fat may find contextual support from two factors: (1) the addition of the adverb מְאֹד, "very," in verse 17, and (2) the description of Ehud's short sword (probably 13–18 inches long) being buried inside the king's belly (vv. 21–22), suggesting that his waistline was quite large. However, both of these points may be countered: (1) the phrase בָּרִיא מְאֹד could simply be translated, "very robust," or "very well-fed" (Stone 2009, 651), and (2) the text does not necessarily say that the sword was buried inside the king. On the contrary, some understand the final clause of verse 22 as describing the blade coming out the king's back. See our discussion below. Stone argues that a blow to the lower abdomen, to kill a victim quickly and quietly, would have to sever the aorta. Furthermore, the blade "must travel at a rather sharp upward angle" (2009, 659). So even if the blade did not come out Eglon's back, this would not imply that he was obese.

5. The temporal indicator וַיְהִי, "and it so happened," in verse 18a marks the transition from the prologue (which gives the preliminaries) to the central

18b he dismissed the people who had carried it. (*sequential*)
19a **But he went back once he reached the carved images at Gilgal**. (*contrastive*)[6]
19b He said: (*sequential*)[7]
19c *"I have a secret message for you, O king."*
19d Eglon replied: (*sequential*)
19e *"Shh!"*
19f All his attendants left. (*consequential*)
20a **When Ehud approached him**, (*circumstantial*)[8]
20b **he was sitting in his upper room all by himself**. (*synchronic*)
20c Ehud said: (*sequential*)
20d *"I have a message from God for you."*
20e So he rose up from his seat. (*consequential*)
21a Ehud reached with his left hand, (*sequential*)[9]
21b pulled the sword from his right thigh, (*sequential*)
21c and drove it into Eglon's belly. (*sequential*)
22a The handle went in after the blade (*sequential*)[10]

---

scene of the narrative (where the plot reaches its peak).

6. The disjunctive clause in verse 19a contrasts Ehud's movements with those of the servants.

7. The dialogue in verses 19–20 slows the story down and helps build the drama. We already suspect what Ehud intends to do and have some idea of how his left-handedness may help him. But how will he get the king isolated and how will he ever be able to escape?

8. The disjunctive clauses in verses 20a, 24a, and 26a, all of which have Ehud as the stated or implied subject, divide the central scene into distinct parts. In verses 18–19 Ehud makes sure he is alone with the king, in verses 20–23 he maneuvers the king into a vulnerable position and then assassinates him, in verses 24–25 the focus turns to the king's servants, and verse 26 reports Ehud's successful escape. The structure in verses 20ab and 24ab (where disjunctive clauses are paired) indicates synchronism of action. In verse 26a the disjunctive clause signals a shift in focus back to Ehud; the disjunctive clause in verse 26b is circumstantial, being subordinate to the main clause that follows.

9. Once the king rises from his throne, the story rushes along in headlong fashion as eight *wayyiqtol* forms appear in rapid succession, interrupted by one brief subordinate explanatory clause in verse 22b. The descriptive details in verse 22 tend to slow the pace ever so slightly, but they also "drive home the point" (!) of the finality of the king's death.

10. If this sword was indeed the Naue Type II variety (see note on v. 16b above), then it would have lacked a cross guard, explaining how the hilt would have entered after the blade. Stone 2009, 662.

22b and the fat closed around the blade, for Ehud did not pull the sword out of his belly. (*sequential*)

22c He went out into the vestibule. (*sequential*)

23a Then Ehud went into the outer area, (*sequential*)

23b closed the doors of the upper room behind him, (*sequential*)

23c **and locked them**. (*complementary*)[11]

24a **When he had left**, (*circumstantial*)

24b **Eglon's servants** entered (*synchronic*)

24c and looked. (*sequential*)

24d They saw the doors of the upper room were locked. (*dramatic*)[12]

24e So they said: (*consequential*)

24f *"He must be relieving himself in the upper room."*

25a They waited so long they became embarrassed. (*sequential*)

25b **They saw that he did not open the doors of the upper room**. (*dramatic*)

25c So they took the key (*consequential*)

25d and opened them. (*sequential*)

25e **They saw their master lying dead on the floor**. (*dramatic*)

26a Now **Ehud escaped while they delayed**. (*dramatic shift in focus*)

26b **When he passed by the carved images**, (*circumstantial*)

26c he escaped to Seirah. (*sequential*)

27a When he arrived there, (*transitional*)[13]

27b he blew a trumpet in the Ephraimite hill country. (*sequential*)

27c The Israelites went down with him from the hill country. (*sequential*)

27d **Now he was in the lead**. (*circumstantial or supplemental*)[14]

---

11. The *waw* + perfect construction in verse 23c is complementary (shutting and locking a door are actions that typically go together; cf. 2 Sam. 13:18), but it may also indicate the climactic act in the sequence and signal a transition in focus. See Longacre 1994, 71–72.

12. The three disjunctives in verses 24d, 25b, and 25e (all beginning with וְהִנֵּה, "and look") dramatically invite the audience to share the servants' perspective. They also tend to slow the pace of the story (after all Ehud needs time to escape) and resolve the tension. The servants' slow reaction and initial failure to suspect anything already suggest what we are told in verse 26—Ehud is about to get away with murder. See Amit 1999, 192–94.

13. The temporal indicator וַיְהִי, "and it so happened," in verse 27a marks the transition to the epilogue, which tells how Ehud followed up his daring deed by mustering Israelite troops and defeating the Moabites.

14. The disjunctive clause in verse 27d facilitates the transition from the hurried actions described in verse 27 to Ehud's speech reported in verse 28b.

28a He said to them: (*resumptive-sequential*)
28b *"Follow me, for the* LORD *has handed your enemies, Moab, over to you."*
28c So they followed him down, (*consequential*)
28d captured the fords of the Jordan opposite Moab, (*sequential*)
28e **and did not allow anyone to cross**. (*complementary*)[15]
29a They struck down about ten thousand[16] Moabites at that time, all of whom were strong, capable warriors. (*sequential*)[17]
29b No one escaped. (*complementary*)[18]

30a So Moab was subdued that day under the hand of Israel, (*summarizing*)
30b and the land was undisturbed for eighty years. (*concluding*)
31a **After Ehud came Shamgar son of Anath**; (*supplemental*)[19]
31b he killed six hundred Philistines with an oxgoad (*summarizing*)[20]
31c and, like Ehud, delivered Israel. (*consequential*)

OUTLINE

Prologue: A Deliverer Arrives (3:12–17)
  Israel sins (3:12a)

The *wayyiqtol* form following the speech (v. 28c), which repeats the verb יָרַד, "go down" (cf. v. 27c), sets the scene in motion again.

15. The clause in verse 28e (introduced with *waw* + a negated perfect) complements the preceding statement; capturing the fords and not allowing anyone to escape are related actions.
16. On the large number mentioned here, see the commentary above on 1:4. As noted there, it is difficult to accept this figure at face value. One possibility is that the Hebrew term אֶלֶף, traditionally understood as a numeral (a "thousand"), actually refers to a contingent of troops, at least in some contexts. Boling, taking this approach, translates the phrase עֲשֶׂרֶת אֲלָפִים, traditionally "ten thousand," as "ten contingents" in verse 29 (1975, 85). Another option is that such large numbers are hyperbolic. See Fouts 1997, 377–88, and 2003, 283–99.
17. The phrases "at that time" (v. 29a) and "that day" (v. 30a) distance us from the events and signal closure, which is provided by the chronological note in verse 30b.
18. Verse 29b (introduced with *waw* + a negated perfect) complements what precedes; it gives more specific information about Moabite casualties and, by stating that no one escaped, has an emphatic function.
19. The disjunctive clause in verse 31a introduces an appendix that is supplemental to the Ehud narrative.
20. Verse 31b is a summary statement of Shamgar's exploits.

The Lord punishes (3:12b–14)
The Lord responds to Israel's cry (3:15a)
Ehud's got something "up his sleeve" (3:15b–17)
Main Event: Down with the Oppressor (3:18–26)
  Maneuvering Eglon into position (3:18–20)
  Executing the plot (3:21–23)
  A deadly delay (3:24–25)
  Negotiating the escape (3:26)
Epilogue: Liberating Israel (3:27–30)
  Finishing the job (3:27–29)
  Peace restored (3:30)
Appendix: Snapshot of a Philistine Killer (3:31)

LITERARY STRUCTURE

A reference to Israel's doing evil also marks the beginning of the second cycle (3:12–30) within this central section of the book. Like the preceding Othniel narrative, the story unfolds as follows: (1) Israel's apostasy (v. 12), (2) the Lord's discipline through a foreign oppressor (vv. 12–14), (3) Israel's cry (v. 15), (4) the Lord's deliverance (vv. 15–29), (5) conclusion (v. 30).

While there is a structural correspondence with the Othniel account, there is also a major difference. As Andersson observes, the account of Othniel is a "report-narrative"; it tells us what happened without including "scenic parts or dialogues." The Ehud story is a "narration-narrative" that shows us what transpired. Andersson explains that the focus becomes the "human level," while "the ultimate, transcendental level fades into the background." He adds: "Othniel is never allowed to take the stage but is reduced to a mere agent or functionary, while Ehud is a hero with almost romantic traits. He is the unexpected protagonist who defeats a physically superior but intellectually inferior enemy by his courage and cleverness" (Andersson 2001, 41).

Structurally the story has a prologue (vv. 12–17), a central scene where the plot reaches its peak (vv. 18–26), and an epilogue (vv. 27–30). The story begins with the recurring introductory formula (v. 12, "The Israelites again did evil before the Lord"). The central scene begins with the temporal indicator וַיְהִי, literally, "and it was," (v. 18). The disjunctive clauses in verses 20a, 24a, and 26a, all of which have Ehud as the stated or implied subject, divide the central scene into distinct parts. The epilogue begins with וַיְהִי (v. 27) and ends with the recurring concluding formula, "and the land was undisturbed" (v. 30b).

EXPOSITION

Prologue: A Deliverer Arrives (3:12–17)

Israel continued to disobey the Lord. There is no specific reference to idolatry at this point in the narrative, but usage of the expression "do evil in the eyes of the Lord" strongly suggests this was the case (see 2:11).[21]

Because of Israel's sin, the Lord gave them over to Eglon, king of Moab, who allied with the Ammonites and Amalekites and conquered the City of the Palms. The description suggests the city is Jericho (see Deut. 34:3 and 2 Chron. 28:15), but 1 Kings 16:34 indicates that Jericho was not rebuilt until the time of King Ahab in the ninth century B.C. (see as well Josh. 6:26, but note 2 Sam. 10:5).[22] Perhaps the Moabites established an outpost there without rebuilding the city *per se*.[23] The reference to Amalekite involvement in Eglon's campaign is sadly ironic, for Moses had instructed Israel to annihilate the Amalekites because of the way they had treated God's people (Deut. 25:17–19, cf. Exod. 17:8–16). Israel's failure in this regard was coming back to haunt them.

Eglon was a more menacing figure than Cushan-Rishathaim, for he lived in a neighboring state, just across the Jordan River, rather than in a distant land. Eglon allied with two other hostile nations. His hold on Israel was stronger and lasted longer than that of Cushan-Rishathaim. The Lord "sold" (literal translation) Israel into the latter's hand so that they were forced to serve this king of Aram for eight years. However, the Lord "moved Eglon . . . against Israel"[24] so that he was able to defeat (נכה, "smite, strike") them, gain a foothold in the

---

21. Perhaps the subsequent reference to "the carved images at Gilgal" (v. 19) is also instructive, but we do not know if Israel or the Moabites set up these idols. The idols seem to mark the boundary between Israelite soil and the territory near Gilgal occupied by the Moabite invaders.

22. According to Judges 1:16, the Kenites had temporarily settled in the City of the Palms following their entry into the land with the Israelites.

23. For a critique of this proposal see Moore 1895, 92. Wood identifies Garstang's "Middle Building" at Jericho with Eglon's palace. He observes that the archaeological evidence suggests "a well-to-do occupant involved in administrative activities." He adds: "Yet, the building complex is isolated, with no evidence for a town to rule over." See Wood 2003, 271–72.

24. The *piel* of the verb חזק (v. 12) here means either "make strong (physically)" (BDB, 304) or "encourage" (*HALOT*, 303). If the former, then the Lord strengthened Eglon militarily, prompting him to attack Israel. If the latter, then perhaps the Lord encouraged him more directly to launch a military campaign against Israel.

land itself, and exercise suzerainty over Israel for eighteen years, ten years longer than Cushan-Rishathaim. The reference to Israel "being subject to" (literally, "serving") a foreign king is ironic, for the prologue earlier informed us that the people "served" foreign gods (2:11, 13, 19; 3:6). Once more the punishment fits the crime (see v. 7).

Once again the Lord responded positively to Israel's cry by providing a deliverer (vv. 9, 15). The narrator gives his name (Ehud), a distinguishing physical characteristic (his left-handedness), and his family and tribal background (son of Gera the Benjaminite).

The phrase "left-handed" (literally, "bound in the right hand") cannot refer to an actual impediment or physical defect. Surely, as Moore points out, the seven hundred Benjaminite slingers described in 20:16 as "bound in the right hand" were not handicapped! (Moore 1895, 94; cf. Halpern 1988b, 40–41). The phrase is an idiom reflecting how these men differed from the norm—they were left-handed. Halpern suggests that the phrase does not refer to mere left-handedness, but rather to a specially trained left-handed or even ambidextrous warrior. He theorizes that the Benjaminites trained such warriors by restricting the use of their right hand at an early age so they could use their left hand with facility in battle. The practice is attested elsewhere in antiquity. As Halpern explains, left-handed warriors had an advantage in hand-to-hand combat and, given the construction of ancient city gates, left-handed slingers also had a distinct advantage when attacking the gates (Halpern 1988a, 35, and 1988b, 40–43).[25]

Ehud's left-handedness proved to be of great importance in his plot to kill the Moabite king. Because he was left-handed Ehud strapped his sword on his right thigh, contrary to the norm. Thus Eglon never suspected that Ehud was reaching for a weapon when he slipped his left hand under his garment to draw his sword. By the time Ehud drew the weapon, it was too late for the king to alert the guards. Ehud's identification as a Benjaminite is ironic, for the name *Benjamin* means "son of the right hand." Yet Ehud is left-handed! This "son of the right hand" is not what he appears to be on the surface.

Ehud's tribal identity is also important for another reason. When he is paired with the Judahite Othniel (cf. 1:9–20) as a model of

---

25. See also King and Stager 2001, 234. They explain: "For greater security, entry through the outer to the inner gate was gained via a dogleg right turn. In this way besiegers carrying the shield in the left hand were exposed to assaults from the defenders of the city." But lefthanded warriors would be able to carry their shields in their right hand, allowing them to protect themselves more readily from attackers on the city wall.

leadership, one sees an ideal of tribal unity consistent with Judah's self-sacrificing love for his brother Benjamin (see Genesis 44). However, this ideal is shattered as the larger story develops. Benjaminites subsequently violate a helpless Judahite (19:1–2, 18), precipitating a civil war in which Judah leads the charge against the Benjaminites (20:18). Ironically, included in the Benjaminite army are seven hundred left-handers who, like Ehud, can skillfully use a deadly weapon, but, in contrast to Ehud, use their skill against their fellow Israelites rather than foreign enemies.[26]

Israel sent their tribute payment, which was so large it had to be carried by several men (see v. 18), to Eglon via Ehud. But Ehud had something up his sleeve! He made a two-edged sword, probably about eighteen inches long, which he strapped to his right thigh and concealed under his outer garment.[27] He intended to give Eglon his tribute and more![28] There is no reference to God instructing Ehud to do this, let alone any indication that the Lord's spirit was at work (in contrast to Othniel). This silence, rather than suggesting divine disapproval, may emphasize that human initiative, when coupled with faith, is not necessarily antithetical to God's program. Ehud seized the opportunity

---

26. The tension between Benjamin and Judah continues when Saul opposes David and when Shimei, like Ehud a Benjaminite "son of Gera," curses David (2 Sam. 16:5; see also 19:16, 18; 1 Kings 2:8). The hostility between David and Shimei stands in stark contrast to the unified goal and purpose of Othniel and Ehud. Schneider (2000, 47–48) contrasts Ehud with Othniel, but she rightly observes that Ehud serves as a foil for the less admirable Benjaminites that appear later in the history. She states: "The book presents a decent judge from the tribe of Benjamin early in the narrative to highlight the extent of the downward spiral, especially by the tribe of Benjamin, exhibited in the book's final stories" (47).

27. As Halpern observes, the double-edged blade would allow the sword "to slice cleanly into the flesh" (1988b, 43). If גֹּמֶד is a unit of measure (a cubit), then the sword could have been as short as 13 inches (short cubit) or as long as 18 inches (standard cubit). However, Stone (2009, 660–63) has challenged this understanding of the word. See the note on the translation of v. 16b above.

28. O'Connell sees "made for him/himself" as ambiguous by intention (1996, 95–96). Elsewhere the idiom עָשָׂה לוֹ, is usually reflexive ("make/prepare for oneself," see Josh. 5:3; 2 Sam. 15:1; 1 Kings 1:5; 22:11; Jon. 4:5; Song 3:9; 1 Chron. 15:1; 2 Chron. 28:24; 32:27, 29), but occasionally it can mean "make/prepare for someone/something else" (see Gen. 37:3; Exod. 37:2, 11–12, 26–27; Neh. 13:5).

that his appointment as tribute-bearer offered and put his faith into action (see further discussion below).

Before describing the assassination, the narrator tells us paren-thetically that Eglon "was a very well-fed man." Perhaps this was already suggested by the king's name, which, by popular etymology, could be taken to mean "calflike."[29] Why is this detail significant? Eglon was a tyrant who had grown rich at Israel's expense over the past eighteen years. His physical stature symbolizes his greed, for it was the result of a luxuriant and indulgent lifestyle made possible by the wealth extorted from Israel. If we understand, as most do, the phrase בָּרִיא מְאֹד to mean "very fat" or "obese," then there is a touch of humor and expectation at this point in the story. Eglon's bulk would make him immobile and vulnerable to Ehud's skill. Eglon was obviously no longer an agile warrior, but he was about to meet one.[30] True to his name, Eglon would prove to be a calf that had been fattened up for slaughter (Alter 1981, 39; Amit 1999, 184; Brettler 2002, 30–31). On the other hand, if the phrase simply indicates that Eglon is healthy and strong, then it highlights Ehud's courage and daring (Stone 2009, 654, 663). In this case, the name does not have a pejorative connotation, nor does it suggest that he had been fattened for the slaughter, as it were (Stone 2009, 654–57).

Main Event: Down with the Oppressor (3:18–26)

Using dramatic irony to its fullest, the narrator now reports how Ehud used deceit to lure Eglon into a death trap. Ehud's courage and bold-ness are highlighted when he sends away the tribute-bearers. This warrior needs no help! Ehud's cunning is apparent in the way he led Eglon along and maneuvered him into a vulnerable position. He first told Eglon he had a secret message for him, prompting the king to send away his attendants. Eglon was apparently sitting in a chamber ad-joining the audience hall. When dismissed, the attendants went to an outer room adjoining the audience hall. Ehud then entered the chamber where the king was sitting.[31] On the lips of Ehud the phrase דְּבַר־סֵתֶר (v. 19) may be intentionally ambiguous. On the surface it means "a secret message," but דָּבָר can refer more generally to a "matter, affair,

---

29. The ן- ending can be adjectival, abstract, or diminutive. See *IBHS*, 92.
30. On the literary role of the reference to Eglon's appearance, see Webb 1987, 129.
31. See Halpern 1988b, 45–46. 2 Samuel 13 and 1 Kings 1 appear to depict a similar three-part architectural structure. See Halpern (52–54), who in-cludes a diagram of this palace structure.

dealing" (Judg. 18:7, 28) or a "task, mission" (Josh. 2:14). From Ehud's perspective the phrase may refer to his secret task or mission to assassinate the king (Klein 1988, 37).

Once alone with the king in his private room,[32] Ehud informed the king he had a divine oracle for him.[33] As one might expect in an address to a foreign king, Ehud used the general name Elohim, "God," rather than the distinctly Israelite covenantal name Yahweh, "Lord" (Moore 1895, 98).[34] In so doing he also avoided any hint of patriotism, which might have aroused suspicion and put Eglon on the defensive. Eglon rose from his throne in anticipation.[35] He was eager to hear what Ehud had to say, perhaps thinking of Ehud the tribute-bearer as a

---

32. Halpern doubts that the עֲלִיַּת הַמְּקֵרָה (v. 20; see also הָעֲלִיָּה/הָעֲלִיָּה in vv. 23–25) was a separate room. He suggests it was a "platform partitioned by a wood screen" (1988b, 51).

33. The phrase דְּבַר־(הָ)אֱלֹהִים, "word of God" (v. 20), refers elsewhere to a prophetic oracle (see 1 Sam. 9:27; 2 Sam. 16:23; 1 Kings 12:22; 1 Chron. 17:3; see also the similar phrases in 2 Kings 14:25 and Isa. 40:8). In 1 Chronicles 26:32 the phrase לְכָל־דְּבַר הָאֱלֹהִים refers to "all matters pertaining to God." Recall that Ehud, after delivering the tribute, left and then turned back once he reached the idols (v. 19). Perhaps he wanted to make it look like he had received an oracle from one of the gods represented by the images. See Handy 1992, 237, note 12.

34. Block suggests that Ehud's use of Elohim, rather than Yahweh, implies a deficient faith, but this is an overly cynical approach that overlooks the strategic element in Ehud's word choice (1988, 49).

35. Jull argues that Ehud murdered Eglon while the king was defecating in his private toilet. In his view the king stood up because he was shocked that Ehud would invade his private space (1998, 70). However, it seems unlikely that Ehud would risk startling the king in this way when split seconds counted so much. Furthermore, while the murder took place in the king's private room (עֲלִיַּת קֵרָה, v. 20; see also הָעֲלִיָּה/הָעֲלִיָּה in vv. 23–25), this may be distinct from a toilet located within it (חֲדַר הַמְּקֵרָה, v. 24). The servants *thought* the king was in the toilet, but the text gives no evidence this was the case. In fact when Ehud approached, Eglon rose from "the throne" (הַכִּסֵּא, v. 20), which most naturally refers to a royal throne within the private room, not to a toilet. When the servants opened the door to the private room, they immediately saw the king lying on the floor (v. 25). This would be unlikely if he were killed in the toilet, which, as Jull argues, would have been an enclosed structure within the room. Halpern argues that the toilet was not a separate room within the king's chamber (1988b, 45–46). He understands the terminology (הָעֲלִיָּה/הָעֲלִיָּה; עֲלִיַּת הַמְּקֵרָה in v. 20; in vv. 23–25; and חֲדַר הַמְּקֵרָה in v. 24) as having the same referent. Consequently the king would need to close the chamber doors when using

faithful servant and ally. Eglon suspected nothing; on the contrary he was vulnerable and, by standing, had made himself a well-positioned target for a quick sword thrust! Amit, who assumes Eglon was obese, observes: "The king's standing up is very important in light of the disproportion between Ehud's small dagger and the king's great girth. The king's belly, stretched taut when he stood up, enabled Ehud to exploit the advantages of his small, two-edged dagger." She also points out that Ehud's tactics left him a way out if the king did not respond as expected: "If during the first stage the king had not sent away his attendants, or if in the second stage he would not have risen from his chair, Ehud could have withdrawn from his original plan and sufficed with some sort of oracular saying or fictitious secret" (1999, 187–89).

With Eglon looming before him, eager to receive his "message" from God, Ehud moved into action and drove his sword into the king's belly before the tyrant could cry out for help. It is not clear if Ehud buried the weapon inside the king's belly or not. If he did, then this might indicate that Eglon was obese. Assuming this was the case, Amit argues that Ehud was able to pull off a "clean murder" (Amit 1989, 113). After all, if there were any bloodstains on his clothes as he passed the guards on his way out, he would have aroused suspicion and been captured. However, it is possible that the sword went out Eglon's back. Some understand the term הַפַּרְשְׁדֹנָה at the end of verse 22 to refer to the king's back and take the "sword," mentioned in the preceding clause, as the subject. But the verb יָצָא, "go out," is masculine, while חֶרֶב, "sword," is feminine. One expects agreement in gender (see Ezek. 33:4, 6), especially when the subject is supplied from the preceding clause. For this reason, it would be better, if one sees this as referring to the sword going out the king's back, to understand the masculine noun לַהַב, "blade," as the subject of the verb (see *NIV*).[36] Another option

---

the toilet facility, explaining in part the servants' assumption that he was relieving himself.

36. Others understand הַפַּרְשְׁדֹנָה to mean "feces" (cf. Hebrew פֶּרֶשׁ, "feces") and translate, "and the refuse came out" (cf. *NASB*), but the form, which includes a *dalet*, a *nun*, and the directive ending, does not readily allow this interpretation. Barré, who understands this as a reference to Eglon's excrement coming out of the wound, seeks to circumvent these difficulties by relating the term to an Akkadian cognate (*naparšudu*) and by suggesting that the final *he* is due to a morphological assimilation to הַמִּסְדְּרוֹנָה in verse 23a. See Barré 1991, 1–11, as well as Mobley 2005, 81–84. O'Connell (1996, 93) understands "feces" as the implied subject of יָצָא and takes הַפַּרְשְׁדֹנָה as "at the anus," a meaning that Barré's Akkadian etymological connection would seem to allow (see Barré 1991, 2–6).

is that Ehud buried the sword inside the king vertically. Stone argues that a blow to the lower abdomen, to kill a victim quickly and quietly, would have to sever the aorta. Furthermore, the blade "must travel at a rather sharp upward angle" (2009, 659). So even if the blade did not come out Eglon's back, this would not imply that he was obese.

The meaning of the final statement in verse 22 is unclear since the last word (הַפַּרְשְׁדֹנָה) occurs only here in the Hebrew Bible. The term has both the prefixed article and the directive ending, suggesting that it may be a technical architectural term, referring to an area into which Ehud moved after he killed the king. However, since he did not lock the doors of the room until he had moved into another area (see v. 23a), this term would seem to refer to an area near the entrance of the room (but see our comments on v. 23a).

The meaning of the first clause in verse 23 is also problematic because the meaning of the term הַמִּסְדְּרוֹנָה is unclear. Like the noun at the end of verse 22, it has the prefixed article and the directive ending, suggesting it is an architectural term describing the area into which Ehud moved when he left the room. (Note that he locked the doors behind him after he moved into this area.) Perhaps the final clause of verse 22 is a variant of verse 23a (Boling 1975, 86–87; Soggin 1981, 51–52). In this case the two rare nouns both refer to an area outside the king's chamber, either the audience hall or the entrance to it.

There has been some debate over Ehud's escape route.[37] Did he lock the doors of the room from the inside and then leave the room through a back door, window, or latrine?[38] Or, as we have suggested in the preceding paragraph, did he simply leave the room the way he entered, locking the doors behind him? Before proposing an answer, we must examine the statement that he "closed the doors of the upper room behind him" (v. 23b). The verb סָגַר, "close, shut," is used in ten passages with the preposition בְּעַד, "behind, after." Five times the word "door" does not appear after the verb and בְּעַד introduces the object that is "shut in":

Genesis 7:16: וַיִּסְגֹּר יְהוָה בַּעֲדוֹ, "then the Lord shut him (Noah) in"

Judges 3:22: וַיִּסְגֹּר הַחֵלֶב בְּעַד הַלַּהַב, "and the fat closed around the blade"

---

37. The following discussion appears in Chisholm 2009c, 172–75.
38. See Halpern 1988b, 43–60. He argues (56–58) that הַמִּסְדְּרוֹנָה refers to the latrine beneath the king's platform through which Ehud left the king's private area after locking the doors.

Judges 9:51: וַיִּסְגְּרוּ בַּעֲדָם, "and locked themselves in" (literal translation)

1 Samuel 1:6: סָגַר יְהוָה בְּעַד רַחְמָהּ, "the Lord closed up her womb" (literal translation)

2 Kings 4:21: וַתִּסְגֹּר בַּעֲדוֹ, "and she shut him in" (literal translation)

In the other five passages סגר takes "door(s)" as its object and is then followed by בַּעַד in the sense of "behind, after":

Judges 3:23: וַיֵּצֵא . . . וַיִּסְגֹּר דַּלְתוֹת הָעֲלִיָּה בַּעֲדוֹ, "and he went out . . . and shut the doors of the upper room behind him" (literal translation)

2 Kings 4:4: וּבָאת וְסָגַרְתְּ הַדֶּלֶת בַּעֲדֵךְ וּבְעַד בָּנַיִךְ, "go and close the door behind you and your sons"

2 Kings 4:5: וַתֵּלֶךְ מֵאִתּוֹ וַתִּסְגֹּר הַדֶּלֶת בַּעֲדָהּ וּבְעַד בָּנֶיהָ, "so she left him and closed the door behind her and her sons"

2 Kings 4:33: וַיָּבֹא וַיִּסְגֹּר הַדֶּלֶת בְּעַד שְׁנֵיהֶם, "and he entered and closed the door behind both of them" (literal translation)

Isaiah 26:20: בֹּא בַחֲדָרֶיךָ וּסְגֹר דְּלָתְךָ בַּעֲדֶךָ, "Enter your inner rooms! Close your door (singular, *Qere*; *Kethib* has the plural "doors") behind you!"

In 2 Kings 4:4–5, 33 and Isaiah 26:20, "closing the door behind" clearly refers to locking oneself inside the room. For this reason Halpern argues that the statement in Judges 3:23 must refer to Ehud locking himself inside the king's chamber, meaning that he would have had to escape through a window, back door, or latrine (Halpern 1988b, 57). However, in each of the other four texts the statement is preceded by a reference to the subject *entering* the room. Obviously, when one closes a door after entering a room, one shuts oneself in the room. But Judges 3:23 is unique. Here the statement is preceded by a reference to Ehud *going out*. When one closes a door after leaving a room, one is not shutting oneself inside the room.[39] So a close examination of the evi-

39. Halpern takes וַיִּסְגֹּר as a flashback, "he had closed" (in his view, prior to Ehud's leaving through the latrine) (1988b, 57). This is possible (see our

187

dence reveals that there are no precise syntactical parallels to Judges 3:23. However, because the verb "go out" appears, it seems that Ehud locked the doors of the room after he stepped out into an adjoining area (apparently the audience hall).[40] Elsewhere, when one closes a door or gate after leaving (יָצָא), the preposition אַחֲרֵי, "after," is used (Gen. 19:6; Josh. 2:7; Ezek. 46:12). The terminology used in the Ehud story may be an ironic twist on the idiom "enter (בּוֹא) and close behind (סָגַר בַּעַד)." One might have expected Ehud to enter, close the door behind him (to assure secrecy?), kill the king, and then escape by an alternate route, as Halpern suggests. Instead the text depicts him coming (בָּא, v. 20) to Eglon, killing him, leaving, and then closing the door behind him (v. 23) as he goes out (וַיֵּצֵא, v. 23). Oddly enough, the only place the

---

discussion of vv. 15–17), but it is not the most natural way of explaining the *wayyiqtol* sequence here. His proposed interpretation is necessary *if* the collocation סָגַר דֶּלֶת בַּעַד must mean "lock oneself in," but the use of יָצָא, "go out," in the preceding clause sets this text apart from other passages, where entry into a room is described.

40. The lock was apparently a tumbler lock (known as an Egyptian lock). King and Stager explain how such locks worked: "A wooden box containing loose pins was attached to the inside of the door above the wooden bolt, or lock case, into which the pins drop when the bar is moved to locked position. To unlock the door the key is inserted into a slot in the bolt until the matching teeth of the key push up the moveable pins so that the sliding bolt can be drawn. When the key is withdrawn, the bolt can be secured by sliding it horizontally into a position in which the pins drop from the box into the slots of the bolt. To make the tumbler locks more difficult to pick, they were mounted on the inside of the door and reached by passing one's hand and key through a hole in the door." With regard to Ehud's escape, they state: "By putting his hand through the keyhole in the door, Ehud could have slid the bolt of the tumbler lock into place from outside. The servants, then, would have had to fetch the key to unlock the doors" (2001, 31–33). They also include a drawing that shows the construction of such a tumbler lock and how one inserted a key to unlock it. In this scenario Ehud did not need a key to lock the door as he left, but the servants would need one to unlock the door. This answers Halpern's objection that the text makes no mention of Ehud fetching a key before locking the door (1988b, 45). Of course, even if a key were required to lock the door from the outside, it is possible that the narrator streamlines the account in verse 23 to give the impression of a hurried but efficient departure from the scene of the crime. In verse 25 he adds a reference to the servants using the key in order to make narrated time correspond more closely to real time. Along with the obvious references to the servants' delay (vv. 24–25a), this allows Ehud the time he needs to escape.

idiom "enter . . . and close behind" appears in this story is in verse 22, where the handle of Ehud's dagger "enters" Eglon's stomach and the fat "closes behind" it. As far as the text is concerned, Ehud did not shut himself into the king's chamber, but his sword was shut in the king's belly! These ironic linguistic twists that deviate from normal patterns mirror Ehud's deceptive, daring deed, which was performed "outside the lines," as it were. The text gives no indication that Ehud closed the doors when he entered the king's chamber. (After all, this might have aroused suspicion on the king's part.) Rather than killing the king behind closed or locked doors, Ehud apparently murdered Eglon with the doors open. He only closed and locked them after his daring deed was accomplished and he had left the chamber!

But how could Ehud lock the doors of the room without being seen and arousing suspicion? As verse 24 indicates, this audience hall separated the king's chamber from an outer room where the king's servants were waiting. The construction at the beginning of verse 24 indicates synchronic action. As Ehud passed by the servants in the outer room, they reasoned correctly that his business with the king was finished, so they entered the audience hall located between the outer room and the king's chamber. The verb בָּאוּ implies that they entered a room, but this could not have been the king's chamber, for its doors were locked and they only entered it later (v. 25). This indicates that there was a room separating the king's chamber from an outer area where they were waiting during Ehud's interview with the king. So Ehud could have locked the doors of the king's chamber without being seen. He would have then left the audience hall, walked right past the guards in the outer area, and left the same way he came in.[41]

While Ehud left the palace and headed for safety, Eglon's servants remained outside the king's chamber. Like their naïve king, they failed to suspect trouble until it was way too late. They did not bother to check on the king until Ehud was gone. Even then they assumed the closed doors meant the king was relieving himself in the toilet located in his chamber (v. 24, cf. חֲדַר הַמְּקֵרָה).[42] The odor of the deceased king's intermingled blood, intestines, and feces undoubtedly contributed to this conclusion. Their air of certainty (cf. Hebrew אַךְ, "surely") only empha-

---

41. For a concise description of Ehud's movements within the palace, see Mobley 2005, 91–92.
42. The statement מֵסִיךְ הוּא אֶת־רַגְלָיו (v. 24) means literally, "he was covering his feet (i.e., with his garments)" (cf. 1 Sam. 24:4). (See BDB, 697; *HALOT*, 754). It is apparently an idiomatic euphemism for urination/defecation, comparable to the English expression, "dropped his drawers."

sizes their dullness. They waited and waited, but when the king did not open the doors, they became embarrassed.[43] Finally they entered the chamber, only to find their master sprawled out dead on the floor.[44] In the meantime Ehud took advantage of their delay and escaped. When he passed the idols near Gilgal (see v. 19)[45] he was back in Israelite territory and he proceeded on to the Ephraimite hill country.[46]

Epilogue: Liberating Israel (3:27–30)

In contrast to the Moabites, Ehud did not delay. With the Moabite king dead, Ehud was ready to exploit their lack of leadership. When

---

43. The verb יָחִילוּ (v. 25) appears to be from a hollow root חיל/חול. BDB (297) defines it here as "be in severe pain, anguish" (from anxious longing). *BHS* textual note "a" labels the reading of the text doubtful and suggests that we read instead וַיְיַחֲלוּ (a *piel* form from the verbal root יחל) or וַיּוֹחִילוּ (a *hiphil* form from the same root, יחל). (*HALOT*, 311, 407, favors the latter emendation.) In either case the form would be translated, "they waited." (A similar problem occurs in Gen. 8:10, 12 where *BHS* note "a" suggests emending "וַיָּחֶל," "and he was in anguish" [??] to "וַיְיַחֶל, "and he waited.") יחל does occur with עַד, "until," elsewhere (see 1 Samuel 10:8; Job 14:14), but חיל/חול does not. If the *hiphil* form of יחל is original, the MT consonantal text either has the prefix vowel defectively written or has accidentally omitted a *waw* after the *yod* prefix by virtual haplography (*yod* and *waw* are very similar in later script phases). If the piel of יחל is original, then MT has inverted the second *yod* (the initial root letter after the verbal prefix) and the *khet*.
44. In this context the active participle נֹפֵל (v. 25) does not mean, "was falling." (It is highly unlikely that Eglon's body remained standing for such a long time and then tumbled to the floor just as the servants walked in!) Followed by אַרְצָה, "to the ground," and in conjunction with מֵת, "dead," נֹפֵל carries the nuance, "was lying prostrate on the ground." (See Judg. 4:22, where נֹפֵל is also followed by מֵת. In 1 Samuel 5:3–4 and 2 Chronicles 20:24 it occurs with אַרְצָה.) This is probably a metonymic use of the verb "fall," where the term actually refers to the effect of falling. Lindars (1995, 151) calls this "the pregnant meaning" of the form (see as well Judg. 19:27; 1 Sam. 31:8).
45. As Amit observes, "the sculptured stones also served as a kind of security border; after Ehud had passed this place, he felt that he had left the danger zone" (1999, 187). For a discussion of the possible literary significance of these stones, see Mobley 2005, 93–99. Mobley proposes they are more than simply boundary markers. He suggests they give the story "mythic potential" and conjure up an image of entering the underworld (99).
46. The precise location of Seirah is not certain, but verse 27 suggests it was located in the Ephraimite hill country.

he arrived in Ephraim, he blew a horn as a signal for Israel to gather. "Blew" in verse 27 and "drove" in verse 21 translate the same Hebrew verb (תקע). The wordplay links Ehud's two decisive actions. He killed the oppressive king and he then followed up on that deed. The horn blast rallied Israel to finish what Ehud had started. These two actions were the defining moments in Ehud's revolt and are linked together as part of a whole. Standing "before them" as the Israelite leader who had disposed of Moab's leader, Ehud challenged Israel to follow him.[47]

He guaranteed victory, promising that Yahweh, the covenant God of Israel, had already given (נתן) the enemy into their hands (v. 28). The very common idiom "give into the hand of" (נָתַן בְּיַד) means "to deliver over to the power of," or "to enable to conquer." Ehud used the perfect form here to describe a future action or state. The action, though not completed in reality, is described as such from Ehud's perspective for dramatic effect. He wished to emphasize to his troops that victory was a "done deal." This dramatic future use of the perfect נָתַן appears elsewhere in Judges in rhetorically charged rallying cries (Judg. 4:14; 7:15) and divine oracles of deliverance (Judg. 1:2; 7:9; 18:10; see also Josh. 6:2; 8:1). It is used once in a response to an omen where the interpreter wishes to emphasize the disaster that the sign symbolizes (Judg. 7:14). Ehud's battle cry echoes the Lord's earlier commission to Judah (Judg. 1:2); as such it is a significant expression of faith.[48]

---

47. In verse 28 *BHS* note "a" suggests, with support from Greek witnesses that attest to the original Septuagintal reading, altering רִדְפוּ, "follow," to רְדוּ, "go down." They observe that the clause immediately following the quotation says "they went down (וַיֵּרְדוּ) after" Ehud, rather than "they followed after him." אַחֲרֵי, "after," occurs only four times with ירד, "go down," in the Old Testament, but it follows רדף, "follow," 45 times (see, for example, Judg. 1:6; 4:16; 7:23; 8:5, 12). A scribe could have easily substituted the more common expression for the relatively rare one. However, the phrase "follow after" (רָדַף אַחֲרֵי) is used 43 times of pursuing someone with hostile intent. Only once is it used in a non-hostile sense of "follow after" (see 2 Kings 5:21, where Gehazi runs after Naaman). In a context where Ehud is leading his men, it is unlikely a scribe would substitute this idiom. Though rarely used of a non-hostile action, the expression רָדַף אַחֲרֵי is attested in this sense and should be retained in verse 28. It is more likely that the Septuagint translator harmonized the reading to the immediately following context.

48. Block questions the degree of Ehud's faith and suggests that his words "need not have been anything more than a rallying slogan" (1988, 49). This view is overly cynical and based on the false assumption that Ehud's deeds have a "Canaanite" quality about them.

The use of the expression נָתַן בְּיַד in Judges is instructive. In 4:14 the declaration is made by Deborah; in 7:14–15 it is spoken by the man whom Gideon overheard talking and then by Gideon himself. In 11:30 the tone of certainty disappears as Jephthah prefaces his vow with the condition, "If you give the Ammonites into my hands" (literal translation). Later, in a tragic reversal, the Philistines declare that their god has given Samson into their hands (16:23–24). A clear progression is discernible. Ehud, a model of faith and leadership, is confident of God's ability. So is Deborah, but oddly enough, she, a woman, must stir up the hesitant male leader Barak. Equally hesitant Gideon also gains such confidence, but only after receiving a confirmatory vision. With Jephthah the statement changes from a cry of faith to a condition prefaced with "if." When Samson is captured, the Philistines' god takes the Lord's place in the formula, which is now uttered by boastful pagans, not a courageous Israelite leader. The decline is obvious and the stark contrast between Ehud and Samson highlights how far Israel had fallen.

Israel followed Ehud to the Jordan River, where they captured the fords in order to prevent any of the Moabite occupational force to escape to their homeland. The Israelite army then killed ten thousand Moabite soldiers, who are described as "strong, capable warriors," undoubtedly to emphasize the magnitude of Israel's victory. The word translated "strong" can also carry the nuance "robust, well-fed"; this may suggest that the Moabites, like their well-fed king, had prospered at Israel's expense. Unlike Ehud, who was able to escape from Moab after killing Eglon (v. 26), none of the Moabite soldiers were able to escape from Ehud and his men. The word repetition highlights the contrast, as well as the Israelite victory.

The narrative concludes with a notice that Israel experienced peace for eighty years, twice as long as the period of rest following Othniel's victory. On the surface this appears to be a positive sign, but we are soon disappointed.

How are we to assess Ehud's murderous deed? (See Chisholm 2011.) Ehud's use of deception and violence may be repugnant to our modern sensibilities and ideas of propriety, but this would probably not have been the case for an ancient Israelite audience (see Deist 1996, 269). As Webb observes, this account is satiric, even comic (1987, 129–31).[49]

---

49. See also Brettler 2002, 33–37; and Christianson 2003, 64. Webb observes: "The grotesquely comic character of the story makes moral judgments irrelevant. We are clearly meant to identify with the protagonist and to enjoy the sheer virtuosity of his performance" (1987, 131). This statement

It is crafted to appeal to Israel's disdain for the Moabites.[50] The utter humiliation of greedy, naïve Eglon would make the account of Ehud's exploits that much sweeter for an ancient Israelite audience that had experienced the oppressive hand of this king for many years.

But some view Ehud's actions in a negative light. Klein views Ehud as "less than honorable." She emphasizes the relative lack of divine involvement in the story, in contrast to the report of Othniel's deeds (1988, 40). Block, while acknowledging God's involvement in Ehud's revolt, nevertheless views Ehud's "treachery and brutality" as having a "Canaanite" quality (Block 1988, 49, and 1999, 171). O'Connell makes a distinction between political and theological perspectives in evaluating ethical behavior. He argues that the satirical flavor of the text reflects the "tribal-political standpoint" of Judges, rather than the (correct, in his view) "deuteronomic evaluation that 'everyone did what was right in one's own eyes'" (1996, 280, note 43).

Wong makes a particularly strong case for the view that Ehud's actions must be viewed in a negative light. He asks rhetorically if "the fundamental incongruity between Ehud's restriction in the right hand and his core identity as a 'son of the right-handers'" hints "at another set of incongruity [*sic*] equally significant with respect to the plot, namely, the incongruity between Ehud's use of deceptive tactics to assassinate, and his core identity as a deliverer raised up by YHWH." He adds, "the incongruity revealed by the wordplay may carry deeper symbolic significance in portraying Ehud as someone whose actions and choices are liable to fall short of the standard expected of him on the basis of who he is. . . . because the tactics he used likewise fell short

---

goes too far when it claims that the story's "comic character . . . makes moral judgments irrelevant." The comic element, when viewed as a celebration of divine justice, is actually quite appropriate.

50. Chalcraft contends that the details of the accounts in Judges 3–5 "do not cast any reflection on the characters of either Ehud or Jael," but, rather, depict the enemies as "sub-human." This in turn gives the stories a "heroic dimension" and justifies the killers' actions (1990, 183). Chalcraft also asserts that Ehud's actions "serve to highlight the stupidity of the enemy" (184). See as well Handy 1992, 233–46. Handy contends that the story is not history, but a joke that takes the form of "ethnic humor." Handy seems offended by the story's tone (244–46), but its comic, even nationalistic, tone has its place when one understands the story as a celebration of divine justice told in a cultural context where people were viewed not so much as individuals, but corporately as part of the ethnic group to which they belonged.

of the standard expected of a deliverer raised up by YHWH" (2006a, 119–20).

Wong demonstrates that the accounts of Joab's assassinations of Abner and Amasa have parallels with the Ehud story. Both Ehud and Joab employed deceit to kill their victims. Joab asked to speak with Abner in private and then killed his unsuspecting victim (2 Sam. 3:27; cf. Judg. 3:19). Later he killed Amasa with a left-handed sword thrust as he grabbed Amasa's beard with his right hand (2 Sam. 20:9–10). The description of how Joab had strapped his sword to his side (2 Sam. 20:8) is very similar to the description of Ehud given in Judges 3:16 (Wong 2006b, 399–403).[51] Wong also establishes the priority of the Judges passage and shows that Joab's deeds are presented in a negative light by the author of 2 Samuel (2006b, 403–10). He concludes: "If Joab's two assassinations are indeed meant to be understood negatively, then by virtue of the fact that each makes allusions to Ehud, one can infer that there must have been aspects of Ehud's assassination that were also viewed negatively by the author of the Joab accounts. And since the allusions seem to concentrate especially on the use of deception, one can only conclude that this use of deception by Ehud must have been what was viewed negatively by the author of the Joab accounts" (2006b, 410).

Is this anti-Ehud sentiment justified? Marais responds to Klein: "In her view Yahweh can only be good and cannot be associated with treacherous conduct, but what if the text itself contains this paradox? Should this paradox be explained and smoothed away with modern, Western logic, or should it be allowed to stand as a paradox?" (1998, 96). Indeed the Lord is not above using deception and brutality when he deems such tactics to be appropriate (though we would not want to imply, as Marais does, that this is somehow contrary to God's goodness).[52] The revolt against oppressive Eglon, when viewed as an act initiating a war of liberation, was such an occasion. Seen in this light, the taunting, almost nationalistic tone of the story, while certainly reflecting cultural custom, may be viewed as a celebration of God's power to vindicate his own (see Ps. 58:10–11).

As we have tried to show in our earlier exegetical remarks, the

---

51. For a list of parallels between Ehud's assassination of Eglon and Joab's murder of Amasa, see Cartledge 2001, 627.

52. See, for example, Jehu's divinely instigated bloodbath against the house of Omri, which used both deception and violence (2 Kings 9–10), and Samson's spirit-energized murder of thirty Philistine men (Judg. 14:19). On the subject of divine deception in general see Chisholm 1998a, 11–28.

narrator presents Ehud's victory over the Moabite army in a positive light and links it with the assassination of Eglon through wordplay. Ehud himself saw his actions as the work of God (5:28). As Schneider points out, Ehud acted "for the Israelite deity, not for his own glory or credit" (2000, 52).[53] By the end of the story one is convinced that God's providence is the unseen force driving Ehud's actions and giving them success. (Webb 1987, 131–32; and Amit 1999, 172–73, and 1989, 97–123).

As for the apparent lack of direct divine involvement in Ehud's revolt, it is true that there is no reference to God instructing Ehud to kill Eglon, let alone any indication that the Lord's spirit was at work (in contrast to Othniel). This silence, rather than suggesting divine disapproval, may emphasize that human initiative, when coupled with faith, is not necessarily antithetical to and may even facilitate God's program (a theme that is apparent in the book of Ruth). Ehud seized the opportunity that his appointment as tribute-bearer offered and put his faith into action. Bowman observes: "The narrator does not explicitly state that the spirit of God is given to either Ehud or Deborah." He adds: "Yet, both successfully deliver Israel from the oppression of its enemies, and both voice their own conviction that God gave them their victories." Bowman concludes: "Even though both of these judges credit God with the victory (3:28; 4:9), their stories stress the importance and necessity of the human involvement in the achievement of success" (Bowman 1995, 36–37).

Furthermore, it is important to recognize that empowerment by the Spirit of Yahweh is not a barometer in the Former Prophets of how a character or his actions should be assessed. Certainly Othniel, a recipient of the Lord's Spirit (3:10), is presented positively, even paradigmatically. But it is Othniel's unhesitating action and God-given victory, not necessarily the reception of the Lord's Spirit, that constitutes the paradigm. Gideon, Jephthah, and Samson were also empowered by the Lord's Spirit (6:34; 11:29; 13:25; 14:6, 19; 15:14), yet all three are

---

53. See as well Andersson's hermeneutical analysis of the debate over how we are to understand Ehud's actions (2001, 44–49). He concludes that the approach of O'Connell and Klein is "disturbing" because it allows the "larger text" to give "the narrative a new meaning that cannot be harmonized with its narrative meaning" (49). For his theoretical discussion of what constitutes a "disturbing" interpretation, see p. 19. For a response to Andersson, see Wong 2006a, 119–24.

presented as deficient leaders, despite their divine enablement.[54] The same proves to be the case with Saul (1 Sam. 10:6, 10; 11:6) and, dare we say, David (1 Sam. 16:13). All are flawed leaders whose stories end in tragedy to varying degrees. On the other hand, nowhere in the Former Prophets is the Lord's Spirit said to empower Joshua, Caleb, Deborah, or Samuel, all of whom are viewed positively.[55]

Despite the fact that there is no mention of Ehud, in contrast to Othniel, being empowered by the Lord's Spirit, the narrator does link the two together in such a way as to suggest that they form a paradigmatic tandem. The statement "the Lord raised up a savior" (וַיָּקֶם יהוה מוֹשִׁיעַ) appears in both accounts (3:9, 15), but is absent in the following accounts of the judges. The expression echoes the statement in the prologue that the Lord "raised up judges" who "saved" the people (2:16, 18). The title "savior" (מוֹשִׁיעַ) is used only of Othniel and Ehud.[56]

It is also noteworthy that there are literary parallels between Ehud and Jael, who is viewed in a positive light (5:24) despite her deception: (1) Both Ehud and Jael made their victims think they were loyal subjects and lured them into a defenseless position. (2) Ehud and Jael killed the leader of the enemy behind closed doors. (3) The same Hebrew verb (תקע) is used to describe Ehud's deadly sword thrust and Jael's fatal hammer blow (cf. "drove" in 3:21 and 4:21). (4) The fallen corpses of Eglon and Sisera are described in almost identical terms (cf. וְהִנֵּה אֲדֹנֵיהֶם נֹפֵל אַרְצָה מֵת, literally, "and look, their lord was falling

---

54. In fact, in the case of Gideon and Jephthah, they both exhibit lack of faith immediately after receiving the Spirit!

55. The Pentateuch may indicate that Joshua possessed the divine Spirit, though the evidence is ambiguous. In Numbers 11 seventy elders receive the divine Spirit (vv. 25–26), but Joshua seems to be distinct from this group (vv. 28–29). Numbers 27:18 may indicate Joshua possessed the divine Spirit, but the Hebrew text reads simply רוּחַ, with no article. Deuteronomy 34:9 states that Joshua was full of "a spirit of wisdom," but this is not identified as the divine Spirit. As for Caleb, Numbers 14:24 describes him as possessing "another spirit," but there is no indication this is the divine Spirit. Deborah and Samuel were prophets, so we can assume that the Lord's Spirit was energizing them in this regard, but the text does not specifically state this as if to highlight it as paradigmatic for leadership.

56. The hiphil participle is used of the Lord in 6:36, and of the men of Ephraim in 12:3, but not of another individual judge. A hiphil finite verbal form of ישע is used several times of judges (2:16, 18; 3:31; 6:14–15; 8:22; 13:5). Rather than undercutting our point, however, the frequent usage of the finite form highlights the fact that the substantival participle is applied only to Othniel and Ehud and appears to place them in a distinct category.

to the ground, dead," in 3:25b with וְהִנֵּה סִיסְרָא נֹפֵל מֵת, literally, "and look, Sisera was falling, dead," in 4:22b).[57] If we use Wong's method of interpreting an earlier character's actions in light of allusions to that character in the description of a later character, these parallels suggest that Ehud, like Jael, should be assessed positively.[58] Jael was blessed in contrast to cursed Meroz, because she participated in the liberation of Israel. When face–to–face with Israel's enemy she acted decisively, in contrast to Meroz (and some of the other tribes, as well as hesitant Barak). This decisive participation is patterned after Othniel and Ehud. Ehud in particular showed great daring as the sole participant, at least initially.

There are also parallels between the account of Ehud's assassination of Eglon and David's victory over the Philistine champion Goliath. Both do the unexpected and unconventional, and strike down an imposing enemy.[59] But beyond these general similarities there are intertextual echoes that suggest conscious linking on the part of the editor(s) of the Former Prophets: (1) The collocations שָׁלַח יָד (Judg. 3:21; 1 Sam. 17:49) and לָקַח חֶרֶב (Judg. 3:21; 1 Sam. 17:51) are used of both Ehud's and David's actions and are clustered only in these two passages in the Hebrew Bible. (2) The expression נָתַן יָד is used of the Lord delivering over the enemy in both passages (Judg. 3:28; 1 Sam. 17:47). (3) The idiom נָפַל אֶרֶץ is used to describe the demise of the enemy in both passages (Judg. 3:25; 1 Sam. 17:49).

As for the parallels between Ehud and Joab, another explanation may better account for the allusions in 2 Samuel. Following the lead of Schneider, we argued earlier that Ehud is a foil for the Benjaminites who appear later in the history (in both Judges and 2 Samuel).[60] We observed that the ideal of Israelite leaders from Judah and Benjamin defeating foreign enemies (cf. 1:9–20; 3:7–30) is shattered in the epilogue when Benjaminites violate a helpless Judahite (19:1–2, 18), precipitating a civil war in which Judah leads the charge against the Benjaminites (20:18), including their left-handed slingers (20:16). Like

---

57. Webb notes some of these parallels (1987, 137). See also Assis 2006, 116–17.

58. I owe this insight to my former student, Dr. Andrey Muzhchil.

59. Eglon should not be viewed as an obese, immobile, easy target, but as a robust, imposing warrior. See Stone, 2009, 649–63. On David's unconventional use of the sling when close combat was expected, see Halpern, 2001, 10–13.

60. See our comments on 3:15 regarding Ehud's tribal affiliation, as well as the footnote that concludes that paragraph.

Ehud, these Benjaminites can skillfully use a deadly weapon, but, in contrast to Ehud, they use their skill against their fellow Israelites rather than foreign enemies. Schneider states: "The book presents a decent judge from the tribe of Benjamin early in the narrative to highlight the extent of the downward spiral, especially by the tribe of Benjamin, exhibited in the book's final stories" (2000, 47). The conflict between Benjamin and Judah continues when Saul opposes David and when Shimei, like Ehud a Benjaminite "son of Gera," curses David (2 Sam. 16:5; see also 19:16, 18; 1 Kings 2:8).

Joab's assassination of Abner contributes to this theme of conflict between the two tribes. As such, Joab stands in contrast to Ehud. Furthermore, when, following the civil war within Judah precipitated by Absalom, Joab killed his own relative Amasa, it is apparent that the intertribal conflict portrayed prior to this in the history had spread to the tribe of Judah and threatened the stability of the nation. The significance of the link between Ehud and Joab is not so much in the similarity of the actions themselves (the description of which establishes a parallel), but in the contrast between the objects of those actions and in their goal. Ehud killed a foreign oppressor in order to deliver Israel; Joab of Judah struck down a Benjaminite, escalating the conflict begun in Judges 20, and then killed one of his own relatives. The point is not that Joab should have been killing foreign oppressors; after all, circumstances had changed since Ehud's time. There was no need to be killing anybody, especially from personal motives of greed as in the case of Joab. Ehud killed to liberate a nation; Joab's killing was strictly to promote his own interests and protect his position as David's general. The literary allusions to Ehud in the Joab accounts highlight the tragic contrast between them and remind the reader how far Israel had fallen from the days when leaders like Othniel and Ehud rid the nation of foreign oppressors. If Ehud and Joab really were "separated at birth," as Wong suggests, then Joab, not Ehud, gets to play Romulus!

To summarize, the narrator presents Ehud in a thoroughly positive light and links him with Othniel to form a paradigmatic tandem. Only of these two is it said, "the Lord raised up a savior," and only these two are designated by the title "savior." While there is no reference to Ehud, in contrast to Othniel, being empowered by the Lord's Spirit, this is not an indication that Ehud is flawed. It simply illustrates the importance of human initiative and faith in the outworking of the divine purpose. In Judges–Samuel empowerment by the Lord's Spirit is not a barometer of how a character or his actions should be assessed. Some leaders are presented in a negative light despite being empowered by the Spirit, while others are depicted positively, despite the absence of any reference to Spirit empowerment. There are indeed similarities between Ehud's assassination of Eglon and Joab's murderous deeds, but this does not cast Ehud in a negative light. The key to understanding the significance of the allusion is not the similarity of action (which merely establishes the link), but rather the contrasting objects. Ehud killed a foreign oppressor and delivered a nation; Joab killed a Benjaminite, escalating tribal conflict, and his own flesh and blood, contributing to the disintegration of the Davidic royal court. In addition to the intertextual connections between Ehud and Joab, there are also links between Jael, who is presented positively, and Ehud, both of whom use cunning to rid Israel of tyrannical rule, as well as David and Ehud. In short, Ehud is a model of courage born out of faith in Yahweh. He sees himself as—and is more than willing to be—an instrument of divine deliverance. In contrast to later judges, he displays and expresses absolute confidence in Yahweh. Together with Othniel he provides a paradigm of leadership in Israel.

Appendix: Snapshot of a Philistine-Killer (3:31)

An appendix to the Ehud narrative briefly describes the exploits of another deliverer, Shamgar, who killed six hundred Philistines. The note informs us that foreigners were threatening Israel from the west, as well as the north (cf. 3:8) and east (cf. 3:13), thereby reminding us of Israel's vulnerability in a hostile world and of their absolute dependence on God.

Shamgar's chronological relationship to Ehud and Deborah is uncertain. According to 3:30, the land experienced eighty years of peace after Ehud's victory over the Moabites. Ehud probably died within this period and, if so, the people's apostasy may very well have started during the eighty-year period (cf. 4:1). It is difficult to see oppression and warlike activity coming within this period of peace, unless "the land" in 3:30 refers only to the portion the Moabites had dominated (Jericho, Gilgal, and Ephraim). In Judges "the land" can sometimes refer to a portion of the land (see 1:2, where "the land" is Judah's allotted territory; cf. as well 6:4 and 18:30, where it refers to the northern kingdom), but at other times it refers to the entire promised land (cf. 2:1–2, 6). If "the land" refers to Israel in a general sense in 3:30, then the Philistine and Canaanite oppressions (3:31; 4:2–3) probably came right at the end of the eighty-year period. If Shamgar was a contemporary of Deborah (see 5:6), his attack on the Philistines may have been concurrent with the events recorded in chapters 4–5. On the other hand, if Ehud's death (4:1b) occurred at the end of the eighty-year period of peace, then it is possible that Shamgar's activity took place during the Israelite apostasy and/or oppression, but before Barak's victory, which ushered in another period of peace (5:31b). It is important to note that Shamgar's victory was not followed by a period of peace (cf. 3:31). Though his victory saved Israel from the Philistine threat, Israel's sin prompted a more devastating oppression in the north. In this scenario, Shamgar can still be viewed as roughly contemporary with Deborah.

This brief notice contains several peculiar elements. Shamgar's name is of foreign (perhaps Hurrian, but possibly Canaanite) (Day 2000, 133), not Israelite, origin and his identification as "son of Anat" has a pagan ring to it, for Anat was a Canaanite goddess of love and war. The designation "son of Anat" is actually inscribed on Phoenician arrowheads as "an honorific military title" rather than a "literal patronymic" (Day 2000, 134–35).[61] There is no mention of God's raising him up or empowering him, but perhaps this is implied by the word "too" (גַּם), which seems to link him with the divinely appointed Ehud. The Lord's statement in 10:11, in which he refers to personally delivering Israel from the Philistines, may also allude to Shamgar's deeds, for 3:31 is the only passage in the book prior to chapter 10 that mentions a deliverance from Philistines (Webb 1987, 132–33). Shamgar's weapon, an oxgoad, while apparently quite effective in the hands of the right man, is also unconventional.

What is one to make of this? Why did an apparent foreigner, armed with a *farm* implement, have to deliver Israel? Were there not any full-fledged Israelites up to the task? There may be a subtle hint here of trouble in Israel. Perhaps there has been a decline in leadership now that Othniel and Ehud have passed off the scene. Our suspicions are realized in chapters 4–5, which tell of a woman judge-prophet who has to prod an Israelite general into fighting and of a non-Israelite woman who, like Ehud, kills an enemy leader.

---

61. See also Shupak 1989, 517–25. Shupak suggests Shamgar was an *apiru* mercenary in the employ of Pharaoh and that his deliverance of Israel was a "collateral" effect of Egyptian military operations in the region, not a purposeful action (524). See as well Craigie 1972a, 239–40. Hess challenges this view (2003, 27–28). For other evidence that the name may have been a military title, see Younger 2002, 130; and Mobley 2005, 27–31. Snyman challenges the view that Shamgar was a professional warrior, arguing that Shamgar's use of a farm implement indicates he was "a farmer at war," not "a farming warrior." In Snyman's estimation, viewing Shamgar in this way heightens the ethnic humor of the account in that a mere farmer humiliates the Philistine army (2005, 125–29).

However, the reference to Shamgar's apparent foreignness, rather than having a purely negative intent, may also emphasize more positively that the Lord's "chosen means" of deliverance "may not be easy to predict or explain" (Webb 1987, 133). This theme of unpredictability emerges clearly in chapters 4–5 where women, including the non-Israelite Jael, take the lead in Israel's deliverance. While a decline in male leadership is certainly disconcerting, it does not tie the Lord's hands. Also, whether a full-fledged Israelite or not, Shamgar's obvious courage contributes to the ideal of leadership being presented in chapter 3. In addition Shamgar serves as a foil for Samson, who also wipes out large numbers of Philistines with an unconventional weapon (see 15:15–16).[62]

Shamgar may also have a more subtle function in relation to the Deborah-Barak account that follows. If the narrator, with polemical design, likens the exploits of Jael to those of the warlike Canaanite goddess Anat,[63] then the reference to Shamgar as "son of Anat" may be a somewhat tongue-in-cheek foreshadowing of what is to come. Anat's "son" had appeared; "Anat" herself would soon arrive![64] In chapter 5 the Lord comes in Baal-like style to defeat the kings of Canaan and demonstrate his sovereignty. Like Baal he has a female ally—an "Anat" as it were!

MESSAGE AND APPLICATION

Thematic Emphases:

Israel's worship of foreign gods prompted God to subject them to an oppressive foreign invader, but in response to Israel's suffering, God raised up a deliverer, Caleb's son-in-law Othniel, whose exploits are already known by readers of Judges (cf. 1:13). When God's spirit empowered Othniel, he acted decisively without laying down any conditions (in contrast to Barak and Gideon), seeking any special assurances

---

62. For comparisons and contrasts between the two, see Klein 1988, 129.

63. See the commentary on Judges 4–5 below, specifically the section entitled "Thematic Emphases" following our comments on 5:31.

64. For more on the possible parallels to Canaanite texts, see Dempster 1978; 33–53; Taylor 1982, 99–108; Alter 1985, 46; and Ackerman 1998, 59–61. Echols (2008, 123–31), on the one hand, objects to the use of mythological materials to illuminate Judges 5. Davidson, on the other hand, attempts to show that all of the characters in Judges 4–5 correspond to deities from the Canaanite myths (Jael = Anat, Deborah = Athtart, Barak = Baal, Sisera = Yam, and Jabin = El) (2005, 43–57). His thesis, however imaginative and creative, is unconvincing.

(cf. Gideon and Jephthah), or foolishly cavorting with the enemy (cf. Samson).

The stability resulting from Othniel's victory was disturbed when Israel rebelled, prompting God to subjugate them to another foreign oppressor. The Lord again responded to Israel's cry by giving them a deliverer named Ehud. Like his predecessor Othniel, Ehud also contributes to the ideal of leadership presented in this chapter. Though he was not directly commissioned or supernaturally empowered, his faith (cf. 3:28) motivated him to seize the opportunity granted him by God's providence. Israel's situation was dire, and Ehud used the means and opportunity available to him to deliver his people from bondage. With cunning and courage he advanced God's program, demonstrating that God rewards human initiative and courage when it is coupled with faith.

The brief notice of Shamgar's success reminds us that God sometimes accomplished his purposes through unlikely means, in this case an apparent foreigner with a peculiar name and an unconventional weapon who may not have even realized he was being used by God. This motif of the unlikely hero will become more prominent as the story unfolds.

Exegetical idea: *God disciplined his sinful people, but, when they cried for help, he rescued them by raising up effective deliverers—empowering one with his spirit, rewarding another's courageous faith, and providentially using the exploits of an unlikely foreigner.*

Theological Principles
The Othniel and Ehud accounts illustrate one of the main themes of the prologue (see especially in 2:6–3:6): When the covenant community experiences failure, they are at fault, not God. God confronts sin in the covenant community and disciplines his rebellious people by subjecting them to humiliating defeat. Yet he responds compassionately to their suffering and intervenes on their behalf.

In accomplishing his purposes God typically uses human instruments. God's ability to deliver his people through individuals demonstrates his superiority to his enemies and proves he is worthy of his people's trust and devotion.

Divine involvement may be more apparent in some cases than in others. As illustrated by Othniel, God sometimes intervenes directly, but at other times his involvement is less visible. He provided Ehud in response to the people's cry, but the text stops short of saying that he empowered Ehud with his spirit. Yet the story indicates that Ehud, whose faith engendered cunning and bravery, was certainly the right man for the job. The brief notice of Shamgar's success mentions nothing of divine involvement, suggesting his exploits were directed by a veiled divine providence. But this Philistine-killer's agenda, perhaps unwittingly, matched God's purposes.

Theological idea: *The Lord disciplines his rebellious people, but he is predisposed to save them when they cry for help. God sometimes accomplishes deliverance through human instruments, intervening in a variety of ways and demonstrating that he is superior to his enemies and deserving of his people's devotion.*

Homiletical Trajectories
(1) The accounts in chapter three, like each of the stories in the book's central section, support the theme of God's faithfulness, highlighted in the prologue (see our discussion of the homiletical trajectories for 2:6–3:6). They also demonstrate God's absolute superiority to the enemies of his people. Whether he intervenes directly through his spirit or operates providentially, he can defeat his enemies. He often accomplishes his purposes through human instruments, sometimes in surprising and unexpected ways.

(2) Like the prologue, these accounts also remind us that God expects his people's full devotion. Unfaithfulness arouses God's anger. As objects of divine anger and discipline, his people lose the security and blessing that could be theirs. The Ehud story is particularly instructive in this regard. As one reads the story, the Moabites come across as over-fed, brutish dolts who are easily victimized by Ehud's cunning and daring. Yet to read the story strictly as nationalistic humor misses the point. After all, the Moabites subjugated Israel for eighteen long years. How could that be? The text's answer is sobering. God's people can experience such humiliation when they are unfaithful to him. The enemy is merely an instrument of divine discipline, easily vanquished by God's power. Israel should never have had to suffer such humiliation. Their sin, not Moab, was the real enemy. When God's people sin, they forfeit divine blessing and become vulnerable to the enemy.

(3) As we move into the accounts of the individual judges, the leadership theme becomes more prominent, allowing us to develop the third of our homiletical trajectories. Set in their larger canonical context, these stories make an important contribution to Israel's understanding of leadership. Joshua and Caleb were models of the ideal

Israelite leader; they trusted God to fulfill his promises. They provide a paradigm of leadership and illustrate what great things God can accomplish for his people through leaders who rely on him. Othniel is a paradigmatic character who, like Joshua and Caleb, becomes a foil for the failed leaders described in subsequent chapters. Ehud's story is particularly instructive, for it shows that God need not directly intervene to win the victory. Armed with a dagger, a plan, and his faith, Ehud seized the moment afforded him by divine providence. The task was not without its obstacles; some might even call his plan foolhardy. But Ehud exhibited foresight (his plan took into account contingencies) and daring, for he was undoubtedly conscious of God's ability to give him success (see 3:28).

As we consider preaching ideas for 3:7–31, we have more than one option. If we focus on the theocentric element in the passage (note the exegetical and theological ideas above) and combine the first and second homiletical trajectories, we might state our *preaching idea* as follows: *Though God may allow us to suffer the humiliating consequences of our sin, he is willing to deliver us and is able to do so in ways that demonstrate his power and his right to our loyalty and worship.*

While this theocentric focus is certainly true to the text, one senses that it fails to develop the full applicational potential of the passage, especially its leadership theme (note the third homiletical trajectory above). In this regard it is Ehud who takes center stage in this chapter. His story highlights the human dimension in the outworking of God's purposes and reminds us, as noted above, that God rewards human initiative and courage when it is coupled with faith. If we focus on Ehud as an exemplary character, another *preaching idea* emerges, which we might state as follows: *Confident that our faithful God seeks what is best for his covenant community and is superior to all opposition, we should exhibit courageous faith as we seek to advance the cause of God's kingdom.* A corollary of this would be: *By faith we should be willing to advance God's purposes by courageously seizing the opportunities granted to us by God's providence, confident that he is able to overcome seemingly overwhelming odds.* Of course, in developing this idea it will be important to describe what courageous faith looks like today (it is no longer demonstrated by assassinating oppressive kings!) and to identify how God is advancing his kingdom at the present time (today's battles are spiritual, not physical, cf. Eph. 6:10–18).

JUDGES 4:1–5:31

A Hesitant General and a Heroic Woman

TRANSLATION AND NARRATIVE STRUCTURE[1]

4:1a The Israelites again did evil before the LORD (*initiatory*)[2]
1b **after Ehud's death.** (*circumstantial*)[3]
2a So the LORD turned them over to Jabin, king of Canaan, who ruled in Hazor. (*consequential*)
2b **The general of his army was Sisera**; (*supplemental*)[4]

---

1. For a survey of the extensive recent research on Judges 4–5, see Mayfield 2009.
2. This next major episode in the macrostructure begins with the formulaic report, "The Israelites again did evil before the Lord" (see 3:7, 12). The *wayyiqtol* form initiates the action, but it is also sequential at the macrostructural level. It introduces a historical account that postdates the story of Ehud recorded in the previous chapter.
3. The disjunctive clause in verse 1b is circumstantial-temporal, informing us that the rebellion described earlier in the verse took place after Ehud's death.
4. The supplemental disjunctive clause in verse 2b introduces us to Sisera, who plays an important role in the following story. The accompanying disjunctive clause in verse 2c provides further information about this character's place of residence.

2c **he lived in Harosheth Haggoyim**. (*supplemental*)
3 The Israelites cried out to the LORD, for Sisera had nine hundred iron chariots and he cruelly oppressed the Israelites for twenty years (*resumptive-consequential*).[5]

4 **Now Deborah, a prophetess, wife of Lappidoth, was serving as a judge in Israel at that time.** (*introductory-backgrounding*)[6]
5a **She would sit under the Date Palm Tree of Deborah between Ramah and Bethel in the Ephramite hill country.** (*introductory-backgrounding / specifying*)[7]
5b The Israelites would come up to her to have their disputes settled. (*complementary*)
6a Deborah sent messengers (*initiatory*)[8]
6b and summoned Barak son of Abinoam from Kedesh in Naphtali. (*sequential*)
6c She said to him: (*sequential or specifying*)
6d *"Is it not true that the LORD God of Israel is commanding you? 'Go, march to Mount Tabor! Take with you ten thousand of men from Naphtali and Zebulun![9]*
7 *Meanwhile I will bring Sisera, the general of Jabin's army, to you at the Kishon River, along with his chariots and huge army. I have handed him over to you.'"*

---

5. The final clause of verse 3 begins with a disjunctive structure (*waw* + subject + verb), but it seems to be an extension of the preceding causal clause. See Genesis 2:5b.
6. The disjunctive clause in verse 4 introduces a new character, who plays an important role in the story to follow. This clause marks the transition to the story proper (the account of Israel's deliverance from oppression) and provides background information for the narrative.
7. The disjunctive clause in verse 5a gives more specific background information about Deborah's role as judge. The *wayyiqtol* form in verse 5b does not initiate the story; it complements the preceding statement.
8. The *wayyiqtol* form in verse 6a initiates the action of the story proper.
9. On the large number mentioned here, see the commentary above on 1:4. As noted there, it is difficult to accept this figure at face value. One possibility is that the Hebrew term אֶלֶף, traditionally understood as a numeral (a "thousand"), actually refers to a contingent of troops, at least in some contexts. Boling, taking this approach, translates the phrase עֲשֶׂרֶת אֲלָפִים, traditionally "ten thousand," as "ten contingents" in verse 6 (1975, 92). Another option is that such large numbers are hyperbolic. See Fouts 1997, 377–88, and 2003, 283–99.

8a Barak said to her: (*sequential*)

8b "*If you go with me, I will go; but if you do not go with me, I will not go.*"

9a She said: (*sequential*)

9b "*I will indeed go with you. But you will not gain fame on the expedition you are taking, for the LORD will turn Sisera over to a woman.*"

9c Deborah got up (*sequential*)

9d and went with Barak to Kedesh. (*sequential*)

10a Barak summoned men from Naphtali and Zebulun to Kedesh. (*sequential*)

10b Ten thousand men followed him. (*sequential*)[10]

10c Deborah went up with him as well. (*sequential or reiterative*)[11]

11a **Now Heber the Kenite had moved away from the Kenites, the descendants of Hobab, Moses' father-in-law**. (*supplemental*)[12]

11b He settled near the tree in Zaanannim near Kedesh. (*sequential*)[13]

12a Sisera heard that Barak son of Abinoam had gone up to Mount Tabor (*resumptive-sequential*),

13 so he ordered all his chariotry—nine hundred iron chariots—and all the troops he had with him, to go from Harosheth Haggoyim to the Kishon River. (*consequential*)

14a Deborah said to Barak: (*sequential*)

14b "*Spring into action, for this is the day the LORD has handed Sisera over to you. Has the LORD not taken the lead?*"

14c So Barak quickly went down from Mount Tabor (*consequential*)

---

10. With regard to the number of troops involved, see the note on verse 6 above.

11. Verse 10c seems to merely repeat verse 9d; if so it is reiterative. However, it is more likely that verse 10c describes movement from Kedesh (where Barak went to muster his forces, v. 10a) to Tabor. Note that verse 12 assumes Barak has gone up (עָלָה) to Tabor from Kedesh. This same verb is used of Deborah's movements in verse 10c (cf. וַתַּעַל, "went up") in contrast to verse 9d (where וַתֵּלֶךְ, "went," from הלך, is used).

12. Verse 11, introduced by a disjunctive ("Now Heber"), provides parenthetical information which, though interrupting the narrative (note that vv. 10 and 12–13 focus on the deployment of forces), promises to be significant in the unfolding story and raises the reader's curiosity.

13. The *wayyiqtol* form in verse 11b introduces a clause that is sequential to the preceding supplemental clause. See Genesis 31:34 and Judges 1:16bc; 4:5b; 7:13.

14d **with ten thousand men following him**. (*circumstantial*)

15a The LORD routed Sisera, all his chariotry, and all his army before Barak with the edge of the sword. (*sequential*)

15b Sisera jumped out of his chariot (*sequential*)

15c and ran away on foot. (*sequential*)

16a **Now Barak chased the chariots and the army all the way to Harosheth Haggoyim**. (*dramatic shift in focus*)[14]

16b Sisera's whole army died by the edge of the sword; (*sequential*)

16c **not even one survived**. (*complementary-reiterative / emphatic*)[15]

17a **Now Sisera ran away on foot to the tent of Jael, wife of Heber the Kenite, for Jabin, king of Hazor, and the family of Heber the Kenite had made a peace treaty**. (*dramatic shift in focus*)

18a Jael came out to welcome Sisera. (*sequential*)

18b She said to him: (*sequential*)

18c *"Stop and rest, my Lord! Stop and rest with me! Don't be afraid!"*

18d So Sisera stopped to rest in her tent (*consequential*)

18e and she put a blanket over him. (*sequential*)

19a He said to her: (*sequential*)

19b *"Give me a little water to drink, for I am thirsty."*

19c She opened a goatskin container of milk (*sequential*)

---

14. The disjunctive clause in verse 16a shifts the focus from the fleeing Sisera back to the victorious Barak (see Buth 1994, 140). Disjunctive clauses perform this same function in verses 17a (shifting the focus back to Sisera), 22a (shifting the focus back to Barak), and 22f (shifting the focus to the dead Sisera). This series of disjunctive clauses also has a structural function in the discourse. The disjunctive clause in verse 16a ("Now Barak") marks the transition from the battle *per se* to its aftermath. In verses 17–21 the fleeing Sisera (cf. v. 15b) becomes the focus as the scene shifts from the general region mentioned in verse 16 to the tent of the aforementioned Heber (cf. v. 11). A disjunctive clause ("Now Sisera") marks this shift in scene. In verse 22a, also introduced by a disjunctive clause (literally, "Now look"), the focus returns to the pursuing Barak (cf. v. 16), who arrives at Heber's tent to find that a woman has already disposed of the evil enemy general. The final disjunctive (v. 22f) provides closure for the scene. The description of Sisera's murder is thus bracketed by references to Barak's pursuing the enemy (cf. vv. 16, 22), highlighting the fact that the glory of killing the Canaanite general escaped him (cf. v. 9), despite his earnest efforts.

15. The switch to the perfect in verse 16c is expected after the negative particle. The clause is asyndetic; this is not surprising given its complementary-reiterative (and therefore emphatic) function.

19d and gave him some milk to drink. (*sequential*)
19e Then she covered him up again. (*sequential*)
20a He said to her: (*sequential*)
20b "Stand watch[16] at the entrance to the tent. If anyone comes along and asks you, 'Is there a man here?' say, 'No.'"
21a Then Jael, wife of Heber, took a tent peg in one hand (*sequential*)
21b and a hammer in the other. (*complementary*)
21c She snuck up on him (*sequential*)
21d and drove the tent peg through his temple (*sequential*)
21e right into the ground (*sequential*)
21f **while he was asleep** (*circumstantial*)[17]
21g from exhaustion; (*supplemental-explanatory*)[18]

---

16. Scholars find the masculine singular form of the imperative problematic. Boling emends the form to an infinitive absolute, which he understands as having imperatival force here (1975, 98). Block suggests, among other options, "since Sisera was a general, accustomed to ordering men, the form may be habitual, reflecting his persistent illusions of control" (1999, 207, n. 266). The most likely explanation is that an original עמדי (the feminine singular) was corrupted to עמד (the masculine singular form) by virtual haplography. In the third century B.C. the letters *dalet* and *yod* were easily confused. Compare, for example, ומריד in the MT version of 2 Samuel 22:48 with ומרדד in the 4Q Sam. version of the passage. See Ulrich 1978, 76.

17. The circumstantial clause in verse 21f tells us what we suspect (cf. v. 19), namely, that she was able to kill him in this manner because he had fallen asleep. However, by delaying reference to this, the narrator adds to the drama of the deed. As we read the actions described in verse 21a–d, we may suspect that Sisera is asleep, but we are not completely sure of this. This downplaying of Sisera's vulnerability makes Jael's deed appear even more heroic and courageous.

18. The *wayyiqtol* form in verse 21g introduces a clause that is subordinate to the preceding circumstantial clause and gives the explanation for his falling asleep so readily. For other examples of a *wayyiqtol* clause having an explanatory function, see Numbers 1:48 and Isaiah 39:1.
    Moore (*Judges*, 126) emends the form to an adjective וְיָעֵף, "(now he was asleep) and exhausted" (1895, 126). Lindars prefers to derive the verb from a root ʿyp or ʿwp meaning "to faint, swoon" and translates "and he collapsed" (1995, 203–4). In this case the *wayyiqtol* form is (con)sequential in relation to the previous וַיִּצְנַח, literally, "and it descended." For other examples of this proposed pattern, namely, *wayyiqtol* (1) + disjunctive clause (with the structure *waw* + independent pronoun + participle) + *wayyiqtol* (2) (in sequence with the preceding *wayyiqtol*), see 2 Samuel 11:4; 13:8; 2 Kings 2:18; 6:30.

21h and he died. (*resumptive-consequential*)

22a **Now Barak was chasing Sisera**. (*dramatic shift in focus*) [19]

22b Jael came out to welcome him. (*sequential*)

22c She said to him: (*sequential*)

22d *"Come here and I will show you the man you are searching for."*

22e So he went with her (*consequential*)

22f **and there was Sisera lying dead** (*dramatic shift in focus*)[20]

22g **with the tent peg through his temple**. (*circumstantial*)

23 So that day God humiliated Jabin, king of Canaan, before the Israelites. (*summarizing*)[21]

24 Israel's power continued to overwhelm Jabin, king of Canaan, until they did away with Jabin, king of Canaan. (*consequential*)

5:1 In that day Deborah and Barak son of Abinoam sang this song: (*flashback*)

2 *"When the leaders took the lead*[22] *in Israel,*

---

19. The disjunctive clause in verse 22a dramatically invites the audience to share an observer's perspective (note הִנֵּה).

20. The disjunctive clause in verse 22f dramatically invites the audience to share Barak's perspective (note הִנֵּה, literally, "and look"). On the perspective here, see Assis 2005b, 8. With its tone of finality, it also signals closure for the central narrative unit.

21. The epilogue (vv. 23–24), though linked to the preceding narrative by a *wayyiqtol* form, is marked by a shift in subject ("God") and the phrase "in that day." The use of the divine name "God" rounds off the narrative of Israel's deliverance. The account was set in motion when Deborah announced the word of Yahweh, the God of Israel (v. 6); it concludes with the statement that this same God won the victory just as he had promised. The threefold reference to Jabin, king of *Canaan*, links these concluding verses to the introduction (cf. v. 2, note that Jabin is called "king of *Hazor*" in v. 17) and establishes an inclusio for the entire narrative.

22. The meaning of the Hebrew expression (בִּפְרֹעַ פְּרָעוֹת) is uncertain. For a survey of opinions, see Lindars 1995, 223–27. The next line refers to the people who responded to Barak's summons to war, so a reference to the leaders who issued the summons would provide a natural poetic parallel. In verse 9 the leaders (Heb. חוֹקְקֵי) of the people and these same volunteers stand in poetic parallelism, so it is reasonable to assume that the difficult Hebrew term פְּרָעוֹת (v. 2a) is synonymous with חוֹקְקֵי of verse 9 (see Lindars 1995, 227). Miller (2008, 650–54) argues that this is a reference to the Egyptian pharaohs who exercised authority in Canaan during the twelfth century BC. He translates the expression literally, "when the Pharaohs

> *When the people answered the call to war—*[23]
> *Praise the LORD!*
> 3 *Hear, O kings!*
> *Pay attention, O rulers!*
> *I will sing to the LORD!*
> *I will sing to the LORD God of Israel!*
> 4 *O LORD, when you departed from Seir,*
> *when you marched from Edom's plains;*
> *the earth shook,*
> *the heavens poured down—*
> *the clouds poured down rain.*
> 5 *The mountains trembled*[24]
> *before the LORD, the One of Sinai;*[25]
> *before the LORD God of Israel.*
>
> 6 *In the days of Shamgar son of Anath,*
> *in the days of Jael caravans disappeared;*
> *travelers had to go on winding side roads.*
> 7 *Warriors*[26] *were scarce,*

---

pharaohed," (that is, "ruled") and suggests that the narrator coined the verb (p. 654).

23. Or, "When the people offered themselves willingly," both here and in verse 9 below. The *hithpael* stem of נדב is used in 2 Chronicles 17:16 of those who volunteered for military service and in Nehemiah 11:2 of those who voluntarily agreed to settle in Jerusalem. In several texts it describes willing contributions to the building of the temple (1 Chronicles 29:5–6, 9, 14, 17 [of the temple project in David's time], and Ezra 1:4; 2:68; 3:5 [of the second temple project]).

24. Or "quaked." The translation assumes the form נָזֹלּוּ from the root זלל "quake" (see *HALOT*, 272). Cf. the Septuagint, Syriac Peshitta, and Targum. See Isaiah 63:19 and 64:2 for other occurrences of this form. Some understand the verb as נזל, "flow" (with torrents of rain water).

25. In parallelism with the title "God of Israel," the phrase זֶה סִינַי is best taken as an epithet, "the One of Sinai." This use of the demonstrative pronoun is attested in Amorite, Ugaritic, and the proto-Sinaitic inscriptions, as well as in Old South Arabic and Arabic. See *HALOT*, 264, as well as Albright 1936, 30; Cross 1962, 238–39, 255; Lipinski 1967, 198, note 3; Echols 2008, 21; and Butler 2009, 137–38.

26. The meaning of the Hebrew noun פְּרָזוֹן is uncertain. Some understand the meaning as "leaders" or "those living in rural areas." The singular noun appears to be collective (note the accompanying plural verb). For various options see Lindars 1995, 237–38; and Echols 2008, 25–26.

they were scarce in Israel;
until you[27] arose, Deborah,
until you arose as a motherly protector in Israel.

8   *God chose new leaders,*
then fighters appeared in the city gates;
but, I swear, not a shield or spear could be found,
among forty thousand in Israel.[28]

9   *My heart went out to Israel's leaders,*
to the people who answered the call to war.
Praise the LORD!

10   *You who ride on light-colored female donkeys,*
who sit on saddle cloths,
you who walk on the road, pay attention!

11   *Hear the sound of those who divide the sheep[29] among the*
watering places;
there they tell of the LORD's victorious deeds,
the victorious deeds of his warriors in Israel.
Then the LORD's people went down to the city gates—

12   *Wake up, wake up, Deborah!*
Wake up, wake up, sing a song!
Get up, Barak!
Capture your prisoners of war, son of Abinoam!

13   *Then the survivors came down[30] to the mighty ones;*

---

27. The translation assumes that the verb is an archaic second feminine singular form. See Lindars 1995, 238; and Echols 2008, 26–28. On the archaic form involved see GKC, 121, para. 44h. Though Deborah is named as one of the composers of the song (v. 1), she is also addressed within it (v. 12). Many understand the verb as first person singular, "I arose."

28. Or "forty contingents." See the commentary above on 1:4. As noted there, it is difficult to accept such figures at face value. One possibility is that the Hebrew term אֶלֶף, traditionally understood as a numeral (a "thousand"), actually refers to a contingent of troops, at least in some contexts. Boling, taking this approach, translates "forty contingents" in verse 8 (1975, 102). Another option is that such large numbers are hyperbolic. See Fouts 1997, 377–88, and 2003, 283–99.

29. The meaning of the Hebrew word is uncertain. Some translate "those who distribute the water" (*HALOT*, 344). For other options see Lindars 1995, 246–47.

30. The translation assumes a repointing of the verb as a perfect or imperfect/ preterite form of ירד, "go down." See Echols 2008, 32. The form as pointed in MT appears to be from רדה, "rule." See GKC, 188, para. 69g.

    the Lord's people came down to me as[31] warriors.

14   *They came from Ephraim, who uprooted Amalek,[32]*
    They follow after you, Benjamin, with your soldiers;
    From Makir leaders came down,
    from Zebulun came the ones who march carrying an officer's staff.

15   *Issachar's leaders were with Deborah,*
    The men of Issachar supported Barak,
    Into the valley they were sent under Barak's command;
    Among the clans of Reuben there was intense heart searching.

16   *Why do you remain among the sheepfolds,*
    listening to the shepherds playing their pipes for their flocks?
    As for the clans of Reuben—there was intense heart searching.

17   *Gilead stayed put beyond the Jordan River,*
    As for Dan—why did he seek temporary employment in the shipyards?[33]
    Asher remained on the seacoast,
    he stayed put by his harbors.

18   *The men of Zebulun were not concerned about their lives;*
    Naphtali charged on to the battlefields.

19   *Kings came, they fought,*
    the kings of Canaan fought,
    at Taanach by the waters of Megiddo;
    but they took no silver as plunder.

20   *From the sky the stars fought,*

---

31. The translation assumes the preposition *bet* prefixed to "warriors" has the force of "in the capacity of." For this use of the preposition, see GKC, 379, para. 119i.

32. The words "they came" are supplied. The text reads literally, "From Ephraim their root in Amalek." Because of the difficulty of the text, many prefer to follow one of the ancient versions or emend the text. For proposals see Lindars 1995, 252–53. The translation proposed here repoints שָׁרְשָׁם (traditionally "their root") as a *piel* verb form with enclitic *mem*. The preposition -בְּ on עֲמָלֵק, "Amalek," introduces the object (see Job 31:12 for an example of the construction). Ephraim's territory encompassed the hill country of the Amalekites (Judg. 12:15).

33. The text reads literally, "Dan—why did he live as a resident alien, ships." The verb גּוּר usually refers to taking up residence outside one's native land. Perhaps the Danites, rather than rallying to Barak, were content to move to the Mediterranean coast and work in the shipyards. For further discussion, see Lindars 1995, 262; and Bartusch 2003, 128–36.

from their pathways they fought against Sisera.
21 *The Kishon River carried them off,*
 The river confronted them[34]—*the Kishon River.*
 Step on the necks of the strong![35]
22 *Then the horses'*[36] *hooves pounded the ground,*
 his stallions galloped madly.
23 *'Call judgment down on Meroz,' says the* LORD's *messenger,*
 'Be sure to call judgment down on those who live there,
 because they did not come to help in the LORD's *battle,*
 to help in the LORD's *battle against the warriors.'*

24 *The most rewarded of women should be Jael,*
 the wife of Heber the Kenite.
 She should be the most rewarded of women who live in tents.
25 *He asked for water,*
 she gave him milk;
 in a bowl fit for important men,
 she served him curds.
26 *Her left hand reached for the tent peg,*
 her right hand for the workmen's hammer.
 She "hammered" Sisera,
 she shattered his skull,
 she smashed his head,
 she drove the tent peg through his temple.
27 *Between her legs he collapsed,*

---

34. Possibly "the ancient river," but it seems preferable in light of the parallel line (which has a verb) to emend קְדוּמִים (attested only here) to a verb with pronominal object suffix (קִדְּמָם, "confronted them"). For discussion see Echols 2008, 38.

35. This line is traditionally taken as the poet-warrior's self-exhortation, "March on, my soul, in strength!" The translation offered here (a) takes the verb (a second feminine singular form) as addressed to Deborah (cf. v. 12), (b) understands נֶפֶשׁ in its well-attested sense of "throat, neck" (cf. Jon. 2:6), (c) takes the final *yod* on נֶפֶשׁ as an archaic construct indicator (rather than a suffix), and (d) interprets עֹז, "strength," as an attributive genitive (the phrase literally reads, "necks of strength," or "strong necks"). For fuller discussion and various proposals, see Lindars 1995, 270–71.

36. The Hebrew text as it stands has a singular noun, but if one moves the prefixed *mem* from the beginning of the next word to the end of סוּס, "horse," the expected plural form is achieved. Another possibility is to understand an error of scribal haplography here, in which case the letter *mem* should appear in both places.

he went limp, he was lifeless;
between her legs he collapsed, he went limp,
in the spot where he collapsed,
there he went limp—violently murdered.

28 *Through the window she looked,*
  Sisera's mother cried out through the lattice,
  'Why is his chariot so slow to return?
  Why are the hoofbeats of his chariot-horses delayed?'
29 *The wisest of her ladies answer,*
  indeed she even thinks to herself,
30 *'No doubt they are gathering and dividing the plunder—*
  a girl or two for each man!
  Sisera is grabbing up colorful cloth,
  he is grabbing up colorful embroidered cloth,
  two pieces of colorful embroidered cloth,
  for the neck of the plunderer!'
31a *May all your enemies perish like this, O Lord!*
  But may those who love him shine like the rising sun at its
  brightest!"

31b The land was undisturbed for forty years. (*concluding*)

OUTLINE
The Story of the Battle (4:1–24)
  Prologue: Sin and Oppression (4:1–3)
    Israel sins (4:1)
    The Lord punishes his people (4:2)
    Israel cries out to the Lord (4:3)
  Main Event: A General Meets His Waterloo (4:4–22)
    What's wrong with this picture? (4:4–5)
    The Lord commissions Barak (4:6–7)
    Barak's underwhelming response (4:8)
    Deborah's rebuke (4:9)
    Preliminaries to battle (4:10–13)
    Deborah jump-starts Barak (4:14)
    The Lord routs the enemy (4:15–16)
    Ehud and Shamgar show up in women's attire (4:17–22)
  Epilogue: Israel over Canaan (4:23–24)
    A battle won (4:23)
    A tyrant defeated (4:24)
Celebrating the Victory in Song (5:1–31a)

LITERARY STRUCTURE

Once again a reference to Israel's sin marks the beginning of a new cycle. As in the previous cycles the plot develops as follows: (1) Israel's apostasy (4:1), (2) the Lord's discipline through a foreign oppressor (vv. 2–3), (3) Israel's cry (v. 3), (4) the Lord's deliverance (vv. 4–24), (5) conclusion (5:31b). Unique to this cycle is the inclusion of a lengthy poem celebrating the Lord's victory and the accomplishments of his human instruments (5:1–31a).[37]

The juxtaposition of narrative and poetic accounts of the victory reminds us of Exodus 14:1–15:21, which reports and celebrates the Lord's defeat of Pharaoh's army at the Red Sea. The similarity may be more than coincidental, for there are other literary and thematic parallels between Exodus 14–15 and Judges 4–5, suggesting the narrator of Judges viewed the Lord's defeat of Sisera as a reactualization of his mighty victory over Pharaoh. The parallels include:[38]

---

37. For a succinct comparison and contrast of the prose and poetic accounts, as well as a helpful survey of scholarly opinion on their origin and relationship, see Block 1999, 175–85. For more detailed studies of the accounts, see Soden 1989; Younger 1991, 109–45; and Butler 2009, 158–77. For a discussion of various views pertaining to the literary genre of Judges 5, see Brettler 2002, 66–74. For ancient Near Eastern parallels to the "triumph hymns" of Exodus 15 and Judges 5, see Kitchen 2003, 218–19.

38. For a detailed study of similarities and dissimilarities between Exodus 14–15 and Judges 4–5, see O'Connell 1996, 134–37. For a lengthy comparison of Exodus 15 and Judges 5, see Hauser 1987, 265–84. Echols (2008, 102–16) sees a marked contrast between Judges 5 and Exodus 15 (as well as 2 Samuel 22 = Psalm 18, and Habakkuk 3). He argues that these other texts highlight the Lord's role as deliverer, while Judges 5, at least in its supposed original form, prior to an alleged liturgical revision, focuses on the human heroes (115–16). Echols may well be correct that Yahweh is not highlighted as directly or as extensively in Judges 5 as in the victory

(1) Both accounts emphasize the strength of the enemy's horses and chariotry (Judg. 4:3, 7, 13, 15–16; 5:22, 28; cf. Exod. 14:9, 17–18, 23, 28; 15:1, 4, 19).

(2) The waters of the Kishon River, like those of the Red Sea, are the Lord's instrument of destruction (Judg. 5:21; cf. Exod. 15:6, 10).

(3) In both instances the Lord confused/routed (הָמַם) the enemy (Judg. 4:15; cf. Exod. 14:24).

(4) In both instances the enemy was totally destroyed, as the language of Judges 4:16 (לֹא נִשְׁאַר עַד־אֶחָד), "not even one was left," and Exodus 14:28 (לֹא־נִשְׁאַר בָּהֶם עַד־אֶחָד) "not even one of them remained," makes clear.

There are also parallels between Judges 4–5 and other parts of Exodus. Judges 4–5 views the Lord's battle with the enemy as a struggle for kingship over his people (note especially Judg. 5:3, 19), as does the Exodus account (Exod. 5:1–2, cf. 14:5, 8; 15:18). The same Hebrew word (לחץ) describes the oppressive deeds of both Jabin and Pharaoh (cf. Judg. 4:3 with Exod. 3:9).

This next major episode in the macrostructure begins with the formulaic report, "the Israelites again did evil before the Lord" (see 3:7, 12). The prologue (vv. 1–3) gives background information for the following story. The disjunctive clause in verse 4 introduces a new character, who plays an important role in the story. This clause marks the transition to the story proper (the account of Israel's deliverance from oppression) and provides additional background information for

---

songs Exodus 15, 2 Samuel 22 = Psalm 18, and Habakkuk 3. But even if we were to agree that Yahweh's involvement is diminished here, such a suppression of divine intervention, at least relatively speaking, is a motif throughout Judges. Yahweh works through human instruments, often behind the scenes or with minimal intervention in human affairs (see Bowman 1995; cf. Butler 2009, lxxxi–lxxxiii). So this feature does not necessarily reflect some type of redactional process. On the contrary, it is consistent with what we see elsewhere in the book's present form. Echols' study, like all diachronic analyses, deals in speculative reconstruction that inevitably yields tenuous conclusions. The fact is that the text as it stands does highlight Yahweh's role in the battle and, because of its prominence in the song's introduction, provides a theological frame for understanding all that follows. Amit even argues that the Lord is the main hero of the story; the human participants are merely his instruments in delivering Israel (1987, 99–104). Similarly, Weitzman (not cited by Echols) observes: "it is God who deserves Israel's praise first and foremost, because it was his intervention in the battle that made victory possible" (1997, 32). As such, the song promotes "allegiance to God."

the narrative. The story proper has four scenes: the commissioning of Barak in the Ephraimite hill country (vv. 6–9), the deployment of troops near the Kishon (vv. 10–13), the battle account (vv. 14–16), and the murder of Sisera (vv. 17–22). In verses 17–21 the fleeing Sisera (see v. 15b) becomes the focus as the scene shifts from the general region mentioned in verse 16 to the tent of the aforementioned Heber (see v. 11). A disjunctive clause marks this shift in scene. In verse 22a, also introduced by a disjunctive clause, the focus returns to the pursuing Barak (see v. 16), who arrives at Heber's tent to find that a woman has already disposed of the evil enemy general. The description of Sisera's murder is thus bracketed by references to Barak's pursuing the enemy (see vv. 16, 22), highlighting the fact that the glory of killing the Canaanite general escaped him (see v. 9), despite his earnest efforts. The disjunctive clause in verse 22f dramatically invites the audience to share Barak's perspective (note הִנֵּה, literally, "and look"). With its tone of finality, it also signals closure for the story proper. The epilogue (vv. 23–24) is marked by a shift in subject (God) and the phrase "in that day." The threefold reference to Jabin, king of *Canaan*, links the concluding verses to the introduction (see v. 2) and establishes an inclusio for the entire narrative. The repetition of יָד, "hand," also links the prologue and epilogue. According to verse 2, the Lord gave the Israelites into "the hands of Jabin" (literal translation); now the "hand of the Israelites" (literal translation) prevailed over Jabin (v. 24) (van Wolde 1995, 241).

The literary structure of the poem in chapter 5 may be outlined as follows: (1) a poetic account of the victory (vv. 1–23), (2) a blessing upon Jael (vv. 24–27), (3) a taunt of Sisera's mother (vv. 28–30), and (4) a concluding imprecation and prayer (v. 31a). Verse 31b, with its reference to the land experiencing peace for forty years, concludes the narrative begun in chapter four.

The structure of the poetic account is as follows: (1) heading and introduction to poetic account, part I (vv. 1–2a), (2) call to praise/listen (vv. 2b–3) and theophanic hymn (vv. 4–5), (3) completion of poetic account, part I (vv. 6–9a), (4) renewed call to praise (vv. 9b–11a), (5) introduction to poetic account, part II (v. 11b), (6) address to Deborah and Barak (v. 12), (7) completion of poetic account, part II (vv. 13–22), (8) curse of Meroz (v. 23).[39]

---

39. For a defense of the literary unity of the song, see Vincent 2000, 61–82. Vincent sees the structure of the poem differently than I do. He divides the poem into two panels (vv. 2–8, 9–22); he proposes that section one (vv. 2–8) parallels section two (vv. 9–22) (73–76). Other structural analyses of

As one can see from the outline, the poetic account is interspersed with other literary forms. The temporal clauses in verse 2a begin the account, but it is interrupted by the call to praise/listen and the theophanic hymn, which constitutes the praise promised in verse 3. The name Yahweh appears at or near the beginning of both the summons and the hymn (cf. vv. 2b and 4a) and the compound name Yahweh, God of Israel concludes both (cf. vv. 3b and 5b). The temporal clauses at the beginning of verse 6 resume the poetic account begun in verse 2a. The reference to "the people who answered the call to war" in verse 9a forms an inclusio with verse 2a and signals closure for the first part of the account, which focuses on the background of the oppression and battle. The renewed call to praise (v. 9b) separates the two major sections of the poetic account, the second of which is introduced with "then" in verse 11b. As in verse 2, this part of the account is interrupted (by the address to the singers, v. 12; cf. vv. 2b–5), and then resumed by "then" at the beginning of verse 13. (Other verbal links connect vv. 11b and 13. Note "went/came down" and "the Lord's people.") The second part of the poetic account focuses on the mustering of the tribes and the battle. Verses 22–23 close the account, with the introductory "then" signaling an inclusio with verses 11b/13 and the concluding reference to the "warriors" providing a verbal link with verse 13. (Like v. 13, vv. 22–23 begin with אָז, "then," and conclude with בַּגִּבּוֹרִים, "against the warriors.") The curse of Meroz, which again raises the issue of tribal participation (cf. vv. 11b/13–18), rounds out the second part of the account by forming a thematic bracket around the battle scene of verses 19–22. Verse 23 also provides a transition to what follows, for the curse of Meroz supplies a dark backdrop for the blessing of Jael.

Indeed, verses 23–30 are a study in contrasts. The curse against unwilling Meroz contrasts sharply with the blessing on able and willing Jael. The juxtaposition of the blessing and taunt contrasts the reality of Sisera's death and the cunning of his female assassin with his mother's fantasies of victory and the pseudo-wisdom of her female attendants.

---

the poem include Blenkinsopp 1961, 61–76; Butler 2009, 124–29; Coogan 1978, 143–66; and Globe 1974, 493–512. For a proposed chiastic structure in verses 14–24 that highlights the theme of participation and nonparticipation, see Wong 2007b, 14–15. For a survey of form-critical research on the poem, see Echols 2008, 9–11. Echols also provides a thorough discussion of the literary unity of the song (64–92). He concludes that an original poem has been "liturgically reworked" (90). For a critique of Echols, see above.

The concluding imprecation/prayer (v. 31), which is introduced by
כֵּן, "so, thus," is linked to the introductory verses of the poem (v. 4) by
the vocative "O Lord," which also binds the imprecation and prayer
together.[40]

EXPOSITION

The Story of the Battle (4:1–24)

Prologue: Sin and oppression (4:1–3). After Ehud's death, the next generation of Israelites again sinned against the Lord.[41] Idolatry is not
mentioned specifically, but the following poem (cf. 5:8) may allude to
such practices precipitating the crisis.

As in the days of Othniel (cf. 3:8), the Lord gave (literally, "sold")
his people into foreign hands. This time the oppressor was Jabin, a
Canaanite king of Hazor, located in northern Israel in the tribal region of Naphtali.[42] Jabin's army commander, Sisera, who led a force
of nine hundred iron chariots, was the instrument of oppression.[43] He
lived in Harosheth Haggoyim, meaning "Harosheth of the nations," a
fact that reminds us of the Lord's decision to leave the nations in and
near the land to test Israel (cf. 2:21–3:4).[44] Because Jabin and Sisera
lived within Israel's allotted territory, they were more of a menace than

---

40. Wong (2007b, 17) proposes a chiastic structure for verses 25–31 in which
    the theme of the "triumph" and vindication of those who love the Lord (vv.
    25–27, 31b) forms a ring around the theme of the "dashed hopes" and "de-
    struction" of his enemies (vv. 28–30, 31a).
41. On the grammatical structure of 4:1b, see Amit 1999, 79.
42. Jabin is called "king of Canaan." For a study of the use of the term *Canaan*
    in ancient Near Eastern literature and in the Merneptah Stele in partic-
    ular, see Sparks 1998, 94–124 (a chapter entitled "Merneptah's Stele and
    Deborah's Song").
43. The figure nine hundred has an authentic ring to it. Thutmose III, in his
    account of the battle of Megiddo, claims to have captured 924 chariots from
    his Asiatic enemies. See *COS* 2:12. In his account of his campaign against
    a western coalition, Shalmaneser III of Assyria reported that the king of
    Damascus had 1200 chariots and the king of Hamath seven hundred. See
    COS 2:263. An ivory plaque from Megiddo dating to the thirteenth century
    BC portrays Canaanite chariots in action. See Yadin 1963, 242–43, 255.
44. Sisera may have ruled as a governor over this area. Harosheth-Hagoyyim
    probably refers not to a town, but to the wooded forests in the Galilee
    region. See Aharoni 1979, 221, 223, and Aharoni and Avi-Yonah 1977, 47.
    For a different view, see Block 1999, 190.

Cushan-Rishathaim, from distant Aram-Naharaim, or Eglon, from the Transjordanian state of Moab, had been.

Years before, Joshua had defeated another King Jabin of Hazor who, like his successor, had a huge number of horses and chariots at his disposal. On that occasion the victorious Joshua burned the enemy chariots and hamstrung the horses as a vivid object lesson that Israel's God was superior to such weapons and that Israel did not need them to succeed in battle. Joshua then burned Hazor and destroyed every living thing within the city (cf. Josh. 11:1–11). Undoubtedly successes like this enabled Joshua to say to the tribe of Joseph: "Though the Canaanites have iron chariots and though they are strong, you can drive them out" (Josh. 17:18b; literal translation). How far Israel had fallen from the days of Joshua! A kingdom again existed in the Hazor region, another Jabin had arisen, and Canaanite iron chariots were oppressing and intimidating God's people. Israel's sin had resurrected, as it were, conquered foes from the past![45]

The description of this oppression suggests it was more severe than those that preceded it. In the Othniel narrative Cushan-Rishathaim never appears as the subject of a verb; we are simply told that the Lord sold his people into the king's hands and that Israel then served the king (3:8). The Ehud narrative, in addition to attributing the oppression to the Lord and noting that Israel served Eglon, attributes hostile actions to the Moabite king, but stops short of actually using a verb meaning "oppress" (3:12–14). However, this narrative specifically declares that Sisera "cruelly oppressed" Israel for a period of twenty years (which is longer than either of the earlier oppressions). The verb

---

45. Some scholars argue that Joshua 11 and Judges 4 are two versions of one tradition. See, for example, Burney 1970, 81, and Moore 1895, 109. Others suggest that the references to Jabin and/or Hazor in Judges 4:2, 17 are later scribal additions influenced by Joshua 11. See, for example, Boling 1975, 94. However, the differences between the two accounts suggest they record distinct historical events. See Petrovich 2008, 495–99. The name Jabin may well have been a dynastic name or title (comparable to Pharaoh or Ben-Hadad) and Hazor may have been repopulated following Joshua's victory. See Wood 1995, 83–85; Block 1999, 188–89; Soden 1989, 272–77; Kitchen 2003, 213; Chavalas and Adamthwaite 1999, 95; and Petrovich 2008, 497–99. An Akkadian tablet from Hazor, dating to the mid-second millennium, mentions a king Ibni, a name also attested at Mari. Dever, observing that Ibni "is the *exact* linguistic equivalent of Hebrew 'Yabin'," suggests that the Bible preserves the memory "of an Ibni (that is, a Yabin) dynasty at Hazor, stretching all the way back to the Middle Bronze Age centuries earlier" (2003, 68).

used (לחץ) also appears in the Exodus account (Exod. 3:9), suggesting that Sisera's treatment of Israel was on a par with Pharaoh's. The adverb "cruelly" (בְּחָזְקָה, literally, "with force") emphasizes the severity of the oppression, while the reference to nine hundred iron chariots conjures up a rather terrifying mental image and suggests the apparent invincibility of the oppressor.

Main event: A general meets his Waterloo (4:4–22). In the earlier cycles Israel's cry is immediately followed by a reference to the Lord's providing a deliverer (cf. 3:9, 15). Not so here, where a portrait of a female prophet-judge replaces the expected report of divine intervention. This is disconcerting, for one wonders how a female judge could possibly thwart the powerful Sisera and his chariot force. The structure of the text highlights the contrast between Deborah and Sisera. Soden outlines the parallelism as follows (1989, 95):

> A. Sisera was the captain of Jabin's army (v. 2)
>   B. He lived in Harosheth Haggoyim (v. 2)
>   C. Israel cried out to the Lord (v. 3)
>   D. He was oppressing Israel for twenty years (v. 3)
> A' Deborah was a prophetess (v. 4)
>   D' She was judging Israel at that time (v. 4)
>   B' She sat in the hill country of Ephraim (v. 5)
>   C' Israel went up to her for judgment (v. 5)

Deborah seems an unlikely candidate for the task of national deliverer, but this should not diminish our confidence in the Lord's ability to rescue his people, for he had already accomplished his salvation through unlikely means (namely, Ehud and Shamgar) (Sternberg 1987, 272–73).

Deborah's appearance as Israel's leader also fuels the fires of suspicion ignited by the description of Shamgar at the end of the previous chapter. The brief account of Shamgar's deeds contains some oddities and raises some questions, but the narrator's portrayal of Deborah is even more peculiar and begins to confirm our suspicions about the state of Israelite leadership. While there is precedent for a female prophet (Exod. 15:20; see also 2 Kings 22:14 and Neh. 6:14), Deborah's role as judge comes as a real surprise, for nowhere else before or after this do we find a woman functioning in such a leadership position in Israel.[46]

---

46. Exodus 18:21–22 indicates men were to serve as judges. According to 2 Kings 11:3, the wicked Athaliah ruled Israel for six years, but she was not approved by God and her reign was a dark blot on Israel's history.

Her role seems far different from that of Acsah, the only other woman to have appeared in the book prior to this. The text highlights the oddity of the situation by its very word choice and syntax. It reads literally, "Now Deborah, a woman,[47] a prophetess, the wife of Lappidoth—she[48] was judging Israel at this time."[49] The statement compels one to ask:

---

47. It is rare to have a proper name followed by the undetermined absolute (i.e., non-suffixed, non-construct) form אִשָּׁה, "woman" (in addition to Judg. 4:4, see 1 Kings 11:26). The absolute form אִשָּׁה is followed by an appositional substantive giving a more specific categorization (cf. "a woman, a prophetess" in Judg. 4:4) in the collocations "a woman, a nurse" (Exod. 2:7); "a woman, a prostitute" (Lev. 21:7: Josh. 2:1; Judg. 11:1; 16:1; Prov. 6:26; Jer. 3:3: Ezek. 16:30; 23;44); "a woman, an adulteress" (Prov. 30:20); "a woman, a concubine" (Judg. 19:1) and "a woman, a widow" (2 Sam. 14:5; 1 Kings 7:14; 11:26; 17:9–10). As one can see, the precise collocation employed in Judges 4:4 is rare, making one think the narrator is drawing attention to Deborah's gender. However, the expression "a woman, a prophetess," does have a parallel in the collocation "a man, a prophet" (Judg. 6:8), raising the possibility that it is simply idiomatic.

48. The collocation of אִשָּׁה, "woman," as a nominative absolute resumed by the third feminine singular pronoun הִיא, "she," is rare (see Gen. 3:12; Prov. 31:30).

49. Since the name Lappidoth appears to be feminine plural, some suggest it is not the proper name of Deborah's husband, but a common noun meaning "flames, torches." Taking it as an abstract noun/attributive genitive, one could then translate the phrase "fiery one" or "spirited woman." For a discussion of this view see Schneider 2000, 66–67; and Davidson 2007, 260–61, note 193. However, the linguistic evidence militates against this proposal. The construct form אֵשֶׁת, "woman/wife of," occurs fifty-seven times with a proper name as genitive. Forty-seven times it occurs with a common noun following it, usually a relational term (master, son, father, brother, neighbor, etc.). Once it is followed by an appositional genitive (1 Sam. 28:17). On several occasions an attributive genitive (often an abstract plural) follows (see Deut. 13:6; 28:64; Ruth 3:11; Prov. 5:18; 9:13; 11:16; 12:4; 21:9, 19; 25:24; 27:15; 31:10; Isa. 54:6; Jer. 13:21; Hos. 1:2; Mal. 2:14–15), but such a collocation never appears in a narrative framework. Thirty times the construction proper name + "wife of" + proper name occurs. The precise construction used in Judges 4:4 (proper name + appositional common noun + "wife of" + noun) appears only here and in 2 Kings 22:14/2 Chronicles 34:22, where we read of "Huldah, the prophetess, the wife of Shallum." This parallel suggests Lappidoth is a proper name in Judges 4:4. Most likely Lappidoth is an abstract noun that was, in the case of Deborah's husband, employed as a proper name. Male proper names ending in וֹת-, though relatively rare, are attested: יְרִימוֹת (Jerimoth), מְרָיוֹת (Meraioth), מְשִׁלֵּמוֹת (Meshillemoth), מִקְלוֹת (Mikloth), נָבוֹת (Naboth), נְבָיוֹת

"Why was a *woman* judging? Were not any men available to accomplish this typically male task? Had the Calebs, Othniels, and Ehuds all disappeared? While the text does not necessarily condemn this state of affairs, the situation is definitely less than ideal and, as we shall see, indicative of a problem that becomes more apparent as the chapter and book unfold.

Block argues that the traditional view of Deborah as a judge is incorrect. He contends she was not a legal functionary who held court and adjudicated civil disputes. Rather she was strictly a prophetic figure to whom the people were looking for some resolution to the foreign oppression they were experiencing. He points out that the verb "to judge" (שׁפט) does not refer in the book of Judges to a legal function *per se*, but more generally to a leadership role that included a military dimension (Block 1994, 229–53, and 1999, 195–97).

It is true that the verb שׁפט usually seems to have a more general meaning, "lead, deliver" in Judges (Judg. 3:10; 10:2–3; 12:7–9, 11, 13–14; 15:20; 16:31; see also 1 Sam. 4:18; 7:6; 2 Kings 15:5; 23:22) (Rozenberg 1975, 77*–86*).[50] However, when one considers linguistic and broader contextual evidence, the traditional view of Deborah as a judge proves to be preferable. In light of usage in Judges, the collocation שׁפט אֶת could very well express the general idea, "govern, lead" in 4:4, but it should be noted that elsewhere it can refer to settling legal disputes (Exod. 18:13, 22, 26; Deut. 18:16; 1 Sam. 7:15–17; 1 Kings 3:9). No matter what shade of meaning one assigns to the verb in verse 4, the use of the phrase לְמִשְׁפָּט (literally, "for the judgment") in verse 5 points to a legal function. Block understands לְמִשְׁפָּט as referring to a prophetic oracle assuring deliverance.[51] However, the phrase usually appears in contexts where formal legal activity is occurring and cases are being adjudicated (see Num. 35:12; Deut. 17:8; Josh. 20:6; 2 Sam.

(Nebaioth), רָמוֹת (Ramoth, see Ezra 10:29, *Qere*), שְׁלֹמוֹת (Shelomoth), טַבָּעוֹת (Tabbaoth). Because the name means "torches, flashes," some have suggested that Lappidoth is an alternative name for Barak, "lightning bolt," and that Deborah and Barak were a husband and wife team. See Boling 1975, 95; and Hess 2003, 33–34. This speculative proposal is unlikely.

50. One should note, however, that the term does have a legal connotation in 11:27, where God's role as "Judge" is viewed as legal in nature. See our discussion of the term in the introduction to the commentary, in the section entitled, "What was the Role of the 'Judges'?"

51. Spronk proposes a similar view, "the people of Israel come to Deborah to receive with her help a divine oracle" (2001b, 236). See as well Ackerman 1975, 11–12.

15:2, 6; Ps. 9:7; Isa. 41:1; 54:17; Mal. 3:5).[52] In other instances it refers to proper agricultural technique (Isa. 28:26), justice in the form of deliverance and vindication (Ps. 76:9; Isa. 59:11), and fair legal treatment (Jer. 30:11; 46:28).[53] The collocation does not refer to an oracle of deliverance.[54]

---

52. See B. Johnson, "מִשְׁפָּט," in *TDOT* 9:89.

53. Unfortunately only in Judges 4:4 is the expression collocated with עלה, "go up." However, לְמִשְׁפָּט, literally, "for judgment," is collocated with another verb of motion (בוֹא, "come") in 2 Samuel 15:2, 6, where it refers to coming before a judge for adjudication.

54. The closest we come to such an idea is in Psalm 76:9 and Isaiah 59:11, where the expression is used with reference to the outworking of divine justice as God delivers his people from oppressors. One could argue that the phrase in Judges 4:5 is metonymic, substituting the effect (God's just intervention) for the cause or catalyst (God's oracular promise of intervention).

In attempting to make his case that מִשְׁפָּט, "judgment," refers to a divine answer to Israel's cry, Block develops several lines of argument, only some of which can be evaluated here (1994, 239–44). (1) He shows how the term is closely related to the verb צעק, "cry out" in several contexts (cf. Judg 4:3). But in the various texts he cites, מִשְׁפָּט, while referring to a response, has a legal connotation and refers to a fair decision. See 1 Kings 3:28; 20:40; Job 19:7, as well as *HALOT*, 651; BDB, 1048. (2) He argues that מִשְׁפָּט can refer to an oracle when used with reference to the Urim and Thummim (Exod 28:30; Num 27:21). A better gloss might be "decision, answer, opinion" (cf. Johnson, "מִשְׁפָּט," in *TDOT* 9:88). Even if an oracle is involved, the meaning here is technical and contextually restricted. Consequently one wonders if these texts have any relevance to our understanding of the term in Judges 4. (3) He suggests that the verb עלה in Judges 4:5 has a technical sense of "go up to inquire," citing alleged parallels in Judges 20:18, 23, 27. But in Judges 20 a *wayyiqtol* form of עלה is followed by a *wayyiqtol* (not infinitival) form of שאל, "inquire." They are actions in sequence; there is no indication of purpose in any formal linguistic sense. In verse 23 the verb "and they wept" appears between "they went up" and "they inquired." In verses 26–27 several verbs intervene ("they entered," "they wept," "they sat," "they fasted," "they offered up"). Judges 4:5 is different; here the prepositional phrase לְמִשְׁפָּט, "for judgment," follows "they went up," indicating purpose. As noted in the text, this collocation never means "for an oracle, message, response" elsewhere, but usually refers to legal adjudication. (4) He proposes that many texts, including Judges 13:12; 1 Samuel 2:13; 8:10–11; 2 Kings 1:7; and several passages in the Latter Prophets, use מִשְׁפָּט "in similar ways," apparently meaning with reference to an oracle. However, in none of these texts is the meaning proposed by Block the most natural way of understanding the

In the broader context of Deuteronomy and the Former Prophets the legal function of judges (שֹׁפְטִים), including kings (see 2 Sam. 15:4 in this regard), is well-attested (see especially Deut. 16:18; 17:9, 12; 19:17–18; 21:2; 25:1–2; 1 Sam. 7:15–17; 2 Sam. 15:4; 1 Kings 3:9, 28). When Samuel appointed his sons as judges, their role was clearly legal, as the reference to their accepting bribes and perverting justice indicates (1 Sam. 8:1–5). The most reasonable interpretation of Judges 4:4–5 is that Deborah was exercising a dual role of prophet and judge, much like Samuel did at a later time.[55] S. Niditch merges the two roles into one, that of "decision maker." She states: "The judge can offer decisions, whether to go to war or how to conduct the battle (e.g., Deborah, Ehud, Gideon), and his or her advice is followed because it is believed to be God-sent knowledge. This oracular capacity also allows him or her to adjudicate more mundane matters, to 'judge' in a more workaday fashion" (2008, 2).

Deborah's status as a judge foreshadows the role she plays in the narrative. As Stek observes: "Her announced status as judge (v. 4), to whom 'the Israelites go up for judgment' (v. 5), identifies her as the

---

word. (a) The phrase מִשְׁפַּט־הַנַּעַר, literally "the rule(s) of/for the boy," refers in Judges 13:12 to the regulations which the boy was to follow to fulfill his Nazirite status. These included abstaining from intoxicating drinks and unclean food, as implied in the angel's instructions to Manoah's wife (v. 14). See Johnson, "מִשְׁפָּט," in *TDOT* 9:96. Similarly in 1 Samuel 10:25 the phrase מִשְׁפַּט הַמְּלֻכָה, literally "the rule(s) of kingship," refers to the regulations the king was to follow, which are outlined in Deuteronomy 17:14–20. See Klein 1983, 100. (b) In 1 Samuel 2:13 וּמִשְׁפַּט introduces a disjunctive clause that gives a specific example of the generalizing statement made in verse 12b. מִשְׁפָּט refers most naturally to the practice outlined in verses 13b–14; it carries the force of "custom, practice" (cf. BDB, 1049) or perhaps "claim" (*HALOT*, 651). (c) In 1 Samuel 8:9, 11 מִשְׁפַּט הַמֶּלֶךְ most naturally refers to the policies, legal claim (cf. *HALOT*, 651), or rights (cf. Johnson, "מִשְׁפָּט," in *TDOT* 9:92) of the typical king, as outlined in 1 Samuel 8:11–17. (d) In 2 Kings 1:7 מִשְׁפָּט refers to the prophet's appearance, as the messengers' response clearly indicates (v. 8). See *HALOT*, 652; Johnson, "מִשְׁפָּט," in *TDOT* 9:96. (e) In the proposed examples from the Latter Prophets, מִשְׁפָּט refers to a formalized, legal accusation (Hos. 5:1), the principles of justice (Isa. 28:6; Mic. 3:1; Mal. 2:17), judicial decision-making (Isa. 28:6), a legal dispute (Isa. 41:1), justice as vindication (Isa. 59:9, 11, 14–15), or one's legal right (Ezek. 21:32 [Eng. v. 27]), but *not* to an oracular message.

55. Her position "under the Date Palm Tree of Deborah" probably relates primarily to her prophetic status. Apparently divine revelation was sometimes associated with sacred trees. Note the reference to the "oak tree of the diviners" in Judges 9:37.

source of justice where the wronged in Israel can secure redress and the oppressed relief. In context, it awakens expectations that she will also deliver the oppressed tribes from Jabin's harsh rule" (1986, 62). Ironically, this one who settled disputes within Israel on behalf of the oppressed would set in motion God's program for delivering his oppressed nation.

In her prophetic capacity Deborah summoned Barak, who was from the tribe of Naphtali. Her message to Barak consists of an introductory messenger formula, a command, and an assurance of victory. Deborah's message came from Yahweh, the God of Israel, a title that emphasizes the Lord's position as the king of Israel. (Note the same emphasis in several other texts where the title appears. See Exod. 5:1; Judg. 5:5; 6:8–10; 11:23.) The message came as a divine command.[56] Barak had no option but to obey. He was to muster ten thousand men from the northern tribes of Naphtali and Zebulun and lead them to Mt. Tabor. The Lord himself would draw the powerful enemy army to the Kishon River and deliver them into Barak's hands. "Bring" (v. 7) and "march" (v. 6) translate the same Hebrew verb (מָשַׁךְ), emphasizing that the Lord's action would be in concert with that of Barak; both would contribute to the same divine strategy.[57] At the same time, the Lord's active role in the battle would be dominant. Barak would simply receive the enemy into his hands; the outcome of the battle did not depend on his prowess.

Our worst suspicions are confirmed in verse 8. Barak, whose name means "lightning-flash," is anything but a firebolt from the sky.[58] In contrast to Joshua, who obeyed God's military commands to the letter (cf. Josh. 10:40; 11:12, 15), Barak answered God's command with a

---

56. The Hebrew text reads literally, "Has the Lord God of Israel not commanded?" This question does not imply that Barak had been negligent in carrying out an earlier command. Rather this form of question is an idiom emphasizing that a command is being issued through the question (see Josh. 1:9; Ruth 2:9; 2 Sam. 13:28). See Moore 1895, 117–18.

57. See Stek 1986, 63–64; and Murray 1979, 169. Murray observes: "This parity of Barak's action with Yahweh's imports an element of the favoured hero into the initial characterization of Barak."

58. Scham observes: "The implications of Barak's name—'lightning'—for a military leader must be viewed as positive but endowing Barak with the characteristics of lightning seems slightly derisive considering his part in the story. He may be swift in answering Deborah's call (Judg. 4:6–7) but his reluctance to do battle without her (4:8) implies an indecisive and recalcitrant personality that belies the quick impulsiveness that his name suggests" (2002, 51).

conditional sentence! Perhaps he focused on the Lord's description of Sisera's army, rather than the promise. (Note "chariots" and "huge army" in v. 7; the latter refers to a "horde, multitude.") In contrast to Othniel and Ehud, men of faith who saw a challenge and responded courageously and decisively, Barak demanded the support of a woman. Israelite male leadership had fallen on hard times; no wonder a woman had to fill the office of judge!

Barak's request was probably motivated by a desire for continued divine guidance (after all, Deborah was a prophetess).[59] However, one does not respond to a divine command and promise with the words "if" or "I will not." God had given assurance of victory; Barak's hesitation was inexcusable. Deborah assured Barak of her presence, but also informed him that his hesitation and weak faith had caused him to forfeit the full glory of the victory.[60] The Lord would deliver the Canaanite general into the hands of a woman. At this point one suspects that Deborah is referring to herself, but there is more to the story (Amit 1987, 92–93; Fokkelman 1999, 85).

The referent of "the way that you are going" (v. 9; literal translation) is not entirely clear. NIV assumes that it refers to the hesitant manner in which Barak responded to God's command. In this case, Deborah rebuked him explicitly and attributed the loss of glory directly to his hesitancy. However, a better option (see NIV margin) is to take the referent as the military campaign upon which Barak was about to embark. In this case the rebuke and reason for the loss of glory are implied, not direct. The linguistic evidence strongly favors this option. Elsewhere when the preposition עַל, "upon," is collocated with דֶּרֶךְ,

---

59. On Barak's motive, see Block 1999, 199. The LXX attempts to give a motive for Barak's demand; it adds at the end of verse 8: "For I know not the day in which the Lord prospers the messenger with me." For a discussion of the text-critical issues, see O'Connell 1996, 458–60. Ackerman argues that the LXX contains the original text and is not a secondary addition (1975, 10). Fewell and Gunn suggest Barak was setting up a test (1990, 398). If Deborah were willing to go along and jeopardize her life, then her prophetic word could be taken as authentic and reliable.

60. Yee speaks of the "shaming" of Barak in this passage (1993, 115–16). See also Butler 2009, 98. For a much more sympathetic view of Barak, see Olson 1998, 780. He argues that the language of the text is intentionally ambiguous and does not necessarily present Barak in a negative light. For an even more positive view of Barak's actions, see Wilcock 1992, 62–64. He contends that Barak's deferring to Deborah is a mark of faith.

"way," it consistently has a locative ("upon") or directive ("toward"), not causal, force.[61]

True to her word, Deborah accompanied Barak, first to Kedesh, where Barak mustered his army (vv. 9d–10a), and then up to Tabor (vv. 10c, 12). After recording Deborah's promise that she would go with him, the text twice says that she accompanied him. The repetition highlights Barak's lack of confidence by reminding us of his earlier conditional statement.

The developing story line is suddenly suspended (v. 11). At first this parenthetical comment about Heber the Kenite seems irrelevant and disruptive to the flow of the narrative. However, the original audience would know enough about Israelite storytelling style to realize this tidbit of information would prove to be important in the unfolding plot.[62] This Heber would somehow play a role in the approaching battle. But how so? Does his identity as a Kenite mean he was on Israel's side (cf. 1:16), or does his departure from Kenite territory to northern Israel suggest the possibility that he had defected to the Canaanites? We must wait and see.

When Sisera heard that Barak had massed his troops at Mt. Tabor, he summoned his nine hundred iron chariots and huge infantry force to the nearby Kishon River, which runs through a valley that was well-suited for chariot warfare. Verse 13 is written from the perspective of the casual observer, who sees the massive Canaanite force moving into a strategic battle location, but does not detect the invisible hand of God drawing it to its demise (cf. v. 7).

With the armies in place, Deborah commanded Barak to charge and assured him that the victory was his[63] because the Lord had marched

---

61. See, for example, Genesis 38:21; 1 Samuel 24:3; 26:3; 1 Kings 20:38; Ezra 8:31, where the expression עַל הַדֶּרֶךְ, means "on the way, road." The idiom דֶּרֶךְ אֲשֶׁר הָלַךְ, "way which (one) is going" usually refers to a literal journey (Gen. 35:3; 42:28; Deut. 1:31, 33; Josh. 3:4; 24:17; 1 Kings 13:9, 17; Neh. 9:12, 19; Jer. 42:3). Twice it is used figuratively of one's lifestyle or general behavioral pattern (Judg. 2:17; 2 Kings 21:21), but it does not refer elsewhere to one's manner of behavior in a specific situation. Only here is the active participial form used in the construction (the perfect is used eight times, the imperfect six times). This might refer to Barak's present hesitancy, or, more likely it has an imminent future force, referring to the mission upon which he was to embark.

62. In this regard see Sternberg 1987, 280. On the rhetorical strategy of the placement of verse 11, see Murray 1979, 179–83.

63. The assuring words of verse 14 essentially repeat the promise of verse 7, but seem to contradict Deborah's statement that the Lord would hand Sisera over to a woman, rather than Barak (cf. v. 9). As the story unfolds

ahead of him into battle (v. 14).[64] This time Barak responded like a lightning bolt and swept down into the valley with his soldiers. The Lord, in fulfillment of his ancient promise (Exod. 23:27), routed the enemy (v. 15), just as he had done in the days of Moses and Joshua (cf. Exod. 14:24 and Josh. 10:10, where the same verb is used of the Lord's victories).[65] At this point we are not told specifically how the Lord accomplished this, but chapter 5 gives a clue. Barak's hurricane of steel put the Canaanites to the sword, chasing them all the way to Sisera's home in Harosheth-Haggoyim and permitting no survivors to escape.

However, Sisera himself was still running loose. He got down from his chariot, escaped from the battlefield on foot, and made his way to the home of the aforementioned Heber.[66] As noted above, Heber's identity as a Kenite may have led us to believe he was an ally of Israel (cf. 1:16), but we are now informed that he was actually on Jabin's side.[67] The news is disconcerting, for it means that Sisera had apparently found asylum and might live to fight again.

When Heber's name is introduced in verse 11, the first-time reader undoubtedly suspects that he, like Sisera and Deborah, will play a significant role in the story. Unlike modern theater programs, which provide a list of all the characters so the audience can orient themselves prior to the start of the play, Hebrew narrative tends to formally introduce characters at the point where they appear in the story line. If a character is central to the story, he or she is often introduced at the very

---

we see that both are true. Verses 7 and 14 refer by synecdoche (Sisera stands for his troops) to Sisera's army, while verse 9 refers specifically to Sisera.

64. The concept of a deity marching ahead of his appointed leader also appears in the Tel Dan Inscription (A5), where the author states that his god Hadad went before him into battle. See Athas 2005, 212–13. For Assyrian parallels to this motif, see *COS*, 2:161, note 5.

65. The verb used, הָמַם, "to rout," may be a play on הָמוֹן, used in verse 7 to describe Sisera's horde of soldiers. The wordplay draws attention to the Lord's sovereignty over even the most powerful human forces. He does not fear a horde (הָמוֹן); on the contrary he routs (הָמַם) them!

66. The repetition of the verb יָרַד, "go down," in verses 14–15 highlights the contrast between Barak and Sisera, as well as the reversal in "the situation between the armies" (Assis 2005b, 6). Barak was on foot, while Sisera was leading his imposing chariot force. Yet despite this "disadvantage," Barak went down from Mount Tabor to attack Sisera, the Lord intervened, and Sisera went down from his chariot to flee from Barak.

67. Margalith theorizes that Jabin may have hired Heber to protect commercial routes from bandits (1995, 633).

beginning, just before the action is initiated (cf. Judg. 13:2; 17:1; 19:1b). At other times, character introductions are embedded within the story line. We then expect the character to appear immediately or shortly thereafter. For example, after describing the Canaanite oppression, the narrator of Judges formally introduces Deborah (4:4–5), who then immediately initiates the action in this new episode (4:6). In the same way, after describing the Ammonite oppression (10:6–16), the narrator formally introduces Jephthah (11:1–3), who soon thereafter enters the story line (v. 5). The old man of Gibeah appears on the scene, is formally introduced, and then immediately enters the story line (19:16–17). But Heber is a "no-show" in the drama. Instead his wife Jael, unmentioned in verse 11, takes center stage. At the literary level she supplants Heber. This foreshadows how she will supplant Barak as the hero of the story.[68]

Ostensibly an ally of Sisera, Jael treated the general as if he were both her master and son. Her actions and words seem to express her devotion. She came out to meet the general, invited him to accept her hospitality, addressed him as "my lord," repeated her invitation, and gave him an assuring word. When he accepted her invitation and entered her tent, she began to show almost motherly concern (Niditch 1993, 114; Alter 1985, 48). She covered him up,[69] responded to his request for water

---

68. See Chisholm 2009c, 176. I originally made this point in an oral presentation at the 2006 national meeting of the Evangelical Theological Society in Washington, D. C. Butler cites this earlier unpublished version (2009, 100), which was subsequently revised and published in *JSOT*.

69. The noun שְׂמִיכָה occurs only here in the Hebrew Bible. It is normally understood as referring to a cover of some kind, an interpretation which makes excellent sense in the context and in the collocation with the *piel* form of כסה, "to cover." It may derive from the root סמך, which has, according to von Soden, an Akkadian cognate meaning "cover over" and nominal derivatives referring to a "covering" (*HALOT*, 759; *TDOT* 10:278). For a discussion of how it has been interpreted in the ancient versions, see Lindars 1995, 198.

Van Wolde sees sexual connotations here (as in 5:27); she understands the statement וַתָּבוֹא אֵלָיו, "she went to him" (4:21; literal translation) as playing off the idiom בּוֹא אֶל, "go to," which can refer to sexual intercourse (1995, 245). See also Assis 2004, 84. But this need not mean that she had a sexual encounter with Sisera, who was undoubtedly too tired for such activity (Matthews 2004, 72).

Reis thinks otherwise (2005, 29–32). She argues that Jael seduced Sisera in order to weaken and kill him. She interprets much of the language as overtly sexual and recreates an erotic scene in Jael's tent. She builds her case on a tenuous understanding in 4:18 of שְׂמִיכָה, which she interprets as a verbal noun, meaning "laying on," that refers to Jael's body

by giving him some tasty and refreshing milk, and then covered him again.[70]

But the plot takes a surprising turn and Deborah's earlier prediction about Sisera dying at the hand of a woman comes into sharper focus.[71] Jael's offer of milk was not an expression of kindness or loyalty, but a devious act designed to make the general entirely defenseless before her. As the exhausted general slept before her, she moved into

---

in a dominant coital posture. Because the verb כסה appears not once, but twice (v. 19), Reis argues that Jael had intercourse with Sisera a second time "to deplete her guest, leaving him sleepy and vulnerable" (31). Reis' proposal is problematic for at least three reasons: (1) Nouns of this morphological pattern (אָאִיאָה) can on occasion express verbal ideas, but several of them refer to concrete entities. (Note especially חליצה, "equipment, stripped from a man," יריעה, "tent curtain," פתיחה, "sword, dagger," צחיחה, "bare land," צניפה, "headband," צפירה, "thread, wreath," קשׁיטה, "a weight, used for money," and רפידה, "back of a chair.") (2) The presence of the article suggests a concrete item is in view. Here it probably indicates that the object is present in the mind of the speaker (see GKC, 407, para. 126q-r [our text cited]; *IBHS*, 243). Often in such cases the item is one that typically appears in the situation being described—a woman's blanket or garment would typically be present in her tent. (3) Furthermore, a syntactical analysis of the construction used in verse 18b militates against her interpretation. The Hebrew collocation used here does not behave as Reis suggests, nor did Jael. For a detailed discussion of the syntactical issues, see Chisholm 2010b. Butler (2009, 105), after surveying the literature available to him at the time of writing, concludes: "One can see sexual intimations here without having to find actual sexual acts described or even hinted at."

Wilkinson proposes an emendation that divides the form בַּשְּׂמִיכָה into two words, בְּשֶׂם, "perfume," and וַיֵּכָה (an apocopated *qal wayyiqtol* from the root כהה, "grow faint") (1983, 512–13). She translates verse 18b "as she overwhelmed him with perfume," and then takes the reconstructed verb with verse 19a: "He grew faint and said to her . . . " This picture of Sisera being overcome by the smell of perfume borders on the bizarre. As Lindars (1995, 198) politely observes, Wilkinson's proposal, "though ingenious, scarcely carries conviction."

70. The milk, in addition to being tasty and refreshing, would also make him sleepy. See Burney 1970, 93.
71. On the surprise element in the episode, see Berlin 1983, 70–1. She points out that the narrator is able to surprise us because the story is "under-narrated." Jael's actions are described, but we are "never given Jael's point of view—none of her perceptions, thoughts, or motivations." On the ambiguity that characterizes the narrator's presentation of Jael, see Amit 1987, 97.

action, grabbing a tent peg and hammering it through Sisera's head into the ground, killing him instantly.[72] In the meantime Barak arrived too late for the kill, but in plenty of time to see Sisera's corpse sprawled out on the floor with a tent peg sticking through his temple.[73]

Jael's invitation to Barak to "come here" (לֵךְ, v. 22) echoes Deborah's earlier charge to him (v. 6, לֵךְ). His failure to respond properly to Deborah's command to fight caused him to forfeit the glory of killing Sisera. Now he receives an invitation to enter the tent so Jael can show him the corpse of the one he has been pursuing. In verse 6, second person verbs (Barak as subject) follow לֵךְ, for Barak is being called to action. But here a first person verb (Jael as subject) follows: Jael is active, Barak is a mere observer of what she has done (Murray 1979, 172–73).

There may be another hint of irony in verse 22 in the non-sexual use of the expression "and he went to her" (וַיָּבֹא אֵלֶיהָ). In the other eight uses of this expression (third masculine singular form of בוא collocated with the preposition אֶל, with a third feminine singular suffix) in the Old Testament, sexual contact is always in view (Gen. 29:23; 30:4; 38:2, 18; Judg. 16:1; Ruth 4:13; 2 Sam.12:24; Ezek. 23:44). But here in the case of Barak it has no such force, perhaps mirroring the fact that a woman has usurped Barak's role as the story's hero (cf. 4:9). He has been, as it were, emasculated literarily. He "goes in to" a woman, but not to express his manhood. On the contrary, he finds that a woman has accomplished what he, a man, should have done.[74] This

---

72. The specific reference to Jael's hand in verse 21 (and again in 5:26) is ironic, for Deborah had prophesied that the Lord would give Sisera into the hand of a woman (see v. 9, which reads literally, "for the Lord will sell Sisera into the hand of a woman").

73. The meaning of רַקָּה, traditionally understood as "temple" (v. 21), has been debated. Apart from this account (see v. 22, as well as 5:26), the term occurs only in the Song of Solomon (4:3; 6:7), where it refers to a part of the face hidden by the beloved's veil and likened to a slice of pomegranate, perhaps the cheek. Boling suggests the upper neck may be in view (1975, 98), while Halpern opts for the throat (1988b, 100, note 10). However, Lindars argues that the parallelism with "head" in 5:26 strongly suggests that the skull or temple is the referent here (1995, 202).

74. Based on the use of the collocation elsewhere, Reis argues that the expression describes Barak having sexual relations with Jael. In her view Jael had already seduced Sisera, not once but twice. (2005, 29–32; see our discussion above). Reis argues that Jael, whom she characterizes as a "habitual gadabout" and "loose woman" (citing Prov. 7:11), also seduced Barak, right in the shadow of Sisera's corpse (34–37). In this case, Reis

would not be the only place where the narrator uses irony to develop the theme of Jael's usurpation of Barak's heroic role. He uses Heber, who is introduced (4:11) but never appears in the story, to highlight this theme (Chisholm 2009c, 175–76).

The text never reveals Jael's motives.[75] Was she defending her honor?[76] Had her sentiments, in contrast to her husband's, been pro-Israelite all along? (Boling 1975, 97) Or did she simply realize that common sense and expediency now demanded that her clan transfer its allegiance from defeated Sisera to Israel? (Fewell and Gunn 1990, 396; Pressler 2002, 158) We cannot be certain. For the narrator her actions, not motives, are what really count.[77]

The numerous parallels between the Ehud/Shamgar and Jael narratives make it clear that the narrator is depicting Jael as another Ehud/Shamgar, albeit of the female variety. The parallels include: (1) Both Ehud and Jael made their victims think they were loyal subjects and lured them into a defenseless position. (2) Ehud and Jael killed the leader of the enemy behind closed doors. (3) Like Shamgar, Jael employed an unconventional weapon. (4) Neither Shamgar nor Jael appears to be a full-fledged Israelite. (5) The same Hebrew verb

suggests that this portrayal of Jael simply reflects the fact that the Bible is "xenophobic" and typically depicts "non-Israelite women" as "ipso facto, immoral" (36). Reis stresses that the collocation elsewhere refers to sexual contact and therefore must have the same force here (34).

But Reis' appeal to the use of the collocation is misleading. In each of the other passages there is a clear contextual indicator that the expression refers to intimate contact. For a detailed refutation of Reis' interpretation of the syntax, see Chisholm 2013.

Here בּוֹא אֶל, following הלך, simply refers to entering her home, an action that is necessary for him to be able to see the fallen Sisera. In short, the collocation does not behave in this context as Reis suggests, nor did Jael.

75. For a summary of proposals see Hamilton 2001, 122–23.
76. Matthews argues that Sisera violated the code of hospitality in several ways. By drawing attention to these violations the narrator justifies Sisera's murder and provides Jael with a motive for killing him. He states: "By approaching her tent, Sisera has shown himself in violation of custom and Jael's invitation can then be taken as a subterfuge to lead him to his death, using the hospitality code as a cover for her actions," which from this point on are designed to "preserve her life and her honor" (1991, 16; see as well Matthews 2004, 68–73).
77. Assis sees the narrator's silence regarding Jael's ("Yael's") motives as highlighting divine providence. He writes: "the concealment of Yael's motives leave [sic] an impression of wonder at such divine intervention" (2004, 88).

(תָּקַע) is used to describe Ehud's deadly sword thrust and Jael's fatal hammer blow (cf. "drove" in 3:21 and 4:21). (6) The fallen corpses of Eglon and Sisera are described in almost identical terms (cf. the statement וְהִנֵּה אֲדֹנֵיהֶם נֹפֵל אַרְצָה מֵת, literally, "and look, their lord was falling to the ground, dead," in 3:25b with וְהִנֵּה סִיסְרָא נֹפֵל מֵת, literally, "and look, Sisera was falling, dead," in 4:22b).[78]

Epilogue: Israel over Canaan (4:23–24). The conclusion reminds us that this victory belonged ultimately to God. The name *God (Elohim)* is appropriate for the conqueror of the Canaanites, because the pagans knew the Lord by this generic name for deity (see 1:7; 3:20; 7:14; 16:17). In the battle at the Kishon River, Jabin discovered the identity of the real sovereign King and God. The verb "humiliated" (כָּנַע) forms a soundplay on the name Canaan (כְּנַעַן), used three times here in the phrase "king of Canaan," and also draws attention to God's sovereignty over the hostile Canaanites. Israel followed up this victory by suppressing Jabin's strength until they eventually destroyed his power.[79]

Celebrating the Victory in Song (5:1–31)

Israel was willing to fight (v. 2a), but the Lord was the real victor in the battle and was deserving of praise. The address to kings and rulers (v. 3) sets the tone for the entire poem. Yahweh's battle with the Canaanites was a test of power to determine whether King Jabin of Canaan or Yahweh would rule over Israel (see v. 19). This song of victory was appropriate because all kings needed to know of the royal splendor and power of victorious Yahweh, the God of Israel.[80]

---

78. Webb notes some of these parallels (1987, 137). See also Assis 2006, 116–17.
79. It is not certain if the Israelites actually destroyed Hazor at this time. For contrary opinions, see Hoffmeier 2007, 243–46 (Hazor was not destroyed at this time), and Wood 2007, 255–56 (Hazor was destroyed at this time).
80. Commenting on the opening verses of the victory song, Weitzman observes: "it is God who deserves Israel's praise first and foremost, because it was his intervention in the battle that made victory possible" (1997, 32). As such, the song promotes "allegiance to God." Hauser sees the defeated kings of Canaan as the addressee here: "Since the only kings around at this point in Israel's history would have been the kings of the Canaanites, whom Israel had just defeated, these Canaanite rulers are being sarcastically told to listen while praises are sung to the God who has just defeated them. This has the effect not only of putting down the Canaanite kings, but also of praising Yahweh and thanking him for the victory" (1987, 269). Contrary to Hauser and others, Echols argues that Judges 5 was originally

The theophanic hymn depicts the Lord as marching from Seir and Edom in the south.[81] Since he is subsequently called "the One of Sinai," the implication is that he is coming from Sinai to fight for his people. The God of Moses, who once revealed his might at Sinai, was still alive and well!

The titles "the One of Sinai" and the "God of Israel," emphasize that he is Israel's Lord. At Sinai the Lord established his covenant with Israel and exhibited his power as a victorious warrior. As Israel stood shaking at the base of the mountain, the Lord thundered away and hurled lightning bolts, demonstrating his sovereignty over the elements of the storm. It comes as no surprise, then, to find storm motifs in Deborah's theophanic description of the warrior Yahweh. As he marched to the aid of his people, the earth and mountains shook and the heavens poured down water. Unless the language is purely stereotypical, it seems to imply that the Lord used a storm to defeat the Canaanite forces at the Kishon River (see vv. 20–21).

The opening verses of the poetic account recall that in the days of Shamgar and Jael the roads in Israel were unsafe and travel was restricted. On the basis of the description in verses 6–7, as well as the invitation to the caravaneers in verses 10–11, Schloen concludes that the Canaanite oppression of the highland tribes involved the disruption of caravan trade. He states: "Through extortion of exorbitant tolls, or even outright plunder, Sisera and his Canaanite allies had stifled caravan traffic through the plain of Jezreel, provoking the Israelite

---

a "heroic victory song" designed to praise its human characters, not the Lord (2008, 198). Only later was it given a more theological emphasis, but even then, the "theological adaptation has not completely obscured the Song's original purpose—the celebration of the heroes—and result [*sic*] is a poem which praises both the heroes and Yahweh" (200). For a critique of Echols, see above.

81. The theophanic hymn (vv. 4–5) displays a chiastic structure: (A) "O Lord, when you departed from Seir, when you marched from Edom's plains; (B) the earth shook, (C) the heavens poured down—(C') the clouds poured down rain. (B') The mountains trembled (A') before the Lord, the God of Sinai; before the Lord God of Israel." See as well Globe 1974, 504; Gray 1988, 425, note 8; Vincent 2000, 78–79; and Younger 2002, 149. Other theophanic descriptions exhibit similar concentric patterns, including Psalms 18:5–20; 29:5–9; and tablet 11, lines 96–106, of the Gilgamesh epic. On Psalm 18 and Gilgamesh, see Chisholm 1983, 48–50, 378–79, respectively. On Psalm 29 see my NET Bible study note on Psalms 29:7 (First Beta Edition 2001, 932, note 1; Second Beta Edition 2003, 885, note 15; and First Edition 2005, 938, note 21), as well as Venter 2004, 237–38.

highlanders into a war to protect their economic interests" (1993, 20). Enemies threatened the cities, and Israel was unprepared militarily. But in the midst of this chaotic situation, God provided new leaders.[82] One of these was Deborah, who was like a protective mother to Israel, "passionately committed to Israel's well-being."[83] When she issued the prophetic call to war, many among the people volunteered. The renewed call to praise is appropriately addressed to travelers, because the roads were once again safe for commerce due to the Lord's deliverance of his people through the army of Israel (called here his "victorious deeds," v. 11).

Under the leadership of Deborah and Barak, the people of the Lord gathered for war. Several tribes (or subtribal groups) are singled out, including Ephraim, Benjamin, Machir (the firstborn of Manasseh, see

---

82. The meaning of verse 8a is notoriously difficult to determine. The text reads literally: "He chose gods, new; then לָחֶם gates." In the first clause some take *Israel* as the subject of the verb, *gods* as object, and *new* as an adjective modifying *gods*. This yields the translation, "(Israel) chose new gods." In this case idolatry is the cause of the trouble alluded to in the context (see Deut. 32:17). However, one may take *God* as subject of the verb and *new* as substantival, referring to the new leaders raised up by God (see v. 9a). For a survey of opinions and a defense of the latter view, see Lindars 1995, 239–40. The interpretation of the second clause is difficult because the second word (לָחֶם) appears only here. Interpretations and emendations of the Hebrew text abound (see Lindars 1995, 240). Perhaps we should repoint the form as a participle לֹחֵם (from the verbal root לחם, "fight"), used substantivally and collectively. We may then translate: "Then fighters (were) in the gates." This would refer to the military leaders or warriors mentioned in the preceding line and in verse 9. For other occurrences of the *qal* of לחם, see Psalms 35:1; 56:2–3.

83. See Ackerman 1998, 43, as well as Dempster 1978, 47, and Bronner 2004, 79–82. The term "mother" is used here in a metaphorical sense, probably connoting protection and tender care. The term is used in a similar manner in two Northwest Semitic inscriptions dating to the ninth–eighth centuries B.C. King Kilamuwa, in describing how he helped his people, declared: "To some I was a father. To some I was a mother. To some I was a brother . . . They were disposed (toward me) as an orphan is to his mother." King Azitawadda boasted: "Ba'l made me a father and a mother to the Danunites." See *COS*, 2:148–50. Another possibility is that the term "mother" points to Deborah's prophetic status (see Block 1999, 226). The corresponding term "father" is used of male prophets, apparently in their prophetic role of giving advice. See 2 Kings 2:12; 6:21; 13:14, as well as 2 Kings 8:9, where King Ben-Hadad is called the prophet's "son." Joseph, in his role as adviser to the king, is called Pharaoh's "father" in Genesis 45:8.

Josh. 13:31; 17:1), Zebulun, Issachar, and Naphtali (see vv. 14–15a, 18). This list is interrupted by a list of other tribes who refused to join in the campaign, including Reuben, Gilead (which probably refers to Gad, see Josh. 13:24–25), Dan, and Asher (vv. 15b–17).[84] The structure of the text appears to highlight their nonparticipation by bracketing verses 15b–17 with references to participating tribes (O'Connell 1996, 117; Wong 2007b, 6–7). Dan's and Asher's lack of participation comes as no surprise (see 1:31–32, 34), but Reuben's and Gilead's/Gad's failure to join the alliance is especially disturbing. In the days of Joshua these tribes, whose allotted territory was east of the Jordan, had supported the other tribes in their invasion of the land (see Josh. 1:12–15; 4:12; 22:1–9), but now they had abandoned their brothers across the Jordan. It is likely the four nonparticipants were motivated by economic interests that differed from those of the highland tribes that participated in the battle (Stager 1988, 227–32; Schloen 1993, 29–30).

On the surface the poem seems to differ from the prose account with regard to the number of tribes involved in the Israelite coalition against Sisera. Chapter four mentions only Naphtali and Zebulun (vv. 6, 10), while the poem adds Ephraim, Benjamin, Makir (= Manasseh) and Issachar. Soden suggests that tribal participation is a peripheral issue in chapter four, so only the main combatants, Naphtali and Zebulun, are mentioned (cf. 5:18). However, in chapter five tribal involvement becomes a main theme, so we get a more detailed survey of how various tribes responded to the crisis (Soden 1989, 252–56). Soden cites similar varying lists of combatants in the Kadesh inscriptions of Rameses II, indicating that this type of variation is not unique in ancient battle accounts (1989, 254–55, note 18).

Halpern argues that chapter four is the product of interpretive reflection on chapter five (1988b, 79–82).[85] According to Halpern, the poem stops short of saying that the additional four tribes were actual participants in the battle. They merely came down to the city gates (v. 11), apparently to await news of the battle's outcome. While they showed greater concern than the tribes mentioned in verses 15b–17, they stopped short of joining Barak's forces. The actual combatants, Naphtali and Zebulun, are identified in verse 18, which corresponds to the description in chapter four. Brettler calls Halpern's view "very farfetched." He asks: "How likely is it that a later reader of Judges 4 would think that only Zebulun and Naftali participated in the battle (4:6),

---

84. On Reuben's failure to participate, see Crown 1967, 240–42.
85. Leuchter (2010, 258) concurs with Halpern's view and calls it "still compelling."

based on a misreading of 5:14–17 that suggests that the other tribes waited at the gates (5:11), and only Zebulun and Naftali risked their lives (v. 18)?" He then adds; "This is especially unlikely since Zebulun is mentioned along with Ephraim, Benjamin, and Machir in 5:14; thus if Zebulun fought, it is likely that these other tribes or groups did as well" (2002, 75).

The list of volunteers (and interested bystanders, if Halpern is correct) is encouraging in one respect, for these same tribes were singled out as partial failures in chapter one (see vv. 21, 27–30, 33). At the same time, the list of participating tribes numbers only six, making it one short of the symbolically significant number of completeness. At this point one fears the tribal alliance is not entirely adequate, especially if Halpern is correct and it consists of two active participants and four interested, but essentially inactive, parties.

The reference to the "kings of Canaan" in verse 19 reminds us again (see v. 3) that this battle was a test of power in which the Lord demonstrated his superiority to the Canaanites (and their god Baal). The plural likely refers to Jabin's subjects among the Canaanite city-states who answered their lord's call to war and marshaled their forces under Sisera in anticipation of acquiring rich spoils (Burney 1970, 144).[86]

Though the Israelite tribal alliance (numbering as many as six or as few as two) was less than complete, the Lord's supernatural power made victory certain. Indeed the stars of the heavens and the Kishon River joined the battle against Sisera, making up for any deficiency on the Israelite side![87]

Verses 20–21, when viewed in light of the earlier theophanic description (vv. 4–5), provide a hint as to how the Lord accomplished the victory. The Lord came in the storm and caused a torrential downpour. The stars of the heavens, associated with the Lord's assembly elsewhere in the Old Testament and viewed as sources of rain in ancient cosmology, showered rain down upon the enemy.[88] The ground grew

---

86. Vassals were required to give military support to their suzerain. See, for example, the treaty between Ashurnirari V of Assyria and Mati'ilu of Arpad. See Pritchard 1969, 532–33.

87. The Lord's supernatural intervention (vv. 20–21) is highlighted in the structure of the text by its placement between descriptions of the enemy's defeat and retreat (vv. 19, 22). See Wong 2007b, 7–8.

88. For texts describing the stars as members of the Lord's heavenly assembly or army, see Job 38:7; Isaiah 40:26; Daniel 8:10. In 1 Kings 22:19 the phrase "host of heaven" is used of the Lord's assembly. Elsewhere this expression refers to the heavenly luminaries, including the stars and planets. See

muddy and the Kishon overflowed, making the Canaanite chariots use-less (Yadin 1963, 256). To escape from the battle site at Taanach (see v. 19) to their home in the north, the panic-stricken Canaanites had to cross the swelling Kishon, which swept many of them away along with their chariots and horses.[89] The terrified survivors who happened to make their way northward were easy pickings for the pursuing Israelite forces.

In true poetic fashion verses 21b–22 recreate some of the emotion and images of the enemy's retreat. Aided by the Lord's supernatural intervention, each Israelite soldier found the courage and strength to pursue the enemy, whose powerful horses frantically dashed for safety, their hooves pounding the turf in anticipatory mimicry of Jael's mighty deathblow![90] The Hebrew verb הלם is translated "pounded" in verse 22 and "hammered" in verse 26.

After this exciting battle account, verse 23 brings us back to the grim reality (see vv. 15b–17) that not all in Israel rose to the challenge. The Lord's angel, who had appeared earlier to confront wrongdoing and announce punishment (see 2:1–5), pronounced a curse upon the in-habitants of Meroz for their unwillingness to help in the Lord's battle. Why Meroz is singled out is not certain; this town may epitomize all who refused to join the alliance, or it may serve as an object lesson to warn others of the eventual consequences of failing to participate in the war of liberation.

Willing, able, and energetic Jael stands in stark contrast to un-willing, passive, and accursed Meroz (vv. 24–27). She receives a special

---

Deuteronomy 4:19; 17:3; 2 Kings 17:16; 21:3, 5; 23:4–5; 2 Chronicles 33:3, 5. A Ugaritic text (*CTA* 3 B 40–41) appears to view the stars as sources of rain. For the transliterated text and translation see Gibson 1978, 48. On the imagery employed in verses 20–22, see Weinfeld 1984, 124–31; Craigie, 1969, 262–63, and 1977, 33–38. Sawyer suggests that the back-ground for the language is a total eclipse of the sun (1981, 87–89). The reference to the stars fighting also reminds one of the miraculous star mentioned by Thutmose III in a battle account. The king reported that Amun-Re miraculously caused a star to approach the enemy: "A star ap-proached, coming to the south of them. The like had not happened before. It shot straight toward them (the enemy), not one of them could stand" (*COS* 2:17).

89. On the problem of identifying the precise geographical location of the battle, see Soden 1989, 277–80.

90. Craigie proposes a *double entendre* here, suggesting that אַבִּירָיו, "his stal-lions," also refers sarcastically to the fleeing Canaanite officers (1972, 352–53).

blessing for her loyalty to Israel and the Lord. When opportunity came her way she marshaled her cunning and strength to destroy the enemy general.

This poetic account abridges and streamlines the earlier narrative in some respects, but also highlights Jael's cunning and effectiveness through additional information and the poetic device of repetition.[91] In the poem we read nothing of Sisera's arrival or of Jael's initial gestures of apparent concern. Instead the focus is on her offer of milk. The narrative tells how she gave him milk when he asked for water; the poem adds that she brought him curdled milk in a bowl fit for a noble, which he must have seen as an obvious gesture of loyalty.[92] The poem mentions nothing of Jael's tucking Sisera into bed; instead it focuses on the deadly deed. The narrative account uses only one verb to describe the murder stroke (see 4:21); the poem employs four synonyms, emphasizing the deadly force of the blow and forcing us to replay it in our minds.[93] The narrative, while describing how the peg went through his skull into the ground, notes simply that he died (4:21–22); the poem uses seven finite verbal forms (כרע and נפל appear three times each, and שכב once) to emphasize the efficiency and finality of the deed (Hauser 1987, 278).[94] The repetition serves to "slow the action almost to a standstill in order to allow the audience to vent their hatred of the Canaanites as they savor Sisera's fall" (Hauser 1987, 278–79).[95] It also repeats the location of his death ("between her legs") to set up an ironic connection with verses 28–30 (on which, see below), and concludes

---

91. According to Soden, such selectivity is typical in poetic texts that accompany narratival accounts in ancient Near Eastern literature (1989, 25–74). See as well Howard's remarks regarding Exodus 14–15 (1993, 28).

92. Hauser sees "a juicy irony" in Sisera's request for water: "Sisera, whose forces had been defeated because he had too much water (v. 21), now must beg a bit of water from a woman" (1987, 273).

93. There is rhyme in the Hebrew text of verse 26b: note the *ah-a'-ah-o // ah-ah-o* vocalic pattern. The third feminine singular verbs also have the same vocalic pattern. The final *mem* of the first verbal root is repeated in the second verbal root, the *mem-khet* combination appears at the beginning of the second and third verbal roots, and the *khet* of the second and third roots appears at the beginning of the fourth verbal root.

94. Cross and Freedman regard שכב and נפל in verse 27a as variants. In their reconstruction only six verb forms appear in verse 27 (1975, 15, 19).

95. The verbal repetition is comparable to a film director visually repeating a key action to seal it vividly in the mind of the viewer.

with a resounding passive form, "murdered" (שָׁדוּד, literally, "violently destroyed, devastated").[96]

The narrative informs us that Jael killed Sisera while he was fast asleep (4:21),[97] but the poem depicts her deed as a heroic military act. It makes no reference to Sisera sleeping (though v. 25b might suggest as much) and describes Jael's actions as an aggressive attack—she grabs her weapons and strikes. It then depicts Sisera as slumping to his knees and falling to the floor, as if she struck him down while he stood before her.[98] Rather than trying to harmonize the accounts at the literal, factual level, it is probably better to see the poem as a creative figurative version of the story designed to magnify Jael and to lampoon the Canaanite general, whose capitulation to Jael's deceit was tantamount to being defeated by her in hand-to-hand combat.[99] For a warrior to die at the hands of a woman was considered utterly humiliating

---

96. Fokkelman points out that the passive participle, unlike the seven intransitive perfects used before it, draws attention to the "agent looming behind the destruction" (1995, 622).

97. For dramatic effect, the narrator delays this detail, including it in a disjunctive clause that follows a sequence of five *wayyiqtol* verb forms describing the murder.

98. See Gray 1986, 260. Boling attempts to circumvent the problem by taking verse 27a as a flashback to Sisera's arrival at the tent that describes him collapsing in exhaustion at Jael's feet (1975, 115). This is not the most natural way of reading verse 27, which clearly describes the effect of the fatal blow mentioned in verse 26. Houston calls Boling's proposal "ingenious," but adds: "we have to say that it is not, on the face of it, very likely that anyone would have thought of reading the verse in that way who did not have the prose at hand" (1997, 541). Soden ("Judges 4 and 5," 267) says that the language of verse 27 "emphasizes the destruction of Sisera," rather than describing "simply a narration of his bodily movements" (1989, 267). It is "not as concerned with the posture of Sisera as it is with his subjection and defeat" (229). While the text's language certainly emphasizes the subduing of Sisera, the presence of "between her legs" suggests that he fell, slumping between her legs. As Halpern says, the use of נָפַל "implies a collapse" (1988b, 83). If taken literally, this is difficult to reconcile with the picture of a sleeping Sisera given in 4:21. On the other hand the image of Jael attacking an upright man with hammer and tent peg is bizarre at best (Halpern 1988b, 82). Bos envisions Sisera sitting with his back to Jael (1988, 52). In any case the image appears to be a literary construct designed to flaunt Jael's heroism and taunt the defeated enemy.

99. On the basis of the terminology used in the text, as well as ancient Near Eastern parallels, Globe argues "the main point" of verse 27 "is to describe

(see Judg. 9:54), but in this case it was appropriate, for the fleeing Sisera is viewed as cowardly.[100]

The scene suddenly changes from Jael's tent floor to Sisera's palace (vv. 28–30). The image of stone-dead Sisera's shattered, bloody skull fades from our mind's eye and we see the general's mother peering out her window in anticipation of her son's return.[101] At first we may feel some sympathy for this concerned mother, but sympathy quickly turns to utter disdain as we discover that she was as greedy for plunder and as insensitive to Israelite suffering as the oppressive Canaanite kings (see v. 19) (Hauser 1987, 276; Fokkelman 1995, 623–24).

This scene taunts Sisera's mother (and all the greedy Canaanites she represents) through a combination of dramatic irony and sarcasm (Hauser 1987, 276–77). As noted earlier, Jael treated Sisera as a mother would, tucking him in and giving him a bowl of milk. However, this motherly treatment was a ploy designed to expose the general's jugular. Jael's motherly charade and deadly cunning stand in contrast with the genuine maternal concern and naïveté displayed in this scene. While the real mother pined away for her absent son, a pretend "mother" destroyed him. The reference to the assurances of the "wisest of her ladies" is also sarcastic, for the supposed wise advice amounts to sheer fantasy, due to Jael's cunning. Sisera's mother's expectation that the warriors are grabbing "a girl (Hebrew רַחַם a term which refers to

---

the conquest of an enemy using the language of military defeat" (1975a, 366).

100. Globe writes: "Now Sisera had shamefully fled from the melee, preferring not to fight to the death like Naphtali and Zebulun. Even worse, he fell before a simple nomad—and a woman at that—who killed him without the aid of a soldier's weapons. In verse 27 the poet employs the language of conquest in battle to point out the disparity between the heroic ideal and the circumstances of Sisera's death. . . . Verse 27, like the rest of Judges v 23–31, is imbued with the elation of a victorious people, and with their contempt for a culturally superior, but spoiled and cowardly enemy" (1975a, 366–67).

101. Ackerman argues that the image of Sisera's mother peering through the window is designed to evoke an image of the Canaanite goddess Asherah (1998, 155–60). This proposal, though creative, falters however, for it assumes that Sisera's mother has the status of queen mother. The text does not cast Sisera in the role of king (he is Jabin's general), nor does it call his mother a queen. For Ackerman's attempt to circumvent these difficulties, see pp. 131–33. For a survey of the literary and artistic evidence for the woman at the window motif in the ancient Near East, see O'Connor 1986, 284–85, note 25.

the female genitals)[102] or two" to satisfy their lust is dripping with sarcasm, for Sisera lies raped as it were at the feet of a woman.[103]

In verses 28–30 the poet seems aware of what happened in Sisera's palace in the aftermath of the battle and even knows what Sisera's mother was thinking! It is easy for modern readers to gloss over this, because we are accustomed to having access to all events through the seemingly ubiquitous news reporters scattered throughout every corner of the world. But how would an Israelite poet gain access to the kind of information recorded in verses 28–30? Perhaps Israelites later became aware of a lament composed by Sisera's mother or some Canaanite palace poet. But it seems more likely that the Israelite poet created a typical scene—a mother trying to calm her fears as she anxiously awaits the return of her son from battle. The poet does so to taunt the defeated Canaanites and to enhance the irony of this would-be-rapist being murdered in the tent of a woman (Hackett 2004, 358–59).

The concluding imprecation once again puts the victory in perspective (v. 31). Jabin, Sisera, and the Canaanite kings were *God's enemies*, not just the oppressors of his people. Deborah and Barak appropriately prayed that all God's foes might meet a similar demise, their imprecation being an Old Testament version of "thy kingdom come."

The imprecation is balanced by a prayer on behalf of those who "love" the Lord.[104] "Love" here has its covenantal sense of loyalty and devotion demonstrated by obedience to God's commands and the repudiation of idols (cf. Exod. 20:6; Deut. 6:5; 7:9; Josh. 22:5; 23:11). The comparison to the bright rising sun suggests splendor, vigor, and perhaps vindication. The reference to the sun's strength (cf. בִּגְבֻרָתוֹ) may have militaristic connotations, suggesting an image of the Lord's

---

102.The term sounds coarse, and may be intended as such. See Patterson 1981, 142, and Bledstein 1993, 41. However, it is possible that the word is merely idiomatic. In the Mesha (Moabite) inscription, it refers to captive female servants (see *COS* 2:138) and in Ugaritic it is used in a non-derogatory manner of the goddess Anat (see Gibson 1978, 77). For a survey of the term's usage outside of Hebrew, see T. Kronholm, "רֶחֶם," in *TDOT* 13:454–55.

103.See Ackerman 1998, 130–1; and Watson 1984, 311. On the sexually suggestive language in verse 27, see R. Alter 1985, 43–49; and Niditch 1989, 47–51 (cf. 2008, 81). The reference to "a girl or two" is ironic, for two "girls" brought about Sisera's demise. Deborah was the catalyst for Israel's victory over Sisera's army and Jael murdered the general. See Ackerman 1998, 131, and Olson 1998, 789.

104.Note the assonance between אֹיְבֶיךָ,"your enemies," and אֹהֲבָיו, "those who love him."

faithful followers as victorious over their enemies.[105] The account ends with a reference to the land having peace for forty years, suggesting that once again the nation's equilibrium has been restored (see 3:11).

MESSAGE AND APPLICATION

Thematic Emphases:
Rebellion once more brought oppression, but this time the enemy arose from within the boundaries of the promised land. In response to Israel's cry, the Lord authorized his prophetess Deborah to commission Barak for battle. Though Barak enjoyed great success, he failed to display the courageous faith of Joshua, Caleb, Othniel, and Ehud. When God challenged him to prepare for battle, he hesitated and answered God's command with a conditional sentence. In contrast to Othniel, who charged into battle to win Acsah's hand in marriage, Barak demanded the military support of a woman before going to war and consequently forfeited to another woman the full glory that should have been his as Israel's military leader. Ironically a woman, Jael, carried on the warrior ideal established in chapter three. By the end of the Barak narrative, one senses that Israel had taken a step backward, at least in terms of the quality of male leadership. Fortunately two courageous women rose to the occasion and compensated for Barak's weakness.[106] Nevertheless, the necessity of women playing a militaristic, rather than inspirational, role was symptomatic of a leadership crisis in Israel and did not bode well for the future. This dilution of leadership continued until, by the end of the book, there was a leadership void that contributed to social chaos and spiritual decline (Chisholm 1994b, 39).

At the same time, God demonstrated that his hands are not tied by a leadership crisis. He can bring deliverance from unexpected quarters, whether by a man with a pagan-sounding name carrying only an oxgoad, or the wife of the enemy's ally armed only with some milk, a hammer, and a tent peg. He also has at his disposal irresistible allies in

---

105. The term גְּבוּרָה, "strength," is often used of the might of warriors. See BDB, 150.
106. Sternberg observes that Barak had only "a junior partnership in a female enterprise" (1987, 283). Van Wolde demonstrates that the narrative depicts Deborah and Jael as active, while Barak is relatively passive (1995, 242–44).

the cosmic realm (in this case the stars of the heavens and the Kishon River), making the military efforts of mere human rulers futile.[107]

The battle at the Kishon proved more than just the Lord's superiority to human kings. Through his self-revelation in the storm, the Lord also demonstrated that he, not Baal, was the true warrior-king and deserved the sole allegiance of his people. The Canaanites believed that Baal, the god of fertility and the storm, was king among the gods (under the ultimate authority of the high god El). With the aid of the goddess Anat, Baal had defeated the chaotic sea and death. He maintained order in the world, defended his people, and, as lord of the storm, was the source of human fertility and agricultural prosperity. This is why Israel found Baal so appealing (cf. 2:11, 13; 3:7; 6:25–32; 8:33; 10:6, 10). However, at the Kishon, the Lord once again revealed himself as lord of the storm, coming to deliver his people in Baal-like style.[108] Like Baal, the Lord even had a female ally in Jael. The irony is apparent. The pagan worshipers of Baal and Anat were destroyed by the God of the storm and by his female ally![109] When all is said and done, the Lord's enemies should realize that it is suicidal to challenge his royal authority and his people should worship him, not Baal or any other would-be king, as the real Lord of the cosmos who controls their destiny.

Exegetical idea: *Responding to his sinful people's pain, the Lord commissioned Barak to deliver his people from the Canaanite oppression he had brought upon them as discipline for their sin. Despite Barak's hesitant response, the Lord gave Israel a great victory, using the forces of nature and an unlikely human instrument to demonstrate his royal power and superiority to the Canaanites and their god Baal.*

---

107. Amit demonstrates that the Lord is the main hero of the story; the human participants are merely his instruments in delivering Israel (1987, 99–104). For a contrary opinion, see Echols 2008. For a critique of Echols, see above.

108. See Chisholm 1994a, 267–83. In the Ugaritic myths, Baal's appearance in the storm to do battle shakes the earth's high places (mountains) (cf. Judg. 5:4–5). See Gibson 1978, 65.

109. See our comments on Shamgar (3:31), as well as the studies by Dempster 1978, Taylor 1982, Alter 1985, and Ackerman 1998 cited above. Echols (2008, 123–31) objects to this use of mythological materials to illuminate Judges 5.

Theological Principles

Some of the theological principles that emerged earlier are apparent in this literary unit as well: (a) Sin brings divine discipline and makes God's people vulnerable to their enemies. (b) God confronts his people's sin, but he also intervenes on their behalf when they cry out in pain. (c) God uses human instruments, sometimes in unexpected ways, to accomplish his purposes.

God's kingship is the dominant theological theme of this story. He defeated the kings of Canaan and demonstrated his superiority to their god Baal by using the storm as his weapon. He alone is deserving of his people's allegiance. The New Testament also depicts God as the warrior-king who fights and defeats his enemies, but in the New Testament the battle is primarily spiritual in its dimension. The enemies are not flesh-and-blood Canaanites, but spiritual forces headed up by the Adversary, Satan (Eph. 6:10–18).[110] Yet in the eschaton, Jesus, the King of kings and Lord of lords, will annihilate all of his foes in heaven and on earth (Rev. 17:13–14; 19:11–16).

Theological idea: *When humans are weak and hesitant, God can still accomplish his purposes, even through unlikely instruments, for he alone is the mighty king who is compassionate toward his people and worthy of their devotion.*

Homiletical Trajectories

(1) God is the compassionate, incomparable king (cf. 1 Tim. 1:17; 6:15) who intervenes on behalf of his people and defeats their enemies. In winning victories he may intervene in power (as he did in the storm) or use unlikely instruments (such as a woman armed only with a tent peg and hammer). Because he alone is the king, God's people must look to him as their sole source of security. Of course, in the context of the New Testament, God does not guarantee physical protection in the here-and-now, but he does promise that nothing, not even physical death, can separate us from his love in Christ Jesus (Rom. 8:31–39).

(2) As in the story of Ehud, Israel's sin brings humiliation and makes the covenant community vulnerable. A related theme emerges in chapter 5. Israel is no longer united; some tribes fail to rally to the aid of their

---

110. For studies of the divine-warfare motif in the Bible and how the New Testament nuances the theme, see Longman and Reid 1995; and Boyd 1997.

brothers in their time of need.[111] Apparently Israel's assimilation to Canaanite culture eroded the tribes' sense of uniqueness. In the same way, if the Church becomes like the world, its sense of uniqueness will be weakened, as will the bond that unites Christians together.

(3) The leadership ideal established in the earlier stories becomes tainted in this account. God wins the victory through Barak, but Barak's hesitancy is disturbing and is a portent of things to come. Ineffective leaders lack adequate faith and need crutches. They forfeit the full success that could be theirs. Yet God is not limited by such failure; he accomplishes his purposes through unlikely, seemingly powerless instruments, who act with what assets they have, however limited they may seem.

Preaching idea: *We need not hesitate to carry out God's purposes, for he is the great king who is capable of defeating his enemies, through even the most unlikely of instruments, and is worthy of our full devotion.*

This preaching idea focuses on the first homiletical trajectory and reflects the primary theme of this passage. However, the other trajectories yield complementary *preaching ideas:* (1) *When the covenant community wavers in its loyalty to God, we may be plagued by flawed leaders and a lack of unity and common purpose.* (2) *If we hesitate to carry out God's purposes, we may experience a diluted form of success and miss the full blessing that could have been ours.* If one desires to preach a sermon on chapter five that is distinct in some ways from a message on chapter four, one might highlight the second part of the first idea listed above, namely the lack of unity and common purpose that is so evident in chapter five (see Wong 2007b). Another option would be to focus on God's sovereign power over the natural elements (see 5:4–5, 20–21) and the polemical dimension discussed above. A *preaching idea* might be: *Because our great king is superior to every false god and is fully capable of advancing his purposes on earth, he deserves our complete devotion.*

---

111. Wong (2007b) argues that the poem is primarily "a polemic against Israelite non-participation in military campaigns against external enemies" (p. 20), not a victory song.

JUDGES 6:1–8:32

The Lord Wins Another Victory through a Hesitant Hero

TRANSLATION AND NARRATIVE STRUCTURE

6:1a The Israelites did evil before the LORD. (*initiatory*)

1b So the LORD handed them over to Midian for seven years. (*consequential*)

2a The Midianites overwhelmed Israel. (*focusing*)

2b **Because of Midian the Israelites made shelters for themselves in the hills, as well as caves and strongholds**. (*supplemental*)[1]

3a **Whenever the Israelites planted crops**, (*characterizing*)[2]

---

1. The disjunctive clause in verse 2b focuses on the effects of the oppression mentioned in verse 2a. It begins an extended section (vv. 2b–6a) that provides background information pertaining to the Midianite oppression.

2. Verse 3 extends the supplemental section by giving further background information. It elaborates on verse 2a and gives insight into the action described in verse 2b. Verse 3 is introduced with וְהָיָה, literally, "and it was," which is then extended by another *weqatal* form (וְעָלָה, literally, "and he went up"). The verb זָרַע, "planted," provides a condition, with the next verb (וְעָלָה) giving the inevitable consequence. If one takes "plant" as metonymic for "grew," the clauses may be viewed as synchronic. (It is obvious from v. 4

249

3b **the Midianites, Amalekites, and people from the east
would move against them.** (*characterizing-sequential*)[3]

4a They attacked them (*characterizing-sequential*)[4]

4b and devoured the land's crops all the way to Gaza.
(*characterizing-sequential*)

4c **They would leave nothing to eat in Israel, not even sheep,
oxen, or donkeys.** (*reiterative-emphatic*)[5]

5a **When they invaded with their cattle and tents, they were
as thick as locusts.** (*supplemental / characterizing*)[6]

5b **You could not even count them and their camels.**
(*specifying-emphatic*)[7]

---

that the Midianites did not attack while the Israelites planted, but waited
until the crops had grown.) This appears to be another example of *weqatal*
expressing what Longacre calls "a customary, script-predictable routine."
The presence of אִם in verse 3a supports this. The particle, which is used
here with the perfect in a narratival context, has the force of "when" or
"whenever." (For examples of this use of the particle [our text included],
see BDB, 50.) See Longacre 1994, 56, and his comments on Judges 2:18–19
(64–65). This use of the construction can be seen as an extension of what
Longacre calls "a how-it-was-done" "procedural discourse."

3. In MT there is a third *weqatal* construction near the end of verse 3 (see
וְעָלוּ, literally, "and they went up"), but the form seems unduly repetitive
(see וְעָלָה, literally, "and he went up," earlier in the verse) and is probably dittographic (note עָלָיו, literally, "against him," which immediately
follows).

4. The *wayyiqtol* forms in verse 4ab extend the supplemental interlude. They
are sequential in relation to what immediately precedes and also have a
characterizing function: Israel would plant—Midian would invade, attack,
and destroy the crops.

5. In verse 4c the negated imperfect (used here of customary action) com-
plements/reiterates verse 4b (see Judg. 3:29; 4:16, though the perfect is
employed in these earlier examples). The clause is also emphatic, for it
further illustrates the extent of the Midianite oppression (even the livestock were taken).

6. Verse 5a provides further background information, explaining why the
destruction described in verse 4 was so thorough. The first verb (יַעֲלוּ, literally, "they would go up," is a customary imperfect (note the preceding
כִּי, "when," used temporally here in a subordinate clause). The following
perfect with *waw* (following the *Qere*) carries the same customary force
(see Gen. 2:6).

7. The disjunctive clause in verse 5b gives a more detailed description of
the vast size of the invaders and therefore has an emphatic function. The
narrator overwhelms us with his verbal portrait of the Midianites.

5c   They came to devour the land. (*focusing*)[8]

6a   Israel was severely weakened because of Midian. (*consequential*)[9]

6b   So the Israelites cried out to the LORD. (*resumptive-consequential*)

7   When the Israelites cried out to the LORD because of Midian, (*transitional-reiterative*)[10]

8a   the LORD sent a prophet to the Israelites. (*sequential*)

8b   He said to them: (*sequential*)

8c   *"This is what the LORD God of Israel says, 'I brought you up from Egypt and took you out of that slave house.*

9   *I rescued you from Egypt's power and from the power of all who oppressed you. I drove them out from before you and gave their land to you.*

10   *I said to you, "I am the LORD your God! Do not worship the gods of the Amorites, in whose land you are now living!" But you have disobeyed me.'"*

11a   The angel of the LORD came (*initiatory*)[11]

11b   and sat down under the terebinth tree in Ophrah owned by Joash the Abiezrite. (*sequential*)

---

8. The *wayyiqtol* clause in verse 5c has a focusing function. Repeating the verb בּוֹא, "come" (see v. 5a), it informs us that the Midianites' purpose in coming in such force was to devour the land (the verb שׁחת, "devour," is repeated, see v. 4b).

9. The *wayyiqtol* clause in verse 6a is consequential in relation to verse 4c and serves as a nice conclusion to the entire supplemental section begun in verse 2b. (Note the repetition of "because of Midian" in verses 2b and 6a. The phrase serves as an inclusio for the supplemental section.) Verse 6a is also consequential in relation to verse 2a and facilitates the transition back into the prologue's main story line, which resumes in verse 6b.

10. The temporal indicator (וַיְהִי) at the beginning of verse 7 formally marks the transition from the report of oppression (vv. 1–6) to the prophetic message (vv. 7–10). See van Midden 1999, 56. This transition is also facilitated by verbal repetition (note "the Israelites cried out to the Lord" in both v. 6b and v. 7a).

11. The introduction to this new episode is not marked formally (v. 11 begins with a *wayyiqtol* form), but the appearance of a new character ("the angel of the Lord") signals a transition.

11c **At the time Joash's son Gideon was threshing wheat in a winepress so he could hide it from the Midianites**. (*circumstantial*)[12]

12a The angel of the Lord appeared to him (*sequential*)

12b and said to him, (*sequential*)

12c *"The Lord is with you, courageous warrior!"*

13a Gideon said to him, (*sequential*)

13b *"Pardon me, sir, but if the Lord is with us, why has such disaster overtaken us? Where are all his miraculous deeds about which our ancestors told us? They said, 'Did the Lord not bring us up from Egypt?' But now the Lord has abandoned us and handed us over to Midian."*

14a Then the Lord turned to him (*sequential*)

14b and said, (*sequential*)

14c *"You have the strength. Deliver Israel from the power of the Midianites! Have I not sent you?"*

15a Gideon said to him, (*sequential*)

15b *"But Master, how can I deliver Israel? Just look! My clan is the weakest in Manasseh, and I am the youngest in my family."*

16a The Lord said to him, (*sequential*)

16b *"I will indeed be with you! You will strike down the whole Midianite army."*

17a Gideon said to him, (*sequential*)

17b *"If you really are pleased with me, then give me a sign as proof that it is really you speaking with me.*

18a *Do not leave this place until I come back with a gift and present it to you."*

18b The Lord said, (*sequential*)

18c *"I will stay here until you come back."*

19a **Now Gideon went** (*introductory*)[13]

19b and prepared a young goat, along with unleavened bread made from an ephah of flour. (*sequential*)

19c **He put the meat in a basket** (*supplemental*)[14]

---

12. The disjunctive clause in verse 11c is circumstantial in relation to the preceding main clause. It tells us what Gideon was doing when the angel arrived and sat down.

13. The disjunctive clause in verse 19a marks a shift in scene from the initial dialogue to the report of the sacrifice.

14. The disjunctive clause in verse 19c is asyndetic; it gives supplemental information about Gideon's preparations. It is complemented by the accompanying disjunctive clause in verse 19d.

19d **and the broth in a pot**. (*complementary*)
19e He brought the food to him under the terebinth tree (*resumptive-sequential*)
19f and presented it to him. (*sequential*)
20a The angel of God said to him, (*sequential*)
20b *"Put the meat and unleavened bread on this rock, and pour out the broth."*
20c Gideon did as instructed. (*sequential*)
21a The angel of the LORD extended the tip of the staff that he had in his hand, (*sequential*)
21b and touched the meat and the unleavened bread. (*sequential*).
21c Fire flared up from the rock (*sequential*)
21d and consumed the meat and unleavened bread. (*sequential*)
21e **The angel of the Lord then disappeared**. (*concluding*)[15]
22a Gideon realized that he was the angel of the LORD. (*sequential*)
22b So Gideon said, (*consequential*)
22c *"Oh no! Master, LORD! I have seen the angel of the LORD face-to-face!"*
23a The LORD said to him, (*sequential*)
23b *"You are safe! Do not be afraid! You are not going to die!"*
24a Gideon built an altar for the LORD there, (*sequential*)
24b and named it, "The LORD is on friendly terms with me." (*sequential*)
24c **To this day it is still there in Ophrah of the Abiezrites**. (*concluding*)[16]

25a That night (*introductory-backgrounding*)[17]
25b the LORD said to him, (*initiatory*)
25c *"Take the bull from your father's herd, as well as a second bull, one that is seven years old.[18] Pull down your father's Baal altar and cut down the nearby Asherah pole.*

---

15. The disjunctive clause in verse 21e concludes the scene and marks the transition from the report to the final dialogue between Gideon and the Lord. Buth (1994, 142), though acknowledging that the function of the clause may be structural, prefers to see this as a "dramatic pause."
16. The asyndetic disjunctive clause in verse 24c gives the episode formal closure.
17. In verse 25a, וַיְהִי introduces the next episode by supplying background information and signaling a time change. See van Midden 1999, 56–57.
18. The Hebrew text reads literally, "Take the bull of the ox which belongs to your father, and/even (?) the second bull, seven years old." It is not clear

26 *Then build an altar for the LORD your God on the top of this*
    stronghold according to the proper pattern. Take the second bull
    and offer it as a burnt sacrifice on the wood from the Asherah
    pole which you cut down."

27a So Gideon took ten of his servants (*consequential*)
27b and did just as the LORD had told him. (*sequential*)
27c Now he was too afraid of his father's family and the men of the
     city to do it in broad daylight, (*supplemental-qualifying*) [19]
27d so he waited until nighttime (*consequential*).
28a When the men of the city got up the next morning,
     (*resumptive-sequential*)
28b **they saw the Baal altar pulled down,** (*dramatic*)[20]
28c **the nearby Asherah pole cut down,** (*complementary*)
28d **and the second bull sacrificed on the newly built altar**.
     (*complementary*)
29a They said to one another, (*sequential*)
29b *"Who did this?"*
29c They thoroughly investigated the matter (*sequential*)
29d and concluded, (*sequential*)
29e *"Gideon son of Joash has done this thing."*
30a So the men of the city said to Joash, (*consequential*)
30b *"Bring out your son, so we can execute him. He pulled down the*
     Baal altar and cut down the nearby Asherah pole."
31a But Joash said to all those who confronted him, (*sequential*)
31b *"Must you fight Baal's battles? Must you rescue him? Whoever*
     takes up his cause will die by morning. If he really is a god, let

---

if this refers to two bulls or to one. See the commentaries for discussion of
interpretive options and proposed alternate readings. Boling attempts to
make sense of MT, translating, "that's right, the second one, seven years
old" (1975, 134). Some emend שֵׁנִי to שָׁנֵי, "fully grown" (cf. *HALOT*, 1604).
Emerton argues that שֵׁנִי means "finest" here, not "second" (1978, 54*-55*).
For further discussion of the issue see Rudman 2000, 97–103.

19. In verse 27c, וַיְהִי introduces a supplemental clause that qualifies the pre-
    ceding statement by informing us that Gideon was afraid of the towns-
    people. This explains why he carried out the Lord's orders during the
    nighttime (v. 27b). (For other examples of supplemental clauses intro-
    duced by וַיְהִי, see 1 Kings 18:4 and 1 Chron. 11:6b.)
20. The disjunctive clause in verse 28b, introduced by וְהִנֵּה, literally, "and look,"
    has a dramatic function, inviting the audience to view the scene through
    the eyes of the townspeople. The accompanying disjunctive clauses com-
    plement the lead clause by filling out the description of the scene.

> *him fight his own battles. After all, it was his altar that was pulled down."*

32a That very day he named him Jerubbaal, saying, (*sequential*)

32b *"Let Baal fight with him,*[21] *for he pulled down his altar."*

33a **All the Midianites, Amalekites, and the people from the east were assembled**. (*introductory-backgrounding*)[22]

33b They crossed the Jordan River (*initiatory*)

33c and camped in the Jezreel Valley. (*sequential*)

34a **The Lord's spirit took control of Gideon**. (*dramatic shift in focus*)[23]

34b He blew a trumpet (*sequential*),

34c summoning the Abiezrites to follow him (*complementary*).

35a **He sent messengers throughout Manasseh** (*supplemental*)[24]

---

21. Endris (2008, 176) suggests that the name Jerubbaal should be understood to mean, "Baal will contend (for himself)." But the quotation in verse 32, introduced by לֵאמֹר, indicates otherwise. In the collocation רִיב + בְּ- the preposition never has a reflexive force. On the contrary, on two other occasions the preposition introduces the one against whom one contends (Gen. 31:36 [Jacob contends with/against Laban]; Hos. 2:4 [the children being addressed are urged to contend with/against their mother]). Furthermore, the explanatory clause within the quotation, introduced by כִּי, indicates that Gideon, the understood subject of נָתַץ, "tore down," is the antecedent of the pronominal suffix on the form בּוֹ. Endris does not include the explanatory clause within the quotation, but instead collocates it with the verb "called." He translates: "Therefore, on that day he was called Jerubbaal, that is, 'Baal will contend', because he pulled down his altar." This understanding of the syntax is possible (cf. Gen. 18:15, but note as well Exod. 15:1; 1 Sam. 23:27; Zech. 8:23). However, the closest syntactical parallel to what we find here suggests otherwise. In Judges 16:18 we also find the sequence קָרָא + לְ- + object of preposition + לֵאמֹר + verb (volitional form) + כִּי. In this case the explanatory clause, introduced by כִּי, is part of the quotation.

22. The disjunctive clause at the beginning of verse 33 sets the stage for the new episode and brings us back to the problem raised in the prologue. It also provides background information for the story to follow. See van Midden 1999, 57.

23. The disjunctive clause in verse 34a appears to shift the focus from the enemy side to Israel. The juxtaposition with verse 33 highlights the fact that the approaching battle is really between the enemy and the Lord.

24. The disjunctive clauses in verse 35 provide supplemental information about what Gideon did once he was energized by the Lord's spirit. However, the style utilized here foreshadows the delay that will be caused by

35b and summoned them to follow him as well (*sequential*).

35c **He also sent messengers throughout Asher, Zebulun, and Naphtali,** (*supplemental*)

35d and they came up to meet them.[25] (*sequential*)

36a Gideon said to God, (*sequential*)

36b *"If you really intend to use me to deliver Israel, as you promised, then give me a sign as proof.*

37 *Look, I am putting a wool fleece on the threshing floor. If there is dew on just the fleece, and the ground around it is dry, then I will be sure you will use me to deliver Israel, as you promised."*

38a It happened as he requested. (*sequential*)

38b He got up the next morning, (*focusing*)[26]

38c and squeezed the fleece. (*sequential*)

38d Enough dew dripped from it to fill a bowl. (*sequential*).

39a Gideon said to God, (*sequential*)

Gideon's hesitancy. Once the Lord's spirit comes upon Gideon (v. 34a), the narrative appears to gain momentum (note the two *wayyiqtol* clauses in v. 34bc). But then the disjunctive in verse 35a tells of more preparations. The *wayyiqtol* in verse 35b seems to get the story rolling again, but the clause is simply sequential to verse 35a and does not return us to the mainline. The narrative is bogged down by another disjunctive in verse 35c. The story seems to get started with the *wayyiqtol* in verse 35d, but, as in verse 35b, it is simply sequential in relation to the disjunctive clause that immediately precedes. A *wayyiqtol* clause does return us to the mainline in verse 36a, but here a verb of speech is used. As in the case of Barak (see Judg. 4:8–9), dialogue replaces action as a hesitant character seeks assurances of victory. Bluedorn suggests that the disjunctive clauses in verse 35 might "indicate the narrator's evaluation that Gideon's extended recruitment is not the consequence of his calling anymore but rather forms a contrast to his clothing with the spirit and his subsequent recruitment of his clan" (2001, 112).

25. The Hebrew text reads, "and they went up to meet them." The subject of the plural verb and the antecedent of the third masculine plural pronoun are not certain. The text may be saying that the men of Asher, Zebulun, and Naphtali went up to meet the messengers. Another option is to emend the plural pronominal suffix to third masculine singular and read, "and they went up to meet *him*" (i.e., Gideon). See the *BHS* apparatus, note "d."

26. The *wayyiqtol* clauses in verses 38b and 40b have a focusing or specifying function; each begins a more detailed description of what is described in the preceding clause.

39b *"Please do not get angry at me, when I ask for just one more sign.*
Please allow me one more test with the fleece. This time make just
the fleece dry, while the ground around it is covered with dew."

40a That night God did as he asked. (*sequential*)

40b Just the fleece was dry (*focusing*)

40c **and the ground around it was covered with dew.**
(*contrastive-concluding*)[27]

7:1a Jerubbaal (**that is, Gideon**) [*supplemental*] along with all his
men got up the next morning (*initiatory*)[28]

1b and they camped near the spring of Harod. (*sequential*)

1c **The Midianites were camped north of them near the hill**
of Moreh in the valley. (*supplemental*)[29]

2a The LORD said to Gideon, (*resumptive-sequential*)

2b *"You have too many men for me to hand Midian over to you.*
Israel might brag, 'Our own strength has delivered us.'

3a *Now, announce to the men, 'Whoever is shaking with fear may*
turn around and leave Mt. Gilead.'" [30]

3b Twenty-two thousand men went home;[31] (*sequential*)

3c **ten thousand remained.** (*contrastive*)[32]

4a The LORD spoke to Gideon again, (*sequential*)

---

27. The disjunctive clause in verse 40c clearly contrasts with the preceding
statement, but it may also signal closure for the scene.

28. The introduction to this new scene is not marked formally (v. 1 begins with
a *wayyiqtol* form), but the shift from nighttime (see 6:40) to morning signals a transition, as does the brief switch to the name Jerubbaal. See van
Midden 1999, 57.

29. The supplemental disjunctive clause in verse 1c also has a dramatic function, for it brings us back to the main problem facing Gideon (see 6:33) and
maintains the tension of the plot.

30. The MT reading "Mount Gilead" in verse 3 is unlikely for geographical
reasons. See the commentaries for proposed emendations.

31. On the large number mentioned here, see the commentary above on 1:4.
As noted there, it is difficult to accept such figures at face value. One possibility is that the Hebrew term אֶלֶף, traditionally understood as a numeral
(a "thousand"), actually refers to a contingent of troops, at least in some
contexts. Boling, taking this approach, translates "twenty-two units" and
"ten units," respectively, in verse 3 (1975, 142). Another option is that such
large numbers are hyperbolic. See Fouts 1997, 377–88, and 2003, 283–99.

32. Disjunctive clauses are used in verses 3c, 6b, and 8b to contrast the situation or action described with what immediately precedes.

4b   *"There are still too many men. Bring them down to the water and I will thin the ranks some more. When I say, 'This one should go with you,' pick him to go; when I say, 'This one should not go with you,' do not take him."*

5a   So he brought the men down to the water. (*consequential*)

5b   Then the LORD said to Gideon, (*sequential*)

5c   *"Separate those who lap the water as a dog laps from those who kneel to drink."*

6a   Three hundred men lapped; (*sequential*)[33]

6b   **the rest of the men kneeled to drink water.** (*contrastive*)

7a   The LORD said to Gideon, (*sequential*)

7b   *"With the three hundred men who lapped I will deliver the whole army and I will hand Midian over to you. The rest of the men should go home."*

8a   The men who were chosen took supplies and their trumpets, (*sequential*)

8b   **but Gideon sent all the rest of the men of Israel back to their homes;** (*contrastive*)

8c   **he kept only three hundred men.** (*summarizing*)[34]

8d   **Now the Midianites were camped down below in the valley.** (*concluding*)[35]

9a   That night (*introductory-backgrounding*)[36]

9b   the LORD said to Gideon, (*initiatory*)

9c   *"Get up! Attack the camp for I am handing it over to you.*

10   *But if you are afraid to attack, go down to the camp with Purah your servant*

11a   *and listen to what they are saying. Then you will be brave and attack the camp."*

---

33. The Hebrew text adds here, "with their hand to their mouth," which makes no sense if the lappers are being compared to dogs (cf. v. 5c). We have omitted the phrase because it is probably a late, misplaced explanatory gloss. If one were to include the phrase, it would fit best at the end of verse 5 or at the end of verse 6 as a description of how those who kneeled drank. For a fuller discussion see the commentary below.

34. The disjunctive clause in verse 8c contrasts with what precedes, but it also serves a summarizing function.

35. The concluding disjunctive clause (v. 8d) has a structural function (it forms an inclusio for the scene, see v. 1), as well as a dramatic role. (The Midianites are not going away!)

36. A temporal indicator (וַיְהִי) and a reference to nighttime in verse 9a mark the beginning of this new scene.

11b So he went down with Purah his servant to where the sentries were guarding the camp. (*consequential*)

12a **Now the Midianites, Amalekites, and people from the east covered the valley like a swarm of locusts**. (*supplemental*)[37]

12b **Their camels could not be counted; they were as innumerable as the sand on the seashore.** (*specifying-emphatic*)[38]

13a When Gideon arrived, (*resumptive-sequential*)

13b there was a man telling another man about a dream he had. (*dramatic*)[39]

13c The man said, (*specifying*)

13d *"Look! I had a dream. I saw a stale cake of barley bread rolling into the Midianite camp. It hit a tent so hard it knocked it over and turned it upside down. The tent just collapsed."*

14a The other man said, (*sequential*)

14b *"Without a doubt this symbolizes the sword of Gideon son of Joash, the Israelite. God is handing Midian and all the army over to him."*

15a When Gideon heard the report of the dream and its interpretation, (*transitional*)[40]

15b he praised God. (*sequential*)

15c Then he went back to the Israelite camp (*sequential*)

15d and said, (*sequential*)

15e *"Rise up for the LORD is handing the Midianite army over to you!"*

16a He divided the three hundred men into three units. (*sequential*)

16b He gave them all trumpets and empty jars with torches inside them. (*sequential*)

17a He said to them, (*sequential*)

17b *"Watch me and do as I do. Watch closely! I am going to the edge of the camp. Do as I do!*

---

37. The supplemental disjunctive clause in verse 12a keeps the tension of the plot before us. (See vv. 1c, 8d.)

38. The disjunctive clause in verse 12b extends the parenthetical section, but also heightens the tension by emphasizing the vast size of the Midianite horde.

39. The disjunctive clause in verse 13b is dramatic and invites us to see and hear (note וְהִנֵּה) what Gideon and Purah witnessed.

40. A temporal indicator (וַיְהִי) in verse 15a marks a transition to a new scene.

18 *When I and all who are with me blow our trumpets, you also
    blow your trumpets all around the camp. Then say, 'For the LORD
    and for Gideon!'"*

19a Gideon took a hundred men to the edge of the camp at the
     beginning of the middle watch, (*sequential*)

19b **just after they had changed the guards**. (*supplemental*)[41]

19c They blew their trumpets as they broke[42] the jars they were
     carrying. (*resumptive-sequential*)

20a All three units blew their trumpets (*focusing*)[43]

20b and broke their jars. (*complementary*)[44]

20c They held the torches in their left hand (*focusing*)[45]

20d **and the trumpets in their right**. (*complementary*)

20e Then they yelled, (*sequential*)

20f *"A sword for the LORD and for Gideon!"*

21a They stood in order all around the camp. (*sequential or
     flashback*)[46]

21b The whole army ran away; (*sequential*)

21c they shouted (*focusing*)[47]

---

41. The asyndetic disjunctive clause in verse 19b gives supplemental informa-
    tion about exactly when the attack was launched.

42. The infinitive absolute וְנָפוֹץ, literally, "and broke," is used here of an action
    that is complementary to what precedes. See GKC, 345, para. 113z.

43. The *wayyiqtol* clause in verse 20a may be taken as sequential if the other
    two units blew their trumpets and broke their jars (v. 20b) *after* the first
    contingent. It seems more likely (note the reference to "three units") that
    verse 20a has a focusing function, informing us that all three units, per-
    haps on signal, blew their trumpets together from the outset.

44. The *wayyiqtol* clause in verse 20b may be sequential in relation to verse
    20a (if they all broke their jars after beginning to blow the trumpets) or
    complementary (if they broke the jars as they began to blow; cf. v. 19c).

45. The *wayyiqtol* clause in verse 20c is focusing in function as it explains
    more precisely circumstances surrounding the actions described in verse
    20ab. The disjunctive clause in verse 20d has a complementary or circum-
    stantial function. As they held the torches in the left hand, they held the
    trumpets in the right.

46. The *wayyiqtol* clause in verse 21a is most likely sequential, describing how
    they remained in formation after performing the actions described earlier.
    However, it is possible that this is a flashback, describing how they had
    already moved into formation prior to blowing the trumpets, breaking the
    jars, and shouting.

47. The *wayyiqtol* clause in verse 21c (literally, "and they shouted") is focusing;
    verse 21d is complementary—they shouted as they ran from the battle. It
    is difficult to know if רוץ, "run," and נוס, "flee," are intended to be distinct

21d as they fled. (*complementary*)

22a When the three hundred men blew their trumpets,
(*reiterative-focusing*)[48]

22b the LORD caused the Midianites to attack one another with their
swords throughout the camp. (*sequential*)

22c The army fled to Beth Shittah on the way to Zererah,
as far as the border of Abel Meholah near Tabbath.
(*resumptive-sequential*)

23a Israelites from Naphtali, Asher, and Manasseh answered the
call (*sequential*)

23b and chased the Midianites. (*sequential*)

**24a Now Gideon sent messengers throughout the Ephraimite
hill country and they announced,** (*introductory*)[49]

24b *"Go down and head off the Midianites. Take control of the fords
of the streams all the way to Beth Barah and the Jordan River."*

24c So all the Ephraimites assembled, (*consequential*)

24d and took control of the fords all the way to Beth Barah and the
Jordan River. (*sequential*)

25a They captured the two Midianite generals, Oreb and Zeeb.
(*sequential*)

25b They executed Oreb on the rock of Oreb (*sequential*)

25c and Zeeb they executed in the winepress of Zeeb.
(*complementary*)[50]

25d They chased the Midianites. (*sequential*)

---

in meaning or synonymous since they are collocated only in this passage.
Boling defines רוץ as "jump up" and translates "awoke with a start" (1975,
147). See also Soggin 1981, 144. Burney prefers to emend וַיָּרָץ, "ran" to
וַיִּיקַץ, "awoke" (1970, 217–18). In either case there would be a sequential
order of events: they jumped up/awoke, shouted, and fled.

48. The *wayyiqtol* clause in verse 22a is reiterative; it takes us back to the action described in verse 20a. It is also focusing in that it introduces a brief
parallel account of the victory that moves beyond what an observer would
have seen and gives a theological explanation for what happened (v. 22b).
Verse 22c then resumes where the previous account left off (v. 21d, note
"fled" in both) and completes both accounts.

49. The disjunctive clause in verse 24a marks the beginning of this new episode. Buth (1994, 140–41) speaks of a "break in temporal succession from
the previous verb."

50. The disjunctive clause in verse 25c describes an action (the execution of
Zeeb) that complements that of the preceding clause (the execution of
Zeeb's partner, Oreb).

25e **Then they brought the heads of Oreb and Zeeb to Gideon, who was now on the other side of the Jordan River.** (*introductory*)[51]

8:1a The Ephraimites said to him, (*sequential*)

1b *"Why have you done such a thing to us?" You did not summon us when you went to fight the Midianites!"*

1c They argued vehemently with him. (*sequential*)

2a He said to them, (*sequential*)

2b *"Now what have I accomplished compared to you? Even Ephraim's leftover grapes are better quality than Abiezer's harvest!*

3a *It was to you that God handed over the Midianite generals, Oreb and Zeeb! What did I accomplish to rival that?"*

3b **When he said this, they calmed down.** (*concluding*)[52]

4a Now Gideon went to the Jordan River (*initiatory-flashback*)[53]

4b and he crossed over[54] with his three hundred men, who, though exhausted, were still chasing the Midianites. (*sequential*)

---

51. The disjunctive clause in verse 25e marks a movement within the episode and introduces the final scene; the Ephraimites' pursuit of Midian leads them to Gideon.

52. The final clause (8:3b), introduced by the temporal particle אָז, "when," + the perfect, marks the end of the episode. The construction appears rarely in a narrative framework. It appears to have a concluding function in Genesis 4:26; Exodus 4:26; 2 Samuel 21:17. The construction can also have introductory (1 Kings 8:12; 2 Kings 14:8; 2 Chron. 8:12, 17), supplementary (Josh. 10:33; 1 Kings 9:24; 22:49), resumptive-sequential (Judg. 13:21), and emphatic functions (2 Sam. 21:18; 1 Chron. 15:2; 2 Chron. 24:17).

53. The *wayyiqtol* clause in verse 4a marks the transition to a new episode. Actually this verse flashes back chronologically to an event that preceded the events recorded in the previous episode. Verse 4ab describes Gideon and his men crossing the Jordan, while 7:25 assumes they have already done so.

54. In the Hebrew text a participle (עֹבֵר, literally, "crossing") appears followed by a personal pronoun and an add-on subject. After a *wayyiqtol* clause, the syntax is unprecedented. For this reason it seems preferable to emend the participle to a *wayyiqtol* form, וַיַּעֲבֹר, "and he crossed over" (see Burney 1970, 227). The collocation third masculine singular *wayyiqtol* + third masculine singular independent pronoun + add-on subject is attested elsewhere (see Gen. 31:21; Josh. 8:10; Judg. 7:11; 1 Sam. 18:17; 19:18; 27:2; 28:8). The closest parallel to this emended form of Judges 8:4 is in 1 Samuel 27:2, which reads literally: "So David arose and crossed over, he and the six hundred men who were with him to Achish."

5a He said to the men of Succoth, (*sequential*)

5b *"Give some loaves of bread to the men who are following me, because they are exhausted. I am chasing Zebah and Zalmunna, the kings of Midian."*

6a The officials of Succoth said, (*sequential*)

6b *"You have not yet overpowered Zebah and Zalmunna. So why should we give bread to your army?"*

7a Gideon said, (*sequential*)

7b *"Since you will not help, after the* LORD *hands Zebah and Zalmunna over to me, I will thresh your skin with desert thorns and briers."*

8a He went up from there to Penuel (*sequential*)

8b and made the same request. (*sequential*)

8c The men of Penuel responded the same way the men of Succoth had. (*sequential*)

9a He also threatened the men of Penuel, warning, (*sequential*)

9b *"When I return victoriously, I will tear down this tower."*

10a **Now Zebah and Zalmunna were in Karkor with their armies.** (*introductory*)[55]

10b **There were about fifteen thousand**[56] **survivors from the army of the eastern peoples;** (*supplemental*)[57]

10c **One hundred and twenty thousand sword-wielding soldiers had been killed.** (*complementary*)[58]

---

55. The disjunctive clause in verse 10a switches our focus to the fleeing enemy and marks a transition to the next scene within the episode.

56. On the large number mentioned here, see the commentary above on 1:4. As noted there, it is difficult to accept such figures at face value. One possibility is that the Hebrew term אֶלֶף, traditionally understood as a numeral (a "thousand"), actually refers to a contingent of troops, at least in some contexts. Boling, taking this approach, translates "fifteen contingents" in verse 10 (1975, 153). Another option is that such large numbers are hyperbolic. See Fouts 1997, 377–88, and 2003, 283–99.

57. Verse 10bc gives supplemental information about the condition of the enemy army. The two clauses are complementary in that the first gives the number of survivors, the second the number of casualties.

58. On the extremely large number used here, see the commentary above on 1:4. As noted there, it is difficult to accept such figures at face value. One possibility is that the Hebrew term אֶלֶף, traditionally understood as a numeral (a "thousand"), actually refers to a contingent of troops, at least in some contexts. Boling, taking this approach, translates "a hundred and twenty sword-wielding contingents" in verse 10 (1975, 153). Another

11a Gideon went up the road of the nomads east of Nobah and Jogbehah (*initiatory*)
11b and ambushed the army (*sequential*)
11c **while they were unprepared**. (*circumstantial*)[59]
12a When Zebah and Zalmunna ran away, (*sequential*)
12b Gideon chased them (*sequential*)
12c and captured the two Midianite kings, Zebah and Zalmunna. (*sequential*)
12d **He had surprised their entire army**. (*summarizing-concluding*)[60]
13   Gideon son of Joash returned from the battle by the pass of Heres. (*initiatory*)
14a He captured a young man from Succoth (*sequential*)
14b and interrogated him. (*sequential*)
14c The young man wrote down for him the names of Succoth's officials and city leaders—77 men in all. (*sequential*)
15a He approached the men of Succoth (*sequential*)
15b and said, (*sequential*)
15c *"Look what I have! Zebah and Zalmunna! You insulted me, saying, 'You have not yet overpowered Zebah and Zalmunna. So why should we give bread to your exhausted men?'"*
16a He grabbed the leaders of the city, along with some desert thorns and briers; (*sequential*)
16b he then "threshed" the men of Succoth with them. (*sequential*)
17a **He tore down the tower of Penuel** (*complementary*)[61]
17b and executed the city's men. (*complementary*)[62]
18a He said to Zebah and Zalmunna, (*initiatory*)
18b *"Describe for me the men you killed at Tabor."*
18c They said, (*sequential*)
18d *"They were like you. Each one looked like a king's son."*

---

option is that such large numbers are hyperbolic. See Fouts 1997, 377–88, and 2003, 283–99.

59. The disjunctive clause in verse 11c describes a circumstance surrounding the ambush. When Gideon launched the attack, the enemy was unprepared and taken by surprise. The Hebrew text reads literally, "And the army was secure."

60. The disjunctive clause in verse 12d has a summarizing tone and provides closure for the scene.

61. The disjunctive clause in verse 17a complements verse 16; it describes how Gideon carried out his threat against Penuel (see v. 9) after fulfilling his warning to Succoth (see v. 7).

62. Verse 17b could be sequential, but it more likely complements the previous clause by describing another element in Penuel's punishment.

19a He said, (*sequential*)

19b *"They were my brothers, the sons of my mother. I swear, as sure as the* LORD *is alive, if you had let them live, I would not kill you."*

20a He ordered Jether his firstborn son, (*sequential*)

20b *"Come on! Kill them!"*

20c **But the youth was too afraid to draw his sword, because he was still young.** (*contrastive*)[63]

21a Zebah and Zalmunna said to Gideon, (*sequential*)

21b *"Come on, you strike us, for a man is judged by his strength."*

21c So Gideon killed Zebah and Zalmunna, (*consequential*)

21d and he took the crescent shaped ornaments that were on the necks of their camels. (*sequential*)

22a The men of Israel said to Gideon, (*initiatory*)

22b *"Rule over us—you, your son, and your grandson. For you have delivered us from Midian's power."*

23a Gideon said to them, (*sequential*)

23b *"I will not rule over you, nor will my son rule over you. The* LORD *will rule over you."*

24a Gideon continued, (*sequential*)

24b *"I would like to make one request. Each of you give me an earring from the plunder you have taken."*

24c (He said this because the Midianites had golden earrings, for they were Ishmaelites.)[64]

25a They said, (*sequential*)

25b *"We are happy to give you earrings."*

25c So they spread out a garment, (*sequential*)

25d and each one threw on to it an earring from his plunder. (*sequential*)

26a The total weight of the golden earrings he requested came to 1700 gold shekels. (*supplemental-descriptive*)[65]

---

63. The clause in verse 20c (introduced with *waw* + negated perfect) contrasts Jether's response with his father's command.

64. The words "he said this" are supplied in the translation. In the Hebrew text this clause is actually subordinate (note כִּי) to "Gideon said" at the beginning of the verse. It explains why Gideon made the specific request recorded here.

65. The descriptive statements in verse 26 are best taken as supplemental. The first is introduced with וַיְהִי, the second with a prepositional phrase.

26b **This was in addition to the crescent-shaped ornaments, jewelry, and purple clothing worn by the Midianite kings, and the necklaces on the camels**. (*supplemental*)

27a Gideon used it to make an ephod, (*resumptive-sequential*)

27b which he put in his hometown of Ophrah. (*sequential*)

27c All the Israelites prostituted themselves to it there. (*sequential*)

27d It became a snare to Gideon and his family. (*concluding*)

28a So the Israelites humiliated Midian; (*summarizing*)

28b **the Midianites' fighting spirit was broken**. (*complementary*)

28c The land was undisturbed for forty years during Gideon's time. (*concluding*)

29a Then Jerubbaal son of Joash went home (*flashback-resumptive*)[66]

29b and settled down (*sequential*)

30 **Gideon fathered seventy sons through his many wives**. (*supplemental*)[67]

31a **His mistress, who lived in Shechem, also gave him a son**, (*supplemental*)

31b whom he named Abimelech. (*sequential*)

32a Gideon son of Joash died at a very old age (*resumptive-sequential*)

32b and was buried in the tomb of his father Joash located in Ophrah of the Abiezrites. (*concluding*)

OUTLINE

Prologue: The Same Old Story (6:1–10)
    Israel sins (6:1a)
    The Lord punishes (6:1b–5)
    Israel cries out to the Lord (6:6)
    The Lord sends a prophet (6:7–10)
Main Events: From Coward to King (6:11–8:27)
    The Lord Chooses a Deliverer (6:11–32)
        Getting a skeptic's attention (6:11–24)
        Taking baby steps (6:25–32)
    Time for the Ultimate Test (6:33–7:23)
        Facing off with the enemy (6:33–35)

---

66. The *wayyiqtol* clause in verse 29a flashes back chronologically to where verse 26b left off.

67. The disjunctive clauses in verses 30 and 31a provide supplemental information that contributes further to the narrator's negative portrait of Gideon. This information has a foreboding quality about it.

LITERARY STRUCTURE

The reference to Israel's doing evil signals a new narrative cycle within the book's central section (cf. 3:7, 12; 4:1). The plot develops as follows: (1) Israel's apostasy (6:1a), (2) the Lord's discipline through a foreign oppressor (6:1b–6a), (3) Israel's cry (6:6b–7), (4) prophetic accusation (6:7–10), (5) the Lord's deliverance (6:1–8:27), (6) conclusion (8:28–32). New to this cycle is the prophetic accusation separating Israel's cry from the report of deliverance.[68]

The literary structure of this cycle includes a prologue (6:1–10), a main narrative consisting of six episodes (6:11–8:27), and an epilogue (8:28–32). The prologue (6:1–10) has two subunits, the report of oppression (vv. 1–6) and the prophetic message (vv. 7–10). The temporal indicator (וַיְהִי) at the beginning of verse 7 formally separates the two sections, while verbal repetition (note "the Israelites cried out to the Lord" in both v. 6b and v. 7a) links them thematically and formally.

The limits of episode one are marked by an inclusio (note the references to Ophrah and the Abiezrite[s] in both vv. 11 and 24) (Webb 1987, 148–49). A disjunctive clause at the end of verse 24 also facilitates closure for the entire episode. The episode divides into three scenes: introductory dialogue (vv. 11–18), report of Gideon's sacrifice (vv. 19–21),

---

68. Lee sees 6:6–7:11 as being comprised of two "narrative strands" that are combined in 6:1–6 and recombined in 7:12–14 (2002, 65–86). However, his strand A, which focuses on Midian's advance, appears in only one verse (6:33), while strand B, which focuses on Israel's/Gideon's situation, appears in the rest of the text. One wonders whether a single verse can constitute a "strand." It seems more likely that the disjunctive clause in 6:33 serves as a structural marker that appears to signal a transition back to the story's macroplot (the Midianite crisis).

and concluding dialogue (vv. 22–24). The disjunctive clause at the beginning of verse 19 marks the transition from the initial dialogue to the account of the sacrifice, while the disjunctive clause at the end of verse 21 brings the report to its conclusion.

A temporal indicator and reference to nighttime introduce the second episode in the narrative. The episode can be divided into two scenes (vv. 25–27, 28–32), corresponding to the references to nighttime (the appearance of לַיְלָה, "night," near the beginning of v. 25 and at the end of v. 27 forms an inclusio for vv. 25–27) and to morning (v. 28a) (Assis 2005a, 43). The verb שָׁכַם, "got up," and the הִנֵּה, literally, "look," clause in verse 28 also signal a shift from Gideon's nighttime deed to its aftermath. The repetition of the words בַּעַל, "Baal," נתץ, "pulled down," and מִזְבֵּחַ, "altar" (vv. 28 and 32), provides an inclusio for the second scene. (These same terms are clustered in v. 30b, just before the pivotal point where the subject shifts from the townspeople to Gideon's father.)

Episode three, the account of the battle proper, contains five scenes. The first (6:33–35) begins with a disjunctive clause (v. 33) reminding us of the larger problem that was introduced in verses 1–10 and has been lurking in the background. Three more disjunctive clauses (vv. 34–35) lay the foundation for what follows. The stage seems to be set for a battle, but Gideon is not quite ready for that step yet. Instead he seeks confirmation of success. This second scene displays two panels, each of which reports Gideon's request (vv. 36–37, 39) and God's response (vv. 38, 40).

Shifts in name (note Jerubbaal) and focus (the narrator describes the location of the Israelite and Midianite campsites) mark the transition to scene three (7:1–8). The disjunctive clauses in the second half of verse 8 signal closure for the scene. The reference to the location of the Midianite camp forms an inclusio with verse 1. Apart from the frame (vv. 1, 8b), the scene consists of four subunits, each of which is introduced by the words, "the Lord said to Gideon" (vv. 2–3, 4–5a, 5b–6, 7–8a).

A temporal indicator and reference to nighttime (v. 9a, cf. 6:25) introduce scene four (7:9–14), which describes how the Lord gives Gideon further confirmation of success. The references to God's giving the enemy into Gideon's hands (vv. 9, 14) form an inclusio for the scene. The central parenthetical disjunctive clause (v. 12) functions as a pivot between the Lord's instructions (vv. 9–11) and Gideon's response (vv. 13–14).[69]

In scene five (7:15–23), which is introduced by a temporal indicator,

---

69. On the dramatic function of verse 12, see Lee 2002, 80.

the long-awaited battle finally arrives. The scene consists of Gideon's instructions and preparations (vv. 15–18), and the battle account proper (vv. 19–23), which is introduced by a description of Gideon's army's movements (v. 19a).

The fourth episode (7:24–8:3), introduced by a disjunctive clause, describes the Ephraimite contribution to the battle and their dispute with Gideon. Verses 24–25 report Gideon's invitation and the Ephraimites' positive response. In 8:1–3 Gideon resolves a conflict with the Ephraimites, who were offended because they had not been summoned to war earlier. The final clause, introduced by אָז, "when," reports the resolution.

In episode five (8:4–21) we read of Gideon's attempt to track down the Midianite chieftains Zebah and Zalmunna and the remnants of their army. The episode has two parallel panels and four distinct scenes. In verses 4–9 the men of Succoth and Penuel refuse to support Gideon, for they are not convinced that he will emerge victorious. The disjunctive clause at the beginning of verse 10, which informs us of the Midianite chieftains' location and troop strength, introduces the next scene in the narrative—Gideon's surprise attack and final victory. The disjunctive clause at the end of verse 12 rounds off the scene. Verses 13–17, which describe how Gideon fulfilled the threats he made against Succoth and Penuel, correspond to verses 4–9. Verses 18–21, which describe the execution of Zebah and Zalmunna, correspond to and complete verses 10–12.

The sixth and final episode (8:22–27), though closely linked with the preceding (note the introductory *waw*-consecutive and the reference to the Midianite jewelry in v. 26 [cf. v. 21]), is marked by a change in subject (the men of Israel now speak) and theme (kingship).

The conclusion (8:28–32) contains an expected formulaic summary about deliverance and peace (v. 28, cf. 3:11, 30; 5:31b), but also provides information concerning Gideon's family, death, and burial (vv. 29–32). The references to Joash, Ophrah, and the Abiezrite(s) form an inclusio for the entire Gideon narrative (cf. 6:11) and contribute to its closure. (Though this cycle of the book's central section begins in 6:1, Gideon, its main character, is not introduced until 6:11.) At the same time, this information lays the foundation for the following section by mentioning Abimelech, his seventy half-brothers, and Shechem.

EXPOSITION

Prologue: The Same Old Story (6:1–10)
The Midianite oppression described in these verses was shorter than

the periods of subjugation mentioned prior to this (which were eight, eighteen, and twenty years in length, respectively), but it was still severe enough.[70] Though it was shorter in duration, it was more intense than these other oppressions.[71] Rather than simply demanding tribute from Israel, the Midianites, along with the Amalekites and other easterners, invaded the land en masse, destroyed the ready-to-harvest crops, and forced the Israelites to hide out in the mountains, leaving the nation severely weakened.[72] The repetition of the verb שׁחת, "devour" (vv. 4–5) highlights the invaders' destructive force. In the second instance the text suggests their primary purpose was to destroy the land (note the infinitival form לְשַׁחֵתָהּ). Of course, this reflects the Israelites' perspective. As far as they were concerned, the Midianites destroyed their crops, but the Midianites' purpose in coming probably was to feed themselves and their cattle.

There are also several ironic elements in these verses. The same phrase used in 3:10 to describe Othniel's victory over Cushan-Rishathaim (וַתָּעׇז יָדוֹ עַל, literally, "and his hand was strong against," is used in 6:2 of Midian's subjugation of Israel.[73] The comparison of the Midianite hordes to locusts, while emphasizing their numerical strength and capacity to destroy, may echo the covenantal curse of Deuteronomy 28:38. Finally, the appearance of the Amalekites is ironic for Moses had instructed Israel to annihilate the Amalekites because of the way they had treated God's people (Deut. 25:17–19, cf. Exod. 17:8–16). Once more (see 3:13) Israel's failure in this regard was coming back to haunt them.

In prior cycles God responded to Israel's cry by sending a deliverer (3:9, 15) or announcing his intention to deliver (4:6). The pattern changes here. God did indeed intend to deliver Israel from its misery (cf. 6:14, 16), but before expressing this intention he sent a prophet to confront the nation with the reason for its troubles.[74] In this way God

---

70. On the authenticity of the references to the Midianites in the Judges period, see Kitchen 2003, 213–14.
71. As noted above in our discussion of the chronology of Judges, it may also be that the smaller number is one of the literary signals that a second panel begins here in the structure of the book's central section.
72. The verb דלל, "be weakened" (v. 6), is used elsewhere of individuals who have lost their strength (Pss. 79:8; 116:6; 142:6), of faded glory (Isa. 17:4), and of dried up streams (Isa. 19:6).
73. In 6:2 *Midian* appears as a genitive after *hand*, whereas in 3:10 a pronominal suffix is attached to *hand*.
74. Martin draws attention to the predominance of the first person in the message. The prophet is the messenger, but the Lord "is the primary character within the speech itself" (2007, 119).

reminded his people that he would not always automatically deliver them from their suffering (Webb 1987, 145). At some point they had to come to grips with the underlying issue of their unfaithfulness.

Like the angel at Bokim (cf. 2:1), the prophet reminded Israel of God's gracious past deeds (vv. 8–9).[75] Their covenant God had rescued them from all their oppressors and had enabled them to conquer the promised land. The oppressors of verse 9 are apparently those kingdoms that conquered Israel following the time of Joshua and have been mentioned earlier in Judges—the Moabites, Amalekites, Ammonites, and Canaanites. (See 1 Sam. 10:18.) The sequence in verse 9 is logical, not chronological. The first half of the verse refers to divine deliverance from oppressors—all the way from Egypt to the present, while the second half of the verse looks back at the initial conquest under Joshua. (See Josh. 24:18.)

The prophet next recalled God's basic demand for loyalty and then concluded with a brief, but to-the-point accusation (v. 10, cf. 2:2b). He does not quote any one text exactly, but seems to combine and summarize several passages. Prior to Judges the precise form "I am the Lord your God" [with אֲנִי as the first-person pronoun and a plural pronominal suffix attached to "God"] appears in several texts.[76] Nowhere else do we read the specific prohibition "Do not worship (literally, "fear") the gods of the Amorites" (the phrase "gods of the Amorites" occurs elsewhere only in Josh. 24:15), but the words do capture the essence of several earlier warnings.[77]

Main Events: From Coward to King (6:11–8:27)

The Lord Chooses a Deliverer (6:11–32)

Getting a skeptic's attention (6:11–24). The angel of the Lord (who last

---

75. For a list of intertextual links between the prophet's message and earlier, as well as later, passages, see Butler 2009, 197–98. See as well Martin 2007. Martin identifies four major themes in the speech (Exodus, land, fear, and hearing) (119–31), and also draws several connections between the speech and the following story of Gideon (131–36).
76. Exodus 6:7; 16:12; Leviticus 11:44; 18:2, 4, 30; 19:3–4, 10, 25, 31, 34, 36; 20:7, 24; 23:22, 43; 24:22; 25:17, 38, 55; 26:1, 13; Numbers 10:10; 15:41; Deuteronomy 29:6.
77. See Deuteronomy 6:13–14; 13:1–11; Joshua 24:14–18. Assis makes a good case that the language of verses 8–10 echoes the Decalogue (Exod. 20:2–3) (2005a, 23–24).

appeared in 2:1–5; cf. also the reference in 5:23) met Gideon while the latter was hard at work threshing in a winepress, where he hoped he could hide his wheat from the ravenous Midianites.[78] The words "courageous warrior" are proleptic and designed to inspire confidence.[79] The angel's assurance of God's enablement and casting of Gideon in a military role already imply the nature of the divine commission.

Gideon, like Moses before him, balked at the suggestion that God might want to use him as his instrument. Prefacing his reply with the polite "pardon me, sir" (literally, "but my lord," בִּי אֲדֹנִי, cf. Exod. 4:10, 13), he questioned the reality of God's presence and altered the personalized "with you" (v. 12, the second person pronoun is singular) to a collective "with us." Gideon argued that circumstances proved that the Lord had abandoned Israel and given the nation over to Midian. His argument is correct as far as it goes. God had temporarily abandoned his people, but only because they had sinned against him (Deut. 32:15). Gideon gave no indication of understanding this important fact, nor did his recalling of God's "miraculous deeds" have any impact on his perspective.

In verse 14 the Lord himself begins to speak directly to Gideon, as opposed to verses 12–13, where the angel and Gideon speak of the Lord in the third person.[80] Some see the Lord and his angel as interchangeable in this narrative and equate the two. However, there are indications within the narrative that the Lord and his angel are distinct.[81]

---

78. On the identity of the messenger/angel, see the commentary above on 2:1.

79. Another option is that the phrase does not have a military connotation here, but rather identifies Gideon as a leading citizen of the community. See Ruth 2:1, where the phrase is used of Boaz. Note as well the remarks of Boling 1975, 131.

80. Verse 14 states that the Lord "turned to" Gideon (cf. וַיִּפֶן אֵלָיו). The expression פָּנָה אֶל can mean "turn toward" in a purely literal, physical sense or "turn toward" in a metonymic sense, that is, "pay attention to, be gracious to" (cf. 2 Kings 13:23) (see BDB, 815; *HALOT*, 937). When used in a literal manner, the expression sometimes appears to mean, "look at closely" (cf. Exod. 16:10; Num. 12:10; 16:42; 2 Chron. 20:24; 26:20). The closest syntactical parallel to Judges 6:14, where the next clause begins with וַיֹּאמֶר, "and said," is in Numbers 12:10–11, where Aaron looks closely at Miriam (cf. וַיִּפֶן, "and turned"), apparently in a literal sense, and then speaks to Moses (cf. וַיֹּאמֶר).

81. Boling speaks of a "three-way conversation" here (1975, 131). Reinhartz addresses this issue at length, but is unwilling to commit to a position. She feels that the text offers no clues as to whether or not the Lord and the angel are one and the same or distinct entities (1998, 174–75). Savran

The switch to the first person ("Have I not sent you?") suggests the Lord is now speaking, as does Gideon's form of address (he uses אֲדֹנִי, "Master," in v. 15; as opposed to אֲדֹנִי, "my lord," in v. 13).[82] Later, after the angel disappears, the Lord and Gideon continue to carry on a dialogue (vv. 21–23). In addressing the Lord, Gideon refers to the angel in the third person.[83]

The Lord was not dissuaded by Gideon's arguments and delivered the formal commission, making explicit what was implied in his greeting. Focusing on the words "you have the strength" (v. 14) rather than the assurance of God's presence (v. 12), Gideon, like Moses (Exod. 3:11; 4:10), questioned his suitability for the task. After all, his clan was the least significant in Manasseh and he was the youngest (צָעִיר) in his family. Gideon's apparent ignorance of the patriarchal traditions is striking. Anyone familiar with those accounts will recall that God can take the youngest and seemingly insignificant and elevate them to great prominence (see Gen. 25:23; 48:13–20).

In response to Gideon's argument that he was not qualified for the job, the Lord personally assured Gideon of his presence, using words virtually identical to those spoken to Moses (Exod. 3:12), Joshua (Josh. 1:5), and the patriarchs (Gen. 26:3; 31:3). With God's enablement Gideon would completely destroy the Midianite horde.[84]

The parallels between Gideon and Moses are instructive for understanding Gideon's commission.[85] Throughout this narrative the Lord focused on what he wanted to accomplish through Gideon the individual, not the nation as a whole. (Note especially 6:12, 14, 16; 7:9,

---

does not see the Lord and the messenger as distinct. On the contrary, he states: "In the narrative theophany traditions, when YHWH and the *malakh* appear in the same text, there is no essential difference between them" (2005, 128).

82. Some textual witnesses do read אֲדֹנִי, "my lord," in both verses, however. But it is likely that original differing readings were harmonized in transmission.

83. One can detect this same distinction between the Lord and his angel in Exodus 3. The angel gets Moses' attention (v. 2) and the Lord then speaks to him (vv. 4ff.). In Genesis 21:17–19 it is also possible to distinguish between God and his angel.

84. The phrase כְּאִישׁ אֶחָד, literally, "as one man" (v. 16) emphasizes the collective unity of a large group. See Numbers 14:15; Judges 20:8, 11; 1 Samuel 11:7; 2 Samuel 19:15.

85. On the parallels between Gideon's commissioning and the call of Moses (Exodus 3), see Webb 1987, 148; Klein 1988, 51; and especially Wong 2007a.

14.) In fact, in chapter 7 he made Gideon reduce his forces to a mere three hundred men. Apparently God wanted to demonstrate the reality of Joshua's observation once more (see Josh. 23:10) and prove again to his people that he was able to accomplish great victories against overwhelming odds. Just as he used lowly Moses to defeat the great Egyptian empire, so he wanted to use Gideon to deliver Israel from the Midianites. But Gideon, like Moses at the burning bush, was not yet capable of grasping or accepting this.

Of course these promises of the divine presence and victory were only of value if the Lord was really speaking. Gideon was not going to rush into action without verifying that the speaker was indeed the Lord.[86] He asked for a verifying sign and then requested that the Lord stay put while he went to retrieve an appropriate gift for his guest. It is not clear if Gideon intended to offer a sacrifice *per se*. The Hebrew word מִנְחָה (v. 18) can refer to a gift offered as a sign of goodwill or submission (Gen. 33:10; 43:11, 15, 25–26; 1 Sam. 10:27). In the Genesis passages the gift is designed to appease someone whom the offerer knows he has offended. Perhaps Gideon wanted to be ready to appease the Lord if and when he proved his identity. Of course, the term may have a sacrificial connotation as well.[87]

Gideon brought a freshly prepared young goat along with some unleavened bread and goat's broth. It is not certain if the goat was intended to be a tasty meal (Gen. 27:9), a valuable gift (Gen. 38:17), a sign of renewed devotion (Judg. 15:1), a worthy sacrifice (Judg. 13:19), or some combination of these options. The angel, who had been

---

86. As translated by NIV, Gideon's statement in verse 17 is a request for the Lord to prove his identity. In this case -שֶׁ has the sense of "that." See Isaiah 38:7, which reads literally, "and this is to you *the sign* from the Lord *that* (אֲשֶׁר) the Lord will do this thing which he has spoken." Perhaps verse 17b should be emended to read as follows: שָׁאַתָּה הַמְדַבֵּר עִמִּי, "that you (are) *the* one speaking with me." The article on the participle could have been lost by haplography (note the final *he* on the preceding form). See Moore 1895, 187. The statement can be paraphrased as follows to bring out its meaning more clearly: "Give me a sign to show that it is really you (Yahweh) that is speaking to me." Though the Lord did not directly identify himself as such, his promise "I will indeed be with you" was a tip-off as to his identity. Boling takes the relative -שֶׁ, in the sense of "pertaining to what" and translates: "produce for me a sign pertaining to what you are telling me" (1975, 132). In this case Gideon is not asking the Lord to prove his identity, but to assure him that he really will enjoy the success announced in verse 16.

87. Note the use of the *hiphil* of נגשׁ, "approach," at the end of verse 19 and then compare Leviticus 2:8; Amos 5:25; and Malachi 2:12; 3:3.

watching silently since his initial greeting (v. 12), instructed Gideon to place the meat and bread on a nearby rock and to pour out the broth. When the angel touched the meat and bread with his staff, fire flared up from the rock and consumed the food. The angel then disappeared. The devouring fire had an important function in the Lord's developing relationship with Gideon. It provided the requested sign (v. 17), communicated his acceptance of Gideon, demonstrated his supernatural power, and proved that his "miraculous deeds" (v. 13) were not something restricted to Israel's distant past.[88]

Having received the sign he requested, Gideon now realized that he was speaking to the Lord himself and had seen the Lord's angel. For the first time he used the name *Yahweh* in addressing his divine visitor (in v. 15 he uses only אֲדֹנָי, "Master"; here he joins that title with the divine name *Yahweh*). The first word from his mouth ("Oh no!", Hebrew אֲהָהּ) reflects great emotional distress (see Josh. 7:7; Judg. 11:35). He was convinced that any mere mortal who saw the Lord's angel face-to-face would not live to tell about it (see Gen. 32:30; Judg. 13:22). The Lord quickly relieved his fears, assuring him that all was well and that he would not die. Gideon responded in genuine worship by building an altar for the Lord. He gave the altar an appropriate name, "The Lord is on friendly terms with me" (literally, "Yahweh is peace," that is, peaceful, friendly), which echoes the Lord's reassuring words to him (v. 23).[89] This act of building and naming an altar places Gideon in line with the ancient patriarchs (Gen. 8:20; 12:7–8; 13:18; 26:25; 33:20; 35:7) and with Moses (Exod. 17:15).

Taking baby steps (6:25–32). The Lord is a jealous God who demands the exclusive worship of his people. It is not enough to build an altar to the Lord, if one leaves the altar of a competing god standing. In their initial encounter the Lord forced Gideon to recognize his presence and power and brought him to the level of genuine worship. Next he pushed Gideon one step further and demanded that he display his loyalty by destroying his father's Baal altar and Asherah symbol. He instructed Gideon to tear down the pagan altar, build a new altar to the Lord in

---

88. It is not certain why the narrator refers to "the angel of God" in verse 20 rather than "the angel of the Lord" as in verses 11, 21–22. This may be a simple case of interchangeable or synonymous readings. Note also the use of two different terms for "rock" in verses 20–21. For a rhetorical explanation for the variation in divine names, see our comments on verses 36–40 below.
89. On the significance of the name of the altar, see Burney 1970, 193.

a prominent place, and offer up one of his father's bulls as a burnt offering, using the wood from the Asherah pole for fuel.

Enlisting the help of ten servants, Gideon obeyed the Lord's command, but he did not yet display the same degree of courage that would characterize his later exploits. Fearing the repercussions of his actions, he carried out the Lord's instructions at night, rather than during the daytime when everyone could see him. Gideon's apprehension is testimony to Israel's spiritual corruption (the whole town seems to be quite attached to this pagan altar) and heightens the dramatic tension of the narrative. This is not simply a story about one man turning to God. His renewed devotion will meet with opposition and he will come into conflict with his own community.

Morning's light brings with it a surprise for the townspeople. Hebrew הִנֵּה, "look," invites us to view the scene through their eyes. When they arrived at the pagan cult site, they saw the effects of Gideon's nighttime efforts. As we already suspect, Gideon's activity could not be kept secret. When the townspeople discovered he was the culprit, they demanded that his father Joash hand him over for execution. Their words are sadly ironic and symptomatic of their apostasy. Gideon had obeyed the Law of Moses (Exod. 34:13; Deut. 7:5; cf. Judg. 2:2), but a whole Israelite town was ready to kill him for it.

Though Joash owned the pagan altar, his attachment to his son seems to outweigh his devotion to Baal. His words may even indicate he had become skeptical of Baal's power. The introductory questions suggest that Baal should not need men to fight his battles for him. The next statement is quite bold. Joash declared that whoever tried to vindicate Baal would end up dead by morning.[90] Was this simply a warning to the crowd that Joash would kill anyone who tried to lay a hand on Gideon? Or, was he implying that Baal would kill anyone who dared to defend his honor, as if he were incapable of vindicating himself? (Assis 2005a, 47–48) Or, was his faith in Baal shaken, causing him to suggest sarcastically that Baal's defenders would end up dead by morning because their god lacked the power to defeat the attacks of his enemies? After all, the reality of the broken altar suggested as much! In his final statement Joash argued that a god ought to be able to defend his own honor when someone smashes his altar. He should not need the help of mere men. Joash then boldly gave his son a new

---

90. When used with the preposition -לְ, the verb רִיב means "contend for." See Job 13:8.

name, *Jerubbaal*, and declared, "Let Baal fight with him."[91] Baal's subsequent failure to defend his honor (though see chapter nine and our
comments in this regard) demonstrated his weakness and unworthi-
ness to be worshiped by Israel.

Time for the Ultimate Test (6:33–7:23)

Facing off with the enemy (6:33–35). Having reported Gideon's call and
initial act of faith, the narrator now returns to the larger problem facing
Israel—the oppressive Midianites and their allies (v. 33, cf. vv. 1–6).
Harvest season had arrived (v. 11) and the eastern hordes had come as
usual to destroy the Israelites' crops (vv. 3–5). But the Lord raised up a
deliverer (vv. 11–32) whom he enveloped (לבֵשׁ, "clothe") with his spirit
(v. 34).[92] The involvement of God's spirit offers great hope, for not since
the time of Othniel had God so empowered an Israelite warrior (cf.
3:10 and note the absence of references to the spirit in the Ehud and
Barak narratives). Like Ehud (3:27), Gideon blew a trumpet signaling
a battle, and then, like Barak (4:10), he summoned an army from the
nearby Israelite tribes.[93]

Hesitating again (6:36–40). The stage is set for the battle and one
anticipates an account of how the Israelites, led by their divinely

---

91. The NIV translates, "they called," but the verb is singular and Gideon's
father, who speaks in verse 31, is most naturally understood as its subject. The precise meaning of the name (which combines a verb with its
subject) is uncertain. The verbal element (יָרֶב > יָרוּב) appears to be an
imperfect ("Baal will fight"), not a jussive. One expects the imperfect to
be יָרִיב, since the root is ריב, not רוב, but perhaps the name preserves an
archaic form of the latter (the root does seem to be attested in the *Kethib*
of both Judg. 21:22 and Prov. 3:30). The name is apparently a case of a
popular etymology; it sounds like the statement, "let Baal fight" (which
uses the distinctly jussive form יָרֶב). For a detailed survey and analysis of
the various roots that have been proposed for the form יָרֶב (which include
רבב, ירה, ירב, ריב and רבה), see Bluedorn 2001, 101–4. Bluedorn concludes
that the verb probably derives from רבב, "increase, be numerous," and
that the name is here a soundplay on ריב, "to contend."
92. For a discussion of the syntactical issues in verse 34, see Waldman 1989,
163–67. Block sees this empowerment as the reason why the Israelites
responded so readily to his summons (1999, 271–72).
93. Manasseh, Asher, Zebulun, and Naphtali are specifically mentioned; Issachar, which came out to aid Barak (see Judg 5:15), is conspicuous by its
absence (cf. 1:27–36).

empowered general, routed the easterners. But the narrative does not deliver what we expect. Instead we discover that Gideon still had doubts about the success of the mission and about the Lord's capability and reliability.[94] Prefacing his remarks with the word "if" (אִם; cf. 4:8; 6:17), Gideon asked for a confirming sign to prove that the Lord would deliver Israel through him as he had promised. He claimed that if God gave him this confirmation, he would "be sure" (literally, "know") that God's promise was dependable. However, when the Lord responded positively to Gideon's request for a sign, Gideon was still not satisfied. He asked for a second sign; God patiently complied.

Gideon's choice of signs was not arbitrary or random. The tests were designed to demonstrate the Lord's control of the dew.[95] This

---

94. Most assess Gideon's request in a negative light, though one must admit that the text itself leaves it to the reader to decide which of Gideon's actions should be attributed to the divine spirit and which should not. In this regard Exum asks, "Is he no longer under the influence of the spirit when he asks for a sign or does the spirit not obviate the need for a sign?" (1992, 164, note 7). Olson draws attention to the fact that the empowerment by the spirit leaves Gideon essentially unchanged. He states: "Before the Spirit of the Lord comes upon him, Gideon is cowardly, hesitant, and secretive (6:11–33). After the Spirit of the Lord has come upon him (6:34), Gideon does not change" (1998, 767; see also p. 802.) Noting that the spirit's presence does not have a positive effect on Jephthah or Samson as well, Olson concludes: ". . . Othniel embodies the ancient ideal of a faithful judge empowered in a special way by the Spirit of the Lord. But when the divine Spirit gradually reappears in later judges, the Spirit is no longer a positive force. In the hands of unfaithful leaders like Gideon, Jephthah, and Samson, the divine Spirit becomes ineffectual and ultimately dangerous and destructive in the extreme" (767–68). Olson seems to imply that the spirit is a malevolent force in these later, post-Othniel accounts, or at least a powerful force that can be used for good or bad by the one who possesses it. If this is his intent, this viewpoint must be challenged. Gideon's story demonstrates that possession of the divine spirit does not automatically make one a paradigm of faith. God provides the capacity to act in faith, but human freedom remains operative and can thwart the spirit's positive influence. *Despite* the spirit's empowerment, Gideon lapses into doubt. The same is true of Jephthah (see our comments below on Judg. 11:29–40). In Samson's case, the actions prompted by the spirit should not be viewed in a negative light (see our comments below on Judg. 14:19).

95. Some suggest that the first test, in contrast to the second, did not entail a miracle because wool retains more moisture than soil. See, for example, Boling 1975, 141, as well as Beck 2008, 37. But Gideon did not ask that the wool simply be wetter than the ground; he asked that the wool be wet

is significant because in Canaanite thinking the storm god Baal controlled the rain and the dew. In one Ugaritic legend Baal's weakness results in the disappearance of rain and dew (Gibson 1978, 115). One of Baal's daughters is even named "Dew" ("Tallaya") (Gibson 1978, 46, 48). Gideon had destroyed Baal's altar, depriving him of sacrifices. Gideon's own father had challenged Baal to "fight" with his son. Indeed Gideon's new name, *Jerubbaal*, made him a potential and likely target for one of Baal's lightning bolts. By seeing a demonstration of God's sovereignty over the dew, an area supposedly under the control of Baal, Gideon could be assured that he was insulated from Baal's vengeance (Woods 1994, 68–69; Standaert 1996, 199–200).

Verses 33–35 lead us to believe that Gideon will be an Othniel, Ehud, and Barak all rolled into one. Instead he proved to be even more cautious and reluctant than Barak. The quality of Israelite male leadership was steadily declining. Nevertheless God's patience with Gideon is a hopeful sign and a reminder that when God decides to deliver his people he will do so, even if he must use the most unlikely heroes.

One of the oddities of verses 36–40 is the use of the divine name *Elohim* ("God"), rather than *Yahweh* ("Lord"). Though some see the shift as evidence of different literary sources (for example, Moore 1895, 198), a better explanation is available. At this point in the story Gideon had regressed. His faith in Yahweh, the ever-present God who helps those whom he commissions (v. 16; cf. Exod. 3:12), was wavering. Gideon knew by this point he was dealing with a deity, but he was not yet sure of this God's reliability. In light of Gideon's insufficient faith, the name *Yahweh* is not appropriate here. The use of the more general name for deity reflects Gideon's limited, partially developed perspective.[96]

---

and the ground *dry* (חָרֶב). Certainly one would expect the ground to still be damp early in the morning, when Gideon got up (v. 38), especially when one considers the large amount of moisture that Gideon squeezed from the fleece. Given the properties of wool, God's response to the second test may have been more impressive than his response to the first, but both involved alteration of natural processes and may be classified as miracles. It is not clear why Gideon asked for the easier test first, but his proposal of an even more difficult test following the first miracle is consistent with his character as revealed in the story.

96. Block also sees a rhetorical purpose in the narrator's choice of divine names (1999, 273). He observes: "The narrator apparently recognizes the incongruity of the situation by deliberately referring to God by the generic designation Elohim rather than his personal covenant name Yahweh." Block suggests that this rhetorical device reflects Gideon's confusion. He

If this proposal is valid for verses 36–40, then we may be able to explain why *Elohim*, not *Yahweh*, is used back in verse 20. Yahweh, the covenant God of Israel, initiated a relationship with Gideon and promised to protect and enable him. Yet by the end of their initial encounter Gideon was doubtful. He used אֲדֹנָי, "Master," but not *Yahweh*, in addressing the Lord (v. 15) and requested a sign (v. 17). Because Gideon's lack of faith is highlighted at the end of the first scene of the story's first episode, it is quite appropriate that the first reference to the deity in the episode's second scene is *Elohim*. The use of *Elohim* (see "angel of God") in verse 20 reflects Gideon's perspective. He was not yet convinced he was speaking with Yahweh or that the angelic messenger came from Yahweh. However, once the Lord gave him a sign, he was willing to use the name *Yahweh* (vv. 22, 24). The name *Yahweh* is appropriate in verses 25–34, where Gideon obeys the Lord's command and is energized by his spirit, but not in verses 36–40, where Gideon essentially questions whether Yahweh really has called him.

Reducing the army to a remnant (7:1–8). The use of the name *Jerubbaal*, in addition to marking a transition in the narrative, may also signal Gideon's renewed faith. From this point on Gideon, though still somewhat apprehensive (see 7:10–11), acts mightily, as he did when he destroyed the Baal altar and received the name Jerubbaal (6:25–32).[97]

The location of the Israelite campsite near the spring of Harod is

---

states, "Apparently Gideon has difficulty distinguishing between Yahweh, the God of the Israelites, and God in a general sense." See as well Polzin 1980, 170; and Assis 2005a, 54.

97. For a similar attempt to explain the significance of the name here, see Boling 1975, 144. Assis, also taking a literary approach to the variation in names, states: "The use of both names here indicates the internal tension related to Gideon's struggle against the Midianites. When he set out for battle some saw him as Jerubbaal—a man who will be punished by the Baal; others saw him as Gideon—a deliverer sent by God. This increases the tension prior to commencement of the combat: what will the results of the battle be and which expectation will be fulfilled?" (2005a, 57) Proposing a literary motive for the use of the names Gideon and Jerubbaal in the narrative marks a radical departure from the way the phenomenon has normally been handled. For a survey of the way the issue has been approached, see Emerton 1976, 289–312. For another attempt to deal with the issue from a diachronic critical perspective, see Auld 1989, 263–67. He proposes, "the Gideon story is an example of late biblical narrative" (263). He concludes, "the extended narrative of Gideon/Jerubbaal as we find it in the MT . . . represents a retelling of an earlier story, known to the writers

ironic. The name Harod sounds like the Hebrew verb חרד, "tremble, be terrified," and its related adjective חָרֵד, "trembling." The very name hints at the emotional state of Gideon's army (see v. 3, where the adjective is used), but it also foreshadows what divinely energized Gideon will do to the Midianites (cf. 8:12, where "surprised" translates the causative form of the verb חרד).[98]

We now discover that Gideon's mustering of an army (6:34–35) was premature. The Lord did not intend to deliver Israel through a large army, for Israel might then attribute their victory to their own power and skill. Instead the Lord wanted to work through a greatly reduced force so that there would be no doubt about the supernatural source of the deliverance. This should come as no surprise, for an unlikely hero theme has already appeared in the book and God's commissioning of Gideon indicated he would use Gideon the individual, not an army (see 6:12–16, where second person singular forms dominate in the Lord's address to Gideon).

In retrospect, we must ask: Was Gideon's enlisting support to tear down the altar (6:27) and his summoning an army symptomatic of his weak faith? A quick reading of 6:34–35 might lead one to believe that the spirit prompted him to call for support, but is this really the case? (After all, most do not attribute his next action, requesting a sign, to the spirit's leading.) It is likely that the summoning of an army was actually a step away from faith that culminated in the request for a sign.[99] Perhaps the Lord even intended for Gideon to perform a Samson-like individual act of heroism that would ignite a war, comparable to what Jonathan did on a later occasion (see 1 Samuel 14).

The Lord implemented a two-part plan to reduce the size of the army. All who were afraid were urged to depart. Not surprisingly, twenty-two thousand of Gideon's thirty-two thousand men left. Announcing that the army was still too large, the Lord devised yet another scheme to trim the army's size. When the men went down to the water to drink, Gideon was to separate those who lapped like a dog and those who knelt and scooped up water with their hands. The Lord

---

of the books of Samuel, about Jerubbaal, father of Abimelech" (265–66). See as well Mobley 2005, 122–24.

98. Klein relates the name to Gideon's fearful state (1988, 56).
99. In this regard see Bluedorn 2001, 112–13. In defense of Gideon, one might point to Ehud and Barak, both of whom summoned armies. But Ehud summoned an army only after performing a bold, individual deed, and Barak was specifically told to do so by the Lord's prophet (see 4:6).

chose those who lapped, for they numbered only three hundred, and sent the rest of the men home.

As it stands, the Hebrew text of verses 5b–6 makes little sense. It reads literally: "Everyone who laps with his tongue from the water as a dog laps, put him by himself, as well as everyone who kneels to drink. And the number of those who lapped with their hand to their mouth was three hundred men, and all the rest of the army knelt to drink water." Verse 5 seems to distinguish two groups, dog-like lappers and kneelers, but verse 6 contrasts those who "lap" by putting their hand to their mouth (dogs don't do this!) with kneelers. The simplest solution is to view the phrase "with their hands to their mouths" as originally an explanatory, marginal gloss that has been accidentally put into the text at the wrong place. It was probably originally designed to explain how the kneelers drank. It fits well at the end of verse 5: "Separate those who lap the water with their tongues like a dog from those who kneel down to drink *with their hands to their mouths*. Three hundred men lapped; all the rest got down on their knees to drink." Or one could place it at the end of verse 6: "Separate those who lap the water with their tongues like a dog from those who kneel down to drink. Three hundred men lapped; all the rest got down on their knees to drink *with their hands to their mouths*" (cf. Burney 1970, 210; Moore 1895, 202; Boling 1975, 145).

Is there some significance to the different drinking postures? Perhaps those who knelt and scooped water with their hand were more alert and therefore more suitable warriors. In this case, by sending them away and choosing the lappers, the Lord decided to use the least likely group (Boling 1975, 145–46). On the other hand, one could view the lappers' action as indicative of their trust in the Lord; they saw no need to be alert when drinking since the Lord was on their side (Burney 1970, 211–12). Moore presents, but rejects, the view that the lappers' dog-like behavior indicated they were "rude, fierce men" who were more fit for battle (1895, 202).[100] These explanations seem contrived. The Lord probably chose this test because he knew only a handful of men would lap like a dog. Scooping water with one's hands is the more normal way of drinking from a stream. It is unlikely that their drinking posture implies anything about the character of the men. The test is simply designed to reduce the army to a mere remnant.

The reference to the three hundred men taking up their trumpets

---

100. Daube entertains the idea that the lappers' action "symbolizes a lapping of the enemy's blood." This does not merely depict them as fierce, but also foreshadows their victory (1956, 156–58).

(v. 8) is a seemingly minor point that gains greater significance upon further observation. The absence of any reference to weapons catches one's attention. One already suspects this battle will be won in a very unconventional manner, and the reference to trumpets confirms this. One is left wondering, "How will these trumpets come into play in the following narrative?" As we shall see, they have an important role to play and, when blown by Gideon's men, serve to link this account with another famous episode in Israel's history.

Reassuring the general (7:9–14). The introductory temporal reference ("That night") marks the transition to a new scene and also links the following account with earlier nighttime events (Klein 1988, 58–59; van Midden 1999, 59–60). Gideon destroyed the Baal altar at night because he was afraid of the townspeople (6:27). The tests with the fleece (6:36–40), which testified to Gideon's wavering faith and apprehension, were conducted at night. Now God confronted Gideon at night. He urged him to charge into battle, but also offered him an opportunity to receive one more confirmatory sign, if he was still afraid. By pushing Gideon to attack by night, God intended to transform his earlier nighttime fears and doubts into faith and victory.

Gideon's decision to take God up on his offer revealed his lingering fear. Gideon arrived with his servant at the outskirts of the camp and was confronted with the vast size of the enemy army. If ever there were a time to get cold feet, this would have been it! But just as Gideon arrived, he overheard one sentry relating a dream to another. The threefold הִנֵּה, "look,"—used once by the narrator and twice by the Midianite storyteller—highlights the significance of the dream and its imagery. In his dream the sentry saw a stale/moldy[101] cake of barley bread come rolling into the Midianite camp and overturn an entire tent.[102] His comrade was quick to interpret its significance. The bread symbolized Gideon's "sword," that is, his military strength, and the toppling of the tent depicted his imminent victory over Midian.[103] The

---

101. On the meaning of Hebrew צְלִיל, see Boling, who derives the term from an Arabic root meaning "become dry" (1975, 146). See as well *HALOT*, 1025.

102. A *weqatal* verbal form introduces the last clause of the storyteller's dream report, perhaps highlighting this action, which has already been mentioned just before this.

103. Pressler suggests that the barley bread, being "an agricultural product . . . symbolized the Israelite farmers" (2002, 176). The text, of course, says the bread symbolized Gideon's "sword," but his army of farmers could be viewed metaphorically as his "sword." Mobley sees ironic reversal in the

use of נפל, "fall," to depict the tent's collapse should strike the reader as more than coincidental, for this same word was used to describe the fallen Eglon (3:28) and Sisera (4:22; 5:27). The dream report suggests that Midian's fate would be like that of these earlier oppressors. The man even confirmed the Lord's reassuring promise. The words "God is handing Midian and all the army over to him" (v. 14; the perfect verbal form is used, emphasizing the certainty of the event) virtually repeat the Lord's declaration in verse 9: "I am handing it over to you" (a perfect verbal form is used, as in v. 14). Even though Gideon was insignificant and an unlikely hero, he would, through God's enablement, do something as seemingly impossible as a cake knocking over a tent.

God's dealings with Gideon mirror Gideon's earlier actions (as recorded in chapter 6). Using the word אם, "if," Gideon initially requested a miraculous sign from God (6:17). Having received his sign and having mustered a large army, he then asked for further confirmation through two tests involving a fleece (6:36–40). Once more he prefaced his remarks with the word "if" (v. 36). But then the Lord took away the army, doing so through a two-part plan involving testing and observation (7:1–8, cf. 6:36–40). Then, using Gideon's favorite word "if," the Lord granted him a final confirmatory sign (7:9–14). The structure is chiastic: (a) Gideon asks for and receives a sign (6:17–21), (b) Gideon gathers an army and seeks confirmation of God's promise through two tests (6:34–40), (b') God dismantles the army through two tests (7:1–8), (a') God offers Gideon a confirmatory sign (7:9–14). Note that the initial sign occurred in broad daylight, while the final sign occurred at night. Gideon's tests occurred at night; God's tests took place during the day.

Responding to the challenge (7:15–23). The dream report finally elevated Gideon to the place where God wanted him to be. He worshiped on the spot, returned to the camp, and issued a battle cry (v. 15) that echoed the Lord's earlier command to him (v. 9). Like Ehud and Deborah before him (cf. 3:28; 4:14), he was now convinced the Lord's power was adequate. Working with what God had made available to him, he began to exercise leadership and devised a scheme for defeating the enemy.[104]

At this point Gideon's progression seems complete. At first he

---

imagery: "This is our first reversal: Israel, Midian's meal ticket according to Judges 6:4–5, transmogrifies into a great round loaf of bread that bowls over the Midianite camp" (2005, 132).

104. Gideon's command in verse 17, in which he emphasizes through repetition that the soldiers must follow his lead, attests to his newly found confidence and sense of leadership. In this regard see Klaus 1999, 74–75.

needed confirmation that the supernatural being speaking to him was indeed Yahweh. Receiving the requested sign, he built an altar to affirm his belief that Yahweh desired to have a peaceful relationship with him (6:17–24). Yahweh then commanded him to destroy the Baal altar, forcing him to demonstrate his allegiance. When Gideon obeyed, he received the divine spirit. However, Gideon then regressed, asking for signs to confirm the divine promise. By sending the bulk of the army away, the Lord forced him to expect something miraculous. The dream report gave final confirmation of that miracle. Gideon was now a full-fledged worshiper who was willing to put his faith into action. He instructed his men to use the battle cry, "For the Lord and for Gideon" (v. 18), suggesting that his allegiance was with the Lord and that he was the Lord's instrument of war.[105]

Armed only with trumpets and torches (which were temporarily placed in earthenware jars to disguise the approach and to keep the flames from being extinguished by the wind) (Burney 1970, 208),[106] Gideon's men blew their trumpets on cue, revealed their flaming torches and shouted, "A sword for the Lord and for Gideon!" The addition of the word "sword" (cf. v. 20) shows that Gideon's men shared his ingenuity, for it would have suggested to the surprised Midianites that the attackers were fully armed.

---

105. McCann suggests Gideon is guilty of "self-assertion" and "seems willing to take at least some of 'the credit' . . . for the victory" (2002, 67–68). See also Claassens 2001, 61; Block 1999, 282, who detects "some ambiguity here," and Olson 1998, 803, who states, "Gideon claims a piece of the spotlight along with God." Olson argues that a comparison of Gideon's battle cry with Joshua 6:16 supports this interpretation. Unlike Gideon, Joshua gave credit for his victory solely to the Lord. In defense of McCann's proposal, it is true that God wanted Israel to recognize him as their deliverer (7:2) and that Israel subsequently attributed the victory to Gideon (8:22). Consequently one could argue that Gideon's battle cry (7:18) betrayed a proud attitude and contributed to the misunderstanding that occurred. However, given wavering Gideon's hesitancy up to this point, it seems more likely that the battle cry is his declaration of full allegiance to the Lord. Furthermore, from the outset of the story God cast Gideon in the role of Israel's deliverer (6:12, 14, 16). In his pre-battle instructions to his troops, Gideon made it clear the Lord would be the author of the victory (7:15) and he gave the Lord the credit for Israel's success after the battle (8:3, 7).

106. The torches were apparently used to set the Midianite tents on fire. See Yadin 1963, 259. He draws attention to a relief depicting the Assyrians setting fire to Arab tents (451).

The prominence of the trumpets cannot be missed. The word שׁוֹפָר, "trumpet," appears eight times in verses 8, 16–22, and the verb תקע, "blow," is used six times in verses 18–22. The use of this verb to describe one of the decisive acts in Gideon's victory links the account with earlier acts of deliverance recorded in the book (cf. 3:21, 27; 4:21). The blowing of trumpets also reminds one of the Lord's great victory over Jericho, when the Israelites blew trumpets outside the city's walls as a prelude to God's miraculous intervention (cf. Joshua 6). The parallelism is probably not coincidental—the Lord was renewing his mighty deeds in Gideon's day, in response to the reluctant hero's earlier question (cf. 6:13).

Finishing the Job (7:24–8:21)

Enter Ephraim (7:24–8:3). With the battle won and the panic-stricken enemy in full flight, Gideon mobilized the nearby tribes (vv. 23–24). (In light of 7:2, we must ask if he was justified in doing so.)[107] He sent messengers ahead to the Ephraimites, asking that they guard the fords of the Jordan to prevent the enemy from escaping. The Ephraimites captured not only the fords, but also two of the Midianite chieftains, Oreb and Zeeb, whose very names (meaning "raven" and "wolf," respectively) remind us that the Midianite hordes had preyed on Israel and, like a scavenger, spared very little. The Ephraimites executed Oreb and Zeeb and then sent their heads to Gideon as tangible proof of their commitment to the cause.

This brief portrait of brotherly cooperation within the tribe of Joseph, which reminds one of Moses' blessing (Deut. 33:17), is quickly marred by dissension. The Ephraimites were displeased that Gideon did not summon them for battle earlier (cf. 6:35). Exercising admirable leadership ability and demonstrating a commitment to tribal unity, Gideon restored their sense of honor and deflated their anger by flattering them and acknowledging their important role in the battle.[108]

107.See Klein, who interprets this and his subsequent actions in a negative light (1988, 61). See also Block 1999, 283.

108.Why did Gideon use the name *Elohim* (God), rather than *Yahweh* (Lord) when speaking to the Ephraimites (v. 3)? Perhaps he did so because God had demonstrated his sovereignty over the nations. See our earlier remarks on 4:23. This, of course, assumes that *Elohim* is the original reading. A few Hebrew manuscripts, the Septuagint, and the Vulgate have/assume *Yahweh* here, a reading that Boling (1975, 150–51) and Burney (1970, 227) prefer.

Gideon's mustering of the Ephraimites reminds one of Ehud's enlisting the support of Ephraim in his revolt against Moabite oppression (see 3:27). However, that earlier account gives no hint of any tension within the Israelite ranks, in contrast to the Gideon narrative, where an intertribal squabble threatens to mar Israel's great victory.

Tracking down the oppressors (8:4–21). This next episode has both a primary and secondary story line. Its primary concern is Gideon's pursuit of the Midianite kings (מְלָכִים) Zebah and Zalmunna. (Oreb and Zeeb are called chieftains or princes, שָׂרִים.) At the same time, a secondary story line concerns Gideon's relationship with the uncooperative towns of Succoth and Penuel.

Gideon persistently and successfully tracked down Zebah and Zalmunna and routed the remnant of their army. This verb translated "surprised," used in 8:12 in the *hiphil* stem (הֶחֱרִיד), literally means, "he caused to tremble." It describes the effect of Gideon's surprise attack on the Midianites. Its use here is ironic, for in 7:3 an adjective (Hebrew חָרֵד) from the same verbal root describes twenty-two thousand of Gideon's frightened soldiers assembled at the spring of Harod (חֲרֹד, meaning "trembling"). The repetition of the root draws attention to the role reversal that characterizes the story. Before the battle Israel's army was trembling, but in the end the Midianites were overcome with terror.

Gideon executed the two kings. At first he was willing to let them live, but when he discovered they had murdered his brothers at Tabor, he was compelled to seek vengeance. He offered his oldest son, Jether, the glory of the kill, perhaps to humiliate his victims. But Jether, like the Gideon of earlier chapters, was not up to the task.[109] Gideon, who had been transformed into a mighty warrior (cf. 6:12), executed the defiant kings and avenged his family. As Webb notes, Jether is a foil that "points up the contrast between Gideon as he was and Gideon as he now is" (1987, 151–52).

This concern for vengeance is a prominent theme in the secondary story line as well, where Gideon does not show the same commitment to unity that he did when dealing with the Ephraimites. When the princes of Succoth refused to show hospitality to Gideon's tired troops and questioned whether he would be successful, he promised to punish them once the campaign was over. When Penuel treated him the same

---

109. Jether's name could be taken to mean, at least by popular etymology, "remnant"—reminding us that the Midianite kings had decimated Israel and Gideon's family.

way, he promised to tear down the city tower when he returned in victory. Gideon was true to his word. He took special pains to make sure that all of the princes of Succoth were punished,[110] and, in addition to tearing down the tower of Penuel,[111] killed its male citizens.[112]

How should one evaluate Gideon's actions? On the surface they seem justified. Both towns were within Gadite territory (on Succoth, see Josh. 13:27) and were probably occupied by Israelites. If so, in light of the earlier curse on Meroz (cf. 5:23), one could judge their failure to cooperate with Gideon as reprehensible and deserving of severe punishment.

Gideon's words to the men of Succoth in verse 15, when compared to what they actually said (v. 6), give us insight into his assessment of their actions. When Gideon and his men arrived in Succoth the first time, he asked for provisions, pointing out that his men were exhausted (v. 5). The city officials rejected their request, saying: "You have not yet overpowered Zebah and Zalmunna. So why should we give bread to your army?" (v. 6)[113] When Gideon returned victoriously

---

110. Mobley sees an echo of Lamech (Gen 4:23–24) here (2005, 120, 160, note 12). Lamech boasted that he would be avenged seventy-seven fold, while Gideon carried out vengeance against the seventy-seven leaders of Succoth.

111. Mobley observes that the verb נתץ, "tear down," is used of both Gideon's tearing down the Baal altar (6:28, 30) and the tower at Penuel (8:17) (2005, 144). Does the repetition have thematic significance? Is there a contrast between the two actions? Perhaps the repetition draws attention to how Gideon's focus has changed from being God's instrument for cleansing Israel to seeking personal vengeance. (See Assis 2005a, 94.) Or are the incidents parallel in some way, perhaps suggesting that the uncooperative men of Penuel were worthy of the same fate as Baal's detestable altar?

112. The Hebrew text reads in verse 16b: "He made known with them the men of Succoth." The verb form וַיֹּדַע is a causative hiphil from ידע "know." One could translate, "he used them (the thorns and briers) to teach the men of Succoth a lesson." However, several ancient versions (Septuagint, Syriac Peshitta, and Latin Vulgate) assume the verb is וַיָּדָשׁ, "and he threshed," from דּושׁ, "thresh," which is used in verse 7. In this case the following בָּהֶם, "with them," refers to the thorns and briers just mentioned. See Amos 1:3, where the preposition -בְּ is collocated with דּושׁ and introduces the instrument used in threshing. In this case one may translate Judges 8:16b: "and he threshed the elders of Succoth with them" (i.e., the aforementioned thorns and briers).

113. The men of Succoth ask, literally, "Are the hand(s) of Zebah and Zalmunna now in your hand?" The reference to the hands of Zebah and Zalmunna may allude to the practice of dismembering enemy corpses and taking

288

with Zebah and Zalmunna in tow, he confronted the leaders of Succoth and reminded them of their earlier words: "Look what I have! Zebah and Zalmunna! You insulted me, saying, 'You have not yet overpowered Zebah and Zalmunna. So why should we give bread to your exhausted men?'" (v. 15). He characterized their earlier statement as an insult. Even more importantly, he changed their actual statement by substituting "exhausted men" for "army." In this way he emphasized the crisis his men were facing at the time of the request (the narrator agrees with his assessment, see v. 4), highlighted the insensitivity of the men of Succoth, and made it clear that he was justified in punishing them.

Why did Gideon treat Succoth and Penuel so harshly, after he had shown such great diplomacy with the Ephraimites? Ephraim was more than ready to support him in battle. Their concern was simply their honor. Succoth and Penuel, on the other hand, showed no willingness to support the armies of Israel against their oppressors.[114]

At the same time, the account is disturbing. Except for being a name spoken by Gideon (vv. 7, 19), the Lord disappears from the story (Claassens 2001, 64, 67–68). The civil strife that follows the battle is symptomatic of Israel's lack of unity and foreshadows even worse civil discord.[115] Gideon seemed more willing to show mercy to Zebah and Zalmunna than he did his own countrymen (Klein 1988, 62).[116] He exe-

---

body parts as trophies of war (see 1 Sam. 17:54). A Ugaritic myth depicts the victorious warrior goddess Anat as dismembering her foes and then attaching heads and hands to her belt as trophies: "Head(s) were like balls beneath her, palm(s) above her like locusts, palm(s) of warrior(s) like avenging grasshoppers. She did stick the heads on her waist, did bind the palms to her sash." See Gibson 1978, 47. Egyptian and Assyrian reliefs show warriors removing the hands of enemy corpses and piling them up in front of scribes so that an accurate casualty count could be taken. See Yadin 1963, 260.

114. Malamat theorizes that Gideon had made a treaty with Succoth and Penuel. When they refused to supply his army, they broke the treaty, explaining why Gideon treated them so harshly. As parallels he cites two Hittite treaties where the vassal was responsible for supplying the suzerain's army. He also cites a Hittite treaty where breach of covenant results in the death of the entire male population of a city (2004, 69–71).

115. As McCann points out, Abimelech's destruction of Shechem's stronghold (מִגְדָּל) is reminiscent of Gideon's actions at Penuel, the tower (מִגְדָּל) of which he tore down (2002, 74). See also Brown 2000, 200.

116. This foreshadows Israel's treatment of Benjamin (cf. Judges 20–21). See Wong 2006a, 125–31.

cuted the Midianite kings only when he discovered they had murdered
his brothers. In fact, one can see a desire for personal vengeance as the
primary motive in each of the violent actions attributed to Gideon in
this chapter (vv. 16–17, 21).[117] It appears that Gideon was more committed to personal vengeance than the Lord's cause. By treating his
Israelite opponents so harshly, while showing a lenient attitude toward
the real enemy (a leniency which we do not see in Ehud or Jael), he set
a misleading example for a nation that seemed more willing to fight
their brothers than the Canaanites and other foreigners.

Gideon Rejects the Crown—or Does He? (8:22–27)

Gideon's military success made him a likely candidate for king in the
eyes of the people.[118] After all, even the Midianite kings acknowledged
that he possessed a princely appearance (v. 18).[119] Their comment foreshadows what transpires in verses 22–27. The people asked Gideon to
establish a royal dynasty and attributed the victory directly to him,
making no mention of God.[120] Gideon rejected the offer, reminding
them that the Lord was their king. One might interpret this as a cop-
out. After all, Moses anticipated a day when Israel would have a king
(Deut. 17:14–20). Furthermore the absence of royal authority contributed to social chaos (Judg. 17:6; 21:25). However, the people's reference
to Gideon saving them must have been a red flag for Gideon, for prior
to the battle the Lord had addressed this very issue and made it clear
he wanted the credit as Israel's savior. Gideon must have sensed the
people's request was shortsighted and contained an implicit rejection
of the Lord, so he refused their offer, at least officially.[121]

---

117. See McCann 2002, 69, as well as Claassens 2001, 64; and Wong 2006a,
166–68.

118. McCann suggests that Gideon's actions in dealing with Succoth may in
part explain why the people were so eager to enthrone him as their king
(2002, 69). See also Assis 2005a, 103.

119. When Gideon asked the Midianites about the appearance of the men they
had killed at Tabor, they replied, "They were like you. Each one looked like
a king's son" (8:18). In other words, they suggested that Gideon looked like
the son of a king, that is, a prince.

120. Some argue that Gideon himself planted the seed for this when he instructed his troops, prior to the battle, to shout "For the Lord and for
Gideon." See our discussion of this issue in the commentary on 7:15–23.

121. See Gerbrandt 1986, 127–28. On the other hand, Younger criticizes Gideon
for not affirming that the Lord was the one who had saved them (2002,
204). He argues that Gideon, by allowing the people's statement to stand
uncorrected, actually endorsed their viewpoint.

Some argue that Gideon really did accept the people's offer. Davies states: "Gideon's words are not a refusal: they are rather a protestation: a protestation of the kind of kingship he would exercise, an avowal that his kingship and that of his family will be so conducted as to eliminate any personal and tyrannical element, and to permit of the manifestation of the divine rule through his own" (1963, 157; cf. van Midden 1999, 65–66). Davies points to other alleged examples of polite statements veiling one's true motive (Genesis 23; Exod. 4:13–14; 2 Samuel 24) and to the following context, where Gideon, though having apparently refused kingship, acts like a king (Davies 1963, 154–57). However, the text never refers to the people making Gideon king and Abimelech's allusion to an oligarchical arrangement among Gideon's sons (9:2) indicates the absence of a dynastic succession, suggesting that Gideon had not become king, at least in an official sense or in the manner the people envisioned (Loewenstamm 1980, 440).

Nevertheless, Gideon's subsequent actions do seem to belie his words.[122] He asked each Israelite to give him a golden earring from his plunder.[123] From the gold he then fashioned an ephod, as if he were ready to assume some type of priestly function.[124] In Exodus 28:4–6 and several other texts, an ephod is described as a priestly or cultic garment. In some cases an ephod is used to obtain a divine oracle (1 Sam. 23:9; 30:7). In Judges 8:26 the ephod is made of gold and is described as being quite heavy (somewhere between 35–75 lbs.) (Burney 1970, 236; Block 1999, 299–300). It was apparently a cultic image or

---

122. Fokkelman suggests that Gideon's "fascination with royalty" emerges in verse 21 with the reference to his taking the crescent-shaped ornaments from the necks of the Midianite camels (1999, 148). The narrator, by drawing attention to this action, reflects Gideon's point of view: "The narrator has promoted them [the Midianite "baubles"] to a position equal to that of the execution, because they represent the field of vision of the grasping Gideon and are the objects of his obsession." See also Assis 2005a, 106–07.

123. Verse 24 identifies the defeated Midianites as "Ishmaelites." This same identification occurs in Genesis 37:25–36; 39:1. Rather than being evidence for different literary sources, the variation is better explained at a rhetorical-linguistic level. See Revell 2001, 74–75. Revell proposes that "Ishmaelite" in Judges 8:24 identifies "a specific characteristic of people otherwise called 'Midianite,'" namely their bedouin-like nature (75, note 16).

124. Halpern argues that Gideon "rejected monarchy," but appropriated "the authority of a priest" (1978, 85).

object, probably used for oracular purposes.[125] Block suggests the term may refer here to the ornamental garment placed on a cultic image, making it a metonymy for an idol (Block 1999, 300). Giving Gideon the benefit of the doubt, we could assume he had good intentions. Perhaps he wanted to give the people a tangible reminder of the Lord's past intervention or desired to consult the Lord on a regular basis.[126] But Davies is probably closer to the truth, when he argues that Gideon's desire to have an ephod betrayed his royal aspirations. He points out that both Saul and David used a priestly ephod for oracular purposes (1 Sam. 14:3, 18 [LXX]; 23:9; 30:7) (Davies 1963, 157). Perhaps the ephod points to a royal priesthood of sorts.

Whatever his motives may have been, this ephod became an object of worship for the idol-prone Israelites and a "snare" to Gideon and his family (v. 27). The use of the term מוֹקֵשׁ, "snare," which refers to the worship of other gods in Deuteronomy 7:16 and Judges 2:3, suggests that Gideon's family became idolaters. It is ironic that Gideon, the one who destroyed the Baal altar in Ophrah, now replaces it with another idolatrous object of worship (Assis 2005a, 110).

One can detect a parallel between Gideon and Aaron, who fashioned a calf from the golden earrings of the people and, though well-intentioned, led Israel into idolatry (see Exodus 32).[127] The comparison to Aaron is ironic, for at the beginning of the story Gideon was cast in the role of a new Moses. Like Moses, Gideon had been transformed from a reluctant servant into the Lord's instrument of deliverance, but

---

125. See Miller 2000, 56, 67. For lengthy discussions of the ephod in the Old Testament, see Burney 1970, 236–43; de Vaux 1965, 2:349–52; and Bray 2006, 112–18.

126. See Webb 1987, 152–53, as well as Amit 1999, 98, 261–62. Olson suggests that Gideon, having rejected the offer of kingship, "constructs the ephod as a mechanical device for divine oracles so that he will not need to take responsibility for guiding the affairs of the nation" (1998, 809). Endris (2008, 178) argues that the ephod was dedicated to Baal, not Yahweh, because the text states that Israel "prostituted" themselves to it and that it became a "snare" to them. Both the verb זנה, "prostitute," and the noun מוֹקֵשׁ, "snare," are used elsewhere in Judges (cf. 2:17 and 2:3, respectively) of worshiping other gods. Certainly the ephod was treated as an idol by Gideon, his family, and Israel, but it is not certain if it was associated with Baal. The statement in 8:33 may suggest that Israel returned to Baal worship *following* Gideon's death, but the verb שׁוב could be translated "continued" there (see below).

127. Gunn 1987, 114; McCann 2002, 70; Olson 1998, 809; Wong 2007a, 543–44.

now, like Moses' brother Aaron, he had naïvely and unwisely led Israel astray.[128]

Epilogue: Trouble Brewing (8:28–32)

The conclusion to the story both satisfies and disturbs. On the positive side, verse 28 tells us that Midian was subdued (cf. 3:30; 4:23) and that a period of peace (forty years in duration, cf. 3:11; 5:31) followed Gideon's victory. The statement that Midian "did not raise its head again" (v. 28, literal translation) is humorous when seen in the light of 7:25, where we are informed that the Midianite chieftains Oreb and Zeeb literally lost their heads at the hands of the Ephraimites. Verse 29 refers to Gideon by the name Jerubbaal, reminding us that Gideon was the Lord's instrument in his ongoing attack on Baalism. Gideon's return home as a conquering hero, his living to a "very old age," and his burial in his father's tomb (v. 32) highlight the weakness of the Canaanite god, who never did contend with the one who desecrated his altar, at least during Gideon's lifetime (but see chapter 9).

However, the conclusion also has its disturbing side. Verses 30–31 inform us that Gideon, despite officially turning down an

---

128. Amit argues that 8:27b is probably a "late addition" and not part of the original story (2001, 28–30). She suggests that the editor responsible for it "was a zealot, who came across the mention of the ephod, was uncertain as to its meaning, assumed it was a pagan image, and condemned Gideon." According to Amit, "this condemnation does not accord with the rest of the story." It contradicts verse 35, which speaks of "all the good" Gideon had done for Israel. However, the statement in verse 35 need not mean that *everything* Gideon did was good. Rather than being an assessment of Gideon's career based on all of his actions (the narrative as a whole gives this), verse 35 looks at matters from Israel's perspective (the focus is Israel's response to Gideon). They showed ingratitude to one who had delivered them from oppression. The phrase "all the good" refers to Gideon's military leadership and the ensuing peace that it brought to the land (v. 28). This is also Jotham's focus when he accuses the people of Shechem of repaying his father's good with evil (9:16–17). Bluedorn suggests that the positive presentation of Gideon in verse 35 sets up a contrast with Abimelech, who plays such an important role in chapter nine (2001, 201). He writes: "Hence it seems once more that the narrator deliberately refers to Gideon as a man of good deeds and perhaps even as a good leader at the outset of the Abimelech narrative to establish a contrast to Abimelech's bad leadership and his and the Baalists' evil deeds as recorded in that narrative. Gideon is characterized as anti-Baalist . . . ."

offer of kingship, nevertheless acted like a king.[129] He married many wives, had a concubine on the side,[130] and named the son he fathered through this concubine Abimelech, which means, "my father is king."[131] Furthermore, Gideon's kinglike accumulation of wives (like his accumulation of gold) was in direct violation of the Deuteronomic rules governing kingship (Deut. 17:17).

By the end of the story one senses that very little of spiritual significance had been accomplished. Israel had found relief from oppression, but the people did not recognize the Lord as their savior and king, the spirit of idolatry was alive and well, and a faulty view of kingship had taken root. What will happen if Gideon's sons decide to accept the people's offer and grasp hold of the royal model that their father rejected in word yet imitated in deed? The next section of the book answers that question for us.

MESSAGE AND APPLICATION

Thematic Emphases
Israel's rebellion again brings a foreign invader into the land. God continues to show mercy to his suffering covenant people. However, the

---

129. For a full treatment of this theme, see Block, *Judges, Ruth*, 299–304.
130. The precise status of a concubine (פִּילֶגֶשׁ) is not entirely clear. For recent discussions, see K. Engelken, "פִּילֶגֶשׁ," in *TDOT*, 11:550–51, and Schneider 2000, 128–30. On the one hand, concubines are distinguished from wives, but, on the other hand, in Judges 19–20 the Levite's concubine seems to have the status of at least a secondary or lesser wife. The Levite is called her husband (19:3; 20:4) and his relationship to the woman's father is that of father-in-law to son-in-law (19:4–5). In Judges 9:18 Jotham calls Abimelech's mother a "female slave" (אָמָה). The term אָמָה can be used of a secondary wife (cf. Gen. 21:10–13 with 16:3).
131. We cannot be entirely certain that this name reflects Gideon's view of his own status, but, as Block observes, "the self-service we have witnessed in Gideon's behavior makes it difficult to resist the conclusion that the name Abimelech reflects the human father's perception of his own status in Israel" (1999, 304). As Block points out, no matter what Gideon's intention may have been, it is clear that his son Abimelech seeks to make the implications of his name a reality. Assis is more confident about Gideon's motives: "The fact that he calls his son 'Abimelech' (= my father is king) shows that Gideon sees him as the son of a king and one way or the other he sees himself as king" (2005a, 113). See as well Wong, who points out that mothers typically name a son in the Hebrew Bible (2006a, 169–71). It is relatively rare for a father to do so.

prophetic accusation that precedes the story of divine deliverance reminds us that there is an underlying moral issue that must sooner or later be addressed. One gets the distinct impression that a time may come when God will not respond to Israel's cry (cf. 10:6–16).

Israel's persistence in sin produces a leadership void. When the Lord calls Gideon, the latter takes Barak's hesitancy to new depths. Yet the Lord patiently develops faith in the heart of his chosen servant. He first convinces Gideon of his identity as Yahweh, the God of Moses who desires to help his people. He then requires Gideon to demonstrate his loyalty in the face of severe opposition from his own countrymen. When Gideon later regresses and questions Yahweh's ability, the Lord patiently accommodates himself to Gideon's tests and offers him further confirmation of his promises. Gideon's development reaches its final stage when he is forced to place his full trust in the Lord's power. Gideon finally steps to the forefront as God's warrior and once again the Lord demonstrates that he can accomplish great things through even the most unlikely instruments. In fact, the darker the backdrop, the more vivid and remarkable a divine display one can expect. Against overwhelming odds, God delivers in a way that should leave no doubt about his sovereignty and right to Israel's sole worship.

Nevertheless, when God's people become entrenched in paganism, spiritual blindness can keep them from responding properly to his self-revelation. When Gideon destroys Baal's altar with no repercussions from the Canaanite god, his own countrymen are ready to kill him. When the Lord puts the enemy to flight, some are concerned only with individual honor, while others refuse to recognize God's hand at work. When the battle is finally over, the people attribute the victory to Gideon, not to the Lord, and quickly turn what could have been a tangible reminder of God's presence into an idol.

Even Gideon dilutes his success by giving priority to personal vendettas, making unwise leadership decisions, and allowing success to go to his head. As noted above, his concern for personal vengeance could send a false message and provide a misleading example. Despite knowing the people's and his own family's penchant for idols, he makes an ephod which quickly becomes an object of worship. By marrying many wives and giving one of his sons a royal name, he acts as if he is a king. While giving lip-service to the Lord's kingship, his actions contradict his words and set the stage for new depths of civil strife and chaos. By the end of Gideon's career, we can see some obvious cracks in the foundation of Israelite society. In the story to follow these cracks widen and threaten to bring the whole structure tumbling to the ground.

Exegetical idea: *Israel's persistence in sin created a climate of spiritual blindness and insensitivity, but God once more showed compassion to his people and accomplished a great victory through hesitant Gideon. The Lord patiently developed Gideon's faith. However, God's purposes were compromised when Gideon lost focus of his mission, made naïve and unwise leadership decisions, and allowed his lifestyle to contradict a theologically correct message.*

Theological Principles

The book's recurring theological principles are present in this literary unit: (a) Sin brings divine discipline and makes God's people vulnerable to their enemies. (b) God confronts his people's sin, but he also intervenes on their behalf when they cry out to him. (c) God utilizes human instruments, sometimes in unexpected ways, to accomplish his purposes.

God's kingship, a prominent theme in Judges 4–5, is apparent here as well. Through Gideon, the Lord attacks Baal's altar. Gideon's father challenges Baal to defend his interests, but Baal remains silent throughout the story as Gideon wins a series of victories against overwhelming odds.

Theological idea: *Persistence in sin creates a climate of spiritual blindness and insensitivity, but during such times God continues to show compassion to his people and can accomplish great things through unlikely instruments. In such dark times the Lord can patiently develop hesitant people into heroes of faith. However, God's purposes can be compromised when his chosen instruments lose focus of their mission, make naïve and unwise leadership decisions, and allow their lifestyle to contradict a theologically correct message.*

Homiletical Trajectories

(1) God is the compassionate king. Even when his people continue to drift from him, he remains active in their experience and seeks to win back their allegiance. He shows up their false gods for what they really are and demonstrates his ability to protect his people. He is superior to all other so-called gods and is deserving of his people's undivided loyalty and worship.

(2) When the covenant community becomes assimilated to the surrounding pagan culture, it can develop an irrational attachment to false gods and fail to see God's hand at work. When God acts in the world, the covenant community is apt to bestow honor on God's human

instruments rather than the One who is truly worthy of their praise. As the community becomes more pagan in its outlook, it loses its sense of unity and common purpose. Petty self-interest and pride can threaten to tear the community apart.

(3) Even in less than ideal conditions God chooses to accomplish his purposes through human instruments. Potential leaders raised in a pagan environment are susceptible to cynicism and likely to possess deficient faith.[132] Yet God is willing to work with such people and mold them into effective instruments through whom he accomplishes great things. However, such individuals may be prone to put personal honor first and to make unwise decisions that foster paganism and threaten the community's unity (see the sequel to Gideon's story in 8:33–10:5).

Preaching idea: *Even in times of spiritual darkness, we should realize that God is accomplishing his purposes, often through hesitant, weak people. We should be willing to carry out God's purposes, trusting him to develop our faith in the process. When we achieve God-given success, however, we must be careful not to undermine God's work by losing focus, making unwise decisions, or acting inconsistently with our profession of faith.*

Because the Gideon story is so lengthy, the exegetical, theological, and preaching ideas encompass several related themes and may seem overly long and unwieldy. It is certainly valid and probably desirable to preach a sermon over the entire story, highlighting its interrelated themes. But prior to or after doing so, one may also focus on each of the homiletical trajectories and develop a *preaching idea* for each one:

(1) *In spiritually dark times, when God may seem absent, we must remember that our compassionate and incomparable God remains concerned for his covenant community and committed to accomplishing his purposes through us.*

(2) *In spiritually dark times, when God may seem absent, we must make sure that we do not (a) grow cynical about his concern for his people, (b)*

---

132. It should be apparent to the reader, in light of our comments above on 6:36–40, that we interpret Gideon's test with the fleece in a negative light as a symptom of his weak faith. If this is the case, his fleece test should not be viewed as a model or pattern for us to following in seeking to discern the will of God!

embrace the gods of our culture, (c) glorify God's human instruments, rather than God himself, or (d) succumb to self-interest and pride.

(3) In spiritually dark times, when God's people tend to be cynical and lack faith, we should be willing to carry out God's purposes, trusting him to develop our faith. When we achieve God-given success, however, we must be careful not to undermine God's work by losing focus of our purpose, making unwise decisions, or acting inconsistently with our profession of faith.

Since Gideon's journey of faith is so prominent in the plot line of the story, one could develop a sermon series around it, with God's patience being an important subtheme. This series is rooted in the third trajectory above.[133] The *preaching ideas* for such a series might be formulated as follows:

(1) Faith awakened: In spiritually dark times, when God may appear to be absent, cynicism can become a barrier to faith, but we must be willing to carry out God's purposes, because he assures us of his enabling presence (6:1–24).

(2) Faith challenged: God may challenge us to demonstrate our faith by asking us to risk opposition (6:25–32).

---

133. The hermeneutical basis for developing this sermon series is as follows: (1) The plot line of the story focuses on the development and compromise of Gideon's faith. (2) This plot line is related to the book's third major theme, focusing on leadership (cf. the third homiletical trajectory). (3) In the corporate thinking of ancient Israel, the nation's leaders represent the nation and, as such, become a model (whether positive, negative, or somewhere in between) for the nation. The model of Gideon's faith, first developed and then compromised, becomes instructive for the nation. (4) For the nation to succeed as a corporate entity, it must, like Gideon, carry out God's purposes in faith, and, unlike Gideon, not compromise its faith and success in the afterglow of victory. But a corporate entity is comprised of both leaders and other individuals, who must in faith obey God and avoid the pitfalls of Gideon. Once we think in terms of the Gideon story being a model for the covenant community, its leaders, and its other individual members, we can justify holding up Gideon as an example (both positive and negative) for the new covenant community (the Church), its leaders, and its other individual members.

(3) *Faith needing assurance: When our faith wavers and we prefer to walk by sight, God may patiently give us added assurance, but he will still require that we trust in him alone for success (6:33–7:14).*

(4) *Faith blossoming: When in faith we carry out God's purposes, we experience his enabling presence in remarkable ways (7:15–23).*

(5) *Faith unappreciated: When in faith we experience God-given success, we may face opposition and criticism from those who fail to appreciate what God has accomplished (7:24–8:3).*

(6) *Faith compromised: When in faith we achieve God-given success, we must be careful not to undermine God's work by losing focus of our purpose, making unwise decisions, or acting inconsistently with our profession of faith (8:4–32).*

JUDGES 8:33–10:5

Seeds of Discord Bring a Harvest of Chaos

TRANSLATION AND NARRATIVE STRUCTURE

33a After Gideon died, (*introductory-backgrounding*)

33b the Israelites continued to prostitute themselves to the Baals. (*initiatory*)

33c They made Baal-Berith their god. (*focusing*)[1]

34 **The Israelites did not remain true to the Lord their God, who had delivered them from all the enemies who lived around them**. (*complementary*)[2]

35 **They did not treat the family of Jerubbaal (that is, Gideon) fairly in return for all the good he had done for Israel**. (*summarizing-proleptic*)[3]

---

1. The *wayyiqtol* clause in verse 33c has a focusing function after the general statement that precedes. It specifies which deity the Israelites worshiped.

2. Verse 34 (which begins with *waw* + a negated perfect) has a complementary function. It gives the flip side (ingratitude) of the idolatry described in verse 33.

3. Verse 35 (which begins with *waw* + a negated perfect) is a proleptic summary. The following episode will tell exactly how the Israelites were unfair to Jerubbaal's descendants.

9:1a Now Abimelech son of Jerubbaal went to Shechem to see his mother's relatives. (*initiatory*)

1b He said to them and to his mother's entire extended family, (*sequential*)

2 *"Tell all the leaders of Shechem this, 'Why would you want to have seventy men, all Jerubbaal's sons, ruling over you, when you can have just one ruler? Recall that I am your own flesh and blood.'"*

3a His mother's relatives spoke on his behalf to all the leaders of Shechem (*sequential*).

3b The leaders were drawn to Abimelech, for they said, (*sequential*)

3c *"He is our close relative."*

4a They paid him seventy silver shekels out of the temple of Baal-Berith. (*sequential*)

4b Abimelech used the silver to hire some lawless, dangerous men (*sequential*)

4c and they became his followers. (*consequential*)

5a He went to his father's home in Ophrah (*sequential*)

5b and murdered on one stone his half-brothers, the seventy legitimate sons of Jerubbaal. (*sequential*)

5c Only Jotham, Jerubbaal's youngest son, escaped, because he hid. (*supplemental-qualifying*)[4]

6a All the leaders of Shechem and Beth Millo assembled (*resumptive-sequential*)

6b and then went (*sequential*)

6c and made Abimelech king by the oak tree near the pillar in Shechem. (*sequential*)

7a When Jotham heard the news, (*initiatory*)

7b he went (*sequential*)

7c and stood on the top of Mount Gerizim. (*sequential*)

7d He spoke loudly to the people below: (*sequential*)

7e *"Listen to me, leaders of Shechem, so that God may listen to you!*

8 *The trees were determined to go out and choose for themselves a king. They said to the olive tree, 'Be our king!'*

9 *But the olive tree said to them, 'I am not going to stop producing my oil, which is used to honor gods and men, just to sway above the other trees!'*

10 *So the trees said to the fig tree, 'You come and be our king!'*

---

4. The *wayyiqtol* clause in verse 5c qualifies the preceding statement by noting an exception to the action just described. It also prepares us for the next episode in the story (see v. 7).

11　*But the fig tree said to them, 'I am not going to stop producing my sweet figs, my excellent fruit, just to sway above the other trees!'*

12　*So the trees said to the grapevine, 'You come and be our king!'*

13　*But the grapevine said to them, 'I am not going to stop producing my wine, which makes gods and men so happy, just to sway above the other trees!'*

14　*So all the trees said to the thornbush, 'You come and be our king!'*

15　*The thornbush said to the trees, 'If you really want to choose me as your king, then come along, find safety under my branches! Otherwise may fire blaze from the thornbush and consume the cedars of Lebanon!'*

16　*Now, if you have shown loyalty and integrity when you made Abimelech king, if you have done right to Jerubbaal and his family, if you have properly repaid him—*

17　*My father fought for you, he risked his life, and delivered you from Midian's power.*

18　*But you have attacked my father's family today. You murdered his seventy legitimate sons on one stone and made Abimelech, the son of his female slave, king over the leaders of Shechem, just because he is your close relative.*

19　*So if you have shown loyalty and integrity to Jerubbaal and his family today, then may Abimelech bring you happiness and may you bring him happiness!*

20　*But if not, may fire blaze from Abimelech and consume the leaders of Shechem and Beth Millo! May fire also blaze from the leaders of Shechem and Beth Millo and consume Abimelech!"*

21a　Jotham ran away to Beer (*sequential*)

21b　and lived there to escape from Abimelech his half-brother. (*sequential*)

22　Abimelech commanded Israel for three years. (*initiatory*)

23a　Then God sent a spirit to stir up hostility between Abimelech and the leaders of Shechem, (*sequential*)

23b　and the leaders of Shechem became disloyal to Abimelech. (*consequential*)

24　He did this so the violent deaths of Jerubbaal's seventy sons might be avenged and Abimelech, their half-brother who murdered them, might have to pay for their spilled blood, along with the leaders of Shechem who helped him murder them.[5]

25a The leaders of Shechem, in rebellion against him, put bandits in the hills, (*focusing*)[6]

25b and they robbed everyone who traveled by on the road. (*sequential*)

25c But Abimelech found out about it. (*sequential*)

26a Gaal son of Ebed came through Shechem with his brothers. (*initiatory*)[7]

26b The leaders of Shechem placed their trust in him. (*sequential*)

27a They went out to the field, (*sequential*)

27b harvested their grapes, (*sequential*)

27c squeezed out the juice, (*sequential*)

27d and celebrated. (*sequential*)

27e They came to the temple of their god (*sequential*)

27f and ate, (*sequential*)

27g drank, (*complementary*)

27h and cursed Abimelech. (*complementary*)

28a Gaal son of Ebed said, (*focusing*)

28b *"Who is Abimelech and who is Shechem, that we should serve him? Is he not the son of Jerubbaal, and is not Zebul the deputy he appointed? Serve the sons of Hamor, the father of Shechem! But why should we serve Abimelech?*

29a *If only these men were under my command, I would get rid of Abimelech!"*

29b He challenged Abimelech, (*sequential*)

29c *"Muster your army and come out for battle!"*

30a When Zebul, the city commissioner, heard the words of Gaal son of Ebed, (*sequential*)

30b he was furious. (*sequential*)

---

5. The words "he did this" are supplied in the translation. In the Hebrew text this entire verse is actually subordinate (note the infinitive construct at the beginning of the verse and the absence of a main clause) to "God sent" (v. 23).

6. The *wayyiqtol* clause at the beginning of verse 25 picks up on the statement in verse 23b and gives a more detailed description of how the Shechemites were disloyal to Abimelech.

7. The introduction of a new character (Gaal) in verse 26a marks a new scene in the episode, even though the *wayyiqtol* clause formally links the statement to what precedes.

31a So he sent messengers to Abimelech, who was in Arumah, reporting, (*consequential*)

31b *"Beware! Gaal son of Ebed and his brothers are coming to Shechem and inciting the city to rebel against you.*

32 *Now, come up at night with your men and set an ambush in the field outside the city.*

33 *In the morning at sunrise quickly attack the city. When he and his men come out to fight you, do to him what you can."*

34a So Abimelech and all his men came up at night (*consequential*)

34b and set an ambush outside Shechem, dividing into four units. (*sequential*)

35a When Gaal son of Ebed came out (*sequential*)

35b and stood at the entrance to the city's gate, (*sequential*)

35c Abimelech and his men got up from their hiding places. (*sequential*)

36a Gaal saw the men (*sequential*)

36b and said to Zebul, (*sequential*)

36c *"Look, men are coming down from the tops of the hills."*

36d But Zebul said to him, (*sequential*)

36e *"You are seeing the shadows on the hills—it just looks like men."*

37a Gaal again said, (*sequential*)

37b *"Look, men are coming down from the very center of the land. A unit is coming by way of the oak tree of the diviners."*

38a Zebul said to him, (*sequential*)

38b *"Where now are your bragging words, 'Who is Abimelech that we should serve him?' Are these not the men you insulted? Go out now and fight them!"*

39a So Gaal led the leaders of Shechem out (*sequential*)

39b and fought Abimelech. (*sequential*)

40a Abimelech chased him (*sequential*)

40b and Gaal ran from him. (*sequential*)

40c Many Shechemites fell wounded at the opening of the gate. (*sequential*)

41a Abimelech went back to Arumah; (*sequential*)

41b Zebul drove Gaal and his brothers out of Shechem. (*sequential*)

42a The next day (*introductory-backgrounding*)[8]

42b the people came out to the field. (*initiatory*)

---

8. Verse 42a, which begins with וַיְהִי, marks a transition to a new scene. Gaal has left and a new day dawns.

42c When Abimelech heard they would do this, (*flashback*)[9]
43a he took his army, (*sequential*)
43b divided them into three units (*sequential*)
43c and set an ambush in the field. (*sequential*)
43d He watched (*sequential*)
43e **and the people were coming out of the city.** (*dramatic*)[10]
43f So he attacked (*sequential*)
43g and struck them down. (*sequential*)
44a **Now Abimelech and his unit attacked** (*focusing*)[11]
44b and blocked the entrance to the city's gate, (*sequential*)
44c **while the remaining two units then attacked all the people in the field** (*complementary*)[12]
44d and struck them down. (*sequential*)
45a **Abimelech fought against the city all that day.** (*dramatic shift in focus*)[13]
45b He captured the city (*sequential*)
45c **and killed all the people in it.** (*complementary*)[14]
45d Then he leveled the city (*sequential*)
45e and spread salt over it. (*sequential*)

---

9. Verses 42c–43e cannot be in strict chronological sequence with verse 42b, because verse 43e describes the people leaving the city, something that is reported as fact in verse 42b. It is best then to see verse 42c as a brief flashback with verses 42d–43d describing what happened prior to the people coming out (vv. 42b, 43e). We must assume that Abimelech heard of the Shechemites' plans to go out to the field sometime before the dawning of the new day and set up his ambush during the night or in the early morning hours.

10. The disjunctive clause in verse 43e (introduced by וְהִנֵּה, "look") is dramatic, inviting us to view the scene through Abimelech's eyes (note "he saw" just prior to this).

11. Verse 44a, introduced by a disjunctive clause, begins a more detailed account of the first phase of the battle described in verse 43fg. See Moore 1895, 263.

12. The disjunctive clause in verse 44c complements verse 44a. It describes what the other two military units were doing while Abimelech and his unit blocked the city gate. One could even view the juxtaposed disjunctive clauses (vv. 44a and 44c) as synchronic.

13. The disjunctive clause in verse 45a shifts the focus back to Abimelech (cf. v. 44ab) after the description of what the two units were doing (v. 44cd).

14. The disjunctive clause in verse 45c describes an action complementary to the capture of the city, mentioned in the preceding clause.

46a   When all the leaders of the Tower of Shechem heard the news, (*sequential*)

46b   they went to the stronghold of the temple of El-Berith. (*sequential*)

47   Abimelech heard that all the leaders of the Tower of Shechem were in one place. (*sequential*)

48a   He and all his men went up on Mount Zalmon. (*sequential*)

48b   He took an ax in his hand (*sequential*)

48c   and cut off a tree branch. (*sequential*)

48d   He put it on his shoulder (*sequential*)

48e   and said to his men, (*sequential*)

48f   *"Quickly do what you have just seen me do!"*

49a   So each of his men also cut off a branch (*consequential*)

49b   and followed Abimelech. (*sequential*)

49c   They put the branches against the stronghold (*sequential*)

49d   and set fire to it. (*sequential*)

49e   All the people of the Tower of Shechem died—about a thousand men and women. (*sequential*)

50a   Abimelech moved on to Thebez; (*initiatory*)

50b   he besieged (*sequential*)

50c   and captured it. (*sequential*)

51a   **Now there was a fortified tower in the center of the city**, (*introductory*)[15]

51b   so all the men and women, as well as the city's leaders, ran into it (*initiatory*)

51c   and locked the entrance behind them. (*sequential*)

51d   Then they went up to the roof of the tower. (*sequential*)

52a   Abimelech came (*sequential*)

52b   and attacked the tower. (*sequential*)

52c   When he approached the entrance of the tower to set it on fire, (*sequential*)

53a   a woman threw an upper millstone down on his head (*sequential*)

53b   and shattered his skull. (*sequential*)

54a   So he quickly called to the young man who carried his weapons, (*consequential*)

---

15. The disjunctive clause in verse 51a, in addition to giving supplemental information, signals movement within the scene from the city proper to the fortified tower.

54b *"Draw your sword and kill me,*[16] *so they will not say, 'A woman killed him.'"*

54c So the young man stabbed him (*consequential*)

54d and he died. (*consequential*)

55a When the Israelites saw that Abimelech was dead, (*sequential*)

55b they went home. (*consequential*)

56 God repaid Abimelech for the evil he did to his father by murdering his seventy half-brothers. (*summarizing*)

57a **God also repaid the men of Shechem for their evil deeds.** (*complementary*)[17]

57b The curse spoken by Jotham son of Jerubbaal fell on them. (*concluding*)

10:1a After Abimelech's death, Tola son of Puah, grandson of Dodo, from the tribe of Issachar, rose up to deliver Israel. (*initiatory*)[18]

1b **He lived in Shamir in the Ephraimite hill country.** (*supplementary*)

2a He led Israel for twenty-three years, (*sequential*)

2b then died (*sequential*)

2c and was buried in Shamir. (*sequential*)

3a Jair the Gileadite rose up after him; (*initiatory*)[19]

3b he led Israel for twenty-two years. (*sequential*)

4a He had thirty sons who rode on thirty donkeys. (*supplemental-descriptive*)[20]

4b **They possessed thirty cities.** (*supplemental*)

4c **To this day these towns, which are in the land of Gilead, are called Havvoth Jair.** (*supplemental*)

---

16. As in 1 Samuel 17:51, the *polel* of מות, "die," is used of the actual death blow, in contrast to the initial blow that leaves the victim fatally wounded. For the latter Judges 9:54 uses הרג, "kill" (referring to the fatal consequences of the blow on the head with the stone), while 1 Samuel 17:50 uses the *hiphil* of מות (for the fatal consequences of the blow on the head with a slingstone).

17. The disjunctive clause in verse 57a is complementary to verse 56. Both Abimelech (v. 56) and the Shechemites (v. 57a) got what they deserved.

18. The phrase "after Abimelech's death" (v. 1) and the introduction of a new character signal the transition to the epilogue.

19. The phrase "after him" (v. 3a) and the introduction of a new character signal the transition to the second report within the epilogue.

20. Verse 4 contains three supplemental clauses. The first is a descriptive statement introduced with וַיְהִי (see 8:26), the second is disjunctive, while the third begins with a prepositional phrase.

5a   Jair died (*resumptive-sequential*)
5b   and was buried in Kamon. (*sequential*)

OUTLINE

Prologue: Israel Persists in Baal Worship (8:33–35)
Main Event: The Rise and Fall of "King" Abimelech (9:1–57)
    Abimelech murders his brothers (9:1–6)
    Jotham appeals for justice (9:7–21)
    A curse cracks a skull (9:22–57)
Epilogue: Stability Restored (10:1–5)

LITERARY STRUCTURE

The story of Abimelech is the sequel to the Gideon narrative. Together with 6:1–8:32, it forms one large literary unit parallel to 3:7–11, 12–31; 4:1–5:31; 10:6–12:15; and 13:1–16:31. In 8:33, the sequel is introduced by וַיְהִי, a reference to Israel's persistence in Baal worship. The prologue sets the stage for the main narrative by giving the background for Abimelech's rise to power, while the epilogue records how a semblance of stability was restored to the land following his death, but not without negative repercussions.

The main narrative has three episodes. A reference to Abimelech marks the transition from the prologue to the first episode. Verses 1–6 tell how Abimelech formed an alliance with the citizens of Shechem and murdered his brothers. References to Abimelech and Shechem appear in verses 1 and 6, as does the verb הלך, "go," forming an inclusio for the unit. Verses 7–21 record Jotham's parable. References to Jotham's movements bracket the unit. In both the introduction and conclusion to his speech he addresses Shechem's nobles (בַּעֲלֵי שְׁכֶם, vv. 7b, 20). Abimelech again becomes the focus of the narrative in verse 22, which introduces the third episode. This long account begins and ends with statements about the Lord's intervention (vv. 23–24, 56–57). The main portion of the episode (vv. 25–55) tells how the Lord providentially brought about Abimelech's demise and Shechem's destruction. This section is divided into three scenes. The first deals with Gaal's rebellion (vv. 26–41). After Gaal's departure (v. 41), a second scene begins with וַיְהִי (v. 42a) and the dawning of a new day. With Abimelech's movement from Shechem to Thebez (v. 50), a new scene begins, though it is not formally introduced.

EXPOSITION

Prologue: Israel Persists in Baal-Worship (8:33–35)

Following Gideon's death, Israel returned to (or continued in?) Baal worship. More specifically, they worshiped Baal-Berith (literally, "Baal of the covenant"), a local manifestation of the Canaanite storm god.[21] Perhaps the name suggests that Israel's covenantal allegiance had shifted (Bluedorn 2001, 198–99). In so doing they "did not remain true to" (literally, "they did not remember") the Lord (see Deut. 8:18), who had delivered them from the various enemies that surrounded them. The passage refers to the earlier accounts in the book. The Lord delivered Israel from northern foes (Aram-Naharaim and Hazor), eastern peoples (Moab and Ammon), westerners (Philistines), southerners (Amalek), and the Midianites (who lived east and south of Israel).

Israel's ingratitude toward the Lord was mirrored in their inappropriate treatment of Gideon's sons, whom the people murdered. The name *Jerubbaal* appears in verse 35 and nine times in chapter 9, whereas the name *Gideon* is completely absent. Perhaps this choice of names serves to highlight the irony and absurdity of Israel's actions. Gideon's experience demonstrated the Lord's power and Baal's weakness. Gideon delivered Israel from terrible oppression through the Lord's power. He also desecrated Baal's altar at Ophrah and then carried a name with him through most of his adult life that was a challenge and an affront to the Canaanite deity. Baal's failure to contend with Gideon was evidence of his weakness. Nevertheless, Israel rejected the Lord and his chosen servant Gideon in exchange for Baal, proving once again that sin is truly irrational!

Main Event: The Rise and Fall of "King" Abimelech (9:1–57)

Abimelech murders his brothers (9:1–6). The situation described in 8:30–31 had all the potential for a severe power struggle. Gideon, despite turning down the people's offer of kingship, acted like a king by

---

21. See M. J. Mulder, "בַּעַל," in *TDOT*, 2:194. Some have suggested that Baal-Berith was the witness or guardian of a covenant between Shechem and other city-states, while others understand Baal-Berith as a party to a covenant with his worshipers. Clements concludes that the title "points more towards a divine covenant between the local Baal and certain citizens of Shechem than to a covenant in which Baal acted as the guardian of a local political compact" (1968, 21–32, especially p. 31). For further discussion see our comments below on El-Berith (Judg. 9:46).

marrying many wives and fathering seventy sons.[22] When he also fathered a son by a Shechemite concubine, he brought into the world a potentially jealous and dangerous rival for his seventy sons. By naming this son *Abimelech* ("my father is king"), Gideon revealed his own hidden aspirations and left the son with a false and potentially self-destructive legacy.[23]

When Abimelech grew up, he took his name seriously and decided to make its implications a reality. Appealing to the fact that he was a blood relative (through his mother) of the Shechemites, he proposed that it would be more efficient for one man, rather than seventy men, to rule over Shechem.[24] Of course, the argument is absurd. Abimelech appealed to ties of blood and brotherhood as he plotted the death of his brothers (Boogaart 1985, 55, note 8). Impressed by his appeal to their close blood ties, the Shechemites declared their allegiance to Abimelech by giving him seventy pieces of silver (corresponding to the number of Abimelech's half-brothers) from the temple reserves of their god Baal-Berith. Abimelech took the money and hired a group of "lawless, dangerous men" as his royal guard.[25] He then went to Ophrah and

---

22. Younger suggests that Gideon must have had between fourteen and thirty wives (2002, 209, note 84). The number seventy is probably nonliteral and symbolic. See Block, who suggests the number is "idealized" and draws parallels to biblical references to seventy sons (Gen. 46:27; 2 Kings 10:1–7), sons/grandsons (Judg. 12:14), elders (Exod. 24:1), and kings (Judg. 1:7) (1999, 303). He also lists extrabiblical parallels in the Panammu inscription and in the Ugaritic myths, where El's consort Athirat (= Asherah) has seventy sons. (For the text, see Gibson 1978, 63.) Genesis 10 lists seventy nations, over which the sons of God (= the Lord's heavenly assembly) rule (Deut. 32:8, DSS and LXX). This implies that the assembly, like the Ugaritic pantheon, numbers seventy. The figure has to be at least an approximate number in 9:5, for if Abimelech killed all seventy of his half-brothers, how do we explain the presence of Jotham following the execution? See as well Fensham 1977, 113–15, and Parker 1997, 84–85.

23. Van Midden goes so far as to see the naming of Abimelech as Gideon's way of appointing his successor (1999, 66–67). Fokkelman writes: "The boundless ambition of Abimelech, whose name ominously enough means 'my father is king,' exposes the desire which was smoldering in Gideon's subconscious, and is its enlargement and fulfillment" (1999, 130).

24. The implication is that Gideon's sons had assumed some type of leadership position over Shechem, or at least were threatening to do so. See Schneider 2000, 136.

25. The Hebrew text describes these men as רֵיקִים וּפֹחֲזִים, literally, "empty and reckless." "Empty" is used elsewhere of a group of mercenaries/bandits (Judg. 11:3), a kind of person who would indecently expose himself (2 Sam.

slaughtered his half-brothers on one stone.[26] Jotham, the youngest, escaped and went into hiding. Meanwhile Abimelech returned to Shechem, where the nobles of the city crowned him king. The seeds planted by Gideon had taken root. Israel (cf. v. 22) now had as its king a murderer who was financed from the treasury of a pagan god and was supported by a gang of thugs. The whole scenario is Canaanite to the core. Of all the characters who have appeared thus far in the pages of Judges, Abimelech most resembles the Canaanite king Adoni-Bezek, who had mutilated and humiliated seventy rival kings (cf. 1:7a). Abimelech went even farther, murdering his seventy brothers.

6:20), and men who supported a coup against a king (2 Chron. 13:7). פחז, "be reckless," and its derivatives are used elsewhere of turbulent water (Gen. 49:4) and prophets who abused their office (Jer. 23:32; Zeph. 3:4). Such mercenary groups appear elsewhere in Israel's early history. Judges 11 tells how Jephthah gathered to himself "lawless men" whom he organized into a small army, presumably to rob and plunder (v. 3). They possessed such military power that the Gileadites, when threatened by the Ammonites, bargained for their services (vv. 4–11). David's activities as a refugee provide a parallel as well. 1 Samuel 22:2 states that "all those who were in trouble or owed someone money or were discontented" (a total of about four hundred men) gathered to David at Adullam. They hired themselves out to Achish of Gath, who gave them Ziklag as a base of operations (1 Sam. 27:6). From there they conducted marauding raids into nearby areas (1 Sam. 27:8–11). Rezon son of Eliada, who rebelled against Hadadezer of Zobah in the time of Solomon, gathered a band of rebels around him and actually occupied and controlled Damascus (1 Kings 11:23–25). These groups resemble the *habiru*, mercenaries mentioned in the Amarna letters who disturbed Canaan in the early fourteenth century B.C. The *habiru* were organized in small groups, probably consisting of 50–100 men. See Greenberg 1955, 75–76. For a sociological analysis of the groups called "empty men" in Judges–Samuel, see Mobley 2005, 36–38.

26. Mobley suggests this "was probably a stone butchering table where blood and other fluids could be drained from carcasses" (2005, 151). He explains: "Presumably, Abimelech does not want the blood of his brothers to fall to the ground, where it would 'cry out,' arousing a response" from an avenging God (cf. Gen. 4:10). He adds: "Working in this realm of taboo and custom, Abimelech captures and disposes of the blood, as if it were possible to avoid the consequences of his crime through ritual." For other examples of the primitive belief that shed blood polluted the ground, see Frazer 1975, 36–37.

But God was watching, and he would repay Abimelech, just as he did Adoni-Bezek (cf. 1:7b).[27]

There is tragic irony in this account of Abimelech's attack against his brothers. Though Gideon was dead and gone, it appears at this point that Baal finally did contend with the one who had torn down his altar. After all, Abimelech's murderous attack on Gideon's family was financed from a Baal temple. Baal had seemingly struck down Gideon's seventy sons, ironically through the instrumentality of another of Gideon's sons. This may explain in part why the name *Jerubbaal* is used exclusively in chapter nine when reference is made to Gideon.

The fact that this enthronement occurred in Shechem is also tragically ironic, for it was in Shechem, where Joseph's bones were eventually buried (Josh. 24:32), that Joshua led Israel in a covenant renewal ceremony and set up a stone under a terebinth tree (אֵלָה) as a perpetual reminder of what had occurred there (see Josh. 24:26.) Abimelech's enthronement took place beside an oak tree (אֵלוֹן) and a pagan pillar (reading הַמַּצֵּבָה in v. 6b). Many years before Jacob had buried the family's idols in Shechem under a terebinth tree (אֵלָה) (see Gen. 35:4). A town that was traditionally associated with renewed loyalty to the Lord had now become the site of an enthronement that represented a blatant rejection of God's authority (Davis 1990, 122, note 2).

The ethnic makeup of the Shechemites is not entirely clear.[28] The prologue states that the Israelites began worshiping Baal-Berith and provides a proleptic summary statement of what will transpire in chapter nine. Thus it seems to view the people of Shechem as Israelite. However, Gaal's appeal to the Shechemites in 9:28 suggests that they were descendants of Hamor, ancestor of the Canaanite ruler Shechem who once lived in the city (see Genesis 34).[29] Perhaps the population was both Israelite and Canaanite; in fact it likely contained a racially mixed element (see 3:5–6). Gaal's rhetoric, while probably not genealogically precise, stressed the city's Canaanite roots, epitomized by

---

27. On the parallels between Abimelech and Adoni-Bezek, see Wong 2006a, 204–06.
28. See Schneider 2000, 135, for a helpful discussion of the issue.
29. Moore recognizes the tension, but offers no resolution (1895, 236). He states: "The author of 8:33 evidently assumes that the people of Shechem were Israelites, and generalizes the local worship of Baal-berith into a defection of Israel as a whole. Nothing is clearer, however, in ch. 9 than that the population of Shechem was Canaanite; the insurrection fomented by Gaal is a rising of the native inhabitants against the rule of the half-Israelite Abimelech."

its very name. When Israelites intermix with the native population, bloodlines get obscured and competing claims to rulership can clash!

Jotham appeals for justice (9:7–21). When the news of Abimelech's enthronement reached Jotham, he ascended Mt. Gerizim and proclaimed a message to the nobles of Shechem. The reference to the "top" of Mt. Gerizim must not be taken too literally. He probably took up a position on the lower slope of Gerizim where he could be heard by those below and from which he could make a quick escape.[30] The location is ironic, for it was on Mount Gerizim that half the tribes of Israel stood for the recital of the covenantal blessings following the invasion of the promised land (Josh. 8:33; cf. Deut. 11:29; 27:12) (Davis 1990, 122; Brown 2000, 208). The mountain was traditionally associated with the blessing of God; now it would be the site of a curse that would tear the nation's social fabric in pieces.

Jotham began his speech with a fable about the trees (which symbolize the people of Israel and of Shechem in particular) seeking a king.[31] One by one the most likely candidates for royalty—the olive tree, fig tree, and grapevine—turn down the offer. Their main concern is to yield their produce for the benefit of gods and men, not to sway in the wind (cf. Isa. 7:2) as king over the trees.[32] Finally the trees turn in desperation to the thornbush, which is clearly unqualified to rule over the trees. The thornbush tentatively agrees to the deal, but emphasizes that the

---

30. Moore 1895, 246; Burney 1970, 272; Boling 1975, 172. See as well Crisler 1976, 138–39.
31. Schöpflin prefers to call the fable a "metaphorical narrative." According to Schöpflin, it is similar to other such narratives in the prophetic literature and casts Jotham in the role of a prophet who opposes a sinful king (2004, 17–22).
32. While אֱלֹהִים most often refers to the one true God (see 9:7), it can also refer to the pagan gods. Verses 9 and 13 appear to reflect the polytheistic thinking of the culture at this time. Jotham depicts the pagan gods in a very anthropomorphic manner as being anointed with oil and as getting drunk on wine (cf. Isa. 24:7–9). In the Ugaritic myths the goddess Anat bathes in the oil of a peace offering (Gibson 1978, 48). Other myths depict the gods as drinking wine at feasts. See, for example, Gibson 1978, 48, 58. One text tells how the high god El hosted a banquet for the gods. While the moon god Yarih crawled around under the tables like a dog, the other gods drank wine until they were inebriated and the floor was covered with their excrement. See Margalith 1979–80, 65–120.

trees must take refuge in its shade.[33] The statement is absurd, for the thornbush is incapable of casting any significant shadow.[34] This offer of power has obviously gone to the thornbush's head, for it then warns that if the trees do not follow through on their offer, it will destroy even the grandest of them—the cedars of Lebanon—with fire.[35] The fable draws attention to Abimelech's arrogance, utter lack of qualifications, inability to provide genuine protection, thirst for power, and destructive potential.[36] It also highlights the stupidity of the Shechemites, who thought a thornbush (an inadequate ruler like Abimelech) could actually provide them with shade (security) (Hamilton 2001, 136).

Jotham confronted the Shechemites with their treatment of Jerubbaal's family. If they had dealt fairly with his father, they were certainly deserving of a blessing, but such a prospect was absurd because of their murderous deeds. Still maintaining a tone of objectivity, he then presented the alternative.[37] If they had not treated Jerubbaal fairly, Jotham prayed that Abimelech and the Shechemites would destroy one another. The language of the curse is very similar to the words spoken by the thornbush to the trees (v. 15). The implication is that the Shechemites, like Jotham's brothers, would be victimized

---

33. "Shade" (צֵל) is a metaphor in the Hebrew Bible and in ancient Near Eastern literature for a ruler's sovereign authority and protection. See Isaiah 30:2; Ezekiel 31:6, 12, 17 and for Akkadian literature *CAD*, 16:190–92, 242–43. For other pertinent references, see J. Schwab, "צֵל," *TDOT*, 12:379, note 78. This idiomatic use can be traced back to early times. In a Sumerian hymn Shulgi boasted, "his protecting shadow stretches out over the land." See Shulgi hymn B, line 355, in Castellino 1972, 66–67.

34. Tatu argues that the Hebrew term (אָטָד) refers to a thorny tree, not a mere bush (2006, 105–24). He contends that the *Zizyphusspina-Christi* is the most likely candidate. If this is the case, then the statement is not as exaggerated as we suggest.

35. As Moore points out, it was probably fairly common for brush fires to begin among thorns and then spread to fields and forests (1895, 249). See Exodus 22:6; Isaiah 9:18.

36. In its literary context the parable denounces Abimelech, not kingship in some abstract sense. For a helpful discussion of this issue, see Gerbrandt 1986, 129–34. See as well Assis, who concludes: "Jotham's fable is not a pro or anti-monarchic declaration. It is a censure of Abimelech's egocentric personality, his unsuitability for the office of king, and the egotistical motives of the citizens of Shechem in making him king" (2005a, 153).

37. On the structure of verses 16–20, see Ogden 1995, 304–06. As he points out, the first condition is really just a foil for the second. The structure mirrors the thornbush's proposal in verse 15.

by Abimelech's destructive capacity, which in the end would cause the power-hungry thornbush itself to go up in smoke.

A curse cracks a skull (9:22–57). Jotham fades from the scene, escaping to Beer, while Abimelech ruled for three years over Israel.[38] The reference to Israel is surprising, for up to this point the narrative has led us to believe this was simply a local affair involving Shechem and its environs. Perhaps all Israel came to recognize Abimelech as its leader, but the language may reflect the pan-Israelite idiom of the book (see the discussion of this in the introduction to the commentary). The notice is at first a bit alarming, for it suggests that Abimelech was growing more successful and that Jotham's curse may fall harmlessly to the ground.

But the narrator does not keep us in suspense very long. In verse 23 we see God directly intervening by sending a spirit to stir up hostility between Abimelech and Shechem.[39] Verse 24 then informs us that God's purpose in doing so was to avenge the shed blood of Jerubbaal's seventy sons. The name *Elohim* (God) is used here and in verses 56–57 because God appears in this chapter as the righteous, sovereign judge. The name *Yahweh* is hardly appropriate, for Israel had rejected him (cf. 8:34) and the loyalty (חֶסֶד) that was to characterize covenantal life had disappeared (cf. 8:35) (Webb 1987, 158; Polzin 1980, 174–76). This incident is just one of several in which God employs the services of an evil spirit to expedite judgment upon sinners (1 Sam. 16:14; 18:10; 19:10; 1 Chron. 21:1 [cf. 2 Sam. 24:1]). The expression "evil spirit" need not mean that the spirit was itself demonic or evil. The Hebrew term רָעָה can refer to moral evil, but it can also refer to disaster, harm, or calamity in a non-moral sense. If the word is given the latter sense here,

---

38. The verb שָׂרַר, "govern," a denominative from שַׂר, "prince," is used only here in Judges. According to Schneider, the word choice indicates that "the text questions the legitimacy of Abimelech's reign" (2000, 142–43). At the very least, it distinguishes him from other Israelite leaders described in the book. Assis suggests its use may be "designed to describe Abimelech's monarchy as working along the lines of monarchy in the Near Ancient East, which is regarded with disfavour in several biblical accounts" (2005a, 154).

39. Irony is apparent here, for in earlier episodes God sends his spirit to empower his chosen deliverers (see 3:10; 6:34). Here he must send an "evil spirit" (literal translation) to destroy a man who threatens the well-being of Israel. See Klein 1988, 70.

the expression may simply mean that the spirit was sent to bring harm and calamity upon the objects of God's anger.[40]

The spirit began his mission by inciting the Shechemites to rebel against Abimelech. The Shechemites decided to rob travelers and merchants as they passed by the city on the trade routes. In some way, probably financially, this harmed Abimelech, who eventually received a report of the Shechemites' rebellion.[41]

This is the second in a series of reports that God providentially used to bring about Shechem's demise. The report of Abimelech's enthronement (cf. וַיַּגִּדוּ, from נגד, "tell, report") prompted Jotham to pronounce a curse on Shechem (v. 7). Here another report (note וַיֻּגַּד, v. 25) informed Abimelech of Shechem's treacherous actions. Zebul sent messengers to Abimelech telling him of Gaal's attempted coup, prompting Abimelech to come to Shechem (v. 31). According to verse 42, the movements of the Shechemites were reported (וַיַּגִּדוּ) to Abimelech, causing him to press the attack against the city itself. Finally, in verse 47, Abimelech learned (cf. וַיֻּגַּד) that the nobles had fled to the city tower, so he set it on fire, killing a thousand Shechemites.

In bringing about the destruction of Shechem, God used two characters, Gaal son of Ebed and Zebul, the governor of the city. Gaal (whose name can be related by popular etymology to a verb גָּעַל, "abhor, loathe") is a loathsome individual who is every bit as repulsive as Abimelech.[42] His social status is uncertain, though he identified with the citizens of Shechem and its Canaanite ancestry (see v. 28). At any rate, the "leaders of Shechem" (v. 26; this is a better translation of בַּעֲלֵי שְׁכֶם than NIV's "citizens") looked to him for protection from Abimelech. It happened to be the time of the grape harvest. The

---

40. For a helpful discussion in this regard, see Block 1999, 323–24. Even if the spirit is viewed as demonic in nature, this need not impugn the goodness of God himself, for the Old Testament makes it clear that he will on occasion resort to deceit when judging sinners. In this case, the demonic spirit would be an instrument or agent of divine retribution. See Moore 1895, 253, as well as Chisholm 1998a.

41. On the possible socio-economic background of the conflict between Abimelech and the Shechemites, see Steinberg 1995, 60–61, and Heffelfinger 2009, 288–89.

42. His full name could be taken to mean "Loathsome, son of a slave." See Schneider 2000, 143. This may be a derogatory literary name, given by the narrator to reflect his character. See Gray 1986, 307. Assis suggests that the designation "son of Ebed" ("son of a servant"), when coupled with the earlier reference to Abimelech as the son of a concubine, shows that the Shechemites "always support people who are unworthy" (2005a, 159).

Shechemites gathered their grapes and then celebrated the harvest in the temple of their god (Baal-Berith?).[43] Emboldened by wine, they cursed Abimelech (v. 27).[44] Gaal challenged Abimelech's authority and boasted that he would "get rid of him" if only the Shechemites would support him militarily.[45] Gaal's appeal to closer kinship ties mirrors the argument Abimelech used to win Shechem's support (see vv. 1–3). Zebul (meaning "prince"), Abimelech's governor in Shechem, reported Gaal's words to Abimelech and advised him to launch a surprise attack against the city. Abimelech followed his advice, surprised Gaal and the Shechemites, routed them in battle, and drove them back into the city. Having played their role in the drama, Gaal and his clan were driven from the city by Abimelech's loyal deputy, Zebul.

The next day the people of Shechem, naïvely thinking that the conflict was over, went out to their fields (Younger 2002, 227).[46] Abimelech's honor was not yet vindicated, however. He divided his troops into three

---

43. The suffixed form of אֱלֹהִים, "god," is used in verse 27 as a so-called plural of respect. Though the plural of respect most often refers to Israel's God, it can on occasion refer to a foreign god. See, among other texts, Judges 11:24; 1 Samuel 5:7; 1 Kings 18:24. In a recent study of אֱלֹהִים Burnett argues that the plural form should be understood as a "concretized abstract plural, according to which the nominal plural form expresses an abstraction in reference to an individual or thing that holds a particular status named by the abstract category in question. Thus the plural of the noun 'god' occurs with the meaning 'deity'" (2001, 53). On the use of אֱלֹהִים as a concretized abstract plural for national patron deities, see Burnett, 65–66. He states: "In connection with the concept of the patron deity, 'ĕlōhîm designates the god who stands in special relationship to a particular individual, group, territory, or nation."

44. The use of the verb "cursed" (קלל) is striking, for God was already implementing Jotham's "curse" (see קִלֲלַת יוֹתָם, v. 57) against Abimelech. Ironically, the Shechemites' cursing of Abimelech epitomizes their rebellion, which is what lures Abimelech to Shechem and leads eventually to his demise, in fulfillment of Jotham's curse.

45. The meaning of Gaal's initial question in verse 28 is not entirely clear. Certainly it does not equate Abimelech with Shechem. It is likely that Shechem stands here for its citizens, many of whom were apparently descendants of Hamor. One may paraphrase: "Who is Abimelech (a halfbreed descendant of an Israelite father) and who are the Shechemites (Canaanite descendants of Hamor), that we (Canaanites) should serve him?" See our earlier comments on the ethnicity of Shechem and the rhetorical nature of Gaal's appeal.

46. Burney thinks they were coming out to resume their attacks on caravans (see v. 25) (1970, 285). Another possibility is that עַם refers here to the

companies (cf. 7:16) and launched an attack. Abimelech took one unit and blocked the city gate, isolating the Shechemites who were in the field. Meanwhile the remaining two units attacked the people in the field.[47] Abimelech invaded the city, killed its people, and spread salt on its fields.[48] This last action was probably symbolic and performed in conjunction with a curse of infertility (see Deut. 29:23; Jer. 17:6; Zeph. 2:9).[49]

Shechem's nobles retreated to the city stronghold, which is associated with the temple of El-Berith (literally, "God of the covenant").[50] Abimelech got some branches from nearby Mount Zalmon, boldly

---

Shechemite army, which may have come back out expecting to resume hostilities.

47. Verse 44a reads literally, "And Abimelech and the heads which were with him attacked and stood at the gate of the city." The plural "heads" (רָאשִׁים) is problematic here, for verse 43 says that Abimelech divided his force into three "heads" (i.e., units) and verse 44b says that two of these "heads" attacked the people in the field. For this reason it is better, following the Vulgate and some Greek witnesses, to read the singular רֹאשׁ, "head," in verse 44a. See Burney 1970, 285; and Moore 1895, 264. If one retains the plural, then verse 44 would have to be understood as follows: Initially Abimelech and his three units rushed to the gate and cut off the retreat of those who had gone out to the field. Two units then attacked the people in the field, while one unit remained guarding the gate.

48. In verse 45 "the city" probably refers to the lower city, which was distinct from the stronghold (see v. 46). See Burney 1970, 286; and Boling 1975, 180. Soggin prefers to see the Tower of Shechem as a "distinct outpost" of Shechem, "administratively autonomous" with its own temple (1981, 192–93).

49. See Burney 1970, 285, as well as Gevirtz 1963, 52–62. In the Sefire treaty a curse upon Arpad states: "May Hadad sow in them salt and weeds, and may it not be mentioned again." See Fitzmyer 1967, 15, 53. In 639 B.C. the Assyrian king Ashurbanipal scattered salt over the territory of Elam following his victory there. See Roux 1966, 303.

50. On the structure of this citadel see Yadin 1963, 261. Wood observes that "the temple of Baal-Berith" (v. 4), "Beth Millo" (vv. 6, 20), "the temple of their god" (v. 27), "the tower of Shechem" (vv. 46–47, 49), and "the temple of El-Berith" (v. 46) "all appear to be the same structure at Shechem" (2003, 277). Following the lead of others, he identifies the temple found at Shechem with the one mentioned in Judges 9 and associates the evidence for a destruction of the city in the Iron Age I period with Abimelech's attack on the city (pp. 278–80). Miller observes that a rebellion occurred at Shechem in 1125 B.C., probably led by a subchief at Arumah (2005, 119–20).

charged up to the wall of the stronghold, piled the wood against it, and set it on fire, killing about a thousand people.[51] The thornbush had consumed the cedars (cf. v. 15) and the first part of Jotham's curse had been realized (v. 20).

The reference to the temple of El-Berith is puzzling, for earlier we read of a temple to Baal-Berith in Shechem (see v. 4). In Canaanite mythology El and Baal were distinct deities. El was the high god who ruled over the divine assembly and imparted authority to the storm god Baal. If this distinction is maintained here, then the city apparently contained a temple for each god and swore allegiance to both.[52] This would mark another ironic twist in the conflict between Gideon (that is, Jerubbaal) and Baal. As noted earlier, Baal seemed to strike back at his antagonist Jerubbaal through Abimelech (see our comments on vv. 1–6). But now this same Abimelech destroys the very Baal temple that initially financed his takeover (this is implied in v. 45) and even goes one step farther. Not only was Baal's temple burned to the ground, but El's temple did not even escape Abimelech's fury. In his providential control of events, the Lord turned Baal's attack on Jerubbaal into a humiliating defeat for both Baal and El by using the same instrument of destruction employed by Baal!

Day prefers not to distinguish Baal and El in Judges 9; he regards the two names as variants, with *El* perhaps being used in a generic sense ("god"). He points out that 8:33 associates this deity with the Baals and that the wine festival mentioned in 9:27 is most naturally seen as a celebration for Baal, not El. In this case, the temples mentioned in verses 4 and 46 are one and the same and verses 46–49 describe a direct attack upon Baal's Shechemite shrine, the very temple that had financed his rise to power (Day 2000, 69–70).[53]

---

51. McCann suggests that Gideon's destruction of the tower (מִגְדָּל) of Penuel (8:9, 17) foreshadowed Abimelech's attacks on the strongholds (מִגְדָּל) at Shechem and Thebez (9:46, 48–49, 51–52) (2002, 74).

52. In the Ugaritic legend of Aqhat, references to the "house of Baal" (*bt b'l*) and the "house of El" (*bt 'il*) appear in poetic parallelism. See Gibson 1978, 104 (*CTA* 17 i 32–33; ii 21–22); *COS* 1:344–45. Ugarit contained separate temples for Baal and Dagon. See Kitchen 2003, 403.

53. Bluedorn is not certain if אֵל is a proper noun or a common noun here (2001, 254–55). If it is a common noun, Bluedorn suggests "the narrator now focuses more generally on the Canaanite deities as *gods*" (emphasis his). If a proper noun, "the reference builds on the implication that Baal has failed to protect the Shechemites (cf. 9:42–45), so that they recognize that Baal is less powerful than YHWH and seek refuge in El's temple." He adds, "In all cases, the reference to אֵל בְּרִית [in 9:46] prepares for the

Lewis argues just the opposite. He contends that El Berith is the Canaanite deity El and that the phrase Baal-Berith (8:33; 9:4) should be understood as a title for El, meaning "lord of the covenant." He reasons that it is unlikely that the city would have had more than one patron deity and that El is a more likely candidate for this position than Baal (1996, 401–23; cf. Block 1999, 305–06). If this is indeed the case, then the polemical element is more indirect and subtle than if Baal were in view. Gideon attacked Baal, one of El's sons.[54] Gideon's father then gave him the name Jerubbaal, a challenge to Baal to defend his interests. In retaliation Baal's father El attacked the sons of Jerubbaal, ironically through the instrumentality of Abimelech, another of Jerubbaal's sons. But then, in an ironic twist, this same instrument of destruction, energized by the spirit sent by Israel's God, attacked and destroyed El's temple.[55]

Abimelech was not satisfied with the destruction of Shechem. He attacked the town of Thebez, probably because it had allied with

---

demonstration that the Canaanite gods are like Baal powerless gods who are unable to keep their covenant and protect their temple and their worshipers from being killed in the fire, which—if אל refers to Baal—has even been kindled by his own representative (9.49)."

54. In the Ugaritic texts both Dagan (= biblical Dagon) and El are identified as Baal's father. This does not mean that these two deities should be equated, nor does it indicate there were competing traditions. The most likely explanation is that Dagan was considered Baal's literal father, but that El can also be called Baal's father because he was the patriarch of the gods who stood at the head of the divine genealogical tree. He may have been viewed as Baal's grandfather. For a discussion of Baal's parentage that develops the arguments and conclusion presented here, see Day 2000, 89–90. For a thorough analysis of various views on the relationship between El and Dagan, see Feliu 2003, 300–02. Feliu concludes: "It is clear that there were two 'Semitic' pantheons in Syria." One is headed by Dagan "in inner Syria" and the other by El "on the coast." He argues that the "two traditions merged in Ugarit," where Dagan is the father of Baal. He points out that "Dagan had a cult and presence in the liturgy of Ugarit, which shows that both gods were considered equal but not assimilated, that is to say, they kept their own status and character even though their profile and position in their respective pantheons were practically identical. Dagan, however, was always perceived as a god foreign to Ugarit, as shown by the two references to Dagan of Tuttul in the text corpus of the coastal metropolis" (p. 302).

55. If one follows this line of argumentation, then the text polemicizes against El as well as Baal. Smith contends, "there are no biblical polemics against El" (2002, 33). Perhaps that statement needs to be qualified.

Shechem, and Abimelech needed to reestablish his authority in the region.[56] The people of Thebez fled into a tower and climbed up to the roof. Abimelech exhibited the same bold recklessness he did at Shechem as he stormed the tower to set it on fire.[57] However, his past successes had bred vulnerability and this time his daring was his undoing. An unidentified woman threw a millstone down from the tower and cracked open Abimelech's skull.[58] The text emphasizes her singularity (v. 53, אֶחָת, "one") and the verb "threw" suggests a heroic act of strength comparable to that of a warrior (Janzen 1987, 35, 37, note 6).[59] The irony of this should not be missed. Abimelech murdered his

---

56. It is possible, of course, that bloodthirsty Abimelech's appetite for violence was not yet satisfied. McCann states: "For no apparent reason, other than that violence tends to become a way of life, Abimelech proceeds to attempt to do at Thebez what he had done at Shechem" (2002, 74). Miller states, "there is no logical reason for Abimelech to follow the destruction of Shechem with an expedition . . . against a low-level site in the Tirzah system" (2005, 120). Tirzah and Shechem were two of five distinct "zones of occupation" or "polities" in the north-central highlands during this time (2005, 29–30, 99–100). However, Heffelfinger, utilizing Miller's chieftainship model, offers two possible reasons for Abimelech's assault on Thebez (2009, 289). She suggests that "the sub-chiefs at Thebez" may "have begun to revolt, perhaps because of the success of the Shechemites' raids in destroying Abimelech's role as distributor of luxury goods," or that Abimelech may have been "attempting to conquer new territory in order to increase his access to luxury goods with which to engage in external trade and thus ensure the future loyalty of his other sub-chiefs after suppressing the Shechemite rebellion."

57. For reliefs showing such assaults upon a city's citadel see Yadin 1963, 346–47.

58. According to Herr and Boyd, the upper millstone was "a loaf-shaped hand grinder" that "could be grasped easily in one hand" and was probably 0.5 to 1.5 feet in length. It was used in conjunction with "a saddle quern . . . a concave stone that was about 1.5 to 3 feet long and 0.5 to 1.5 feet wide." Such stones were typically made from black basalt (2002, 37, cf. King and Stager 2001, 95).

59. Janzen and many others envision the woman dropping, rather than throwing the millstone, but apparently they assume that a larger type of stone was used. Based on archaeological evidence, Herr and Boyd argue that the type of millstone used by the woman would have weighed four to nine pounds and could have been easily thrown (2002, 62). Moore (*Judges*, 268) states that the upper millstone probably weighed about 25–30 pounds, but the type of stone he envisioned the woman using did not become popular until much later (1895, 268; cf. Herr and Boyd 2002, 37).

brothers on one stone (v 5; אֶבֶן אֶחָת); now he meets his demise when a solitary woman hurls a single stone on his head (Boogaart 1985, 51).

Vain and arrogant to the very end, Abimelech quickly instructed his servant to run him through with a sword so that people would not remember him as one who was killed in battle by a woman. The text informs us that "he died," but there is no record of his being buried. This omission contrasts with the obituaries that appear elsewhere in this literary unit (i.e., 6:1–10:5; cf. 8:32; 10:2, 5).[60] The description of Sisera's death (cf. 4:21) provides the closest stylistic parallel to the account of Abimelech's death. In both cases וַיָּמָת, "and he died," appears in a consequential clause after a verb describing a violent action (cf. וַתִּתְקַע . . . וַתִּצְנַח, literally, "and she drove . . . and it fastened," in 4:21, and וַיִּדְקְרֵהוּ, literally, "and he stabbed him," in 9:54).

A comparison of this account with Sisera's death is instructive. In the earlier account a woman (Jael) delivered the land from a *foreign* oppressor; here a woman delivers the land again, once more, ironically, by a fatal blow to the head with an unconventional weapon (cf. 5:26 with 9:53). However, this time the oppressor is *Israelite*. Gooding remarks: "Things have seriously deteriorated when the bondage from which Israel has to be delivered in this fashion is no longer bondage to some foreign power but a bondage to one of Israel's own number who, instead of being a deliverer of Israel, has installed himself as a tyrant, and is maintaining his tyranny by ruthless destruction" (1982, 74*–75*). The quality of Israelite leadership had steadily regressed as the brave warrior Othniel was replaced by hesitant Barak and unwise and timid Gideon, who in turn gave way to the "anti-judge" Abimelech, a power hungry and bloodthirsty initiator of civil discord.[61] The changing roles of the women are symptomatic of this decline. Unlike Acsah, who inspired worthy and brave deeds, women were forced to assume the role of warrior, first to deliver the nation from a foreign oppressor (Sisera) and then from a power hungry countryman (Abimelech).

This portion of the narrative ends where it began (cf. vv. 23–24) with a theological commentary on the events recorded in the chapter. By providentially bringing about Abimelech's death and Shechem's destruction, God was repaying them for what they did to Gideon's sons.

---

60. See as well the obituaries that appear in later literary units (12:7, 10–11, 15; 16:31). The obituary of the paradigmatic leader Othniel does not contain a reference to burial either, but in his case the reference to his death is preceded by a note that the land had rest (3:11; cf. 8:28, 32), another telling omission in the conclusion to the Abimelech account.

61. On Abimelech as an "anti-judge," see Assis 2005a, 172.

In so doing he also demonstrated once more that he is the just king over the earth, who carries out justice on behalf of individuals who have been wronged and are powerless before their oppressors. When they appeal to his justice by uttering a curse, he will bring that curse to fulfillment.[62] The "curse" of Jotham refers here to the words of verse 20, which can be understood as an appeal to the divine Judge to annihilate Shechem and Abimelech for their unjust, murderous deeds.

In his curse Jotham called for Abimelech and the lords of Shechem to destroy each other by fire (v. 20). When Abimelech burned down the stronghold of Shechem, killing one thousand Shechemites who had taken refuge there, the first part of the curse was fulfilled in a literal manner. However, the second part of the curse, where the lords of Shechem destroy Abimelech by fire, did not seem to be fulfilled literally. However, there is more here than meets the eye. Thebez was probably an ally of Shechem and Hebrew אִשָּׁה, "woman" (v. 53) sounds like אֵשׁ, "fire" (Fokkelman 1992, 38–39). The אֵשׁ that destroyed Abimelech came in the form of an אִשָּׁה, showing again that God often works through unexpected means when carrying out his purposes. Though the fulfillment was not literal, the curse was realized in a way that brought added shame to the murderer Abimelech.

As Boogaart demonstrates, there are striking parallels between the accounts of Abimelech's and Gaal's conspiracies that contribute to the theme of poetic justice. He explains: "after the decisive intervention of God, the original evil of conspiracy returns to haunt Abimelech and the men of Shechem. Regarding Abimelech: just as Shechem had conspired with him against its rightful rulers, the house of Jerubbaal, so Shechem later conspired with Gaal against him; just as Abimelech had emphasized his close ties with the men of Shechem at the expense of the sons of Jerubbaal, so Gaal emphasized his close ties with Shechem at the expense of Abimelech. Regarding the men of Shechem: just as they had responded to Abimelech and had revolted against the house of Jerubbaal, a revolt which they carried to a successful conclusion, so they responded to Gaal and revolted against Abimelech. Their second revolt, however, proved to be their downfall, setting events in motion that brought about not only the death of Abimelech, but their own as well" (1985, 51).

Epilogue: Stability Restored (10:1–5)
The story of Abimelech is a fast-paced account filled with action and

---

62. On the other hand, God ignores and does not bring unjust or undeserved curses to pass. See Proverbs 26:2.

violence. It tells how chaos engulfed the nation as a power-hungry ruler sought to establish a Canaanite style of rule within the nation. By the end of the account, the reader needs relief, both literarily and emotionally. The epilogue provides this by giving a rather capsulized and pedestrian account of the careers of Abimelech's successors, Tola and Jair, and by indicating that some semblance of order was reestablished in Israel and Transjordan (Klein 1988, 83; Olson 1998, 820; Beem 1991, 150–51). The reference to Tola's delivering Israel reminds one of earlier judges (cf. 3:9, 15, 31; 6:14; 7:7; 8:22). The reference to Jair's numerous offspring suggests that God had bestowed his blessing on Israel's leader (McCann 2002, 76–77; Beem 1991, 152).

However, the epilogue also has its disturbing elements. The earlier formulaic conclusion, which mentioned the land having peace (3:11, 30; 5:31; 8:28), does not appear here or later.[63] Abimelech's quest for power marked a transition for Israel. Genuine peace was no longer a reality. The reference to Jair's thirty sons has a Gideon-like aura about it (cf. 8:30), for it suggests that Jair had multiple wives (Younger 2002, 239).[64] Furthermore these sons rode on donkeys (v. 4), giving them a princelike aura (cf. 2 Sam. 13:29; 16:2) that suggests a dynastic tendency and a consolidation of power that could prove detrimental to the Israelite social order (Younger 2002, 239; Nelson 2007, 355). It seems that Gideon, despite his rejection of kingship, had set a precedent for kinglike behavior that mirrored the pagan culture, not God's ideal (see Deut. 17:17). In Tola's delivering Israel we hear an echo of Gideon, the one who delivered his people, but in Jair's numerous children we hear a different echo of Gideon, the one who planted the seeds of discord.

---

63. As noted earlier, this does not mean that the sequence is chronological. The Jephthah and Samson accounts may actually overlap chronologically with earlier accounts (see the discussion of the book's chronological framework above, as well as Chisholm 2009a, and Chisholm 2010d). Furthermore, the epilogue appears to record events that occurred at the very beginning of the Judges period. It appears that the transition from the land having rest to the absence of rest and then to the chaos described in the epilogue has a rhetorical function.

64. The Hebrew term בָּנִים, "sons," could conceivably include grandsons or descendants in general, but 12:14, where "sons" (בָּנִים) and "grandsons" (בְּנֵי בָנִים, "sons of sons") are clearly distinguished, suggests that Jair's sons, not descendants in general, are in view in 10:4.

MESSAGE AND APPLICATION

Thematic Emphases

The story of Abimelech is a reminder of what can happen to God's people when they become ungrateful and their leaders act unwisely and inconsistently. Gideon declared the Lord's kingship, but sent a false signal to both the people and his son when he acted like a typical Canaanite king. Abimelech took his father's actions to new depths and exploited the people's faulty view of kingship and rejection of the Lord. Even when some semblance of peace was restored, Jair carried on Gideon's kinglike ways.

However, the Lord remains sovereign even during the worst of times. He preserved Jotham and brought his justified curse to pass. In the process he intervened supernaturally (by sending a spirit to stir up strife) and manipulated people and circumstances in order to accomplish his just purposes. Through a series of reports he drew Abimelech to Shechem and brought about the destruction of that sinful city. By giving Abimelech temporary success, the Lord placed him in a vulnerable position where his daring became his downfall. By using a woman armed with a millstone to kill Abimelech, the Lord once more showed he can accomplish his purposes through unlikely instruments. Following Abimelech's death, the Lord providentially restored some semblance of order to Israel through the judges Tola and Jair.

Exegetical idea: *When unwise and inconsistent Gideon planted the seeds of discord, chaos resulted as his son, the power-hungry megalomaniac Abimelech, tried to become Israel's king. He and the people who supported him brought conflict and violence to the covenant community, but God punished the perpetrators and restored a semblance of order to the land. Unfortunately, Gideon's bad example of acting in a kinglike manner was perpetuated by Jair.*

Theological Principles

Kingship in the hands of the wrong person is dangerous. The epilogue to Judges makes the point that a king could have prevented the moral chaos that engulfed Israel during the Judges period (cf. 17:6; 18:1; 21:25). But the account of Abimelech's aborted attempt to become king shows that not just any king would do. Israel needed a king like the one depicted in Deuteronomy 17:14–20, not a power-hungry tyrant.

The Lord is the real king of his people. In the ancient Near East, kings were responsible for promoting and maintaining justice in their realm, at least ideally (Weinfeld 1995). This chapter reveals Yahweh the just king in action as he intervenes supernaturally and providentially to vindicate his servant Gideon by bringing Jotham's curse to pass.

In the account of Abimelech the Lord once more demonstrates his superiority to the Canaanite god Baal. When Baal finally does strike at Jerubbaal, his effort blows up in his face, leaving the pagan temple(s) of Shechem in ruins.

Theological idea: *When unwise and inconsistent leaders plant the seeds of discord, chaos can be the result as power-hungry megalomaniacs move into the leadership void. Such leaders and the people who find them attractive can bring misery to God's people, but God is just and will punish those who abuse others and who spread strife through the covenant community. Even so, the negative example of an unwise leader often lives on in his successors.*

Homiletical Trajectories

The Abimelech story is actually part of one large literary unit (6:1–10:5); it is the sequel to Gideon's story. Since it describes events that occurred after Gideon's death, it may be treated separately for homiletical purposes. Nevertheless, one should recognize its relationship to what precedes. The story of Abimelech, as well as the brief notice about Jair, illustrate how unwise leadership decisions can have destructive long-range consequences for the covenant community.

(1) The Lord is the ultimate King of his people and will not allow power-hungry imposters or false gods to usurp his position. He faithfully fulfills his royal responsibility of dispensing justice. Acting both directly and providentially, he brings down those who commit murderous deeds and threaten to destroy the covenant community.

(2) When the covenant community becomes paganized, it looks to the wrong kind of people to lead it and ends up being torn by dissension.

(3) Power-hungry opportunists threaten to destroy the covenant community. They inevitably elevate themselves, rather than God. But God opposes such individuals and those who follow them (cf. 3 John 9–11).

Preaching idea: *When we embrace the attitude of the pagan culture in which we live, power-hungry opportunists sometimes seize leadership and spread conflict, but God opposes such people and will hold them accountable for their abusive, self-serving behavior.*

If we focus on the first trajectory, a *preaching idea* might be: *We can be confident that our just God, in response to the prayers of innocent victims, will punish those who abuse others and spread discord through the covenant community.* Another way of developing this idea would be as follows: *If your pagan attitudes and actions are threatening God's covenant community by promoting conflict, you had better watch out for "falling rocks"! If power-hungry pagans are causing chaos in your little corner of God's covenant community, appeal to and trust in our just and sovereign God for deliverance and vindication.*

If we focus on the second and third trajectories, a *preaching idea* might be: *We must remain faithful to God, for embracing pagan attitudes and turning to pagan practices and leaders is self-destructive and does severe harm to God's covenant community.*[65]

---

65. For an exposition of the Abimelech story, entitled "The Thornbush Who Wanted to Rule the Forest," see Chisholm 1998b, 248–55.

JUDGES 10:6–12:15
Triumph Turns to Tragedy

TRANSLATION AND NARRATIVE STRUCTURE

6a   The Israelites again did evil before the Lᴏʀᴅ. (*initiatory*)
6b   They worshiped the Baals and the Ashtar idols, as well as the gods of Syria, Sidon, Moab, the Ammonites, and the Philistines. (*focusing*)[1]
6c   They abandoned the Lᴏʀᴅ (*complementary*)[2]
6d   **and did not worship him**. (*complementary*)[3]
7a   So the Lᴏʀᴅ was furious with Israel (*consequential*)
7b   and turned them over to the Philistines and Ammonites. (*sequential*)

---

1. The *wayyiqtol* clause in verse 6b focuses on how specifically the Israelites did evil (v. 6a).
2. The *wayyiqtol* clause in verse 6c describes Israel's rebellion from a complementary angle. By doing evil and pursuing other gods (v. 6ab), Israel essentially abandoned the Lord.
3. Verse 6d, comprised of a negated perfect with objective suffix, complements the preceding statement. Abandoning the Lord and failing to worship (literally, "serve") him are two sides of the same coin.

8a   They ruthlessly oppressed[4] the Israelites that year. (*sequential*)

8b   **(For eighteen years they oppressed all the Israelites living east of the Jordan in Amorite country in Gilead).** (*parenthetical*)[5]

9a   Then the Ammonites crossed the Jordan to fight with Judah, Benjamin, and Ephraim. (*sequential*)

9b   Israel suffered greatly. (*consequential*)

10a So the Israelites cried out to the LORD, (*consequential*)

10b *"We have sinned against you. We abandoned our God and worshiped the Baals."*

11a The LORD said to the Israelites, (*sequential*)

11b *"Did I not deliver you from Egypt, the Amorites, the Ammonites, the Philistines,*

12   *the Sidonians, Amalek, and Midian when they oppressed you? You cried out to me, and I delivered you from their power.*

13   *But since you abandoned me and worshiped other gods, I will not deliver you again.*

14   *Go and cry out to the gods you have chosen! Let them deliver you from trouble!"*

15a But the Israelites said to the LORD, (*sequential*)

15b *"We have sinned. Do to us as you see fit, but deliver us today."*

16a They threw away the foreign gods they owned (*sequential*)

16b and worshiped the LORD. (*complementary*)[6]

16c Finally the LORD tired of seeing Israel suffer so much. (*sequential*)

17a The Ammonites assembled (*initiatory*)

17b and camped in Gilead; (*sequential*)

17c the Israelites gathered together (*complementary*)[7]

---

4. Two similar sounding *wayyiqtol* forms are joined here for emphasis. I have treated them as one in the translation and clause analysis. On the question of the subject of the verbs, see the discussion below.

5. The syntax of verse 8b is notoriously difficult. The translation assumes this is an asyndetic temporal clause with ellipsis of the verb (the words "they oppressed" are supplied). See fuller discussion in the commentary below.

6. The *wayyiqtol* clause in verse 16b complements the preceding statement. Throwing away idols and worshiping the Lord are two related aspects of Israel's spiritual renewal.

7. The description of the Israelites' action in 10:17c is not necessarily sequential to what precedes. If the troop movements were concurrent, which seems likely, it complements the description of the Ammonite deployment (v. 17ab).

17d and camped in Mizpah. (*sequential*)
18a The leaders of Gilead said to one another, (*sequential*)
18b *"Who is willing to lead the charge against the Ammonites? He
     will become the leader of all who live in Gilead!"*
11:1a Now Jephthah the Gileadite was a brave warrior.
     (*supplemental*)[8]
1b   **His mother was a prostitute,** (*supplemental*)[9]
1c   and Gilead was his father. (*complementary*)
2a   Gilead's wife also gave him sons. (*complementary*)
2b   When his wife's sons grew up, (*sequential*)
2c   they made Jephthah leave (*sequential*)
2d   and said to him, (*complementary*)
2e   *"You are not going to inherit any of our father's wealth, because
     you are another woman's son."*
3a   So Jephthah fled from his half-brothers (*consequential*)
3b   and lived in the land of Tob. (*sequential*)
3c   Lawless men joined Jephthah's gang (*sequential*)
3d   and traveled with him. (*sequential*)
4a   Some time after this, (*introductory-backgrounding*)[10]
4b   the Ammonites attacked Israel. (*initiatory / resumptive*)
5a   When the Ammonites attacked Israel, (*transitional-reiterative*)
5b   the leaders of Gilead asked Jephthah to come back from the land
     of Tob. (*sequential*)
6a   They said, (*focusing*)
6b   *"Come, be our commander, so we can fight the Ammonites."*

---

8. The disjunctive clause in 11:1a introduces a new character (Jephthah),
    who plays a prominent role in the narrative to follow.
9. The disjunctive clause in verse 1b provides supplemental information
    about this new character that is important to understanding the following
    narrative. The *wayyiqtol* clauses in verses 1c and 2a complement verse 1b
    by providing further background information essential to understanding
    the irony of what follows. On the chronological flashback involved in verse
    1c, see Buth 1994, 144.
10. In relation to verse 3, verse 4ab (introduced with וַיְהִי, which is followed by
    a temporal phrase and a *wayyiqtol* clause) appears to begin a new scene.
    But it also picks up where 10:17 left off and resumes the main narrative
    after the parenthesis about Jephthah. Verse 5a reiterates verse 4 as it
    makes the transition back into the narrative where 10:18 left off. After
    the introductory וַיְהִי, it contains a temporal clause that is circumstantial
    to the *wayyiqtol* clause in verse 5b. Putting 10:17–18 and 11:4–5 together,
    the chronological order appears to be: (a) 10:17 // 11:4 = 11:5a, (b) 10:18, (c)
    11:5b.

7a   Jephthah said to the leaders of Gilead, (*sequential*)

7b   *"But you hated me and made me leave my father's house. Why do you come to me now, when you are in trouble?"*

8a   The leaders of Gilead said to Jephthah, (*sequential*)

8b   *"That may be true, but now we pledge to you our loyalty. Come with us and fight the Ammonites. Then you will become the leader of all who live in Gilead."*

9a   Jephthah said to the leaders of Gilead, (*sequential*)

9b   *"Alright! If you take me back to fight the Ammonites and the* Lord *gives them to me, I will be your leader."*

10a   The leaders of Gilead said to Jephthah, (*sequential*)

10b   *"The* Lord *will judge any grievance you have against us, if we do not do as you say."*

11a   So Jephthah went with the leaders of Gilead. (*consequential*)

11b   The people made him their leader and commander. (*sequential*)

11c   Jephthah repeated the terms of the agreement before the Lord in Mizpah. (*sequential*)

12a   Jephthah sent messengers to the Ammonite king, saying, (*initiatory*)

12b   *"Why have you come against me to attack my land?"*

13a   The Ammonite king said to Jephthah's messengers, (*sequential*)

13b   *"Because Israel stole my land when they came up from Egypt— from the Arnon in the south to the Jabbok in the north, and as far west as the Jordan. Now return it peaceably!"*

14   Jephthah sent messengers back to the Ammonite king (*sequential*)

15a   and said to him, (*sequential*)

15b   *"This is what Jephthah says, 'Israel did not steal the land of Moab and the land of the Ammonites.*

16   *When they left Egypt, Israel traveled through the desert as far as the Red Sea and then came to Kadesh.*

17   *Israel sent messengers to the king of Edom, saying, "Please allow us to pass through your land." But the king of Edom denied the request. Israel sent the same request to the king of Moab, but he was unwilling to cooperate. So Israel stayed at Kadesh.*

18   *Then Israel went through the desert and bypassed the land of Edom and the land of Moab. They traveled east of the land of Moab and camped on the other side of the Arnon; they did not go through Moabite territory (the Arnon was Moab's border).*

19   *Israel sent messengers to Sihon, the Amorite king, king of
      Heshbon, and said to him, "Please allow us to pass through your
      land to our land."*

20   *But Sihon did not permit Israel to pass through his territory.*[11] *He
      assembled his whole army, camped in Jahaz, and fought with
      Israel.*

21   *The LORD God of Israel handed Sihon and his whole army over
      to Israel and they defeated them. Israel took all the land of the
      Amorites who lived in that land.*

22   *They took all the Amorite territory from the Arnon in the south to
      the Jabbok in the north, from the desert in the east to the Jordan
      in the west.*

23   *Since the LORD God of Israel has driven out the Amorites before
      his people, Israel, do you think you can just take it from them?*

24   *You have the right to take what Chemosh your god gives you, but
      we will take the land of all whom the LORD our God has driven
      out before us.*

25   *Are you really better than Balak son of Zippor, king of Moab? Did
      he dare to quarrel with Israel? Did he dare to fight with them?*

26   *Israel has been living in Heshbon and its nearby towns, in Aroer
      and its nearby towns, and in all the cities along the Arnon for
      three hundred years! Why did you not reclaim them during that
      time?*

27   *I have not done you wrong, but you are doing wrong by attacking
      me. May the LORD, the judge, judge this day between the
      Israelites and the Ammonites!"'*

28   **But the Ammonite king disregarded the message sent by
      Jephthah.** *(concluding-qualifying)*[12]

29a   The LORD's spirit empowered Jephthah. *(initiatory)*
29b   He passed through Gilead and Manasseh *(sequential)*
29c   and went to Mizpah in Gilead. *(sequential)*[13]

---

11. For a defense of the traditional Hebrew text here and of the translation
    "permit" for האמין, see Novik 2009, 577–83.

12. The negated clause in verse 28 is not merely sequential, because it marks
    a disruption of the dialogue pattern established in verses 12–15. It is best
    labeled concluding, since it terminates the diplomatic stage and signals
    a transition to the battle, and qualifying, since it makes the point that
    Jephthah's negotiations proved futile.

13. Jephthah seems to have been at Mizpah when he sent the messengers
    to the Ammonite king (cf. v. 11). Perhaps verse 29bc describes how he

29d **From Mizpah in Gilead he approached the Ammonites**.
(*concluding*)[14]

30a Jephthah made a vow to the LORD, (*flashback*)[15]

30b saying, (*focusing*)

30c *"If you really do hand the Ammonites over to me,*

31 *then whoever is the first to come through the doors of my house to meet me when I return safely from fighting the Ammonites——he will belong to the LORD and I will offer him up as a burnt sacrifice."*

32a Jephthah approached the Ammonites to fight with them, (*resumptive-reiterative*)

32b and the LORD handed them over to him. (*sequential*)

33a He completely annihilated them from Aroer all the way to Minnith—twenty cities in all, even as far as Abel Keramim! (*sequential*)

---

went through Gilead and Manasseh to recruit troops and then returned to Mizpah. See Block 1999, 365; and Burney 1970, 318–19. However, 10:17 gives the impression that the Israelite army was already assembled at Mizpah and simply needed an able leader. See Moore 1895, 298. Furthermore, it seems unlikely that Jephthah, having agreed to lead the army, would leave deployed battle lines to do further recruiting. However, apparently the two armies had been deployed for quite some time, at least long enough for the elders to seek out Jephthah and retrieve him from Tob. Perhaps Jephthah, thinking he needed more warriors, took a chance that conflict would not break out immediately.

14. The disjunctive clause in verse 29d appears to mark a transition to the actual battle account. This view of its function finds support in verse 32a, where the statement is repeated and followed by a reference to the battle proper. The repetition in verse 32a gives the impression that the narrative has been interrupted and the battle unnecessarily delayed by the negotiations described in verses 30–31. Dawson views the final clause of verse 29 as the conclusion to what he calls the "aperture section" of the battle episode (1994, 159). Whether one calls it introductory (to the battle proper) or concluding (to the prologue to the battle proper), it clearly marks a boundary within the scene.

15. The *wayyiqtol* clause in verse 30a appears to carry on the action within this scene, but the resumptive nature of verse 32a (cf. v. 29d) suggests this may not be an ordinary sequential account of events. Verses 30–31 can be viewed as a flashback embedded within the main narrative. Another option is that verses 29d and 32a describe Jephthah's approach as a two-stage process. In this case verse 30a is initiatory and verse 32a sequential.

33b The Ammonites were defeated by the Israelites. (*summarizing*)[16]

34a When Jephthah came home to Mizpah, (*initiatory*)
34b **there was his daughter coming out to meet him, dancing to the rhythm of tambourines.** (*dramatic*)[17]
34c **She was his only child;** (*supplemental*)[18]
34d **except for her he had no son or daughter.** (*complementary-emphatic*)[19]
35a When he saw her, (*transitional-sequential*)[20]
35b he ripped his clothes (*sequential*)
35c and said, (*sequential*)
35d "Oh no! My daughter! You have completely ruined me! You have brought me disaster! I made an oath to the LORD, and I cannot break it."
36a She said to him, (*sequential*)
36b "My father, since you made an oath to the LORD, do to me as you promised. After all, the LORD vindicated you before your enemies, the Ammonites."
37a She then said to her father, (*sequential*)
37b "Please grant me this one wish. For two months allow me to walk through the hills with my friends and mourn my virginity."
38a He said, (*sequential*)
38b "You may go."
38c He permitted her to leave for two months. (*sequential*)
38d She went with her friends (*sequential*)

---

16. The *wayyiqtol* clause in verse 33b summarizes the outcome of the battle and facilitates the transition to a new scene that takes place at Jephthah's home (v. 34).
17. The disjunctive clause in verse 34b (introduced with וְהִנֵּה, "and look") has a dramatic function. We see the scene unfold through an eyewitness. Dawson sees the appearance of Jephthah's daughter as the "peak event" in the episode (1994, 159). On the role of הִנֵּה here see Fuchs 2000, 181.
18. The disjunctive clause in verse 34c provides supplemental information that heightens the tension created by the appearance of Jephthah's daughter.
19. The asyndetic disjunctive clause in verse 34d essentially repeats the preceding clause. It heightens the tension to an almost unbearable degree by emphasizing that this is his only child.
20. The clause in verse 35a (introduced with וַיְהִי and a temporal clause) signals a transition within the scene (cf. 2:4a), as the focus shifts from Jephthah's daughter to Jephthah. The clause introduces an action that is sequential, but not as important as the action that follows (cf. 2:4a).

38e and mourned her virginity as she walked through the hills.
(*sequential*)

39a After two months (*introductory*)[21]

39b she returned to her father, (*initiatory*)

39c and he did to her as he had vowed. (*sequential*)

39d **She had never experienced intimate relations with a
man**. (*concluding*)[22]

39e This gave rise to a custom in Israel: (*supplemental or
consequential*)[23]

40 **Every year Israelite women commemorate the
daughter of Jephthah the Gileadite for four days**.
(*supplemental-specifying*)

12:1a The Ephraimites assembled (*initiatory-flashback*)[24]

1b and crossed over to Zaphon. (*sequential*)

1c They said to Jephthah, (*sequential*)

1d *"Why did you go and fight with the Ammonites without asking us
to go with you? We will burn your house down right over you."*

2a Jephthah said to them, (*sequential*)

2b *"My people and I were entangled in controversy with the
Ammonites. I asked for your help, but you did not deliver me
from their power.*

3 *When I saw that you were not going to help, I risked my life and
advanced against the Ammonites, and the LORD handed them
over to me. Why have you come up to fight with me today?"*

4a Jephthah assembled all the Gileadites (*sequential*)

4b and they fought with Ephraim. (*sequential*)

4c The Gileadites defeated Ephraim, because the Ephraimites had
insulted them, saying, *"You Gileadites are refugees in Ephraim,
living within Ephraim's and Manasseh's territory."* (*sequential*)

---

21. The וַיְהִי at the beginning of verse 39, which is followed by a temporal prepositional phrase, marks a transition to the culminating event of the scene.

22. The disjunctive clause in verse 39d gives somber and tragic closure to the
scene and episode.

23. The *wayyiqtol* clause in verse 39e, which can be viewed as a consequence
of what precedes, gives additional information that is then filled out in
verse 40.

24. It is likely that this episode occurred in the aftermath of the battle, before
the death of Jephthah's daughter. For this reason verse 1a, in addition
to initiating the new scene, may be viewed as a flashback. See Gunn and
Fewell 1993, 117.

5a   The Gileadites captured the fords of the Jordan River opposite
      Ephraim. (*sequential*)

5b   **Whenever an Ephraimite fugitive said**, *"Let me cross over,"*
      (*supplemental-characterizing*)[25]

5c   the Gileadites asked him, *"Are you an Ephraimite?"* (*sequential*)

5d   If he said, *"No,"* (*sequential*)

6a   then they said to him, *"Say 'Shibboleth.'"* (*sequential*)

6b   If he said, *"Sibboleth,"* (*sequential*)

6c   **and could not pronounce the word correctly,**
      (*complementary*)

6d   they grabbed him (*sequential*)

6e   and executed him right there at the fords of the Jordan.
      (*sequential*)

6f   On that day forty-two thousand Ephraimites[26] fell dead.
      (*summarizing*)[27]

7a   Jephthah led Israel for six years; (*concluding*)

7b   then he died (*sequential*)

7c   and was buried in his city in Gilead. (*sequential*)

---

25. The structure of verses 5b–6e requires special attention. The וַיְהִי, literally,
    "and it was," clause at the beginning of verse 5b introduces a supplemental
    section that gives a detailed account of what happened at the fords of the
    Jordan (v. 5a) and explains in part why the Ephraimite casualties were so
    high (v. 6f). The *waw* + non-consecutive perfect is an off-line construction
    that introduces a brief section outlining the procedural details of what
    happened at the fords. Note the use of the imperfect verbal form (func-
    tioning in a customary manner) in the following temporal clause (כִּי יֹאמְרוּ,
    literally, "when they would say"). After this the typical sequence of events
    at the fords is given with the use of *wayyiqtol* forms, though an imperfect
    appears in the negated, specifying clause in verse 6c.

26. This figure seems inordinately high. See the commentary above on 1:4. As
    noted there, it is difficult to accept such figures at face value. One possi-
    bility is that the Hebrew term אֶלֶף, traditionally understood as a numeral
    (a "thousand"), actually refers to a contingent of troops, at least in some
    contexts. Boling, taking this approach, translates the phrase "forty-two
    Ephraimite contingents" in verse 6 (1975, 211). Another option is that such
    large numbers are hyperbolic. See Fouts 1997, 377–88, and 2003, 283–99.

27. The *wayyiqtol* clause in verse 6f provides closure for the entire episode by
    summarizing the Ephraimite casualties (note "on that day"), including the
    total number of Ephraimites who fell in battle (v. 4) and at the fords (vv.
    5–6).

8   After him Ibzan of Bethlehem led Israel. (*initiatory*)[28]
9a   He had thirty sons. (*supplemental-descriptive*)[29]
9b   **He arranged for thirty of his daughters to be married outside his extended family,** (*supplemental*)
9c   **and he arranged for thirty young women to be brought from outside as wives for his sons.** (*supplemental-complementary*)
9d   He led Israel for seven years; (*reiterative-focusing*)[30]
10a then he died (*sequential*)
10b and was buried in Bethlehem. (*sequential*)
11   After him Elon the Zebulunite led Israel for ten years. (*initiatory*)
12a Then Elon the Zebulunite died (*sequential*)
12b and was buried in Aijalon in the land of Zebulun. (*sequential*)
13   After him Abdon son of Hillel the Pirathonite led Israel. (*initiatory*)
14a He had forty sons and thirty grandsons who rode on seventy donkeys. (*supplemental-descriptive*)[31]
14b He led Israel for eight years. (*reiterative-focusing*)[32]
15a Then Abdon son of Hillel the Pirathonite died (*sequential*)
15b and was buried in Pirathon in the land of Ephraim, in the hill country of the Amalekites. (*sequential*)

OUTLINE

Prologue: The Lord's Patience Runs Short (10:6–16)
  Israel sins (10:6)
  The Lord punishes (10:7–9)
  Israel cries out to the Lord (10:10)
  The Lord rejects Israel's cry (10:11–14)
  Israel gets desperate (10:15–16)

---

28. Within the epilogue, the phrase "after him" (vv. 8, 11, 13) and the introduction of a new character signal the transition from one report to another.
29. Verse 9 contains three supplemental clauses. The first (introduced with וַיְהִי) is a descriptive statement about Ibzan's sons, the second and third, which have a disjunctive structure and complement each other, elaborate on Ibzan's family situation.
30. The *wayyiqtol* clause in verse 9d is reiterative and gives the specific length of Ibzan's rule (see v. 8a).
31. Verse 14a (introduced by וַיְהִי) gives supplemental information about Abdon's family.
32. The *wayyiqtol* clause in verse 14b is reiterative and gives the specific length of Abdon's rule (see v. 13a).

Main Event: Bargaining and Killing (10:17–12:7)
  An outcast becomes a general (10:17–11:11)
  Jephthah gives a history lesson (11:12–28)
  A foolish vow spells death for a daughter (11:29–40)
  Celebration turns to civil war (12:1–7)
Epilogue: Order Restored (12:8–15)

LITERARY STRUCTURE

The stereotypical reference to Israel's apostasy ("the Israelites again did evil before the Lord") marks the beginning of this new section. The pattern of sin-punishment-painful cry appears again, but this time the Lord is reluctant to send relief, even though for the first time in the book the cry to the Lord is accompanied by an acknowledgement of sin. Only after Israel puts away their idols does the Lord relent. A lengthy account of Israel's deliverance follows, but it is marred by Jephthah's foolish vow and by a civil war.

The prologue (10:6–16) provides the background (the Ammonite oppression of Israel and of Gilead in particular) for the main event (Jephthah's war with Ammon). References to Israel serving other gods/the Lord bracket the unit (Webb 1987, 42). The first episode (10:17–11:11) in the story proper tells how Israel chose Jephthah to be its military leader. The unit begins and ends with references to Mizpah. The story line is interrupted by a flashback in 11:1–3 (note the introductory disjunctive clause) that provides details about Jephthah (Webb 1987, 42). The story resumes in 11:4, picking up where 10:18 left off. The second episode (11:12–28) records Jephthah's messages to the Ammonite king, the king's response, and Jephthah's counter-response. The third episode (11:29–40), which gives the account of the battle and its aftermath, consists of two scenes. The first (vv. 29–33) describes Jephthah's battle with the Ammonites (vv. 29, 32–33) and his vow to the Lord (vv. 30–31). The second scene (vv. 34–40), which is marked by a return to Mizpah after the battle, relates the tragic aftermath of Jephthah's vow.[33] A parenthetical etiological remark (v. 40) closes the scene. The final episode (12:1–6) tells of the civil war which followed Jephthah's victory and concludes with Jephthah's epitaph (v. 7) The epilogue consists of accounts of minor judges (vv. 8–15), slows the literary

---

33. Verses 34–39 display a chiastic structure: (A) narrated events (vv. 34–35a), (B) Jephthah speaks (v. 35b), (C) the daughter speaks (v. 36), (C') the daughter speaks (v. 37), (B') Jephthah speaks (v. 38a), (A') narrated events (vv. 38b–39). See Trible 1984, 98–99.

pace, and indicates that some semblance of order was reestablished after the turmoil surrounding Jephthah's career.

EXPOSITION

Prologue: The Lord's Patience Runs Short (10:6–16)

The preceding Gideon-Abimelech narrative cycle clearly illustrates Israel's obsession with Baal. Consequently it comes as no surprise to read here that Israel "worshiped the Baals and Ashtar idols." What is alarming is the report that they also worshiped the gods of Aram, Sidon, Moab, the Ammonites, and Philistines. Nothing like this was reported in the earlier cycles, though the introductory general summary of the period forewarned the reader of this development (cf. 2:12). Religious apostasy is never static; it tends to spiral downward and become increasingly pagan. Israel's unfaithfulness angered the Lord and prompted him to deliver the nation over to Philistine and Ammonite invaders, who applied pressure on Israel from the west and east, respectively (v. 8a). (The Ammonites, as one would expect, oppressed those Israelites living in Gilead east of the Jordan, and this oppression actually lasted for eighteen years [v. 8b]). In addition to subduing Transjordan, the Ammonites crossed the Jordan and invaded the territory of Judah, Benjamin, and Ephraim (v. 9).

The syntax of verse 8 is problematic, as well as its relationship to verse 7. The Hebrew text reads literally, "They shattered and crushed the Israelites in that year, eighteen years all the Israelites who were beyond the Jordan in the land of the Amorites who are in Gilead." As it stands, the text separates "in that year" from "eighteen years." (Note the disjunctive *athnaq.*) The phrase "in that year" most naturally refers back to the action described in verse 7. The rhetorical point of "in that year" would then be that foreign oppression was the immediate consequence of the Lord's anger.[34] In this case the text would seem to make a distinction between (a) a Philistine-Ammonite invasion in the year the Lord was angry and handed the Israelites over to these enemies and (b) an eighteen-year period of oppression (presumably Ammonite) centered in Transjordan. If so, one could assume that the Philistine oppression was relatively short-lived and not sustained,

---

34. When the phrase "in that year" appears elsewhere, it always refers to the time period of an event described immediately before (see Gen. 26:12; 47:17–18; Deut. 14:28; Josh. 5:12; Jer 28:1, 17; 2 Chron. 27:5).

since the Ammonites receive the narrator's focus from verse 8b on-ward.[35] To summarize, in this case we have the following chronological scenario: The Lord was angry with Israel and handed them over to the Philistines and Ammonites (v. 7), who that very same year oppressed Israel (v. 8a). Parenthetically, we are told that this oppression lasted in Gilead for eighteen years (v. 8b). Continuing the story line of verses 7–8a, the narrator informs us that the Ammonites crossed the Jordan and invaded tribal regions located there (v. 9), prompting the events recorded in verses 10–16. By verse 17, the scene has shifted to the eighteenth year mentioned in verse 8b, for Jephthah's great victory and subjugation of Ammon (11:32–33) brought an end to the oppression.

The two verbs used to describe the Ammonites' treatment of Israel sound the same in Hebrew (וַיִּרְעֲצוּ וַיְרֹצְצוּ, literally, "they shattered and crushed"). The repetition of sound and the movement from the basic (*qal*) verbal stem to the emphatic or repetitive (*poel*) stem emphasize the severity of Israel's defeat.[36]

Israel cried out to the Lord, acknowledging their sin and confessing

---

35. There is no verb in verse 8b, so to understand this as a clause one must assume an ellipsis here and supply the verb from the preceding clause (note that NIV supplies "they oppressed" here). If verse 8b is a clause (and not just appositional; see below), it is a rare asyndetic type where a temporal indicator of some kind provides parenthetical information that may function structurally to signal closure or a transition (cf. 6:24; 17:6; 21:25). In this case it would signal the transition in focus from a general oppression (note the references to Philistines and Israel) to a more localized situation in Transjordan.

    Since there is no verb in the second half of verse 8, one could argue that שְׁמֹנֶה עֶשְׂרֵה refers to "the eighteenth year." See Boling 1975, 191–92. The expression שְׁמֹנֶה עֶשְׂרֵה שָׁנָה can be taken as "eighteen years" (see Judg. 3:14; 2 Kings 24:8) or as "eighteenth year" (2 Kings 22:3; 23:23; 2 Chron. 35:19; Jer. 32:1). Elsewhere the latter is preceded by the preposition *bet*, but in Judges 10:8 this is unnecessary since the preposition appears with the preceding phrase, to which "eighteenth year" may be taken as appositional. Note also the absence of the preposition in the phrase "and (in) the thirteenth year" in Genesis 14:4b. In this case, "the eighteenth year" would have to be appositional to "in that year." But the context provides no point of reference.

36. The verb רעץ, "shatter," occurs only here and in Exodus 15:6, where it describes how the Lord's hand shattered the Egyptians. The verb רצץ, "crush," occurs frequently in the *qal* stem, but only rarely in the *piel* (see 2 Chron. 16:10; Job 20:19; Ps. 74:14) or *poel* (only here) stems. This suggests that the switch to the more emphatic repetitive form in the second verb is by design.

they had forsaken their God in favor of the Baals (v. 10).[37] This seems to be a significant advance, for earlier stories record no such confession. While they may have confessed their sins on these earlier occasions (see 1 Sam. 12:9–11 and our earlier discussion on Judg. 3:7), any reference to such confession was suppressed literarily. Consequently, the inclusion of a confession here grabs the reader's attention and sets the reader up for the surprising divine response recorded in verses 11–14.

The Lord's patience was running short. In the first three cycles he responded favorably to Israel's cry. In the Gideon cycle, he delayed deliverance and sent a prophet to confront the people with the root cause of their suffering (6:7–10). Here in 10:11–14 delay turns to outright refusal. He reminded Israel of all the times he had delivered them from foreign oppressors.[38] As if to imply that he could not take their confession seriously, he refused to rescue them this time. With a note of sarcasm he urged them to seek deliverance from the foreign gods they had chosen.

By reminding them of how he had delivered them from the numerous surrounding people groups, including the Ammonites, Philistines, and Sidonians, the Lord hinted at his superiority to the deities of these nations. Israel was worshiping these gods (v. 6), but in their confession of sin (v. 10) they mentioned only the Baals, who were distinct from these other deities (cf. v. 6). In his response the Lord mentions the "other gods" (v. 13) whom the people had "chosen" (v. 14), hinting at the inadequacy of their confession, which mentions only the Baals.

Israel refused to take "no" for an answer. They again confessed their sin and declared their willingness to submit to some other form of discipline, if only the Lord would deliver them from the present crisis. To demonstrate their sincerity, they put away the "foreign gods" (not just the Baals!) and served the Lord.

How did the Lord respond? The usual interpretation of verse 16b is that the Lord softened at this point (see, for example, Moore 1895,

---

37. The concept of corporate confession is at home in the second millennium B.C., as Kitchen demonstrates with parallels from ancient Ugarit and elsewhere (2003, 404–05).

38. Verse 11b appears to be textually corrupt. As it stands, the Hebrew text reads literally, "Is it not from Egypt and from the Amorite and from the sons of Ammon and from the Philistines?" A verb appears to be missing. Scholars sometimes insert הוֹשַׁעְתִּי אֶתְכֶם or הִצַּלְתִּי אֶתְכֶם, "(Did) I (not) deliver/rescue you . . .?" However, both of these verbs typically appear with מִיַּד, "from the hand of," not simply מִן, "from" (cf. v. 12b). See the discussions in Moore 1895, 281–82, and Burney 1970, 296.

281). According to this view, the term עָמָל (translated "misery" in NIV) is taken as a reference to Israel's suffering under the heavy hand of their oppressors (cf. vv. 8–9).[39] The Lord became exasperated over their condition and decided to intervene.[40]

Some scholars challenge this interpretation, arguing that the text instead describes how the Lord was exasperated with Israel's hypocritical efforts to win back his favor (Polzin 1980, 177–78; Block 1999, 348–49; and Younger 2002, 244–45). In dealing with עָמָל, Block starts with the basic sense of "hard work, effort," and then extends the meaning here to refer to "their confessional and sacrificial attempts to win divine favor" (1999, 349). This specific nuance is not attested elsewhere for the word. A more likely option, mentioned by Block, is that עָמָל has a moral/ethical nuance here, a meaning that is well-attested for the term elsewhere.[41] In this case, the nation's persistent evil, not the hypocrisy of their repentance, is in view (Janzen 2005, 347).

No matter how one understands verse 16, the text does stop short of saying, at least directly, that Israel's repentance prompted God to intervene. Perhaps this suggests, especially in light of verses 11–14, a continuing skepticism on God's part with regard to Israel's sincerity (Janzen 2005, 348). But it is possible, in light of subsequent developments, that Israel's repentance opened the door for God's compassion. Indeed in the following account, the Lord's spirit energizes Jephthah for battle (11:29) and the Lord gives the Ammonites into Jephthah's hand (11:32).

Verses 11–12 refer to past oppressions at the hands of several nations. The reference to Egypt looks back to the time prior to the Exodus. The book does not mention a deliverance from Amorite oppression *per se*. Since the term sometimes designates the inhabitants of Canaan, it could refer here to the Canaanite oppressors of Judges 4–5 (Burney 1970, 297). The Ammonites were allies of Eglon; the Amalekites aided

---

39. This nuance of meaning is well-attested elsewhere. See BDB, 765 (no. 1).

40. The Hebrew expression used to describe God's response (וַתִּקְצַר נַפְשׁוֹ, literally, "his spirit was short") is used elsewhere of impatience and emotional fatigue (see Num. 21:4; Judg. 16:16; Zech. 11:8). According to Fretheim, the use of this expression in Judges 10:16 depicts God as suffering with his people (1984, 129). Building on Fretheim's observation, McCann states that "God's quality of life is diminished" by his people's suffering (2002, 79).

41. See BDB, 765 (no. 2), which offers the gloss "trouble, mischief," for this usage of the word. It should be noted, however, that BDB lists our verse under their first category of meaning, which they gloss as "trouble" in the sense of "one's own suffering."

both Eglon and the Midianites. A Philistine oppression is alluded to in 3:31, but there are no references to a Sidonian oppression. As for Maon, some prefer to read "Midian" with the Old Greek (Burney 1970, 297–98). However, it is not readily apparent how the corruption would have occurred. *Maon* is clearly the more difficult reading and its presence, coupled with the absence of any reference to Midian earlier in the list, would have invited an editorial change (Moore 1895, 280; Boling 1975, 192–93). If one retains the reading of the Hebrew text, it is possible that the Meunites are in view, though they appear elsewhere only at a much later time in Israel's history (see 1 Chron. 4:41; 2 Chron. 20:1 [LXX]; 26:7).

Main Event: Bargaining and Killing (10:17–12:7)

An outcast becomes a general (10:17–11:11). In the eighteenth year of the Ammonite oppression in Transjordan (mentioned in 10:8b), the Ammonites assembled for war in Gilead. We are not told what prompted the Ammonite military action; they already exercised control over the Israelites (v. 8b). Judges 6:1–6 may provide an analogy. There we are told that Midian exercised control over Israel for seven years, yet they conducted annual military actions.

In the face of the Ammonite threat, the Israelites living in Gilead gathered for battle at Mizpah, but had no general to lead their armies.[42] Desperate for leadership, they promised a rulership position (ראש, "leader," 10:18) to anyone who was willing to assume military responsibility for the upcoming battle.

At this point the narrator suspends the story and introduces the individual who would eventually lead the Gileadite forces. His name is Jephthah, a Gileadite whom the narrator characterizes as a mighty warrior. He was a son of Gilead by a prostitute. Gilead's legitimate sons drove Jephthah away, insisting that he not share in their inheritance.[43] Jephthah fled to the land of Tob, located north of Gilead, gathered some

---

42. For a helpful map of the military operations described in the Jephthah narrative, see Aharoni and Avi-Yonah 1977, 55 (map 78).

43. According to Marcus, Jephthah's brothers used legal channels to disinherit him on grounds that he was adopted (1990, 105–13). He shows how the terminology used by Jephthah to describe what the elders did to him (cf. 11:7) reflects ancient Near Eastern adoption contracts. Of course, the statement that Gilead "fathered" (*hiphil* of ילד) Jephthah (11:1) is problematic for his view. Marcus argues that Gilead did literally father Jephthah, but because of Jephthah's mother's status (prostitute), Gilead adopted

men around him, and apparently became a mercenary of sorts. It was undoubtedly during this period that he acquired his reputation as a warrior.[44]

A first-time reader, while undoubtedly sympathetic to Jephthah's plight as an underdog and outcast, should have some serious reservations about his qualifications, for Jephthah resembles Abimelech in certain respects. Neither man was a full-fledged son (Abimelech's mother was a second-class wife of Gideon; Jephthah's mother was a prostitute) and both gathered around them "lawless men" (cf. 11:3 with 9:4).[45]

Having introduced the hero of the coming battle, the narrator returns to the main story line in 11:4. No one in the Gileadite army was up to the leadership task, so the elders of Gilead (the same group as the "leaders" mentioned in 10:18?) asked Jephthah to command their army (note קָצִין, "commander," v. 6).[46] At first Jephthah was hesitant to help those who had rejected him in the past.[47] His objection may have been a subtle way of suggesting they reverse their earlier legal decision and restore his inheritance (Marcus 1989, 95–100). Perhaps he was

---

Jephthah to legitimize his paternity. He then theorizes that the brothers' lawsuit against Jephthah contested the legitimacy of the adoption.

44. Gilead cannot be the same individual mentioned in Numbers 26:29 and Joshua 17:3. That Gilead, a descendant of Manasseh, was the grandfather/ancestor of a man who lived at the same time as Joshua, and we know from Judges 11:26 that Jephthah lived many years after the time of the conquest. Apparently the Gilead mentioned in 11:3 was a prominent or well-known Gileadite who perhaps was named after his illustrious ancestor.

45. For comparisons and contrasts between the two men, see Klein 1988, 83–84. Claassens does not see the "lawless [literally, empty] men" in a negative light (1996, 110). Based on the use of the phrase in 1 Samuel 22:2, she concludes that they "were not necessarily people without good morals, but rather people who, due to some disaster or misfortune, had lost everything." She adds: "To surivive [sic] such people sometimes had to resort to stealing, plundering and mercenary service."

46. Gunn and Fewell suggest that the elders' treatment of Jephthah (rejecting him and then inviting him to return as their deliverer) mirrors Israel's attitude toward the Lord. They rejected him, but then turned to him when trouble came (1993, 114).

47. Actually verse 2 says that his half-brothers drove him away, but in verse 7 Jephthah accuses the elders of having done so. The relationship between his half-brothers and the elders is not entirely clear. It is likely that the elders legally authorized the decision of the half-brothers. See Marcus 1990, 106.

also suggesting they make their offer more attractive (Wong 2006a, 172). The elders did just that. They improved their offer by promising a position of rulership (note רֹאשׁ, "leader," 11:8) as a reward for leading the army. This position was part of the original general offer (cf. 10:18), but was omitted from their initial invitation to Jephthah (cf. 11:6). Apparently the elders tried to acquire Jephthah's services at the lowest possible price, but he successfully manipulated them into offering more.[48] Jephthah agreed to their terms and they swore an oath that solidified the agreement.[49] Having sealed the deal, Jephthah came to Gilead, where the elders made him ruler (רֹאשׁ) and military commander (קָצִין) on the spot.[50] Jephthah got a better deal than he expected. He expected to be made ruler after victory was achieved (v. 9).[51] Perhaps the elders wanted to assure him they were serious so that he would not get "cold feet" and withdraw from his commitment.[52]

---

48. For a discussion of the negotiations, see Webb 1987, 52–53. See as well Craig 1998, 76–85.

49. Verse 9 is sometimes translated as a question (see NIV), in which case Jephthah was questioning their sincerity. However, there is no interrogative marker in the Hebrew text. It is more likely that he simply summarized the terms of the agreement. They then ratified the terms by oath (v. 10). See Moore 1895, 287–88. According to Marcus, the statement at the beginning of verse 9 (literally, "If you bring me back") has legal connotations and refers to their reinstating his inheritance (1989, 99–100).

50. For a discussion of the distinction between the two terms, see Willis 1997, 33–44. Marcus argues that the terms are purely synonymous. He contends that the only issue at stake is Jephthah's inheritance and that he was not bargaining for a higher position (1989, 95–100).

51. Berman understands Jephthah's response as proof that he was reluctant to accept their offer. Only when the battle was won and God's favor demonstrated, would he accept their offer (2004, 96–102).

52. Some writers have drawn parallels between the account of the Gileadites' bargaining with Jephthah (10:17–11:11) and the account of Israel's encounter with God in 10:6–16. See, for example, Polzin 1980, 178; and Webb 1987, 54, both of whom see contrasts between the accounts. Berman, however, sees a close connection between the Lord and Jephthah (2004, 102–14). He draws seven points of contact (106–09): (1) Israel suffers oppression from the Ammonites, but fails to appeal to the obvious savior because they have rejected him prior to the crisis. (Berman makes the point that Israel suffered for eighteen years before finally turning to the Lord for deliverance.) (2) The people appeal to "the rejected, yet potential, savior" out of desperation. (3) The initial pleas are inadequate. (4) The potential savior rejects the pleas. (5) The people make a second offer to the savior. (6) The supplicants emphasize their sincerity. (7) Each savior

The episode concludes by reporting, "Jephthah spoke all his words before the Lord in Mizpah" (v. 11b; literal translation). The precise meaning of this statement is unclear. Perhaps the text is simply noting that once chosen as Gilead's leader, Jephthah recognized the Lord's authority and brought all of his concerns before him. "His words" may even refer to the messages recorded in the following verses, the second of which appeals to the Lord as judge.[53] However, it seems more likely that the phrase "his words" refers to Jephthah's earlier summary of the agreement (v. 9) (Moore 1895, 288; Gray 1986, 316; and Webb 1987, 53). In this case verse 11 informs us that he formalized the agreement in the Lord's presence.

At this point in the story the reader feels some emotional relief. Though Jephthah was similar to Abimelech on the surface, the differences outweigh the similarities. While both were desirous of rulership, Jephthah did not actively pursue it, nor did he resort to murder to achieve it. Unlike Abimelech, who was more than willing to be financed by money from a pagan temple treasury, Jephthah appears to be a worshiper of the Lord.

Jephthah gives a history lesson (11:12–28). Jephthah initially sought to resolve the conflict with Ammon by peaceful means. He asked why the Ammonite king marched against Gilead. The Ammonite king claimed that the land between the Arnon and Jabbok, which Israel conquered when they came into the area in the time of Moses, was rightfully his. He demanded that Jephthah give it back peaceably.

---

responds, but with hesitancy. These points of contact yield the following plot structure in both stories (110): (1) "The savior is unjustly rejected." (2) "The oppressed people fail to appeal to the savior in time of distress because he has long since been rejected." (3) "The supplicants make an inadequate and insincere appeal to the savior in order to address the Ammonite problem." (4) "The savior rejects the appeal out of a sense of betrayal." (5) "Desperate, the supplicants make a second round of offers to woo the savior." (6) "Though wary of the insincerity of the supplicants, the savior elects to grant salvation." What is the point of this parallelism? Berman concludes (111) that the focus of 10:17–11:11 is "cast on a central biblical theme: assessing and concretizing the strained relationship between God and his wayward covenantal partner, Israel." He adds: "The very real and concrete dimension of Jephthah's abuse stands as a metaphor for Israel's treatment of God in chapter 10."

53. When the phrase דִּבֶּר לִפְנֵי, "speak before," is used elsewhere (Exod. 6:12; Num. 36:1; 1 Kings 3:22; Esth. 8:3), the speaker is seeking some special consideration from a superior party.

The Ammonite king's interpretation of history was incorrect. Jephthah reminded him of the facts, demonstrating that Israel's claim to the territory was a valid one. As Jephthah asserted, Israel did not take land from Moab or Ammon (the sons of Lot). After the Israelites left Egypt, they eventually came to Kadesh, where they asked permission from the kings of Edom and Moab to pass through their lands. When these kings refused, Israel bypassed their lands and traveled to the east of them. When they approached the kingdom of Sihon the Amorite, they asked his permission to pass through his lands, but he refused and marched against Israel.[54] Israel fought and defeated the Amorites, capturing all the land between the Arnon and Jabbok. Jephthah's rehearsal of history highlights two facts: (1) Israel did not initiate wars of conquest with the eastern peoples. They cooperated fully with Edom and Moab, and only fought the Amorites when they refused Israel passage and initiated a war. (2) At the time when Israel took the region, it belonged to Sihon the Amorite, not the Ammonites. Other texts make it clear that the Ammonite kingdom was located to the east of Sihon's and that Israel did not venture into it (Num. 21:24), because the Ammonite border was fortified and, more importantly, the Lord prohibited them from doing so (Num. 21:24; Deut. 2:19, 37).[55]

Having spelled out the facts, Jephthah developed his argument as follows: (1) Since the Lord transferred the region in question from Sihon to Israel, the Ammonites had no right to claim it. They should have been content with ancient divine decisions about national boundaries.[56] (2) The Ammonite king should follow the example of Balak of Moab, who, when thwarted in his attempt to bring a curse on Israel, refused to attack Israel and returned to his home (see Numbers 22–

---

54. For a theological interpretation of Sihon's obstinance, see Deuteronomy 2:24–35.
55. Jephthah's version of Israel's approach to the land follows the Numbers 20–21 account (see also Deuteronomy 2). Numbers 33:37–49 appears to give an alternate tradition. For an attempt to harmonize the traditions, see Merrill 1987, 86–89.
56. Jephthah spoke of Chemosh as if he were on a par with the Lord. This does not necessarily mean he was polytheistic or that he recognized the Lord as a mere local deity. He may have been merely assuming the Ammonite king's perspective for the sake of argument. See Hamilton 2001, 144. For a contrary opinion, see Younger, who charges Jephthah with "theological error" (Younger 2002, 256). Gray sees this as "a classic expression of Israelite henotheism, the recognition and worship of Yahweh only in Israel and the admission of the existence and authority of other gods among their worshippers" (1986, 317).

24). He claimed no right to the conquered territory. (3) Israel had been occupying the region in question for three hundred years, but the Ammonites had not tried to take it.[57] This was odd, especially if Israel had stolen it from them in the first place. Their failure to invade the region for so long a period suggested they had never viewed it as originally theirs prior to this king's bogus claim.

Why did Jephthah refer to Chemosh as the Ammonite god (note "your god" in v. 24)? Other texts, as well as the extrabiblical Mesha (Moabite) inscription, associate Chemosh with Moab (Num. 21:29; 1 Kings 11:7, 33; 2 Kings 23:13; Jer. 48:7, 13, 46), while Milkom is identified as the god of the Ammonites (1 Kings 11:5, 7, 33; 2 Kings 23:13).[58]

It is possible, as Boling suggests, that Ammon had subdued Moab and that the Ammonite king now regarded himself as heir of all lands formerly held by Moab (1975, 203–04). Originally Moab, not Sihon or Ammon, had owned the disputed territory, meaning that Chemosh was originally the god of the region.[59] However, Chemosh had long ago relinquished claim to the area (when Sihon the Amorite took it from Moab), while the Lord had long ago established jurisdiction over it (by taking it from Sihon and giving it to Israel). Both sides must abide by the decisions of the gods that had stood firm for three hundred years. Even if the Ammonite king claimed to be the new suzerain over Moab and heir to territory ruled by Chemosh, the facts of history invalidated his claim.

Since the text gives no indication that Ammon had conquered Moab, however, a less complicated explanation may be preferable. Rather than proposing a historical-cultural explanation for linking the king of Ammon with Moab's god, it would be better to view Jephthah's statement as purely rhetorical. The Ammonite king was claiming land that his people had never controlled, as Jephthah's history lesson makes clear. Moab and then Sihon had controlled it before Israel conquered it. By speaking to the Ammonite king as if he were a Moabite king, Jephthah sarcastically reminds him that he could claim the land only if he were Moabite. But even if he were a Moabite, the king could only

---

57. For a discussion of Jephthah's use of the figure three hundred, see the introduction.
58. Aufrecht argues that El was actually the chief god of the Ammonites, though he acknowledges that Milkom was popular (1999, 159). For a critique of this view, see Hess 2007, 272, note 116.
59. According to Numbers 21:26–29, Sihon took the region in question from Moab.

claim what Chemosh granted and the Moabite god had surrendered this area long ago.

Of course, as noted above, there is an even simpler solution to the problem. Younger argues that Jephthah was ignorant of the facts and mistakenly thought Chemosh was the Ammonite deity (2002, 256–57). It might seem unlikely that one who had lived in Transjordan in proximity to Ammon and Moab would be ignorant of such a basic fact, but he may have indeed been confused on this matter.

Jephthah concluded his case by declaring his innocence and accusing the Ammonite king of wrongdoing. He then appealed to the Lord as the adjudicator in the dispute. He seemed confident he would be vindicated and that the just nature of his cause guaranteed victory. However, the king rejected Jephthah's arguments (v. 28), making a conflict inevitable.

A foolish vow spells death for a daughter (11:29–40).[60] The Lord's spirit came upon Jephthah, moving him to advance against the Ammonites (v. 29). At this point everything looks fine. It appears that the Lord had responded to Jephthah's appeal for justice and was ready to vindicate his people's claim to the land. However, as in Gideon's case, empowerment by the spirit does not automatically ensure faith or negate the human will. Jephthah was not yet completely confident of victory. Demonstrating extreme caution and apparently wanting to leave nothing to chance, he made a vow to the Lord. He promised to give an offering if the Lord gave him a victory. There was nothing inherently wrong with promising a sacrifice in exchange for divine intervention. Making a vow to a deity in a prayer for deliverance was a typical response to a crisis in this culture. A prayer discovered at ancient Ugarit promises the god Baal an offering (or perhaps offerings) if he drives an enemy away from the city's gates (cf. *COS*, 1:283–85; Pardee 2001, 232). In Numbers 21:2 the Israelites vowed to place all the cities of the Negev under the ban in exchange for a victory in battle.[61] Hannah vowed to dedicate her child to the Lord's service if he would only deliver her from the oppressive taunts of Peninnah (1 Sam. 1:11). In con-

---

60. Much of the following discussion on verses 29–40, and on Jephthah's vow in particular, appears in Chisholm 2010c.

61. Steinberg provides an outline showing the structural parallels between Jephthah's vow and the vow recorded in Numbers 21:2. In both cases a sacrifice is promised, but in Numbers 21:2 it comes from the spoils of victory as part of the *ḥērem*, while in Jephthah's case the sacrifice is the victor's own daughter (1999, 123).

trast to these legitimate vows, Jephthah's vow was wrong because it was inappropriate in the context it was given and, more importantly, because of the nature of the offering it promised (Exum 1992, 50).

Though cautious bargaining was perhaps necessary when dealing with the Gileadites (cf. 11:4–11), Jephthah did not need to bargain with the Lord, for he was the champion of a just cause (vv. 12–28) and was already energized by the divine spirit (v. 29).[62] Like Barak and Gideon (cf. 4:8; 6:17, 36–37), his use of "if" prior to the battle testifies to his uncertainty about its outcome.[63] Webb comments on the irony of the vow: "Ironically, after resting his case confidently with Yahweh

---

62. Prior to the vow Jephthah demonstrated a great deal of savvy in his use of words, but now, at this strategic turning point in the story, his words prove to be his downfall. On the theme of "the awful and sustaining power of words" in the story, see Exum 1993b, 131–36.

63. In Judges when אִם, "if," is followed by the imperfect, as in verse 30, the particle is usually conditional and the imperfect hypothetical (see 4:8, 20; 6:37; 13:16; 14:12–13; 16:7, 11, 13). The only apparent exception to this is in 15:7, where the context indicates אִם has the force of "since" and the imperfect is customary or present progressive. One may translate, "If you continue to act like this . . .," but since Samson immediately carried out his vow without apparently giving the Philistines opportunity to change (v. 8), the NIV rendering ("Since you've acted like this") is preferable. The NIV translates 21:21, "When the girls of Shiloh come out," but the hypothetical nuance of the imperfect may be retained (see NASB). On the basis of custom and past experience, the elders anticipated the young women would come out to dance, but their words leave open the possibility they might not do so. The closest parallels to Jephthah's vow are in 14:12 and 16:11. In both passages, as in 11:30–31, the protasis has the conditional אִם followed by the infinitive absolute and imperfect, while the apodosis, introduced by a *weqatal*, states a promise or guaranteed outcome if the action proposed in the protasis is realized. Trible suggests that the presence of the infinitive absolute in Jephthah's vow signals his uncertainty and insecurity (1984, 96). By using this emphatic form, he appears to be "pushing the bargaining mode of discourse to its limit." However, in two of the three other cases where a vow is introduced by a formula utilizing a *wayyiqtol* form of נדר, "swear," the infinitive absolute appears before the imperfect (cf. Num. 21:2; 1 Sam. 1:11, in contrast to Gen. 28:20). (See as well 2 Sam. 15:8, where a *qatal* form appears in the introductory formula and an infinitive absolute [cf. *Qere*] precedes the *yiqtol* verb in the protasis.) So the syntax appears to reflect the vowing idiom, rather than some unique emphasis on Jephthah's part. In these other vows אִם is conditional and the imperfect is hypothetical. For a study of these texts see Marcus 1986, 18–21.

the judge (11.27), Jephthah now slips a bribe under the table" (1987, 64).[64] Olson argues that this bribe violated an important principle of Deuteronomic Law. He maintains that the vow was inappropriate "*in this particular context*" because it was a "bribe" designed "to influence the divine judge in the context of a court case." He explains: "Jephthah has himself set up the conflict with the Ammonites as a court battle with the Lord as judge (11:27). According to Deuteronomy's laws, any bribes or gifts to judges are strictly prohibited lest they unduly influence the judges' decisions (Deut. 16:19). This prohibition is grounded in Israel's understanding of God, who 'is not partial and takes no bribe' (Deut 10:17 NRSV). Thus Jephthah's vow in itself violates a deeply held Israelite norm in regard to the prohibition of gifts or bribes to judges" (1998, 832).

Exum is not as confident about the standard interpretation of Jephthah's actions, reflected in our comments above (1992, 49–50). She suggests the text's gaps make it possible that "Jephthah makes his vow under the influence of Yhwh's spirit." She adds that the vow's "position between the coming of the spirit of Yhwh upon Jephthah and the victory renders it impossible to determine whether victory comes as the result of the spirit, or the vow, or both." However, Webb points out that the vow is clearly marked as an "interruption," for verse 32 picks up where verse 29 left off (1987, 62–63).[65] Webb concludes that the text's structure indicates that "while the victory is *causally* related to Jephthah's endowment with the Spirit it is only *incidentally* related to the vow" (emphasis his).

The description of the promised sacrifice (v. 31) also attests to Jephthah's sense of desperation and lack of confidence, for it suggests he was willing and maybe even intending to sacrifice a human being to God, apparently thinking that such a radical proposal would guarantee

---

64. At the same time, Webb (64–65) argues that Jephthah was not aware of what the reader knows, namely, that the Lord's spirit had energized him. Trible assumes that Jephthah was aware of the spirit's involvement. She writes, "Jephthah himself does not evince the assurance that the spirit of Yahweh ought to give. Rather than acting with conviction and courage, he responds with doubt and demand" (1981, 60–1). Block is noncommittal; he writes: "Whether or not Jephthah was aware of his divine empowerment is not clear" (1999, 365).

65. Note especially the disjunctive clause at the end of verse 29 and the resumptive clause at the beginning of verse 32 (where the verb עבר, "approach," is repeated).

divine support.[66] The text uses a masculine singular participle with the prefixed article, followed by a relative pronoun and third masculine singular verb (literally, "the one going out who goes out"). The substantival masculine singular participle (הַיּוֹצֵא, literally, "the one going out") is used elsewhere of inanimate objects (Num. 21:13; 32:24) as well as persons (Jer. 5:6; 21:9; 38:2). In each case context must determine the referent. The use of the infinitive לִקְרָאתִי, "to meet me," is not determinative by itself, for it can be used of animals as well as people (see Judg. 14:5; Job 39:21). However, with the exception of Job 39:21, the collocation of the infinitive לִקְרָאת, "to meet," and the verb יצא, "go out" is used of persons, not animals. The construction of Iron Age houses would allow for an animal to come through the doors of a house,[67] but one must ask: "Did animals typically greet returning conquerors?" (Bal 1988a, 45; Amit 1999, 88). It was far more likely that a woman would greet him (see 1 Sam. 18:6) (Fuchs 2000, 183; Steinberg 1999, 125). Of course, all of these considerations are academic. No matter what Jephthah's intention may have been at the time of the vow, the fact that he actually did offer up his daughter indicates the language of the vow

---

66. According to 2 Kings 3:27, the Moabite king Mesha, in an effort to save himself from the attacking Israelite army, offered his firstborn son as a "burnt sacrifice" (עֹלָה). The same term is used in Jephthah's vow (Judg. 11:31b). In fact the syntactical construction is the same in both texts: *hiphil* of עלה + suffixed pronoun functioning as direct object + עֹלָה functioning as an adverbial accusative. (In Gen. 22:13 the preposition -לְ appears before עֹלָה, but it is omitted in both Judg. 11:31 and 2 Kings 3:27.) There may be further evidence for human sacrifice even earlier than Mesha's time. According to Hess, an Egyptian relief from Medinet Habu dating to the 13th century B.C., "depicts citizens of Ashkelon within their besieged walls raising incense burners to their deities and lifting up smaller figures, perhaps children who are about to be hurled to their deaths or in some other manner to be sacrificed for the salvation of their city" (2007, 136; see also pp. 224–25, where he correlates this evidence with the account of Jephthah's sacrifice). See as well Logan 2009, 668–69, for a survey of evidence of human sacrifice in Canaanite culture.

67. See Boling 1975, 208, contrary to Moore 1895, 299–300. See also King and Stager, who point out that livestock occupied the ground floor of the typical pillared house in Iron Age Israel (2001, 34). A drawing of such a house appears on p. 29 of their book. Miller, describing the typical house in the highlands of Palestine during the period 1200–1000 BC, observes, "One of the first-floor rooms was a court for the animals" (2005, 98). Brichto seems to overlook this fact. He comments: "Animals come out of barn sheds and paddocks, not out of a house's doors" (1992, 211.)

was fluid enough to encompass human beings, including women.[68] He was willing and maybe intending to make a human offering from the very beginning, though he apparently did not expect his daughter to meet him first (Cartledge 1992, 179–80). Jephthah's brand of Yahwism had been tainted by the paganism around him.

The Lord gave Jephthah a great victory over the Ammonites that broke the back of their oppressive rule over Israel. The use of כ͏ַֿﬧﬨﬨ in verse 33 recalls earlier victories that ended oppression (cf. 3:30; 4:23; 8:28). Jephthah devastated (literally, "struck down [with] a very great striking down") twenty Ammonite towns (v. 33). The only time this emphatic construction is used in the Former Prophets prior to this is in Joshua 10:20 (see also v. 10, though מְאֹד is omitted there) to describe Israel's annihilation of the Canaanite coalition at Gibeon. The narrator may allude to this event to emphasize the extent of Jephthah's victory and to depict Jephthah as being a new Joshua of sorts, at least militarily. The text also states that the Lord gave the Ammonites into Jephthah's hand (11:32; cf. 12:3), an expression that is used earlier of victories that brought deliverance from oppression (3:10; 4:7, 14; 7:7, 14–15). Jephthah's victory was decisive and thorough. Yet there may be an ominous sign here. Prior to this in Judges, when enemies were subdued, the land experienced rest (3:30; 4:23/5:31; 8:28), but no such statement follows in verse 33 or later in the story.

Indeed triumph quickly turned to tragedy. When Jephthah returned victoriously from the battle, his daughter, his only child, was the first to come through the front doors to meet him. She danced and played a tambourine in celebration of her father's victory, but was greeted by an act of mourning and shocking news as her father tore his clothes and told her of his rash vow.[69] Jephthah's daughter insisted that her father keep his vow. In a patriarchal society, perhaps she had

---

68. Jephthah did not object to offering his daughter on the basis of the gender of the form used in the vow. From his perspective the masculine form was fluid enough to include a female.

69. The text does not say he told her the content of the oath, but her response in verse 36 suggests he may have done so (cf. Gunn and Fewell 1993, 116), unless, of course, she suspected the worst on the basis of his agitated response to her arrival (cf. Trible 1984, 102–03). Jephthah used the verb עכר, "to trouble," to describe how she had brought him ruin (v. 35). (Note that he uses the infinitive absolute before the finite form of the verb for emphasis.) This verb is also used in Joshua 7:25 to describe how Achan brought trouble upon Israel. The place of Achan's execution is called the Valley of Achor (Trouble). In both accounts a great Israelite victory was turned into an occasion for sorrow by one man's lack of wisdom.

no other option. But perhaps her insistence that her father keep his vow illustrates how deeply pagan thinking had permeated the minds of the people at this stage in Israel's history. As Janzen observes, "his daughter agrees with him, parroting his faulty reasoning," perhaps indicating that she "accepts the same foreign (and therefore wrong) assumptions about sacrifice that her father does" (2005, 347–48).

Jephthah's daughter asked that she be allowed to mourn her virginity for two months. Jephthah granted her request and she mourned with her friends for the specified period of time, after which he fulfilled his vow by offering her as a burnt sacrifice. A great divine victory was remembered instead as an occasion to mourn the death of a young woman who was the victim of her father's and a whole culture's assimilation to paganism.[70]

Because of the emphasis on the daughter's virginity in verses 37–39, some argue that Jephthah did not sacrifice his daughter, but instead devoted her to a life of celibacy as a servant of the Lord.[71] According to this view, the apodosis in verse 31 would have to offer alternatives, "He will belong to the Lord *or* I will offer him up as a burnt sacrifice."[72] In

---

70. See Webb, who points out how Jephthah's vow swallows up the story (1987, 62–63). What should have been an account of a victory followed by a celebration turns instead into a tragic story of an only-daughter's death. The interruption of the battle scene by the report of the vow (vv. 30–31) signals the unraveling of the story.

71. For a survey of the history of interpretation of the Jephthah story, see Gunn 2005, 133–69. For a study of how Judges 11:30–40 has been treated in Jewish and historical-critical circles, see Rottzoll 2003, 210–30. For a brief survey of some Christian readings of the story see Thompson 2002, 49–61. Houtman examines some ways in which the story has been treated in Christian devotional literature (2005, 167–90). Robinson also discusses various ways in which the details have been understood in the history of interpretation (2004, 331–48). Begg analyzes Josephus' version of the Jephthah story (2006). For further analysis of historical Jewish interpretation, see Valler 1999 and Kramer 1999. Beavis (2010) suggests intertextuality between the story of Jephthah's sacrifice of his daughter and Mark's account of the raising of Jairus' daughter.

72. The structure of the entire apodosis is unique. The initial וְהָיָה (v. 31a) introduces the apodosis, "then (it will be)." It is followed by a substantival participle (הַיּוֹצֵא, literally, "the one going out'), a relative clause (with relative pronoun, imperfect, prepositional phrase, and infinitive construct), and a temporal clause (with preposition, infinitive construct, and two prepositional phrases), but there is no predicate complementing הַיּוֹצֵא. One expects an imperfect verbal form to appear (see Josh. 7:15; 1 Kings 19:17; Isa. 24:18). Instead another וְהָיָה appears; it seems to provide the

other words, if a human came through the doors, then Jephthah would commit him/her to the Lord's service (much like Hannah did Samuel), but if an animal came through the doors, he would offer it up as a whole burnt offering to the Lord.[73] However, this understanding of the

---

complement for the initial participle. One may translate literally: "Then [it will be] the one coming out, who comes out from the doors of my house to meet me when I return in peace from the Ammonites, [then he] will become the Lord's . . . "

73. Some take a different approach. Brichto, appealing to the law of the firstborn in Exodus 13:11–13, argues that Jephthah intended to offer an animal from the very beginning (1992, 213–14). When his daughter appeared, Jephthah had to redeem her by offering an animal in her place. But this meant she belonged to the Lord and could not be married. He writes: "If Jephthah's daughter now belonged to YHWH, she could not be given or taken in marriage. By cloistering her off from contact with any male, Jephthah would have 'executed upon her the vow he had taken'" (214).

Reis offers a unique interpretation (2002, 105–30). She proposes that Jephthah vowed to offer the first servant who met him *as if* he/she were a burnt offering. In other words the language is metaphorical (114). In her view Jephthah was trying to motivate the men of Gilead to support him in the upcoming battle. He promised to dedicate a servant to the Lord in the sense that he would pay a redemption price for the person, releasing him/ her from the ordinary responsibilities of work. (For a woman this would include the "work" of bearing children.) By showing his willingness to absorb such a financial loss, Jephthah was demonstrating to the Gileadites that he was a generous man, willing to share the spoils of victory with his men, and he was also suggesting that the victory would prove to be lucrative. There would be plenty of servants among the spoil, making it easy to replace the one dedicated (114–15). According to Reis, Jephthah's daughter knew about the vow and purposely greeted him first. Why? Reis argues it was customary for women to greet victorious warriors. Jephthah's daughter, a spoiled child in Reis's view, perhaps assumed her father would iron out any problems related to the vow (126). But Reis then suggests that the daughter may have acted in order to "defy convention and continue to be the one and only love of an extremely indulgent father than become some man's first wife" (126). When her father responded in anger, she decided to undo the consequences. She made a foray into the mountains to appeal to local pagan gods to intervene on her behalf, but to no avail (126). In this scenario Israelite women do not mourn what happened to Jephthah's daughter (v. 40), but celebrate "her choice of independence and self-determination" and triumph in "one young woman's achievement of autonomy" and "her success in shaping her own life" (127). Reis's proposed explanation for Jephthah's daughter's motivation seems far-fetched.

syntax is questionable, for the *waw* before the second clause is more naturally taken here as sequential or as explicative, specifying exactly how the one coming through the doors would become the Lord's.[74] When the construction used in the apodosis of the vow (conjunction + perfect verbal form followed by another conjunction + perfect verbal form)[75] appears elsewhere in Joshua, Judges, and Samuel, the second verb gives a sequential or consequential action, provides a complementary idea, or specifies the preceding action, but it never gives an alternative.[76] This strongly suggests that Jephthah's daughter became the Lord's *by being* sacrificed to him as a whole burnt offering or that she was formally declared to be the Lord's and then, *as a consequence*, sacrificed to him.

The language of the vow's fulfillment must also be considered. In verse 39 the statement "she did not know a man" (literal translation) is a disjunctive, not a consecutive, clause.[77] The disjunctive clause is

It transforms an ancient Israelite young woman who, like virtually every other woman in this patriarchal society, would have accepted her primary life's role as entailing marriage and motherhood, into a very modern, westernized-looking, spoiled brat who manages to escape the responsibilities of work and childbearing and in so doing becomes the poster child for her fellow feminists!

74. The expression "belong to the Lord" (הָיָה לַיהוָה) is neither a technical phrase for sacrifice (though see Lev. 23:18) nor for dedicating a person to the Lord. It can be used of sacrifices (Lev. 23:18, 20; 27:32), priests (1 Kings 2:27), altars (Isa. 19:19), memorials (Isa. 55:13), and worshipers (Mal. 3:3).

75. We do not refer to cases where a perfect with *waw* introduces an apodosis after a perfect with *waw* in the protasis (see, for example, Judg. 1:12; 1 Sam. 17:9).

76. See, among others, Joshua 1:15; 4:3; 6:18; 7:9; 20:4; 23:12, 16; 24:20; Judges 2:18; 4:6, 20; 6:18; 11:8; 13:3; 16:7, 11, 17; 19:9; 21:21; 1 Samuel 1:22; 2:15, 35; 4:9; 6:8; 8:20; 9:8, 19; 10:3–4, 6; 12:14; 14:34; 15:3; 16:2, 23; 17:35, 46; 19:2–3; 23:2, 23; 25:5, 31; 31:4; 2 Samuel 6:22; 7:10, 12; 9:10; 11:15; 12:11, 16, 22; 14:3, 26; 15:2, 5, 14, 25; 17:2, 9, 17. Judges 16:17 is particularly noteworthy because within the apodosis a first person perfect verbal form follows a third person form (note וְסָר, "would leave") as in Judges 11:31b. The second verb is consequential or reiterative-complementary in its relationship to the first (Samson's loss of strength makes him weak, just like other men). See also Genesis 34:15–16 and Exodus 18:16, where the apodosis of a conditional sentence has at least two perfects (each with the prefixed conjunction) describing sequential or complementary actions, but not alternatives.

77. As Moore points out, the pronoun הִיא, "she," would not be inserted before the negated verb if this clause were part of the basic narratival framework (1895, 303).

both preceded and followed by *wayyiqtol* clauses. This same basic syntactical structure (*wayyiqtol* clause + disjunctive clause with independent pronoun and perfect verbal form + *wayyiqtol* clause) appears in several other passages. In these examples, the disjunctive clause is usually contrastive (Gen. 32:23–24 [Eng, 22–23]; 42:8–9; Judg. 3:18–19; 9:17–18; 10:12–13; 1 Kings 19:3–4; 2 Kings 5:24–25). In Judges 16:20–21 the disjunctive clause appears to be explanatory (literally, "he thought . . . for he did not know"), in 1 Samuel 25:37–38 it is either clarifying or consequential (literally, "His heart failed him, that is/so that he became like a stone"), and in 1 Kings 1:41 it is circumstantial or parenthetical (literally, "they heard it while they finished eating" or "they heard it—now they had finished eating"). The action or condition described in the disjunctive clause is concurrent with or subsequent to that of the preceding *wayyiqtol* clause, with the possible exception of 1 Kings 1:41. Unlike so many of these structurally parallel texts, the disjunctive clause in Judges 11:39 is not contrastive. Of the various options the following would seem to fit best:

(1) parenthetical: "He did to her as he had vowed—now she had never known/did not know a man."[78]

(2) consequential: "He did to her as he had vowed and consequently she never knew a man." This would allow the celibacy view, but it fits the sacrificial view as well. When her father offered her up as a burnt offering, she died a virgin, depriving her of an opportunity to be a wife and mother, the expectation and desire of the typical Israelite young woman in this patriarchal culture.[79]

In either case the text's emphasis on her virginity highlights the tragedy of the event by reminding us of her unrealized potential. Her anonymity in the story may also contribute to its tragic dimension. By dying prematurely, she was unable to carry on a genealogical line; the family name died out with her, as it were.[80]

---

78. In this case it is not clear if the perfect has a past perfect or simple past function.

79. See the insightful comments of Brown 2000, 230–31.

80. See Reinhartz 1998, 121. She observes: "Anonymity focuses attention on her stage of life and the concept of loss: loss of life, loss of posterity." At the same time, by suppressing her name and simply calling her Jephthah's daughter, the narrator keeps reminding us of Jephthah's power over her in this patriarchal context and of the magnitude of Jephthah's loss. Exum states: "The father's name is remembered but the daughter's is not. Ultimately the text withholds autonomy from Jephthah's daughter. It confines her voice within patriarchal limits, using it to affirm patriarchal authority . . . ." (1992, 68). See also Steinberg 1999, 126.

Did Jephthah have any other option than to sacrifice his daughter? According to Block, he had two alternatives. First, Block suggests that Jephthah could have spared his daughter and "brought the curse upon himself" (1999, 377). However, it is unlikely that Jephthah would have thought in such individualistic terms. He probably would have assumed that any curse falling on him would have a corporate dimension and that his daughter would be judged along with him. Either way his daughter was doomed. After all, the Hebrew Bible is replete with examples of judgment encompassing an individual's children. For example, the Lord warned his enemies that their sin would have negative consequences for their family throughout their lifetime (Exod. 20:5; 34:7; Num. 14:18). Dathan's, Abiram's, and Achan's innocent children died along with their sinful parents (Num. 16:27, 32; Josh. 7:24). David, with the Lord's approval, allowed the Gibeonites to execute Saul's seven sons because of their father's crimes against that city (2 Sam. 21:1–9, 14). The Lord also took the lives of four of David's sons because of his sin against Uriah (2 Sam. 12:5–6, 10; cf. 12:14–15; 13:28–29; 18:15; 1 Kings 2:25).[81]

Second, Block argues that Jephthah "could have followed the Mosaic Torah and paid twenty shekels to the priest at the central shrine as compensation for the life of his daughter" (1999, 377).[82] He adds: "Leviticus 27:1–8 regulates cases in which one person vows another, that is, devotes a person to the sanctuary for sacred service and then for reasons unspecified finds it impossible or impractical to fulfill the vow" (377). However it is unlikely that the Levitical law cited by Block is applicable in Jephthah's situation. As Block admits, Jephthah's situation is different in that he promised a burnt offering. Block nevertheless cites the rabbinical principle of *qal wāḥômer* and states, "a rule that applied in a lesser case would certainly apply in a more serious case involving the very life of a human being" (377). This seems far less than certain.

Contrary to Block's proposal, Niditch views Jephthah's vow as unredeemable because it was made in the context of war. She compares

---

81. For a detailed study of the theme of corporate judgment in the Hebrew Bible, see Kaminsky 1995.
82. This view seems to reflect the interpretation of the Targum. See Younger 2002, 265 (including note 57); he states that Jephthah was "tragically" ignorant of the law of redemption. Contrary to what Block states, Leviticus 27:5 suggests that the conversion price for Jephthah's daughter (if she was between the ages of five and twenty) would have been ten shekels, not twenty.

the language and syntax of Jephthah's vow (Judg. 11:30–31) to "the vow of *ḥērem*" in Numbers 21:2–3, and is convinced the institution of חֵרֶם underlies Jephthah's war vow (1993, 33–34; see also Logan 2009, 665–85). Following Niditch's lead, one could argue on the basis of Leviticus 27:28–29 that Jephthah was unable to redeem his daughter because she had been devoted (note the use of the verb חרם, "dedicate," in vv. 28–29) to the Lord (see also Logan 2009, 682). However, it is unlikely that this law is relevant to our reading of the story because the root חרם does not appear with reference to Jephthah's vow.[83]

Janzen offers a better, and simpler, alternative. He points out that the Deuteronomistic History makes it clear that "obeying is better than sacrificing." Against the background of the Deuteronomic law, "the question of child sacrifice is hardly a borderline issue" (2005, 345). He states: "Jephthah's vow should never have been made in the first place since it was, in reality, an illegal bribe; yet after it was made, Jephthah was certainly under no obligation to fulfill it and thus augment his sin. Obeying is better than sacrificing here because, as in the case of Saul, Jephthah had a direct command from Yhwh—in his case in the form of Deuteronomic law—that obviated the sacrifice. In

---

83. Logan (2009, 665–85) contends that Jephthah's action, when viewed in its historical and cultural context, would have been viewed as commendable. Her argument is unconvincing, because, as noted above, it is based on the faulty notion that Jephthah's vow must be understood in light of the institution of חֵרֶם, when in fact the term is not used here. She argues that ancient readers would understand and agree that Jephthah's war vow would have to be fulfilled. But she overlooks the fact that this war vow is presented as a bribe to the Lord, in violation of Deuteronomic law (see above). Her proposal that the language of Judges 11:30, 36, 39 echoes Numbers 21:2 and 30:2 is convincing, but she misinterprets the significance of those intertextual connections. She states that "to educated Israelites," familiar with the Numbers traditions, the intertextual citations "would have been recognized as legal arguments advanced to convince them that Jephthah's act was not only sanctioned but also mandated by God" (680). On the contrary, the echoes have an ironic function here. Jephthah's vow (v. 30), while constructed like that of Numbers 21:2, is a perversion of the war vow because of its pagan (offering a human sacrifice) and illegal (equivalent to a bribe) nature (see above). His daughter tragically adhered to an ancient principle of vow-keeping (v. 36; cf. Num. 30:2) in a context where the principle was invalidated by the nature of the vow. Finally, the narrator's observation that he fulfilled his vow (v. 39), in words that echo Numbers 30:2, simply adds to the tragic irony of the scene, rather than giving legal sanction to his actions.

Dtr's eyes, when Israel wishes to sacrifice, it has an obligation to do so in a manner that does not, unlike the sacrifices of Saul, the Elides and Jephthah, contradict the will of YHWH" (345–46). In other words, if Jephthah had understood the Lord's priorities and commands, he would have realized that fulfilling his vow simply compounded his crime. Of course, therein lies the problem. After all, if he had known the Law, he would have not promised God a human sacrifice in the first place! Jephthah's ignorance compounds the tragedy, for his daughter's life could and should have been spared in accordance with the principle that obedience supercedes sacrifice.

Some are understandably troubled by the narrator's apparent neutrality.[84] Fuchs goes even further, arguing that Jephthah's indictment of his daughter (v. 35), while not necessarily reflecting the narrator's point of view, is allowed to stand "as the only explicit evaluation of the daughter's actions" (2000, 186–87). The silence of the narrator and of God makes Jephthah out to be a victim. She also contends (190) that the daughter's relatively calm and reasoned response (v. 36) endorses and justifies Jephthah's point of view. In short, she argues that the narrational style is designed to protect both Jephthah and the Lord from criticism (193).

An analysis of point of view is in order. Berlin speaks of "three senses in which the term point of view can be applied" (1983, 47). (1) The "perceptual point of view" is "the perspective through which the events of the narrative are perceived." In our story the narrator is content to take the stance of a neutral observer and report the events objectively. He also reports, through quoted material, the perspectives of Jephthah and his daughter. (2) The "conceptual point of view" is "the perspective of attitudes, conceptions, world view." (3) The "interest point of view" is "the perspective of someone's benefit or disadvantage." In this story the narrator's focus is on Jephthah.

Because the narrator's focus of interest is Jephthah, the seemingly objective perceptual perspective actually reflects a father's perspective, perhaps to create sympathy for Jephthah and highlight the tragic and ironic dimension of what happened. But this need not mean that the narrator blames Jephthah's daughter. Jephthah's words display a realistic quality; when people face the consequences of their foolish behavior, they often try to place the blame elsewhere. Pressler calls his response "a classic case of blaming the victim" (2002, 204). Perhaps the contrast between Jephthah's irrational accusation and his daughter's obedient demeanor highlights his folly, as well as her vulnerability.

---

84. See, for example, Exum 1990, 422, and Römer 1998, 37.

Assis points out that "Jephthah's egocentricity does not allow him to see his daughter's tragedy" (2005a, 216).

We suggest that the narrator's conceptual point of view is that of the Deuteronomic law, familiarity with which he assumes on the part of his readers. As Römer points out, Deuteronomy forbids human sacrifice in no uncertain terms (12:29–31; 18:10) (1998, 30). Perhaps, in light of this, the narrator felt it unnecessary to offer moral commentary on Jephthah's act. Sometimes, as photographic journalism has demonstrated, simple depiction is more effective than verbiage. The words of Bal, used with reference to the scene of the dead concubine in Judges 19, are applicable here: "Vision is a mode of speech in this horror-story" (1993, 222). The simple, stark words, "he did to her as he had vowed" (v. 39) stimulate the imagination and conjure up an appalling image that prints the words "guilty" over the perpetrator of this holocaust.

The wider context of the story must also be taken into account (McCann 2002, 83–85.) The book of Judges traces the changing roles of women in conjunction with the deterioration in male leadership. Against this background, Jephthah's daughter is definitely a sympathetic figure, while Jephthah's folly marks a further descent in leadership.[85]

The early chapters of Judges present an ideal of male leadership, especially through the portrait of Othniel. Unfortunately later judges, who were plagued by deficient faith (Barak, Gideon, Jephthah) and/or lack of wisdom (Gideon, Jephthah, Samson), failed to live up to this ideal.[86] By the end of Samson's story, Israel's greatest warrior was reduced to a helpless and vulnerable female role, much like the Canaanite general Sisera earlier in the book. By the end of the book, there are no leaders present. Instead Israelite men war with each other and cause untold suffering for Israelite women.

The changing roles of the women vis-à-vis the male leaders contribute to this account of Israel's societal decline. In contrast to Acsah, who inspired mighty deeds, women were soon forced into other roles.

---

85. See Chisholm 1994b, a summary of which appears in the introduction to this commentary, entitled, "What Role Do the Female Characters Play?"

86. Wong argues that one can detect a weakness of faith in Samson as well (cf. 15:18). In fact, Samson's weakness comes *after* a God-given victory, in contrast to earlier judges, who expressed weakness of faith *prior* to victory (2006a, 163–65). Wong also proposes that one can detect an "increasing prominence" in "self-interest as motivation" for action as one moves from Gideon to Jephthah to Samson (165–76). This contributes to the theme of deteriorating leadership in the book's central section.

Due to Barak's weak faith and Gideon's lack of wisdom, Deborah, Jael, and the unnamed woman in Thebez assume the role of warriors, demonstrating the same courage, cunning, and prowess as the earlier heroes Othniel, Ehud, and Shamgar. As the male leaders continued to lose effectiveness and then disappeared altogether, the highly valued and heroic women of the early chapters step aside for the brutalized victims of the later chapters.

With Jephthah's sacrifice of his daughter, the crisis in Israelite leadership during this period is evident. After the chaos produced by Abimelech, the Yahweh-worshiping Jephthah appears to restore quality leadership to Israel. But it is shocking to see that even a Yahweh-worshiper has become so paganized in his thinking that he would resort to human sacrifice to assure success. The radically changing role of the story's major female character draws attention to the continuing decline in the quality of male leadership and in the society's spiritual discernment. In the earlier stories women heroically delivered the nation from oppressors; now an Israelite woman becomes an innocent victim of her own father's lack of faith and wisdom.[87] In contrast to Acsah, who received from her father Caleb a husband and a blessing in the form of life-giving springs, Jephthah's unnamed daughter (unnamed to emphasize that she did not help carry on a genealogical line?) is doomed to a brief life of infertility culminating in a hideous death (Pressler 2002, 207).[88] To make matters even worse, Jephthah's slaughter of his own flesh and blood foreshadows his battle with Ephraim (his brothers, if he was from the tribe of Manasseh) and in turn the bloody civil war described in the book's final chapters in which many Israelite women,

---

87. Claassens makes a strong case for seeing wisdom themes in the Jephthah story (1997, 211). She states: "In view of these wisdom elements, it is possible that Jephthah is portrayed as someone who was *not* wise, somebody whose example therefore was *not* to be followed. This notion is particularly compelling considering that the wisdom tradition . . . implies that wisdom can commonly be associated with *speech*, especially in societies which are orally inclined. A person was considered wise when he/she knew *what* to say and even more important *when* to say it . . . . Consequently it can be said that Jephthah's behaviour is that of a *foolish* person" (emphasis hers). See as well Claassens 1996, 114, where she contends that the main theme of the story is "*the danger of impulsive speech*, so often warned against by Israelite sages" (emphasis hers).

88. In this regard note also the sharp contrast between childless Jephthah and the so-called minor judges (mentioned both before and after the Jephthah story), who had numerous offspring (10:4; 12:9, 14). See Mullen 1993, 156, note 97.

like Jephthah's daughter, became victims of a misplaced oath and male brutality (Exum 1990, 423, 430).[89] The image of Jephthah's daughter weeping as she walked over the hills (v. 38) foreshadows the nation's weeping during and in the aftermath of the war with Benjamin (20:23, 26; 21:2) (McCann 2002, 87).

Janzen demonstrates that the story of Jephthah's sacrifice illustrates the "most important motif" of the Deuteronomistic History, namely, "when Israel worships like foreigners, it will act like foreigners" (2005, 341). In the literary sequence of the story, Jephthah's pagan sacrifice is followed by the Ephraimites' invasion of Gilead, which mimics the Ammonite invasion at the beginning of the story (Janzen 2005, 352–53).

But what of God's silence? While puzzling and even disturbing, it need not be interpreted in some fatalistic manner to mean that he required fulfillment of the vow or approved of the sacrifice.[90] Just because Jephthah ostensibly made his offering to God does not mean that God desired it or found it acceptable (see Mic. 6:6–8). Nevertheless, the reality is that God grants humans the freedom to act against his antecedent (or, in this case, moral) will.[91] Certainly one wishes God had spoken from the sky, as he did to Abraham, and prevented Jephthah from offering his daughter. However, God typically does not intervene to prevent immoral human acts, even when they seem to be done in his name. Commenting on this story, Bowman observes: "When human freedom to act in destructive ways is exercised, God does not intervene and compromise the exercise of this freedom. Instead the deity allows divine power to be constrained" (1995, 37; cf. McCann 2002, 86–87).

This is, of course, not the only instance in Judges where God is a silent, seemingly absent, observer while an atrocity is committed. How could God stand idly by and allow the men of Gibeah to perpetrate such a horrific crime against the Levite's concubine? Unterman sees God's silence as evidence that Gibeah was "a town abandoned by God" (1980, 164). He attempts to demonstrate that Judges 19 contains verbal echoes of "the Binding of Isaac" (Gen. 22) (161–64; cf. Trible 1984, 80). The narrator intends to contrast God's intervention for Isaac with his

---

89. Of course, the foreshadowing is at the literary level only, for the events of chapters 20–21 appear to have occurred chronologically *before* Jephthah's conflict with the Ephraimites.

90. See Römer, who cites Ecclesiastes 5:3–4 (1998, 37–38), and Janzen 2005, 344–46.

91. For an insightful discussion of this point, see Lewis 1979, 52–53.

silence in Gibeah in order to highlight the fact that Gibeah was "a town unfit for man or God" (164). Perhaps the report of God's silence in Judges 11 facilitates a contrast between the paganlike Jephthah, who proposed to offer to God a human sacrifice as an illegal bribe, and the faithful Abraham, who responded in unwavering obedience to God's seemingly irrational demand that he sacrifice the son of promise.

But this still fails to account adequately for the *fact* of God's silence. Bowman addresses the problem of God's silence in Gibeah from a theological angle: "Like that of Jephthah's daughter, this story suggests that a human act of self-preservation results in innocent suffering. When human beings are irresponsible in exercising their freedom, God does not intervene. Instead God allows divine power to be constrained." He adds: "The Epilogue thus confirms and intensifies the emerging portrait of God in Judges, one in which the deity refrains from intervention in order to preserve the exercise of human freedom, even if that exercise results in innocent victims. It also confirms and intensifies the emerging portrayal of human beings as flawed in the exercise of their freedom. The narrator's portrayals stress human responsibility, not divine accountability, and emphasize responsible human interaction, not responsive divine intervention" (1995, 41).

To summarize, God's silence should not be interpreted to mean that he required fulfillment of the vow or approved of the sacrifice. Just because Jephthah ostensibly made his offering to God does not mean that God desired it or found it acceptable. God grants humans the freedom to act against his moral will and typically allows the consequences of those free moral actions to unfold without intervening.

Recognizing this fact should prompt us to think long and hard about actions we contemplate, because we cannot assume God will intervene and prevent negative consequences or collateral damage. God has granted us the dignity of causality, for better or worse. Possessing this freedom gives us genuine power to impact God's world, either positively or negatively, but it also carries with it grave responsibility. In contrast to Jephthah, we must make sure we know God's standards and act accordingly. Otherwise, our actions may prove to be horrifying and bring frightening and tragic consequences.

Celebration turns to civil war (12:1–7). Both personal tragedy and civil strife marred Jephthah's victory over the Ammonites. After the battle, the Ephraimites marshalled their forces, crossed the Jordan, and confronted Jephthah. They accused him of not calling them to the battle and threatened to burn his house down. Jephthah denied the accusation, pointing out that the Ephraimites had refused to respond to his call for help.[92] Jephthah then attacked the Ephraimites, routed them, and wiped out their survivors as they attempted to cross the Jordan to return home. Forty-two thousand Ephraimites died.

The account of the Gileadite-Ephraimite civil war has an important literary role in the book. It is parallel to the earlier accounts of Ehud's mustering the Ephraimites for battle and to Gideon's encounter with them following his victory over the Midianites (cf. 7:24–8:3). Ehud received full cooperation from Ephraim (3:27–29), but Gideon's relationship with them was rocky. The Ephraimites criticized Gideon for not calling for their help sooner, but Gideon was able to appease them and prevent a war. Jephthah received no cooperation from Ephraim and made no attempt to appease them. Perhaps he was justified in his actions (if they really did refuse to come when called) and they actually threatened him with violence. Jephthah treated them with the same lack of compassion as Gideon had shown to Succoth and Penuel. Despite Jephthah's great victory, it is obvious that the social fabric of the covenant community was continuing to deteriorate. Ephraim seemed more willing to fight his own brother (assuming that many of the Gileadites were from the tribe of Manasseh) than Israel's common enemy. The same kind of hatred that characterized Joseph's brothers (Genesis 37) had now ripped apart the family of Joseph. As disturbing as all this seems, Jephthah's war with Ephraim foreshadows another civil war described in the book's final chapters (19–21).[93] His dealings with Ephraim also contrast with those of Ehud, highlighting the disintegration and strife that was ruining the covenant community. In this regard Gooding observes: "Ehud with the Ephraimites takes the fords of Jordan against the Gentile enemy and slaughters them. Jephthah adopts precisely the same tactics with equal success. Unfortunately he uses them not against the Gentile enemy but against his fellow nationals, the Ephraimites" (1982, 74*).[94]

Fortunately for Israel, the nation was spared total chaos. The civil

---

92. Mehlman, noting the absence of any reference to such a summons earlier in the account, suggests that this was a bargaining ploy and that Jephthah had not really summoned them. However, he admits, "some things happened that were not related in the biblical account" (1995, 78). If the Ephraimites' claim was correct, then Jephthah's actions are reprehensible (Wong 2006a, 180).

93. See Wong 2006a, 125–31; and Olson 1998, 837. Trible understands verses 1–6 as exalting Jephthah and thus misses the foreshadowing function of the story (1984, 107).

94. See also Amit 1999, 89; and Jobling 1995, 110–11.

strife that followed Gideon's victory culminated in the chaotic reign of Abimelech, who terrorized the land for three years (cf. 9:22) before God brought about his demise and restored a forty-five year period of order (10:1–5). No new Abimelech rose up out of the clash between Gilead and Ephraim. Jephthah led Israel for six years (12:7), and his death was followed by twenty-five more years of relative stability (cf. vv. 8–15).

Epilogue: Order Restored (12:8–15)
As before (cf. 10:1–5) the brief list of so-called minor judges gives the reader an emotional break after the action-packed account that precedes it. The emphasis on numerous offspring and intermarriage with others might suggest that Israel was experiencing a degree of unity and divine blessing, though we do not read of genuine peace being restored (see our comments on 10:1–5). This stability seems to have extended throughout the land, for judges from the three major geographical areas are singled out—Ibzan from Bethlehem in the south (vv. 8–10), Elon from Zebulun in the north (vv. 11–12), and Abdon from the more centrally located Ephraimite hill country (vv. 13–15).

However, there is something disturbing about these reports. The references to numerous offspring (vv. 9, 14) force us to reflect once more on the tragedy of the preceding account, where Jephthah's only child is killed (Mullen 1982, 199). Furthermore, these children were presumably born from numerous wives, suggesting these leaders had a harem (Gray 1986, 322; Younger 2002, 277). In addition to this, the image of Abdon's sons and grandsons riding on donkeys (v. 14, cf. 10:4) has a royal aura about it (cf. 2 Sam. 13:29; 16:2), suggesting a dynastic tendency and a consolidation of power that could prove detrimental to the Israelite social order (Younger 2002, 278; Nelson 2007, 355). Even the reference to intermarriage is ambiguous. The Hebrew text simply states, "thirty daughters he sent away to the outside and thirty daughters he brought in for his sons from the outside" (v. 9). It is usually assumed that this refers to intermarriage with other Israelite clans. This view may be correct (see Deut. 25:5), but it is possible that intermarriage with Canaanites could be included (see Judg. 3:6, though different verbs are employed there).[95]

Olson observes that this list, when compared to earlier material

---

95. Schneider raises the issue of the text's ambiguity and suggests that intermarriage with foreigners may have been involved (2000, 188). See also Nelson 2007, 355–56.

about "minor judges," focuses "on their personal lives and individual concerns rather than the national welfare" (1998, 764). He points out that Shamgar (3:31) and Tola (10:1) delivered Israel, but all we read of here are children and donkeys. Actually, as Olson notes, this movement is already evident in the first list in 10:1–5, where the notation about Tola's salvific work (10:1–2) is followed by a description of Jair's sons and their donkeys (10:3–5). Furthermore the judges in the second list serve for twenty-five years cumulatively, in contrast to Tola (twenty-three years) and Jair (twenty-two years), who served for forty-five years cumulatively. Olson writes: "The relative shortness of their tenures corresponds to the relative brevity of the judgeships of Jephthah [six years] and Samson [twenty years], indicating again a sense of decreasing effectiveness as leaders" (764). He concludes: "The concern for Israel's national welfare among the early judges has been gradually diluted into personal agendas, individual familial concerns, and trivial pursuits among the last judges" (765; see as well his comments on 819–20, 839–40).

MESSAGE AND APPLICATION

Thematic Emphases
Persistent and escalating paganism made the Lord cynical about his people's sincerity and reluctant to deliver them, but once more his great mercy eventually prompted him to respond to their suffering. As we have seen throughout the book, the Lord was able and willing to accomplish his purposes through unlikely instruments (in this case an outcast son of a prostitute). Yet paganism tainted the covenant community and robbed the Lord's great deeds of their impact. Jephthah's vow, born out of deficient faith, turned a victory into a tragedy and Ephraim's petty self-interest and pride turned an occasion for celebration into a civil war. When God's people became contaminated by paganism, even their best leader fell far short of the ideal. Rather than uniting behind the Lord and celebrating his redemptive acts, Israel was once more stained by internal conflict.

Exegetical idea: *Persistent ingratitude alienated God from his people. God was predisposed to show compassion to his people, but he brought them relief only when they radically repudiated their sin. Even when God intervened, the contaminating effects of paganism were still evident in the community and in Jephthah. Jephthah's deficient faith diluted his victory and Ephraim's pride, coupled with Jephthah's offended honor, led to civil war.*

Theological Principles

One of the book's recurring themes is evident again in this story: Sin brings divine discipline and makes God's people vulnerable to their enemies. Yet God's response to his people's pain is different this time, reminding us that he is not predictable and cannot be manipulated. God is compassionate, but he will sometimes withhold that compassion until his people come to grips with just how serious their sin is. His initial refusal to respond to their cry, even though it was accompanied by a confession of sin, forced Israel to confront the heart of the issue and demonstrate their loyalty in a tangible way by getting rid of their idols. Despite his initial reluctance to respond to Israel's cry, the Lord once again exhibited compassion.

The Lord's kingship, one of the book's ongoing themes, is apparent in this story as well. Jephthah's speech emphasizes that Israel's history is the outworking of the Lord's sovereign decisions and actions. As in the past (cf. 10:11–12), the Lord once again demonstrates his ability to deliver his people from hostile enemies.

Theological idea: *Persistent ingratitude can alienate God from his people. God is predisposed to show compassion to his people, but sometimes he will bring them relief only when they radically repudiate their sin. Even when God intervenes, the contaminating effects of paganism are sometimes still evident in the community and its leaders. Deficient leaders can dilute God's blessing, and pride can lead to conflict within the covenant community.*

Homiletical Trajectories

(1) This story, like those that precede it, illustrates God's commitment to his people. As usual, he confronts their sin by implementing disciplinary measures. He is willing to show compassion, but we should not assume that relief comes if we simply push the right buttons and say we are sorry for our misdeeds. Persistent sin must be confronted in a genuine, sometimes even radical, manner. This involves recognizing that the Lord alone is the source of salvation. Genuine repentance in turn opens the door to God's compassion, which prompts him to intervene.

(2) Like earlier stories, this account also illustrates how assimilation to the surrounding pagan culture results in the covenant community losing its sense of unity and common purpose. Petty self-interest and pride can tear the community apart.

(3) As the covenant community becomes more like the pagan world

around it, the leaders who emerge in the community may display some frightening pagan traits. God can use such flawed leaders to accomplish his purposes, but their deficient faith may turn triumph into tragedy and their deficient wisdom may prove inadequate to promote and sustain unity within the community.

Preaching idea: *Persistent ingratitude can so alienate us from God that he will bring relief only when we radically repudiate our sin. Even then, the contaminating effects of our pagan culture are sometimes still evident in our community and its leaders. Deficient leaders can dilute God's blessing, and pride can lead to conflict within the community.*

This preaching idea reflects the Jephthah story as a unified whole. If we focus on the first trajectory, a *preaching idea* might be: *God must sometimes discipline us when we sin, but we should not assume that relief comes if we simply push the right buttons and say we are sorry for our misdeeds. We must confront persistent sin in a radical manner.*

If we focus on the second and third trajectories, a *preaching idea* might be: *When we embrace the surrounding pagan culture, we can lose our sense of unity and common purpose, allowing petty self-interest and pride to tear the covenant community apart. During such times, we must be especially vigilant, for the leaders who emerge among us may display some frightening pagan traits. God can use such flawed leaders to accomplish his purposes, but their deficient faith may turn triumph into tragedy and their deficient wisdom may prove inadequate to promote and sustain unity within the community.*

JUDGES 13:1–16:31

Samson: Lion Killer with a Sweet Tooth

TRANSLATION AND NARRATIVE STRUCTURE

13:1a The Israelites again did evil before the LORD, (*initiatory*)

1b   so the LORD handed them over to the Philistines for forty years. (*consequential*)

2a   There was a man from Zorah, from the Danite tribe,[1] (*introductory*)[2]

2b   **whose name was Manoah**. (*supplemental*)[3]

2c   **His wife was infertile** (*supplemental*)

2d   **and childless**. (*reiterative*)

3a   The LORD's messenger appeared to the woman (*initiatory*)[4]

---

1. מִשְׁפָּחָה, "clan," is used here of the tribal group of Dan (see as well 18:2, 11; cf. 17:7, where it is used of the tribe of Judah). The word appears to refer to a clan within a larger tribal group in 9:1; 18:19; and 21:24.

2. Verse 2a marks the transition to the story proper and provides background information for the narrative.

3. The disjunctive clauses in verse 2bc give additional information about key participants in the story to follow.

4. The *wayyiqtol* clause in verse 3a initiates the story proper. Verse 1 initiates a new literary unit in the macrostructure. Compare the structure of 13:1–3 with 4:1–6.

3b and said to her, *(sequential)*
  "You are infertile and childless, but you will conceive and have a son.

4 *Now be careful! Do not drink wine or strong drink,[5] and do not eat any food that will make you ritually unclean.*

5 *Look, you will conceive and have a son. You should not cut his hair, for the child will be dedicated to God from birth. He will begin to deliver Israel from the power of the Philistines."*

6a The woman went *(sequential)*
6b and said to her husband, *(sequential)*
6c *"A man sent from God came to me. He looked like God's messenger—he was very awesome. I did not ask him where he came from, and he did not tell me his name.*

7 *He said to me, 'Look, you will conceive and have a son. So now, do not drink wine or strong drink and do not eat any food that will make you ritually unclean. For the child will be dedicated to God from birth until the day he dies.'"*

8a Manoah prayed to the LORD, *(sequential)*[6]
8b *"Excuse me, Master. Please allow the man sent from God to visit us again, so he can teach us how we should raise the child who will be born."*

9a God heard Manoah's prayer. *(sequential)*
9b God's messenger visited the woman again, *(sequential)*
9c **while she was sitting in the field**. *(circumstantial)*
9d **But her husband Manoah was not with her.** *(supplemental)*
10a The woman ran quickly *(resumptive-sequential)*
10b and told her husband, *(sequential)*
10c *"Come quickly, the man who visited me the other day has appeared to me."*
11a So Manoah got up *(consequential)*
11b and followed his wife. *(sequential)*
11c When he met the man, *(sequential)*

---

5. There is some debate over the referent of the term שֵׁכָר. Some regard it as beer (Borowski 1987, 92), but it is more likely that the term refers to a grape product. See King and Stager, who suggest it is the pomace of the grape distilled into a type of brandy (2001, 101–03). Another option is that it refers to date palm wine (Walsh 2000, 200–02).

6. In the Hebrew text there is a *wayyiqtol* clause attached ("and he said"); it has a specifying function in relation to the preceding verb "he prayed."

11d he said to him, (*sequential*)

11e *"Are you the man who spoke to this woman?"*

11f He replied, (*sequential*)

11g *"Yes."*

12a Manoah said, (*sequential*)

12b *"Now, when your announcement comes true, how should the child be raised and what should he do?"*

13a The LORD's messenger told Manoah, (*sequential*)

13b *"Your wife should pay attention to everything I told her.*

14 *She should not drink anything that the grapevine produces. She must not drink wine or strong drink, and she must not eat any food that will make her ritually unclean. She should obey everything I commanded her to do."*

15a Manoah said to the LORD's messenger, (*sequential*)

15b *"Please stay here awhile, so we can prepare a young goat for you to eat."*

16a The LORD's messenger said to Manoah, (*sequential*)

16b *"If I stay, I will not eat your food. But if you want to make a burnt sacrifice to the LORD, you should offer it."*

16c (He said this) because Manoah did not know that he was the LORD's messenger.[7]

17a Manoah said to the LORD's messenger, (*sequential*)

17b *"Tell us your name, so we can honor you when your announcement comes true."*

18a The LORD's messenger said to him, (*sequential*)

18b *"You should not ask me my name, because you cannot comprehend it."*

19a Manoah took a young goat and a grain offering (*sequential*)

19b and offered them on a rock to the LORD. (*sequential*)

19c **The Lord's messenger did an amazing thing** (*circumstantial*)[8]

19d **as Manoah and his wife watched.** (*synchronic*)

---

7. In the Hebrew text this final clause is actually subordinated to what precedes (note כִּי, "because"). It explains why the angel said what he did.

8. The juxtaposed disjunctive clauses in verse 19cd indicate synchronic action (see 3:20, 24). Verse 19c should be emended to read as a disjunctive clause. See our remarks on this verse in the commentary that follows. Within their context, these disjunctive clauses draw attention to the angel's action and mark a transition within the scene.

20a As the flame went up from the altar toward the sky, (*focusing-circumstantial*)[9]

20b the LORD's messenger went up in it (*focusing*)

20c **while Manoah and his wife watched.** (*circumstantial*)

20d They fell face down to the ground. (*consequential*)

21a **The Lord's messenger did not appear again to Manoah and his wife.** (*supplemental*)[10]

21b **Then Manoah realized the visitor had been the Lord's messenger.** (*resumptive-sequential*)

22a Manoah said to his wife, (*sequential*)

22b *"We will die for sure, because we have seen God."*

23a But his wife said to him, (sequential)

23b *"If the LORD wanted to kill us, he would not have accepted the burnt offering and the grain offering from us. He would not have shown us all these things, or just now have spoken to us like this."*

24a Manoah's wife gave birth to a son (*sequential*)

24b and named him Samson. (*sequential*)

24c The child grew (*sequential*)

24d and the LORD empowered him. (*sequential*)

25 The LORD's spirit began to control him in Mahaneh Dan between Zorah and Eshtaol. (*sequential*)

14:1a Samson went down to Timnah, (*initiatory*)

1b where a Philistine woman caught his eye. (*sequential*)

2a When he got home, (*sequential*)

2b he told his father and mother, (*sequential*)

2c *"A Philistine woman in Timnah has caught my eye. Now get her as my wife."*

3a But his father and mother said to him, (*sequential*)

3b *"Certainly you can find a wife among your relatives or among all our people. You should not have to go and get a wife from the uncircumcised Philistines."*

3c But Samson said to his father, (*sequential*)

---

9. Verse 20a begins a more focused description of what the amazing act (v. 19c) entailed. It is also circumstantial in relation to the statement that follows. Verse 20b has a focusing function in relation to verse 19c; it describes specifically the amazing deed performed by the angel.

10. Verse 21a is supplemental; verse 21b relates consequentially to verse 20 and is best labeled resumptive-sequential (note אָז, "then"). See Chisholm 2010a, and our remarks in the commentary.

3d   *"Get her for me, because she is the right one for me."*

4a   **Now his father and mother did not realize this was the Lord's doing, for he was seeking an opportunity to stir up trouble with the Philistines.** (*supplemental*)

4b   **At that time the Philistines were ruling Israel.** (*supplemental*)

5a   Samson went down to Timnah. (*initiatory*)

5b   When he approached the vineyards of Timnah,[11] (*sequential*)

5c   **he saw a roaring young lion attacking him.** (*dramatic*)

6a   The Lord's spirit empowered him (*sequential*)

6b   and, as easily as one would tear a young goat, he tore the lion in two (*sequential*)

6c   **with his bare hands.** (*circumstantial*)

6d   **But he did not tell his father or mother what he had done.** (*supplemental*)

7a   Samson continued on down to Timnah. (*initiatory*)

7b   When he spoke to the woman, (*sequential*)

7c   he considered her to be just the right one. (*sequential*)

8a   Some time later, when he went back to marry her, (*sequential*)

8b   he turned aside to see the lion's remains. (*sequential*)

8c   **He saw a swarm of bees in the lion's carcass, as well as some honey.** (*dramatic*)

9a   He scooped it up with his hands (*sequential*)

9b   and ate it as he walked along. (*sequential*)

9c   When he returned to his father and mother, (*sequential*)

9d   he offered them some (*sequential*)

9e   and they ate it. (*sequential*)

9f   **But he did not tell them he had scooped the honey out of the lion's carcass.** (*supplemental*)

---

11. The Hebrew text says, "Samson went down with his father and mother to Timnah. When they approached, . . ." Verse 6b states that Samson did not tell his parents about his encounter with the lion (vv. 5b–6a), but verse 5a gives the impression they would have seen the entire episode. One could assume that Samson separated from his parents prior to the lion attack, but the Hebrew text does not indicate this. It seems more likely that the words "with his father and his mother" were accidentally copied into the text, perhaps under the influence of verse 4a, where the same phrase appears. An original singular verb ("he approached") may have been changed to the plural form ("they approached") after the words "his father and his mother" were accidentally added to the text.

10a Then Samson's father accompanied him down to Timnah for the marriage. (*initiatory*)

10b Samson hosted a party there, for this was customary for bridegrooms to do. (*sequential*)

11a When the Philistines saw he had no attendants, (*transitional-sequential*)[12]

11b they gave him thirty groomsmen (*sequential*)

11c who kept him company. (*consequential*)

12a Samson said to them, (*sequential*)

12b *"I will give you a riddle. If you really can solve it during the seven days the party lasts, I will give you thirty linen robes and thirty sets of clothes.*

13a *But if you cannot solve it, you will give me thirty linen robes and thirty sets of clothes."*

13b They said to him, (*sequential*)

13c *"Let us hear your riddle."*

14a He said to them, (*sequential*)

14b *"Out of the one who eats came something to eat;*
out of the strong one came something sweet."

14c They could not solve the riddle for three days. (*sequential*)

15a On the fourth day (*transitional-circumstantial*)[13]

15b they said to Samson's bride, (*sequential*)

15c *"Trick your husband into giving the solution to the riddle. If you refuse, we will burn up you and your father's family. Did you invite us here to make us poor?"*

16a So Samson's bride cried on his shoulder (*consequential*)

16b and said, (*sequential*)

16c *"You must hate me; you do not love me. You told the young men a riddle, but you have not told me the solution."*

16d He said to her, (*sequential*)

---

12. Verse 11a, which introduces the Philistines into the scene and marks a transition within the scene, is sequential to verse 10b, but it describes an action that is not as important as what follows in verse 11b (cf. 2:4; 11:35).

13. In reading "fourth day" we follow the Septuagint; MT has "seventh day." See the commentary below. Verse 15a is a brief temporal indicator that is circumstantial to what follows. It is also transitional, for it signals a shift in the scene from the preliminary dialogue to a significant event that will lead to the Philistines' discovering the answer to the riddle. Broida (2010, 17) states that a "dramatic pause surrounds" verse 14; she sees a new scene introduced in verse 15.

16e "Look, I have not even told my father or mother. Do you really
expect me to tell you?"

17a She cried on his shoulder until the party was almost over.
(*sequential*)

17b Finally, on the seventh day, (*transitional-circumstantial*)[14]

17c he told her because she had nagged him so much. (*sequential*)

17d Then she told the young men the solution to the riddle.
(*sequential*)

18a On the seventh day, before the sun set, the men of the city said
to him, (*sequential*)

18b "What is sweeter than honey?
What is stronger than a lion?"

18c He said to them, (*sequential*)

18d "If you had not plowed with my heifer,
you would not have solved my riddle."

19a The LORD's spirit empowered him. (*sequential*)

19b He went down to Ashkelon (*sequential*)

19c and killed thirty men. (*sequential*)

19d He took their clothes (*sequential*)

19e and gave them to the men who had solved the riddle.
(*sequential*)

19f He was furious (*supplemental-explanatory*)[15]

19g and went back home. (*sequential*)

20 Samson's bride was then given to his best man. (*sequential*)

15:1a Sometime later, during the wheat harvest,
(*introductory-backgrounding*)

1b Samson, taking a young goat as a gift, went to visit his bride.
(*initiatory*)

1c He said to her father, (*sequential*)

1d "I want to have sex with my bride in her bedroom."

1e **But her father would not let him enter.** (*contrastive*)[16]

2a Her father said, (*sequential*)

---

14. Like verse 15a, the brief temporal indicator in verse 17b is both circumstantial to the following clause and transitional in the scene. It introduces the peak event, Samson's divulging of his secret.

15. Verse 19f gives the reason why Samson did not stay with his wife, but returned home (v. 19g).

16. The clause in verse 1e (introduced by a negated perfect) contrasts the father's response with Samson's request.

2b *"I really thought you absolutely despised her, so I gave her to your best man. Her younger sister is more attractive than she is. Take her instead."*

3a Samson said to them, *(sequential)*

3b *"This time I am justified in doing the Philistines harm!"*

4a Samson went *(sequential)*

4b and captured three hundred jackals *(sequential)*

4c and got some torches. *(sequential)*

4d He tied the jackals in pairs by their tails *(sequential)*

4e and then tied a torch to each pair. *(sequential)*

5a He lit the torches *(sequential)*

5b and set the jackals loose in the Philistines' standing grain. *(sequential)*

5c He burned up the grain heaps and the standing grain, as well as the vineyards and olive groves. *(sequential)*

6a The Philistines asked, *(sequential)*

6b *"Who did this?"*

6c They were told, *(sequential)*

6d *"Samson, the Timnite's son-in-law, because the Timnite took Samson's bride and gave her to his best man."*

6e So the Philistines went up *(sequential)*

6f and burned her and her father. *(sequential)*

7a Samson said to them, *(sequential)*

7b *"Because you did this, I will get revenge against you before I quit fighting."*

8a He struck them down, slaughtering them.[17] *(sequential)*

8b Then he went down *(sequential)*

8c and lived for a time in the cave in the cliff of Etam. *(sequential)*

9a The Philistines went up *(sequential)*

9b and invaded Judah. *(sequential)*

9c They arranged for battle in Lehi. *(sequential)*

10a The men of Judah said, *(sequential)*

10b *"Why do you attack us?"*

10c The Philistines replied, *(sequential)*

10d *"We have come up to take Samson prisoner so we can do to him what he has done to us."*

---

17. The Hebrew text reads literally, "he struck them, calf against thigh, (with) a great slaughter."

11a Three thousand men from Judah went down to the cave in the cliff of Etam (*sequential*)[18]

11b and said to Samson, (*sequential*)

11c *"Do you not know that the Philistines rule over us? Why have you done this to us?"*

11d He said to them, (*sequential*)

11e *"I have only done to them what they have done to me."*

12a They said to him, (*sequential*)

12b *"We have come down to take you prisoner so we can hand you over to the Philistines."*

12c Samson said to them, (*sequential*)

12d *"Promise me you will not kill me."*

13a They said to him, (*sequential*)

13b *"We promise! We will only take you prisoner and hand you over to them. We promise not to kill you."*[19]

13c They tied him up with two brand new ropes (*sequential*)

13d and led him up from the cliff. (*sequential*)

14a **When he arrived in Lehi,** (*circumstantial*)[20]

14b **the Philistines shouted as they approached him.** (*synchronic*)

14c The LORD's spirit empowered him. (*sequential*)

14d The ropes around his arms were like flax dissolving in fire (*sequential*)

14e and they melted away from his hands. (*sequential*)

15a He happened to see a solid jawbone of a donkey. (*sequential*)

15b He grabbed it (*sequential*)

15c and struck down a thousand men. (*sequential*)[21]

---

18. On the number mentioned here, see the commentary above on 1:4. As noted there, it is difficult to accept such figures at face value. One possibility is that the Hebrew term אֶלֶף, traditionally understood as a numeral (a "thousand"), actually refers to a contingent of troops, at least in some contexts. Boling, taking this approach, translates "three contingents" in verse 11 (1975, 237). Another option is that such large numbers are hyperbolic. See Fouts 1997, 377–88, and 2003, 283–99.

19. In both cases "we promise" is an attempt to bring out the emphatic force of the infinitive absolute.

20. The juxtaposed disjunctive clauses in verse 14ab indicate synchronic action.

21. On the number mentioned here, see the commentary above on 1:4. As noted there, it is difficult to accept such figures at face value. One possibility is that the Hebrew term אֶלֶף, traditionally understood as a numeral (a "thousand"), actually refers to a contingent of troops, at least in some

16a Samson then said, (*sequential*)

16b *"With the jawbone of a donkey I have left them in heaps;*
with the jawbone of a donkey I have struck down a thousand
men."

17a When he finished speaking, (*transitional-circumstantial*)

17b he threw the jawbone down (*sequential*)

17c and named that place Ramath Lehi. (*sequential*)

18a He was very thirsty, (*sequential*)

18b so he cried out to the LORD (*consequential*)

18c and said, (*specifying*)

18d *"You have given your servant this great victory. But now must I*
die of thirst and fall into the hands of the uncircumcised?"

19a So God split open the basin at Lehi (*consequential*)

19b and water flowed out from it. (*consequential*)

19c When he took a drink, (*sequential*)

19d his strength was restored (*sequential*)

19e and he revived. (*consequential*)

19f **For this reason he named it En Hakkore, which remains**
in Lehi to this very day. (*supplemental-explanatory*)[22]

20 Samson led Israel for twenty years during the days of Philistine
prominence. (*concluding*)

16:1a Samson went to Gaza. (*initiatory*)

1b There he saw a prostitute (*sequential*)

1c and went in to have sex with her. (*sequential*)

2a The Gazites were told,[23] (*sequential*)

2b *"Samson has come here."*

2c So they surrounded the town[24] (*consequential*)

---

contexts. Boling, taking this approach, translates "a whole contingent" in
verse 15 (1975, 237). Another option is that such large numbers are hyperbolic. See Fouts 1997, 377–88, and 2003, 283–99.

22. Verse 19f (introduced by עַל־כֵּן, ("for this reason, therefore") provides an
etiological note that is supplemental to the story line. The narrator's supplemental note explains how the site received its name.

23. The Hebrew text reads literally, "To the Gazites, saying." An introductory
verb is missing. With the LXX we add "and it was reported."

24. The Hebrew text reads simply "And they surrounded." The rest of the
verse suggests that "the town" is the object, not "the house." Though they
knew he was in the town, apparently they did not know exactly where he
had gone. Otherwise, they could have just gone into or surrounded the
house and would not have needed to post guards at the city gate. For further discussion see the commentary.

2d   and hid all night at the city gate, waiting for him to leave. (*sequential*)
2e   They relaxed all night, thinking, (*focusing*)[25]
2f   *"He will not leave until morning comes; then we will kill him!"*
3a   Samson spent half the night with the prostitute, (*flashback*)[26]
3b   then he left in the middle of the night. (*sequential*)
3c   He grabbed the doors of the city gate, as well as the two posts, (*sequential*)
3d   and pulled them right off, bar and all. (*sequential*)
3e   He put them on his shoulders (*sequential*)
3f   and carried them up to the top of a hill east of Hebron. (*sequential*)

4a   After this (*introductory-backgrounding*)
4b   Samson fell in love with a woman who lived in the Sorek Valley. (*initiatory*)
4c   **Her name was Delilah.** (*supplemental*)
5a   The rulers of the Philistines went up to visit her (*resumptive-sequential*)
5b   and said to her, (*sequential*)
5c   *"Trick him! Find out what makes him so strong and how we can subdue him and humiliate him. Each one of us will give you eleven hundred silver pieces."*
6a   So Delilah said to Samson, (*sequential*)
6b   *"Tell me what makes you so strong and how you can be subdued and humiliated."*
7a   Samson said to her, (*sequential*)
7b   *"If they tie me up with seven fresh bowstrings that have not been dried, I will become weak and be just like any other man."*
8a   So the rulers of the Philistines brought her seven fresh bowstrings that had not been dried (*sequential*)

---

25. Verse 2e has a focusing function as it describes more specifically what the Philistines did as they waited for Samson during the night.
26. Verse 3 involves a flashback; the actions described occurred within the time frame depicted in verse 2. After Samson arrived at the prostitute's house, the men of Gaza set an ambush for him "all night" long and made no move to capture him during the night (v. 2). The actions described extend from the time when they became aware of his presence until morning. However, using a *wayyiqtol* verbal form, verse 3 informs us that Samson stayed with the prostitute until the "middle of the night" and then arose and left the city, apparently without the guards noticing!

8b   and they tied him up with them. (*sequential*)

9a   **While they were hiding in the bedroom,** (*circumstantial*)

9b   she said to him, (*sequential*)

9c   *"The Philistines are here, Samson!"*

9d   He snapped the bowstrings as easily as a thread of yarn snaps when it is put close to fire. (*sequential*)

9e   **The secret of his strength was not discovered.** (*summarizing*)

10a   Delilah said to Samson, (*sequential*)

10b   *"Look, you deceived me and told me lies. Now tell me how you can be subdued."*

11a   He said to her, (*sequential*)

11b   *"If they tie me tightly with brand new ropes that have never been used, I will become weak and be just like any other man."*

12a   So Delilah took new ropes (*sequential*)

12b   and tied him with them (*sequential*)

12c   and said to him, (*sequential*)

12d   *"The Philistines are here, Samson!"*

12e   (**The Philistines were hiding in the bedroom.**) (*supplemental*)

12f   But he tore the ropes from his arms as if they were a piece of thread. (*resumptive-sequential*)

13a   Delilah said to Samson, (*sequential*)

13b   *"Up to now you have deceived me and told me lies. Tell me how you can be subdued."*

13c   He said to her, (*sequential*)

13d   *"If you weave the seven braids of my hair into the fabric and secure it with the pin to the wall, I will become weak just like any other man."*[27]

14a   So when he was asleep, (*sequential*)

---

27. The Hebrew text of verse 13d reads simply, "He said to her, 'If you weave the seven braids of my head into the fabric.'" The translation above essentially follows the LXX. The last clause in both Vaticanus and Alexandrinus differs slightly from the syntax in verses 7 and 11. Both Vaticanus and Alexandrinus have χαι ασθενησω χαι εσομαι ως εις των ανθρωπων, "and I will be weak and I will be as one of the men," in verses 7 and 11. This corresponds to Hebrew וְחָלִיתִי וְהָיִיתִי כְּאַחַד הָאָדָם in both verses. In verse 13 Vaticanus has χαι εσομαι ως εις των ανθρωπων ασθενης, while Alexandrinus has χαι εσομαι ασθενης ως εις των ανθρωπων. Though the word order differs, both can be translated, "and I will be weak as one of the men."

14b Delilah took the seven braids of his hair, (*sequential*)

14c wove them into the fabric, (*sequential*)

14d fastened it with the pin to the wall,[28] (*sequential*)

14e and said, (*sequential*)

14f *"The Philistines are here, Samson!"*

14g He woke up (*sequential*)

14h and tore away the pin of the loom and the fabric. (*sequential*)

15a She said to him, (*sequential*)

15b *"How can you say, 'I love you,' when you will not share your secret with me? Three times you have deceived me and have not told me what makes you so strong."*

16a She nagged him every day (*transitional-sequential*)[29]

16b and pressured him (*reiterative-emphatic*)[30]

16c until he was sick and tired of it. (*consequential*)

17a Finally he told her his secret. (*consequential*)

17b He said to her, (*specifying*)

17c *"My hair has never been cut, for I have been dedicated to God from the time I was conceived. If my head were shaved, my strength would leave me; I would become weak, and be just like all other men."*

18a When Delilah saw that he had told her his secret, (*sequential*)

18b she sent for[31] the rulers of the Philistines, saying, (*consequential*)

18c *"Come up here again, for he has told me his secret."*

---

28. The Hebrew text omits verse 14a–c. The translation above follows the LXX (Vaticanus) in verse 14a–d: και εγενετο εν τω κοιμασθαι αυτον και ελαβεν Δαλιδα τας επτα σειρας της κεφαλης αυτου και υφανεν εν τω διασματι και επηξεν τω πασσαλω εις τον τοιχον. Alexandrinus differs in some respects: και εκοιμισεν αυτον Δαλιδα και εδιασατο τους επτα βοστρυχους της κεφαλης αυτου μετα της εκτασεως και κατεκρουσεν εν τοις πασσαλοις εις τον τοιχον. In verse 14d the Hebrew text has simply, "and she fastened (it) with the pin." Vaticanus has και επηξεν τω πασσαλω εις τον τοιχον in verse 14d, adding "into the wall" (cf. also Alexandrinus).

29. The *wayyehi* in verse 16a, which is followed by a temporal clause, carries on the sequence of action, but it also marks a significant transition in the episode. Prior to this Samson has resisted her efforts to find the secret of his success, but now he will begin to weaken (v. 16c) and then give in (v. 17).

30. The *wayyiqtol* clause in verse 16b reiterates what has just been said, apparently for emphasis. It also heightens the drama of the episode by stressing how determined she became.

31. The Hebrew text has two verbs here, "she sent and she summoned."

18d So the rulers of the Philistines went up to her,[32] (*consequential*)
18e carrying the silver in their hands. (*focusing*)
19a She made him go to sleep on her lap (*sequential*)
19b and then called a man in (*sequential*)
19c to shave off[33] the seven braids of his hair. (*sequential*)
19d She made him vulnerable[34] (*consequential*)
19e and his strength left him. (*consequential*)
20a She said, (*sequential*)
20b *"The Philistines are here, Samson!"*
20c He woke up (*sequential*)
20d and thought, (*sequential*)
20e *"I will do as I did before and shake myself free."*
20f **But he did not realize that the Lord had left him.**
 (*supplemental-explanatory*)[35]
21a The Philistines captured him (*sequential*)
21b and gouged out his eyes. (*sequential*)
21c They brought him down to Gaza (*sequential*)
21d and bound him in bronze chains. (*sequential*)
21e He became a grinder in the prison. (*sequential*)

---

32. The Hebrew text of verse 18d begins with וְעָלוּ, "and they went up," a *weqatal* form. While the relatively rare *weqatal* construction is attested elsewhere where one expects a *wayyiqtol* form (see Judg. 3:23), what the function of the construction would be in this case is not clear. It is preferable in this instance to read a *wayyiqtol* form וַיַּעֲלוּ, "and they went up," a reading that is attested in many Hebrew manuscripts (see *BHS* note 18b). The MT reading probably suffers from virtual haplography here; the letters *waw* and *yod* are very similar in some script phases. The translation assumes the *wayyiqtol* reading and classifies the function of the clause accordingly.

33. The Hebrew text reads, "and she shaved off." The point seems to be that Delilah acted through the instrumentality of the man she summoned (Soggin 1981, 254).

34. The Hebrew text reads, "She began to humiliate him." Rather than referring to some specific insulting action on Delilah's part after Samson's hair was shaved off, this statement probably means that through the devious actions just described she began the process of Samson's humiliation which culminates in the following verses. The language is tragically ironic, for the Philistines used this same verb in their instructions to Delilah (v. 5, "Find out what makes him so strong and how we can subdue him and humiliate him.") and Delilah echoed this in her initial request (v. 6, "Tell me what makes you so strong and how you can be subdued and humiliated").

35. The supplemental disjunctive clause in verse 20f explains why Samson made the previous statement.

22 His hair began to grow back after it had been shaved off. (*sequential*)

23a The rulers of the Philistines gathered to offer a great sacrifice to Dagon their god and to celebrate. (*introductory*)

23b They said, (*sequential*)

23c *"Our god has handed over to us Samson, our arch-enemy."*[36]

24a When the people saw him,[37] (*sequential*)

24b they praised their god, saying, (*sequential*)

24c *"Our god has handed over to us our enemy, the one who ruined our land and killed so many of us!"*

25a When they got good and silly, (*transitional-sequential*)[38]

25b they said, (*sequential*)

25c *"Call for Samson so he can entertain us!"*

25d So they summoned Samson from the prison (*sequential*)

25e and he entertained them. (*sequential*)

25f They made him stand between two pillars. (*sequential*)

26a Samson said to the young man who held his hand, (*sequential*)

26b *"Position me so I can touch the pillars that support the temple. Then I can lean on them."*

27a Now the temple was filled with men and women, (*supplemental*)[39]

---

36. This translation is an attempt to bring out the force of the plural, which appears to be a plural of degree or a concretized abstract plural. See the note in the commentary for a more detailed discussion of the point.

37. Most interpret this as a reference to Samson, but this seems premature, since verse 25 suggests he was not yet standing before them. Consequently some prefer to see this statement as displaced and move it to verse 25 (Burney 1970, 387). It seems more likely that the pronoun refers to an image of Dagon.

38. The *wayyehi* in verse 25a, which is followed by a temporal clause, carries on the sequence of action, but it also marks a transition in the episode from the preliminaries (vv. 23–24) to the main event, which will prove to be the Philistines' demise.

39. The disjunctive clauses in verse 27 have an important role in the narrative. Viewed collectively the three statements highlight the degree of Samson's humiliation, but they also prepare us for the magnitude of his victory. Verse 27bc has a specifying-emphatic function (cf. 6:5b; 7:12b). Each statement adds additional details that heighten the drama and draw attention to the magnitude of the event. Verse 27b informs us that the leaders were present, while verse 27c tells us that there were even people on the roof of the temple.

27b **and all the rulers of the Philistines were there**. (*specifying-emphatic*)

27c **There were three thousand men and women on the roof watching Samson entertain**. (*specifying-emphatic*)

28a Samson called to the LORD,[40] (*resumptive-sequential*)

28b *"O Master, LORD, remember me! Strengthen me just one more time, O God, so I can get swift revenge against the Philistines for my two eyes!"*

29a Samson took hold of the two middle pillars that supported the temple (*sequential*)

29b and he leaned against them, with his right hand on one and his left hand on the other. (*sequential*)[41]

30a Samson said, (*sequential*)

30b *"Let me die with the Philistines!"*

30c He pushed hard (*sequential*)

30d and the temple collapsed on the rulers and all the people in it. (*consequential*)

30e He killed many more people in his death than he had killed during his life. (*supplemental-descriptive*)[42]

31a His brothers and all his family went down (*sequential*)

31b and brought him back.[43] (*sequential*)

31c They buried him between Zorah and Eshtaol in the tomb of Manoah his father. (*sequential*)

31d **He had led Israel for twenty years**. (*concluding*)[44]

OUTLINE

Miracle Baby (13:1–25)
    Israel rebels (13:1)
    Birth announcement (13:2–5)
    Details matter (13:6–7)
    Manoah meets an angel (13:8–23)

---

40. The Hebrew text actually has two verbs, "he called . . . and said."

41. I have taken אֶחָד בִּימִינוֹ וְאֶחָד בִּשְׂמֹאלוֹ, literally, "one in his right hand and one in his left hand," as a compound adverbial accusative, rather than compound circumstantial clauses.

42. The *wayyiqtol* clause in verse 30e gives supplemental information that highlights the magnitude of Samson's final accomplishment.

43. The Hebrew text has two verbs here, "and they lifted him up and brought (him) up."

44. The disjunctive clause in verse 31d pulls down the curtain on Samson's career.

"Sunny" arrives (13:24–25)
A Wedding Without a Honeymoon (14:1–20)
    Samson picks a wife (14:1–4)
    Lion killer (14:5–6)
    Samson likes sweets (14:7–9)
    Samson loses a bet (14:10–18)
    Samson pays off a debt (14:19–20)
Samson Gets Revenge (15:1–20)
    Playing with fire (15:1–8a)
    Showdown at Jawbone Hill (15:8b–20)
Femmes Fatales (16:1–22)
    Samson flirts with disaster (16:1–3)
    Disaster flirts back (16:4–22)
Tragedy and Triumph (16:23–31)
    "Sunny" dies in darkness (16:23–30)
    Death notice and epitaph (16:31)

LITERARY STRUCTURE

Another reference to Israel doing evil before the Lord (13:1) introduces the next and final major literary unit of the book's central section. The report of Israel's lapse into sin and God's disciplinary judgment sets the stage for the story of Samson, which consists of five episodes. The account of Samson's birth, which is bracketed by references to Zorah and the tribe of Dan (13:2, 25), informs us of God's purpose for Samson.[45] Within this episode are four scenes: the angel's encounter with Manoah's wife (vv. 2–5), her report to her husband (vv. 6–7), the angel's second visit (vv. 8–23), and the child's birth and development (vv. 24–25). Chapter 14 tells of Samson's unconsummated marriage to a Philistine woman. References to Samson (or, in one case, his father) "going down" mark distinct movements within this episode (cf. 14:1, 5, 7, 10, 19). Chapter 15 records the conflicts with the Philistines that the aborted marriage produced. In 15:1, the temporal indicator (וַיְהִי) separates the report of the failed marriage (chapter 14) from the series of events comprising its sequel (chapter 15). Again a reference to Samson "going down" (15:8b) divides this episode into two scenes.[46] The reference to Samson's leading Israel for twenty years (15:20) seems to bring the entire story to a happy ending, but we quickly discover this is not

---

45. For other indicators of closure in verses 24–25, see Broida 2010, 15. Yet, as she points out, they anticipate what is to follow, so the verses have a transitional function as well.
46. For other indicators of closure in verses 7–8, see Broida 2010, 18–19.

the case. The premature conclusion is not misplaced, however, for rhetorically it signals that Samson's career is as good as over. All that remains is humiliation and death. Chapter 16 tells of Samson's downfall (vv. 1–22) and his death and burial (vv. 23–31). There are two episodes in verses 1–22: Samson's visit to the Philistine prostitute at Gaza (vv. 1–3) and his entrapment by Delilah, which leads to his imprisonment in Gaza (vv. 4–22, cf. v. 21). A disjunctive clause (v. 23) introduces the final episode in the story, which concludes with an epitaph and disjunctive clause reporting the length of Samson's career as judge (v. 31).

EXPOSITION

Miracle Baby (13:1–25)

Israel rebels (13:1). For the sixth time in this section of the book of Judges, we read that the Israelites "did evil before the Lord." No specifics are given, but we can assume that idolatry was involved. The Lord handed his rebellious people over to the Philistines for forty years, the longest single period of oppression mentioned in the book (and one reminiscent of the wilderness wandering period).[47]

Unlike earlier cycles, the narrator does not report that Israel cried out to the Lord. The omission is odd, but the reason for it becomes apparent as the story unfolds. The people had come to accept the Philistines as their overlords and no longer desired relief. Even when Samson demonstrated tremendous military capability, his fellow Israelites failed to rally around him. In fact they criticized his efforts and handed him over to the enemy (cf. 15:9–13) (Webb 1987, 163). However, despite Israel's acceptance of their condition, God intended to intervene. The omission of any reference to Israel crying out sets the stage for the story to follow, which tells how God began to deliver a people who did not seek deliverance through a deliverer who failed

---

47. In the introduction to the Jephthah account, we read of a Philistine oppression (10:7), but the narrator never states specifically that it ended or continued. The subsequent narrative, which focuses exclusively on the Ammonites, may imply that the Philistine oppression was short-lived. At any rate, 13:1 seems to assume that earlier Philistine oppression had ended, for when Israel again sinned after the period of Jephthah and his successors, the Lord delivered Israel into the hands of the Philistines.

to see himself as such. The stylistic variation signals the overall incongruity and irony of the story.[48]

Birth announcement (13:2–5). The narrator introduces a man named Manoah, a Danite who resided in Zorah.[49] He also observes that Manoah's wife was sterile and childless.[50] At this point anyone familiar with biblical history cannot help but think of the recurring barren-mother type scene (Brown 2000, 239). Sarah (Gen. 11:30), Rebekah (Gen. 25:21), and Rachel (Gen. 29:31) are all described in similar terms (Olson 1998, 845).[51] God miraculously opened the wombs of these barren women and enabled them to give birth to sons (Isaac, Jacob, Joseph and Benjamin) who played an important role in the history of the covenant community. When the Lord's angel appears and announces that Manoah's wife would bear a son (vv. 3, 5), we expect this child will have a significant role to play, perhaps on a par with Isaac himself, whose birth was also announced in a special manner (Genesis 17–18).

After announcing the child's birth, the angel instructed Manoah's wife to follow a diet fit for a Nazirite (cf. Num. 6:3–4), for her son would

---

48. See Chisholm 2009c, 177. I originally made this point in an oral presentation at the 2006 national meeting of the Evangelical Theological Society in Washington, D. C. Butler cites this earlier unpublished version (2009, 322), which was subsequently revised and published in *JSOT*.

49. The formulaic introduction also appears in Judges 17:1; 1 Samuel 1:1; 9:1. On its significance as a linking device at the macrostructural level, see Chisholm 1994b, 46–47.

50. The adjective עֲקָרָה, "barren, childless," should not necessarily be understood in a technical gynecological sense. It describes a childless woman who, based on observation, was viewed as incapable of bearing children (cf. Gen. 11:30; 25:21; 29:31; Exod. 23:26; Deut. 7:14 [where the masculine form also appears]; 1 Sam. 2:5; Job 24:21; Ps. 113:9; Isa. 54:1).

51. For a thorough analysis of Judges 13 as a type scene, see Johnson 2010. He identifies seven elements in "the son of a barren woman" type scene: "(1) a statement describing the woman's barrenness; (2) an attempt by the woman or her spouse to obtain children; (3) the promise of the son; (4) information about the promised child; (5) a reaction (usually doubt) to the promise; (6) the birth of the son; and (7) the naming of the son" (272). Additionally there are two "minor recurring elements" in these scenes: "(1) the command to name the son; and (2) a statement of the son's prosperity" (272). In Judges 13 six of the main elements are present; the second element (the "attempt to acquire a son") is missing. The second of the two minor elements is also present (273–83, 286).

be consecrated to God as a Nazirite from birth. He also made it clear that the child's primary task would be military—he would "begin to deliver Israel from the power of the Philistines" (v. 5). This is surprising, for one might think God would have abandoned Israel by now. In the preceding cycle he was reluctant to respond to Israel, even when they confessed their sins (10:6–16). Now, when they had not even cried out to the Lord, he decided to deliver them. His sovereign and spontaneous decision to do so reminds us that he would never forsake his covenant people, no matter how apathetic they became.

The Lord's announcement that he would cause a childless woman to give birth is also significant in light of the preceding Jephthah narrative. The last act of "worship" recorded prior to this was Jephthah's sacrifice of his daughter out of misplaced devotion to the Lord. Here the Lord corrects that faulty view by demonstrating his desire to give children to his people, not take them away. He delights in making the barren woman a mother, not in his worshipers making potential mothers childless.

The precise timing and nature of Samson's conception are unclear.[52] NIV (note "you will conceive" in vv. 5, 7) assumes that Samson's mother would conceive sometime after her encounter with the angel, presumably after having marital relations with Manoah. In this view the angel's statement in verse 3 ("you are infertile") is a straightforward assessment of her condition at the time of the encounter and the predicate adjective הָרָה, literally, "pregnant," in verse 5 is understood as future (equivalent to וְהָרִית, "you will conceive," in v. 3).[53] The syntactical structure of verses 3–5 may favor this interpretation. Elsewhere when הִנֵּה נָא, literally, "look" (v. 3), is collocated with וְעַתָּה, "now" (v. 4), הִנֵּה נָא introduces the logical basis for an argument, while וְעַתָּה introduces the logical consequence (see Gen. 27:2–3; 2 Kings 5:15). Manoah's wife's impending conception and pregnancy (v. 3) necessitates that she observe a strict diet (v. 4). Verse 5 then begins with כִּי, "for," which is most naturally understood as an explanation for the instructions in verse 4 (cf. the following uses of the collocation וְעַתָּה + imperative(s) + כִּי: Gen. 20:7; Num. 22:6; 1 Sam. 9:13; 20:31; 25:17; 2 Sam. 3:18; 7:29; 13:13; 19:7). If so, then verse 5a is essentially equivalent to verse 3 in that it repeats (for the sake of emphasis) the basis for the instructions in

---

52. The discussion that follows also appears in Chisholm 2009b, 147–50.

53. On the use of the *weqatal* form (cf. וְהָרִית, "you will conceive," v. 3) to express a future development after a nominal sentence indicating a present fact, see *IBHS*, 534 (32.2.4), as well as GKC, 334 (112x) and Joüon-Muraoka, 396–97 (119c).

verse 4.[54] Consequently it appears that וְהָרִית (v. 3) and הִנָּךְ הָרָה, "look you will conceive" (v. 5), have the same temporal force.[55]

However, this is not the only grammatical option for the adjective in verse 5; it is possible to translate "you are pregnant." Several factors seem to favor this: (1) Elsewhere the predicate adjective הָרָה indicates a past condition (from the storyteller's perspective) when used in a narratival framework (1 Sam. 4:19), but it has a present force in quotations within a narratival framework (see Gen. 16:11; 38:24–25; 2 Sam. 11:5; Isa. 7:14 [though this last text is debated]).[56] (2) Elsewhere when suffixed הִנֵּה is followed by a predicate adjective, the adjective indicates a present condition (Gen. 16:11; Song 1:15–16; 4:1).[57] (3) Unlike other accounts where barren women become pregnant, there is no reference in the context to Manoah's wife conceiving (contrast Gen. 21:2; 25:21; 30:23; 1 Sam. 1:20), only to her giving birth to the child (see v. 24). Consequently it is possible that Manoah's wife became pregnant as the angel spoke with her. This could have occurred by a supernatural act, although this need not be the case since conception does not occur immediately after copulation (she could have had relations with Manoah shortly before this).[58]

---

54. However, it is possible that the כִּי at the beginning of verse 5 is emphatic ("surely, indeed"). In this case verse 5 could make an advance on the previous argument by pointing out that she is now pregnant, in fulfillment of the statement in verse 3. See Boling 1975, 220.

55. I owe this insightful syntactical argument to my friend and former student, Dr. Tom Keiser.

56. The form that follows in verses 5 and 7 (וְיֹלַדְתְּ) is difficult (cf. Gen. 16:11 as well). The vocalization appears to be a mixture of an active participle (cf. Isa. 7:14) and a second feminine singular perfect (cf. v. 3). See Joüon-Muraoka, 269 (para. 89j), as well as p. 73 (para. 16g). However, GKC (pp. 223, para. 80d; 276, para. 94f) understands the form as a participle without the helping vowel before the *tav* ending.

57. The same is true when suffixed הִנֵּה is followed by a predicate nominative (cf. Gen. 44:16; 2 Sam. 5:1; Jer. 44:2), with the exception of 2 Chronicles 20:24, where a narrator is the speaker.

58. Several commentators argue that she was pregnant when the angel spoke to her in verse 5. See Block 1999, 402; Boling 1975, 220; Moore 1895, 317; Klein 1988, 111–14. Brettler contends it was the messenger who impregnated her (2002, 44–49, cf. Reinhartz 1998, 98–101; and Margalith 1986a, 400–01). In her report to Manoah (v. 6) she states: "A man sent from God came to me." Brettler points out that the idiom בּוֹא אֶל, "enter to," can have a sexual connotation (see Judg. 15:1; 16:1) and may be translated: "The man of God slept with me" (2002, 45; see Klein 1988, 114; and Margalith 1986a, 400. The *qal* of בּוֹא is collocated with אֶל, and a distinctively

feminine singular suffix, either third or second person, eighteen times, fifteen of which have a sexual connotation [Gen. 29:21, 23; 30:3–4; 38:2, 16, 18; Deut. 21:13; 22:13; Judg. 16:1; Ruth 4:13; 2 Sam. 12:24; Ezek. 16:33; 23:17, 44]. There is no sexual connotation in Judges 4:22 and Ecclesiastes 9:14 [where a city, not a woman is the antecedent of the suffix]; Joshua 2:3 is ambiguous [the subject is plural here, but cf. Ezek. 16:33 and 23:17 in this regard].) While this expression is by no means technical for sexual intercourse, its appearance in a context where conception is a major theme is striking. Usage would also seem to favor an idiomatic use. Elsewhere when a woman uses the idiom "come to me," as Manoah's wife does, it has a sexual connotation. (See Gen. 38:16; 39:14, 17. Josh. 2:4 is ambiguous; the verb there is plural, not singular.) Brettler draws attention to the text's emphasis on the human qualities of the messenger and observes that angelic parentage would account well for Samson's superhuman abilities. He draws a parallel to Genesis 6, where angels cohabit with human women, and suggests post-biblical sources (Josephus and Pseudo-Philo) hint at this interpretation of Samson's birth.

However, a closer look at the immediate context militates against this proposal. In verse 8 Manoah prays that the Lord would allow the man of God "to come again to us" (literal translation). Surely the idiom "come to" does not have a sexual connotation here! Of course one could argue that Manoah, who shows a propensity for confusion elsewhere in the chapter, did not understand the full implications of his wife's statement in verse 6. However, verse 9 informs us that the angel of God, in response to Manoah's request, "came again to" her (literal translation). The action is viewed as repeating the earlier incident (note עוֹד, "again"). Why would he need to have sexual relations with her again if she was already pregnant (cf. v. 5)? (Elsewhere the collocation of a masculine singular form of the *qal* of בּוֹא, "enter," with אֶל, "to," followed by אִשָּׁה, "a woman," has a sexual connotation [cf. Gen. 38:8–9; Judg. 15:1; 1 Chron. 7:23; Prov. 6:29; Ezek. 23:44], but in five cases אִשָּׁה is suffixed or modified by a genitive and clearly refers to a man's wife. In the other example [Ezek. 23:44] it is followed by appositional זוֹנָה and refers to a prostitute. When the definite form הָאִשָּׁה, "the woman," is the object of the preposition, as in Judg. 13:9, there is no sexual connotation, though in both of the other instances the verb is masculine plural, not singular [1 Sam. 28:8; 2 Sam. 17:20].) In verse 10 she simply reports to Manoah that the man "appeared" (נִרְאָה) to her. This suggests that בּוֹא אֶל, "enter to" (v. 9) merely refers to his appearing to her and has no sexual connotation. If so, we can safely assume that בּוֹא אֶל in her initial report to Manoah (v. 6) refers to the man's appearing to her (cf. וַיֵּרָא in v. 3) and nothing more. (The *qal* of בּוֹא and the *niphal* of ראה appear to be interchangeable in 1 Kings 10:12; Ps. 42:3; Isa. 16:12; and Mal. 3:2, though the preposition אֶל is collocated with בּוֹא only in Isa. 16:12.) In short, in this context the Hebrew collocation does not behave as Brettler suggests, nor

Details matter (13:6–7). Manoah's wife reported her experience to her husband. She was not sure of the messenger's identity. She called him a "man sent from God" (i.e., a prophet, cf. Josh. 14:6; 1 Sam. 9:6–10), but suspected he was an angel because of his awesome (נוֹרָא) appearance (v. 6).[59] When reporting the visitor's message, she focused on the angel's instructions about the food and drink she should avoid. She omitted the prohibition about cutting the child's hair (perhaps this was assumed on the basis of his identification as a Nazirite; cf. v. 7b) (Boling 1975, 221) and, more importantly, failed to say anything about his future military role.[60] The latter omission is of great significance. Samson's mother failed to communicate what was most important—her son's divinely appointed destiny.[61] Her response to the angel's message foreshadows Israel's failure to recognize Samson as their God-given deliverer and Samson's own confusion about his role in life.[62]

---

did Manoah's wife. Nevertheless, there may be a subtle dimension to the language that ironically plays off the use of the expression for sexual contact. While the messenger did not actually impregnate Manoah's wife, he did make a prophetic pronouncement that guaranteed she would conceive. He did not "come to" her in a literal sexual sense, but his visit did precede and precipitate her conceiving. The use of this idiom, coupled with the omission of any reference to Manoah's involvement in his wife's pregnancy, highlights the miraculous nature of Samson's conception and birth.

59. Savran notes that this term "nearly always implies divinity" (2005, 136).
60. See Polzin 1980, 183; Alter 1981, 101; and, for a helpful chart, Hamilton 2001, 151.
61. The text does not tell us why she failed to do this. Perhaps she was so excited about having a baby that she overlooked God's purpose in giving her one. Gunn and Fewell suggest other possibilities: "Does she fear to put the idea of a child destined for warfare in her husband's head? Does she hope to thwart the divine purpose? Or does she wish to see divine purpose work out its own way, unencumbered by her husband's control? Of course, more simply, she may be simply blocking her fear, as she trembles for the future of her unborn child" (1993, 68). Savran doubts she deliberately withheld information: "Given her guileless character and the subsequent unimportance of Samson's parents in the rest of the cycle, it is improbable that Manoah was deliberately deceived by his wife" (1988, 83–84).
62. There are additional, seemingly minor variations between the angel's message and Manoah's wife's report. She repeats the angel's instructions, "Do not drink wine or strong drink and do not eat anything unclean" with two slight variations. She omits the command "Be careful" (הִשָּׁמְרִי, cf. v. 4) and uses the feminine form of "unclean" (טְמֵאָה), rather than the masculine form (v. 4). These variations may seem insignificant, but her lack of care in relating the angel's words caused Manoah to be confused and resulted in

Samson's mother also added the words "until the day he dies" to the angel's message (see v. 7b). This is not necessarily implied by the angel's message. Presumably once Samson fulfilled his mission, he would no longer need to follow the Nazirite regimen. When viewed in the light of the aforementioned omissions, this addition has an ominous effect (Kim 1993, 191). Samson's fall would come as a result of his hair being cut (Block 1999, 406) and his story would culminate in his tragic death, rather than the salvation of his people (Alter 1981, 101; Exum 1980, 49).

There is some question about the exact nature of Samson's Nazirite status.[63] According to Numbers 6:1–21, Nazirite vows were voluntary and temporary. Nazirites were to abstain from wine and fermented drinks, and were not allowed to eat grapes or raisins. During the time of their vow of separation, they were prohibited from cutting their hair and from going near a corpse. If someone died suddenly in their presence, they had to shave their hair, present an offering to the Lord, and renew their vow. Following successful completion of the period of separation, an elaborate ritual was prescribed to terminate the vow.[64]

In contrast to Numbers 6, Samson's Nazirite status was imposed on him by the Lord from birth. The only regulation specifically mentioned by the angel pertained to Samson's hair; it was not to be cut. Since the angel prohibited his mother from drinking wine and fermented drinks, one may reasonably assume that the regulation pertaining to such beverages also applied, but this is not actually stated.[65]

Samson not fully understanding the purpose of his calling. Kim suggests that the gender variation with the term "unclean" may simply be "an effort to avoid a danger of monotony" (1993, 190). However, when viewed in light of her other, more significant alterations of the angel's message, this slight change reinforces the narrator's portrayal of her as one who fails to give attention to detail.

63. Discussion of Samson's Nazirite status also appears in Chisholm 2009b, 155–61.

64. For a helpful summary of the regulations pertaining to Nazirites, see Matthews 2004, 134–36.

65. Kim states: "We should be careful not to regard the first two Nazirite prohibitions as pertaining only to the woman. These restrictions also pertain to the boy. The reason for her diet is not simply that she will bear a son but that the boy to be born will become a Nazirite from the womb" (1993, 185). He argues that the causal clause in verse 7 ("for the child will be dedicated to God") clearly indicates that the child's Nazirite status is the reason why she must abstain from drinking wine. One can detect the same logic in verses 4–5.

Nothing is mentioned at all about contact with a corpse, though later incidents in the story take on fuller significance if seen against the background of this regulation (see 14:9; 15:15). The rule pertaining to someone who dies suddenly is problematic in Samson's case. If it was applicable to Samson, then he violated his Nazirite status when he killed the Philistines (14:19; 15:15).[66] But his exploits against the Philistines were spirit empowered. Furthermore, how could Samson possibly begin the deliverance of Israel without killing the enemy? Though apparently Samson did not see himself in the role of Israel's deliverer, this was God's plan for him (13:5). Why would God make Samson a Nazirite and then cast him in a role that inherently necessitated the violation of his Nazirite status? Perhaps one way to harmonize Samson's military exploits with the Nazirite rule would be to argue that Samson should have cut his hair and renewed his Nazirite status after each conflict with the Philistines. However, there is no indication in the angel's instructions or in the ensuing narrative that this was expected.

It seems more likely that the rule pertaining to contact with a corpse did not apply in cases where individuals were lifelong Nazirites. Milgrom, after noting that both Samson and Samuel came in contact with corpses (on the latter, see 1 Sam. 15:33), states: "That they were not bound by such a prohibition can be inferred from the instruction of the angel to Samson's mother. She is enjoined to eschew forbidden food (Judg. 13:14), but nothing is said about contracting impurity from the dead, which, according to the priestly code, would have automatically defiled her embryo (cf. Num. 19:22). Here we must assume that the lifelong Nazirite was subject to the same law as the priest, for whom corpse contamination only suspended his priesthood for a prescribed period of impurity (seven days, as for a layman, inferred from Lev. 22:4) but did not cancel it" (Milgrom 1989, 357).[67]

To summarize, it seems there are three options for interpreting the nature of Samson's Nazirite status: (1) Samson's situation should be interpreted in light of Numbers 6:1–21 in its entirety. All of the rules listed there applied in his case. (2) Only the Nazirite regulations specifically referred to in the angel's instructions were applicable in Samson's case, namely those pertaining to cutting one's hair and to drinking the fruit of the vine. The rule pertaining to contact with a

---

66. If the regulation in Numbers 6:9 also applied to animals, then Samson's killing a lion (14:6) violated this rule as well.

67. Ashley is not certain that Samuel was actually a lifelong Nazirite (1993, 139–40).

corpse did not apply because of the special circumstances of Samson's Nazirite calling. (3) Samson's Nazirite status was different from the situation described in Numbers 6. In Samson's case the only rule pertained to the cutting of his hair.[68]

Manoah meets an angel (13:8–23). Manoah asked the Lord to send the messenger again, so that he might teach them how to raise the boy. The request seems a bit odd, for the messenger made it clear on his first visitation that the child was to be raised a Nazirite. But, as noted above, Manoah must have wondered about the child's purpose in life. God responded to Manoah's prayer and once more sent his angel to Manoah's wife. She retrieved her husband, who verified that this was the same individual who had appeared before to his wife. Given his wife's statement (v. 10), this hardly seemed necessary, but apparently Manoah wanted to be certain.

Manoah asked the angel how the boy should be raised and inquired concerning his son's future work (v. 12), a question that would have been unnecessary if his wife had reported all the angel had said. The angel informed him that his wife must give careful attention to everything he had told her (v. 13).[69] In the Hebrew text "everything" is placed in first position in the sentence for emphasis. The angel then outlined the regulations, but he mentioned only those that Manoah's wife had

---

68. Since the angel did not mention the regulation about touching a corpse, Cartledge argues that this prohibition did not apply in Samson's case. He also points out that the angel, while prohibiting Samson's mother from drinking wine, said nothing about this regulation being applicable to Samson himself. Since Samson got in trouble only when his hair was cut, Cartledge concludes that contact with a corpse and abstention from wine were not part of Samson's Nazirite obligations and that the temporary Nazirite status envisioned in Numbers 6 differs from Samson's permanent condition (1992, 19–20). See also Jonker 1992, 55; Margalith 1986b; 230–32; Emmrich 2001, 71–72; and Bartusch 2003, 162.

69. The *niphal* of שׁמר, when collocated with the preposition מִן, "from," has the force of "pay attention to, beware of." See Genesis 31:29; Exodus 23:21; Deuteronomy 23:9; 1 Samuel 21:4; 2 Kings 6:9; Jeremiah 9:4. The statement in Judges 13:13b refers to more than just adherence to the commands given before; it means she should pay attention to all that the angel said previously, including his comments about the boy's work. In verse 14, where the *qal* of שׁמר, literally, "guard," is collocated with כֹּל, "all," as its object, obedience to prior commands is specifically in view, but verse 13b is broader in its scope than this.

reported to her husband before (cf. v. 14 with vv. 4 and 7).[70] The angel did not mention the information omitted by Manoah's wife in her report—the prohibition pertaining to the boy's hair and the identification of his life's work (cf v. 5).[71] This seems odd, since Manoah specifically asked about the child's work. Apparently the angel expected Manoah's wife to inform her husband about these things, but there is no evidence she ever did. In the story to follow Samson never gives any indication he understood himself to be Israel's deliverer. The angel's reticence fits the story, however. Initially he revealed God's intention to deliver his people, despite their failure to ask for deliverance. But once Manoah's wife, who had not asked to be delivered from her barren condition, overlooked this, it is as if God purposely veiled his intention.[72] He was content to work behind the scenes, delivering a people who did not seek deliverance through a deliverer who failed to see himself as such.

Manoah invited the messenger to stay for a meal, but the angel

---

70. The phrase מִשְׁפַּט־הַנַּעַר, literally, "the rule(s) of/for the boy," refers in verse 12 to the regulations that the boy was to follow to fulfill his Nazirite status. In 1 Samuel 10:25 the phrase מִשְׁפַּט הַמְּלֻכָה, literally, "the rule(s) of kingship," refers to the regulations the king was to follow, which are outlined in Deuteronomy 17:14–20. Block understands מִשְׁפַּט־הַנַּעַר in Judges 13:12 as a reference to the oracle of verses 3–5 (1999, 408), but verse 14 suggests the rules alluded to in the oracle are in view. See Burney 1970, 347; and Kim 1993, 201–02. Block argues that the phrase מִשְׁפַּט הַמֶּלֶךְ, literally, "the practice of the king," refers to an oracle in 1 Samuel 8:9, 11, but it seems more likely that the policies of the typical king, outlined in 1 Samuel 8:10–17, are in view.

71. In fact, he even omits any reference to Samson's Nazirite status (cf. vv. 5, 7). See Exum 1980, 52.

72. It is odd that Manoah's wife, though barren, is not depicted as seeking relief from her condition. Her passive role in the account contrasts with other barren women who seek a child from the Lord, sometimes exhibiting desperation in their pleas and efforts. See Genesis 25:21; 30:6, 24; 1 Samuel 1:9–20. The biblical narrator in Judges 13 does not indicate that the angel's visitation was in response to the prayer of Manoah's wife. She was seemingly resigned to her condition, much like Israel was resigned to being enslaved by the Philistines. They did not ask the Lord for relief, but he decided to deliver them anyway. Kim aptly suggests that the narrator may have "used her barrenness as an analogue for Israel's current situation." He adds, "the woman's barrenness not only provides a fitting background for a miraculous birth but also reflects analogically the pathetic plight of the Israelites who by their apostasy have foreclosed their future" (1993, 181). See as well Greene 1991, 57.

refused.[73] He hinted that a burnt offering might be appropriate and that it should be offered to the Lord. The narrator then explains that it was necessary for the angel to say this because Manoah did not realize he was speaking with the Lord's angel. Stuttering Manoah, who apparently was still confused about the messenger's identity, asked for his name, but the angel informed Manoah that he would not be able to comprehend it, for it was "beyond understanding" (v. 18, literal translation).[74] Some understand the angel to be identifying himself as "Wonderful," but the preceding question suggests otherwise. The Hebrew word is used here with the same sense as in Psalm 139:6, where the feminine form of the adjective describes God's knowledge as being incomprehensible and unattainable (Burney 1970, 349; Moore 1895, 321). As the angel suggested, Manoah sacrificed a young goat as a burnt offering to the Lord, along with a grain offering. The angel ascended in the flame of the sacrificial fire, prompting both Manoah and his wife to fall to the ground and hide their faces.[75] Apparently at this point Manoah finally realized the messenger's identity (v. 21b).[76]

---

73. Kim considers Manoah's possible motives in requesting the angel to stay (1993, 203–04). He concludes, "both ancient oriental hospitality and Manoah's quest for his true identity are sufficient reasons for the invitation."

74. Manoah's response in verse 17 begins in an awkward fashion, reading literally, "Who your name?" One expects him to say, "What is your name?" but he uses the wrong pronoun. Perhaps he started to say, "Who are you?" See Boling 1975, 222. The pronoun מִי, "who," is collocated with שֵׁם, "name," only here, but מָה, "what," appears before this noun in Genesis 32:27; Exodus 3:13; and Proverbs 30:4.

75. Verse 19c has suffered from textual corruption. As it stands, it reads literally: "and doing an amazing thing while Manoah and his wife watched." The subject of the participle מַפְלִא has been accidentally omitted. One may supply the missing subject in one of two ways: (a) הוּא מַפְלִא, "he was . . . ." In this case the pronoun dropped out by partial haplography with the preceding consonants—note the double הו before מפלא. (b) וּמַלְאַךְ יהוה מַפְלִא, "and the angel of the Lord was . . . ." In this case the subject dropped out by homoioteleuton. The scribe's eye jumped from the first יהוה (see לַיהוה, "to the Lord") to the second (in the phrase "the angel of the Lord"). A conjunction was subsequently prefixed to מַפְלִא. For other examples of juxtaposed disjunctive clauses with participial predicates within a narrative framework, see 2 Samuel 3:1 (where the second clause is contrastive) and 15:23 (where the second clause is circumstantial-temporal). It is more common for at least one of the predicates to be a perfect (see, for example, Judg. 3:24; 15:14; 1 Sam. 9:5, 17, 27; 20:41; 2 Sam. 17:24; 2 Kings 2:23).

76. Zakovitch sees an inconsistency in the narrative at this point. According to Zakovitch, verse 21 indicates that Manoah realized the being was the

398

Manoah feared he would die, but his wife correctly reasoned that the Lord would not have accepted their offerings or revealed such truths to them if he intended to kill them.

Manoah's statement in verse 22 requires closer inspection. He declares, literally, "We will surely die because God we have seen!" Since verse 21 informs us that Manoah finally recognized the messenger as the angel of the Lord, it is odd that here he claims to have seen God. This might suggest that the angel and God are to be equated ontologically, but this need not be the case. Having taken so long to recognize the messenger's true identity, perhaps Manoah compensates for his dullness by going to the opposite extreme. This burst of hyperbole is perfectly valid, of course, for the angel represented God and came with full divine authority. When one spoke to him or saw him, it was as if one had spoken with or seen the one who sent him (see Judg. 2:1–3).[77]

Lord's angel only when he failed to reappear. As Zakovitch argues, Manoah would likely have come to this conclusion when he saw the being ascend in the fire (v. 20). So, Zakovitch reasons, verses 19–20 must be secondary to the narrative (1985, 193). However, Zakovitch's premise is wrong. The juxtaposition of the two clauses in verse 21 need not imply a causal or consequential relationship between them. Having noted that the angel ascended in the fire, the narrator interjects a parenthetical note of interest. We could paraphrase: "By the way, he never appeared to them again." With the particle אָז, "then," he resumes the story, indicating that the being's dramatic exit is what convinced Manoah of his angelic status. (See Moore 1895, 324.) There are only a couple parallels to the clausal structure of Judges 13:21 (a clause with negated perfect followed by a clause introduced by אָז with a perfect), but both support our analysis. In 1 Kings 8:11–12 the second clause (v. 12) does not give a consequence of the preceding clause (v. 11), but rather relates consequentially to verse 10. In the same way, Judges 13:21b relates consequentially to verse 20, not to verse 21a (which is parenthetical). In 1 Kings 22:48–49 (vv. 49–50 in the English text) the second clause (v. 49) does not give a consequence of the preceding clause (v. 48b), but rather relates consequentially to verse 48a. Chronologically the order is v. 48a–v. 49–v. 48b. (On the chronological issue here, see Cogan 2001, 500.) In the same way the chronological order in Judges 13:20–21 is verses 20–21b–21a. See Chisholm 2010a.

77. Moore suggests that Manoah uses אֱלֹהִים in the sense of "a god" or "superhuman being" and refers specifically to the angel, not God (1895, 324). He cites 1 Samuel 28:13 as a parallel, where Saul's response to the woman (v. 14, "What about his appearance?") and her reply to his question (v. 14, "An old man is coming up! He is wrapped in a robe!") suggest she uses אֱלֹהִים in verse 13 to refer to an individual. However, in verse 13 אֱלֹהִים appears to be a numerical plural, "gods, spirits," for it is modified by the plural participle

How should we assess the narrator's portrayal of Samson's parents? Manoah's request for an audience with the messenger may seem to indicate that he doubted his wife's credibility, but, as we noted above, her less-than-complete report naturally left him with some unanswered questions about the child's purpose in life.[78] At the same time, he does give evidence of distrusting his wife. His initial question to the angel (v. 11) was unnecessary, given his wife's verification of the messenger's identity (v. 10). Manoah's question about the "rule for the boy's life" also seems unnecessary, since his wife's report made it clear the boy would be a Nazirite. Manoah's spiritual sensitivities are portrayed as dull. Despite his wife's and the angel's hints (vv. 7, 16), he was slow to discern the angel's identity and then drew a wrong conclusion about God's intentions.

As for Manoah's wife, she was more perceptive than her husband (Amit 1993, 148–50). She suspected the messenger was an angel from the very beginning and in the end she corrected her husband's faulty reasoning (Fuchs 2000, 56–57).[79] However, there are several disturbing features about the narrator's presentation of her. Unlike other barren mothers who are supernaturally enabled to bear a son, she is never named.[80] Could this be a hint that her son would never live up to his

---

עֹלִים, "coming up." If so, it apparently refers to a whole group of spirits that ascended from the conjurer's pit, among whom was Samuel (v. 14). Johnston (following the proposal of Hutter) suggests that the medium's statement ("I see spirits coming up") is idiomatic, reflecting an ancient formula used by necromancers when they conjured up underworld gods. In this case the statement probably would mean, "the consultation is successful" or "I have contacted Samuel" (2002, 145–46). If Johnston is correct, this idiomatic usage is not relevant to our understanding of Manoah's use of the term.

78. Schneider seems to miss this point (2000, 199). She suggests that Manoah was "not willing to accept" his wife's words; she argues that Manoah's questioning is not "legitimated" by the text. Likewise Ackerman states that Manoah "either does not believe his wife or is not satisfied with the information provided by his wife" (1998, 112). She adds that Manoah's request for an audience "smacks of hubris." While it is true that Manoah asked for some information already provided by his wife, the omission in his wife's report prompted Manoah to seek clarification about the boy's role in life. See Kim 1993, 195–96.

79. Fuchs contrasts Judges 13 with Genesis 18, comparing Sarah's role in Genesis 18 with Manoah's role in Judges 13 (2000, 57–58).

80. Other features that appear in other barren-woman accounts are absent as well. See Exum 1980, 47–48; Johnson 2010, 274, 286.

potential or take his place among the famed leaders of the covenant community?[81] Furthermore, she did not actively seek deliverance from barrenness and she failed to report to her husband the most significant element in the angel's announcement. She contrasts with Hannah, another barren woman who will soon appear in the unfolding history and miraculously conceive a son. Manoah's wife seemed unconcerned for her own or Israel's deliverance, but Hannah actively sought a child from the Lord and interpreted her deliverance from barrenness as a foreshadowing of the Lord's deliverance of Israel (cf. 1 Sam. 2:1–10).[82]

Through his portrayal of Samson's parents, the narrator seems to be telling us that Samson was entering an environment of spiritual dullness, where people were not attuned to the Lord's purposes and revelation, nor expecting him to intervene in any significant way.[83] Will the boy prove to be a child of his times and fail to realize his destiny? Perhaps more to the point, if his own mother overlooked such an important element in the angel's announcement, how would the child discover the Lord's purpose for his life?

The narrator's use of divine names in this chapter is also significant. The narrator correctly identifies the messenger as Yahweh's angel throughout the narrative (vv. 3, 13, 15–17, 20–21). Likewise, the narrator informs us that Manoah was actually praying and sacrificing to Yahweh (vv. 8, 19). However, the narrator does not use *Yahweh* exclusively. He employs *God* and *the angel of God* in verse 9, probably to reflect the limited perspective of the characters at this point (see vv. 6, 8) (Boling 1975, 221; Johnson 2010, 275). The characters do not share the narrator's perspective until the end of the scene. In his initial

---

81. Of course, her anonymity may simply be a literary device whereby the narrator focuses on her role; she is more typical than personal. However, as Reinhartz observes, her role as mother is downplayed in chapter 13; she is called Manoah's wife and "the woman," but never "mother" (1998, 96). This changes as the story unfolds (see 14:2–6, 9), so perhaps we should not make too much of it. For a positive assessment of her anonymity, see Johnson 2010, 273–74.

82. For these reasons I cannot agree with McCann, who sees Samson's mother as the real hero of the story (2002, 96–97), or with Bronner, who calls her "an ideal Israelite mother" (2004, 30).

83. Olson has a much more positive opinion of Samson's parents (1998, 847). He writes: "The parents of Samson emerge as faithful and obedient models of faith who desire that God 'teach us what we are to do concerning the boy' (13:8)." He compares them to the faithful generation of Judges 2:7, while Samson corresponds to the faithless generation that followed (Judg. 2:10).

visitation, the angel referred to *God,* not *Yahweh* (v. 5). Consistent with this, Manoah's wife called the visitor a *man/angel of God* (v. 6). Manoah prayed to the *Master* (אֲדוֹנָי) and referred to the messenger as *the man of God* (v. 8). When the angel finally used the name *Yahweh* (v. 16), we are specifically told that Manoah had not realized that the visitor was Yahweh's angel. Not until after the sign did Manoah finally recognize the angel's true identity (v. 21). Even then he used a generic name *(God,* v. 22), though his wife corrected his perspective by employing the name *Yahweh* for the first time (v. 23).

"Sunny" arrives (13:24–25). The chapter's final verses report the fulfillment of the angelic birth announcement. Manoah's wife gave birth to a son and named him Samson (שִׁמְשׁוֹן, meaning "sunlike, solar"). How are we to interpret the significance of this name? On the one hand, we might see it positively, as suggesting divine empowerment and deliverance (Webb 1987, 164–65). On the other hand, it may hint at the pagan environment into which he was born, for the sun god was worshiped in Canaan and the town of Beth Shemesh (meaning "house of the sun") was nearby (see 1:33) (Block 1999, 417–18).[84] Block suggests that the name, "if not outrightly pagan is dangerously compromising" (419).

As Samson grew, the Lord blessed him and eventually the Lord's spirit began to stir (or impel) him (cf. 3:10; 6:34; 11:29; though different verbs are used there).[85] We are not told the precise form the blessing took, but it is possible, given Samson's later deeds of supernatural strength, that the verb "blessed" here has the nuance of "empowered, endued with special capacity."[86] The stage is set for Samson to confront the Philistines and begin his life's work of delivering his people from their oppressors.

A Wedding Without a Honeymoon (14:1–20)

Samson picks a wife (14:1–4). Knowing that Samson's destiny was to deliver Israel, we expect the divine spirit (13:25) will move him to initiate some type of military encounter with the Philistines. We read instead

---

84. For evidence of a sun cult in ancient Canaan and Israel see Day 2000, 151–55.

85. The verb פעם occurs only here in the *qal* stem. Elsewhere it appears in the *niphal* and *hithpael* with the meaning "be troubled, disturbed." See Genesis 41:8; Psalms 77:4; Daniel 2:1, 3. The *qal* apparently has an active sense, "trouble, disturb," or in this context "stir up."

86. See the texts listed in *HALOT*, 160, under category one of the *piel*, glossed "to endue someone with special power." See as well Block 1999, 418.

of Samson's intention to marry a Philistine woman. His parents voiced their objection by reminding him that intermarriage with the uncircumcised Philistines was inappropriate. Their concern seems valid and their logic convincing, but then the narrator startles us by informing us that Samson's desire for the woman was "the Lord's doing, for he was seeking an opportunity to stir up trouble with the Philistines."[87] The Lord disapproved of intermarriage with foreigners (see Judg. 3:5), but on this occasion he had a higher purpose that entailed circumventing the norm.[88] As the following story reveals, Samson's emotional involvement with a Philistine woman set the stage for strife between Samson and the Philistines. This strife in turn had the potential to be the catalyst for a war of liberation, which was the Lord's goal all along (see Judg. 13:5).[89]

To exonerate Samson's parents and the Lord, it is tempting to view the Lord's involvement as passive. According to this scenario God simply allowed Samson to follow his selfish, wrong inclinations and then incorporated them into his overall plan, much like he did the sinful deeds of Joseph's brothers.[90] However, the inclusion of the phrase "from the Lord" (literal translation) suggests that the Lord was the driving force behind Samson's behavior. Two texts in particular provide especially relevant parallels. In Genesis 24:50 Laban and Bethuel agree that the arrival of Abraham's servant is "the Lord's doing" (literally, "from the Lord"). In 1 Kings 2:15 Adonijah acknowledges that Solomon's right to rule comes "from the Lord" (literal translation, i.e., by divine decision).[91] This does not mean that the Lord overrode Samson's personality or

---

87. On the narrator's use of temporary gapping here, see Sternberg 1987, 238.
88. For a survey of scholarly opinion on this issue, see Butler 2009, 333–34.
89. This passage is instructive for our understanding of divine providence. God could have directly intervened and destroyed the Philistines as he did Sodom and Gomorrah. But God rarely operates this way. He usually chooses to get involved in more indirect ways through human instruments. As McCann observes, he "works *incarnationally*" (emphasis his), using the "human resources" at his "disposal, flawed as they may be" (2002, 102). Some prefer to understand Samson, not God, as the subject of the pronoun הוא, "he," in verse 4, but this seems highly unlikely. For a critique of this proposal, see Mobley 2005, 188.
90. Klein appears to interpret Judges 14:4 along these lines (1988, 116–17). See as well Younger 2002, 302.
91. See also 2 Chronicles 22:7, where the phrase "from God" refers to how God manipulated the timing of events so as to bring about the downfall of Ahaziah.

natural inclinations, but it does suggest Samson would not have pursued the Philistine woman apart from a divine nudge.[92]

Lion killer (14:5–6). In its present form the Hebrew text of verses 5–6 seems very confusing. According to verse 5, Samson went down to Timnah with his parents. As they approached the vineyards of Timnah, a young lion attacked and Samson, energized by the divine spirit, ripped the lion apart.

According to Strawn, this deed is "remarkable" in three ways: (1) "Since few people tear goat-kids apart—uncooked ones at least—this is impressive enough on its own" (2009, 151). (2) The text highlights the fact "that this tearing is done barehanded," without the aid of a weapon (151). (3) The term כְּפִיר refers to a young lion, more specifically, a nomadic, subadult (between two and three and a half years old) lion that has been driven from the pride. As Strawn points out, *"all male lions become nomadic as subadults"* (155). When such lions "attempt to claim a territory," they "tend to roar more frequently and to be more aggressive" (158). This coincides with the description of the lion encountered by Samson. Strawn concludes that such a roaring, nomadic lion "is perhaps the most dangerous instance of the world's dominant land predator that one could possibly encounter." He adds: *"That* is the kind of lion that Samson encounters and it is *that* kind of lion that he rips apart with ease, with nothing in his hand! How better could the author(s) begin the story of Samson and his remarkable strength" (158; emphasis is his).[93]

The narrator informs us (v. 6) that Samson did not tell his parents of the incident, but verse 5 gives the impression they would have seen the entire episode. One could assume that Samson must have separated from his parents prior to the lion attack,[94] but the Hebrew text does not indicate this. Some Greek witnesses read a singular verb "and *he* approached," while others have "and he turned aside." Boling prefers combining the readings, arguing that the accidental omission

---

92. Brettler demonstrates that chapters 14–15 exhibit themes from wisdom literature (2002, 50–54). With regard to Judges 14:4 he observes: "This idea, that YHWH is really in control, even when people appear to be acting of their own volition, characterizes wisdom literature" (51).

93. Niehaus sees Samson's exploits against the background of "contemporary Assyrian royal claims to have fought lions on the ground, hand to hand, and slaughtered them." (2008, 52).

94. For a brief survey of attempts to explain the text along these lines, see Moore 1895, 330–31.

of the first verb led to a reinterpretation of the second verb as a plural in the MT tradition (1975, 230). Moore, however, regards the reading "and he turned aside" as an early attempt to clarify the text (1895, 333). Another possibility is that the phrase "his father and his mother" has accidentally been copied into the text in verse 5, perhaps under the influence of verse 4 or 6, with the verb "approached" then being altered to a plural to agree with the subject.[95] No matter which textual change we choose, it is apparent that Samson was not with his parents when the lion attacked.

The setting of the episode (the vineyards of Timnah) may be significant. If Samson was bound by the rule pertaining to drinking the fruit of the vine (see Judg. 13:4, as well as Num. 6:3–4), then his approaching a vineyard creates an ominous mood and reminds us that threats to his Nazirite status are lurking in his environment.[96]

What is the significance of Samson's killing the lion? This attack in Philistine territory foreshadows Samson's divinely orchestrated conflicts with the Philistines. Samson's killing the lion foreshadows his victories over the Philistines at Ashkelon and Lehi, where the Lord's spirit also "rushes upon" (צלח) him and enables him to kill his enemies with supernatural ease (see 14:19; 15:14). In both 14:5–6 and 15:14 the phrase "to meet him" (with hostile intent, לִקְרָאתוֹ) follows a verb for roaring/shouting (the human equivalent of a lion's roar) and precedes

---

95. Perhaps in an early manuscript the phrase "his father and his mother" at the beginning of verse 4 appeared on the line immediately above verse 5a and the scribe accidentally inserted it in the latter position. If so, we might call this a vertical dittography.

96. Schneider argues that Samson violated his Nazirite status by approaching the vineyard and suggests this is why he did not tell his parents about the incident (2000, 205). Crenshaw wonders if the lion attack was a warning to Samson that he had ventured too close to the vineyard. Lions appear in two accounts in Kings as instruments of divine punishment against disobedient servants of God (1 Kings 13:24–28; 20:35–36). Crenshaw backs off from this conclusion, however, because Samson, unlike the prophets in Kings, was able to kill the lion (1978, 84). Perhaps Crenshaw's interpretive caution is unwarranted. In Judges 16:1–3 Samson succeeds in Gaza despite his wrongdoing; yet his carelessness foreshadows and leads to his eventual failure. The same could be true in chapter 14, except that here the spirit of the Lord empowers him, while 16:1–3 omits any reference to the spirit. Perhaps more importantly, the fact remains that Samson did not drink the fruit of the vine here and therefore did not violate his Nazirite status. It is more likely that the reference to the vineyard simply contributes to the literary effect and mood of the story.

the reference to the Lord's spirit rushing upon Samson (Exum 1983, 38; Emmrich 2001, 71).

Why did Samson not tell his parents of his accomplishment? We cannot be sure of Samson's motives; perhaps he considered the attack a bad omen that his parents could use in their effort to dissuade him from getting involved with the Philistine woman. At any rate, by informing us of Samson's parents' ignorance of the incident, the narrator once more depicts them as not being fully aware of the degree to which the Lord was involved in Samson's life. This in turn mirrors Samson's own ignorance of his role as a Nazirite and Israel's failure to understand what God was accomplishing through him.

Samson likes sweets (14:7–9). Having finally spoken to his prospective bride, Samson found her to be everything he had anticipated (note the use of the Hebrew verb יָשַׁר, "to be right," in both vv. 4 and 7).[97] Later, on his way to Timnah to marry her, he turned aside to look at the lion he had killed. He found that honeybees had built a hive in the lion's carcass, so he scooped some of the honey up in his hands and ate it.[98] He even took some of it back home and gave it to his parents, though he did not tell them from where it came.

What was the significance of Samson's eating the honey from the lion's carcass? If Samson was bound by the Nazirite rule pertaining to contact with a corpse (see our earlier discussion of this issue), then his actions reveal that he was willing to give his physical appetites priority over his Nazirite commitment. According to Numbers 6:6, a Nazirite was not to "contact a dead body." The Hebrew phrase "dead body" (נֶפֶשׁ מֵת) occurs only in this passage.[99] Numbers 6:7 makes it clear that human corpses are primarily in view. It is not certain that the language includes animals as well. נֶפֶשׁ can refer to animals, and an antonymic expression, נֶפֶשׁ חַיָּה, "living creature," encompasses animals

---

97. The language of the text suggests that sexual desire was not the only motivating factor in Samson's attraction to the woman. See Gunn's response (1992, 231–32) to Bal's interpretation of the story, as well as Greenstein 1981, 249; Sasson 1988, 339, note 2; and Exum 1993a, 70, note 18.

98. The text of verse 8 specifically mentions that he saw a swarm of bees in the lion's carcass. Since bees are depicted elsewhere as dangerous and harmful (see Deut. 1:44; Ps. 118:12; Isa. 7:18), it is possible they were a warning to Samson that he should stay away from the honey. See Kim 1993, 243. If this episode does indeed foreshadow Samson's encounter with Delilah (symbolized by the honey), then the bees, like the lion (vv. 5–6), foreshadow Samson's Philistine enemies (Kim 1993, 243–44).

99. A similar expression, נַפְשֹׁת מֵת, "dead person(s)," appears in Leviticus 21:11.

as well as humans (see Gen. 1:20, 24, 30; 2:7, 19; 9:12, 15–16; Ezek. 47:9). If the law applied to animals as well as humans, then Samson violated a Nazirite regulation by touching honey that was in contact with the lion's carcass (Klein 1988, 129–30; Soggin 1981, 240).[100] Even if he technically did not break the rule in question, the story creates an ominous mood for it shows Samson violating the spirit of the law and coming precariously close to compromising his Nazirite status. Either way, this incident foreshadows the Delilah affair, where Samson decided physical gratification was more important than anything else, even his Nazirite status (Kim 1993, 312–13).

Samson was so enamored with the honey that he took some back to his parents, apparently delaying his trip to Timnah to marry the woman. However, he did not tell them where he got it, perhaps because he did not want them to discover that he had violated the Nazirite rule about touching a carcass. It is possible Samson interpreted his finding the honey on his way to his wedding as a good omen that foreshadowed blessing. Perhaps he viewed it as a symbol of the sexual pleasure about to be his or as an aphrodisiac, appropriately provided just before his wedding (see Song 4:11 and 5:1).[101]

Samson loses a bet (14:10–18). For whatever reason, Manoah decided to accompany his son to Timnah for the wedding. (Verses 8–9 give the impression that Samson was alone on his earlier aborted trip to Timnah.) Following the custom of bridegrooms, Samson held a seven-day wedding banquet, where wine would have abounded.[102] If Samson was bound by the Nazirite rule pertaining to drinking wine, then once

---

100. This assumes, of course, that the Nazirite regulations of Numbers 6 were applicable in his case. To charge Samson with willful violation of his Nazirite status we must also assume that he was aware of the regulations given in Numbers 6. The angel did not mention this particular regulation when he spoke to Samson's mother (Judg. 13:4–5). As noted earlier, Cartledge argues that this omission indicates this prohibition did not apply in Samson's case (1992, 19–20).

101. Niditch observes that honey "is a symbol of fertility in many cultures and an appropriate food eaten on the way to form marriage relations" (2008, 156). In a Ugaritic text honey (*'ar*) and mandrakes (*ddy*) are mentioned as elements in an offering that Baal instructs Anat to make. See Gibson 1978, 49, 51 (texts 3 C 12–14, 3 D 53–54, and 3 D 73–75). Mandrakes (cf. Heb. דּוּדַי) were considered an aphrodisiac (see Gen. 30:14–16; Song 7:14 [English v. 13]).

102. On the possible Greek background of this Philistine wedding feast, see Yadin 2002, 416–18.

again the mood is ominous, for he was in an environment where his Nazirite status could be easily compromised (Schneider 2000, 206; Soggin 1981, 241).[103] One might expect Samson to bring some of his friends as groomsmen, but Samson was fortunate just to have his father in attendance at this foreign wedding. The Philistines provided him with thirty attendants, including a best man (vv. 11, 20).[104]

Samson's greed and lust again surfaced as he challenged the thirty groomsmen to a wager. If they could interpret a riddle within seven days, he would give each of them a new set of clothes. However, if they failed to interpret the riddle correctly, each of them must give him a set of clothes.[105] Because the riddle reflected Samson's own unique experience in finding the honey in the lion's carcass, rather than something common to all men, the Philistines understandably were at a loss to explain its meaning.[106]

---

103. The text never describes Samson as drinking fermented beverages here, so we cannot assume (as Olson 1998, 850, does) that he violated his Nazirite status. See O'Connell 1996, 225, as well as Milgrom 1989, 356. Levine's characterization of Samson as "a carousing adventurer, reveling in wine, women, and song" is not entirely accurate—women and song yes, but there is no proof from the text that he drank intoxicating beverages (1993, 230). Greene argues that the wording of 14:10 suggests Samson did partake of strong drink (1991, 64–65). However, the text simply says that he held a feast, as was the custom of bridegrooms. Contrary to what Greene argues, this does not necessarily imply "that Samson's behaviour was the same as any other man's," which would have included drinking wine. However, it does depict him as being in a seemingly compromising position and flirting with danger.

104. At the beginning of verse 11 the Hebrew text reads, "when they saw." The Old Greek apparently read, "when they feared" (understanding the root to be ירא, rather than ראה). In this case the Philistines are portrayed as wary of Samson. See Emmrich 2001, 73, note 24.

105. Yadin, appealing to the Greek background of this Philistine wedding, argues that Samson's saying is not a riddle, but a "capping song" in which Samson recites the first verse of a poem and challenges his opponents to "cap" it with the appropriate second verse (2002, 419). Yadin contends that this explanation better accounts for the use of the term חִידָה (which refers elsewhere to a saying or parable, not a riddle) and the use of the verb הִגִּיד (which means "tell, recount," not "solve, explain").

106. Galpaz-Feller correctly observes: "This riddle truly cannot be solved, because it refers to a rare and unusual occurrence. Someone who has not experienced it cannot discover what is hidden within it" (2006b, 111–12). The riddle has two parallel statements, the second of which gives more detailed descriptions: "Out of one who eats came something to eat" and "out

Samson seems to possess great cunning, but he overlooked two important facts—the Philistines' ingenuity and, more importantly, his own vulnerability to female charm. The Philistines threatened to murder Samson's bride and her family if she did not coax from him the solution to the riddle. For the remainder of the banquet she desperately pleaded with Samson to tell her the answer to the riddle.[107] There is a hint of trouble in verse 16, where the bride aligns herself with the Philistines (note "my people") and Samson implies that his relationship to his parents supercedes his relationship to her (Greene 1991, 65). He finally gave in, she reported the answer to the groomsmen,

---

of the strong one came something sweet" (v. 14). To solve the riddle one must explain the referents of its two metaphors: "one who eats/the strong one" and "something to eat/something sweet." The Philistines express their solution in two questions that use the second line of Samson's poetic couplet. They identify its referents in reverse order: "What is sweeter than honey? What is stronger than a lion?" (v. 18) (Both sides were trying to put their poetic prowess on display.) Samson's indignant response clearly shows the Philistines were correct.

Despite the straightforward nature of the riddle and its solution, scholars have concocted creative interpretations of the riddle that supposedly yield hidden, deeper meanings that in some cases are sexual in orientation. We will not take the time here to list, describe, or interact with them, since they unnecessarily complicate matters. For a survey of such views see Schipper 2003, 339–53. Rather than moving to the end of the spectrum marked simplicity, Schipper opts to muddy the waters by concluding: "I have only briefly sketched out various solutions to show that the surrounding narrative obscures the riddle's meaning and resists any attempt by the reader to locate an unambiguous solution and perform a final act of completion" (353). Contrary to Schipper's statement, the narrative does not obscure the riddle's meaning. However, Schipper's conclusion does illustrate nicely the capacity of modern scholarship to obscure what is transparent by overinterpreting a text.

107. It is probably better to follow the Old Greek and read "on the fourth day" in verse 15a. This harmonizes better with the preceding reference to three days (v. 14) and with the portrait of the woman given in verse 17. *NIV*'s translation "the whole seven days" in verse 17 is misleading. The Hebrew text simply reads, "(for) the seven days," meaning for the remainder of the seven-day banquet period, starting on the fourth day. See Boling 1975, 231. Moore prefers to retain "seventh" in verse 15 and emend "three" in verse 14 to "six" (1895, 335). But verse 17 gives the impression she had been nagging him about this prior to the seventh day. Kim resolves the problem by arguing that the numbers three and seven are not used literally here (1993, 257–58).

they won the wager by solving the riddle just before the deadline, and Samson accused them of cheating.[108]

Samson pays off a debt (14:19–20). Soured by the Philistines' devious behavior, humiliated Samson was finally at a point where the Lord could effectively use him. The divine spirit rushed upon him, just as he did earlier when the lion attacked (see v. 6), and Samson murdered thirty men of Ashkelon, took their clothes, and used them to pay off his debt to the Timnite groomsmen. Rather than consummating the marriage, he angrily returned home, and the Timnite woman was given instead to the best man at the wedding. While the narrator's statement about the Timnite woman's marriage might suggest closure for the story, one suspects this is just the beginning of Samson's dealings with the Philistines, for the death of thirty Ashkelonites does not even begin to relieve Israel from Philistine oppression.

Samson's murderous act, prompted by the spirit of the Lord, is problematic for many modern readers. However, like Ehud's assassination of Eglon, it should not be viewed in isolation. Ehud's murderous deed initiated a war of liberation against the oppressive Moabites. Likewise, Samson's murderous deed should be viewed as an act of war against the oppressive Philistines. From the very beginning of the story we know the Lord intended to deliver Israel from the Philistines through Samson (Judg. 13:5). The narrator later informs us that the Lord nudged Samson in the direction of the Philistines in order to ignite a conflict (14:4). Having laid the foundation for strife, the Lord's spirit empowered Samson to inaugurate the war.[109] This does not mean

---

108. The statement "if you had not plowed with my heifer" emphasizes that they had used a source of information that should have been off-limits to them. Heifers were used for farm work (see Borowski, 1987, 52), but one typically used one's own farm animals, not another man's.

109. Downplaying the divine spirit's role in this event, Younger accuses Samson of "murder and larceny" (2002, 304). Olson contends that the Lord's spirit "impels Samson to act powerfully but with unthinking impulse, violence, and faithlessness" (1998, 767). In Samson's experience the spirit is "no longer a positive force" (768). On the contrary, "the divine Spirit becomes ineffectual and ultimately dangerous and destructive in the extreme" (768). According to Olson, the spirit prompts Samson to kill the lion (14:6) and in so doing to break "the nazirite prohibition of touching a corpse or eating anything unclean" (850–51). He also empowers Samson to murder the Ashkelonites and to steal their clothing, thus violating two commandments of the Decalogue (Deut. 5:17, 19). However, as noted above, it is not certain if the rule pertaining to touching corpses applied in Samson's case.

that Samson understood his actions in this light. This is where Ehud and Samson contrast. Ehud was very much aware that he was leading a war of liberation. As we have noted above, Samson was unaware of his role as God's deliverer; he was simply expressing his indignation at being cheated. But Samson's very human, selfish response to Philistine trickery becomes a weapon of war in the Lord's hand.

Samson Gets Revenge (15:1–20)

Playing with fire (15:1–8a). The Timnite woman still had a place in Samson's heart. At the time of the wheat harvest (late April—late May), when people would be celebrating the land's fertility for another year and a vigorous youth's romantic impulses might be especially strong (see Gen. 30:14; Ruth 2:23), Samson took a young goat and visited the Timnite woman.[110] Not knowing that her father had given the woman to another man, Samson requested that he be allowed to have marital relations with his "wife." Her father refused, explaining that he had given her to another man because he thought Samson "despised" her.[111] To appease Samson he offered his younger daughter, who, in his opinion, was even more attractive than her older sister. Samson would have none of it.[112] Instead he declared his innocence in the matter and warned that he would make the Philistines pay for taking his property from him. Some might debate whether or not he was justified in killing the Ashkelonites, but this time Samson was sure his rights had been violated. Though he had left the wedding in a rage and had failed

---

Even if it did, it is not certain that the rule pertained to animal corpses. Furthermore, given Samson's calling to be a warrior, it is doubtful that Numbers 6:9 applied in his case. As for Samson's alleged violations of the commandments prohibiting murder and theft, these rules would not apply to acts of holy war.

110. Boling suggests the gift of a goat may have been "the ancient counterpart of the box of chocolates" (1975, 234). However, others suggest that it may have been payment for her services (cf. Gen. 38:17–19) (see Kim 1993, 268).

111. As Boling points out, the terminology may suggest divorce (1975, 234–35). See also Galpaz-Feller 2006b, 125. Note also the father's use of emphatic infinitives absolute. Polzin translates his statement, "I must insist that you certainly divorced her!" (1980, 189)

112. Gunn states: "To Samson, the marriage was not just a marriage of convenience, nor the Timnite's daughter just a beautiful face. The woman was one who was 'right in his eyes.' To Samson the father's speech smacks of inexcusable casualness" (1992, 236).

to consummate the marriage, as far as he was concerned the Timnite woman belonged to him.

In avenging himself Samson once more performed a superhuman deed, though this time his actions are not directly attributed to the divine spirit. He caught three hundred foxes (or perhaps jackals),[113] somehow tied them "in pairs by their tails," fastened torches to each pair, and set them loose in the Philistines' harvest-ripened fields (see v. 1), destroying their crops, vineyards, and olive groves.[114] The destruction of the Philistines' crops foreshadows the destruction of the temple of Dagon, the Philistine god of grain (see 16:23–30).

Samson's actions enraged the Philistines and set the stage for a major conflict. When the Philistines found out that Samson was the arsonist, they burned to death the Timnite woman and her father. We do not know if this form of execution was common among the Philistines (see 14:15). In this case the Philistines probably viewed it as appropriate, for they considered the man and his daughter to be partially responsible for their crops being burned. Samson announced his intention to seek revenge and then gave them a thorough beating.[115]

Showdown at Jawbone Hill (15:8b–20). After his great victory, Samson retreated to a cave located in the Cliff of Etam. In the meantime Philistine troops gathered at Lehi. When the Judahites inquired as to why the Philistines had marshalled their forces, the Philistines told them they were seeking revenge against Samson. Rather than rallying behind Samson and fighting for their independence, three thousand Judahites proceeded to Etam, reminded Samson that the Philistines must be treated with the respect due overlords, accused him of jeopardizing their safety, and informed him that they intended to hand him over to the Philistines. Samson protested his innocence, but his quarrel was not with his fellow Israelites. He bargained with them, making them swear that they would only bind him, not kill him. When the Philistines saw Samson bound, they came racing toward him,

---

113. See Margalith 1985, 225–26. On the difficulty of distinguishing between the fox and jackal, see M. J. Mulder, "שׁוּעָל," in *TDOT*, 14:537–38.

114. Gunn argues that Samson's "action is more commensurate with the injury" than his earlier murder of the thirty men (1992, 236). He explains: "the Philistines have taken away his woman, who would bear his seed, so he will take away the fruit of the Philistines' fields."

115. The meaning of the idiom "calf to thigh" in verse 8 is unclear. The phrase מַכָּה גְדוֹלָה, literally, "a great slaughter," appears earlier in Joshua 10:10, 20 and Judges 11:33.

whooping with joy and the anticipation of revenge. But once again the Lord's spirit rushed upon him, enabling him to snap the ropes. He grabbed a nearby jawbone from a donkey's carcass (compromising his Nazirite status?) and, with an efficiency that would make Shamgar smile (cf. 3:31), killed a thousand Philistines.

Quite pleased with his achievement, Samson composed a little poem that capsulizes the magnitude of the deed, discarded his makeshift weapon on the battlefield, and named the place Ramath-Lehi, "Jawbone Height/Hill" to commemorate his victory.[116] The precise meaning of the second half of the poem's first line is debated. The phrase is traditionally interpreted "a heap, two heaps," referring to the heaps of enemy corpses lying before him.[117] Several other options have been proposed, including among others: (a) "I have made donkeys of them" (NIV),[118] (b) "I have thoroughly skinned them,"[119] (c) "I have mightily raged against them."[120]

This poetic utterance is significant literarily, for it suggests that Samson seems to have gotten the last word in his ongoing conflict with the Philistines. He had formulated his riddle as a poetic doublet (14:14); the Philistines employed the same style when they offered the solution to the riddle and gained the upper hand (14:18). Samson's lame response to their trickery also appears as a poetic doublet (14:19). Now Samson, having wiped out an entire Philistine army, celebrated his victory with a quatrain (or compound doublet). Samson was the only one left composing poetry and this time it was a victory song! However, this is not the end of the story. This war of words continues in chapter 16, where the Philistine rulers celebrate their capture of Samson with a thanksgiving song structured as a poetic doublet (see v. 23), which is

---

116. NIV "and the place was called" is misleading. Samson is most naturally understood as the subject of the verb "named" in verse 17. The verb is active, literally, "he called," not passive, and there is no need to assume an indefinite subject here.

117. See Boling 1975, 239. Some prefer to emend the forms to an infinitive absolute followed by a perfect and translate "I have totally piled up." See Soggin 1981, 247; and Gray 1986, 333.

118. See Burney 1970, 373. In this case חֲמֹרָתִים is emended to חֲמַרְתִּים, a denominative verb from חֲמוֹר, "donkey."

119. See *HALOT*, 330. In this case חֲמוֹר חֲמֹרָתָיִם is emended to חָמוֹר חֲמַרְתִּים, an infinitive absolute and finite verb cognate to an Arabic verb meaning "scrape."

120. This option is discussed by Boling (1975, 239). It reads an infinitive absolute and finite form (with enclitic *mem*) from the root חמר, "foam, ferment, boil up."

then echoed by the people, who expand it into a declaration of praise arranged as a poetic triplet (v. 24). Samson again has the last word, but it comes in the form of a prayer and death wish, not a victory song (vv. 28, 30).

Killing a thousand Philistines with a donkey's jawbone was evidently hard work, even for one empowered by the Lord's spirit. Samson's thirst overpowered him, prompting him to pray to the Lord. For the first time in the story, the narrator depicts Samson as being conscious of a divine presence. Though the narrator tells us that Samson prayed to Yahweh, Samson himself, at least in the account, did not use this name, but only addressed God with the personal pronoun "you." Samson acknowledged God's role in the victory,[121] but his main concern was his physical need and his fear of falling into the hands of the Philistines, whom he referred to with the derogatory "uncircumcised." The narrator then informs us that God miraculously provided water, which revived Samson.[122] He uses the generic name *Elohim*, rather than *Yahweh*, perhaps highlighting Samson's failure to use the covenant name. An etiological observation follows, noting that the spring was subsequently named En Hakkore, "Spring of the One who Calls/ Prays."

The story appears to end happily with the report that Samson led Israel for twenty years. Elsewhere a reference to the length of a judge's

---

121. Samson affirmed: "You have given your servant this great victory." These words may suggest a nascent understanding of his role as Israel's deliverer, but we should not read too much into the statement. The self-designation "your servant" may simply be polite or reflect his awareness of his Nazirite status, and the term תְּשׁוּעָה most likely refers to Samson's personal victory over/deliverance from the Philistines in the battle (cf. the first person verb forms in v. 16). It need not carry the connotation "national deliverance." For other examples of the collocation of תְּשׁוּעָה and the verb נתן, "give," see 2 Kings 5:1; Psalms 144:10; Isaiah 46:13. For the collocation נתן בְּיַד־עֶבֶד, literally, "give into the hand of a servant," see Genesis 32:17 and 2 Chronicles 34:16; in both texts it seems to mean "commit to the care of."

122. The text says that God broke open the מַכְתֵּשׁ that was in Lehi. The term is derived from the verbal root כתש, "to pound, strike" (*HALOT*, 507). In Proverbs 27:22 מַכְתֵּשׁ is used of mortar, while in Zephaniah 1:11 it refers to a market district in Jerusalem. The referent in Judges 15:19 is unclear. Block understands the referent to be a seam in a rock (1999, 447), while *HALOT* (583) glosses the term "molar" (of the jawbone). Since the מַכְתֵּשׁ is transformed into a spring, the term may refer to a basin or hollow located on the hill or ridge (cf. v. 17).

career signals closure and is followed by a reference to his death (10:2, 5; 12:7, 9b–10a, 11b–12a, 14b–15). The omission of such a notation here is striking. But the narrator has a strategy. Samson's death will be outlined in detail, rather than briefly noted. Chapter 16 provides the account of his death, before repeating the notation about the length of his career. The truncated summary in 15:20 leaves us with the expectation of death and burial and creates an ominous mood for the story to follow. Rather than simply giving Samson an epitaph, the narrator describes his death as that of the naïve victim of his own weaknesses. Samson would enter the vestibule of death and never come out.[123] His carelessness in dealing with the Philistines, a cavalier approach to the Nazirite regulation regarding his hair, and his obsession with satisfying his physical passions would conspire to bring about his demise.

Femmes Fatales (16:1–22)

Samson flirts with disaster (16:1–3). In the previous episode Samson seems to have taken a step toward God and begun to fulfill his destiny. We hope he has learned that cavorting with the enemy can get one into a great deal of trouble. Unfortunately the story now takes a sharp turn for the worse, as the narrator reports how Samson foolishly went to Gaza to visit a prostitute.

The Philistines, who had not forgotten what Samson did to them, were bent on killing him. Apparently not knowing exactly where Samson had gone, they surrounded the entire town with guards.[124]

---

123. See Chisholm 2009c, 178–79. I originally made this point in an oral presentation at the 2006 national meeting of the Evangelical Theological Society in Washington, D. C. Butler cites this earlier unpublished version (2009, 345), which was subsequently revised and published in *JSOT*.

    If the placement of the truncated concluding formula in 15:20 is a rhetorical device, this means that it should not be used to construct theories of the text's composition and literary evolution, as so many have done. See, for example, Burney 1970, 338; Boling 1975, 240; Brettler 2002, 42; and Mobley 2005, 183–84. For a discussion of the issue, see Amit 1999, 266–67, note 54.

124. We assume the verb "they surrounded," has "the town" as its implied object; no object appears in the Hebrew text. It is unlikely they surrounded the prostitute's house, for in this case it would not have been necessary to guard the gate or even to wait around for Samson to finish what he came to do. It is more likely that the rumor of his arrival spread throughout the town, but that no one knew his exact whereabouts. Boling translates the verb וַיָּסֹבּוּ "they gathered around" (1975, 245). See 2 Samuel 18:15,

They focused their attention on the city gate, where they set an ambush.[125] Knowing that the gates would be closed at night, they patiently waited until morning, for they assumed that was when Samson would attempt to leave.

Perhaps Samson suspected that the Philistines would try to trap him, or maybe he just had his fill of the prostitute's charms. At any rate, he decided to leave the city in the middle of the night. Moving past the unsuspecting guards at the gate, he tore loose the doors, posts, and bar of the gate, lifted them to his shoulders, and carried them all the way to a hill near distant Hebron, close to forty miles away.[126] His removal of the city gate, a symbol of security, foreshadows the widespread death that would overtake this same city by the end of the chapter (Polzin 1980, 191).

How was Samson able to leave the city in this manner without rousing the Philistines? Boling suggests that the structure of the gate complex would have facilitated Samson's escape because the guards would probably have been inside one of the adjoining rooms (1975, 248). Block, on the other hand, argues just the opposite (1999, 450). He finds it difficult to believe that Samson could have walked through the tunnel-like opening inside the gate without being noticed, for guardrooms

---

where, as in Judges 16:2, the verb has no object and is combined with a following verb. The text there reads literally, "And ten young men, the armor bearers of Joab, gathered around and struck down Absalom." The men of Gaza, apparently not knowing Samson's exact whereabouts, assembled at the gate and set an ambush for him.

125. The reference to the Philistines setting an ambush (cf. וַיֶּאֶרְבוּ, literally, "and set an ambush," in v. 2) foreshadows the Delilah episode, where the Philistines again set an ambush for Samson (cf. הָאֹרֵב, literally, "the ambush," in vv. 9 and 12). See Galpaz-Feller 2006b, 134.

126. On the structure of gates in ancient Israel, see King and Stager 2001, 234–36. For a discussion of the different types of bars used on city gates, see E. Otto, "שַׁעַר," in *TDOT*, 15:372. Based on archaeological and biblical evidence, Barrick estimates the gates would have weighed anywhere from 5,350 to 10,700 pounds. If one includes the bar and bronze plating, the weight would have been doubled. The distance from Gaza to Hebron is 36 miles as the crow flies and the ascent in elevation about 3200 feet. To move 5,350 pounds a distance of 36 miles in 18 hours would take about 28.5 horsepower (Barrick 1976, 83–93). It is not clear why Samson took the gate to Hebron. Kim suggests that he did so "to humiliate the Judahites for their cowardice" in handing him over to the Philistines (1993, 306). He adds: "And it must have shamed the Judahites to see the gate of Gaza . . . carried to Hebron as a striking spoil of war and demonstration of victory."

lined both sides of the opening. Margalith, who understands the story as an aetiological legend, explains that to remove the doors, Samson would have had to remove the lintel, upon which rested the upper wall. This would have caused the whole wall to collapse (1987, 68–69). It is difficult to believe this would have escaped the attention of the guards! Amit prefers to look at the event from a rhetorical angle. She recreates the scene: "The Philistines 'kept whispering to each other' all night long, planning to capture and kill Samson, while he slipped out of the city at midnight right under their noses. This means that they were still plotting away in whispers when he was already gone with their city gate on his shoulders. Moreover, he must have performed this presumably noisy exploit . . . extremely quietly." She concludes that the narrator purposely mocks the Philistines (2001, 7–8).

What is the literary function of this brief account? As suggested above, the episode informs us that Samson had not changed significantly; he remained careless and driven by his physical appetites. The absence of the Lord's spirit is noteworthy, though it is obvious that Samson still possessed supernatural strength. In short, this account, while impressing us with another remarkable demonstration of Samson's strength and implying that God was still at work in Samson's life, has a foreboding quality to it. The Philistines were intent on destroying Samson. But they were dimwitted and did not seem to pose a real danger to Samson. Yet a real threat to Samson's well-being did remain. Despite his strength, he remained vulnerable to female charms. Would this weakness somehow allow the Philistines to get the upper hand, as they did in Timnah? What would happen if a woman ever became his enemy? (Crenshaw 1978, 91).

Worse yet, Samson's visit to the prostitute casts him in the role of a fool destined for destruction. The truncated concluding formula in 15:20 has already programmed us to expect some reference to Samson's death. We know from wisdom literature that prostitutes reside in the gateway to death (Prov. 6:26; 7:24–27; 23:27). Despite Samson's feeble efforts to display wisdom and his flair with words (see Judg. 14:14, 18; 15:16), the narrator depicts him as one who violates a cardinal wisdom doctrine.[127] This does not bode well for his future.

---

127. Brettler develops many parallels between Judges 14–15 and wisdom literature (2002, 50–54). However, oddly enough, he argues that wisdom motifs are absent from chapter 16 (54)! On the contrary, the strong wisdom flavor of chapters 14–15 sets the stage for the folly of chapter 16. Mobley sees this account as largely positive and misses its foreboding character (2005, 190–91).

Disaster flirts back (16:4–22). By now we expect episodes in Samson's story to revolve around women. Consequently we should not be surprised to read that Samson fell in love.[128] Yet this is the first time the narrator uses the word "love" to describe Samson's attraction to women (Vickery 1981, 69).[129] One wonders if this deeper emotional involvement will make him even more vulnerable than he proved to be at Timnah.[130] The woman's name (Delilah) is given,[131] but we are not told her status[132]

---

128. Like its English counterpart, the Hebrew verb אהב, "to love," has a broad spectrum of meaning, ranging from mere physical attraction to loyal devotion. Here it refers primarily to physical-emotional attraction. For other examples of this use, see Genesis 34:3 (of Shechem's love for Dinah), 2 Samuel 13:1, 4, 15 (of Amnon's love for Tamar), and 1 Kings 11:1 (of Solomon's love for his many foreign wives). The term can also be used of a woman's romantic attraction to a man (1 Sam. 18:20; of Michal's love for David).

129. In Judges 14:16 the Timnite woman accuses Samson of not loving her, but the narrator never actually states that Samson "loved" her. Ironically, in the Delilah account it is never stated that Delilah loves Samson (Klein 1993b, 63).

130. Samson undoubtedly loved the Timnite woman; he revealed the answer to the riddle in response to her challenge that he did not love her (cf. Judg. 14:16). Yet only here does the narrator state that Samson loved a woman. Exum observes: "The narrator's statement that Samson loved Delilah is, I think, not a sign that this is the first time Samson has loved, but rather a signal that this time is going to be especially important—a fatal attraction" (1993a, 82).

131. The name Delilah may mean "with dangling curls" or "flirtatious," see *HALOT*, 222. Younger relates the name to an Akkadian cognate meaning, "to praise, glorify" (2002, 315, note 70). In this case the name may suggest Delilah was praiseworthy, perhaps because of her physical beauty. Hess proposes a derivation from a root meaning, "to be weak, poor, low" (2003, 35). This variety of opinion suggests we do not really know the derivation for sure and should probably not make the meaning of Delilah's name an issue in exposition.

132. Smith observes: "It is often assumed that Delilah was a prostitute, but the text nowhere states that she was (although this assumption itself says something about interpreters) (1999, 94)." Smith is correct regarding the text, but her parenthetical comment sounds jaded and cynical. The assumption made by interpreters is understandable, albeit unproven, in light of the brief account of Samson's escapades that immediately precedes! Her precise identity is not as important as her literary function. Whether or not she was a prostitute in reality, her appearance as Samson's lover right after an unambiguous reference to a prostitute invites a comparison. Klein

or if she was an Israelite or Philistine.[133] Her precise ethnic identity is not of primary importance; what really matters is her allegiance, which she was willing to sell for the right price.[134] The Philistine rulers, probably five in number, representing the Philistines' five major cities, made her a monetary offer she could not refuse, promising her 1100 shekels apiece if she could discover the secret of Samson's strength.[135]

---

observes that her "activities split the 'prostitute'-male relationship into two: one man 'loves' her, another (actually 'others') pay her" (1993b, 62).

133. Klein is convinced Delilah was a Philistine: "I can discover no basis for inferring Delilah to be Israelite, and there is at least the suggestion that she is Philistine. After his disdain of his parent's charge that he find a woman of his own people and his subsequent escapades with non-Israelite women (the Timnite woman and the prostitute of Gaza), Samson's love for Delilah and her association with Philistines are consistent with his earlier behavior, all of which strongly supports that she is not an Israelite and is a Philistine" (1993b, 62, note 1).

134. See Weitzman 2002, 161–62. The reference to her home being in the Valley (or wadi) of Sorek (literally, "valley/wadi of the vine") may be ominous, if indeed Samson was to avoid the fruit of the vine. See Segert 1984, 458. Klein suggests a subtle symbolism in the name. Wadis can become "virtual torrents" when it rains, and the fruit of the vine, though "pleasant," can cause "dangerous loss of control." Thus "Delilah is mingled with uncontrolled 'torrents' and control-eroding wine, both strongly suggestive of overwhelming passions" (1993b, 61).

For a sympathetic reading of Delilah's motives and actions see Amit 2002, 59–76. Amit traces the history of interpretation (in her view largely misinterpretation) of Delilah in both Jewish and Christian literature and art. She contends that Delilah was an Israelite who saved her tribe (Judah) from the Philistine threat by helping the Philistines capture Samson. She turned the money she received from the Philistines over to her tribe to help them "recover from the depredations that Samson had caused" (75). In response to Amit, one may agree that some interpreters have engaged in speculation and unwarranted gap-filling in their treatment of Delilah. However, the narrator is not as reticent as Amit contends (59) and her interpretation of the text is just as marred by unwarranted gap-filling as the studies she criticizes. While others may have embellished the narrator's portrait of Delilah, Amit turns it on its head, making for a topsy-turvy rereading of the story. For a survey of other positive treatments of Delilah, see Smith 1999, 109–11.

135. Younger shows this was an astronomical figure (2002, 316, note 75). If ten shekels was the average annual wage (cf. Judg. 17:10), then 5500 shekels was 550 times this figure. If we assume for illustrative purposes that the annual average wage today is $25,000, then 5500 shekels would be equivalent to fifteen million dollars in modern currency.

The Philistines' instructions to her are foreboding. They told Delilah to "trick" (Hebrew פָּתִי) Samson (v. 5). At the Timnite wedding the Philistines used this same verb form (פַּתִּי) when they demanded that Samson's bride-to-be "trick" him (14:15).[136] The Timnite woman succeeded. Will Delilah?

The story of Samson's seduction (vv. 6–21) displays four panels and effectively uses repetition and variation to build suspense and highlight Samson's stupidity.[137] It may be outlined as follows:

Panel 1 (vv. 6–9)
Delilah's request (v. 6)
Samson's response (v. 7)
The failed plot (vv. 8–9)

Panel 2 (vv. 10–12)
Delilah's complaint and request (v. 10)
Samson's response (v. 11)
The failed plot (v. 12)

Panel 3 (vv. 13–14)
Delilah's complaint and request (v. 13)
Samson's response (v. 14a)
The failed plot (v. 14b)

Panel 4 (vv. 15–21)
Delilah's complaint and request (vv. 15–16)
Samson's response (v. 17)
The successful plot (vv. 18–21)

In verses 13–14 the Septuagint preserves the original text. The Hebrew text reads: "(13) Delilah then said to Samson: 'Up to now, you have deceived me and told me lies. Tell me how you can be subdued!' He said to her: 'If you weave the seven braids of my hair into the fabric.' (14) So she fastened (it) with the pin and said to him, 'The Philistines

---

136. See Schneider 2000, 220; and Ackerman 1998, 232. The verb פָּתָה, "trick,"
is related etymologically to פֶּתִי, "simple-minded, naïve," a term used in
Proverbs of the naïve youth who is lured into sexual promiscuity that leads
to his death (see Prov. 7:7). Such naïve persons fail to see the consequences
of their behavior (Prov. 1:32; 22:3; 27:12). See Chisholm 2009c, 178–79.
137. For a helpful study of the pericope's structure, see Exum 1997, 39–46.

are here, Samson.' He woke up from his sleep and tore away the pin of the loom and the fabric." (literal translation)

The Septuagint has a longer version of the account. The words in italics reflect the additional material appearing in the Septuagint (Vaticanus version): "(13) Delilah said to Samson: 'Up to now you have deceived me and told me lies. Tell me how you can be subdued.' He said to her: 'If you weave the seven braids of my hair into the fabric *and se-cure (it) with the pin to the wall, I will become weak just like any other man.' (14) So when he was asleep Delilah took the seven braids of his hair, wove (them) into* the fabric, fastened (it) with the pin *to the wall*, and said: 'The Philistines are here, Samson!' He woke up from his sleep and tore away the pin of the loom and the fabric."

The Hebrew text has been shortened by an accidental error. Note that the last word before the Septuagint plus is הַמַּסָּכֶת, "the fabric" (underlined in the translation above for easy recognition). This same word appears at the end of the plus, suggesting that a scribe's eye jumped from the first instance of the word to the second, resulting in the omission of the intervening words.[138]

Contextual factors support the longer version. In the shorter version Samson's explanation seems truncated and incomplete, especially when compared to the explanations he gives Delilah both before (vv. 7, 11) and after this (v. 17). Furthermore in the shorter version Delilah's response does not correspond to Samson's directions, contrary to the pattern we see before (vv. 8, 12) and after (v. 19) this. In a paneled narrative like this (vv. 6–9, 10–12, 13–14, 15–22), one expects structural symmetry in the panels leading up to the climax, where structural deviation is then common. The longer version provides the symmetry one expects and is contextually more compatible.

There are several reasons why Delilah might have believed the false explanations Samson offered in the first three panels. The suggestion that he could be subdued by seven fresh bowstrings (v. 7) has

---

138.See Burney 1970, 380. This type of scribal mistake is well-attested elsewhere. See Klein 1974, 27–29. The omission of the phrase אֶל הַקִּיר, "to the wall," in the Hebrew text of verse 14d may be due to virtual homoioteleuton. A scribe's eye could have skipped from the final *dalet* on the preceding word (בַּיָּתֵד, "with the pin") to the very similar *resh* on the end of הַקִּיר, "the wall," resulting in the omission of the prepositional phrase. While using the Greek text to reconstruct the original reading, Moore rejects the references to the pin being secured into the wall, arguing that this reflects a misunderstanding of the weaving process (1895, 353–54; cf. Burney 1970, 381).

an authentic ring to it, for seven is a highly symbolic number that might suggest magical or supernatural power. In the second panel he advised the use of "new" (i.e., strong) ropes and placed the emphatic infinitive absolute (cf. "tightly") before the verb "tie," suggesting an element of certainty. In the third panel he again used the number "seven," presented a substantially different plot involving his hair, and offered more detailed instructions that she might have thought were too elaborate to be a hoax.[139]

As is typical with paneled stories of this type, several literary variations from the repetitive pattern of the earlier panels mark out the culminating panel as distinct. In the fourth panel Delilah's argument is far more persuasive than before as she questions the sincerity of Samson's love for her and nags him day after day. We already know Samson was vulnerable to this kind of argumentation and suspect the worst. The Timnite woman employed the same tactic and the narrator uses the same verb to describe her persistence (14:16–17).[140] Possibly Samson sensed this denial of genuine love might result in the withholding of sexual favors. The narrator's observation that her nagging tired him "to death" (literal translation) hints at the final outcome of her efforts and is dripping with irony, for his capitulation to her nagging would lead to his death.

Samson's response is also far different in the final panel. Rather than using the simple pattern, "If . . ., I will become weak and be just like any other man," he now prefaced his response with an authentic explanation about his personal background, changed the verb form in the protasis of the conditional sentence to a perfect (he used the imperfect earlier), added the words "my strength would leave me," and changed "like any other man" to "like all other men."[141]

---

139. On the construction of looms and the technique of weaving, see King and Stager 2001, 152–58. They discuss (p. 157) how Delilah could easily have woven Samson's hair into the warp of her loom.

140. The verb צוק lies behind "nagged" in 14:17 and 16:16. On the correlation between the texts, see Ackerman 1998, 232; Exum 1997, 44; and Galpaz-Feller 2006b, 178. Galpaz-Feller states: "When one observes Samson's conduct with Delilah and compares it with the account of his relations with the woman from Timnath, it would appear at first that these are two versions of the same story. By telling the story in this manner, the author chooses to emphasize that Samson has learned nothing from his experience. He repeats the mistakes of his past in an obsessive and patterned manner."

141. NIV does not reflect this last variation. In the accidentally shortened Hebrew text, the third panel (v. 13) has no statement about Samson

Delilah's response to Samson's explanation and the Philistines' response to her report also differ significantly in the fourth panel. This time, the narrator informs us, Delilah was absolutely convinced he was telling the truth, and her words to the Philistines reflect that. They too seemed sure she was right, for they arrived with their money in hand.

The shaving of Samson's hair violated his Nazirite status. If one understands Samson as bound by all the regulations of Numbers 6 (see our earlier discussion), then the shaving of his hair may have been the last in a series of violations of the Nazirite rules. He had touched the honey from the lion's carcass, attended a wedding banquet, touched the jawbone of a dead donkey, and killed a lion and several Philistines. If one assumes that the Nazirite regulation about corpses applied to animals as well as humans, that Samson drank some wine at the wedding,[142] and that his battle exploits placed him in the situation envisioned in Numbers 6:9, then he had violated all but one of the Nazirite rules prior to his encounter with Delilah. When his hair was shaved, this was the straw that broke the camel's back.[143]

However, this view requires some assumptions that are not necessarily supported by the text. It is possible that none of the actions prior to the Delilah incident violated the Nazirite code, at least technically speaking. The law about corpses may not have applied to animals, the text never says that he actually drank the prohibited beverages, and the situation described in Numbers 6:9 may not have applied to one whom God has commissioned to fight battles. So it is possible that Samson had not violated any of the Nazirite rules prior to the incident with Delilah. In this case the incident involving the animal corpse and Samson's appearance at the wedding may contribute to the story by creating an ominous mood where threats to Samson's Nazirite status lurk in his environment.

Of course, one could take an intermediate position. Perhaps Samson violated the rule about contact with a corpse when he ate the honey, but did not violate any of the other rules prior to the incident with Delilah. In this case, God was patient with him and willing to overlook the initial violation of Nazirite ritual. It is possible that

---

becoming as weak as any other man. This change in wording in verse 17 is also reflected in the Alexandrinus and Vaticanus versions of the Septuagint, though they differ slightly from each other.

142. See the discussion above in our comments on Judges 14:10.

143. Olson ("Judges," 842) argues that Samson broke "all three nazirite vows by eating unclean food, drinking alcohol, and cutting his hair" (1998, 842; cf. Brown 2000, 245–46; and Wong 2006a, 92–96).

Samson was not even aware of this regulation, since the angel did not mention it. But when Samson told Delilah the secret of his strength, he went too far. His long hair was the distinguishing feature that marked him out as a special servant of God. In fact, the only Nazirite rule the angel drew to his mother's attention was the regulation about his hair remaining unshaven. As noted above, when he told Delilah the secret of his success, he did more than violate a rule; he rejected his role as God's servant. For the second time in the story, in a far more telling way, he gave priority to his own gratification, rather than his divine calling. God was compelled to respond decisively.[144]

A second view of Samson's Nazirite status is that he was bound only by the rules pertaining to drinking wine and shaving his hair. If we assume he broke one of the rules by drinking at the wedding, then the shaving of his hair broke the second rule, violated his Nazirite status, and brought God's discipline. However, as we have already noted, the text does not actually say he drank wine. This would explain why he was not disciplined until his hair was shaven, for only at that point was his Nazirite status compromised.

A third view, as noted earlier, is that the only regulation applicable in Samson's case pertained to his hair. If so, it is understandable why God withdrew his strength when Samson's hair was shaved off. As Samson confessed to Delilah, his long hair was a unique visible reminder of his special relationship to God. His identity and destiny were inextricably linked to his long hair. He should have suspected that Delilah intended to betray him.[145] Delilah's initial request (v. 6) does not hide her intentions. In fact it essentially repeats the Philistines' instructions (v. 5).[146] Delilah's lack of subtlety makes her appear naïve. Perhaps Samson could not bring himself to admit that Delilah, the object of his affection, would really betray him. When she persisted in seeking the secret to his strength and followed his instructions each time as if to subdue him, maybe he interpreted her actions as playful kidding. Of course, if the Philistines actually appeared on the first two occasions, he should have realized her intentions were malicious. However, the text states that they were hiding in the bedroom (vv. 9, 12) and does not actually say that they tried to subdue Samson. Perhaps they waited to see if the scheme worked and when he demonstrated his

---

144. See the insightful discussion in Webb 1987, 169–70.
145. See Ackerman 2000, 35. She calls Samson a "witless lout." Bledstein prefers the term "dodo" (1993, 49). She characterizes him as "all brawn, little brain aside from street smarts with riddles" (p. 50).
146. On Delilah's direct approach see Klein 1993b, 63–64.

strength, they stayed hidden or slipped out the back door. If so, then Samson never actually saw them and probably concluded Delilah was just playing. Noting that Samson never questioned Delilah's motives, Schneider states; "Samson was either so naive as not to see what was happening, or so arrogant and confident in his strength that he had no fear" (2000, 222). He was probably both naïve and arrogant, but there is a more basic, elemental explanation for Samson's apparent stupidity. His sexual addiction blinded him to reality, causing him to overlook the obvious as he insanely pursued sexual gratification.[147] He told Delilah the secret of his strength, as if to say, "Your happiness and my sexual satisfaction are more important than my divine calling." To keep Delilah he was willing to become as weak as all other men. This was a blatant rejection of his Nazirite status. God did not tolerate this attitude and withdrew his energizing strength from Samson, at least temporarily.

But if one takes this view, then what is the point of the earlier incidents in the story (approaching the vineyard, coming in contact with the lion's corpse, attending the wedding festival, killing Philistines) that echo the Nazirite regulations of Numbers 6? Perhaps the earlier incidents contribute to the overall incongruity and irony of the story. This is a story about a deliverer who never discovers his purpose in life and ends up beginning the deliverance of a people who never ask to be delivered. As such the story takes place within a framework of incongruity and irony. The story is filled with incongruities, including, among others: (1) Israel does not ask for deliverance, but God decides to deliver them anyway. (2) God decides to supernaturally enable a barren woman to conceive, even though she does not ask for a child. (3) When told her son's purpose in life, the mother fails to share the information with her husband Manoah. (4) When Manoah, who is understandably confused about his son's role, asks for clarification, the angel does not give him a straightforward answer, but simply says that his wife should remember everything she was told. (5) Manoah's wife gives birth to Samson, though the text makes no reference to her husband having relations with her prior to or after the angel's visit. (6) When the Lord's spirit begins to move Samson, he goes to Timnah and picks out a Philistine wife, seemingly in violation of the Lord's standard regarding intermarriage with foreigners. (7) When Samson's parents understandably object to him becoming romantically involved

---

147. Klein is closer to the truth of the matter when she suggests that Delilah may have believed "that love not only makes lovers blind but also stupid" (1993b, 63–64).

with a Philistine woman, the narrator informs us the Lord was behind this strange development. (8) When Samson ignites a potential war with the Philistines, his own countrymen arrest him and hand him over to the enemy. Within this framework the incidents that echo the Nazirite regulations fit well. Samson is a Nazirite, but not the usual type. He parades through the story seemingly violating or nearly violating Nazirite regulations right and left. However, he has not really done so, because only one rule applies in his case. This incongruity is exactly what one expects in this story, which might be subtitled, "What's Wrong with This Picture?"

When the Philistines captured Samson with Delilah's help, Israel's story had come full circle from the earlier account of Jael and Sisera. On that earlier occasion Israel's ally Jael lured a *foreign* general to his death; now the Philistines' ally Delilah has lured the greatest of *Israel's* warriors to his demise. Samson is in the role of Sisera, and Delilah in the role of Jael.[148]

When viewed in light of this parallel, the third panel in Samson's encounter with Delilah (16:13–14) takes on fuller significance. In that panel Samson moved ominously closer to the truth by focusing on his hair (Crenshaw 1978, 94; Exum 1997, 44). The words תָּקַע, "fasten," and יָתֵד, "pin," contribute to this ominous mood, for both also appear in the account of Sisera's murder (Olson 1998, 858). Jael killed the Canaanite general by pounding (תִּקַע) a tent peg (יָתֵד) through his head as he slept within her private quarters (4:21). Here we see Samson tossing around these same words, as he was ready to fall asleep in the private quarters of a woman whose allegiance was with his enemies. The narrative seems to be going out of its way to suggest he was on the brink of becoming another Sisera.

The Philistines gouged out Samson's eyes,[149] bound him in chains, and forced him to do woman's work.[150] The reference to the Philistines

---

148. See Chisholm 1994b, 43–44; and Schneider 2000, 223–24. Both Webb (1987, 164) and Klein (1988, 137) note verbal and thematic parallels between the two stories. For parallels between Delilah and Jael, see Ackerman 2000, 36–41.

149. For examples of putting out the eyes as a form of punishment in the ancient Near East, see Galpaz-Feller 2006b, 201–03.

150. Block aptly observes: "from the perspective of the Philistines, there is ironic justice in Samson grinding grain, since he had destroyed so much of their crop" (1999, 462, note 423). Mesopotamian texts also mention this form of punishment. See van der Toorn 1986, 248–51. Exodus 11:5; Job 31:10 and Isaiah 47:2 suggest that grinding was typically done by women. Lamentations 5:13 describes the people's disgrace and humiliation following the

binding (אסר) him in chains is especially ironic, for this same verb was used earlier to describe various attempts to subdue him.[151] The men of Judah bound him with ropes (15:10, 12–13), and Delilah tied him up with bowstrings (16:7–8) and then with new ropes (16:11–12), but in each instance he tore them off. But this time, having lost his special Nazirite status along with his hair, he was subdued.

His career appeared to be at a tragic end.[152] The one named "sun-like" (see 13:24) now lived in a world of darkness. At first he appeared to be destined for greatness, for his supernatural conception seemingly placed him in line with the great patriarchs Isaac, Jacob, and Joseph. In many respects he resembled the first judges. Like Othniel, he was divinely empowered and did not hesitate to attack the enemy. His delight in riddles, especially ones that others could not possibly solve on their own, suggested a capacity for cunning, much like Ehud possessed. Like Shamgar, he was able to slaughter hundreds of Philistines single-handedly, even with an unconventional weapon. Yet an embarrassing lack of wisdom brought about his downfall. Like the naïve fool portrayed in Proverbs, his sexual drives caused him to act rashly and without foresight. Following the pattern of Barak, Gideon, and Jephthah, his use of the word "if" (see 16:7, 11, 13, 17; as well as 14:12–13) signaled his weakness. Their use of conditional sentences pointed to their weak faith; in Samson's case, his use of conditional sentences was a symptom of his carelessness and folly.[153] Like the naïve and unsuspecting Sisera, he was duped by a woman behind closed doors and ended up humiliated.[154]

However, this story is full of ironic twists and surprises. One might assume Samson's loss of strength meant that God had abandoned him for good, but the narrator hints this may not be the case when he

---

Babylonian invasion. Included in the description is a portrait of young men being forced to "toil at the millstones."

151. On the importance of the binding theme in the story, especially as it appears in the speeches, see Klein 1993b, 64–65.

152. Is it merely coincidental that Zedekiah, the last king of Judah, was treated like Samson? 2 Kings 25:7 states the Babylonians "put out his eyes, bound him with bronze shackles, and took him to Babylon." At that point Judah and its king were humiliated like Samson and appeared to have come to a tragic demise. But to an exilic audience Samson's story offers encouragement, for Samson's blinding was followed by the defeat of the enemy. In the same way, Zedekiah's humiliation would be a prelude to the downfall of Babylon. See Brettler 2002, 58.

153. For a more detailed discussion of this point see Chisholm 1994b, 43.

154. There are also parallels to the Ehud story. See Handy 1992, 242–44.

observes that Samson's hair began to grow again (v. 22). If God were through with Samson, why would the narrator tell us this? Perhaps we (and the Philistines!) have jumped to conclusions and Samson still has a future. After all, without his eyesight, Samson's Achilles heel—an eye for women (see 14:1; 16:1)—had been eliminated.[155] Furthermore, the location of Samson's prison—Gaza—reminds us of the time when he uprooted and carted off Gaza's gate, suggesting that this city was not secure as long as he was around.

Tragedy and Triumph (16:23–31)

Having subdued their greatest enemy, the Philistines decided to celebrate their victory by holding a sacrificial feast for their patron deity Dagon, the god of grain.[156] The Philistine rulers praised Dagon for

---

155. Galpaz-Feller observes: "Vision is deceptive. Samson cannot see reality until he is blinded" (2006b, 210). She adds: "His vision deceives him and leads to his decline. When he is blind, Samson sees and understands better" (212). For her discussion of "the motif of deceptive vision" in the Samson story, see pp. 207–13.

156. Dagon appears to have been the chief deity of the Philistines. See 1 Samuel 5:1–7 and 1 Chronicles 10:10. Though an older interpretation understood him to be a fish god, it is more likely that he was a weather-fertility deity responsible for crops. In Ugaritic *dgn* means "grain," and the storm-god Baal is called Dagon's son. For a discussion of the Old Testament and extrabiblical evidence pertaining to this deity, see Day 2000, 85–90. Day thinks that "grain" is probably a secondary meaning for *dgn* in Ugaritic and that the term is etymologically related to a verbal root "be cloudy, rainy" (87–88). According to Day, "the earliest sources do not particularly connect Dagon with the grain, though they do suggest that Dagon was a storm god, and of course a storm god is implicitly a fertility god, whence the corn would derive" (88). Singer prefers to see Dagan/Dagon as fundamentally "an earth and vegetation deity." He considers any storm characteristics "as no doubt secondary" (1992, 437). Singer argues that evidence from the Bible, Amarna, and Canaanite inscriptions indicates that Dagan/Dagon was not a native Canaanite deity. He writes: "The cumulative evidence from various sources leads to the inevitable conclusion that the Philistines and the other Sea Peoples who settled in Palestine did *not* encounter Dagon as one of the gods of the land, and obviously could not have adopted his cult in their new land" (439, emphasis his). Singer asks, "If so, how did Dagon become the main god of the Philistines?" He considers it possible that they adopted him from the Phoenicians or that they "encountered and adopted the cult of Dagan/Dagon" in Syria before they moved south into Canaan and "brought Dagon with them" (439–40).

delivering their arch-enemy Samson into their hands.[157] The people essentially repeated this affirmation of praise, but expanded it by substituting a description of Samson for his name. They viewed Samson as one who had devastated their land (see 15:5) and killed many of their people. This declaration of praise was the Philistines' response to Samson's victory song (15:16). Would the victorious Philistines have the last word?

As the Philistines grew merrier, they decided to add insult to injury. They brought Samson out of prison so he could parade before them and entertain them.[158] Perhaps they found it amusing to see this once

---

For a thorough study of the evidence pertaining to this deity, see Feliu 2003.

157. The rulers use a plural in describing Samson as their enemy (note אוֹיְבֵינוּ). If this is a so-called plural of degree, it would have the force of "enemy *par excellence*" or "arch-enemy." Burnett prefers to understand such plurals as "concretized abstract plurals." He points out that some of these plural forms "can be used in reference to a single individual or object that is exemplary of the quality named and to which a corresponding status applies" (2001, 21–22). In this case the plural may carry the nuance "the one who is to us hostility personified." Even so, the use of the plural, as opposed to the singular, suggests some degree of rhetorical emphasis.

158. Halton (2009, 61–64) suggests that there is a pun in verse 25, involving שׂחק, used in the *piel* stem in the sense of "entertain," and the verb שׁחק, "to crush." The early "graphical ambiguity" of the text, where the sibilants were not distinguished, "facilitates this pun" (63). In his view there is latent comedy in the text, as well as a dual perspective: "The author of this pericope used the ambiguity of the verb in Judg 16:25, 27 to articulate two points of view. The masoretic tradents follow the perspective of the festive Philistines as they vocalized שׂחק to convey the notion that Samson's captors brought him into the temple in order to entertain them. The second point of view is that of the narrator. The narrator injects an element of dark comedy into this account stating that the Philistines summoned Samson in order to crush themselves" (64).

This proposal, while certainly a testimony to Halton's creativity, is unconvincing for the following reasons: (1) The rarity of the verb שׁחק (it appears four times in the Old Testament) makes the alleged pun overly subtle. (2) One cannot simply focus on the lexical meaning of the verbs in question without considering syntactical factors. The *piel* of שׂחק, "entertain," collocates easily with the following לָנוּ, "for us," but the proposed verb שׁחק, "crush," does not. It would yield a reading "that he may crush for us." But one expects an object with this verb, whether stated (Job 14:19; Ps. 18:43/2 Sam. 18:43) or implied (Exod. 30:36). (3) In its two clearest uses in the Old Testament, the verb שׁחק means "grind, wear down, erode."

great, but now blinded warrior stumbling and groping in the darkness. When the narrator informs us that Samson leaned against the temple pillars, it seems to be nothing more than a realistic extra touch to

---

In Exodus 30:36 it describes the action of grinding spices into powder, while in Job 14:19 it is used of running water wearing away stones. In Psalm 18:43 (English v. 42) it figuratively describes the psalmist's annihilation of his enemies after striking them down; he grinds them up like dust, which is then carried away by the wind (the text reads literally, "I ground them like dust upon the face of the wind"). The parallel text in 2 Samuel 22:43 has simply, "I ground them up like the dust of the earth." Halton appeals to the parallelism in 2 Samuel 22:43, where דקק and רקע are used. דקק means "crush, grind" (*HALOT*, 229). However, it may not be original to the text. It does not appear in 4Q Samuel (where only רקע is used), nor in Psalm 18:43, where only the *hiphil* of the verb ריק, "to empty out," appears. The Psalm 18:43 reading is probably a corruption, but it is uncertain which of the verbs used in 2 Samuel 22:43 lies behind it. The verb רקע seems to refer to the action of stamping upon or beating down clay. If original to the text, it may depict a slightly different image than we see in the first line of the verse. Because of the confused textual situation in Psalm 18:43/2 Samuel 22:43, it is unwise to appeal to 2 Samuel 22:43 as "the text most relevant to Judg 16:25–27" (p. 63). The clearest uses, which should be the most relevant to sober lexical inquiry, suggest the action of grinding or rubbing. Furthermore, as acknowledged by Halton, some cognates of the verb שחק can refer to grinding or rubbing (pp. 62, note 3 [Syriac]; 63, note 10 [Akkadian]). See as well the meaning "rub" attested in Official Aramaic (*DNWSI*, 1121).

True, the verb is used in Psalm 18:43/2 Samuel 22:43 in the context of defeating enemies, but there it depicts actions performed in the aftermath of the victory, not the felling of the enemy *per se*. The structure of verses 33–46 is as follows: divine preparation and enablement for battle (vv. 33–36), pursuit and felling of the enemy (vv. 37–41), consummation of the victory by annihilating the helpless enemy (vv. 42–43), and subjugation of the nations (vv. 44–46). Samson's destruction of the temple is more comparable to felling the enemy, not to final annihilation of a subdued enemy. If the destruction of the temple is viewed as the final, consummative act in Samson's victory over the Philistines, the proposed parallel to 2 Samuel 22:43 might be able to stand, but this seems overly subtle. Furthermore, one must remember that Samson only initiated Yahweh's war against the Philistines; he did not consummate it (cf. Judg. 13:5).

In short, the image of grinding does not facilitate the alleged pun as readily as Halton seems to think. It does not provide a suitable metaphor for the sudden manner in which Samson actually destroyed the temple and, as a military metaphor, it depicts annihilation of the enemy following a victory, not the actual felling of the enemy.

the story—an attempt by a blinded and humiliated man to regain his equilibrium and catch his breath. But then the narrator adds that the temple was so packed to capacity that even the roof was covered with Philistines.[159] Like the earlier reference to Samson's returning hair (v. 22), this observation catches our attention, for we suddenly realize that if somehow Samson could perform another superhuman act of strength (as when he tore up Gaza's gate and carried it away to distant Hebron),

---

159. For a reconstruction of the scene as depicted in the text, see Moore 1895, 360–61. Block, citing an archaeological report by A. Mazar, observes that a Philistine temple at Tell Qasile contained a long room, the roof of which was supported by two pillars almost three meters (approximately 9.8 feet) apart (1999, 466). However, if the pillars were this far apart, Samson would not have been able to touch both pillars at the same time, unless, of course, he was a giant. Based on his exploits of strength, one might assume he had superhuman stature, but the text never indicates this. (For a brief discussion of later Jewish traditions that Samson was gigantic in size, see Mobley, 1997, 229–30.) Margalith finds the description of the temple structure to be problematic: "Palestinian archaeology has so far not discovered any temple buildings large enough to support such a number of spectators, certainly not buildings resting on two central pillars. The houses and temples of that period were roofed with wooden beams and even the cedars of Lebanon could not provide beams for halls larger than 30 x 60 feet; and since the walls of these halls supported the roof there could not have been 'two central pillars upon which the house stood.'" Margalith adds that "the biblical description is reminiscent rather of the famous frescoes of the palace of Knossos, where the motif of the twin pillars forming a chapel or sanctuary appears repeatedly, depicting a crowd of 'thousands' of men and women seated on roofs and watching the sacred games. What these frescoes do not show is that the 'roofs' were actually terraces of the palace" (1987, 70). On the other hand, Kitchen finds the incident as described in the biblical text to be plausible (2003, 216). He acknowledges: "Most typical Palestinian temples, especially local Canaanite designs, had few columns (except sometimes a pair at the entrance), and they offer no light on Samson's last exploit." However, he then adds: "But Philistine temples may have drawn for inspiration on the Aegean world whence they had indubitably come. In Cyprus at Kition was found a series of five temples; in the twelfth century Temples 4 and 5 (particularly the latter) consisted of rectangular roofed halls supported by slim pillars (in pairs in no. 5) with the sanctuary at the rear end and main entrance at one side at the front. If some such structure once stood at Gaza, then after his public performances for his captors, a Samson could have been allowed inside such a temple for a pause, have pulled in the middle pair of columns, and the overweight of people on its roof would have led to its speedy and progressive collapse."

the Philistine throng within and on top of the temple could be in deep trouble (Schneider 2000, 225).

The final verses of the story record the highlight of Samson's tragic career. Samson, the former riddler (14:14) and taunting victor (15:16), was now completely dependent on God, just as he was following the battle at Jawbone Hill when he thought he was dying of thirst (15:18). For the second time in the story he cried out to God. However, this time there was no cute turn of phrase (14:14), poetic bravado (15:16) or brusque sarcasm (15:18). He addressed God more appropriately, even using the covenantal name *Yahweh*. (Prior to this he addressed God as "you" [15:18] and referred to him as *Elohim* [16:17].) He begged to be remembered and strengthened so that he might exact vengeance on the Philistines for taking his eyesight from him. For the second time in the book God answered his prayer, allowing him to push the pillars over and bring the temple crashing down. Ironically, in his death he won his greatest victory, for the narrator informs us that he killed many more Philistines on this one occasion than he had throughout his life.

Despite this great victory, the story is clouded by a tragic element. Even at the end of his life, Samson still did not understand his role as Israel's deliverer. His concern was merely personal vengeance, which motivated him so strongly that he was willing to surrender his own life to achieve it.[160] In the end the scent of death overwhelms the story, as the root מות appears five times in verse 30 (Chisholm 2009c, 179).

The final verse, which informs us of his burial in his father's tomb and of his length of service, pulls the curtain shut. This reverses the order seen elsewhere (cf. our comments on 15:20), where a notation about the length of a judge's career precedes a reference to his burial. The two notations about Samson's length of service (15:20 and

---

160. See Block 1999, 467–68, as well as Greenberg 1983, 12–13. Peels downplays Samson's desire for personal vengeance and attempts to interpret his actions in light of his role as Israel's deliverer (1995, 100–02). However, he seems to overlook the grim reality of Samson's ignorance of his role. There is no evidence in the text that Samson viewed himself as saving Israel. In 15:18 he speaks of his victory as personal and in 16:28 he seeks personal vengeance. Galpaz-Feller also takes an overly optimistic view of Samson's death, calling it "an act of heroism, sacrifice, and redemption" (2006a, 315–25, especially p. 325). However, she does acknowledge that Samson's primary concern is personal revenge. She states: "He knows God's power to save, but this time, too [as in chapter 15], Samson makes a request for himself and not for his people. He asks for strength to take personal revenge as opposed to national revenge" (2006b, 220). On the just nature of Samson's cause and petition, see Jost 1999, 123.

16:31b) end up as bookends for the story of Samson's descent into death (Chisholm 2009c, 179). The references to Zorah and Manoah provide an inclusio for the entire story (see 13:2), while the phrase "between Zorah and Eshtaol" links with 13:25 to form an inclusio for the portion of the story dealing with his career and adult life.

MESSAGE AND APPLICATION

Thematic Emphases
Once more Israel's rebellion resulted in subjugation. But this time the people did not cry out to the Lord; they were resigned to their condition (see 15:11–12). Yet the Lord decided to intervene anyway, giving life to Manoah's wife's barren womb.

Samson failed to understand his role as God's consecrated servant. In her exuberance over her pregnancy, Manoah's wife failed to communicate to her husband Samson's role as Israel's deliverer. Samson gives no evidence that he saw himself in this capacity. His conflicts with the Philistines were motivated by personal vengeance, not by any larger vision.[161] Without an understanding of the significance of his Nazirite status, Samson was willing to place it in jeopardy and eventually succumbed to personal gratification.

In some respects Samson represented Israel (Klein 1988, 116; Olson 1998, 842–43, 860–61; and Webb 1995, 116–17). Despite his miraculous beginning and tremendous God-given potential, he missed his calling to be God's consecrated servant. He became a humiliated prisoner on foreign soil, but in the end was vindicated by God when he desperately begged for divine intervention.

With Samson's death in the rubble of the Philistine temple, the decline in Israelite leadership was complete. Deficient faith and lack of wisdom culminated in spiritual ignorance and utter folly.[162] This leadership void characterized this period of chaos in Israel's history (see chapters 17–21).

God accomplished his purpose (the beginning of Israel's deliverance from the Philistines), despite Samson's shortcomings and Israel's apathy. In the process he again demonstrated his sovereignty and superiority to pagan deities by destroying the temple of a foreign god (cf.

---

161. On vengeance as the motivating force in Samson's conflicts with the Philistines, see Wong 2006a, 174–75.
162. Bledstein observes that Samson's "treatment in the recorded history turns heroism upside down in a lampoon of heroics" (1993, 50).

9:46–49).[163] Samson's great victory in Dagon's temple reminds us that it was God's disfavor with his people, not the power of foreign gods (cf. 16:23–24), that caused them to be humiliated before their enemies.[164]

Exegetical idea: *God was at work among his people, even when they were insensitive to his presence. He accomplished his purpose through unwise Samson, though Samson failed to understand his role as God's deliverer and was motivated by personal gratification and vengeance, not some sense of a higher calling. His failure to understand his role in God's plan led to tragic personal failure and pain, and kept him from enjoying the benefits of God's mighty deeds.*

Theological Principles

Perhaps more than any other story in Judges, the story of Samson illustrates God's sovereign freedom to act as he sees fit. Even when his people seemed content to live under divine discipline and did not ask for divine intervention, God was at work and began to bring them relief despite their apathy and ignorance.

In accomplishing his purposes God can use the most clueless of instruments. In the process he supernaturally energizes his servant (cf. 13:25; 14:6, 19; 15:14), providentially maneuvers him into situations that are advantageous to the realization of the divine goal (cf. 14:4), answers Samson's prayers for help and vengeance (cf. 15:18–19; 16:28), and even exploits Samson's failures (cf. chapter 16).[165] When all is said and done, God demonstrates his commitment to his people and his superiority to their enemies and all so-called gods.

Theological idea: *God is always at work among his people, even when they are insensitive to his presence. He can even accomplish his purposes through unwise instruments who fail to understand their role as his servants and are primarily motivated by personal gratification. However, a failure to understand one's role in God's plan can lead to*

---

163. Mobley sees Samson's capture by the Philistines as foreshadowing the capture of the ark (1 Samuel 4–5) (2005, 205). He compares both to "the Trojan Horse" and observes that Samson, like the ark, "ultimately proves to be an agent of destruction."
164. On the polemical element in chapter 16, see Gunn 1987, 118; Webb 1987, 165–66; and Brettler 2002, 57.
165. For a helpful study of the motif of answered prayer in the Samson story, see Exum 1983, 30–45.

tragic personal failure and pain, and keep one from enjoying the benefits of God's mighty deeds.

Homiletical Trajectories

(1) God is always at work accomplishing his purposes, even when his people are apathetic and clueless. In so doing, he demonstrates his sovereignty, bringing triumph out of tragedy. When the story of Samson is viewed from this perspective, it may be entitled, "A Sovereign God Can Win with His Hands Tied Behind His Back."

(2) Persistence in sin and assimilation to the surrounding pagan culture can make God's people insensitive to his purposes for them. Unfortunately a clueless community fails to experience, appreciate, and enjoy the benefits of God's work in their midst. Subsequent generations, who inherit the story, are the primary beneficiaries.

(3) Even when a leader is used mightily by God, his life can end up in personal tragedy if he makes personal gratification his priority and never understands his role in God's plan. Samson's miraculous conception seemed to foreshadow a great career, but his failure to understand his divinely ordained destiny seriously handicapped him from the start. When we are ignorant of God's larger purposes, we can miss the significance of his work in our lives and give priority to personal gratification. A preoccupation with satisfying our physical appetites, especially when coupled with an unclear vision of our spiritual destiny, can jeopardize our status as God's servants and lead to tragic failure and humiliation.

Preaching idea: *We should be encouraged to know that God is always at work among his people and can accomplish his purposes in far less than ideal circumstances. Yet when we fail to understand our role in God's plan, we can experience personal failure and pain and miss enjoying the benefits of God's mighty deeds.*

This preaching idea reflects the Samson story as a whole literary unit. If we focus on the first trajectory, we can see a silver lining in Samson's tragic story, which illustrates God's ability to accomplish his purposes in less than ideal circumstances. A *preaching idea* for this theme might be: *We should be encouraged to know that God is always at work among his people and can accomplish his purposes in far less than ideal circumstances.*

If we focus on the second and third trajectories, the story is a tragedy in which a specially endowed servant of God, commissioned from birth, fails to achieve his potential and never grasps his purpose in life. A *preaching idea* for this tragic dimension might be: *When we fail to understand our role in God's plan, we can fail morally and experience embarrassment, humiliation, pain, and even premature death.*[166]

---

166. For a sermon that develops Samson's story from this perspective, entitled "Lion Killer with a Sweet Tooth," see Chisholm 1998b, 235–42.

JUDGES 17:1–19:1a

Idols, a Renegade Levite, and a Rival Cult

TRANSLATION AND NARRATIVE STRUCTURE

17:1a There was a man from the Ephraimite hill country
(*introductory-backgrounding*)

1b **whose name was Micah**. (*supplemental*)

2a He said to his mother, (*initiatory*)

2b *"You know the eleven hundred pieces of silver which were stolen
from you, about which I heard you pronounce a curse? Look here,
I have the silver. I stole it, but now I am giving it back to you."*[1]

2c His mother said, (*sequential*)

2d *"May the LORD reward you, my son!"*

3a When he returned to his mother the eleven hundred pieces of
silver, (*sequential*)

3b his mother said, (*sequential*)

---

1. In the Hebrew text the statement, "but now I am giving it back to you,"
appears at the end of verse 3 and is spoken by the mother. But verse 4
indicates she did not give the money back to her son. The statement appears to be misplaced and fits much better in verse 2. It may have been
accidentally omitted from a manuscript, written in the margin, and then
later inserted in the wrong place in another manuscript.

3c *"I solemnly dedicate[2] this silver to the LORD. It will be for my son's benefit. We will use it to make a carved image and a metal image."[3]*

4a When he returned the silver to his mother, (*resumptive-reiterative*)[4]

4b she took two hundred pieces of silver to a silversmith, (*sequential*)[5]

4c who made them into a carved image and a metal image. (*sequential*)

4d They were put in Micah's house. (*sequential*)[6]

5a **Now this man Micah owned a shrine**. (*supplemental*)[7]

5b He had made an ephod and some personal idols (*flashback*)[8]

5c and ordained one of his sons (*sequential*)[9]

5d to serve as his priest. (*sequential*)

---

2. The perfect is understood as instantaneous or performative in function. On the basis of alleged parallels with Greek and Latin curses against thieves, Faraone, Garnand, and López-Ruiz argue that the consecration occurred in the past at the time of the curse in order to motivate a positive response from the deity (2005, 164).

3. The text reads literally, "I solemnly dedicate this silver to the Lord from my hand to my son to make a carved image and a metal image." But this does not mean "to my son (in order for him) to make," because she actually had a silversmith, not her son, make the images (v. 4).

4. The *wayyiqtol* clause at the beginning of verse 4 resumes the narrative after the quotation by repeating in an abbreviated form verse 3a.

5. The Hebrew text has two verbs here, "and his mother took two hundred pieces of silver and gave it to a silversmith."

6. If verse 5 is a flashback, then verse 4d could be taken as the conclusion to the episode.

7. The supplemental disjunctive clause in verse 5a explains why the idols were put in Micah's house (cf. v. 4d).

8. Since Micah apparently already owned a shrine at the time he took the silver, one would assume that the shrine was outfitted with cultic equipment and a priest. Consequently I understand verse 5b-d as a flashback, expanding on the explanatory supplemental clause in verse 5a. However, it is possible that verse 5b-d describes actions that occurred after the idols were placed in Micah's home. In this case verse 5b should be classified as resumptive-sequential, for it picks up the sequence of events after the parenthetical comment (cf. v. 5a).

9. The text reads literally, "and he filled the hand of one of his sons." Likewise, verse 12b reads, "Micah filled the hand of the Levite." Usage elsewhere, especially in Exodus and Leviticus, suggests that the idiom "fill the hand" refers to ordination to priesthood. See Bray 2006, 90–94.

6a   **In those days Israel had no king.** (*concluding*)[10]

6b   **Each man did what he considered to be right.**
(*complementary*)

7a   There was a young man from Bethlehem in Judah.
(*introductory-backgrounding*)[11]

7b   **He was a Levite** (*introductory-backgrounding*)

7c   **who had been temporarily residing among the tribe of
Judah.**[12] (*introductory-backgrounding*)

8a   This man left the town of Bethlehem in Judah to find another
place to live. (*initiatory*)

8b   As he came to the Ephraimite hill country, he made his way to
Micah's house. (*sequential*)

9a   Micah said to him, (*sequential*)

9b   *"Where do you come from?"*

9c   He replied to him, (*sequential*)

9d   *"I am a Levite from Bethlehem in Judah. I am looking for a new
place to live."*

10a   Micah said to him, (*sequential*)

10b   *"Stay with me. Become my adviser and priest. I will give you ten
pieces of silver per year, clothes, and food."*[13]

11a   So the Levite agreed to stay with the man; (*sequential*)

11b   Micah treated the young man as if he were one of his sons.
(*sequential / summarizing*)

12a   Micah ordained the Levite; (*focusing / sequential*)[14]

---

10. The asyndetic disjunctive clause in verse 6a formally concludes the episode. Verse 6b complements verse 6a by explaining that the absence of
effective leadership during the period produced a situation where each
individual did as he pleased. As a unit, verse 6 explains how the appalling
episode just described could have taken place and how one could operate
his own religious shrine without censure.

11. The *wayyehi* clause at the beginning of verse 7 formally introduces the
next episode, while the disjunctive clauses in verse 7bc provide background information for the story to follow.

12. מִשְׁפָּחָה, "clan," is used here of the tribal group of Judah (cf. 13:2; 18:2, 11;
where it is used of the tribe of Dan). The word appears to refer to a clan
within a larger tribal group in 9:1; 18:19; and 21:24.

13. The Hebrew text adds, "and the Levite went." This only makes sense if
taken with "to live" in the next verse. Apparently "the Levite went" and
"the Levite agreed" (v. 11a) are alternative readings that have been juxtaposed in the text.

14. Verse 12a has a focusing function in relation to verse 11b. It begins a more
detailed description of Micah's relationship to the Levite. At the same time

12b the young man became his priest (*consequential*)
12c and lived in Micah's house. (*complementary*)[15]
13a Micah said, (*sequential*)
13b *"Now I know God will make me rich, because I have this Levite as my priest."*
18:1a **In those days Israel had no king**. (*concluding*)[16]

1b In those days the Danite tribe was looking for a place to live, because at that time they did not yet have a place to call their own among the tribes of Israel. (*introductory-new episode / backgrounding*)[17]
2a The Danites sent out from their whole tribe[18] five representatives, capable men from Zorah and Eshtaol, to spy out the land and explore it. (*initiatory*)
2b They said to them, (*specifying*)
2c *"Go, explore the land."*
2d They came to the Ephraimite hill country (*sequential*)
2e and spent the night at Micah's house. (*sequential*)
3a **As they approached Micah's house**, (*circumstantial*)[19]

---

the statement is sequential to verse 11a, suggesting that verse 11b may be viewed as a proleptic summary statement.

15. Verse 12c complements verse 12b. Together they describe the consequences of Micah's hiring the Levite (v. 12a).

16. The disjunctive clause in 18:1a is an abbreviated form of the conclusion to the first episode (cf. 17:6). It formally concludes the episode by explaining how the episode just recorded could have taken place. At the same time the clause also provides background information for the episode to follow.

17. The disjunctive clause in verse 1b formally introduces the next episode and provides background information for the story to follow.

18. מִשְׁפָּחָה, "clan," is used here and in verse 11 of the tribal group of Dan (see as well 13:2; cf. 17:7, where it is used of the tribe of Judah). The word appears to refer to a clan within a larger tribal group in 9:1; 18:19; and 21:24.

19. The Hebrew text of verse 3a reads literally, "they (were) with the house of Micah." Since verse 3c describes them turning aside when they hear the Levite's accent, the preposition עִם must mean "near, close to," in verse 3a. Note the use of this same preposition in verse 22. See BDB, 768, no. 2. The asyndetic disjunctive clause in verse 3a involves a flashback. Verse 2e describes how they spent the night at Micah's home, but the incident recorded in verses 3–5 took place as they approached Micah's house (cf. v. 3, which says they turned aside from their journey when they heard the Levite's accent). Verse 3a is circumstantial in relation to the disjunctive clause that follows in verse 3b. Together they describe synchronic action.

3b   **they recognized the accent of the young Levite**.
     (*synchronic*)

3c   So they stopped there (*consequential*)

3d   and said to him, (*sequential*)

3e   *"Who brought you here? What are you doing in this place? What is your business here?"*

4a   He told them, (*sequential*)

4b   *"Here's what Micah has done for me.*[20] *He hired me and I became his priest."*

5a   They said to him, (*sequential*)

5b   *"Seek a divine oracle for us, so we can know if we will be successful on our mission."*

6a   The priest said to them, (*sequential*)

6b   *"Go with confidence. The* LORD *will be with you on your mission."*

7a   So the five men journeyed on (*sequential*)

7b   and arrived in Laish. (*sequential*)

7c   They noticed that the people there were living securely, like the Sidonians do, undisturbed and unsuspecting. (*sequential*)

7d   **No conqueror was troubling them in any way**.
     (*supplemental*)

7e   **They lived far from the Sidonians and had no dealings with anyone**. (*supplemental*)

8a   When the Danites returned to their tribe in Zorah and Eshtaol, (*resumptive-sequential*)

8b   their kinsmen asked them, (*sequential*)

8c   *"How did it go?"*

9a   They said, (*sequential*)

9b   *"Come on, let's attack them, for we saw their land and it is very good. You seem lethargic, but don't hesitate to invade and conquer the land.*

10   *When you invade, you will encounter unsuspecting people. The land is wide! God is handing it over to you—a place that lacks nothing on earth!"*

11   So six hundred Danites, fully armed, set out from Zorah and Eshtaol. (*sequential*)

12a They went up (*sequential*)

---

20. The Hebrew text reads literally, "He said to them, 'Such and such Micah has done for me and he hired me and I became his priest.'" Though the statement is introduced and presented as a direct quotation, the phrase "such and such" may be the narrator's condensed version of what the Levite really said.

12b and camped in Kiriath Jearim in Judah. (*sequential*)

12c (**To this day that place is called Mahaneh Dan**.
     (*supplemental*)[21]

12d (**It is west of Kiriath Jearim**.) (*supplemental*)

13a From there they traveled through the Ephraimite hill country
     (*resumptive-sequential*)

13b and arrived at Micah's house. (*sequential*)

14a The five men who had gone to spy out the land of Laish said to
     their kinsmen,[22] (*sequential*)

14b *"Do you realize that inside these houses are an ephod, some
     personal idols, a carved image, and a metal image? Decide now
     what you want to do."*

15a They stopped there (*sequential*)

15b and went inside the young Levite's house (which belonged to
     Micah),[23] (*sequential*).

15c They asked him how he was doing, (*sequential*)

16   **while the six hundred Danites, fully armed, stood at the
     entrance to the gate.** (*circumstantial*)

17a The five men who had gone to spy out the land went up;
     (*sequential*)[24]

17b **they broke in** (*emphatic-rhetorical*)[25]

---

21. The name *Mahaneh Dan* means, "Camp of Dan."

22. The Hebrew text has two verbs, "the five men . . . answered and said."

23. In the Hebrew text "Micah's house" is appositional to "the young Levite's
    house."

24. The precise meaning of the verb וַיַּעֲלוּ, "and they went up," is not clear
    in this context. Verse 17a may be a flashback to verse 15b, making the
    point that their entry was a forced one. However, verse 15c, where they
    ask about the priest's well-being (literally, "peace"), makes this unlikely.
    It is more likely that verse 15b describes their initial entry into the house,
    while verse 17ab refers to their entering the inner area of the house, where
    the shrine was apparently located. It is possible that עלה, "go up," is used
    because the shrine was located on the second floor of the house or perhaps
    even on the roof (cf. Jer. 19:13). Another option is that verse 15b describes
    their entry into the compound where the house was located ("house" being
    a synecdoche in this case), while verse 17ab describes their entry into the
    house proper or the shrine. The use of עלה may indicate that the struc-
    ture was on an elevated area within the compound. For a discussion of
    the structure of ancient Israelite houses, see King and Stager 2001, 9–19,
    28–35.

25. In verse 17bc the narrator uses asyndetic perfect verbal forms to create
    a staccato style. This technique is a feature of the impassioned style of

17c **they stole the carved image, the ephod, the personal idols, and the metal image,** (*emphatic-rhetorical*)[26]

17d **while the priest was standing at the entrance to the gate along with the six hundred fully armed men.** (*circumstantial*)

18a **When these men broke into Micah's house** (*reiterative/ circumstantial*)[27]

18b and stole the carved image, the ephod, the personal idols, and the metal image, (*reiterative/sequential*)

18c the priest said to them, (*sequential*)

18d *"What are you doing?"*

19a They said to him, (*sequential*)

19b *"Shut up! Put your hand over your mouth and come with us! You can be our adviser and priest. Wouldn't it be better to be a priest for a whole Israelite tribe than for just one man's family?"*

20a The priest was happy. (*sequential*)

20b He took the ephod, the personal idols, and the carved image (*sequential*)

20c and joined the group. (*sequential*)

---

archaic poetry (Judg. 5:26-27; cf. Exod. 15:8–10, 12–15; cf. GKC, 387 [para. 120h]). It draws attention to the statements, lends rhetorical vividness to the account, and expresses the narrator's agitation. The narrator is so appalled by the Danites' audacity that he departs from the usual reportorial style of connecting verbs with the conjunction. I originally made this point in an oral presentation at the 2006 national meeting of the Evangelical Theological Society in Washington, D. C. Butler cites this heretofore unpublished version (2009, 396). Rendsburg, noting the syntactical oddity, suggests that the "speeded syntax" indicates "the speed with which" the action occurred (1998–99, 10, section 5.5). There may be some merit to this proposal, for the same syntactical style may indicate hurried action as well in 20:43 (see also Josh. 3:16; 1 Sam. 30:20).

26. The items are listed in a different order here than in verse 14 (which reflects the pairings given in 17:3–5). Rendsburg suggests that this change is intentional and gives "a sense of ransacking" (1998–99, 9, section 5.1). The sense of chaos continues in verses 18, where odd syntax is employed in the expression "idol of the ephod," and 20, where one of the items is no longer mentioned (9, section 5.2).

27. In verse 18ab the narrator repeats his description of the Danites' theft. The disjunctive clause in verse 18a is circumstantial in relation to verse 18c, but reiterative in relation to verse 17b. Verse 18b is sequential in relation to verse 18a, but reiterative in relation to verse 17c. The repetition serves a rhetorical purpose. By repeating the description of the crime, the narrator forces his audience to confront the magnitude of the deed.

21a They turned (*sequential*)
21b and went on their way. (*sequential*)
21c They walked behind the children, the cattle, and their possessions. (*sequential*)
22a **After they had gone a good distance from Micah's house**, (*circumstantial*)[28]
22b **Micah's neighbors gathered together** (*synchronic*)
22c and caught up with the Danites. (*sequential*)
23a When they called out to the Danites, (*sequential*)
23b the Danites turned around (*sequential*)
23c and said to Micah, (*sequential*)
23d *"Why have you gathered together?"*
24a He said, (*sequential*)
24b *"You stole my gods that I made, as well as this priest, and then went away. What do I have left? How can you have the audacity to say to me, 'What do you want?'"*
25a The Danites said to him, (*sequential*)
25b *"Don't say another word to us, or some very angry men will attack you, and you and your family will die."*
26a The Danites went on their way; (*sequential*)
26b when Micah realized they were too strong to resist, (*sequential*)
26c he turned around and went home. (*concluding*)

27a **Now the Danites took what Micah had made, as well as his priest**, (*introductory*)[29]
27b and came to Laish, where the people were undisturbed and unsuspecting. (*initiatory*)
27c They struck them down with the sword (*sequential*)
27d **and burned the city**. (*complementary*)[30]

---

28. The asyndetic disjunctive clause at the beginning of verse 22 is circumstantial in relation to the disjunctive clause that follows in verse 22b. Together they describe synchronic action.
29. The disjunctive clause at the beginning of verse 27 formally introduces the next and final episode. At the same time it reiterates what has been said earlier (cf. vv. 17–18, 20), adding the priest to the string of loot! The repetition keeps the magnitude of the Danites' crime before the audience.
30. The disjunctive clause in verse 27d describes an action that complements what precedes it. Killing people and burning buildings were actions that typically went together in ancient warfare.

28a **No one came to the rescue because the city was far from Sidon and they had no dealings with anyone**. (*supplemental*)[31]

28b **The city was in a valley near Beth Rehob**. (*supplemental*)

28c The Danites rebuilt the city (*resumptive-sequential*)

28d and occupied it. (*sequential*)

29a They named it Dan after their ancestor, who was one of Israel's sons. (*sequential*)

29b **But the city's name used to be Laish**. (*supplemental*)

30a The Danites set up the carved image. (*resumptive-sequential*)

30b **Jonathan, descendant of Gershom, son of Moses,[32] and his descendants served as priests for the tribe of Dan until the time of the exile**. (*supplemental*)

31 They set up and worshiped[33] Micah's carved image the whole time God's authorized shrine was in Shiloh. (*reiterative-sequential*)[34]

19:1a In those days (*circumstantial*)

1b **Israel had no king**. (*concluding*)[35]

---

31. The supplemental disjunctive clause in verse 28a explains why the Danites were able to successfully carry out their plot.

32. In the Hebrew text the name *Manasseh* appears, with a suspended *nun*, instead of Moses, which is preserved in a few medieval Hebrew manuscripts and in some Greek witnesses. This alteration of the text was probably made to protect Moses' reputation. See Moore 1895, 401–02; and Burney 1970, 434–35. For a discussion of the identity of the Manasseh intended by the scribal alteration, see Weitzman 1999, 448–60.

33. The Hebrew text says simply, "and they set up," but the temporal note at the end of the verse indicates that the verb שׂים, "set up," must be metonymic here, "set up and worship."

34. Verse 31 reiterates verse 30a, but it also makes the point that this idolatry continued on for generations.

35. The epilogue's recurring formula (cf. 17:6; 18:1; 21:25) appears again in 19:1. The structure of the formula differs in 19:1 in two ways: (1) וַיְהִי occurs before the prepositional phrase, rather than "in those days," and (2) the second part of the formula is וּמֶלֶךְ אֵין בְּיִשְׂרָאֵל, literally, "and a king there was not in Israel." The word order differs from the pattern in the other texts (אֵין מֶלֶךְ בְּיִשְׂרָאֵל, literally, "there was not a king in Israel"). The *wayyehi* clause at the beginning of verse 1 is circumstantial in relation to the following disjunctive clause, which concludes the episode. This verse seems to have a pivotal function, for it provides background information for the story that follows.

OUTLINE

Homemade Religion (17:1–6)
Micah Hires a Pro (17:7–18:1a)
Lookin' for a Home, Gotta' Have a Home (18:1b—19:1a)
    Stealing a shrine and priest (18:1b–26)
    Setting up a rival cult (18:27–19:1a)

LITERARY STRUCTURE

Part one of the book's epilogue tells how the Danites established a rival cult in the distant north. The story may be divided into three episodes: (1) 17:1–6 records how an Ephraimite named Micah established a household shrine. וַיְהִי introduces the episode, while the observation "in those days Israel had no king; everyone did what he considered to be right" concludes it.[36] (2) 17:7–18:1a tells how Micah hired a wandering Levite to be his personal priest. וַיְהִי introduces the episode and the observation "in those days Israel had no king" concludes it.[37] (3) 18:1b–19:1a records how the Danites took Micah's cultic equipment and Levite, conquered land in the distant north, and set up their own rival cult site in their new home. This third episode begins with the introductory "in those days" and ends with the observation "in those days Israel had no king."[38] The episode has two scenes (18:1b–26 and 18:27–19:1a), the second of which is marked out by the introductory disjunctive וְהֵמָּה (v. 27), as well as the shift in location from the hill country of Ephraim to Laish.

EXPOSITION

Homemade Religion (17:1–6)

This story begins with the confession of a thief. An Ephraimite named Micah stole eleven hundred shekels of silver from his mother,[39] but

---

36. The same statement appears as the conclusion to the book's final story (21:25), so it is reasonable to assume that it concludes this first episode as well.

37. This abbreviated version of the summary statement in 18:1 can be taken as concluding the episode (cf. 17:6 and 21:25), introducing the next episode, or as marking a transitional link between the successive episodes. The analogy with 17:6 and 21:25 suggests a concluding function. See Gray 1986, 343; and Hamilton 2001, 164.

38. As with the abbreviated statement in 18:1a, this summary can be taken as concluding, introductory, or transitional.

39. Based on the reference to eleven hundred shekels, as well as other connections between this account and the preceding Samson-Delilah story,

when he heard his mother utter a curse (probably calling down divine judgment on the unknown [to her] culprit), he returned the money and confessed his crime.[40] His mother, who was quick to make solemn statements, called upon the Lord to bless him and solemnly dedicated the silver to the Lord with the intent that an idol/idols (פֶּסֶל וּמַסֵּכָה) would be made from it (v 3).[41] She took two hundred shekels of the returned silver and had a silversmith make the idol/idols, which she placed in her son's house. Micah was apparently the spiritual leader of the family for he had his own personal shrine, complete with an ephod, household idols (תְּרָפִים), and a (non-Levitical) priest (one of his own sons).[42]

There are several textual and grammatical difficulties in this

---

Schneider suggests that Delilah and Micah's mother are one and the same (2000, 231–32). This creative proposal, which follows rabbinical tradition, is overly speculative and not supported by concrete textual evidence. Klein sees a significant literary connection between the stories without resorting to such speculation (1988, 143–44; see as well 1993b, 66–67). She suggests a comparison of the two stories indicates that Micah, who stole eleven hundred shekels from his mother, is depicted as being even more reprehensible than Delilah, who accepted eleven hundred shekels in a business deal.

40. On the basis of alleged parallels with Greek and Latin curses against thieves, Faraone, Garnand, and López-Ruiz suggest that the public curse was designed to frighten the thief into returning the stolen property (2005, 176–77).

41. The Hebrew expression, which literally means "a carved image and a molten image," may be a hendiadys, with both words describing one idol. See Boling, who notes the singular verb וַיְהִי, "and it was," in the last clause of verse 4 (1975, 256). However, as Mueller points out, this is problematic in 18:17–18, where פֶּסֶל and מַסֵּכָה are separated by "ephod and household idols" as if they were distinct items. In 18:20, 30–31 פֶּסֶל appears by itself (2001, 59, 69). Moore, noting these apparent inconsistencies, makes a case for treating מַסֵּכָה as an explanatory gloss throughout chapters 17–18 (1895, 375–76). See also Burney 1970, 409. The isolated reference to פֶּסֶל in verses 20, 30–31 could, on the one hand, be an abbreviated way to refer to one idol. On the other hand, if one assumes that the phrase פֶּסֶל וּמַסֵּכָה refers to separate idols, it is possible, as Schneider suggests, that the Levite left the מַסֵּכָה for Micah (2000, 239). Furthermore, Rendsburg has argued that the syntax is deliberately confused in chapter 18 to reflect the ransacking and chaos that was quickly occurring (1998–99, 8–11, section 5).

42. For a Mesopotamian parallel to Micah's shrine see van der Toorn 1996, 250–51. Micah's shrine is called "a house of God" (בֵּית אֱלֹהִים). The narrator later refers to the authorized cult site at Shiloh as "the house of God"

passage: (1) The preposition -לְ probably has the sense of "from" in verse 2 after the verb "were stolen."[43] (2) The statement "I am giving it back to you" at the end of verse 3, appears to be misplaced. As noted earlier, it should probably be moved to verse 2, right after "I stole it" (Moore 1895, 376; Boling 1975, 255–56).[44] It may have been accidentally omitted from a manuscript, written in the margin, and then later inserted in the wrong place in another manuscript. (3) Verse 4a seems to unnecessarily repeat verse 3a. Apparently it is resumptive after the quotation in verse 3c. (4) "For my son" in verse 3 probably means "for my son's benefit" (by undoing the curse placed upon him and/or by adorning his personal shrine). It does not mean, "so that my son can make an image and idol," for the woman hired a silversmith to do this (v. 4).

Of course, this scene is absurd.[45] Micah (whose name means "Who is like Yah?") and his mother seem to be religious. She cursed, blessed and vowed—all in the space of two verses, and he had his very own home worship center, despite the fact the official cult site was located within Ephraim's territory in Shiloh (cf. 18:31). There are many things wrong with the picture. Micah was a thief (he stole from his own mother!) and idolater whose greed was only outweighed by a strong desire to save his skin. His mother shared his obsession with idols and seemed to think she could manipulate the Lord with her

---

(18:31; בֵּית־הָאֱלֹהִים). Note the presence of the article on the divine name, suggesting the distinctiveness of the site. See Davis 1984, 158.

43. See Boling 1975, 255. On this use of the preposition see *HALOT*, 508, and Sivan, who discusses its use in both Ugaritic and biblical Hebrew (1997, 196).

44. For more radical reconstructions of the text, see Burney 1970, 417–20; and Soggin 1981, 264–65. For a defense of the clause order in the Hebrew text, see Mueller 2001, 54–55. According to Mueller, the text, which depicts the silver being passed between mother and son four times, reflects "the inner confusion of Micah and his mother in the wake of the curse spoken by the mother" (55). See as well Amit 1999, 324, note 18. Note also the translation of Faraone, Garnand, and López-Ruiz (2005, 163). If one follows their approach, it is possible Micah returned the money to his mother (v. 3a), who then gave it back to him (v. 3c, MT) so that she could fulfill the vow she took at the time she uttered the curse (v. 2b). Verse 4 would then reiterate verse 3a, with the remainder of verse 4 describing the fulfillment of the vow. However, according to verse 4, she gave the money (or at least two hundred shekels of it) to a silversmith, not her son.

45. For a helpful study of the incongruities in the description of Micah and his mother, see Block 1999, 478–82.

solemn statements. From her perspective a curse could be turned to a blessing with one quick promise that she would make the Lord an idol/idols! Furthermore, what did she do with the other nine hundred shekels of silver she consecrated to the Lord?[46] Despite all their religiosity, Micah and his mother blatantly violated the law of God and fell under the curse of idolaters. Deuteronomy 27:15 pronounces a curse on anyone who makes a פֶּסֶל וּמַסֵּכָה, literally "a carved image and a molten image," and 1 Samuel 15:23 denounces the sin of having household idols (תְּרָפִים). The reference to an ephod is also alarming, since the only earlier reference in Judges to this divination device is negative (see Judg. 8:27).[47]

Like earlier (11:30–31) and later (21:1, 7, 18) vows, Micah's mother's oath led to nothing but trouble. The image and idol she consecrated to the Lord ended up with the Danites in an idolatrous shrine that rivaled the Lord's official shrine in Shiloh. Micah's mother is a foil for Hannah, who also made a solemn vow to the Lord. However, Hannah's appropriate vow, by which she dedicated her son to the Lord, led to the revival of genuine worship of the Lord in Israel.

The narrator can only shake his head in dismay and remark that the leadership void in Israel had led to anarchy. The statement "Israel had no king" suggests that the presence of a king would have provided

---

46. Faraone, Garnand, and López-Ruiz cite examples from later Greek and Latin curses against thieves in which the victim of the theft (and author of the curse) promises the deity only a portion of the restored money (2005, 172, 176). However, Micah's mother did not specify just a portion in her dedicatory statement; she said, "I solemnly dedicate *this silver*" (literally, "*the* silver," emphasis mine; Faraone, Garnand, and López-Ruiz understand the verb as simple past, "I indeed consecrated"), suggesting she intended to dedicate it in its entirety.

47. Wong suggests there is an intentional allusion to or echo of Gideon's idolatry in the Micah story (2006a, 83–89). In both instances "bizarre" actions occur. After declining kingship with an affirmation that the Lord is king (Judg. 8:23), Gideon collected gold earrings and made an ephod (8:24–27). After Micah's mother dedicated silver to the Lord, she commissioned idols to be made. They ended up in Micah's shrine along with an ephod (17:2–5). Wong observes: "The actions of the protagonists in both cases are equally bizarre and inexplicable. Thus, in the end, all the parallel shows is that although bizarre, the incongruity between action and profession demonstrated by Micah and his mother is not unique after all, since the exact same tendency has also been displayed by one of Israel's judges" (89).

a standard for the nation to follow.[48] Without such a standard, "everyone did what he considered to be right."[49] The statement reflects the Deuteronomic ideal of a king who promotes the law by his teaching and example (Deut. 17:18–20).[50] This would entail regulating the cult (chapters 17–18 describe a cultic violation), ensuring social justice (chapters 19–20 depict social injustice at its worst), and unifying the nation (in contrast to the dissension seen in chapter 21) (O'Connell 1996, 10, 268–304). By suggesting a king was needed, the narrator is already preparing us for later developments in the unfolding history, especially the coming of David, who did what was right in the eyes of

---

48. Niditch suggests the statement "In those days Israel had no king," may be a simple chronological marker, "a way of declaring events to belong to a long-ago past" (1999, 205). She does not view the statement as "a condemnation, anticipating the need for the monarchy," but rather as "an indication that in the old days things were different" (2008, 182). Perhaps the wording in 18:1 and 19:1, both of which omit the reference to each man doing what was right in his eyes, lends support to her thesis. However, it seems that a logical relationship is intended, especially in light of the frequent subsequent references in the history to kings doing what was right in the Lord's eyes (see below), in contrast to what is said about the Judges period. The closest linguistic parallel to Judges 17:6 and 21:25 occurs in 1 Samuel 3:1, where the statement introduced by the temporal formula (literally, "in those days the word of the Lord was rare") logically complements the asyndetic clause, "revelatory visions were infrequent." If 17:6 and 21:25 do indeed suggest that the absence of a king led to anarchy, then the abbreviated statements in 18:1 and 19:1 may be viewed as affirming the same point in an elliptical manner. Within the narrative they briefly remind the reader of the point made toward the beginning of the epilogue (17:6) and at its conclusion (21:25).

49. Olson points out that all Ten Commandments are broken in Judges 17–21 (1998, 864–65). Olson (p. 864) suggests that the statement "everyone did what he considered to be right" (literally, "did what was right in his own eyes") "is functionally equivalent" to the recurring statement that Israel "did what was evil in the eyes of the Lord" (Judg. 2:11; 3:7, 12; 4:1; 6:1; 10:6; 13:1) (864; cf. Wong 2006a, 196).

50. See Gerbrandt 1986, 190–91, as well as Howard 1990, 106–08. For a striking Egyptian parallel to the statement in Judges 17:6, see Greenspahn 1982, 129–30. Butler (2009, 474–75) suggests that "Joshua, the true model of leadership in Israel," is in view here. However, Joshua was not a king. Perhaps he is in view here, but, if so, he would have to be viewed as a pre-royal embodiment or foreshadowing of the ideal king depicted in Deuteronomy 17:14–20.

the Lord (see 1 Kings 11:33, 38; 14:8; 15:5),[51] as well as other devoted kings, including Asa (1 Kings 15:11), Jehoshaphat (1 Kings 22:43), Joash (2 Kings 12:2), Amaziah (2 Kings 14:3), Azariah (2 Kings 15:3), Hezekiah (2 Kings 18:3), and especially Josiah (2 Kings 22:2).

Satterthwaite agrees that Judges 17–21 is "pro-monarchic." He explains: "The 'no king' formula indeed suggests that a king would have prevented some of the wrongs described in the chapters: idolatry, destruction of family life, civil war. However, the impression the chapters leave us with is not of a capable, righteous king, but of various evil situations which stand in need of remedy." He adds: "The chapters should be regarded as setting an agenda: not any king will do, but only a king who will set to rights wrongs such as these" (1993, 87–88).

With respect to the story of Micah in particular, the statement in 17:6 (see also 18:1; 19:1) should be seen against the backdrop of Deuteronomy 12:8, where Moses warned the people not to do what was right in their own eyes with regard to cultic matters.[52] When they entered the land they were to destroy the shrines and idols, and worship the Lord at a site chosen by him. Judges 17 depicts a blatant violation of this and anticipates the cultic reforms of Josiah, who "did what was right in the eyes of the Lord" (literal translation) and reformed the cult according to the Deuteronomic ideal (2 Kings 22:2) (Mueller 2001, 115–16).

Not everyone agrees that the statement in Judges 17:6 is promonarchic. Talmon argues that in Judges "king" (מֶלֶךְ) and "judge" (שֹׁפֵט) are synonymous. Consequently the statements in the epilogue about the absence of a "king" do not anticipate the monarchy, but refer instead to periods within the era of the judges when there was no leader (1969, 135–44, 242). However, while the verb שָׁפַט, "lead, judge, deliver," is used of royal activity, kings and judges are not equated in

---

51. Cundall argues that the pro-monarchic sentiment of the epilogue reflects the Davidic or early Solomonic period, "when the monarchy was functioning more efficiently than was often the case in later centuries." He adds: "The Judges period is shown as the 'dark ages', when there was no unity, no peace, prosperity or security, no justice or righteousness. The Davidic dynasty had secured all these, . . . The high-lighting, by selection and presentation, of the evils of the earlier period constitute therefore a kind of apology for the monarchy" (1969, 180–81).

52. See Mueller 2001, 112–16, as well as O'Connell 1996, 239, 278–79; Mayes 2001, 255; and Wong 2006a, 195–96.

the Former Prophets. In fact 2 Kings 23:22 clearly distinguishes the judges era from that of the kings.[53]

Block argues that Judges 17:6 does not mean or even imply that a king was needed to prevent moral anarchy. Rather than being a pro-monarchic or pro-Davidic statement, it makes the point that Israel was fully capable of sinning without being influenced to do so by a king (1999, 475–76). Rather than portraying kings as moral guides, the subsequent history depicts them as leading Israel into rebellion (483). Dumbrell contends that the negative attitude toward kingship in Judges 8–9 undermines the view that the statement in the epilogue is pro-monarchic (1983, 27–29; cf. Wong 2006a, 201–12). Marais sees a pro-monarchic sentiment in the epilogue, but argues that this positive view has already been deconstructed in the Abimelech story and was undermined by Israel's history, which culminated in the exile, the period that provides the authorial or at least redactional context of Judges. This history proved that the monarchy was no better than the judges (1998, 134–35).

It is true that kingship is presented in a negative light in Judges 8–9 and that the monarchy proved to be ultimately unsuccessful in Israel's subsequent history. But Judges 17–21 does not give kingship a blanket endorsement. Rather, building on Deuteronomy 17:14–20, it views kingship in an idealized sense. Despite the historical failures of the monarchy and the realities of the exile, this ideal is present in 1–2 Kings in the references to certain kings doing what was right in the Lord's eyes (see the texts cited above) and is certainly alive and well in the Latter Prophets.[54]

Another possibility is that the reference to the absence of a king alludes to the people's repudiation of divine kingship.[55] Since the Lord is called Israel's "king" both before and after this (see Deut. 33:5 and 1 Sam. 12:12), this interpretation is possible. However, in Judges the Lord is never called "king" (מֶלֶךְ) *per se*, though he is viewed as ruling over Israel (see מָשַׁל, Judg. 8:23). Furthermore the statement "there was no king in Israel" would be an odd way to say the people did not recognize God as king. After all, God remained king despite their rebellion

---

53. For these and other arguments, see O'Connell's refutation of Talmon's position (269–70, note 3; cf. Wong 2006a, 200–01).

54. Wong objects to this view because the author did not "qualify the term explicitly" (2006a, 211–12).

55. Boling seems to suggest this (1975, 258 [in his discussion of Judg. 18:1], 293 [in his discussion of 21:25], and 294). See also Block 1999, 476; and Wong 2006a, 212–23.

(see 1 Sam. 12:12). Elsewhere the statement "there is no king" (אֵין מֶלֶךְ) means there is no king in fact (Hos. 3:4; 10:3). Nevertheless the statement could be rhetorical and sarcastic in Judges 17–21, reflecting the viewpoint of the people.[56] Furthermore, Wong makes a convincing case that 2 Chronicles 15:3–6 refers to the Judges period as a time when Israel had "no true God nor instructing priest nor the law," because the Lord had responded to their rebellion by forsaking them (2006a, 221). Wong concludes, "rather than speaking of the mere absence of these three things at some particular point in the history of Israel, 15:3 must be referring to the non-honouring of YHWH and instructing priest and the law in Israel during the period of the Judges." He adds: "For in an era when YHWH was already known to Israel and both the priesthood and the law were well established, the only way YHWH and the law could meaningfully be absent from Israelite society would be for them to be absent from the perspective of a society that has chosen to ignore them. Besides, as indicated in 15:4, the fact that YHWH could still be sought and found when His people needed Him shows that the true God was not really absent in the absolute sense, but merely from those who did not honour Him" (2006a, 223).

A final option is to fuse the idealized human king and divine king viewpoints. Since the idealized kingship envisioned in Deuteronomy 17:14–20 is theocratic in nature, it is possible that "king" carries a double meaning in Judges 17:6. Perhaps we could define the "king" referred to here as an idealized king serving as the earthly vice-regent of the divine King Yahweh, as envisioned in Deuteronomy and eventually realized in the Davidic dynasty.

Micah Hires a Pro (17:7–18:1a)

A caption under the next scene might read "Greed Personified." We now read of a Levite who left Judahite territory, journeyed to Ephraim, and stopped at Micah's house. He had been living in Bethlehem (v. 9), which was not one of Judah's Levitical towns (cf. Josh. 21:9–16) (Wong 2006a, 90). We discover later he was a descendant of Gershom son of Moses (18:30), and therefore a member of the Kohathite branch of the Levitical family tree (1 Chron. 23:12–15; cf. Exod. 6:18, 20). Because he was a descendant of Moses, not Aaron, he was to live in Ephraim, Dan, or western Manasseh (Josh. 21:4, 20–26) (Younger 2002, 338–39).[57]

---

56. See our earlier comments on Judges 1:19.
57. The Kohathite descendants of Aaron were assigned to Judah, Simeon, and Benjamin (Josh. 21:4, 9–19). Klein attaches Gershom to the Gershonites, who were assigned to Issachar, Asher, Naphtali, or Manasseh (Josh. 21:6,

When Micah discovered the visitor was a Levite, he offered him a salaried position, including room and board, as his "adviser (literally, "father") and priest." "Father" is a title of honor that may suggest the priest would give advice and protect the interests of the family, primarily by divining God's will, perhaps through the use of the ephod (Boling 1975, 257).[58] The Levite agreed to the contract and settled in with Micah and his family. Micah's primary motive is revealed when he declared that the Lord would make him rich (literally, "be good to") because he had a Levite as his priest. The *hiphil* of יטב may be translated "to prosper, enrich" (see Gen. 12:16). Once more the narrator can only shake his head and remind the reader, "Israel had no king." If they had, they might have realized that one's priestly heritage should not be hired out and that the Lord cannot be manipulated into bestowing his blessings.

Block argues that this portrait of a wandering Levite is a parody on the Deuteronomic legislation pertaining to Levites (Deut. 18:6–8) (1999, 486–87). According to Deuteronomy, a Levite was allowed to move from anywhere in Israel to the cult site chosen by the Lord and to serve there with other Levites.[59] But the Levite in Judges 17 was wandering with no clear goal in mind, apparently hoping he could find some place to make a living. He took a job at a shrine, but not with the Levitical community at the central cult site in Shiloh (see Judg. 18:31). He became a rogue priest engaging in heterodox Yahwism at a private shrine.[60]

There is tragic irony here. This Levite agreed to serve at a shrine

---

27–33) (1988, 152–53), but Gershom son of Moses (a Kohathite) is not the same as Gershon, who was a brother of Kohath (see 1 Chron. 23:6–20).

58. See Genesis 45:8, where Joseph, who was a diviner and interpreter of dreams, is called Pharaoh's "father," and 2 Kings 6:21; 13:14, where a prophet is referred to as a "father." Note also 2 Kings 8:9, where a king identifies himself as a prophet's "son." One of a prophet's main functions was to communicate divine oracles; see 2 Kings 8:9; 13:14–19.

59. Levites who lived away from the central cult site carried out a variety of functions, including making judicial decisions, pronouncing blessings, and giving instructions regarding ritual purification. See Deuteronomy 21:5; 24:8.

60. Miller characterizes "heterodox Yahwism" as involving "(1) the presence of cult objects rejected in more orthodox expressions, (2) the use of unacceptable procedures for discerning the divine will, and (3) the veneration and consultation of the dead" (2000, 51). Micah's shrine included at least the first two of these. Miller (p. 56) suggests that the "household idols" (תְּרָפִים) were actually "ancestor figurines used in necromancy" (56). He draws here

that had a carved image (מַסֵּכָה). Levites had once rallied to defend the Lord's honor and execute those who had worshiped such an image (cf. Exod. 32:4, 8, 25–29). But now, as Wong observes, "by consenting to serve Micah's מסכה, this Levite had in fact turned his back on an honour that had once distinguished his people from the rest of Israel" (2006a, 91).

Lookin' for a Home, Gotta' Have a Home (18:1b–19:1a)

Stealing a shrine and priest (18:1b–26). The narrator turns briefly from the story of Micah and the Levite to introduce the next actors in the unfolding drama, the Danites. He informs us that the Danites were still looking for a home.[61] Judges 1:34 has already informed us that they were beaten back by the Amorites and confined to the hill country. They selected five warriors and sent them from Zorah and Eshtaol (Samson's home territory; see 13:25) on a spying mission to find a place in the land where they might settle. They arrived in Ephraim and, like the Levite before them, stopped at Micah's house.

As they neared Micah's house they recognized the Levite's southern accent and asked how he came to be living in Ephraim (Boling 1975, 263).[62] When they discovered he was a priest, they requested an oracle from God (note the absence of the covenant name *Yahweh*).[63] The Levite glibly sent them away in peace, claiming their journey was "before/in front of Yahweh" (literal translation). Though the Levite uses

---

on the research of van der Toorn 1990, 203–22. See as well K. van der Toorn and T. Lewis, "תְּרָפִים," *TDOT*, 15:777–89.

61. The syntax of verse 1b is difficult. It reads literally, "and in those days the tribe of Dan was seeking for itself an inheritance to occupy, for it had not fallen to him unto that day in the midst of the tribes of Israel by an inheritance." There is no stated subject for the feminine verb form נָפְלָה, "fell." The noun אֶרֶץ, "land," should be supplied or implied as subject on the basis of analogy with Numbers 34:2b, which literally reads, "the land that will fall to you by inheritance," and Ezekiel 47:14b, which literally reads, "and this land will fall to you by inheritance" (see also Ezek. 47:22). This statement does not mean the Danites had been denied an allotment. Rather it points out that they had not yet occupied their allotted territory. See Joshua 19:40–48. For a discussion of the problem see Block 1999, 493–94.

62. Burney disagrees with this view and argues that the Danites knew the Levite personally (1970, 425).

63. Bray states that the Danites "invite Yahweh into their situation" (2006, 36). But the text seems to go out of its way to indicate otherwise. They simply ask that the Levite inquire of God (v. 5; אֱלֹהִים).

Yahweh's name in the formulation of his blessing, there is no reference to his inquiring of Yahweh (Boling 1975, 263). Furthermore his
oracle is ambiguous (Polzin 1980, 198). The phrase "before/in front of
Yahweh" need not be interpreted in a positive sense. In its only other
use in the Hebrew Bible (Prov. 5:21) it simply means that one's actions
are in full view of Yahweh, who examines their moral quality.[64]

With the Levite's blessing, the men journeyed on to Laish, located
in a remote region in the far north, southeast of Sidon and to the east
of Mt. Lebanon. The residents of Laish were prosperous and seemingly
secure, and had little to do with the outside world. The spies returned
home, gave a good report, and encouraged their fellow Danites to attack, assuring them that God (they once more use *Elohim*, not *Yahweh*)
had delivered the land into their hands. Oddly enough, they never specifically named the land they had spied out.[65]

This account exhibits parallels with other biblical stories about
spies investigating an area prior to a military attack (Block 1999, 491–
92; and O'Connell 1996, 235–37). Building on Wagner's form-critical
work, Bauer states that the typical spy story (see Num. 13–14; 21:32–
35; Deut. 1:19–46; Josh. 2; 7:2–4; 14:7–8) contains six elements: (1) the
selection of the spies, (2) the commissioning of the spies, (3) a report of
the execution of the mission, (4) an announcement of the spies' return
and a report of their findings, (5) a declaration of the gift of the land by
Yahweh, and (6) a conclusion (2000, 37–38). Bauer's analysis is problematic in some respects. Not all the texts listed constitute spy stories
per se. In some cases a brief reference to spying out a location is described as a prelude to an attack. Spy stories appear in Numbers 13–14
(a different version of which appears in Deut. 1:19–46) and Joshua 2.
Joshua 7:2–4 may be labeled a brief report, but it is hardly a story. As
for the six elements, the selection of the spies appears only in Numbers
13:1–16 (cf. Deut. 1:23) and what Bauer calls a conclusion is in each
case a distinct episode. The stories do typically include the commissioning of the spies (Num. 13:17–20; Josh. 2:1a; 7:2a), a report of the
execution of the mission (Num. 13:21–25; Deut. 1:24; Josh. 2:1b–22;

---

64. The verb פלס, when used with "path," as it is in Proverbs 5:21, can mean
"make level" (Isa. 26:7), but it can also carry a more neutral connotation,
"consider carefully, examine" (Prov. 4:26; 5:6). Proverbs 5:22–23, which
speak of divine judgment, favor the latter nuance in verse 21. See Boström
1990, 99.

65. This omission has prompted some to emend עֲלֵיהֶם, "against them" (v. 9)
to "to Laish." Some Greek witnesses also add a reference to Laish at this
point. See Burney 1970, 429.

7:2b), an announcement of the spies' return and a report of their findings (Num. 13:26–33; Deut. 1:25; Josh. 2:23–24; 7:3), and a declaration of the gift of the land by Yahweh (Num. 14:6–9; Deut. 1:25, 29–31; Josh. 2:24). Judges 18 contains these typical elements: commissioning of the spies (v. 2a), a report of the mission (vv. 2b–7), and an announcement of the spies' return and their report, which includes a declaration that the land is a divine gift (vv. 8–10).[66]

Despite these formal parallels, there are disturbing oddities about Judges 18:1–10, so much so that Block sees the story as a "parody" of earlier accounts and Bauer labels it "an anti-spy story" (Block 1999, 492; Bauer 2000, 38).[67] In earlier spy stories there is a statement, prior to the sending of the spies, that the land to be explored has been granted by Yahweh (Num. 13:1–2; Deut. 1:20–21; Josh. 1:2–15). No such statement appears in Judges 18 (Bauer 2000, 38).[68] Upon their return the spies claim divine support (v. 10), but this confidence is based on an oracle that was sought almost as an afterthought and was acquired from a rogue priest at an idolatrous shrine.[69] Their description of Laish as "very good" (v. 9) echoes the report of the twelve spies whom Moses sent into Canaan following the Exodus (Num. 14:7; cf. Deut. 1:25). Moses frequently called Canaan the "good land" (Deut. 3:25; 4:21–22; 6:18; 8:7, 10; 9:6; 11:17; cf. also Josh. 23:16). The Danites had already been allotted a portion of this "good land" (Josh. 19:40–48), but they were unable to occupy it (Judg. 1:34; cf. Josh. 19:47). Now they were ready to settle for a substitute "good land" on the outer fringe of Israelite territory, taken from a peaceful, anonymous people rather than the mighty Amorites.

In response to the report, six hundred Danite warriors took their families and possessions (cf. v. 21) and moved northward to conquer Laish.[70] On the way they camped in Mahaneh Dan (cf. 13:25)[71] and then

---

66. Bauer sees the selection of the spies in verse 2a and takes verses 11–31 as a conclusion (2000, 38).

67. For contrasts between Joshua 2 and Judges 18, see Wong 2006a, 55–57.

68. Mueller also notes the absence of divine involvement in the Danites' quest (2001, 66–67).

69. Boling makes the point that they should have sought an oracle prior to their mission (1975, 263).

70. This certainly could not have been the entire tribe. See Block 1999, 503–04.

71. Bauer argues that the reference to Mahaneh Dan has great literary significance. It depicts the Danites as "brutal desperadoes following a path other than that which Yahweh, the God of Israel, had commanded" (2001, section 6.1). By depicting the Danites as camped beyond, rather than in, Kiriath-Jearim, the narrator, reflecting a Judean perspective, portrays

eventually arrived at Micah's house in Ephraim (which appears to have been on a thoroughfare!).[72] A light clicked on in the minds of the spies. They would need to set up a cult site in their new land, so they decided to take Micah's ephod and idols. While their army of six hundred men stood nearby, they broke into his house and stole the cultic objects, after having the audacity to greet the Levite with שָׁלוֹם, "peace"![73] Twice in verses 16–17 (see also v. 11) the six hundred men are described as equipped with weapons. The repetition draws attention to the power wielded by the Danites (Schneider 2000, 239). Marais compares this to "a scene from a Mafia film in which the 'bad guy' always has a body-guard of silent men with guns in the background. They rarely, if ever, speak but their role in the power play is overwhelming" (1998, 138).

When the Levite objected, the Danites told him to keep his mouth shut and offered him a new job as their "adviser (literally, "father") and priest" (v. 19), arguing that it was better to serve a whole tribe than to be one man's personal priest. The Levite, who was delighted at this opportunity to gain greater prestige and make more money, needed little convincing. He quickly grabbed Micah's ephod and idols and gladly became an honorary Danite. Verse 20 states literally, "he went into the midst of the people," emphasizing his new allegiance.

Micah gathered some of his neighbors (probably extended family members, cf. v. 22 with v. 25) and pursued the Danites, who had the gall to question why he had summoned a military contingent and come after them. Appalled by their response, Micah explained that they had stolen his god/gods and his priest (v. 24). The precise referent of אֱלֹהַי אֲשֶׁר־עָשִׂיתִי, "my gods (or "god") that I made," is unclear. In 17:5

---

them as distancing themselves from God's commandments, the tablets of which had once been present in Kiriath-Jearim during the ark's stay there. He also portrays them as distancing themselves from Judah, the "'one true' Israel, which lives in accordance with God's commandments" (section 4.5).

72. As the Danites approached Micah's home, they referred to cultic equipment being in "these houses" (18:14). This probably refers to the numerous houses occupied by Micah's extended family. See van der Toorn 1996, 197–98.

73. The verb לקח, "take," is used five times in chapter 18 to describe how Micah's cult objects were taken from him. The narrator states this four times (vv. 17–18, 20, 27) and Micah once (v. 24). Davis finds this ironic, for the term is used twice in 17:2 to describe how Micah took his mother's silver (1984, 159). As Davis points out, this does not bode well for the Danite sanctuary: "The sanctuary of Dan has its origin in a double theft. What else can come out of it except curse and ruin?"

Micah is said to have "made" an ephod and some household idols. Perhaps in 18:24 he refers to the latter, in which case he was a syncretist. He worshipped Yahweh, but not exclusively. A second option is that the פֶּסֶל, "idol" (or פֶּסֶל וּמַסֵּכָה) is the referent.[74] Micah did not actually make the image(s) (17:4), but perhaps he could speak of himself as doing so because the family finances paid for it/them. If only one idol is in view, it is possible that it was an image of Yahweh and we can translate "my god." A third option is that Micah refers here to both the household idols and the carved/molten image(s).

The Danites did not attempt to justify their actions; as far as they were concerned, "might made right." They told Micah to cease arguing, warning him that any further objections on his part would be met with severe hostility. Characterizing themselves as "very angry" men (v. 25), they threatened to kill Micah and his family.[75] Realizing that he was powerless before such people, Micah gave up and went home, undoubtedly a bit disillusioned. Having a Levite in the house had not turned out to his advantage after all (cf. 17:13); in fact the Levite's presence attracted the Danites to his house in the first place (18:3) and eventually caused him to lose all his cultic objects. So much for undeserved blessings upon idolatrous thieves (see 17:2)! Apparently the Lord's favor could not be assured by glibly reciting a blessing or hiring a Levite.

Setting up a rival cult (18:27–19:1a). The Danites took Micah's cult objects and moved on to Laish.[76] They killed the unsuspecting residents, who had no allies to come to their rescue, and burned the city.[77] The text gives no indication that the people of Laish were one of the groups

---

74. The matter is complicated by the ambiguity of the terminology. Does it refer to one image or two (or more) idol(s)? If the latter, did the Levite take only the carved image, leaving the molten one for Micah? See our earlier note on 17:3.

75. The phrase "very angry" (literally, "bitter of soul") is also used in 2 Samuel 17:8 of David and his warriors, who are compared there to a bear robbed of her cubs. When collocated with נֶפֶשׁ, "soul," the term מַר, "bitter," has a strong emotional connotation. See as well 1 Samuel 1:10; 22:2; Job 3:10; 7:11; 10:1; Proverbs 31:6; Isaiah 38:15; Ezekiel 27:31.

76. Note that the narrator refers simply to "what Micah had made" (v. 27; cf. v. 31), in contrast to Micah, who referred to "my god(s) that I made" (v. 24). Davis argues that the narrator "refuses to dignify such relics by calling them 'gods'" (1984, 159). He sees this as evidence of the narrator's "polemical stance" against the characters of the story.

77. Wong notes that in Ezekiel 38:10–11 attacking unsuspecting people "is characterized as an evil scheme" (2006a, 39, note 35).

the Lord had authorized the Israelites to wipe out (Deut. 20:17). On the contrary, it seems to go out of its way to stress their isolation and suggests that they were distinct from others. If this was indeed the case, then the Danites violated the Deuteronomic war policy, which made it clear that more distant nations were to be treated differently than the native Canaanite population. Israel was to implement genocide against the native peoples (Deut. 20:16–18), but they were to give more distant city-states an opportunity to become Israelite subjects (Deut. 20:10–15). Only if this offer of peace was rejected were the Israelites allowed to attack. Even then, only men were to be killed (Wong 2006a, 39).

The description of the Danite slaughter of Laish (וַיַּכּוּ אוֹתָם לְפִי־חָרֶב), literally, "and they struck them with the mouth of the sword") echoes the prologue, where the men of Judah "struck" Jerusalem "with the mouth of the sword" (1:8) and the men of Joseph did the same to Bethel (1:25). It is ironic that terminology associated with the divinely authorized conquest of the land is here associated with the Danites' unauthorized conquest of a city that lay far to the north of their allotted territory. As Wong observes, "Israel seems subsequently to have lost her ability to apply" the laws regulating the conquest "with understanding and discernment" (2006a, 40).

Bauer calls the Danites' distant northern campaign an "anti-conquest." Building on the work of von Rad and Malamat, he shows that the story of the Danite conquest does not fit the holy war genre and that it differs significantly from pan-Israelite conquest accounts (Bauer 2000, 40–41). Von Rad isolated fifteen elements in the holy-war genre (1991, 41–51). Only three of these appear in Judges 18, and even these three do not conform to the normal holy-war pattern. As Bauer observes, the Danites' "consultation of God has a very dubious character," the "confirmation" of the mission "is apparently groundless," and "the ban is carried out without the ritualistic dimension of the consignment of spoils to Yhwh, but rather as a pure act of violence upon the inhabitants of Laish" (41).[78] Malamat identifies ten points of contact between Judges 18 and earlier accounts of Israel's migration from Egypt to Canaan (1970, 1–16, especially p. 2). Bauer shows that several of these are "inverted" in Judges 18, indicating that the Danite account is really an "anti-story" (2000, 42–46).[79]

---

78. Niditch sees the Danite conquest as reflecting the "ideology of wars of expedience," which requires no "just cause" (1993, 128).

79. Bray argues that the Danite conquest, at least in the original story as he reconstructs it, was legitimate and engineered by Yahweh (2006, 40–41). He contends that the text, when read from a rhetorical-critical

The Danites rebuilt the city and named it after their progenitor.[80] They set up an idolatrous cult with Jonathan, a descendant of

---

perspective, does not condemn their actions and he accuses those who denounce them of being guilty of "anachronistic assumption that the Bible reflects the same values we hold" (37). He hints that such an interpretation may reflect a reader-response hermeneutic. But surely the context sends multiple signals that the Danites' actions should be viewed in a negative light. Their behavior, like the other appalling deeds recorded in the epilogue, illustrates the moral depths reached by Israel during this period. A *rhetorical*-critical reading must reflect the final form of the text. Bray's argument stands or falls on his *redactional*-critical assumption that the statements in 17:6; 18:1a; 19:1; and 21:25 come from a "post-exilic redactor," as does 18:31 (31). The negative view of the Danites reflects a proper rhetorical-critical approach; Bray's view reflects a redactional-critical approach that speculates as to what the "original story" (41) may have meant. Furthermore, apart from the allegedly postexilic additions, one would still have ample reason to view the Danites' actions negatively. The story is filled with irony, especially in its portrayal of the Danite effort as an "anti-spy" story and an "anti-conquest" account. (Bray [whose work was published in 2006] does not list Bauer's article [2000] or Block's commentary [1999] in his bibliography, let alone interact with them.) Bray labels the account a "cultic foundation story" (58). Based on the form-critical evidence he cites (42–58), this may be correct, but, if so, it is another example of how the narrator produces a parody of the normal pattern. Indeed Bray himself identifies significant differences between the Jerusalem cult foundation accounts and the Danite story (50). He states that in the case of the Danites, "the whole story hinges upon the giving of the oracle in Judg 18:6." He sees this event as pivotal in the story: "the narrative has been leading up to this single event, and all subsequent actions of the Danites refer back to it." But, as we attempted to show earlier, Bray has missed the irony of the passage, which describes a bogus oracle given by a bogus priest (see our comments on 18:5–6). Bray also notes that in the Danite account "the cultic objects themselves are not of ancient origin, their only value lies in the fact that they are dedicated to Yahweh; in this story it is the priest who has a high ancestry, and it is this which comes to the fore in the narrative" (50). The cultic objects' lack of antiquity may well be a signal that this is a parody. They may have been dedicated to Yahweh, but they were dedicated by an idolatrous scoundrel! This priest of "high ancestry" dishonors his heritage by serving as an unauthorized cult functionary at idolatrous shrines!

80. For a survey of the archaeological evidence from Laish/Dan, see Wood 2003, 275–77, as well as Kitchen 2003, 211.

Gershom son of Moses (we finally discover the Levite's name) as its priest.[81] His family continued in this capacity all the way to the exile of the northern kingdom in 734–732 B.C. (2 Kings 15:29).[82] The narrator concludes by reminding us that this Danite cult was a renegade worship center, a rival to the legitimate cult site at Shiloh.

MESSAGE AND APPLICATION

Thematic Emphases

Because of persistent paganism combined with a leadership void, Israel became spiritually polluted and torn apart by social anarchy. During the time period depicted in chapters 17–18 Israelites maintained a semblance of religion. They prayed in the Lord's name (17:2),

---

81. Butler observes: "Certainly the Danites trumpeted the fame and family of their priest, but the Jerusalem tradition held on to Aaronic priesthood, not Mosaic. Hiring a Mosaic priest, particularly a stolen Mosaic priest with a shrine of idols, did not meet divine qualifications" (2009, 398). See as well Mueller 2001, 73.

82. The collocation of גְּלוֹת, "exile," with הָאָרֶץ, "the land," is unique. Some suggest emending הָאָרֶץ to הָאָרוֹן, "the ark." In this case the Philistine captivity of the ark would be in view (see 1 Sam. 4:21–22). This would fit nicely with the reference to Shiloh in Judges 18:31, but the reading has no textual support. For a detailed defense of the emendation see O'Connell 1996, 481–83. For a critique of O'Connell's view, see Bray 2006, 22–23. It is odd that verse 30 speaks of the exile terminating Dan's rival cult, while verse 31 focuses on the early period, when worship was centered in Shiloh, and makes no mention of other worship centers prior to the fall of the northern kingdom. See Burney 1970, 414–15. The discrepancy between verses 30–31 probably reflects different stages of redactional activity. The precise phrase בֵּית־הָאֱלֹהִים, "the house of God" (with the article attached to the divine name), apart from this text, occurs only in late texts (primarily in Ezra-Nehemiah and Chronicles) and usually refers to the Jerusalem temple (see, however, 1 Chron. 6:48 [Hebrew v. 33], where the phrase is appositional to "tabernacle"). The Shiloh worship center is called the "house of Yahweh" in 1 Samuel 1:7, 24; 3:15 (see also Judg. 19:18, though the text may be corrupt). It is reasonable to conclude that verse 30b is the product of a redactor working sometime after 734–721 B.C. Verse 31, while originating in an earlier period when Shiloh was still a prominent worship site, was later modernized in its language. For an alternative solution, see Bray 2006, 23. He suggests that verse 30 "may be seen coming possibly from the hand of a Northern refugee at the time of the Assyrian invasions," while verse 31 "is probably best regarded as part of a later, hostile redaction made when the narrative was incorporated into Judges."

dedicated money to the Lord (17:3), desired the Lord's favor (17:13), inquired concerning the divine will (18:5), and pronounced oracles in the Lord's name (18:6). It is a telling commentary, however, that the Lord is mentioned only in quotations, not in the narrative framework of the story (Davis 1984, 159). He is essentially absent from the story as a character. Though the characters speak of him, their actions do not honor him (McMillion 1999, 242–43). The account is marred by (1) a mother who overlooked her son's greed, thought she could manipulate the Lord with solemn formal statements, and believed the Lord was pleased with idols, (2) a man (Micah) who was obsessed with idols and thought he could gain the Lord's favor by having his very own shrine and priest, (3) a Levite who sold his services to the highest bidder and proclaimed oracles without genuine divine authority, and (4) a group of "very angry" Danites who, though unable to take their divinely appointed land, believed might made right, justified their violent deeds by appealing to a bogus divine oracle, and launched a conquest of territory nowhere near their allotted inheritance.

Marais aptly summarizes the story as follows: "The story of Micah and his Levite thus represents the apostasy and the degeneration of Israelite society as it influences family life and cultic institutions. It is a world where everything is free for the taking by either those who can afford it or those who have the most power. With no eyes to behold and to measure, other than their own, chaos reigns in the world of the judges. Yahweh is absent except for the thwarted visions the characters might have had of Him. He did not act, nor did he speak. He was a mere memory within a curse or a blessing" (1998, 138).

Exegetical idea: *As Israel persisted in paganism and quality spiritual leadership was absent, spiritual confusion and chaos overtook the covenant community as a corrupt and superficial form of religion replaced genuine worship.*

Theological Principles
James 1:27 states that pure religion in God's sight has two basic components: concern for the weak and vulnerable (that is, an ethical dimension that makes the best interests of others a priority) and spiritual purity (defined as keeping oneself unstained by the pagan world and its standards). Judges 17–18 depicts the antithesis of pure religion. The main characters in these chapters are motivated solely by self-interest and greed and approach God in a thoroughly pagan manner.

In this story and the following one, the need for theocratic kingship emerges (17:6; cf. 18:1; 19:1; 21:25). These editorial comments envision the kingship ideal depicted in Deuteronomy 17:14–20 and anticipate the rise of the Davidic monarchy. (For further discussion, see the "Theological Themes" section for 19:1b—21:25 below.)

Theological idea: *When God's people persist in paganism and quality spiritual leadership is absent, spiritual confusion and chaos can overtake the covenant community as a corrupt and superficial form of religion replaces genuine worship.*

Homiletical Trajectories

(1) As noted above, God is present in this story in name only. His absence from the narrative *per se* is striking. Though we know from the book's prologue and stories that God was active throughout the Judges period, his absence here reminds us that his rebellious people forfeit the blessing of God's presence in their experience.

(2) This story illustrates how corrupt the covenant community can become when they embrace a pagan worldview. Selfishness, greed, intimidation, and violence become the order of the day. A renegade, pagan form of religion emerged in Israel at this time. Renegade, paganized religion is characterized by:

(a) a view of God that is pagan to the core (17:1–6). (Micah's mother devalued ethics, the core of genuine worship of the Lord, and tried to manipulate God for her own benefit.)

(b) a greedy spirit that tries to manipulate God for material benefits (17:7–18:1a). (Micah and the Levite are greed personified. They use their religion for financial gain.)

(c) a self-centered attitude that uses power to further its own interests (18:1b–31). (The Danites, while desiring God's stamp of approval on their self-serving efforts, reject God's purposes and ethical standards, and resort to violent methods that have no place for the rights of others.)

(3) The story also reminds us of the importance of godly leadership for the covenant community. The narrator's comment in 17:6 (cf. also 18:1; 19:1) informs us that the paganism evident in the story could have been curtailed or prevented if there had been a leader who promoted covenant fidelity by word and example.

Preaching idea: *When we persist in the paganism of our culture and quality spiritual leadership is absent, a renegade form of religion can* *replace genuine worship, bring spiritual confusion and chaos with it, and prevent us from experiencing the blessing of God's presence.*

One can definitely develop the second trajectory at the homiletical level, focusing in detail on the characteristics of renegade religion, in contrast to the twin pillars of genuine religion as stated in James 1:27. A *preaching idea* for this might be: *We must avoid falling into the trap of renegade religion, which is plagued by (a) a pagan view of God that devalues ethics and attempts to manipulate God, (b) a materialistic attitude, and (c) a self-centered and self-serving use of power.*

TRANSLATION AND NARRATIVE STRUCTURE

19:1c There was a Levite living temporarily in the remote region of the Ephraimite hill country. (*introductory-backgrounding*)

1d He acquired a concubine from Bethlehem in Judah. (*initiatory*)

2a She[1] got mad at him (*sequential*)

2b and went home to her father's house in Bethlehem in Judah. (*sequential*)

2c When she had been there four months, (*sequential*)

3a her husband came[2] after her, hoping he could convince her to return. (*sequential*)

3b **He brought with him his servant and a pair of donkeys**. (*supplemental*)

3c When she brought him into her father's house (*resumptive-sequential*)

3d and the young woman's father saw him, (*sequential*)

3e he warmly greeted him. (*sequential*)

---

1. Literally, "his concubine," that is, the one mentioned in verse 1d.
2. The Hebrew text has two verbs here, "he arose and came."

4a   His father-in-law, the young woman's father, persuaded him to stay, (*sequential*)

4b   so he remained with him for three days. (*consequential*)

4c   They ate (*focusing*)

4d   and drank (*complementary*)

4e   and spent the night there (*focusing*).

5a   On the fourth day (*transitional-circumstantial*)[3]

5b   they woke up early (*sequential*)

5c   and the Levite got ready to leave. (*sequential*)

5d   But the young woman's father said to his son-in-law, (*sequential*)

5e   *"Have a bite to eat for some energy, then you can go."*

6a   So the two of them sat down (*sequential*)

6b   and ate (*sequential*)

6c   and drank together. (*complementary*)

6d   Then the young woman's father said to the man, (*sequential*)

6e   *"Why not stay another night and have a good time!"*

7a   When the man got ready to leave, (*sequential*)

7b   his father-in-law convinced him to stay (*sequential*)

7c   so he remained another night. (*consequential*)

8a   He woke up early in the morning on the fifth day so he could leave, (*sequential*)

8b   but the young woman's father said, (*sequential*)

8c   *"Get some energy. Wait until later in the day to leave!"*

8d   So they ate a meal together. (*sequential*)

9a   When the man got ready to leave with his wife and servant, (*sequential*)

9b   his father-in-law, the young woman's father, said to him, (*sequential*)

9c   *"Look! The day is almost over! Stay another night! Since the day is over, stay another night here and have a good time. You can get up early tomorrow and start your trip home."*

10a   **But the man did not want to stay another night.** (*contrastive*)[4]

10b   He left[5] (*sequential*)

10c   and traveled as far as Jebus (*sequential*)

---

3. The *wayyehi* clause at the beginning of verse 5 marks a transition within the scene from the third to the fourth day.

4. Verse 10a (which begins with a negated perfect) contrasts the man's response with his father-in-law's desire and with his prior willingness to stay on an extra day.

5. The Hebrew text has two verbs here, "he arose and went."

10d **(that is, Jerusalem).** (*supplemental*)
10e **He had with him a pair of saddled donkeys and his wife.** (*supplemental*)

11a **When they got near Jebus,** (*introductory-new scene*)
11b **it was getting quite late** (*introductory-backgrounding*)
11c and the servant said to his master, (*initiatory*)
11d *"Come on, let's stop at this Jebusite city and spend the night in it."*
12a But his master said to him, (*sequential*)
12b *"We should not stop at a foreign city where non-Israelites live. We will travel on toward Gibeah."*
13a He said to his servant, (*sequential*)
13b *"Come on, we will go into one of the other towns and spend the night in Gibeah or Ramah."*
14a So they passed by Jebus (*sequential*)
14b and traveled on. (*sequential*)
14c The sun went down when they were near Gibeah in Benjamin. (*sequential*)
15a They stopped there in order to spend the night in Gibeah. (*sequential*)
15b They came into the city (*sequential*)
15c and sat down in the town square, (*sequential*)
15d **but no one invited them in to spend the night.** (*concluding*)[6]

16a **But then an old man passed by, returning at the end of the day from his work in the field.** (*dramatic shift in focus / new scene*)[7]
16b **The man was from the Ephraimite hill country;** (*supplemental*)
16c **he was living temporarily in Gibeah.** (*supplemental*)
16d **(The residents of the town were Benjaminites.)** (*supplemental*)
17a When he looked up (*resumptive-sequential*)
17b and saw the traveler in the town square, (*sequential*)

---

6. The disjunctive clause at the end of verse 15 signals closure for the scene.
7. The disjunctive clause at the beginning of verse 16 (introduced by וְהִנֵּה, literally, "and look") shifts the focus to a new character and introduces a new scene. It also has a dramatic function as it invites the audience to move inside the story and view the scene as if they were eyewitnesses.

17c the old man said, (*sequential*)

17d *"Where are you heading? Where do you come from?"*

18a The Levite said to him, (*sequential*)

18b *"We are traveling from Bethlehem in Judah to the remote region of the Ephraimite hill country. That's where I'm from. I had business in Bethlehem in Judah, but now I'm heading home. But no one has invited me into his home.*

19 *We have enough straw and grain for our donkeys, and there is enough food and wine for me, your female servant, and the young man who is with your servants. We lack nothing."*

20a The old man said, (*sequential*)

20b *"Don't worry! I will take care of all your needs. But don't spend the night in the town square."*

21a So he brought him to his house (*sequential*)

21b and fed the donkeys. (*sequential*)

21c They washed their feet (*sequential*)

21d and had a meal.[8] (*sequential*)

22a **They were having a good time,** (*introductory*)[9]

22b **when all of a sudden some men of the city, some good-for-nothings, surrounded the house and kept beating on the door.** (*dramatic*)[10]

22c They said to the old man who owned the house, (*sequential*)

22d *"Send out the man who came to visit you so we can have sex with him."*

23a The man who owned the house went outside (*sequential*)

23b and said to them, (*sequential*)

23c *"No my brothers! Don't do this wicked thing! After all this man is a guest in my house. Don't do such a disgraceful thing!*

24 *Here are my virgin daughter and the visitor's wife. I will bring them[11] out and you can abuse them and do to them whatever you like. But don't do such a disgraceful thing to this man!"*

---

8. The Hebrew text reads, "they ate and drank."

9. The asyndetic disjunctive clause at the beginning of verse 22 formally introduces the next scene.

10. The disjunctive clause in verse 22b (introduced by וְהִנֵּה, literally, "and look") introduces new characters into the scene and again (cf. v. 16a) invites the audience into the story.

11. The apparent third masculine plural pronouns in this verse are probably archaic common dual forms, referring to the two women. The book of Ruth displays many such forms. See Boling, *Judges*, 276.

25a **The men refused to listen to him,** (*contrastive*)[12]
25b so the Levite grabbed his wife (*consequential*)
25c and made her go outside to them. (*sequential*)
25d They raped her (*sequential*)
25e and abused her all night long until morning. (*complementary*)
25f They sent her away[13] at dawn. (*sequential*)
26a The woman arrived back at daybreak (*sequential*)
26b and sprawled out on the doorstep of the house where her master was staying until it became light. (*sequential*)
27a When her master got up in the morning, (*sequential*)
27b opened the doors of the house, (*sequential*)
27c and went outside to start on his journey, (*sequential*)
27d **there was the woman, his wife, sprawled out on the doorstep of the house** (*dramatic*)[14]
27e **with her hands on the threshold.** (*circumstantial*)
28a He said to her, (*sequential*)
28b *"Get up, let's leave!"*
28c **But there was no response.** (*contrastive*)[15]
28d He put her on the donkey (*sequential*)
28e and went home.[16] (*sequential*)
29a When he got home, (*sequential*)
29b he took a knife, (*sequential*)
29c grabbed his wife, (*sequential*)
29d and carved her up into twelve pieces. (*sequential*)
29e Then he sent them throughout Israel. (*sequential*)
30a **Everyone who saw the sight** (*characterizing*)[17]

---

12. Verse 25a (which begins with a negated perfect) contrasts the crowd's response with the old man's request.
13. The *piel* of שׁלח is sometimes understood here in the sense of "let her go, released her," but this seems too mild. In 2 Samuel 13:16 Tamar, having been raped by Amnon, objects to being "sent away." Berman understands this to be "an expulsion that expresses his disgust and repulsion" (2004, 66). He sees a similar nuance in Judges 19:25.
14. The disjunctive clause in verse 27d (introduced by וְהִנֵּה, literally, "and look") is dramatic, forcing us to view the hideous, tragic scene through the calloused Levite's eyes. The accompanying circumstantial clause provides a further detail that adds to the tragic dimension of the event.
15. The disjunctive clause in verse 28c contrasts the woman's lack of response with the Levite's command.
16. The Hebrew text has two verbs here, "he arose and went."
17. Verse 30 is introduced with וְהָיָה, literally, "and it was," which is then extended by another *weqatal* form (וְאָמַר, "and said"). This appears to be

30b **said**, (*characterizing-sequential*)
30c *"Nothing like this has happened or been witnessed from the day the Israelites left the land of Egypt until the present day.*[18] *Take careful note of it! Discuss it and speak!"*
20:1a All the Israelites from Dan to Beersheba and from the land of Gilead, left their homes (*initiatory*)
1b and assembled before the LORD at Mizpah. (*sequential*)
2 The leaders of all the people from all the tribes of Israel took their places in the assembly of God's people, which

---

another example of *weqatal* expressing what Longacre calls "a customary, script-predictable routine" (see 6:3ab) (1994, 56). The scene described here was played out in twelve different places as body parts arrived among the respective tribes.

18. Codex A of the LXX has the following additional words: "And he instructed the men whom he sent out, 'Thus you will say to every male of Israel: "There has never been anything like this from the day the Israelites left Egypt until the present day.""' It is possible that these words were accidentally omitted from the Hebrew textual tradition. A scribe's eye could have jumped from the first instance of "until this day" to the second, leaving out the intervening words. In this case if one retroverts και ενετειλατο as a *wayyiqtol* form וַיְצַו, "and he instructed," the construction would involve a flashback to a time before verse 30a. O'Connell wants to retrovert the Greek to וְצִוָּה (a *weqatal* form corresponding to the two that precede) (1996, 484). But flashbacks more commonly occur with *wayyiqtol*, not *weqatal*. Perhaps it is better to treat the plus in LXXA as a variant reading that has been juxtaposed with the reading preserved in the Hebrew text. The final exhortation goes with both variants. In this case the variants are as follows: (1) Everyone who saw the sight said, "Nothing like this has happened or been witnessed from the day the Israelites left the land of Egypt until the present day. Take careful note of it! Discuss it and speak!" (2) And he instructed the men whom he sent out, "Thus you will say to every male of Israel: 'There has never been anything like this from the day the Israelites left Egypt until the present day. Take careful note of it! Discuss it!" Burney reasons that reading two was original (1970, 470). A scribe's eye jumped from "Israel" at the end of verse 29 to "Israel" within the quotation from the Levite, omitting the intervening words. The original text of verses 29e–30ab would have read: "Then he sent them throughout Israel. And he instructed the men whom he sent out, 'Thus you will say to every male of Israel.'" Once the intervening words were omitted, some form of introduction to verse 30c was needed, giving rise to the reading preserved in MT. According to Burney, the use of *weqatal* forms betrays a late date for verse 30ab.

numbered four hundred thousand sword-wielding foot soldiers. (*sequential*)[19]

3a   The Benjaminites heard that the Israelites had gone up to Mizpah. (*supplemental-qualifying*)[20]

3b   Then the Israelites said, (*resumptive-sequential*)

3c   *"Explain how this wicked thing happened!"*

4a   The Levite, the husband of the murdered woman, spoke up, (*sequential*)

4b   *"I and my wife stopped in Gibeah of Benjamin to spend the night.*

5   *The leaders of Gibeah attacked me and at nighttime surrounded the house where I was staying. They wanted to kill me; instead they abused my wife so badly she died.*

6   *I grabbed hold of my wife and carved her up and sent the pieces throughout the territory occupied by Israel, because they committed such an unthinkable atrocity in Israel.*

7   *All you Israelites, make a decision here!"*

8a   All Israel rose up in unison, saying, (*sequential*)

8b   *"Not one of us will go home! Not one of us will return to his house!*

9   *Now this is what we will do to Gibeah. We will attack the city as the lot dictates.*

10   *We will take ten of every group of one hundred men from all the tribes of Israel (and a hundred of every group of a thousand, and a thousand of every group of ten thousand) to get supplies for the army.*[21] *When they arrive in Gibeah of Benjamin they will punish them for the atrocity which they committed in Israel."*

---

19. On the exceptionally large number mentioned here, see the commentary above on 1:4. As noted there, it is difficult to accept such figures at face value. One possibility is that the Hebrew term אֶלֶף, traditionally understood as a numeral (a "thousand"), actually refers to a contingent of troops, at least in some contexts. Boling, taking this approach, translates "four hundred contingents" in verse 2 and "four hundred sword-bearing contingents" in verse 17 (1975, 280–81). Another option is that such large numbers are hyperbolic. See Fouts 1997, 377–88, and 2003, 283–99.

20. The *wayyiqtol* clause in verse 3a has a supplemental-qualifying function. It qualifies the pan-Israelite language in verses 1–2 (note "all the Israelites," "from Dan to Beersheba," "all the tribes") by informing us that the Benjaminites heard about the gathering, implying that they did not attend. This introduces additional tension into the narrative by setting up the potential for civil conflict.

21. On the large numbers mentioned here, see the note at 1:4 above. In 20:10 it is apparent that עֲשָׂרָה, "ten," is one-tenth of מֵאָה, traditionally "one

11 So all the men of Israel gathered together at the city as allies. (*sequential*)

12a The tribes of Israel sent men throughout the tribe of Benjamin, saying, (*sequential*)

12b *"How could such a wicked thing take place?*

13a *Now, hand over the good-for-nothings in Gibeah so we can execute them and purge Israel of wickedness."*

13b **But the Benjaminites**[22] **refused to listen to their Israelite brothers**. (*contrastive*)[23]

14 The Benjaminites came from their cities and assembled at Gibeah to make war against the Israelites. (*sequential*)

15 That day the Benjaminites mustered from their cities twenty-six thousand sword-wielding soldiers, besides seven hundred well-trained soldiers from Gibeah. (*focusing*)[24]

---

hundred." מֵאָה, in turn, is one-tenth of אֶלֶף, traditionally "one thousand," which in turn is one-tenth of רְבָבָה, traditionally "ten thousand."

22. The consonantal Hebrew text (*Kethib*) states literally: "and they were not willing, Benjamin." There is incongruity between the plural verb (אָבוּ, "they were [not] willing") and the following singular subject Benjamin. Many medieval Hebrew manuscripts, supported by the LXX, Syriac, and Targums support the marginal reading (*Qere*) in reading בְּנֵי בִנְיָמִן, "the sons of Benjamin." In this case the plural subject agrees with the plural verb. One could argue that the *Kethib* is a case of a plural verb being employed with a collective proper noun, but a closer look at the literary style of Judges 20–21 makes this unlikely. The proper name Benjamin appears as the subject of a preceding verb three times; each time the verb is singular (20:25, 40; 21:14). In 20:39 the subject Benjamin precedes its verb; the verb is singular. In 20:41 the phrase אִישׁ בִּנְיָמִן, "men [collective singular] of Benjamin" is the subject of a preceding singular verb. Eight times the phrase "sons of Benjamin" appears as the subject of a preceding verb; each time the verb is plural (20:3, 14–15, 21, 31, 32, 36; 21:23). The evidence indicates that the *Kethib's* lack of agreement is incongruous and the *Qere* reading is consistent with the narrator's style. In the *Qere* reading the sequence בני is repeated: בני בנימן. Apparently haplography occurred, with the sequence being written only once instead of twice.

23. Verse 13b (introduced by a negated perfect) contrasts Benjamin's response with Israel's demand.

24. On the large number mentioned here, see the commentary above on 1:4. As noted there, it is difficult to accept such figures at face value. One possibility is that the Hebrew term אֶלֶף, traditionally understood as a numeral (a "thousand"), actually refers to a contingent of troops, at least in some contexts. Boling, taking this approach, translates "twenty-six

16a **Among this army were seven hundred specially trained left-handed soldiers.** (*supplemental*)

16b **Each one could sling a stone and hit even the smallest target.** (*supplemental*)

17a **The men of Israel (not counting Benjamin) had mustered four hundred thousand sword-wielding soldiers,** (*concluding-contrastive / reiterative*)[25]

17b **every one an experienced warrior.** (*supplemental*)

18a The Israelites went up[26] to Bethel (*initiatory*)

18b and asked God, (*sequential*)

18c *"Who should lead the charge against the Benjaminites?"*

18d The LORD said, (*sequential*)

18e *"Judah should lead."*

19a The Israelites got up the next morning (*sequential*)

19b and deployed their forces near Gibeah. (*sequential*)

20a The men of Israel marched out to fight Benjamin; (*sequential*)

20b they arranged their battle lines against Gibeah. (*reiterative-focusing*)

21a The Benjaminites attacked from Gibeah (*complementary*)

21b and struck down twenty-two thousand Israelites that day. (*sequential*)[27]

22a The Israelite army took heart (*sequential*)

22b and once more arranged their battle lines, in the same place where they had taken their positions the day before. (*sequential*)

23a The Israelites went up (*sequential*)

---

sword-bearing contingents" in verse 15 (1975, 281). Another option is that such large numbers are hyperbolic. See Fouts 1997, 377–88, and 2003, 283–99.

25. The disjunctive clause in verse 17a has multiple functions. It contrasts the size of the vast Israelite army with Benjamin's much smaller force; it also reiterates what we were told back in verse 2. It also concludes the opening scene by telling us that each side had deployed its forces. The battle is ready to begin.

26. The Hebrew text has two verbs, "arose and went up."

27. On the large number mentioned here, see the commentary above on 1:4. As noted there, it is difficult to accept such figures at face value. One possibility is that the Hebrew term אֶלֶף, traditionally understood as a numeral (a "thousand"), actually refers to a contingent of troops, at least in some contexts. Boling, taking this approach, translates "twenty-two Israelite contingents" in verse 21 (1975, 281). Another option is that such large numbers are hyperbolic. See Fouts 1997, 377–88, and 2003, 283–99.

23b and wept before the LORD until evening. (*sequential*)
23c They asked the LORD, (*sequential*)
23d *"Should we again march out to fight the Benjaminites, our brothers?"*
23e The LORD said, (*sequential*)
23f *"Attack them!"*[28]
24 So the Israelites marched toward the Benjaminites the next day. (*sequential*)
25a The Benjaminites again attacked them from Gibeah (*complementary*)
25b and struck down eighteen thousand sword-wielding Israelite soldiers. (*sequential*)[29]
26a So all the Israelites, the whole army, went up[30] to Bethel. (*consequential*)
26b They wept (*sequential*)[31]
26c and sat there before the LORD; (*complementary*)
26d they did not eat anything that day until evening. (*complementary*)
26e They offered up burnt sacrifices and tokens of peace to the LORD. (*complementary*)
27a The Israelites asked the LORD— (*sequential*)
27b **(The ark of God's covenant was there in those days**. (*supplemental*)
28a **Phinehas son of Eleazar, son of Aaron, was serving the Lord in those days**.)— (*supplemental*)

---

28. The text reads literally, "go up to him." While this could certainly refer to a military attack (cf. Judg. 1:1; 12:3, 20:30), as we have translated the expression, one must admit that the language is ambiguous. See Lapsley 2005, 53–54.

29. On the large number mentioned here, see the commentary above on 1:4. As noted there, it is difficult to accept such figures at face value. One possibility is that the Hebrew term אֶלֶף, traditionally understood as a numeral (a "thousand"), actually refers to a contingent of troops, at least in some contexts. Boling, taking this approach, translates "eighteen more Israelite contingents" in verse 25 (1975, 281). Another option is that such large numbers are hyperbolic. See Fouts 1997, 377–88, and 2003, 283–99.

30. The Hebrew text has two verbs here, "went up and came to."

31. The *wayyiqtol* clauses in verse 26b-e do not describe actions that are in chronological sequence, but rather list the various cultic activities in which Israel would have engaged that day, some of which must have been done simultaneously.

28b "*Should we once more march out to fight the Benjaminites our brothers, or should we quit?*"

28c The Lord said, (*resumptive-sequential*)

28d "*Attack, for tomorrow I will hand them over to you.*"

29 So Israel hid men in ambush outside Gibeah. (*sequential*)[32]

30a The Israelites attacked the Benjaminites the next day; (*complementary*)

30b they took their positions against Gibeah just as they had done before. (*reiterative-focusing*)

31a The Benjaminites attacked the army, (*complementary*)

31b **leaving the city unguarded**. (*complementary-dramatic*)[33]

31c They began to strike down their enemy just as they had done before—on the main roads (one leads to Bethel, the other to Gibeah) and in the field. About thirty Israelites fell.[34] (*sequential*)

---

32. For detailed clausal analyses of verses 29–48, see Chisholm 1998b, 139–42; Revell 1985, 417–33; and Satterthwaite 1992, 80–89. Though brief, Buth's discussion is also helpful (1994, 143–44, 150–51).

    The structure of verses 29–31 requires careful analysis. Verse 30a, which describes the deployment of Israel's main force, complements verse 29, which informs us that Israel had taken a group of men and set an ambush for Benjamin (cf. v. 33). This action sets this panel apart from previous ones, where we were simply told that Israel marched toward Benjamin's army (vv. 20, 24). Verse 30b essentially repeats the preceding statement, heightening the drama of the event by slowing the pace of the story (cf. v. 20ab). As before, a description of Benjamin's attack complements the reference to Israel's troop movements (cf. vv. 20–21, 24–25). However, this time there is an asyndetic perfect (with a prepositional phrase) reflecting Israel's perspective (v. 31b). Benjamin was boldly attacking as they did before, probably with the expectation of another victory. But, from Israel's strategic standpoint, they were being drawn away from their city, making the city vulnerable to the previously mentioned ambush. In this regard the clause may be viewed as giving a complementary perspective. The asyndetic style reflects the tone of a participant, rather than a mere narrator, so the clause may also be classified as dramatic.

33. As the previous note points out, the asyndetic style reflects the tone of a participant, rather than a mere narrator. We are present at the scene and we suspect, in accordance with the Lord's oracle of assurance (v. 28), that the outcome will be different this time. Unfortunately, some fail to see the rhetorical significance of the stylistic variation and propose emending the perfect to a *wayyiqtol* form, which is what we might have expected (see *BHS* textual note 31a).

34. Verse 31c is actually one long sentence in the Hebrew text. For the sake of English style, the final prepositional phrase (literally, "about thirty men in

32a Then the Benjaminites said, (*sequential*)
32b *"They are defeated just as before."*
32c **But the Israelites said,** (*contrastive*)[35]
32d *"Let's retreat and lure them away from the city into the main roads."*
33a **All the men of Israel got up from their places** (*circumstantial*)[36]
33b and took their positions at Baal Tamar, (*sequential*)
33c **while the Israelites hiding in ambush jumped out of their places west of Gibeah.** (*synchronic*)
34a Ten thousand men, well-trained soldiers from all Israel, then made a frontal assault against Gibeah— (*sequential*)[37]
34b **the battle was fierce.** (*transitional*)[38]
34c **The Benjaminites did not realize that disaster was at their doorstep.** (*supplemental*)
35a The LORD annihilated Benjamin before Israel; (*resumptive-sequential*)
35b the Israelites struck down that day twenty-five thousand and one hundred sword-wielding Benjaminites. (*complementary-focusing*)[39]
36a Then the Benjaminites saw they were defeated. (*concluding*)

Israel") has been treated as a separate sentence in the translation.

35. By juxtaposing Israel's words (v. 32cd) with those of Benjamin (v. 32ab), the narrator continues to contrast the perspectives of the warring sides.

36. The disjunctive clause in verse 33a is circumstantial in relation to verse 33c. Taken together the two clauses indicate synchronic action.

37. On the large number mentioned here, see the commentary above on 1:4. As noted there, it is difficult to accept this figure at face value. One possibility is that the Hebrew term אֶלֶף, traditionally understood as a numeral (a "thousand"), actually refers to a contingent of troops, at least in some contexts. Boling, taking this approach, translates the phrase עֲשֶׂרֶת אֲלָפִים, traditionally "ten thousand," as "ten choice contingents" in verse 34 (1975, 282). Another option is that such large numbers are hyperbolic. See Fouts 1997, 377–88, and 2003, 283–99.

38. The disjunctive clauses in verse 34bc signal a transition in the scene from the conflict to Benjamin's defeat. This is the turning point in the struggle.

39. Verse 35b gives more specific information about the battle (the number of casualties). By describing Israel's actions, it also complements the theological perspective given in verse 35a. On the large figure given, see the note at verse 34. In verse 35 Boling translates "twenty-five contingents (one hundred men)" (1975, 282). We prefer to understand a number of this nature to refer to twenty five contingents and one-tenth of another, that is 25.1 contingents.

36b The Israelites retreated before Benjamin, because they had confidence in the men they had hidden in ambush outside Gibeah. (*flashback-focusing*)[40]

37a **The men hiding in ambush acted quickly** (*dramatic*)[41]

37b and rushed to Gibeah. (*sequential*)

37c They attacked (*sequential*)

37d and put the sword to the entire city. (*sequential*)

38 **The Israelites and the men hiding in ambush had agreed to send up a smoke signal from the city.** (*supplemental*)[42]

39a The Israelites counterattacked. (*resumptive-sequential*)[43]

39b **Benjamin had begun to strike down the Israelites (about thirty Israelites fell)**[44] **for they said,** (*dramatic-flashback: shift in focus*)

39c *"There's no doubt about it! They are totally defeated as in the earlier battle."*

40a **But when the signal, a pillar of smoke, began to rise up from the city,** (*dramatic-flashback: shift in focus*)[45]

40b the Benjaminites turned around (*sequential*)

40c **and saw the whole city going up in a cloud of smoke that rose high into the sky.** (*dramatic*)[46]

41a **When the Israelites turned around,** (*dramatic-flashback: shift in focus*)[47]

---

40. Verses 36b–48 give a parallel, expanded account of verses 33–36a. The *wayyiqtol* clause in verse 36b begins this more focused account and involves a flashback to the time of the Israelite retreat (cf. vv. 32–33).

41. The disjunctive clause in verse 37a has a dramatic function; it shifts our focus from the main battle to the men hiding in ambush.

42. The disjunctive clause in verse 38 is supplemental; it gives information that is pertinent to understanding what transpires after this (vv. 39–41).

43. The *wayyiqtol* clause in verse 39a shifts the focus back to the confrontation with the main Benjaminite force. It flashes back chronologically to where verse 36 left off.

44. For the sake of English style, the prepositional phrase (literally, "about thirty men") has been treated as a parenthesis in the translation.

45. The disjunctive clause in verse 40a shifts the focus back to the scene at the city. It flashes back chronologically to where verse 37 left off.

46. The disjunctive clause in verse 40c (introduced with וְהִנֵּה, literally, "and look") has a dramatic function and invites us to witness the scene with the Benjaminites.

47. The disjunctive clause in verse 41a shifts the focus to the Israelite army. It flashes back chronologically to the event described in verse 39a.

41b the Benjaminites panicked because they could see that disaster was on their doorstep. (*sequential*)

42a They retreated before the Israelites, taking the road to the wilderness. (*sequential*)

42b **But the battle overtook them** (*contrastive*)[48]

42c **as men from the surrounding cities struck them down.** (*circumstantial*)

43a **They surrounded the Benjaminites,** (*focusing-dramatic*)[49]

43b **chased them from Nohah,** (*dramatic-sequential*)

43c **and annihilated them all the way to a spot east of Geba.**[50] (*dramatic-sequential*)

44 Eighteen thousand Benjaminites, all of them capable warriors, fell dead. (*summarizing or sequential*)[51]

45a The rest turned (*complementary*)

45b and ran toward the wilderness, heading toward the cliff of Rimmon. (*sequential*)

45c But the Israelites caught five thousand them on the main roads. (*sequential*)

45d They stayed right on their heels all the way to Gidom (*sequential*)

45e and struck down two thousand more. (*sequential*)

---

48. The disjunctive clause in verse 42b contrasts Benjamin's failure to escape with their desire to do so, reported in verse 42a.

49. The three clauses in verse 43 all begin with a perfect without a *waw*, creating a staccato style that tends to intensify the dramatic tone and highlight the actions. We are no longer reading a report, but are present at the scene witnessing the demise of Benjamin. Unfortunately, some miss the significance of the stylistic variation and propose emending the perfects to the expected, but relatively pedestrian, *wayyiqtol* forms (cf. *BHS* notes 43a, 43b, and 43d). Verse 43 gives a more detailed description of what has been reported in verse 42. See Berman 2004, 58.

50. The Hebrew text has "unto the opposite of Gibeah toward the east." Gibeah may not be correct here, since the Benjaminites retreated from there toward the desert and Rimmon (see v. 44). A slight emendation yields the reading "Geba." For a contrary opinion, see Berman 2004, 59.

51. On the large number mentioned here, see the commentary above on 1:4. As noted there, it is difficult to accept such figures at face value. One possibility is that the Hebrew term אֶלֶף, traditionally understood as a numeral (a "thousand"), actually refers to a contingent of troops, at least in some contexts. Boling, taking this approach, translates "eighteen Benjaminite contingents" in verse 44 (1975, 283). Another option is that such large numbers are hyperbolic. See Fouts 1997, 377–88, and 2003, 283–99.

46   That day twenty-five thousand sword-wielding Benjaminites fell
     in battle, all of them capable warriors. (*summarizing*)[52]
47a Six hundred survivors turned (*resumptive-sequential*)
47b and ran away to the wilderness, to the cliff of Rimmon.
     (*sequential*)
47c They stayed there four months. (*sequential*)
48a **The Israelites returned to the Benjaminite towns**
     (*dramatic-flashback: shift in focus*)[53]
48b and put the sword to them, wiping out the cities, the animals,
     and everything they could find. (*sequential*)
48c **They set fire to every city in their path**. (*concluding*)[54]

21:1a **The Israelites had taken an oath in Mizpah, saying**,
     (*introductory*)[55]
1b   *"Not one of us will allow his daughter to marry a Benjaminite."*
2a   So the people came to Bethel (*initiatory*)
2b   and sat there before God until evening, (*sequential*)
2c   weeping loudly and uncontrollably.[56] (*sequential*)
3a   They said, (*sequential*)
3b   *"Why, O LORD God of Israel, has this happened in Israel? An
     entire tribe has disappeared from Israel today!"*

4a   The next morning (*introductory-backgrounding*)[57]
4b   the people got up early (*initiatory*)
4c   and built an altar there. (*sequential*)
4d   They offered up burnt sacrifices and tokens of peace. (*sequential*)
5a   The Israelites asked,

---

52. See the note on verse 44 above.
53. The disjunctive clause in verse 48a shifts the focus from the Benjaminites
    (v. 47) back to the Israelite army. It also flashes back chronologically to
    where verse 47b left off.
54. The asyndetic disjunctive clause in verse 48c formally marks the conclu-
    sion to this scene.
55. The disjunctive clause at the beginning of verse 1 formally introduces the
    new scene. It flashes back chronologically to the time of the assembly at
    Mizpah (cf. 20:1–17).
56. The Hebrew text reads literally, "and they lifted up their voice(s) and wept
    with great weeping." Both the cognate accusative (בְכִי, "weeping") and the
    attributive adjective גָדוֹל, "great" emphasize their degree of sorrow.
57. The *wayyehi* clause at the beginning of verse 4 marks the transition to a
    new scene.

5b   *"Who from all the Israelite tribes did not assemble before the*
      *L*ORD*?"*

5c   For they recalled that they had made a solemn oath that
      whoever did not assemble before the LORD at Mizpah must
      certainly be executed.[58] *(sequential)*

6a   The Israelites regretted what had happened to their brother
      Benjamin. *(focusing-flashback)*[59]

6b   They said, *(sequential)*

6c   *"Today we cut off an entire tribe from Israel.*

7   *How can we find wives for those who are left? After all, we took*
     *an oath in the L*ORD*'s name not to give them our daughters as*
     wives."

8a   So they asked, *(sequential)*

8b   *"Who from all the Israelite tribes did not assemble before the*
      *L*ORD *at Mizpah?"*

8c   **Now it just so happened no one from Jabesh Gilead had
      come to the gathering.** *(dramatic-supplemental)*[60]

---

58. In the Hebrew text verse 5 is one long sentence in which two quotations
are embedded. The text reads literally: "The sons of Israel said, 'Who is
there who did not go up in the assembly from all the tribes of Israel to
the Lord' for a great oath there was concerning the one who did not go up
before the Lord at Mizpah, saying, 'He must surely be put to death.'"

59. The *wayyiqtol* clause in verse 6a provides the reason why Israel assembled
at Bethel to mourn. It flashes back chronologically to a time before the assembly was called (v. 2). Note how verses 6b–8a give a more detailed report
of their words (cf. v. 5) and how verse 8a is very similar to verse 5a.

60. In verse 8c, which is introduced by וְהִנֵּה, literally, "and look," the narrator
highlights the important fact that Jabesh Gilead had not sent anyone to
the assembly. But which assembly is in view? There are two options: (1)
This could refer to the assembly at Mizpah prior to the battle (20:1–3), for
the people mention this event in the preceding question (v. 8b; cf. v. 5 as
well). In this case verse 9 could refer to (a) a review of the Mizpah mustering that took place at Bethel, or to (b) the roll call that had been taken
at Mizpah prior to the battle. In favor of this latter option is the use of
the *hithpael* of פקד, which appears in 20:17 to describe how the Israelites
mustered their forces at Mizpah prior to the battle. At any rate 21:10 is
set in the time of the post-battle assembly at Bethel. (2) However, another
way of reading verses 8–10 is as follows: Wondering who might have been
missing at Mizpah, the assembly at Bethel took a roll call, found Jabesh
Gilead missing at Bethel, and then attacked the absent city. In this scenario the Israelites assumed that Jabesh Gilead's absence at Bethel meant
they had not come to Mizpah. Perhaps this is correct, but, if verse 8b refers to the assembly at Bethel, the narrator never specifically says Jabesh

9a   When they took roll call, (*resumptive-sequential*)

9b   **they noticed none of the inhabitants of Jabesh Gilead were there.** (*dramatic-reiterative*)[61]

10a   So the assembly sent twelve thousand capable warriors against Jabesh Gilead. (*consequential*)[62]

10b   They commanded them, (*focusing*)[63]

10c   *"Go and kill with your swords the inhabitants of Jabesh Gilead, including the women and little children.*

11a   *Do this: exterminate every male, as well as every woman who has been in bed with a male. But spare the lives of any virgins."*

Gilead was absent at Mizpah. Can we assume that their absence at Bethel implies this? Perhaps not, for almost four months had passed since the end of the battle (cf. 20:47 with 21:13). The clausal analysis above assumes the second scenario. If we follow the first, then we could analyze verses 8c–10a as follows, depending on which option we choose for verse 9:

Option 1a:

  8c Now it just so happened no one from Jabesh Gilead had come to the gathering. (*dramatic-supplemental / flashback*)

  9a When they reviewed the roll, (*resumptive-sequential*)

  9b they noticed none of the inhabitants of Jabesh Gilead were there. (*dramatic*)

  10a So the assembly sent twelve thousand capable warriors against Jabesh Gilead. (*consequential*)

Option 1b:

  8c Now it just so happened no one from Jabesh Gilead had come to the gathering. (*dramatic-supplemental / flashback*)

  9a When they had taken roll call, (*sequential*)

  9b they noticed none of the inhabitants of Jabesh Gilead were there. (*dramatic-reiterative*)

  10a So the assembly sent twelve thousand capable warriors against Jabesh Gilead. (*resumptive-sequential*)

61. The disjunctive clause in verse 9b (introduced by וְהִנֵּה, literally, "and look") is dramatic and reiterates verse 8c.

62. On the large number mentioned here, see the commentary above on 1:4. As noted there, it is difficult to accept such figures at face value. One possibility is that the Hebrew term אֶלֶף, traditionally understood as a numeral (a "thousand"), actually refers to a contingent of troops, at least in some contexts. Boling, taking this approach, translates "twelve contingents" in verse 10 (1975, 289). Another option is that such large numbers are hyperbolic. See Fouts 1997, 377–88, and 2003, 283–99.

63. The *wayyiqtol* clause in verse 10b tells us specifically what the Israelites told the warriors when they sent them on the mission to exterminate Jabesh Gilead.

11b So they did as instructed.[64] (*sequential*)
12a They found among the inhabitants of Jabesh Gilead four hundred young women who were virgins—they had never been in bed with a male. (*focusing*)[65]
12b They brought them back to the camp at Shiloh in the land of Canaan. (*sequential*)
13a The entire assembly sent messengers[66] to the Benjaminites at the cliff of Rimmon (*sequential*)
13b and assured them they would not be harmed. (*sequential*)
14a So the Benjaminites returned at that time, (*consequential*)
14b and the Israelites gave to them the women they had spared from Jabesh Gilead. (*sequential*)
14c **But there were not enough to go around.** (*qualifying*)[67]

15 **The people regretted what had happened to Benjamin because the Lord had weakened the Israelite tribes.** (*introductory-reiterative / flashback*)[68]
16a The leaders of the assembly said, (*sequential*)
16b *"How can we find wives for those who are left? After all, the Benjaminite women have been wiped out."*
17a They said: (*sequential*)

---

64. At the end of verse 11 some Greek witnesses add the words, "'But the virgins you should keep alive.' And they did so." These additional words can be retroverted: וְאֶת־הַבְּתוּלוֹת תְּחַיּוּ וַיַּעֲשׂוּ כֵן. A scribe's eye may have jumped from the *waw* on וְאֵת to the initial *waw* of verse 12, accidentally leaving out the intervening letters. These extra words are represented in the translation above.
65. Verse 12 tells us specifically how the warriors carried out the instruction pertaining to the virgins (cf. v. 11b, as reconstructed from the Greek witnesses). See also verse 23ab.
66. The Hebrew text has two verbs, "sent and spoke."
67. Verse 14c, which begins with a negated perfect, qualifies what precedes it by informing us that the raid on Jabesh Gilead did not yield enough wives for the Benjaminite survivors.
68. The disjunctive clause at the beginning of verse 15 formally introduces the next scene. It is also reiterative (cf. v. 6a) and flashes back chronologically to a time before the events recorded in chapter 21 (see our earlier note on v. 6a). Verse 16 catapults us back into the developing narrative to the point where verse 14bc left off.

17b   *"The remnant of Benjamin must be preserved. An entire Israelite tribe should not be wiped out.*[69]

18   *But we can't allow our daughters to marry them, for the Israelites took an oath, saying, 'Whoever gives a woman to a Benjaminite will be destroyed!'*

19   *However, there is an annual festival to the* LORD *in Shiloh, which is north of Bethel (east of the main road that goes up from Bethel to Shechem) and south of Lebonah."*

20a   So they commanded the Benjaminites, (*sequential*)

20b   "Go hide in the vineyards,

21   and keep your eyes open. When you see the daughters of Shiloh coming out to dance in the celebration, jump out from the vineyards. Each one of you, catch yourself a wife from among the daughters of Shiloh and then go home to the land of Benjamin.

22   When their fathers or brothers come and protest to us, we'll say to them, "Do us a favor and let them be, for we could not get each one a wife through battle. You would only be guilty if you had voluntarily given them wives."[70]

23a   The Benjaminites did as instructed. (*sequential*)

23b   They abducted two hundred of the young women to be their wives. (*focusing*)

23c   They went home[71] to their own territory, (*sequential*)

23d   rebuilt their cities, (*sequential*)

23e   and settled down in them. (*sequential*)

24a   Then the Israelites dispersed from there to their respective tribal and clan territories. (*complementary-flashback,* cf. v. 23c)[72]

---

69. The Hebrew text reads, "An inheritance for the remnant belonging to Benjamin, and a tribe from Israel will not be wiped away." The first statement lacks a verb. Some emend the text to read, "How can an inheritance remain for the remnant of Benjamin?"

70. The Hebrew text reads, "You did not give to them, now you are guilty." The text as it stands makes little sense. It is preferable to emend לֹא, "not," to לוּא, "if." This particle introduces a purely hypothetical condition, "If you had given to them (but you didn't), you would now be guilty." See Moore 1895, 453–54.

71. The Hebrew text has two verbs, "they went and returned."

72. Verse 24a complements verse 23c and flashes back chronologically to the action described there. As Benjamin returned home, the rest of the Israelites dispersed. It is unlikely that they waited for the Benjaminites to rebuild their cities (v. 23de) before dispersing.

24b Each went from there to his own property. (*reiterative*)[73]
25a **In those days Israel had no king**. (*concluding*)[74]
25b **Each man did what he considered to be right**.
  (*complementary*)

OUTLINE

Sodom and Gomorrah Revisited (19:1b–30)
  Retrieving a wife (19:1b–10)
  Stopping in Gibeah (19:11–15)
  Hospitality extended (19:16–21)
  Evil personified (19:22–30)
Bye Bye Benjamin! (20:1–48)
  Considering the evidence (20:1–17)
  Round one to Benjamin (20:18–21)
  Round two to Benjamin (20:22–25)
  Benjamin down and out (20:26–48)
Six Hundred Brides for Six Hundred Brothers (21:1–25)
  Feeling regret (21:1–3)
  Murder and kidnapping (21:4–14)
  Dodging a vow (21:15–25)

LITERARY STRUCTURE

The second part of the book's epilogue may be divided into three episodes: (1) the rape of the Levite's concubine (chapter 19), (2) the civil war between Benjamin and the other Israelite tribes (chapter 20), and (3) the account of how the tribes managed to find wives for the Benjaminite survivors (chapter 21).

The crime in Gibeah precipitated the civil war. The episode has four scenes: (1) the Levite's visit to Bethlehem to retrieve his concubine (19:1b–10; note the introductory וַיְהִי in v. 1b),[75] (2) the Levite's arrival

---

73. Verse 24b is reiterative; perhaps the repetition signals closure for the story.
74. The asyndetic disjunctive clause in verse 25a formally concludes the episode, the epilogue, and the book. Verse 25b complements verse 25a by explaining that the absence of effective leadership during the period produced a situation where each individual did as he pleased. See also 17:6ab.
75. Lapsley notes that the phrase "arose and went" and a reference to saddled donkeys appear in both verses 3 and 10; she suggests the presence of an inclusio (2005, 41). It appears that the scene begins in verse 1, not verse 3, but there is a movement within the scene in verse 3 as the Levite travels to and arrives in Bethlehem. It is possible that verses 1–2 function as a

and inhospitable welcome in Gibeah (vv. 11–15; note the introductory disjunctive/circumstantial clauses in v. 11 and the concluding disjunctive clause in v. 15b), (3) the hospitality of the old Ephraimite (vv. 16–21; note the introductory disjunctive clause in v. 16), and (4) the rape of the concubine (vv. 22–30; note the introductory circumstantial/disjunctive clauses in v. 22 and the concluding וְהָיָה clause in v. 30, which could be taken as introducing the next episode of the story).

The account of Israel's civil war with Benjamin (chapter 20) may be divided into two scenes. Verses 1–17 set the stage for the conflict. The Israelite tribes gathered at Mizpah, heard the Levite's testimony, and decided to confront the Benjaminites. The Benjaminites refused to hand over the culprits and mustered their forces for battle. The disjunctive clause in verse 17, which contrasts the huge size of the Israelite army with the relatively small Benjaminite army, concludes this scene.

The battle account proper appears in verses 18–48. Verses 18–36a display three panels, the structure of which may be outlined as follows:

Panel 1 (vv. 18–21)
Israel seeks divine guidance (v. 18)
Israel prepares for battle (vv. 19–20)
Benjamin attacks (v. 21)

Panel 2 (vv. 22–25)
Israel seeks divine guidance (vv. 22–23)
Israel prepares for battle (v. 24)
Benjamin attacks (v. 25)

Panel 3 (vv. 26–36a)
Israel seeks divine guidance (vv. 26–28)
Israel prepares for battle (vv. 29–30)
Benjamin attacks (v. 31)
Benjamin is tricked and defeated (vv. 32–36a)

Verses 36b–48 parallel and complement verses 29–36a. This section begins (v. 36b) and ends (v. 48) with the movements of the men of Israel. (Note the concluding disjunctive clauses in v. 48.) Disjunctive clause structures and other nonstandard grammatical constructions are used throughout this story to indicate shifts in focus, provide important parenthetical information, and highlight certain events. Verse

---

prologue to the scene, with the scene *per se* being marked out by the inclusio between verses 3 and 10.

36b tells how the main Israelite army retreated before the enemy so that the contingent lying in ambush might invade Gibeah unopposed. Verse 37 (note the introductory disjunctive structure) focuses on the Israelite ambush against Gibeah, while verse 38 parenthetically (note the disjunctive structure) tells of the prearranged signal between the ambush force and the main army. Verse 39a continues verse 36b. The disjunctive clause in verse 39b shifts the focus to Benjamin's response to the movements of the main Israelite army, while verse 40 (also introduced by a disjunctive clause) turns our attention to the smoke rising from Gibeah and Benjamin's response to the sight (note the disjunctive וְהִנֵּה clause midway through the verse). In verse 41 (introductory disjunctive clause again) the main Israelite army turns to charge, causing Benjamin to turn back in panic (vv. 41b–42a). A disjunctive clause (v. 42b) begins the description of Benjamin's defeat, which utilizes three *qatal* (perfect) verb forms (v. 43) before switching to the usual *wayyiqtol* narrative pattern (vv. 44–45). The וַיְהִי clause in verse 46 introduces the concluding section (note that vv. 17b, 35b, and 46b all refer to men who draw the sword).

Chapter 21 describes the aftermath of the battle. It tells how Israel managed to preserve the tribe of Benjamin from extinction by finding wives for the six hundred fugitives hiding at the rock of Rimmon. There are three distinct scenes: Verses 1–3 tell how Israel went to Bethel after the battle and lamented that one entire tribe was nearly extinct (note the disjunctive clause at the beginning of v. 1). Verses 4–14 record the campaign against Jabesh Gilead that yielded four hundred wives for the Benjaminite fugitives. (Note the introductory וַיְהִי and change of temporal setting in v. 4a.) Finally verses 15–25 tell how the remaining two hundred fugitives acquired wives by kidnapping some of the daughters of Shiloh. The scene begins with a disjunctive clause and ends with the Israelites returning to their homes (v. 24). The statement, "In those days Israel had no king; everyone did what he considered right" (v. 25; cf. 17:6) is a fitting conclusion to the epilogue.

EXPOSITION

Sodom and Gomorrah Revisited (19:1b–30)

Retrieving a wife (19:1b–10). This story provides another example of the anarchy that swept over Israel during this leaderless period in the nation's history. The first few verses of the account give background information essential to the story. A Levite (note the thematic connection to chapters 17–18, where a Levite also plays an important role), who was temporarily residing in a remote area of the Ephraimite hill country, acquired a concubine from Bethlehem in Judah. She became angry with him and returned to her father's house in Bethlehem. The Hebrew verb זנה is traditionally interpreted to mean "commit adultery, be unfaithful" (see NIV) but this verb never appears elsewhere with the preposition עַל introducing the party violated by an adulterous act (Burney 1970, 460).[76] Codex Alexandrinus has "she was angry at him;" the verb may be cognate to Akkadian *zenû* "be angry, hate."[77] This quarrel between husband and wife may seem like a minor incident that simply provides necessary background for the following story. But it has an important foreshadowing function. As Niditch points out, the story will trace a progression "from trouble between a man and his wife, to a symbolically potent instance of trouble between anti-social Israelites and the man, which in turn leads to a massive civil war, the disintegration of Israelite society as a whole" (1982, 371).

After four months the Levite went to Bethlehem to try to convince her to come back. The parenthetical note about the Levite's servant and donkeys lends a touch of realism to the story and shows that the Levite does have some means. The concubine's father was glad to meet the Levite and treated him in a very hospitable manner—entertaining him for three days. When the Levite decided to leave on the fourth day, the concubine's father talked him into staying another night.[78] The next morning he urged the Levite to postpone his departure until after-

---

76. The verb is collocated with עַל in Ezekiel 16:15–16, but in verse 15 the preposition has a causal force (literally, "you committed adultery on account of your fame") and in verse 16 it is locative (literally, "you committed adultery upon them" [the high places just mentioned]). In Hosea 9:1 זנה מֵעַל, literally, "commit adultery from upon" is used of Israel being unfaithful to God. The verb can also be collocated with מֵאַחֲרֵי, "from after" (Hos. 1:2), מִתַּחַת, "from under" (Hos. 4:12), and מִן, "from" (Ps. 73:27) to indicate that one has committed adultery against a partner. For a defense of the traditional reading, see Wong 2006a, 108–11. Reis understands the expression זנה עַל in the sense of "whored for him" and argues that the Levite was an ancient Israelite pimp who "was prostituting his wife" (2006, 129). This suggestion borders on the absurd.

77. See *HALOT*, 275, which suggests the connotation "feel repugnance" here, as well as Cohen 1978, 130, and Butler 2009, 407, 418–19. On the lack of the expected apocopation in the third-*he* form, see GKC, 211–12 (para. 75t).

78. The expression "refresh your heart" (literal translation) in verses 5 and 8 also appears in Genesis 18:5, where Abraham treats the angelic visitors with great hospitality.

noon.[79] After the midday meal, he suggested the Levite stay one more night, but the Levite insisted on leaving this time and headed toward Jebus (=Jerusalem) with his concubine.

What is the literary purpose of this first scene? The answer becomes apparent by the end of the chapter. This folksy, realistic introduction to the story stresses the father's hospitable attitude. He simply would not allow the Levite to leave until he was adequately fed and rested. His hospitality will serve as a literary foil to the treatment the Levite receives in Gibeah, for it places the heinous deed of the men of Gibeah against the backdrop of the societal ideal (Block 1999, 527). Of course, irony is also present, for the father's hospitality led to a delayed departure that caused the travelers to turn into Gibeah as night fell (Marais 1998, 138–39).[80]

Stopping in Gibeah (19:11–15). As the Levite approached Jebus, the servant suggested they stop there for the night.[81] The Levite was not willing to do this for he did not trust the Jebusites.[82] Instead he decided to press on to a Benjaminite city, where he expected to be safe. As the sun went down, they arrived in Gibeah and sat down in the city square, where travelers apparently stayed if they had no lodging (cf. Gen. 19:2). The disjunctive clause at the end of verse 15 has a foreboding tone, for it suggests something was wrong in Gibeah. Its citizens did not seem to be concerned about the time-honored principle of hospitality, just epitomized so well by the concubine's father.

---

79. The verb translated "convinced" in verse 7 also appears in Genesis 19:3, where it describes how hospitable Lot insisted that the angels stay with him. It is also used in Genesis 19:9 of the Sodomites' attempt to break down Lot's door.

80. Lapsley draws attention to the concubine's absence in verses 4–10; this seems odd in light of the fact that the Levite's goal in traveling to Bethlehem was to win back her affections (2005, 40–42). Lapsley contends that "the narrator is subtly guiding the reader to evaluate the behavior of the Levite in a critical light" (p. 42).

81. On the important role that temporal setting plays in the story, see Fields 1992. The fact that they arrive in Gibeah at night is ominous, for "night was the time for crime, and thus a time of danger" (p. 31).

82. According to Judges 1:21, the Benjaminites had not been able to dislodge the Jebusites from Jerusalem. Fokkelman shows that the dialogue between the Levite and the servant is arranged in a chiastic structure, with the central element being the Levite's remark about the Jebusites not being of Israel (1999, 110). This highlights his prejudice, but also sets us up for the ironic development to follow.

Hospitality extended (19:16–21). The next scene relieves the tension somewhat. An old man, a temporary resident of Gibeah who, like the Levite, had come from the hill country of Ephraim, approached the travelers and asked about their itinerary. The Levite's response (v. 18) mentions the "house of Yahweh," though the Septuagint has simply "my house" here. Perhaps the Levite intended to visit Shiloh (cf. 18:31) or Bethel (cf. 20:18) before going home, but it is also possible that the Hebrew text reflects a misinterpretation of the first person suffix as an abbreviation for Yahweh (Moore 1895, 415–16).[83] The Levite explained that they had everything they needed, but the old man urged them to spend the night with him, expressed his willingness to feed them, and took them to his house, where they washed their feet and enjoyed a meal.

Perhaps our first impressions are wrong; maybe hospitality was still alive and well. The language of verses 21b–22a even echoes that of verses 6, 8–9, possibly lulling us into thinking the Levite would enjoy the same kind of hospitality in Gibeah as he did in the home of his father-in-law.[84] However, there are some foreboding elements in this account. The travelers' encounter with the old man sounds a lot like the introduction to Genesis 19, where Lot insists that the travelers stay with him, not in the street, and treats his visitors with great hospitality (vv. 1–3). In that case, Lot's hospitality was the calm before the storm. Will the same be the case here? After all, the old Ephraimite, like Lot, was not a full-fledged citizen of the town in which he resided and the reality described in verse 15b still lurks in the background. No native resident of Gibeah reached out to the travelers; perhaps this lack of concern for hospitality was merely a symptom of an even greater evil that was present in the town.

Evil personified (19:22–30). Our worst suspicions are now realized. The men of the city surrounded the house, pounded on the door, and

---

83. Lapsley is not convinced that the Levite is being honest here (2005, 43). She suggests that his statement may be "a mere façade of piety, offered for the consumption of the old man to make the Levite appear more sympathetic." Lapsley also observes that the Levite uses the first person singular "me" in verse 18 when stating that no one had invited them in, while the narrator uses the plural "them" when making the same observation in verse 15. She suggests that the narrator is already depicting the Levite as "one who cares more for himself than he does for those in his care."

84. On the verbal parallels and their thematic significance, see Niditch 1982, 367.

insisted that the old man send out the Levite so they could sexually abuse him.[85] The old man urged them not to do such a disgraceful thing and then, before waiting for a response, desperately offered them his own virgin daughter and the Levite's concubine.[86] Apparently his sense of hospitality toward travelers extended primarily to males! When the men outside refused to listen, the Levite grabbed his concubine and threw her to the wolves, who brutally raped her all night long.[87]

---

85. Basing his opinion on anthropological research, Stone argues that there is more involved here than mere sexual desire. It is also an issue "of power (the men of Gibeah wish to express their power over the Levite) and honor (the men of Gibeah wish to bring dishonor and shame upon the Levite)" (1996, 75–79, especially p. 79). See also Hackett 2004, 361–62; and Niditch 2008. 193. A modern parallel occurs in the homosexual rape scene in the film "Deliverance." See Reis 2006, 138–39.

86. The term נְבָלָה, "disgraceful," is also used of rape in Genesis 34:7, where Dinah's brothers accuse Shechem of violating their sister, and in 2 Samuel 13:12, where Tamar urges her half-brother Amnon not to force himself upon her. For a helpful discussion see Butler 2009, 424.

87. Who turned the concubine over to the rapists—the old man or the Levite? Verse 25 attributes this action simply to "the man." In the immediate context the Levite is called "a man" (v. 1), "the man" (vv. 6–7, 9–10, 28), "the man who was traveling" (v. 17), "the man who came to your house" (v. 22), and "this man" (vv. 23–24). The old man is called "an old man" (v. 16), "the man" (vv. 16, 26), "the old man" (vv. 17, 20, 22), and "the man, the owner of the house" (v. 23). On the surface it seems as if either the Levite or the old man could be the subject in verse 25. Certain factors might favor seeing the old man as the referent. The old man is the subject of two verbs in verse 23 ("went outside and said"), while the Levite has not been the subject of a verb in the narrative framework since verse 18. (He is the subject of the verb "came" in verse 22b, but this is within a quotation.) However, a closer look at the language of the text suggests the Levite was the one who turned the concubine over to the crowd. In verse 23 the old man goes out (יֵצֵא) to the men and speaks to them. There is no indication the Levite or the concubine accompanied him. In fact, the old man promises to "bring out" (v. 24, *hiphil* of יצא) his daughter and the concubine, indicating they were still inside. Since verse 25 describes "the man" sending/bringing the concubine out (*hiphil* of יצא again), one might think that the old man went back into the house and retrieved her. But the text gives no indication of this. It is more likely that the Levite, standing inside the house, heard what the old man had said, saw the crowd's refusal to accept his proposal, and pushed the concubine out to the men, perhaps thinking that the sight of her would change their minds. Stuart, who understands the old man as the referent in verse 25, suggests the Levite was not aware of what was going on and was in a back room (2001, 51–52). Stuart's proposed

In verse 22 NIV gives the impression that this group of thugs did not encompass the entire male population of the town. The Hebrew text (אַנְשֵׁי הָעִיר אַנְשֵׁי בְנֵי־בְלִיַּעַל) has two parts: (a) literally, "the men of the city," and (b) literally, "men who were sons of wickedness." Within (b) the phrase בְנֵי־בְלִיַּעַל, "sons of wickedness" is appositional to the immediately preceding construct form אַנְשֵׁי, "men of," and specifies what type of men they were. This entire expression is appositional to אַנְשֵׁי הָעִיר, "the men of the city." Does (b) specify the more general (a) and refer to the "local hell-raisers" (the phrase is Boling's) among the larger population, or does (b) equate the two groups and characterize the entire male population as wicked?[88] Judges 20:5 (cf. בַּעֲלֵי הַגִּבְעָה, "leaders of Gibeah") seems to include the leaders of the town among the perpetrators, but this is the Levite's version of the story, which may be altered for effect (Webb 1987, 190–91; Wenham 2004, 68). Judges 20:13, which places הָאֲנָשִׁים, "the men," in apposition to בְנֵי־בְלִיַּעַל, "sons of wickedness," is ambiguous. The phrase "sons of wickedness" elsewhere describes the vilest kind of societal and/or moral riffraff (see Deut. 13:13; 1 Sam. 2:12; 10:27; 25:17; 2 Sam. 23:6; 1 Kings 21:10–13).[89]

---

scenario seems unlikely. The old man's reference to "this man" (v. 23) suggests the Levite may have been standing near the door and was visible to the crowd. There are other arguments suggesting the Levite is the subject. The Levite's actions in verse 29 seem to mirror those described in verse 25, suggesting he is the subject in both cases (see our discussion of v. 29). The closest syntactical parallel to verse 25 appears in 2 Samuel 1:11, where we read וַיַּחֲזֵק דָּוִד בִּבְגָדָיו, "and David grabbed his clothes." Here David is both the subject of the verb (*hiphil* of חזק, as in Judg. 19:25) and the antecedent of the pronoun on the object. In the same way it is most natural to take "the man" in Judges 19:25 as both the subject of the verb ("grabbed") and the antecedent of the pronoun on the object ("his wife"). See also Webb 1987, 262, note 25; and Block 1999, 539.

88. Amit (1999, 344) and Block (1999, 535–36) favor the latter position.
89. The term בְלִיַּעַל, "wickedness," appears as a modifier of בֵּן, "son of" (or בְּנֵי, "sons of"), אִישׁ, "man of," אָדָם, "man of," or בַּת, "daughter of." It is used to characterize rebels against God (Deut. 13:14; 1 Sam. 2:12) or against God's chosen king (1 Sam. 10:27; 25:17, 25; 2 Sam. 16:7; 20:1; 2 Chron. 13:7). It describes those who spread dissension or plot evil (1 Sam. 30:22; Prov. 6:12; 16:27; Nah. 1:11; 2:1) and refers to liars or cheaters, often in the context of social injustice (Deut. 15:9; 1 Sam. 2:12; 1 Kings 21:10, 13; Job 34:18; Ps. 101:3; Prov. 19:28). In 1 Samuel 1:16 Hannah is concerned that Eli will take her for a drunken "daughter of Belial" who shows no respect for a holy shrine. In summary, the term is associated with rebellion against authority and with other heinous crimes that result in societal disorder and anarchy. It describes those who oppose God and the moral/

In the morning the battered and dehumanized concubine stumbled back to the house and fell down in the doorway. When the Levite, who is called her "master,"[90] opened the door to leave and continue his trip home, he found her sprawled on the doorway with her hands grasping the threshold.[91] Her posture showed she was desperately seeking shelter when she fell, and it indicates she was too weak to open or even knock on the door.[92] As if nothing had happened, the Levite commanded her

---

ethical order he has established. They show no fear of God and promote chaos and destruction. See Maag 1965, 294–95.

90. In verses 26–27 the plural form of אָדוֹן, "master," is used. If this is a so-called plural of respect or degree, it would emphasize his absolute authority over his concubine. (The plural form also appears in vv. 11–12, where it is used of the Levite's status in relation to his servant.) Burnett prefers to understand the plural form of אָדוֹן as a "concretized abstract plural" that "can be used in reference to a single individual or object that is exemplary of the quality named and to which a corresponding status applies." He suggests the translation "lord(ship)" (2001, 21–22). In this case it would still seem that some degree of emphasis is expressed, as in English when one addresses a superior as "your lordship." On the theme of the concubine's subservience to the Levite and the other men in the story, see Ackerman 1998, 236–39. Stone notes how the woman's role in the story changes abruptly. At the beginning she is active; she leaves the Levite. But then he retrieves her with no indication that she agreed to return. From this point on she is passive, subject to the will of the males in the story. He theorizes that the woman's "initial actions are recounted in part to cast doubt upon the Levite's character" (1996, 73–74). Müllner, who understands the chapter's initial description of the concubine in a sexual sense, states: "Inasmuch as the narrative casts the Levite's wife's acts in a negative light, she is not constructed as a blameless victim" (1999, 138). However, as noted above, the reading in verse 2 is debated and, as Stone suggests, her actions may say more about the Levite than herself. The Levite is the primary focus of the story (note v. 1), while the concubine is an agent, literarily speaking.

91. Ironically, the participial form of נֹפֵל (see v. 27) also appears in Judges 3:25 and 4:22 to describe the fallen enemies Eglon and Sisera, respectively. Though perhaps being overly creative, Bal sees the verb "he opened" (וַיִּפְתַּח) in verse 27 as echoing the name of Jephthah (יִפְתָּח), another male character in the story whose actions led to the death of an innocent female (1993, 223).

92. Reis observes that "her lord and the old host were not waiting up anxiously, keeping watch for any sound of her. They were most likely fast asleep in a drunken stupor after making their hearts merry (v. 22). And with no aid, no tender nursing, no one to care, and probably no will to live, the concubine dies" (2006, 142).

to get up so they could be on their way, but she failed to respond.[93] The Levite threw her on a donkey and returned to his home.

Lapsley points out that the Levite's command to his wife in verse 28 are the first words he has spoken to her in the story. She states: "Recalling once again the Levite's initial intention to speak to the heart of his wife [cf. v. 3], the irony that these are his first words to his wife, spoken to her prostrate form, could not be more stark" (2005, 49). Indeed his first interaction with her in the story was when he threw her to the mob. In this regard, Lapsley notes: "The narrator to this point has taken pains to depict the Levite as utterly indifferent to his wife, despite his initial intention to 'speak to her heart.' Seizing her and throwing her to the mob thus conforms to what we know of his character" (46). In verse 27 the narrator simply calls her "the woman" because she is no longer "defined by her relationships with the men who have abandoned her" (47).

Oddly enough the narrator does not tell us she was actually dead (Polzin 1980, 200).[94] Unlike Judges 3:25 and 4:22, where the participle of נפל, "to fall," is followed by מֵת, "dead," there is no qualifying word in 19:27.[95] The short statement אֵין עֹנֶה, "there was no response" (v. 28) is not a technical expression for death. Elsewhere it simply indicates there was no response to someone's words.[96] Later the narrator refers to her as "the murdered woman" (20:4), but we are forced to ask, "Murdered by whom?" (Schneider 2000, 266–67)[97] The Levite attributes

---

93. On the calloused, matter-of-fact behavior of the Levite, see Lasine 1984, 44–45; Webb 1987, 190; Schneider 2000, 263–64; Exum 1993a, 195–96; and Block 1999, 540–41. Niditch aptly observes that his "insensitivity towards his concubine, his non-communication with her, his selfishness are, in fact, a microcosm of larger community-relationships in Israel. He does not take care of her, the townspeople of Gibeah do not take care of him" (1982, 371).

94. Lasine disagrees with Polzin, arguing, "there is little doubt that *the reader* is meant to conclude that the concubine was dead" (1984, 45).

95. Codex Vaticanus adds, "for she was dead," in verse 28 after the words "and she did not answer," but this is most likely an interpretive gloss. For a contrary opinion see Boling, who argues that כי מתה, "for she was dead," was omitted by homoioteleuton (1975, 276). Josipovici objects on literary grounds to this proposal (1988, 115).

96. See 1 Samuel 14:39; 1 Kings 18:26, 29; Isaiah 50:2; 66:4.

97. Block, observing that the term רצח refers primarily to premeditated murder, suggests this makes it more likely that the Levite actually killed her, for the men of Gibeah intended to rape, not kill (1999, 553). He asks: "If her death was a secondary effect of their violence, would it be called

her death to the mob violence she experienced (20:5), but can we trust his version of what happened? (Webb 1987, 191; Block 1999, 541)

When he got home the Levite cut her body into twelve parts, and sent one part to each of the twelve tribes of Israel as a shocking object lesson of what had occurred.[98] Two of the verbs used in verse 25 reappear here (Trible 1984, 80). In verse 25 the Levite grabbed (*hiphil* of חזק) the concubine and threw her outside; here he grabs (*hiphil* of חזק again) her body to cut it up (Olson 1998, 877–78). In verse 25 the *piel* of שלח, "send," describes how the rapists let the concubine go in the morning; here it describes how the Levite sent her bodily parts to the tribes. Is the verbal repetition coincidental or ironic? When the rest of Israel saw the evidence, they recognized this was the most heinous crime ever committed in Israel and that some type of action was necessary.[99]

The parallels between this story and Genesis 19 are unmistakable.[100]

---

murder?" However, as Block acknowledges, the verb can be used of unpremeditated, accidental killing. Furthermore, the narrator may wish to emphasize that the men of Gibeah, despite their stated intention, were guilty of murder because such a violent act jeopardized the life of the victim. After all, stated motive for an action is not always a legitimate legal defense if that action inherently carries the potential to do more harm than what the perpetrator intended or expected.

98. The Levite's action is similar to that of Saul, who cut a pair of oxen into pieces and sent them throughout Israel with this warning: "Whoever does not go out after Saul and after Samuel should expect this to be done to his oxen!" (1 Sam. 11:7) The Levite may have been communicating a similar warning to the Israelite tribes, perhaps suggesting that they would experience severe divine judgment if they did not execute justice. There are examples in ancient Near Eastern literature of treaty rituals where an animal would be cut up as a warning of what would happen to those who violated the treaty. See Sparks 2005, 444.

99. We should probably assume that some type of explanation accompanied the body parts. However, Exum suggests that the tribes refer specifically to the dismemberment in Judges 19:30 and 20:3 (1993a, 187). Reis argues that the Levite chopped up the woman into twelve parts, symbolizing "the rending and disunion of the twelve tribes of Israel," and sent all twelve pieces of the chopped up body to the tribes in succession (2006, 142–43). She also points out that the Levite, by not immediately burying the concubine, violated the Deuteronomic law (cf. Deut. 21:23) (2006, 145).

100. For charts showing the verbal parallels between Genesis 19 and Judges 19, see Burney 1970, 444–45; O'Connell 1996, 250–52; and Block 1990, 326–31, and 1999, 532–34. For a helpful discussion of the parallels, see Klein 1988, 165–72.

Gibeah had become the new Sodom, populated by thugs who were morally blind. Like Lot, the old man attempted to preserve his honor and follow the law of hospitality by offering two women to the men outside his door. However, in subtle ways, his offer is more calloused than Lot's (Lasine 1984, 39). Lot offered his two daughters; the old man offered his daughter and another man's concubine.[101] Furthermore, Lot told the Sodomites: "Do to them whatever you please" (Gen. 19:8; literally, "do to them according to what is good in your eyes"). The old man uses almost identical words (Judg. 19:24, literally, "do them what is good in your eyes"), but he prefaces this with the words: "I will send them out and you can abuse them."[102]

Lot's and the old man's actions must not be justified by an appeal to cultural norms. Rather in each case their desperation was a symptom of a society that had reached the uttermost moral depths. Something is drastically wrong when men place strict adherence to a societal norm over the life of a fellow human being. After all, as Reis observes, "Men are bound in honor, duty, and affection to protect the weaker and more vulnerable members of their families" (2006, 140).[103]

Of course, the story's shock effect is not limited to the Sodom-like actions of the men of Gibeah or the Lot-like offer of two women to the would-be rapists. The old man actually offered one of his visitors (the female one) to the thugs, and the Levite's cold-hearted selfishness and lack of compassion are chilling. While we certainly sympathize with the Levite's sense of outrage, we must also ask: Was he really fundamentally different from the men of Gibeah? Or, was he tainted by the same disease that had reached its terminal stage in Gibeah? Indeed, as the rest of the story unfolds, we discover that all Israel had become more like Gibeah (and Sodom) than they realized.

One of the notable features of this story is the anonymity of the characters. What is the significance of this? According to Hudson, the

---

101. Despite the old man's offer, only the Levite's concubine is handed over. Stone argues that the crowd accepts this because they want to dishonor the Levite, not the old man (1996, 81–82).

102. The *piel* of the verb עָנָה, "abuse," is used of rape elsewhere (Gen. 34:2; Deut. 22:29; 2 Sam. 13:12, 14, 22, 32; Lam. 5:11).

103. Reis rightly objects to those interpreters who argue that the narrator justifies the actions of the old man and the Levite. She states: "Genesis 19 and Judges 19 are not manuals for how to act in an emergency, nor do they manifest Israelite rules of hospitality or express patriarchal dominance. They exemplify monstrous behavior and breach of God's rules. . . . the text neither suppresses nor endorses the pitiless actions of Lot and the Levite" (2006, 140–41).

narrator uses anonymity in this story (as well as in chapters 20–21) "to epitomize familial, tribal and national deterioration" (1994, 54). He contends that the characters' anonymity universalizes them. He states: "Anonymity gives the implicit impression that *every* individual within Israel was dangerous because every individual was doing right in his or her own eyes" (60). He adds: "Moreover, by viewing the anonymity of the concubine the reader gets the impression that 'every' concubine from Dan to Beersheba could be raped, murdered and dismembered" (60).[104] Hudson argues that anonymity has a second role in these chapters. He points out that Israel during this period "was a world of alienation and annihilation" populated by "the powerful abuser and the powerless victim" (61). In such a context "anonymity parallels the loss of identity and personhood" (59; cf. Block 1999, 518).

In a similar vein Reinhartz, focusing on the concubine, sees the woman's anonymity as "symbolic of her silence, the progressive passivity attributed to her, and the tragic fate with which the story culminates." She adds: "These features combine to efface her identity and her very existence. That this woman is silenced, denied subjectivity, erased, and scattered, both by the men in the story and by the storyteller, is clear. At the very least, anonymity symbolizes this denial of her identity and personhood" (1998, 125).

How could God stand idly by and allow the men of Gibeah to commit this horrific crime against the concubine? Unterman sees God's silence as evidence that Gibeah was "a town abandoned by God" (1980, 164). He attempts to demonstrate that Judges 19 contains verbal echoes of "the Binding of Isaac" (Gen. 22) (161–64; cf. Trible 1984, 80). The narrator intends to contrast God's intervention for Isaac with his silence in Gibeah in order to highlight the fact that Gibeah was "a town unfit for man or God" (164).[105]

Bowman addresses the problem of God's silence from a theological angle: "Like that of Jephthah's daughter, this story suggests that a human act of self-preservation results in innocent suffering. When

---

104. See also Reis, who states: "The technique of namelessness illustrates the disintegration and dehumanization of society while it universalizes the characters in this sordid story. The Levite, the father, the old host, and the men of Gibeah are paradigmatic perpetrators, unforgivable, earning and deserving the contempt of history. And the nameless woman, immortalized, represents every victim—man, woman, or child—of the tyranny of the strong over the weak" (2006, 146).

105. Unterman argues that the narrator does this as part of his anti-Saul polemic.

human beings are irresponsible in exercising their freedom, God does not intervene. Instead God allows divine power to be constrained." He adds: "The Epilogue thus confirms and intensifies the emerging portrait of God in Judges, one in which the deity refrains from intervention in order to preserve the exercise of human freedom, even if that exercise results in innocent victims. It also confirms and intensifies the emerging portrayal of human beings as flawed in the exercise of their freedom. The narrator's portrayals stress human responsibility, not divine accountability, and emphasize responsible human interaction, not responsive divine intervention" (1995, 41). However, as Bowman observes, God is not entirely silent in this story. As in the story of Abimelech, he does not prevent the crime from taking place, but he does eventually intervene as judge, as we shall see (41–42).

Bye Bye Benjamin! (20:1–48)

Considering the evidence (20:1–17). Having seen with their own eyes the gory evidence of the crime, the Israelite tribes gathered in force at Mizpah, located near Gibeah.[106] Because of its fairly central location Mizpah was an ideal spot for the tribes to gather.[107] The language in verses 1–2 is exaggerated, for there was one tribe missing. The Benjaminites, who had received one of the concubine's body parts (19:29), heard about the gathering, but did not go. This hints at their hostile and isolationist attitude toward the other tribes.

When the tribes asked for the details of the crime, the Levite gave them an account of what had happened to him and his concubine in Gibeah. In light of his rather calloused treatment of the concubine the morning after the crime, one suspects the Levite was primarily concerned with his own honor.[108] In his report to the tribes he focused on the mob's treatment of him (note "attacked me . . . to kill me" in v. 5)

---

106. Judges 20:1 speaks of the nation's boundaries being from Dan (in the north) to Beersheba (in the south). On the surface this suggests that the Danite migration described in chapter 18 had already occurred. However, it is possible that the idiomatic phrase simply reflects the geographical reality of a (later) time, when the book was written or put together. The date of the story depends on how one interprets Judges 20:27–28. See our discussion of these verses in the text below.

107. See 1 Samuel 7:5; 10:17. This is a different Mizpah than the one referred to in Judges 10–11.

108. See Stone 1995, 101; as well as Ackerman 1998, 239; Block 1999, 554; and Yee 1995a, 166.

and spoke of the concubine as belonging to him (note "my wife" in vv. 5–6) (Lapsley 2005, 51). He identified the culprits as the "leaders of Gibeah." If this is correct, it speaks volumes about the societal disintegration in Gibeah. But the Levite may have stretched the facts in his zeal to see justice served.[109] The Levite also said that the men of Gibeah wanted to kill him. This is an overstatement, though certainly understandable in light of what happened to the concubine.[110] It may also have been an attempt to diminish his role in the concubine's death.[111] He did not tell the tribal assembly that the men of Gibeah wanted to sexually abuse him or that he turned the concubine over to the mob.[112] But just in case they subsequently found out about that detail of the story, this claim that his life was in jeopardy could be used to justify his behavior. Having conveniently failed to mention how the mob got hold of the concubine, he told how they raped her, causing her death. In describing the crime he used the *piel* of עָנָה, "abused," the term employed by the old man when he offered the women to the crowd (see 19:24).[113] Oddly enough, the tribal representatives did not ask him to fill the logical gap in his testimony at this point. Did they not wonder how an attempt on the Levite's life ended up with his concubine being raped? (Klein 1988, 177)[114] Leaving out the details of how he discovered her body, the Levite told how he cut her corpse into pieces and distributed the body parts throughout the land. He concluded by challenging the tribes to decide on a wise and just course of action.

In a rare display of unity the tribes decided to muster an army and

---

109. See Klein, who considers this aspect of the Levite's report to be a fabrication (1988, 177).
110. Moore defends this statement as essentially correct (1895, 424). Klein calls it "an outright lie" (1988, 177), but this charge seems a bit strong. Stone argues that the Levite's claim makes sense in light of what happened to his concubine (1996, 83).
111. Webb suggests that the Levite, by emphasizing the personal threat, diminished his own responsibility for what happened (1987, 191).
112. On this important point, see Lasine 1984, 49, as well as Exum 1993a, 186; and Reis 2006, 145.
113. This term was not used, however, in the actual narrative of the concubine's rape in Judges 19:25. See Gravett 2004, 284.
114. As Webb observes: "In the absence of further information, what he says could conjure up a totally different scenario from the actual one, namely: his life was threatened; he escaped, but his concubine was caught and raped; he later recovered her body, and so on" (1987, 191).

march against Gibeah.[115] They sent messengers throughout Benjamin explaining what had happened and demanded that the perpetrators of the crime be handed over for execution. However, blood ties were apparently more important to Benjamin than justice. The Benjaminites refused to cooperate with the rest of Israel and gathered their forces to defend Gibeah, even though they were hopelessly outnumbered. The statement in verse 13b, לֹא אָבוּ, "(the Benjaminites) refused to listen," echoes 19:25, where the same expression is used to describe how the men of Gibeah initially rejected the old man's offer of the two women (Matthews 2004, 194).

The reference to the seven hundred left-handed slingers is quite ironic, for this contingent would oppose Israel's armies in the approaching battle, in stark contrast to Ehud, another Benjaminite left-hander who led Israel to a great victory over the Moabites.[116] The notation may be somewhat foreboding, suggesting that Benjamin, though greatly outnumbered, had weapons available that would diminish to some extent their numerical disadvantage.[117]

Round one to Benjamin (20:18–21). Before going into battle Israel went to Bethel, where the ark of the covenant was located and Phinehas the priest ministered (see vv. 27–28), to ask God (*Elohim*, not *Yahweh*, is used) who should lead the army into battle. The Lord replied that Judah was to take the lead. This scene is reminiscent of the book's introduction, where the tribes asked the Lord who should lead them

---

115. On the irony involved see Butler 2009, 440–41. Lapsley writes: "The book that has depicted the chaotic disorganization of the tribes, and that has been pointing toward a time when the tribes would be unified . . . now presents the tribes unified—except, crucially, for Benjamin. And that exception is the root of the irony in the repetitions of 'as one man': the unity evoked by this phrase leads to the worst violence yet in Judges and to a civil war that further wounds and fractures Israel. It is a bogus unity that renders real unity even more remote" (2005, 52).

116. The phrase אִטֵּר יַד־יְמִינוֹ, literally, "bound in his right hand," is used in both Judges 3:15 and 20:16. On the construction and use of the ancient sling, see King and Stager 2001, 228–29. In the hands of a trained warrior, the sling was a deadly long-range weapon. Sling stones found at Lachish are smooth and round, and made of flint; each is six to seven centimeters in diameter (= approximately 2.34–2.73 inches) and weighs approximately 250 grams (= 8.75 ounces). King and Stager estimate one could propel a sling stone at a speed of 160–240 kilometers/hour (= 99.2–148.8 miles/hour).

117. On the figure four-hundred thousand, see the note on the translation of verse 17a above.

against the Canaanites and he picked out Judah. The irony is obvious and tragic. At the beginning of the book, Israel was prepared to unite against the common foe; now at the end of the book the original ideal had failed to materialize, Israel had descended to the moral level of Sodom, and the tribes were forced to take action against one of their own brothers.[118] Any unity between the tribes was "hollow" (Guest 1997, 265).

As noted above, verse 27 indicates the ark of the covenant was at Bethel at this time. This is difficult to harmonize with the following passages: (1) Joshua 18:1, which tells how Joshua set up the tent of meeting (which housed the ark, see Exod. 30:26; 31:7; Num. 7:89; 1 Kings 8:4) in Shiloh, (2) Joshua 22:12–13, which locates Phinehas son of Eleazar (cf. Judg. 20:28) at Shiloh, (3) Judges 18:31, which indicates the house of God was at Shiloh during the period of the judges, and (4) 1 Samuel 4:4, which locates the ark in Shiloh at the time of Eli. Block suggests that the Israelites had transported the ark to Bethel for the occasion as a symbol of God's powerful presence (cf. 1 Samuel 4) (Block 1999, 561; Soggin 1981, 293; Younger 2002, 373). However, the language of the text ("The ark of God's covenant was there in *those days*") suggests that Bethel was the regular location of the ark during the time period when these events occurred.[119] The phrase "in those days" refers in this context to the pre-monarchic era or at least to the period described in chapters 17–21 (see 17:6; 18:1; 19:1; 21:25).[120] Furthermore, if the ark had been taken from its normal place, why would it not be with the Israelites at Mizpah? Merrill suggests that the central cult site moved at some point during this period from Shiloh to Bethel and back (1987, 181, note 93). Since we do not have all of the

---

118. See Marais 1998, 140; Block 1999, 568–69; and McCann 2002, 134–35. Wong points out that the "remarkable similarities" between the "oracular inquiries" in 1:2 and 20:18 actually serve to draw attention to "the stark difference in outcome, thereby forcing an alert reader to look for plausible explanations to account for that difference" (2006a, 34). Due to the contrasting portraits of Judah in the prologue and epilogue, Bledstein sees "the closing of Judges" as "a parody of the opening" (1993, 52).

119. To alleviate this problem Block restricts "those days" to "the days of the first two battles described in vv. 18–25" (1999, 561).

120. As noted in the introduction to the commentary, both the Danite migration and the civil war with Benjamin appear to have occurred very early in the Judges period.

facts about this period, this is certainly possible, but there is no evidence to corroborate it.[121]

The mention of Phinehas may facilitate a literary association with an earlier incident, recorded in Joshua 22:10–34.[122] On that occasion the Israelites heard a rumor of cultic impropriety on the part of the Transjordanian tribes. The western tribes sent Phinehas and ten tribal representatives to investigate the matter. They reminded the eastern tribes of the Achan incident, which demonstrated that the sin of one can have serious repercussions for the entire nation (Josh. 22:20). When the eastern tribes offered a reasonable defense of their actions, they were exonerated and a civil war was averted. But in Judges 20 Phinehas plays no role; his name is merely mentioned in passing. The tribes rush to judgment and make hasty vows. The Benjaminites, unlike the Transjordanian tribes in the earlier story, elevate tribal loyalty above national unity, even when it means harboring criminals. Rather than being reconciled, the participants fight a bloody civil war.[123]

The first day's fighting went poorly for Israel as the Benjaminites attacked and killed twenty-two thousand Israelites. The Israelites encouraged one another and again approached the Lord, this time with great contrition. The defeat had shaken their confidence, so they asked if they should continue the campaign. After all, Benjamin was their brother; perhaps blood ties were more important than the execution of justice. The Lord answered with a brief but assuring word, "Attack them."

121.See the discussion in Bright 1981, 169–70. Some interpreters take בֵּית־אֵל as "house/sanctuary of God" here, rather than a proper name, and understand the referent as Shiloh or Mizpah. (See the sources cited in Moore 1895, 433.) This is unlikely for elsewhere בֵּית־אֵל is a proper name referring to the town of Bethel (see, e.g., Judg. 1:22–23; 4:5), while either בֵּית (הָ)אֱלֹהִים, "house of (the) God," or בֵּית יהוה, "house of Yahweh," is used for the sanctuary of God.

122.Niditch speaks of Joshua 22:10–34 as a "thematic companion piece" to Judges 19–20 (1982, 374). She develops some of the comparisons and contrasts between the two accounts. See also Organ 2001, 203–18; as well as Wong 2006a, 71–74.

123.The site of Shiloh plays a prominent role in both stories. In Joshua 22 the western tribes meet at Shiloh to organize an attack against the Transjordanian tribes (v. 12), but first wisely send Phinehas to secure the facts—peace ensues. However, in Judges 21 the Israelite warriors, having devastated Jabesh Gilead, return to Shiloh with their plunder (v. 12). The leaders then send the two hundred wifeless Benjaminites to Shiloh to kidnap brides. See Wong 2006a, 73–74.

Round two to Benjamin (20:22–25). The second day's fighting was almost as disastrous as the day before, as eighteen thousand Israelites fell before Benjamin. The Israelites came before the Lord en masse (note "all the Israelites" and the addition of "the whole army" in v. 26). Once again they wept, but this time they also fasted and presented sacrifices and peace offerings to the Lord. Apparently the Lord was pleased with this expression of humility, for this time he assured them of victory on the next day.

This raises the question of why the Lord allowed the Israelites to experience defeat on the first two days of the battle. Perhaps he wanted them to humble themselves sufficiently. After all, the beginning of the chapter gives no indication that they sought his guidance in how they should respond to the atrocity. Even when they did consult him, they simply asked who should lead the charge (v. 18). As Webb states, "they are already committed to the war and Yahweh's approval is assumed" (1987, 193). Their initial defeat taught them that divine authorization should be sought before, not during such a grave mission (Marais 1998, 141; Boling 1974, 43).[124] The Lord's delay in giving them victory mirrors their delay in inquiring concerning his will in the matter.

Benjamin down and out (20:26–48). Significant changes occur in this third panel, suggesting that the result of the third day's battle would be much different, in fulfillment of the Lord's oracle. Israel set an ambush outside Gibeah and devised a plot that would exploit Benjamin's aggressiveness and confidence. As the Benjaminites attacked, the main Israelite force retreated, leading the Benjaminites away from Gibeah.

At this point verses 33–36a give a condensed version of the battle, while verses 36b–48 give a more detailed account of how the ambush contributed to Gibeah's downfall.[125] Piecing the accounts together, we

---

124. Olson goes a step further and speaks of Israel's defeat on the first two days of the battle as "God's judgment" (1998, 885). Pressler argues that both the tribal alliance's initial defeat and eventual victory were "chastisement" from God (2002, 253). She suggests that the divine word in verse 28 was a false oracle, like the one referred to in Ezekiel 14:3–8.

125. Brichto calls this literary device "the synoptic/resumptive technique" (1992, 13–14). He explains: "Essentially it is the treatment of one event two times. The first narration of the event . . . is usually *briefer* (hence *synoptic*) than the second" and "is an independent, freestanding literary unit." He adds: "The second treatment or episode, usually longer than the first, may or may not be able to stand by itself." According to Brichto, one may also use the labels "conclusive" and "expansive" for the respective treatments. He explains that the second treatment provides "a more detailed

can reconstruct the battle as follows: When the main Israelite force drew the Benjaminites away from Gibeah, ten thousand crack troops charged into Gibeah, wiped out the residents, and set the town on fire. When the main force saw the smoke going up from the city, they turned on the Benjaminites, who recognized too late they had been tricked.[126] Eighteen thousand Benjaminites died in the battle, while several thousand more ran away. The Israelites chased the fugitives and killed seven thousand warriors. Ironically "caught" in verse 45 translates Hebrew עלל, the same verb translated "abused" in 19:25. The polysemantic wordplay highlights God's poetic justice, for it suggests the Benjaminites received an appropriate punishment for tolerating such a heinous crime (Berman 2004, 62–65).

The theological high point of the account comes in verse 35, which informs us that the Lord was the real victor in the battle. Using the same verb (נגף) employed in Exodus 12 to describe the plague on Egypt's firstborn (vv. 23, 27; see Josh. 24:5, where it is used of all God's plagues on Egypt), the narrator observes that the Lord "annihilated" Benjamin.

When the day was over, more than twenty-five thousand, one hundred (25,100) Benjaminites had died (v. 35; the figure in v. 46 is an approximate number). Six hundred Benjaminites managed to escape and hid out at the rock of Rimmon for four months. In the meantime Israel wiped out the rest of the Benjaminite towns, killing every living thing and setting the towns on fire.

Verse 15 indicates that the Benjaminite army numbered twenty-six thousand troops and an additional seven hundred slingers. They lost twenty-five thousand, one hundred men in battle (cf. v. 35 with vv. 44–46) and an additional six hundred men escaped.[127] What happened to the extra thousand men? The most reasonable explanation is that they were killed during the fighting on the first two days. Moore

---

account (hence *resumptive-expansive*) of how the bottom line of the first episode (hence *conclusive*) was arrived at."

126. According to verse 41, the Benjaminites realized that disaster (רָעָה) had overtaken them. This is the same term used to describe the evil actions of the men of Gibeah (20:12–13; cf. 19:23, where the verbal root appears). Berman, following a suggestion made by Reich, sees an intertextual connection that surfaces the theme of justice ("measure for measure") (2004, 56–57).

127. Verse 35 mentions 25,100 troops, while verse 46 rounds this to twenty-five thousand, the total of the figures given in verses 44 (eighteen thousand), and 45 (five and two = seven thousand). An additional six hundred men are mentioned in verse 47.

and Burney discuss and reject this explanation, arguing that the narrator is too precise and concerned about details to omit such a fact (Moore 1895, 429; Burney 1970, 475). However, the account of the first two days' fighting emphasizes Israel's humiliating defeat. To speak of Benjaminite casualties would diminish the literary effect. In verses 35, 44–47 the narrator's emphasis is the devastating defeat that Benjamin experienced on this one day. Again, to mention the earlier days' casualties at this point is irrelevant to his literary purpose. He allows readers who happen to be concerned with such details to connect the dots for themselves.

There is tragic irony in the description of Israel's victory. In verses 37 and 48 we read how Israel "struck with the mouth of the sword" both Gibeah and the Benjaminite towns. The expression used (נכה לפי־חרב, literally, "strike with the mouth of the sword") was used in the book's prologue to describe Judah's conquest of Jerusalem and Joseph's victory at Bethel (Wong 2006a, 38). But now we hear of Israelites inflicting the same kind of slaughter upon their own countrymen.

The description of the ambush against Gibeah is reminiscent of Israel's ambush of Ai (cf. Joshua 8). In fact, there are numerous verbal parallels between Judges 20:29–48 and Joshua 8:3–29, suggesting that the former alludes to the latter (Wong 2006a, 57–63). Israel treated their own brother, Benjamin, as they had a Canaanite city-state. Worse yet, they killed more Benjaminites than they had Canaanites at Ai (cf. Josh. 8:25 with Judg. 20:46); they burned all of Benjamin's towns, not just the offending city (cf. Josh. 8:28 with Judg. 20:48); and they even killed the Benjaminites' animals, something they did not do at Ai (cf. Josh. 8:27 with Judg. 20:48) (Wong 2006a, 69–70). Wong describes the tragic irony as follows: "Thus, not only had Israel not treated Benjamin with the compassion of brothers, they even dealt with them more harshly than they did to the non-Israelite enemies at Ai. No wonder then, that while the Israelites at Ai had reason to celebrate with covenant renewal after they disposed of an enemy according to YHWH's instructions, the Israelites who fought against Benjamin were left to mourn the consequence of their own action as they gave in to excessive vindictiveness in dealing with a brother." Israel "knew only to superficially copy past strategies of success without understanding how to appropriately apply them in their own context" (2006a, 70).

Six Hundred Brides for Six Hundred Brothers (21:1–25)

Feeling regret (21:1–3). Prior to the battle Israel had taken an oath that they would not allow any of their daughters to marry a Benjaminite

(v. 1, cf. v. 18). When the battle ended, they realized the implications of this hasty vow. An entire tribe was ready to disappear. Six hundred Benjaminite fugitives remained, but without wives to marry the tribe would soon die out. Once more Israel congregated at Bethel (cf. 20:18) and wept before God (cf. 20:23, 26). The reference to the Israelites sitting before God (v. 2; see Elohim), rather than Yahweh (cf. 20:26), may be a subtle signal from the narrator that not all is right (Block 1999, 570). The collocation of נָשָׂא קוֹלָם (literally, "lift their voice") and בָּכָה("weep") in verse 2 is an echo of 2:4, the only other passage in which the expression is used in Judges.[128] At Bokim, Israel wept after being chastised by the Lord's messenger for their disobedience. Here they weep as a result of the consequences of their excesses, just prior to committing atrocities upon Jabesh Gilead and Shiloh. As Wong observes, "both instances involve the entire Israelite community having gathered together to weep over the prospect of a bleak future" (2006a, 40).

The Israelites lamented the near extinction of Benjamin. The force of their question ("Why . . . has this happened in Israel?") is not entirely clear. The form of the question is unique, so there are no parallels to illuminate its significance.[129] The speech function of the question is most likely expressive. It is probably a rhetorical way of saying they wished it had not happened. Contrary to the opinion of some, it is unlikely that they were seeking an answer (though one could be readily given!) or that they were implying God was somehow at fault (cf. Moore 1895, 445; Burney 1970, 570–71). The text later attributes the situation to the Lord (v. 15), but this need not mean that the people were accusing the Lord of inappropriate behavior.[130]

Murder and kidnapping (21:4–14). The next morning they built an

---

128.See Wong, who offers an insightful correlation of the two passages at the thematic level (2006a, 40–41).

129.Interrogative לָמָה, "why," is followed by vocative "Yahweh" in three other texts, but in these cases Yahweh or Yahweh's anger is collocated as subject with a following imperfect verbal form (see Exod. 32:11; Pss. 10:1; 88:15). Here the vocative appears within the sentence, "Why . . . has this happened?" Only in this passage do we find the question לָמָה . . . . הָיְתָה, "Why has this happened?"

130.In verse 15 it is not clear if the statement includes the people's perspective on the cause of Benjamin's demise, or only the narrator's (cf. 20:35). See Block 1999, 573. Elsewhere when the *niphal* of נחם, used in the sense "regret, be sorry," is collocated with כִּי + a perfect verbal form, the subject of both נחם and the verb following כִּי is the same (Gen. 6:6–7; 1 Sam. 15:11, 35), but here the subject changes.

altar and presented sacrifices and peace offerings (cf. 20:26). However, rather than inquiring of the Lord (cf. 20:23b, 27), they devised their own strategy for solving the problem. Prior to the battle they had taken another oath that anyone who did not participate in the battle against Benjamin would be executed. Assuming that Jabesh Gilead had not sent anyone to the battle,[131] they apparently reasoned that this town was not bound by the oath pertaining to marriage. They decided to wipe Jabesh Gilead out, with the exception of any young virgins they could find (cf. Num. 31:7, 17–18). In this way they were able to circumvent their oath, which stated: "Not one of *us* . . . " (Satterthwaite 1993, 82).

When commissioning the warriors to attack Jabesh Gilead, they use the verb חרם (v. 11), a word that has not appeared in Judges since 1:17, which describes how Judah and Simeon annihilated the Canaanites of Zephath and renamed the town Hormah, mimicking the verb חרם. Ironically, apart from Judah's-Simeon's action, the tribes had failed to put the native Canaanites under the ban, but now they implemented this policy of divinely sanctioned war against one of their own towns.[132] The expression "struck with the mouth of the sword" (נכה לְפִי־

---

131. Verse 8b states that Jabesh Gilead had not sent anyone to the assembly. But which assembly is in view? There are two options: (1) This could refer to the assembly at Mizpah prior to the battle (20:1–3), for the people mention this event in the preceding question (v. 8a; cf. v. 5 as well). In this case verse 9 could refer to (a) a review at Bethel of the Mizpah mustering (cf. Block 1999, 574) or to (b) the roll call that had been taken at Mizpah prior to the battle. In favor of this latter option is the use of the *hithpael* of פקד, which appears in 20:17 to describe how the Israelites mustered their forces at Mizpah prior to the battle. At any rate 21:10 is set in the time of the post-battle assembly at Bethel. (2) However, another way of reading verses 8–10 is as follows: Wondering who might have been missing at Mizpah (v. 8a), the assembly at Bethel took a roll call (v. 9a), found Jabesh Gilead missing at Bethel (vv. 8b, 9b), and then attacked the absent city (v. 10). In this scenario the Israelites assumed that Jabesh Gilead's absence at Bethel meant they had not come to Mizpah. Perhaps this is correct, but if verse 8b refers to the assembly at Bethel, the narrator never specifically says Jabesh Gilead was absent at Mizpah. Can we assume that their absence at Bethel implies this? Perhaps not, for almost four months had passed since the end of the battle (cf. 20:47 with 21:13).

132. For a discussion of this from a rhetorical angle, see Wong 2006a, 35–37. He observes "that in contrast to the very beginning of the book where the חרם-laws are appropriately applied, Israel seems subsequently to have lost her ability to apply these laws with understanding and discernment" (40).

חָרַב) appears in the assembly's commissioning of the army (v. 10). This is sadly ironic for this same expression is used in the book's prologue of Judah's slaughter of Jerusalem and Joseph's victory at Bethel (1:8, 25) (Wong 2006a, 38). The military contingent sent to destroy Jabesh Gilead returned from the slaughter with four hundred virgins. Israel made peace with the six hundred Benjaminite fugitives at Rimmon and turned the virgins over to them as wives.

Dodging a vow (21:15–25). Two hundred Benjaminites still needed wives, so the Israelites devised another scheme to solve the problem. They instructed the Benjaminites to go to the annual feast to the Lord in Shiloh, hide in the nearby vineyards, and wait for the daughters of Shiloh to appear. When they came out to dance and celebrate, each of the remaining two hundred Benjaminites was to grab a young woman and take her home to Benjaminite territory as a wife.[133] When the fathers of the women objected, the Israelites would defend the Benjaminite cause and relieve any concern that their oath had been broken. Once again they were able to find a loophole in their oath. The oath said no one would "give" (literal translation) his daughter to a Benjaminite (vv. 1, 18); it said nothing about Benjaminites kidnapping daughters (Satterthwaite 1993, 82). When the time for the feast came, the Benjaminites, freed up by a technicality, followed these instructions and carted off two hundred young women.[134] Like Jephthah's daughter before them, the women's dancing and joy was rudely turned into horror (cf. 11:34).

The irony of all this is tragic. Appalled by the treatment of the Levite's concubine, Israel marched against Benjamin and, with the Lord's help, executed justice against Gibeah for its crimes.[135] However,

---

133.They use the verb חָטַף, "catch" (v. 21), which appears elsewhere only in Psalms 10:9, where it describes how oppressors "catch" their victims, like a lion stalking prey or a hunter trapping animals. The term suggests a violent act against a helpless and unsuspecting victim. See Bach 1998, 11.

134.The narrator describes their action with the verb גָּזַל, which means "tear away, rob" (see, for example, Judg. 9:25). It is used of violently or forcefully seizing what belongs to another. See BDB, 159; J. Schüpphaus, "גָּזַל," in *TDOT* 2:456–57.

135.The Lord had certainly given Israel the victory (cf. 20:28), but it is debatable whether he had "weakened" the Israelite tribes (21:15) to the extent described in chapter 20. It was actually the Israelites' excesses that had left Benjamin almost totally annihilated. It is possible that the כִּי clause in 21:15 reflects the perspective of the people, not the narrator. See Lapsley for a well-reasoned discussion of the options here (2005, 60–61).

rather than consulting the Lord for help in preserving the tribe of Benjamin, they concocted their own plan, which was severely limited in its options due to overexuberance after the battle (cf. 20:48; 21:16) and hasty vows made prior to the battle (the parallel with Jephthah is apparent).[136] They ended up slaughtering and kidnapping helpless women (cf. vv. 10–12, 21–24). As Exum observes, they "repeat on a mass scale the crimes they found so abhorrent in the men of Gibeah" (1990, 431).[137] What began as a war against a Benjaminite town that had violated the wife of a Levite from Ephraim (cf. 19:1) ends with the Israelites authorizing a Benjaminite kidnapping of two hundred young women from the Ephraimite town of Shiloh (Ackerman 1998, 254–55). As Satterthwaite observes, "all the killing . . . carried out with the aim of avenging the concubine's death, has not made Israel any safer a place for women" (1993, 85).

By the end of the book Israel's moral decline is transparently clear. Though we see a society giving lip service to hospitality and justice, its conduct was, as Webb observes, "debased because of the moral blindness and/or perversity of its citizens (including Levites and elders)" (1987, 197). Women, who at the beginning of the book inspired great deeds and played the role of national deliverer, are now raped, slaughtered and kidnapped by their own countrymen.[138] Ironically the brutalization of Israelite women anticipated by Sisera's mother (cf. 5:30) becomes a reality, not through a ruthless foreign conqueror and his soldiers, but through Israelite men.

As earlier (17:6), the narrator can only shake his head in dismay and remark that the leadership void in Israel had led to anarchy (v. 25). As noted above, the statement "Israel had no king" suggests that the presence of a king would have provided a standard for the nation to follow. Without such a standard, "everyone did what he considered to be right."[139]

---

136. On the thematic connection between Jephthah's vow and that of the Israelites at Mizpah, see Wong 2006a, 132–35.

137. On the injustice inherent in Israel's actions, see O'Connell 1996, 262–63. Israel was hesitant to wipe out Benjamin, but they had no qualms about annihilating Jabesh Gilead.

138. On the contrasts between Acsah and the oppressed women of the final chapters, see Klein 1988, 172–73, 190, as well as Wong 2006a, 42–46.

139. See the commentary on 17:6 above for a full discussion of the meaning of this statement.

MESSAGE AND APPLICATION

Thematic Emphases

Israel had persisted in paganism and had no competent, godly leaders to remind them of the Lord's covenant standards. Paul Miller observes: ". . . when the covenant relationship between God and God's people is neglected, the faculty of moral judgment atrophies. It not only becomes impossible to *do* right, it becomes impossible to *know* what is right" (2003, 103). In this spiritual void the covenant community became as morally corrupt as ancient Sodom and was eventually torn apart by conflict. The moral disease infecting Benjamin had contaminated even the male victim of the hideous crime at Gibeah and the men responsible for avenging the wrong. By the end of this story, Israel's attempt to bring the criminals of Gibeah to justice had exploded in their faces. An entire tribe was left decimated and six hundred women were horribly violated. Once again a foolish, misguided oath left death in its wake (cf. 11:29–40), only on a much larger scale.

The passage drips with tragic irony. Though unable to unify in their effort to take the land from the Canaanites, the tribes unified to fight one of their own. Sisera's mother's vision of Israelite women being abused in the aftermath of battle (5:30) became a reality, but the culprits were Israelites, not Canaanites. Benjamin's conflict with Judah (the Levite's concubine was from Judah and Judah led the attack against Benjamin) is antithetical to the brotherly love shown by Judah towards Benjamin in Genesis 44. Worse yet, it foreshadows tensions to come (cf. the Saul-David conflict in 1–2 Samuel).

Exegetical idea: *As God's people persisted in paganism and had no competent, godly leaders to confront them with God's standards, a moral cancer invaded the covenant community, making it capable of the vilest sins. Uncontrollable lust and cruel disregard for the vulnerable and helpless characterized a community contaminated by moral pluralism, where individuals and communities lived by their own self-serving "standards" of right and wrong, rather than by God's covenant principles. God's people desperately needed godly leadership.*

Theological Principles

Like the preceding story, Judges 19–21 depicts the antithesis of pure religion. A moral cancer invaded the covenant community, bringing with it uncontrollable lust and cruel disregard for the vulnerable and helpless. (See the earlier discussion of "Theological Themes" related to 17:1–19:1a.)

511

As in the story of Abimelech (chapter 9), God appears in the role of just king as he defeats the Benjaminites (20:35). Yet the necessity of God acting in punitive judgment was not the ideal. In this story and the preceding one the need for theocratic kingship emerges (21:25; cf. 17:6; 18:1; 19:1). This editorial comment envisions the kingship ideal depicted in Deuteronomy 17:14–20. The presence of such a leader could have prevented the abuses described in the epilogue. Yet the remainder of the history (1–2 Samuel, 1–2 Kings) tells how the monarchy, despite some success in bringing moral order to the land, eventually failed and collapsed as the king went into exile with his people. The royal ideal envisioned in Judges and both the former and latter prophets is ultimately realized through Jesus the Messiah. Though Judges does not ostensibly have a messianic theme, its vision of a royal ideal prepares the way for the developing messianism that follows in the Hebrew Bible.[140]

Theological idea: *When God's people persist in paganism and have no competent, godly leaders to confront them with God's standards, a moral cancer can invade the covenant community, making it capable of the vilest sins. Uncontrollable lust and cruel disregard for the vulnerable and helpless are signs of a community contaminated by moral pluralism, where individuals and communities live by their own self-serving "standards" of right and wrong, rather than by God's covenant principles. God's people desperately need godly leadership.*

Homiletical Trajectories
(1) As the just king of Israel, God works to preserve order in the midst of chaos. He punishes evildoers and those who support them. Yet ideally he purposes to create a community that promotes justice modeled by an ideal leader. (See point three below.)

(2) When the covenant community becomes like the surrounding pagan world, it can sink to unprecedented moral depths. People become lustful and cruel, and will give personal "honor" and pride higher priority than morality and ethics. The community becomes prone to strife that inflicts pain and suffering on innocent and helpless people throughout the community.

---

140. On the nascent messianism in Samuel–Kings, see Satterthwaite 1995, 41–65; and Provan 1995, 67–85.

(3) The covenant community needs godly leadership because sinful people are prone to rebel. It is here that Judges yields a Christotelic theme that should be the capstone of the exposition of the book. The epilogue to Judges anticipates the rise of the Davidic monarchy, but the historical kings ultimately failed. God's ideal leader is Jesus the Messiah, who will establish his kingdom on earth. He is currently ruling over his Church, whose leaders and members are to model the character of their Lord and King.[141]

Preaching idea: *We must reject the paganism of the surrounding culture and seek competent, godly leaders to confront us with God's standards. Otherwise lust and cruelty can contaminate the new covenant community as people live by their own self-serving "standards" of right and wrong, rather than by God's covenant principles.*

If we want to develop the Christotelic dimension, the moral chaos and leadership void described in these chapters (as well as in chapters 17–18) can be used as the dark backdrop against which we point God's people to the messianic hope. A *preaching idea* might be: *Though the covenant community can be contaminated by the pagan culture around it, our King will eventually establish his just rule on earth in which his perfect standard of morality and ethics will displace the injustice produced by human lust and cruelty.*

---

141. I intend this statement to be understood within the framework of so-called progressive dispensationalism, which promotes an "already-not yet" hermeneutic with regard to God's kingdom.

REFERENCES
FOR JUDGES

Abela, Anthony. 2002. "Two Short Studies on Judges 5." *TBT* 53, 133–37.

Ackerman, James S. 1975. "Prophecy and Warfare in Early Israel: A Study of the Deborah-Barak Story." *BASOR* 220 (December), 5–13.

Ackerman, Susan. 1998. *Warrior, Dancer, Seductress, Queen: Women in Judges and Biblical Israel.* New York: Doubleday.

_____. 2000. "What if Judges Had Been Written by a Philistine?" *Biblical Interpretation* 8, 33–41.

Aharoni, Yohanan. 1979. *The Land of the Bible.* rev. ed. Translated and edited by Anson Rainey. Philadelphia: Westminster.

Aharoni, Yohanan, and Michael Avi-Yonah. 1977. *The Macmillan Bible Atlas.* rev. ed. New York: Macmillan.

Ahlström, Gösta w. 1977. "Judges 5:20 f. and History." *JNES* 36, 287–88.

Albrektson, Bertil. 1967. *History and the Gods.* Lund: CWK Gleerup.

Albright, W. F. 1936. "The Song of Deborah in the Light of Archaeology." *BASOR* 62, 26–31.

Alter, Robert. 1981. *The Art of Biblical Narrative.* New York: Basic Books.

_____. 1985. *The Art of Biblical Poetry.* New York: Basic Books.

_____. 1990. "Samson Without Folklore." In *Text and tradition: The*

Hebrew Bible and Folklore, edited by Susan Nidtch, 47–56. Atlanta: Scholars Press.

Amit, Yairah. 1987. "Judges 4: Its Contents and Form." *JSOT* 39, 89–111.

_____. 1988. "The Use of Analogy in the Study of the Book of Judges." In *"Wunschet Jerusalem Frieden": Collected Communications to the XIIth Congress of the International Organization for the Study of the Old Testament, Jerusalem 1986,* edited by Matthias Augustin and Klaus-Dietrich Schunck, 387–95. Frankfurt am Main: Peter Lang.

_____. 1989. "The Story of Ehud (Judges 3:12–30): Form and Message." In *Signs and Wonders: Biblical Texts in Literary Focus,* edited by J. Cheryl Exum, 97–123. Decatur: Society of Biblical Literature.

_____. 1990. "Hidden Polemic in the Conquest of Dan: Judges XVII-XVIII." *VT* 60, 4–20.

_____. 1993. "'Manoah Promptly Followed his Wife' (Judges 13.11): On the Place of the Woman in Birth Narratives." In *Judges,* edited by Athalya Brenner, 146–56. FBC. Sheffield: Sheffield Academic.

_____. 1994. "Literature in the Service of Politics: Studies in Judges 19–21." In *Politics and Theopolitics in the Bible and Postbiblical Literature*, edited by Henning G. Reventlow, Yair Hoffman, and Benjamin Uffenheimer, 28–40. JSOTSup 171. Sheffield: Sheffield Academic.

_____. 1999. *The Book of Judges: The Art of Editing.* Leiden: Brill.

_____. 2000. "Bochim, Bethel, and the Hidden Polemic (Judg 2,1–5)." In *Studies in Historical Geography and Biblical Historiography,* edited by Gershon Galil and Moshe Weinfeld, 121–31. Leiden: Brill.

_____. 2001. *Reading Biblical Narratives.* Minneapolis: Fortress.

_____. 2002. "I, Delilah: A Victim of Interpretation." In *First Person: Essays in Biblical Autobiography,* edited by Philip R. Davies, 59–76. London: Sheffield Academic.

_____. 2003. "Progression as a Rhetorical Device in Biblical Literature." *JSOT* 28, 3–32.

Andersson, Greger. 2001. *The Book and Its Narratives: A Critical Examination of Some Synchronic Studies of the Book of Judges.* Örebro: Örebro University.

_____. 2007. "A Narratologist's Critical Reflections on Synchronic Studies of the Bible: A Response to Gregory T. K. Wong." *SJOT* 21, 2, 261–74.

Asen, Bernhard. 1997. "Deborah, Barak and Bees: *Apis Mellifera,* Apiculture and Judges 4 and 5." *ZAW* 109, 514–33.

Ashley, Timothy R. 1993. *The Book of Numbers*. NICOT. Grand Rapids: William B. Eerdmans.

Assis, Eliyahu. 2004. "The Choice to Serve God and Assist His People: Rahab and Yael." *Bib* 85, 82–90.

_____. 2005a. *Self-Interest or Communal Interest: An Ideology of Leadership in the Gideon, Abimelech and Jephthah Narratives (Judg 6–12)*. VTSup 106. Leiden: Brill.

_____. 2005b. "'The Hand of a Woman': Deborah and Jael (Judges 4)." *The Journal of Hebrew Scriptures* 5:19. doi:10.5508/jhs.2005. v5.a19.

_____. 2006. "Man, Woman and God in Judg 4." *SJOT* 20, 1, 110–24.

Athas, George. 2005. *The Tel Dan Inscription: A Reappraisal and a New Interpretation*. London: T & T Clark International.

Auffret, Pierre. 2002. "En ce Jour-là Debora et Baraq Chantèrent: Ètudes Structurelles de Jg 5,2–31." *SJOT* 16, 113–50.

Aufrecht, Walter. 1999. "The religion of the Ammonites." In *Ancient Ammon,* edited by Burton MacDonald and Randall W. Younker, 152–62. Leiden: Brill.

Auld, A. Graeme. 1975. "Judges 1 and History: A Reconsideration." *VT* 25, 261–85.

_____. 1989. "Gideon: Hacking at the Heart of the Old Testament." *VT* 39, 257–67.

_____. 1998a. "Tribal Terminology in Joshua and Judges." In *Joshua retold: Synoptic Perspectives,* 69–76. Edinburgh: T & T Clark.

_____. 1998b. "What Makes Judges Deuteronomistic?" In *Joshua Retold: Synoptic Perspectives*, 120–26. Edinburgh: T & T Clark.

Ausloos, Hans. 2008. "The 'Angel of YHWH' in Exod. xxiii 20–33 and Judg. ii 1–5. A Clue to the 'Deuteronom(ist)ic Puzzle?'" *VT* 58, 1–12.

Bach, Alice. 1998. "Rereading the Body Politic: Women and Violence in Judges 21." *BibInt* 6, 1–19.

Bal, Mieke. 1988a. *Death and Dissymmetry: The Politics of Coherence in the Book of Judges*. Chicago: University of Chicago Press.

_____. 1988b. *Murder and Difference: Gender, Genre, and Scholarship on Sisera's Death*. Translated by Matthew Gumpert. Bloomington: Indiana University Press.

_____. 1993. "A Body of Writing: Judges 19." In *Judges,* edited by Athalya Brenner, 208–30. FCB. Sheffield: Sheffield Academic.

Barré, Michael L. 1991. "The Meaning of *Pršdn* in Judges III 22." *VT* 41, 1–11.

Barrick, William D. 1976. "Samson's Removal of Gaza's Gates." *BNEAS* 8, 83–93.

Bartusch, Mark W. 2003. *Understanding Dan: An Exegetical Study of a Biblical City, Tribe and Ancestor.* JSOTSup 379. London: Sheffield Academic.

Bauer, Uwe F. W. 2000. "Judges 18 as an Anti-Spy Story in the Context of an Anti-Conquest Story: The Creative Usage of Literary Genres." *JSOT* 88, 37–47.

_____. 2001. "A Metaphorical Etiology in Judges 18:12." *The Journal of Hebrew Scriptures* 3:5. doi:10.5508/jhs.2001.v3.a5.

Beavis, Mary Ann. 2010. "The Resurrection of Jephthah's Daughter: Judges 11:34–40 and Mark 5:21–24, 35–43." *CBQ* 72, 46–62.

Beck, John A. 2008. "Gideon, Dew, and the Narrative-Geographical Shaping of Judges 6:33–40." *BSac* 165, 28–38.

Beem, Beverly. 1991. "The Minor Judges: A Literary Reading of Some Very Short Stories." In *The Biblical Canon in Comparative Perspective,* edited by K. Lawson Younger, William W. Hallo, and Bernard F. Batto, 147–72. Scripture in Context IV. Lewiston: Edwin Mellen.

Begg, Christopher. 2006. "The Josephan Judge Jephthah." *SJOT* 20:2, 161–88.

Ben-Tor, Amnon. 1998. "The Fall of Canaanite Hazor—The "Who" and "When" Questions." In *Mediterranean Peoples in Transition: Thirteenth to Early Tenth Centuries BCE,* edited by Symour Gitin, Amihai Mazar, and Ephraim Stern, 456–67. Jerusalem: Israel Exploration Society.

Berlin, Adele. 1983. *Poetics and Interpretation of Biblical Narrative.* Sheffield: Almond.

Berman, Joshua A. 2002. "The 'Sword of Mouths' (Jud. III 16; Ps. CXLIX 6; Prov. V 4): A Metaphor and Its Ancient Near Eastern Context." *VT* 52, 291–303.

_____. 2004. *Narrative Analogy in the Hebrew Bible: Battle Stories and Their Equivalent Non-Battle Narratives.* VTSup 103. Leiden: Brill.

Binger, Tilde. 1997. *Asherah: Goddesses in Ugarit, Israel and the Old Testament.* JSOTSup 232. Sheffield: Sheffield Academic.

Bledstein, Adrien. J. 1993. "Is Judges a Woman's Satire of Men Who Play God?" In *Judges,* edited by Athalya Brenner, 34–54. FCB. Sheffield: Sheffield Academic.

Blenkinsopp, Joseph. 1961. "Ballad Style and Psalm Style in the Song of Deborah: A Discussion." *Bib* 42, 61–76.

_____. 1963. "Structure and Style in Judges 13–16." *JBL* 82, 65–76.

Block, Daniel I. 1988. "The Period of the Judges: Religious Disintegration Under Tribal Rule." In *Israel's Apostasy and Restoration: Essays in*

Honor of Roland K. Harrison, edited by Avraham Gileadi, 39–57. Grand Rapids: Baker.

———. 1990. "Echo Narrative Technique in Hebrew Literature: A Study in Judges 19." *WTJ* 52, 325–41.

———. 1994. "Deborah Among the Judges: The Perspective of the Hebrew Historian." In *Faith, Tradition, and History: Old Testament Historiography in its Near Eastern Context,* edited by A. R. Millard, James K. Hoffmeier, and David W. Baker, 229–53. Winona Lake: Eisenbrauns.

———. 1997. "Will the Real Gideon Please Stand Up? Narrative Style and Intention in Judges 6–9." *JETS* 40, 353–66.

———. 1999. *Judges, Ruth.* NAC. Nashville: Broadman & Holman.

Bluedorn, Wolfgang. 2001. *Yahweh versus Baalism: A Theological Reading of the Gideon-Abimelech Narrative.* JSOTSup 329. Sheffield: Sheffield Academic.

Bohmbach, Karla G. 1999. "Conventions/Contraventions: The Meanings of Public and Private for the Judges 19 Concubine." *JSOT* 83, 83–98.

Boling, Robert G. 1974. "'In Those Days There Was No King in Israel.'" In *A Light Unto My Path: Old Testament Studies in Honor of Jacob M. Myers,* edited by Howard N. Bream, Ralph D. Heim, and Carey A. Moore, 33–48. Philadelphia: Temple University Press.

———. 1975. *Judges.* AB. New York: Doubleday.

Boogaart, Thomas A. 1985. "Stone for Stone: Retribution in the Story of Abimelech and Shechem." *JSOT* 32, 45–56.

Borowski, Oded. 1987. *Agriculture in Iron Age Israel.* Winona Lake: Eisenbrauns.

Bos, Johanna W. H. 1988. "Out of the Shadows: Genesis 38; Judges 4:17–22; Ruth 3." *Semeia* 42, 37–67.

Boström, Lennart. 1990. *The God of the Sages: The Portrayal of God in the Book of Proverbs.* Stockholm: Almquist & Wiksell.

Bowman, Richard. G. 1995. "Narrative Criticism: Human Purpose in Conflict with Divine Presence." In *Judges and Method: New Approaches in Biblical Studies,* edited by Gale A. Yee, 17–44. Minneapolis: Fortress.

Boyd, Gregory A. 1997. *God at War: The Bible and Spiritual Conflict.* Downers Grove: InterVarsity.

Bray, Jason S. 2006. *Sacred Dan: Religious Tradition and Cultic Practice in Judges 17–18.* LHBOTS 449. New York: T & T Clark.

Brenner, Athalya. 1990. "A Triangle and a Rhombus in Narrative Structure: A Proposed Integrative Reading of Judges IV and V." *VT* 40, 129–38.

_____, ed. 1993. *Judges*. FCB. Sheffield: Sheffield Academic.

_____, ed. 1999. *Judges*. FCBSS. Sheffield: Sheffield Academic.

Brettler, Marc Z. 1989a. "Jud 1,1–2,10: From Appendix to Prologue." *ZAW* 101, 433–35.

_____. 1989b. "The Book of Judges: Literature as Politics." *JBL* 108, 395–418.

_____. 1991. "Never the Twain Shall Meet? The Ehud Story as History and Literature." *HUCA* 62, 285–304.

_____. 2002. *The Book of Judges*. London: Routledge.

Brichto, Herbert C. 1992. *Toward a Grammar of Biblical Poetics: Tales of the Prophets*. New York: Oxford University Press.

Bright, John. 1981. *A History of Israel*. 3rd ed. Philadelphia: Westminster.

Broida, Marian. 2010. "Closure in Samson." *The Journal of Hebrew Scriptures* 10:2. doi:10.5508/jhs.v10.a2.

Bronner, Leila Leah. 1993. "Valorized or Vilified? The Women of Judges in Midrashic Sources." In *Judges,* edited by Athalya Brenne, 72–95. FCB. Sheffield: Sheffield Academic.

_____. 2004. *Stories of Biblical Mothers: Maternal Power in the Hebrew Bible*. Lanham: University Press of America.

Brooks, Simcha S. 1996. "Saul and the Samson Narrative." *JSOT* 71, 19–25.

Brown, Cheryl A. 2000. "Judges." In *Joshua, Judges, Ruth,* edited by J. Gordon Harris, Cheryl A. Brown, and Michael S. Moore, 121–289. Peabody: Hendrickson.

Burnett, Joel S. 2001. *A Reassessment of Biblical Elohim*. SBLDS 183. Atlanta: Society of Biblical Literature.

Burney, C. F. 1970. *The Book of Judges*. Reprinted. New York: KTAV.

Buth, Randall. 1994. "Methodological Collision Between Source Criticism and Discourse Analysis: The Problem of "Unmarked Temporal Overlay" and the Pluperfect/Nonsequential *Wayyiqtol*." In *Biblical Hebrew and Discourse Linguistics,* edited by Robert Bergen, 138–54. Winona Lake: Eisenbrauns.

Butler, Trent C. 2009. *Judges,* WBC. Nashville: Thomas Nelson.

Camp, Claudia V. and Carole Fontaine. 1990. "The Words of the Wise and Their Riddles." In *Text and Tradition: The Hebrew Bible and Folklore,* edited by Susan Niditch, 127–51. Atlanta: Scholars Press.

Campbell, Antony F., and Mark A. O'Brien. 2000. *Unfolding the Deuteronomistic History*. Minneapolis: Fortress.

Campbell, Edward F., Jr. 1983. "Judges 9 and Biblical Archaeology." In *The Word of the Lord Shall Go Forth: Essays in Honor of David Noel*

Freedman in Celebration of his Sixtieth Birthday, edited by Carol L. Meyers and M. O'Connor, 263–71. Winona Lake: Eisenbrauns.

Cartledge, Tony W. 1992. *Vows in the Hebrew Bible and the Ancient Near East.* JSOTSup 147. Sheffield: Sheffield Academic.

_____. 2001. *1 and 2 Samuel.* SHBC. Macon: Smyth & Helwys.

Castellino, Giorgio R. 1972. *Two Shulgi hymns (BC).* Rome: Instituto di Studi del Vicino Oriente.

Chalcraft, David J. 1990. "Deviance and Legitimate Action in the Book of Judges." In *The Bible in Three Dimensions*, edited by David J. A. Clines, Stephen E. Fowl, and Stanley E. Porter, 177–201. JSOTSup 87. Sheffield: Sheffield Academic.

Chavalas, Mark W. and Murray R. Adamthwaite. 1999. "Archaeological Light on the Old Testament." In *The face of Old Testament Studies: A Survey of Contemporary Approaches,* edited by David W. Baker and Bill T. Arnold, 59–96. Grand Rapids: Baker Academic.

Chepey, Stuart D. 2002. "Samson the 'Holy One': A Suggestion Regarding the Reviser's Use of ἅγιος in Judg 13,7; 16,17 LXX Vaticanus." *Bib* 83, 97–99.

Childs, Brevard S. 1963. "A Study of the Formula 'Until this Day.'" *JBL* 82, 279–92

Chisholm, Robert B., Jr. 1983. "An Exegetical and Theological Study of Psalm 18/2 Samuel 22." Th. D. diss., Dallas Theological Seminary.

_____. 1994a. "The Polemic Against Baalism in Israel's Early History and Literature." *BSac* 151, 267–83.

_____. 1994b. "The Role of Women in the Rhetorical Strategy of the Book of Judges." In *Integrity of Heart, Skillfulness of Hands,* edited by Charles H. Dyer and Roy B. Zuck, 34–46. Grand Rapids: Baker.

_____. 1995. "Does God 'Change His Mind?'" *BSac* 152, 387–99.

_____. 1998a. "Does God Deceive?" *BSac* 155, 11–28

_____. 1998b. *From Exegesis to Exposition.* Grand Rapids: Baker.

_____. 2002. "A Rhetorical Use of Point of View in Old Testament Narrative." *BSac* 159, 404–14.

_____. 2007a. "Anatomy of an Anthropomorphism: Does God 'Discover' Facts?" *BSac* 167, 3–20.

_____. 2007b. "Yahweh versus the Canaanite Gods: Polemic in Judges and 1 Samuel 1–7." *BSac* 168, 165–80.

_____. 2009a. "The Chronology of the Book of Judges: A Linguistic Clue to Solving a Pesky Problem." *JETS* 52, 247–55.

_____. 2009b. "Identity Crisis: Assessing Samson's Birth and Career." *BSac* 170, 147–62.

_____. 2009c. "What's Wrong With This Picture? Stylistic Variation as a Rhetorical Technique in Judges." *JSOT* 34.2, 171–82.

_____. 2010a. "A Note on Judges 13:20–21: Sorting Out the Syntax." *JBQ* 38.1, 10–12.

_____. 2010b. "What Went on in Jael's Tent? The Collocation ותכסהו בשׂמיכה in Judges 4, 18." *SJOT* 24.1, 143–44.

_____. 2010c. "The Ethical Challenge of Jephthah's Fulfilled Vow." *BSac* 167, 404–22.

_____. 2010d. "In Defense of Paneling as a Clue to the Chronology of Judges: A Critique of Andrew Steinmann's Reply." *JETS* 53, 375–82.

_____. 2011. "Ehud: Assessing an Assassin." *BSac* 168, 274–82.

_____. 2013. "What Went on in Jael's Tent? (Part Two)." *SJOT* 27.2 (forthcoming).

Christianson, Eric S. 2003. "A Fistful of Shekels: Scrutinizing Ehud's Entertaining Violence (Judges 3:12–30)." *BibInt* 11, 53–78.

Claassens, Julie. 1996. "Notes on Characterisation in the Jephtah Narrative." *JNSL* 22/2, 107–15.

_____. 1997. "Theme and Function in the Jephthah Narrative." *JNSL* 23/2, 203–19.

_____. 2001. "The Character of God in Judges 6–8: The Gideon Narrative as Theological and Moral Resource." *HBT* 23, 51–71.

Clements, Ronald E. 1968. "Baal-Berith of Shechem." *JSS* 13, 21–32.

Cogan, Mordechai. 2001. *I Kings*. AB. New York: Doubleday.

Cohen, Harold R. 1978. *Biblical Hapax Legomena in the Light of Akkadian and Ugaritic*. SBLDS 37. Missoula: Scholars Press.

Cohen-Kiener, Andrea. 1991. "Three Women." *JBQ* 19, 204–05.

Coogan, Michael D. 1975. "A Structural and Literary Analysis of the Song of Deborah." *CBQ* 40, 143–66.

Craig, Kenneth M., Jr. 1998. "Bargaining in Tov (Judges 11, 4–11): The Many Directions of So-Called Direct Speech." *Bib* 79, 76–85.

Craigie, Peter C. 1969. "The Song of Deborah and the Epic of Tukulti-Ninurta." *JBL* 88, 253–65.

_____. 1972a. "A Reconsideration of Shamgar Ben Anath (Judg 3:31 and 5:6)." *JBL* 91, 239–40.

_____. 1972b. "Some Further Notes on the Song of Deborah." *VT* 22, 349–53.

_____. 1977. "Three Ugaritic Notes on the Song of Deborah." *JSOT* 2, 33–38.

Crenshaw, James L. 1978. *Samson: A Secret Betrayed, a Vow Ignored*. Atlanta: John Knox.

Crisler, B. Cobbey. 1976. "The Acoustics and Crowd Capacity of Natural Theaters in Palestine." *BA* 39/4, 128–41.

Cross, Frank M. 1962. "Yahweh and the God of the Patriarchs." *HTR* 55, 225–59.

Cross, Frank M. and David N. Freedman. 1975. *Studies in Ancient Yahwistic Poetry*. SBLDS 21. Missoula: Scholars Press.

Crown, A. D. 1967. "Judges V 15b–16." *VT* 17, 240–42.

Cundall, A. E. 1969. "Judges—An Apology for the Monarchy?" *ExpTim* 81, 178–81.

Daube, David. 1956. "Gideon's Few." *JJS* 7, 155–61.

Davidson, E. T. A. 2005. "Can Sources of *Judges* Be Found in the Ugaritic Myths?" PEGLMBS 25, 43–57.

Davidson, Richard M. 2007. *Flame of Yahweh: Sexuality in the Old Testament*. Peabody: Hendrickson.

Davies, G. Henton. 1963. "Judges VIII 22–23." *VT* 13, 151–57.

Davis, Dale R. 1984. "Comic Literature—Tragic Theology: A Study of Judges 17–18." *WTJ* 46, 156–63.

_____. 1990. *Such a Great Salvation: Expositions of the Book of Judges*. Grand Rapids: Baker.

Dawson, David A. 1994. *Text-Linguistics and Biblical Hebrew*. JSOTSup 177. Sheffield: Sheffield Academic Press.

Day, John. 1985. *God's Conflict With the Dragon and the Sea*. Cambridge: Cambridge University Press.

_____. 2000. *Yahweh and the Gods and Goddesses of Canaan*. Sheffield: Sheffield Academic.

Deist, Ferdinand. 1996. "'Murder in the Toilet' (Judges 3:12–30): Translation and Transformation." *Scriptura* 58, 263–72.

de Moor, Johannes C. 1993. "The Twelve Tribes in the Song of Deborah." *VT* 43, 483–94.

Dempster, Stephen G. 1978. "Mythology and History in the Song of Deborah." *WTJ* 41, 33–53.

de Vaux, Roland. 1965. *Ancient Israel*. 2 vols. New York: McGraw-Hill.

Dever, William G. 2003. *Who Were the Early Israelites and Where Did They Come From?* Grand Rapids: William B. Eerdmans.

_____. 2004. "Histories and Non-Histories of Ancient Israel: The Question of the United Monarchy." In *In Search of Pre-Exilic Israel*, edited by John Day, 65–94. London: T & T Clark International.

de Waard, Jan. 1989. "Jotham's Fable: An Exercise in Clearing Away the Unclear." In *Wissenschaft und Kirche: Festschrift für Eduard Lohse*, edited by Kurt Aland and Siegfried Meurer, 362–70. Bielefeld: Luther-Verlag.

Dillard, Raymond B. and Tremper Longman III. 1994. *An Introduction to the Old Testament*. Grand Rapids: Zondervan.

Dorsey, David A. 1999. *The Literary Structure of the Old Testament.* Grand Rapids: Baker.

Dragga, Sam. 1987. "In the Shadow of the Judges: The Failure of Saul." *JSOT* 38, 39–46.

Drews, Robert. 1989. "The 'Chariots of Iron' of Joshua and Judges." *JSOT* 45, 15–23.

Dumbrell, William J. 1983. "'In Those Days There Was No King in Israel; Every Man Did What Was Right in his Own Eyes.' The Purpose of the Book of Judges Reconsidered." *JSOT* 25, 23–33.

Echols, Charles L. 2005. "The Eclipse of God in the Song of Deborah (Judges 5)." *TynBul* 56.2, 149–52.

_____. 2008. *"Tell Me, O Muse": The Song of Deborah (Judges 5) in the Light of Heroic Poetry.* LHBOTS 487. New York: T & T Clark.

Ellington, John. 1992. "More on *Shibboleth* (Judges 12.6)." *TBT* 43, 244–45.

Emerton, John A. 1976. "Gideon and Jerubbaal." *JTS* 27, 289–312.

_____. 1978. "The 'Second Bull' in Judges 6:25–28." *ErIsr* 14, 52*–55*.

Emmrich, Martin. 2001. "The Symbolism of the Lion and the Bees: Another Ironic Twist in the Samson Cycle." *JETS* 44, 67–74.

Endris, Vince. 2008. "Yahweh versus Baal: A Narrative-Critical Reading of the Gideon/Jephthah Narrative." *JSOT* 33.2, 173–95.

Eslinger, Lyle. 1989. *Into the Hands of the Living God.* Sheffield: Sheffield Academic.

Exum, J. Cheryl. 1980. "Promise and Fulfillment: Narrative Art in Judges 13." *JBL* 99, 43–59.

_____. 1983. "The Theological Dimension of the Samson Saga." *VT* 33, 30–45.

_____. 1989. "The Tragic Vision and Biblical Narrative: The Case of Jephthah." In *Signs and Wonders: Biblical Texts in Literary Focus* edited by J. Cheryl Exum, 59–83. Decatur: Society of Biblical Literature.

_____. 1990. "The Centre Cannot Hold: Thematic and Textual Instabilities in Judges." *CBQ* 52, 410–31.

_____. 1992. *Tragedy and Biblical Narrative.* Cambridge: Cambridge University Press.

_____. 1993a. *Fragmented Women: Feminist (Sub)versions of Biblical Narratives.* JSOTSup 163. Sheffield: JSOT.

_____. 1993b. "On Judges 11." In *Judges,* edited by Athalya Brenner, 131–44. FCB. Sheffield: Sheffield Academic.

_____. 1997. "Harvesting the Biblical Narrator's Scanty Plot of Ground: A Holistic Approach to Judges 16:4–22." In *Tehillah le-Moshe: Biblical and Judaic Studies in Honor of Moshe Greenberg,* edited by Mordechai Cogan, Barry L. Eichler, and Jeffrey H. Tigay, 39–46. Winona Lake: Eisenbrauns.

Faiman, David. 1993. "Chronology in the Book of Judges." *JBQ* 21, 31–40.

Faraone, Chrisopher A., Brien Garnand, and Carolina López-Ruiz. 2005. "Micah's Mother (Judg. 17:1–4) and a Curse from Carthage (*KAI* 89): Canaanite Precedents for Greek and Latin Curses Against Thieves?" *JNES* 64, 161–86.

Feliu, Lluis. 2003. *The God Dagan in Bronze Age Syria.* Translated by Wilfred G. E. Watson. Culture and History of the Ancient Near East 19. Leiden: Brill.

Fensham, Frank C. 1977. "The Numeral Seventy in the Old Testament and the Family of Jerubbaal, Ahab, Panammuwa and Athirat." *PEQ* 109 (July-December), 113–15.

Fewell, Danna N. and David M. Gunn. 1990. "Controlling Perspectives: Women, Men, and Authority of Violence in Judges 4 and 5." *JAAR* 56, 389–411.

Fields, Weston W. 1992. "The Motif of 'Night as Danger' Associated with Three Biblical Destruction Narratives." In *Sha`arei Talmon: Studies in the Bible, Qumran, and the Ancient Near East Presented to Shemaryahu Talmon,* edited by Michael Fishbane and Emanuel Tov, 17–32. Winona Lake: Eisenbrauns.

Fitzmyer, Joseph A. 1967. *The Aramaic Inscriptions of Sefire.* Rome: Pontifical Biblical Institute.

Fokkelman, Jan. 1992. "Structural Remarks on Judges 9 and 19." In *Sha`arei Talmon: Studies in the Bible, Qumran, and the Ancient Near East Presented to Shemaryahu Talmon,* edited by Michael Fishbane and Emanuel Tov, 33–45. Winona Lake: Eisenbrauns.

_____. 1995. "The Song of Deborah and Barak: Its Prosodic Levels and Structure." In *Pomegranates and Golden Bells: Studies in Biblical, Jewish, and Near Eastern Ritual, Law, and Literature in Honor of Jacob Milgrom,* edited by David P. Wright, David N. Freedman, and Avi Hurvitz, 595–628. Winona Lake: Eisenbrauns.

_____. 1999. *Reading Biblical Narrative.* Translated by Ineke Smit. Louisville: Westminster John Knox.

Fouts, David M. 1997. "A Defense of the Hyperbolic Interpretation of Large Numbers in the Old Testament." *JETS* 40, 377–88.

_____. 2003. "The Incredible Numbers of the Hebrew Kings." In *Giving the Sense: Understanding and Using Old Testament Historical Texts,* edited by David M. Howard Jr. and Michael A. Grisanti, 283–99. Grand Rapids: Kregel, 2003.

Frazer, James G. 1975. *Folklore in the Old Testament.* Reprinted. New York: Hart.

Fretheim, Terence. 1983. *Deuteronomic History.* Nashville: Abingdon.

_____. 1984. *The Suffering of God.* Philadelphia: Fortress.

Frolov, Serge. 2007. "Fire, Smoke, and Judah in Judges: A Response to Gregory Wong." *SJOT* 21:1, 127–38.

_____. 2008. "Joshua's Double Demise (Josh. XXIV 28–31; Judg. II 6–9): Making Sense of a Repetition." *VT* 58, 315–23.

_____. 2009. "Rethinking Judges." *CBQ* 71, 24–41.

Fuchs, Esther. 1993. "Marginalization, Ambiguity, Silencing the Story of Jephthah's Daughter." In *Judges,* edited by Athalya Brenner, 116–30. FCB. Sheffield: Sheffield Academic.

_____. 2000. *Sexual Politics in the Biblical Narrative: Reading the Hebrew Bible as a Woman.* JSOTSup 310. Sheffield: Sheffield Academic.

Galil, Gershon. 2004. "The Chronological Framework of the Deuteronomistic History." *Bib* 85, 713–21.

Galpaz-Feller, Pnina. 2006a. "'Let My Soul Die with the Philistines,' (Judges 16.30)." *JSOT* 30, 315–25.

_____. 2006b. *Samson: The Hero and the Man.* Bern: Peter Lang.

Garsiel, Moshe. 1993. Homiletic Name-Derivations as a Literary Device in the Gideon Narrative: Judges VI-VIII. *VT* 43, 302–17.

Geoghegan, Jeffrey C. 2003. "'Until This Day' and the Preexilic Redaction of the Deuteronomistic History." *JBL* 122, 201–227.

Gerbrandt, Gerald E. 1986. *Kingship According to the Deuteronomistic History.* SBLDS 87. Atlanta: Scholars Press.

Gevirtz, Stanley. 1963. "Jericho and Shechem: A Religio-Literary Aspect of City Destruction." *VT* 13, 52–62.

Gibson, John C. L. 1978. *Canaanite Myths and Legends.* 2d ed. Edinburgh: T & T Clark.

Gillmayr-Bucher, Susanne. 2009. "Framework and Discourse in the Book of Judges." *JBL* 128, 687–702.

Globe, Alexander. 1974. "The literary Structure and Unity of the Song of Deborah." *JBL* 93, 493–512.

_____. 1975a. "Judges v 27." *VT* 25, 362–67.

_____. 1975b. "The Muster of the Tribes in Judges 5 11e–18." *ZAW* 86, 169–84.

_____. 1990. "'Enemies Round About': Disintegrative Structure in the Book of Judges." In *Mappings of the Biblical Terrain: The Bible as Text,* edited by Vincent L. Tollers and John Maier, 233–51. Lewisburg: Bucknell University Press.

Gnuse, Robert. 2007. "Abducted Wives: A Hellenistic Narrative in Judges 21?" *SJOT* 21:2, 228–40.

Goldingay John. 2003. *Old Testament Theology, Volume One: Israel's Gospel*. Downer's Grove: InterVarsity.

Gooding, David W. 1982. "The Composition of the Book of Judges." *ErIsr* 16, 70*-79*.

Gravett, Sandie. 2004. "Reading 'Rape' in the Hebrew Bible." *JSOT* 28, 279–99.

Gray, John. 1986. *Joshua, Judges, Ruth*. New Century Bible Ccommentary. Grand Rapids: Wm. B. Eerdmans.

_____. 1988. "Israel in the Song of Deborah." In *Ascribe to the Lord: Biblical and Other Studies in Memory of Peter C. Craigie*, edited by Lyle Eslinger and Glen Taylor, 421–55. JSOTSup 67. Sheffield: Sheffield Academic.

Greenberg, Moshe. 1955. *The Hab/Piru*. New Haven: American Oriental Society.

_____. 1983. *Biblical Prose Prayer*. Berkeley: University of California.

Greene, Mark. 1991. "Enigma Variations: Aspects of the Samson Story Judges 13–16." *VE* 21, 53–79.

Greene, John T. 1989. *The Role of the Messenger and Message in the Ancient Near East*. BJS 169. Atlanta: Scholars Press.

Greenspahn, Frederick E. 1982. "An Egyptian Parallel to Judg 17:6 and 21:25." *JBL* 101, 129–30.

_____. 1986. "The Theology of the Framework of Judges." *VT* 36, 385–96.

Greenstein, Edward L. 1981. "The Riddle of Samson." *Proof* 1, 237–60.

Guest, Pauline D. 1997. "Dangerous Liaisons in the Book of Judges." *SJOT* 11, 241–69.

_____. 1998. "Can Judges Survive Without Sources?: Challenging the Consensus." *JSOT* 78, 43–61.

Guillaume, Philippe. 1998. "An Anti-Judean Manifesto in Judges 1?" *BN* 95, 12–17.

_____. 2000. "Deborah and the Seven Tribes." *BN* 101, 18–21.

_____. 2001. "Dating the *Negatives Besitzverzeichnis* (Judges 1, 27–34): The case of Sidon." *Hen* 23, 131–37.

_____. 2002. "From a Post-Monarchical to the Pre-Monarchical Period of the Judges." *BN* 113, 12–17.

_____. 2004. *Waiting for Josiah: The Judges*. Edinburgh: T & T Clark.

Gundry, Stanley N., ed. 2003. *Show Them No Mercy: 4 Views on God and Canaanite Genocide*. Grand Rapids: Zondervan.

Gunn, David M. 1974. "Narrative Patterns and Oral Tradition in Judges and Samuel." *VT* 24, 286–317.

_____. 1987. "Joshua and Judges." In *The literary guide to the Bible,* edited by Robert Alter and Frank Kermode, 102–21. Cambridge: Harvard University Press.

_____. 1992. "Samson of Sorrows: An Isaianic Gloss on Judges 13–16." In *Reading Between Texts: Intertextuality and the Hebrew Bible,* edited by Danna N. Fewell, 225–53. Louisville: Westminster/John Knox.

_____. 2005. *Judges.* BkBC. Malden: Blackwell.

Gunn, David, and Danna N. Fewell. 1993. *Narrative in the Hebrew Bible.* Oxford: Oxford University Press.

Hackett, Jo Ann. 2004. "Violence and Women's Lives in the Book of Judges." *Int* 58, 356–64.

Hadley, Judith M. 2000. *The Cult of Asherah in Ancient Israel and Judah.* Cambridge: Cambridge University Press.

Hallo, William W. 2004. "New Light on the Story of Achsah." In *Inspired Speech: Prophecy in the Ancient Near East, Essays in Honor of Herbert B. Huffman,* edited by John Kaltner and Louis Stulman, 30–35. JSOTSup 378. London: T & T Clark International.

Halpern, Baruch. 1978. "The Rise of Abimelek Ben-Jerubbaal." *HAR* 2, 79–100.

_____. 1988a. "The Assassination of Eglon." *BRev* (December), 33–41, 44.

_____. 1988b. *The First Historians: The Hebrew Bible and History.* San Francisco: Harper & Row.

Halton, Charles. 2009. "Samson's Last Laugh: The Ś/ŠḤQ Pun in Judges 16:25–27." *JBL* 128, 61–64.

Hamilton, Victor P. 2001. *Handbook on the Historical Books.* Grand Rapids: Baker.

Handy, Lowell. 1992. "Uneasy Laughter: Ehud and Eglon as Ethnic Humor." *SJOT* 6, 233–46.

Hauser, Alan J. 1975. "The 'Minor Judges'—a Re-Evaluation." *JBL* 94, 190–200.

_____. 1987. "Two Songs of Victory: A Comparison of Exodus 15 and Judges 5." In *Directions in Biblical Hebrew Poetry,* edited by Elaine R. Follis, 265–84. JSOTSup 40. Sheffield: JSOT.

Heffelfinger, Katie. 2009. "'My Father is King': Chiefly Politics and the Rise and Fall of Abimelech." *JSOT* 33, 277–92.

Heller, Roy L. 2004. *Narrative Structure and Discourse Constellations: An Analysis of Clause Function in Biblical Hebrew Prose.* HSS 55. Winona Lake: Eisenbrauns.

Hendel, Ronald S. 1996. "Sibilants and *Sibbolet* (Judges 12:6)." *BASOR* 301, 69–75.

Herr, Denise D., and Mary P. Boyd. 2002. "A Watermelon Named Abimelech." *BAR* 28.1, 34–37, 62.

Hess, Richard S. 1997. "The Dead Sea Scrolls and Higher Criticism of the Hebrew Bible: The Case of 4QJudg." In *Scrolls and the Scriptures: Qumran Fifty Years After*, edited by Stanley E. Porter and Craig A. Evans, 122–28. JSPSup 26. Sheffield: Sheffield Academic.

_____. 1999. "Judges 1–5 and Its Translation." In *Translating the Bible: Problems and Prospects*, edited by Stanley E. Porter and Richard S. Hess, 142–60. JSOTSup 173. Sheffield: Sheffield Academic.

_____. 2003. "Israelite Identity and Personal Names from the Book of Judges." *HS* 44, 25–39.

_____. 2007. *Israelite Religions: An Archaeological and Biblical Survey*. Grand Rapids: Baker Academic.

Hoffmeier, James K. 2007. "What is the Biblical Date of the Exodus? A Response to Bryant Wood." *JETS* 50, 225–47.

Houston, Walter J. 1997. "Murder and Midrash: The Prose Appropriation of Poetic Material in the Hebrew Bible (Part II)." *ZAW* 109, 534–48.

Houtman, Cornelis. 2005. "Rewriting a Dramatic Old Testament Story: The Story of Jephthah and his Daughter in Some Examples of Christian Devotional Literature." *BibInt* 13, 167–90.

Howard, David M. 1990. "The Case for Kingship in Deuteronomy and the Former Prophets." *WTJ* 52, 101–15.

_____. 1998. *Joshua*. NAC. Nashville: Broadman & Holman.

Hoyt, JoAnna. 2012. "Reassessing Repentance in Judges." *BSac* 169, 143–58.

Hudson, Don M. 1994. "Living in a Land of Epithets: Anonymity in Judges 19–21." *JSOT* 62, 49–66.

Humphreys, W. Lee. 1989. "The Story of Jephthah and the Tragic Vision: A Response to J. Cheryl Exum." In *Signs and Wonders: Biblical Texts in Literary Focus,* edited by J. Cheryl Exum, 85–96. Decatur: Society of Biblical Literature.

Janzen, David. 2005. "Why the Deuteronomist Told about the Sacrifice of Jephthah's Daughter." *JSOT* 29.3, 339–57.

Janzen, J. Gerald. 1987. "A Certain Woman in the Rhetoric of Judges 9." *JSOT* 38, 33–37.

_____. 1989. "The Root *pr´* in Judges v 2 and Deuteronomy xxxii 42." *VT* 39, 393–406.

Jeter, Joseph R. 2003. *Preaching Judges*. St. Louis: Chalice.

Jobling, David. 1989. "Right-Brained Story of Left-Handed Man: An Antiphon to Yairah Amit." In *Signs and Wonders: Biblical Texts in*

Literary Focus, edited by J. Cheryl Exum, 125–31. Decatur: Society of Biblical Literature.

———. 1995. "Structuralist Criticism: The Text's World of Meaning." In *Judges and Method: New Approaches in Biblical Studies,* edited by Gale A. Yee, 91–118. Minneapolis: Fortress.

Johnson, Benjamin J. M. 2010. "What Type of Son is Samson? Reading Judges 13 as a Biblical Type-Scene." *JETS* 53, 269–86.

Johnston, Philip S. 2002. *Shades of Sheol: Death and Afterlife in the Old Testament.* Downers Grove: InterVarsity.

Jones-Warsaw, Koala. 1993. "Toward a Womanist Hermeneutic: A Reading of Judges 19–21." In *Judges,* edited by Athalya Brenner, 172–86. FCB. Sheffield: Sheffield Academic.

Jonker, Louis C. 1992. "Samson in Double Vision: Judges 13–16 from Historical-Critical and Narrative Perspectives." *JNSL* 18, 49–66.

Josipovici, Gabriel. 1988. *The Book of God: A Response to the Bible.* New Haven: Yale University Press.

Jost, Renate. 1999. "God of Love/God of Vengeance, or Samson's 'Prayer for Vengeance.'" In *Judges,* edited by Athalya Brenner, 117–25. FCBSS. Sheffield: Sheffield Academic.

Jull, Tom A. 1998. "מקרה in Judges 3: A Scatological Reading." *JSOT* 81, 63–75.

Kallai, Zecharia. 1997. "'Dan Why Abides He by Ships'—and the Rules of Historiographical Writing." *JNSL* 23/2, 35–45.

Kaminsky, Joel S. 1995. *Corporate Responsibility in the Hebrew Bible.* JSOTSup 196. Sheffield: Sheffield Academic.

Kamuf, Peggy. 1993. "Author of a Crime." In *Judges,* edited by Athalya Brenner, 187–207. FCB. Sheffield: Sheffield Academic.

Kim, Jichan. 1993. *The Structure of the Samson Cycle.* Kampen: Kok Pharos.

King, Philip J. and Lawrence E. Stager. 2001. *Life in Biblical Israel.* Louisville: Westminster John Knox.

Kitchen, Kenneth A. 2003. *On the Reliability of the Old Testament.* Grand Rapids: William B. Eerdmans.

Klaus, Natan. 1999. *Pivot Patterns in the Former Prophets.* JSOTSup 247. Sheffield: Sheffield Academic.

Klein, Lillian R. 1988. *The Triumph of Irony in the Book of Judges.* JSOTSup 68. Sheffield: Sheffield Academic.

———. 1993a. "A Spectrum of Female Characters in the Book of Judges." In *Judges,* edited by Athalya Brenner, 24–33. FCB. Sheffield: Sheffield Academic.

———. 1993b. "The book of Judges: Paradigm and Deviation in Images of Women." In *Judges,* edited by Athalya Brenner, 55–71. FCB. Sheffield: Sheffield Academic.

_____. 1999. "Achsah: What Price this Prize?" In *Judges,* edited by Athalya Brenner, 18–26. FCBSS. Sheffield: Sheffield Academic.

Klein, Ralph. 1974. *Textual Criticism of the Old Testament: The Septuagint after Qumran.* Philadelphia: Fortress.

_____. 1983. *1 Samuel.* WBC. Waco, TX: Word.

Knauf, Ernst A. 1991. "Eglon and Ophrah: Two Toponymic Notes on the Book of Judges." *JSOT* 51, 25–44.

Kramer, Phyllis S. 1999. "Jephthah's Daughter: A Thematic Approach to the Narrative as Seen in Selected Rabbinical Exegesis and in Artwork." In *Judges,* edited by Athalya Brenner, 67–92. FCBSS. Sheffield: Sheffield Academic.

Laato, Antti. 2003. "Theodicy in the Deuteronomistic History." In *Theodicy in the World of the Bible,* edited by Antti Laato and Johannes C. de Moor, 183–235. Leiden: E. J. Brill.

Lapsley, Jacqueline E. 2005. *Whispering the Word: Hearing Women's Stories in the Old Testament.* Louisville: Westminster John Knox.

Lasine, Stuart. 1984. "Guest and Host in Judges 19: Lot's Hospitality in an Inverted World." *JSOT* 29, 37–59.

Latvus, Kari. 1998. *God, Anger and Ideology: The Anger of God in Joshua and Judges in Relation to Deuteronomy and the Priestly Writings.* JSOTSup 279. Sheffield: Sheffield Academic.

Layton, Scott C. 1997. "Ya'el in Judges 4: An Onomastic Rejoinder." *ZAW* 109, 93–94.

Leder, Arie C. 2002. "Paradise Lost: Reading the Former Prophets by the Rivers of Babylon." *CTJ* 37, 9–27.

Lee, Bernon. 2002. "Fragmentation of Reader Focus in the Preamble to Battle in Judges 6.1–7.14." *JSOT* 97, 65–86.

Leuchter, Mark. 2010. "'Why Tarry the Wheels of his Chariot?' (Judg 5,28): Canaanite Chariots and Echoes of Egypt in the Song of Deborah." *Bib* 91, 256–68.

Levine, Baruch. 1993. *Numbers 1–20.* AB. New York: Doubleday.

Lewis, C. S. 1979. *Mere Christianity.* New York: Macmillan.

Lewis, Theodore J. 1996. "The Identity and Function of El/Baal Berith." *JBL* 115, 401–23.

Lichtheim Miriam. 1976. *Ancient Egyptian Literature, Volume II: The New Kingdom.* Berkeley: University of California Press.

Lilley, J. P. U. 1967. "A Literary Appreciation of the Book of Judges." *TynBul* 18, 94–102.

Lindars, Barnabus. 1979. "The Israelite Tribes in Judges." In *Studies in the Historical Books of the Old Testament,* edited by John A. Emerton, 95–112. VTSup 30. Leiden: E. J. Brill.

_____. 1995. *Judges 1–5.* Edinburgh: T & T Clark.

Lipinski, Edward. 1967. "Juges 5, 4–5 et Psaume 68, 8–11." *Bib* 48, 185–208.

Loewenstamm, Samuel E. 1980. *Comparative Studies in Biblical and Ancient Oriental Literatures.* AOAT 204. Neukirchen-Vluyn: Neukirchener Verlag.

Logan, Alice. 2009. "Rehabilitating Jephthah." *JBL* 128, 665–85.

Longacre, Robert E. 1994. "*Weqatal* Forms in Biblical Hebrew Prose: A Discourse-Modular Approach." In *Biblical Hebrew and Discourse Linguistics,* edited by Robert Bergen, 50–98. Winona Lake: Eisenbrauns.

Longman, Tremper, III, and Daniel G. Reid. 1995. *God is a Warrior.* Grand Rapids: Zondervan.

Maag, V. 1965. "Belijaʻal im Alten Testament." *TZ* 21, 287–99.

MacIntosh, Andrew A. 1985. "The Meaning of *MKLYM* in Judges XVIII 7." *VT* 35, 68–77.

Malamat, Abraham. 1970. "The Danite Migration and the Pan-Israelite Exodus-Conquest: A Biblical Narrative Pattern." *Bib* 51, 1–16.

_____. 2004. "The Punishment of Succoth and Penuel by Gideon in the Light of Ancient Near Eastern Treaties." In *Sefer Moshe: The Moshe Weinfeld Jubilee Volume,* edited by Chaim Cohen, Avi Hurvitz, and Shalom M. Paul, 69–71. Winona Lake: Eisenbrauns.

Marais, Jacobus. 1998. *Representation in Old Testament Narrative Texts.* Leiden: Brill.

Marcus, David. 1986. *Jephthah and His Vow.* Lubbock, TX: Texas Tech University.

_____. 1989. "The Bargaining Between Jephthah and the Elders (Judges 11:4–11)." *JANES* 19, 95–100.

_____. 1990. "The Legal Dispute Between Jephthah and the Elders." *HAR* 12, 105–15.

_____. 1992. "Ridiculing the Ephraimites: The Shibboleth Incident (Judg 12:6)." *Maarav* 8, 95–105.

Margalit, Baruch. 1979–80. "The Ugaritic Feast of the Drunken Gods: Another Look at RS 24.258 (KTU 1.114)." *Maarav* 2/1, 65–120.

_____. 1995. "Observations on the Jael-Sisera Story (Judges 4–5)." In *Pomegranates and Golden Bells: Studies in Biblical, Jewish, and Near Eastern Ritual, Law, and Literature in Honor of Jacob Milgrom,* edited by David P. Wright, David N. Freedman, and Avi Hurvitz, 629–41. Winona Lake: Eisenbrauns.

Margalith, Othniel. 1985. "Samson's Foxes." *VT* 35, 224–29.

_____. 1986a. "More Samson Legends." *VT* 36, 397–405.

_____. 1986b. "Samson's Riddle and Samson's Magic Locks." *VT* 36, 225–34.

_____. 1987. "The Legends of Samson/Heracles." *VT* 37, 63–70.

Martin, Lee R. 2007. "The Intrusive Prophet: The Narrative Function of the Nameless Prophet in Judges 6." *JSem* 16, 113–40.

_____. 2009. "From Gilgal to Bochim: The Narrative Significance of the Angel of Yahweh in Judges 2:1." *JSem* 18, 331–43.

Matthews, Victor H. 1989. "Freedom and Entrapment in the Samson Narrative: A Literary Analysis." *PRSt* 16, 245–57.

_____. 1991. "Hospitality and Hostility in Judges 4." *BTB* 21, 13–21.

_____. 2004. *Judges and Ruth*. NCBC. Cambridge: Cambridge University Press.

Mayes, Andrew D. H. 2001. "Deuteronomistic Royal Ideology in Judges 17–21." *BibInt* 9, 241–58.

Mayfield, Tyler. 2009. "The Accounts of Deborah (Judges 4–5) in Recent Research." *CurBS* 7, 306–35.

McCann, J. Clinton. 2002. *Judges*. Interpretation. Louisville: John Knox.

McCarter, Peter K. 1980. *I Samuel*. AB. New York: Doubleday.

McMillion, Phillip. 1999. "Worship in Judges 17–18." In *Worship and the Hebrew Bible; Essays in Honour of John T. Willis*, edited by M. Patrick Graham, Rick R. Marrs, and Steven L. McKenzie, 225–43. JSOTSup 284. Sheffield: Sheffield Academic.

McNutt, Paula M. 1990. *The Forging of Israel: Iron Technology, Symbolism, and Tradition in Ancient Society*. JSOTSup 108. Sheffield: Almond.

Mehlman, Israel. 1995. "Jephthah." *JBQ* 23, 73–78.

Meier, Sam A. 1988. *The Messenger in the Ancient Semitic World*. HSM 45. Atlanta: Scholars Press.

Merrill, Eugene H. 1987. *Kingdom of Priests*. Grand Rapids: Baker.

Milgrom, Jacob. 1989. *Numbers*. JPSBC. Philadelphia: The Jewish Publication Society.

Miller, Geoffrey P. 1996. "Verbal Feud in the Hebrew Bible: Judges 3:12–30 and 19–21." *JNES* 55, 105–17.

_____. 1998. "A Riposte Form in the Song of Deborah." In *Gender and Law in the Hebrew Bible and the Ancient Near East*, Victor H. Matthews, Bernard M. Levinson, and Tikva Frymer-Kensky, 113–27. JSOTSup 262. Sheffield: Sheffield Academic.

Miller, Paul. 2003. "Moral Formation and the Book of Judges." *EQ* 75, 99–115.

Miller, Patrick D. 1982. *Sin and Judgment in the Prophets*. Chico: Scholars.

_____. 2000. *The Religion of Ancient Israel*. Louisville: Westminster John Knox.

Miller, Robert D., II. 2002. "Deuteronomistic Theology in the Book of Judges?" *OTE* 15, 411–16.

_____. 2005. *Chieftains of the Highland Clans: A History of Israel in the 12th and 11th Centuries B.C.* Grand Rapids: William B. Eerdmans.

_____. 2008. "When Pharaohs Ruled: On the Translation of Judges 5:2." *JTS* 59, 650–54.

Mobley, Gregory. 1997. "The Wild Man in the Bible and the Ancient Near East." *JBL* 116, 217–33.

_____. 2005. *The Empty Men: The Heroic Tradition of Ancient Israel*. New York: Doubleday.

Moore, George F. 1895. *Judges*. ICC. Edinburgh: T & T Clark.

Mosca, Paul G. 1984. "Who Seduced Whom? A Note on Joshua 15:18 // Judges 1:14." *CBQ* 46, 18–22.

Mueller, E. Aydeet. 2001. *The Micah Story: A Morality Tale in the Book of Judges*. New York: Peter Lang.

Mullen, E. Theodore, Jr. 1982. "The 'Minor Judges': Some Literary and Historical Considerations." *CBQ* 44, 185–201.

_____. 1984. "Judges 1:1–36: The Deuteronomistic Reintroduction of the Book of Judges." *HTR* 77, 33–54.

_____. 1993. *Narrative History and Ethnic Boundaries*. Atlanta: Scholars Press.

Müllner, Ilse. 1999. "Lethal Differences: Sexual Violence as Violence Against Others in Judges 19." In *Judges,* edited by Athalya Brenner, 126–42. FCBSS. Sheffield: Sheffield Academic.

Murray, D. F. 1979. "Narrative Structure and Technique in the Deborah-Barak Story (Judges IV 4–22)." In *Studies in the Historical Books of the Old Testament,* edited by John A. Emerton, 155–89. VTSup 30. Leiden: E. J. Brill.

Na'aman, Nadav. 1990. "Literary and Topographical Notes on the Battle of Kishon (Judges iv–v)." *VT* 40, 423–36.

_____. 2005. "The Danite Campaign Northward (Judges XVII-XVIII) and the Migration of the Phocaeans to Massalia (Strabo IV 1,4)." *VT* 55, 47–60.

Nel, Philip. 1985. "The Riddle of Samson (Judg 14,14.18)." *Bib* 66, 534–45.

Nelson, Richard D. 2007. "Ideology, Geography, and the List of Minor Judges." *JSOT* 31, 347–64.

Ng, Aandrew H.-S. 2007. "Revisiting Judges 19: A Gothic Perspective." *JSOT* 32.2, 199–215.

Niditch, Susan. 1982. "The 'Sodomite' Theme in Judges 19–20: Family, Community, and Social Disintegration." *CBQ* 44, 365–78.

_____. 1989. "Eroticism and Death in the Tale of Sisera." In *Gender and Difference in Ancient Israel,* edited by Peggy L. Day, 43–57. Minneapolis: Fortress.

_____. 1990. "Samson as Culture Hero, Trickster, and Bandit: The Empowerment of the Weak." *CBQ* 52, 608–24.

_____. 1993. *War in the Hebrew Bible.* New York: Oxford University Press.

_____. 1999. "Reading Story in Judges 1." In *The Labour of Reading: Desire, Alienation, and Biblical Interpretation,* edited by Fiona C. Black, Roland Boer, and Eris Runions, 193–208. SBL Semeia Studies 36. Atlanta: Society of Biblical Literature.

_____. 2008. *Judges: A Commentary.* OTL. Louisville: Westminster John Knox.

Niehaus, Jeffrey J. 2008. *Ancient Near Eastern Themes in Biblical Theology.* Grand Rapids: Kregel.

Niesiolowski-Spanò, Lukasz. 2005. "Where Should One Look for Gideon's Ophra?" *Bib* 86, 478–93.

Novik, Tavi. 2009. "האמין in Jud 11,20 and the Semantics of Assent." *ZAW* 121, 577–83.

O'Brien, Mark A. 1994. "Judges and the Deuteronomistic History." In *The History of Israel's Traditions: The Heritage of Martin Noth,* edited by Steven L. McKenzie and M. Patrick Graham, 235–59. JSOTSup 182. Sheffield: Sheffield Academic.

O'Connell, Robert H. 1996. *The Rhetoric of the Book of Judges.* VTSup 63. Leiden: Brill.

O'Connor, Michael. 1986. "The Women in the Book of Judges." *HAR* 10, 277–93.

Ogden, Graham S. 1991. "The Special Features of a Story: A Study of Judges 3:12–30." *TBT* 42, 408–14.

_____. 1995. "Jotham's Fable: Its Structure and Function in Judges 9." *TBT* 46, 301–08.

Olson, Dennis T. 1998. "The Book of Judges." In *The New Interpreter's Bible, Volume II,* edited by David L. Petersen, et al., 721–888. Nashville: Abingdon.

Organ, Barbara E. 2001. "Pursuing Phinehas: A Synchronic Reading." *CBQ* 63, 203–18.

Otzen, Benedikt. 1979. "Israel Under the Assyrians." In *Power and*

Propaganda: A Symposium on Ancient Empires, edited by Mogens T. Larsen, 251–6). Copenhagen: Akademisk Forlag.

Pardee, Dennis. 2001. "Ugaritic Science." In *The World of the Arameans III,* edited by P. M. Michèle Daviau, John W. Wevers, and Michael Weigl, 223–54. JSOTSup 326. Sheffield: Sheffield Academic.

Parker, Simon B. 1997. *Stories in Scripture and Inscriptions.* New York: Oxford University Press.

Parunak, H. van Dyke. 1975. "A Semantic Survey of NḤM." *Bib* 56, 512–32.

Patterson, Richard. 1981. "The Song of Deborah." In *Tradition and Testament: Essays in Honor of Charles Lee Feinberg,* edited by John S. and Paul D. Feinberg, 123–60. Chicago: Moody.

Payne, Elizabeth J. 1983. "The Midianite Arc in Joshua and Judges." In *Midian, Moab and Edom: The History and Archaeology of Late Bronze and Iron Age Jordan and North-West Arabia,* edited by John F. A. Sawyer and David J. A. Clines, 163–72. JSOTSup 24. Sheffield: JSOT.

Peels, Hendrik G. L. 1995. *The Vengeance of God: The Meaning of the Root NQM and the Function of the NQM-Texts in the Context of Divine Revelation in the Old Testament.* Leiden: Brill.

Penchansky, David. 1992. "Staying the Night: Intertextuality in Genesis and Judges." In *Reading Between Texts: Intertextuality and the Hebrew Bible,* edited by Danna N. Fewell, 77–88. Louisville: Westminster/John Knox.

Petrovich, Douglas. 2008. "The Dating of Hazor's Destruction in Joshua 11 by Way of Biblical, Archaeological, and Epigraphical Evidence." *JETS* 51, 489–512.

Pettey, Richard J. 1990. *Asherah: Goddess of Israel.* New York: Peter Lang.

Pitard, Wayne T. 1987. *Ancient Damascus.* Winona Lake: Eisenbrauns.

Polzin, Robert. 1980. *Moses and the Deuteronomist: A Literary Study of the Deuteronomic History, Part One.* New York: Seabury.

Pressler, Carolyn. 2002. *Joshua, Judges, and Ruth.* Westminster Bible Companion. Louisville: Westminster John Knox.

Pritchard, James. 1969. *Ancient Near Eastern Texts Relating to the Old Testament.* 3rd ed. Princeton: Princeton University Press.

Provan, Iain. W. 1995. "The Messiah in the Books of Kings." In *The Lord's Anointed: Interpretation of Old Testament Messianic Texts,* edited by Philip E. Satterthwaite, Richard S. Hess, and Gordon J. Wenham, 67–85. Grand Rapids: Baker.

Reinhartz, Adele. 1992. "Samson's Mother: An Unnamed Protagonist."

JSOT 55, 25–37. [This article also appears in *Judges,* edited by Athalya Brenner, 157–70. FCB. Sheffield: Sheffield Academic.]

_____. 1998. *"Why ask my name?": Anonymity and Identity in Biblical Narrative.* New York: Oxford University Press.

Reis, Pamela T. 2002. *Reading the Lines: A Fresh Look at the Hebrew Bible.* Peabody: Hendrickson.

_____. 2005. "Uncovering Jael and Sisera: A New Reading." *SJOT* 19.1, 24–47.

_____. 2006. "The Levite's Concubine: New Light on a Dark Story." *SJOT* 20.1, 125–46.

Rendsburg, Gary A. 1998–99). "Confused Language as a Deliberate Literary Device in Biblical Hebrew Narrative." *The Journal of Hebrew Scriptures* 2:6. doi:10.5508/jhs.1999.v2.a6.

Revell, Ernst J. 1985. "The Battle with Benjamin (Judges XX 29–48) and Hebrew Narrative Technique." *VT* 35, 417–33.

_____. 2001. "Midian and Ishmael in Genesis 37: Synonyms in the Joseph Story." In *The World of the Aramaeans I: Biblical Studies in Honour of Paul-Eugene Dion,* edited by P. M. Michèle Daviau, John W. Wevers, and Michael Weigl, 70–91. JSOTSup 324. Sheffield: Sheffield Academic.

Robinson, Bernard P. 2004. "The Story of Jephthah and his Daughter: Then and Now." *Bib* 85, 331–48.

Römer, Thomas. 1998. "Why Would the Deuteronomists Tell About the Sacrifice of Jephthah's Daughter?" *JSOT* 77, 27–38.

Römer, Thomas and Albert de Pury. 2000. "Deuteronomistic Historiography (DH): History of Research and Debated Issues." In *Israel Constructs its History: Deuteronomistic Historiography in Recent Research,* edited by Albert de Pury, Thomas Römer, and Jean-Daniel Macchi, 24–141. JSOTSup 306. Sheffield: Sheffield Academic.

Ross, James. 1987. "The Prophet as Yahweh's Messenger." In *Prophecy in Ancient Israel,* edited by David L. Petersen, 112–21. Philadelphia: Fortress.

Rottzoll, Alexandra, and Dirk U. 2003. "Die Erzählung von Jiftach und Seiner Tochter (Jdc 11,30–40) in der Mittelalterlich-Jüdischen und Historisch-Kritischen Bibelexegese." *ZAW* 115, 210–30.

Roux, Georges. 1966. *Ancient Iraq.* Baltimore: Penguin Books.

Rozenberg, Martin S. 1975. "The Šōf^eṭîm in the Bible." *ErIsr* 12, 77*-86*

Rudman, Dominic. 2000. "The Second Bull in Judges 6:25–28." *JNSL* 26/1, 97–103.

Ryken, Leland, James C. Wilhoit, and Tremper Longman III, eds. 1998. *Dictionary of Biblical Imagery.* Downers Grove: InterVarsity.

Sasson, Jack M. 1988. "Who Cut Samson's Hair (and Other Trifling Issues Raised by Judges 16)." *Proof* 8, 333–39.

Satterthwaite, Philip E. 1992. "Narrative Artistry in the Composition of Judges XX 29ff." *VT* 42, 80–89.

_____. 1993. "'No king in Israel': Narrative Criticism and Judges 17–21." *TynBul* 44, 75–88.

_____. 2005. "Judges." In *Dictionary of the Old Testament Historical Books,* edited by Bill T. Arnold and H. G. M. Williamson, 580–92. Downers Grove: InterVarsity.

Savran, George W. 1988. *Telling and Retelling: Quotation in Biblical Narrative.* Bloomington: Indiana University Press.

_____. 2005. *Encountering the Divine: Theophany in Biblical Narrative.* London: T & T Clark.

Sawyer, John F. A. 1981. "'From Heaven Fought the Stars' (Judges V 20)." *VT* 31, 87–89.

_____. 1983. "The Meaning of *Barzel* in the Biblical Expressions "Chariots of Iron", "Yoke of Iron", etc." In *Midian, Moab and Edom: The History and Archaeology of Late Bronze and Iron Age Jordan and North-West Arabia,* edited by John F. A. Sawyer and David J. A. Clines, 129–34. JSOTSup 24. Sheffield: JSOT.

Scham, Sandra. 2002. "The Days of the Judges: When Men and Women Were Animals and Trees Were Kings." *JSOT* 97, 37–64.

Scherer, Andreas. 2002. "Simson und Schamgar." *ZAW* 114, 106–09.

Schipper, Jeremy. 2003. "Narrative Obscurity of Samson's חידה in Judges 14.14 and 18." *JSOT* 27, 339–53.

Schloen, J. David. 1993. "Caravans, Kenites, and *Casus Belli*: Enmity and Alliance in the Song of Deborah." *CBQ* 55, 18–38.

Schneider, Tammi J. 2000. *Judges.* Collegeville: Liturgical Press.

Schöpflin, Karin. 2004. "Jotham's Speech and Fable as Prophetic Comment on Abimelech's Story: The Genesis of Judges 9." *SJOT* 18. 1, 17–22.

Schoville, Keith N. 1994. "Canaanites and Amorites." In *Peoples of the Old Testament World,* edited by Alfred J. Hoerth, Gerald L. Mattingly and Edwin Yamauchi, 157–82. Grand Rapids: Baker.

Segert, Stanislav. 1984. "Paronomasia in the Samson Narrative in Judges xiii-xvi." *VT* 34, 454–61.

Sellin, Ernst, and Georg Fohrer. 1968. *Introduction to the Old Testament.* Translated by David E. Green. Nashville: Abingdon.

Shupak, Nili. 1989. "New Light on Shamgar ben `Anath." *Bib* 70, 517–25.

Singer, Itamar. 1992. "Towards the Image of Dagon the God of the Philistines." *Syria* 69, 431–50.

Sivan, Daniel. 1997. *A Grammar of the Ugaritic Language*. Leiden: Brill.

Smith, Carol. 1997. "Samson and Delilah: A Parable of Power?" *JSOT* 76, 45–57.

_____. 1999. "Delilah: A Suitable Case for (Feminist) Treatment?" In *Judges,* edited by Athalya Brenner, 93–116. FCBSS. Sheffield: Sheffield Academic.

Smith, Michael J. 2005. "The Failure of the Family in Judges, Part 1: Jephthah." *BSac* 162, 279–98.

Smith, Mark S. 2002. *The Early History of God: Yahweh and the Other Deities in Ancient Israel*. 2nd ed. Grand Rapids: Eerdmans.

Snyman, Stephanus D. 2005. "Shamgar Ben Anath: A Farming Warrior or a Farmer at War?" *VT* 55, 125–29.

Soden, J. 1989. "Prose and Poetry Compared: Judges 4 and 5 in Their Ancient Near Eastern Context. Ph. D. diss., Dallas Theological Seminary.

Soggin, J. Alberto. 1981. *Judges*. OTL. Translated by John Bowden Philadelphia: Westminster.

_____. 1988. "The Migdal Temple, Migdal Sᵉkem Judg 9 and the Artifact on Mount Ebal." In *"Wunschet Jerusalem Frieden": Collected Communications to the XIIth Congress of the International Organization for the Study of the Old Testament, Jerusalem 1986,* edited by Matthias Augustin and Klaus-Dietrich Schunck, 115–19. Frankfurt am Main: Peter Lang.

Sparks, Kenton L. 1998. *Ethnicity and Identity in Ancient Israel*. Winona Lake: Eisenbrauns.

_____. 2005. *Ancient Texts for the Study of the Hebrew Bible*. Peabody: Hendrickson.

Spronk, Klaas. 2001a. "A Story to Weep About: Some Remarks on Judges 2:1–5 and its Context." In *Unless Someone Guide Me . . . Festschrift for Karel A. Deurloo,* edited by Janet W. Dyk, et al., 87–94. Maastricht: Uitgeverij Shaker.

_____. 2001b. "Deborah, a Prophetess: The Meaning and Background of Judges 4:4–5." In *The Elusive Prophet,* edited by Johannes C. de Moor, 232–42. Leiden: E. J. Brill.

Stadler-Sutskover, Talia. 2002. "The Leading Word and its Roles in Judges 19–21." In *Bible and Computer: The Stellenbosch AIBI-6 Conference,* edited by Johann Cook, 295–307. Leiden: Brill.

Stager, Lawrence E. 1988. "Archaeology, Ecology and Social History: Background Themes to the Song of Deborah." In *Congress Volume: Jerusalem, 1986*, edited by John A. Emerton, 221–34. VTSup 40. Leiden: Brill.

_____. 1989. "The Song of Deborah: Why Some Tribes Answered the Call and Others Did Not." *BAR* 15:1, 51–64.

Standaert, Benoit. 1996. "Adonai Shalom (Judges 6–9): The Persuasive Means of a Narrative and the Strategies of Inculturation of Yahwism in a New Context." In *Rhetoric, Scripture and Theology: Essays from the 1994 Pretoria Conference*, edited by Stanley E. Porter and Thomas H. Olbricht, 195–202. JSNTS 131. Sheffield: Sheffield Academic.

Starke, Robert A. 2002. "Samson—The Last Judge." *Kerux* 17, 3 (Dec), 11–28.

Steinberg, Naomi. 1995. "Social Scientific Criticism: Judges 9 and Issues of Kinship." In *Judges and Method: New Approaches in Biblical Studies,* edited by Gale A. Yee, 45–64. Minneapolis: Fortress.

_____. 1999. "The Problem of Human Sacrifice in War: An Analysis of Judges 11." In *On the Way to Nineveh: Studies in Honor of George M. Landes*, edited by Stephen L. Cook and S. C. Winter, 114–35. ASOR Books, Volume 4. Atlanta: Scholars Press.

Steinmann, Andrew E. 2005. "The Mysterious Numbers of the Book of Judges." *JETS* 48, 491–500.

_____. 2010. "Literary Clues in Judges: A Response to Robert Chisholm." *JETS* 53, 365–73.

Stek, John. 1986. "The Bee and the Mountain Goat: A Literary Reading of Judges 4." In *A tribute to Gleason Archer,* edited by Walter C. Kaiser Jr., and Ronald F. Youngblood, 53–86. Chicago: Moody.

Sternberg, Meir. 1987. *The Poetics of Biblical Narrative*. Bloomington: Indiana University Press.

Stevenson, Jeffery. S. 2002. "Judah's Successes and Failures in Holy War: An Exegesis of Judges 1:1–20." *ResQ* 44, 43–54.

Stone, Ken. 1995. "Gender and Homosexuality in Judges 19: Subject-Honor, Object-Shame?" *JSOT* 67, 87–107.

_____. 1996. *Sex, Honor, and Power in the Deuteronomistic History*. JSOTSup 234. Sheffield: Sheffield Academic.

Stone, Lawson G. 2009. "Eglon's Belly and Ehud's Blade: A Reconsideration." *JBL* 128, 649–63.

Strawn, Brent. 2009. "*kĕpîr 'ărāyôt* in Judges 14:5." *VT* 59, 150–58.

Stuart, Douglas. 2001. *Old Testament Exegesis*. 3rd ed. Louisville: Westminster John Knox.

Sweeney, Marvin A. 1997. "Davidic Polemics in the Book of Judges." *VT* 47, 517–29.

Talmon, Shemaryahu. 1969. "In Those Days There Was No King in

Israel." *Proceedings of the Fifth World Congress of Jewish Studies* 1, 135–44, 242.

Tanner, J. Paul. 1990. "Textual Patterning in Biblical Hebrew Narrative: A Case Study in Judges 6–8." Ph. D. diss., University of Texas.

_____. 1992. "The Gideon Narrative as the Focal Point of Judges." *BSac* 149, 146–61.

Tatu, Silviu. 2006. "Jotham's Fable and the *Crux Interpretum* in Judges IX." *VT* 56, 105–24.

Taylor, J. Glen. 1982. "The Song of Deborah and Two Canaanite Goddesses." *JSOT* 23, 99–108.

Thompson, John L. 2002. "Preaching Texts of Terror in the Book of Judges: How Does the History of Interpretation Help?" *CTJ* 37, 49–61.

Tollington, Janet E. 1998. "The Book of Judges: The Result of Post-Exilic Exegesis?" In *Intertextuality in Ugarit and Israel, Oudtestamentische Studien,* Johannes C. de Moor, 186–96. Leiden: Brill.

Trebolle Barrera, Julio. 1989. "Textual Variants in *4QJudga* and the Textual and Editorial History of the Book of Judges." *RevQ* 54, 229–245.

Trible, Phyllis. 1981. "A Meditation in Mourning: The Sacrifice of the Daughter of Jephthah." *USQR* 31, 59–73.

_____. 1984. *Texts of Terror: Literary-Feminist Readings of Biblical Narratives.* Philadelphia: Fortress.

Ulrich, Eugene C. 1978. *The Qumran Text of Samuel and Josephus.* Missoula: Scholars Press.

Unterman, Jeremiah. 1980. "The Literary Influence of 'the Binding of Isaac' (Genesis 22) on 'the Outrage at Gibeah' (Judges 19)." *HAR* 4, 161–66.

Valler, Shulamit. 1999. "The Story of Jephthah's Daughter in the Midrash." In *Judges,* edited by Athalya Brenner, 48–66. FCBSS. Sheffield: Sheffield Academic.

van der Kooij, Arie. 1995. "'And I also Said': A New Interpretation of Judges II 3." *VT* 45, 294–306.

van der Toorn, Karel. 1986. "Judges XVI 21 in the Light of Akkadian Sources." *VT* 36, 248–53.

_____. 1990. "The Nature of the Biblical Teraphim in the Light of the Cuneiform Evidence." *CBQ* 52, 203–22.

_____. 1996. *Family Religion in Babylonia, Syria, and Israel.* Leiden: Brill.

Van Dijk-Hemmes, Fokkelien. 1993. "Mothers and a Mediator in the

Song of Deborah." In *Judges,* edited by Athalya Brenner, 110–14. FCB. Sheffield: Sheffield Academic.

van Midden, P. J. 1999. "Gideon." In *The Rediscovery of the Hebrew Bible,* edited by Janet W. Dyk, et al., 51–67. Maastricht: Uitgeverij Shaker.

_____. 2001. "A Hidden Message? Judges as Foreword to the Books of Kings." In *Unless Someone Guide Me . . . Festschrift for Karel A. Deurloo,* edited by Janet W. Dyk, et al., 77–85. Maastricht: Uitgeverij Shaker.

van Wolde, Ellen. 1995. "Ya'el in Judges 4." *ZAW* 107, 240–46.

Venter, Pieter M. 2004. "Spatiality in Psalm 29." In *Psalms and Liturgy,* edited by Dirk J. Human and Cas J. A. Vos, 235–50. JSOTSup 410. London: T & T Clark.

Vickery, John B. 1981. "In Strange Ways: The Story of Samson." In *Images of Man and God: Old Testament Short Stories in Literary Focus,* edited by Burke O. Long, 58–73. Sheffield: Almond.

Vincent, Mark A. 2000. "The Song of Deborah: A Structural and Literary Consideration." *JSOT* 91, 61–82.

von Rad, Gerhard. 1991. *Holy War in Ancient Israel.* Translated by Marva J. Dawn. 3rd ed. Grand Rapids: William B. Eerdmans.

Waldman, Nahum M. 1989. "The Imagery of Clothing, Covering, and Overpowering." *JANES* 19, 161–70.

Walsh, Carey E. 2000. *The Fruit of the Vine: Viticulture in Ancient Israel.* HSM 60. Winona Lake: Eisenbrauns.

Washburn, David L. 1990. "The Chronology of Judges: Another Look." *BSac* 147, 414–25.

Watson, Wilfred G. E. 1984. *Classical Hebrew Poetry: A Guide to its Techniques.* JSOTSup 26. Sheffield: JSOT.

Webb, Barry G. 1987. *The Book of the Judges: An Integrated Reading.* JSOTSup 46. Sheffield: Sheffield Academic.

_____. 1995. "A Serious Reading of the Samson Story (Judges 13–16)." *RTR* 54, 110–20.

Weinfeld, Moshe. 1967. "The Period of the Conquest and the Judges as Seen in the Earlier and the Later Sources." *VT* 17, 97–113.

_____. 1984. "Divine Intervention in War in Ancient Israel and in the Ancient Near East." In *History, Historiography and Interpretation: Studies in Biblical and Cuneiform Literatures,* edited by Hayim Tadmor and Moshe Weinfeld, 121–47. Reprint. Jerusalem: Magnes.

_____. 1993. "Judges 1.1–2:5: The Conquest Under the Leadership of the House of Judah." In *Understanding Poets and Prophets: Essays in Honour of George Wishart Anderson,* edited by A. Graeme Auld, 388–400. JSOTSup 152. Sheffield: Sheffield Academic.

_____. 1995. *Social Justice in Ancient Israel and in the Ancient Near East.* Minneapolis: Fortress.

Weitzman, Steven. 1997. *Song and Story in Biblical Narrative: The History of a Literary Convention in Ancient Israel.* Bloomington: Indiana University Press.

_____. 1999. "Reopening the Case of the Suspiciously Suspended Nun in Judges 18:30." *CBQ* 61, 448–60.

_____. 2002. "The Samson Story as Border Fiction." *BibInt* 10, 158–74.

Wenham, Gordon J. 2004. *Story as Torah: Reading Old Testament Narrative Ethically.* North American paperback ed. Grand Rapids: Baker.

Wessels, J. P. H. 1997. "Persuasions in Judges 2.20–3.6: A Celebration of Differences." In *The Rhetorical Analysis of Scripture: Essays from the 1995 London Conference,* edited by Stanley E. Porter and Thomas H. Olbricht, 120–36. JSOTSup 146. Sheffield: Sheffield Academic.

Wharton, James A. 1973. "The Secret of Yahweh: Story and Affirmation in Judges 13–16." *Int* 27, 48–66.

Wiggins, Steve A. 1993. *"A Reassessment of 'Asherah.'"* AOAT 235. Neukirchener-Vluyn: Verlag Butzon & Bercker Kevelaer.

_____. 1993. "Old Testament Dagan in the Light of Ugarit." *VT* 43, 268–74.

Wilcock, Michael. 1992. *The Message of Judges.* BST. Downers Grove: InterVarsity.

Wilkinson, Elizabeth. 1983. "The *Hapax Legomenon* of Judges iv 18." *VT* 33, 512–13.

Williams, Jay G. 1991. "The Structure of Judges 2.6–16.31." *JSOT* 49, 77–85.

Willis, Timothy M. 1997. "The Nature of Jephthah's Authority." *CBQ* 59, 33–44.

Wilson, Michael K. 1995. "'As you like it': The Idolatry of Micah and the Danites (Judges 17–18)." *RTR* 54, 73–85.

Winther-Nielsen, Nicolai. 2002. "Fact, Fiction, and Language Use: Can Modern Pragmatics Improve on Halpern's Case for History in Judges?" In *Windows into Old Testament History,* edited by V. Philips Long, David W. Baker, and Gordon J. Wenham, 44–81. Grand Rapids: William B. Eerdmans.

Wong, Gregory. T. K. 2005. "Is There a Direct Pro-Judah Polemic in Judges?" *SJOT* 19.1, 84–110.

_____. 2006a. *Compositional Strategy of the Book of Judges.* VTSup 111. Leiden: Brill.

_____. 2006b. "Ehud and Joab: Separated at Birth?" *VT* 56, 399–411.

_____. 2006c. "Narratives and Their Contexts: A Critique of Greger Andersson with Respect to Narrative Autonomy." *SJOT* 20, 216–30.

_____. 2007a. "Gideon: A New Moses?" In *Reflection and Refraction: Studies in Biblical Historiography in Honour of A. Graeme Auld,* Robert Rezetko, Timothy H. Lim, and W. Brian Aucker, 529–45. VTSup 113. Leiden: Brill.

_____. 2007b. Song of Deborah as polemic. *Bib* 88, 1–22.

Wood, Bryant G. 1995. "Jabin, King of Hazor." *Bible and Spade* 9, 83–85.

_____. 2003. "From Ramesses to Shiloh: Archaeological Discoveries Bearing on the Exodus–Judges Period." In *Giving the Sense: Understanding and Using Old Testament Historical Texts,* edited by David M. Howard Jr. and Michael A. Grisanti, 256–82. Grand Rapids: Kregel.

_____. 2005. "The Rise and Fall of the 13th-Century Exodus-Conquest Theory." *JETS* 48, 475–89.

_____. 2007. "The Biblical Date for the Exodus is 1446 BC: A Response to James Hoffmeier." *JETS* 50: 249–58.

Woodhouse, Robert. 2003. "The Biblical Shibboleth Story in the Light of Late Egyptian Perceptions of Semitic Sibilants: Reconciling Divergent Views." *JAOS* 123.2, 271–89.

Woods, Fred E. 1994. *Water and Storm Polemics Against Baalism in the Deuteronomic History.* New York: Peter Lang.

Yadin, Azzan. 2002. "Samson's ḤÎDÂ." *VT* 52, 407–26.

Yadin, Yiguel. 1963. *The Art of Warfare in Biblical Lands.* Translated by M. Pearlman. London: Weidenfeld and Nicolson.

Yee, Gale A. 1993. "By the Hand of a Woman: The Metaphor of the Woman Warrior in Judges 4." *Semeia* 61, 99–132.

_____. 1995a. "Ideological Criticism: Judges 17–21 and the Dismembered Body." In *Judges and Method: New Approaches in Biblical Studies,* edited by Gale A. Yee, 146–70. Minneapolis: Fortress.

_____, ed. 1995b. *Judges and Method: New Approaches in Biblical Studies.* Minneapolis: Fortress.

Young, Edward J. 1964. *An Introduction to the Old Testament.* rev. ed. Grand Rapids: William B, Eerdmans.

Younger, K. Lawson. Jr. 1991. "Heads! Tails! Or the Whole Coin?! Contextual Method and Intertextual Analysis: Judges 4 and 5." In *The Biblical Canon in Comparative Perspective: Scripture in Context IV,* edited by K. Lawson Younger, William W. Hallo, and Bernard F. Batto, 109–45. Lewiston: Edwin Mellen.

_____. 1994. "Judges 1 in Its Near Eastern Literary Context. In *Faith,*

Tradition, and History: Old Testament Historiography in its Near Eastern Context, edited by Alan R. Millard, James K. Hoffmeier, and David W. Baker, 207–27. Winona Lake: Eisenbrauns.

_____. 1995. "The Configuring of Judicial Preliminaries: Judges 1.1–2.5 and its Dependence on the Book of Joshua." *JSOT* 68, 75–92.

_____. 2002. *Judges and Ruth.* NIVAC. Grand Rapids: Zondervan.

Yuan, D. A. 2006. "A Proposed Chronology for Judges." Th.M. thesis, Dallas Theological Seminary.

Zakovitch, Yair. 1985. "Assimilation in Biblical Narratives." In *Empirical Models for Biblical Criticism,* edited by Jeffrey H. Tigay, 175–96. Philadelphia: University of Pennsylvania Press.

Zewi, Tamar. 2007. *Parenthesis in Biblical Hebrew.* Leiden: Brill.

RUTH

INTRODUCTION
TO RUTH

In the English Bible the book of Ruth follows Judges. This placement, which reflects the order of books in the Septuagint, makes sense, because the events recorded in Ruth took place during the Judges period.[1] The reference to David at the end of Ruth forms a transition between Judges, which states in its epilogue that Israel desperately needed a king, and 1 Samuel, which tells of the rise of kingship in Israel and the eventual choice of David to rule the nation.[2]

---

1. On the legitimacy of the Septuagint's placement of the book, see Moore 2001, 31, note 8. He concludes, "all the old arguments for the *priority* of one canonical context (MT) *over* another (LXX) are antiquated. On the contrary LXX's canonical order is just as legitimate, just as interesting, and just as authoritative as that of MT" (emphasis his). See also Goswell 2009, 461–62, who concludes that the book of Ruth "works well in all" of its "possible canonical positions" (462).

2. For a discussion of how the book of Ruth may be connected to both Judges and 1 Samuel, see Linafelt 1999, xviii-xxv. It is possible the story's connection with Bethlehem also contributed to its placement after Judges, since both of the stories in the epilogue to Judges mention Bethlehem. In Judges 17 a Levite moves from Bethlehem to Ephraim (v. 7), while in Judges 19 a Levite marries a woman from Bethlehem and then retrieves her from there after she leaves him (vv. 1–2). For a study of this

In the Hebrew Bible the book of Ruth is not located in the Former Prophets (Joshua, Judges, Samuel, Kings); instead it appears in the third section of the canon, the Writings, as one of the five Scrolls (or Megilloth).[3] In some editions (cf. *BHS*) it appears as the first of the Megilloth, right after Proverbs, probably because Ruth epitomizes the worthy wife described in the conclusion to Proverbs (note אֵשֶׁת חַיִל, "worthy wife," in both Ruth 3:11 and Prov. 31:10). However, the book's placement within the Writings is not fixed. Other traditions place the book at the beginning of the Writings before Psalms, or second in the Megilloth after Song of Songs.[4]

LITERARY GENRE

Since the rise of Old Testament form criticism, scholars have assigned various genre labels to the book of Ruth, including folktale, novella, and short story.[5] Such designations often seem arbitrary and those who propose them have at times imposed a preconceived notion of genre upon the text, rather than letting the internal evidence of the text speak for itself. When one examines the book, it seems to be a

---

"Bethlehem trilogy," see Merrill, 1985, 131–33, as well as Moore 2001, 36–37. Contrasting Ruth with Judges 17–21, Moore shows that the themes of Ruth would be relevant to the kingship theme in the historical books (2001, 27–41, especially 36–41). Leder analyzes Ruth's contribution to the overall theme of the historical books (2002, 18–22). He argues that faithfulness to the law is the theme that binds together Joshua–Kings. In Joshua, Israel "commits itself to keep torah and serve the Lord," but in Judges the nation "ignores torah" and "serves and follows other gods." In Samuel, David "brings order to Israel by serving God," but then the "kings serve other gods" during a period of "torahlessness." The book of Ruth sits in the middle of this paneled structure (Joshua–Judges // Samuel–Kings), describing how "torah piety brings fullness to Naomi and Israel's emptiness" (21). For Leder, "the Ruth narrative occupies the center and focal point of a second 'Pentateuch'" (20).

3. The others are Song of Songs, Ecclesiastes, Lamentations, and Esther.
4. For a fuller discussion see Campbell 1975, 33–36. Actually the situation is much more complex than this, with the placement of Ruth varying greatly. See Dearman and Pussman 2005, 59–86. The authors point out that Ruth's placement varies depending on the canonical ordering principle being employed. There are three basic patterns: (1) "literary or nonchronological ordering," (2) "chronological ordering," and (3) a "liturgical arrangement" reflecting the book's use during the Festival of Weeks (60–61).
5. For a brief survey of attempts to label the genre of Ruth, see Bush 1996a, 33–36.

"historical short story."[6] Both the prologue and epilogue suggest it records historical events. The prologue sets the book within the period of the Judges (1:1), while the concluding genealogy (4:18–22) links one of its main characters (Boaz) with a family history that appears in ancient Israel's genealogical records (cf. 1 Chronicles 2; Block 1999, 602). The book is relatively short (85 verses) and it has the classic earmarks of a story—setting, plot structure, characterization, and varying points of view.[7]

After carefully examining the book's plot structure and characterization, Bush (1996a, 46) calls it "an edifying short story" that contains "a problem-based plot" (37). Following a description of the setting, the problem is stated and then developed. It may be summarized as "the death & emptiness of Naomi's life" resulting from the loss of her husband and sons (39). With the introduction of Boaz to the story, the plot moves toward resolution, but not without complications. Resolution comes with the birth of Obed and the recognition that he will serve as Naomi's protector (39–40). Yet, for Bush, the "all-encompassing intent" of the book "is to depict the quality of its characters, not that of a situation or a sequence of events" (42). He contends that it presents Boaz, Ruth, and Naomi "as exemplary characters" and "as models for his readers to emulate." As such, the story "intends to edify as much as to inform and entertain" (46).

Bush is correct about the story's edifying function—Boaz and especially Ruth are certainly exemplary characters. However, he overstates his case with regard to Naomi (45–46). In her case, there is significant character development as she moves from a "bitter" woman filled with despair to a satisfied grandmother. Along the way her view of God changes as well, as she comes to realize that God is her advocate, not her adversary. This change in Naomi's circumstances and perspective is central to the plot and draws attention to an important theme of this story—God's concern for and deliverance of the needy. The label

---

6. The label is Campbell's (1975, 3). Unfortunately, he then opts to call Ruth a "*Novelle*," the content of which he regards as "at least primarily fictional, if not purely so" (3–4). He concludes that the story, while being plausible and a "good guide to life and custom," is "fictional" (10). However, Campbell gives no compelling arguments why one must arrive at this conclusion. On the contrary, there is ample reason to regard it an accurate account of the events it records. Block, after mounting a convincing case for the book's historicity, labels it "an independent historiographic short story" (1999, 602–03).

7. For a fuller discussion of each of these elements, see below.

"edifying short story" may be too restrictive, for it fails to highlight the redemptive theme and theocentric nature of the book.

The book's redemptive theme emerges through its comedic plot structure. Building on the work of Frye, Grant calls the plot structure "comic/monomythic." He adds: "As such, it manifests four literary structural elements as the plot moves from tragedy through anti-romance, and then through comedy to romance" (Grant 1991, 424). He defines romance as "literature that depicts an ideal human society; joy and harmony pervade the atmosphere" (424, note 1). The book of Ruth achieves this level in 4:13–22 (437). By way of contrast, anti-romance "portrays a society in bondage; there is a distinct absence of joy and harmony" (424, note 1). Anti-romance is present in Ruth 1:19b–22 (431). One descends into anti-romance via tragedy, which is inherently "transitional" (424, note 1). The deaths of Elimelech and his sons serve this function in the book of Ruth (425). Finally, "comedy is also transitional and is the opposite of the tragic element in that it pulls the movement up from the bondage of joyless anti-romance into the freedom of joyful romance" (424, note 1). The comic structure of the book of Ruth "begins to unfold" in Ruth 1:22b and culminates in chapter 4 (433). To summarize, in the book of Ruth tragedy brings anti-romance, but in the end romance is achieved via the comic element.[8]

Rather than allowing the internal evidence of the book to dictate his understanding of its genre, Berman imposes the label "legal homily" upon the book on the basis of its alleged dependence on Deuteronomic law. He explains: "the book of Ruth constitutes a legal homily whose plot unfolds according to the sequential order of the legal materials found in Deuteronomy 24, 16–25, 10, and is a comment upon them" (Berman 2007, 23). He builds his case on Fishbane's work on innerbiblical exegesis, as well as studies by Levine and Goulder on the use of the Law in the book of Ruth. After showing that ancient Near Eastern law codes sometimes used "concatenation" (or "associative linking") as a structural device, he attempts to show that the seemingly disparate laws in Deuteronomy 24:16–25:10 can actually be seen as a cohesive unit once "their strategies of linkage" are detected (24).

Berman then tries to demonstrate that the story of Ruth reflects these laws (27–38). He explains the death of Elimelech and his sons against the background of Deuteronomy 24:16 (a prohibition against executing a son for the sins of a father, or a father for the sins of a son),

---

8. Grant explains that "the monomyth is the cyclic composite narrative comprising the four elements just described; it is the archetypal pattern true of all literature" (424, note 1).

arguing that their deaths should be seen as divine punishment. The plight of Naomi and Ruth is addressed by Deuteronomy 24:17–18 (which warns against exploitation of the impoverished, including widows), while Deuteronomy 24:19–21 (laws which command that something be left during the harvest for the impoverished) appears to have some relevance to Ruth's actions in chapter 2. Berman is hard-pressed to integrate Deuteronomy 25:1–4 into his proposed scheme. Indeed he admits: "Ultimately, however, my contention that Ruth constitutes a *sequential* legal homily of the *entire* passage from Deuteronomy 24,16–25,10 will depend upon my capacity to integrate . . . the laws of flogging (25, 1–3) and the injunction against muzzling an ox while threshing (25, 4)" (31). He appeals to a *"sensus plenior"* reading, pointing out that both the flogging law and Boaz's kindness to Ruth, as expressed in Ruth 2:15–16, are concerned with preserving human dignity. As for Deuteronomy 25:4, Berman, following Talmudic tradition, interprets the law nonliterally as a reference to not repressing a "woman's sexual satisfaction" (36).[9] Once this is assumed it is rather easy to relate the law to the laws that follow in Deuteronomy 25:5–10, which in turn have been understood as the background for Boaz's actions in Ruth 3–4.

Berman's proposal, while certainly a glowing testimony to his imagination and creativity, is unconvincing for at least five reasons:

(1) His attempt to link the various laws of Deuteronomy 24:16–25:10 is unpersuasive. He fails to articulate clearly how they are tied together thematically. There may be associative linking of some sort at work here, but even if this is the case, it is very loose and hardly establishes the basis for the tight plot structure we find in the book of Ruth.

(2) Berman's argument that the deaths of Elimelech and his sons were the result of divine punishment cannot be sustained. See our comments on 1:5 below.

(3) It is not clear that the gleaning law of Deuteronomy 24:19 is the background for Ruth 2. The Law legislated that the poor, widows, and resident foreigners be permitted to glean the corners of fields and pick up what the harvesters failed to gather (cf. also Lev. 19:9–10; 23:22). Ruth's request may reflect this, but she did not assume a right to glean. She hoped someone would treat her with favor. When she arrived at the field, she

---

9. For a similar interpretation of this law, see Carmichael 1980, 250–53.

did not claim any legal right, but instead asked for and received permission to glean (Ruth 2:7–8).

(4) Berman's attempt to integrate Deuteronomy 25:1–4 into the plot of the Ruth story is tortuous. Any connection between preserving the dignity of a severely beaten criminal and the self-respect of the honorable Ruth is so loose as to be virtually untied. The attempt to squeeze a sexual connotation out of the ox muzzling law is too speculative to be compelling. Berman is unwise to follow the lead of the ancient interpreters to whom he credits this notion, for it probably says more about their prurient interests than anything else.

(5) Finally, it is unlikely the redemption described in Ruth should be seen against the background of the levirate laws.[10] Boaz was not the brother of Mahlon, nor the brother-in-law of Ruth. Neither Ruth nor Boaz acted under legal obligation (cf. Ruth 3:10–11), in contrast to what we see in the episode recorded in Genesis 38, where Judah's sons were obligated to raise up offspring for their deceased brother, and in the Deuteronomic laws (Deut. 25:5–10), where a brother-in-law was likewise obligated to carry on a deceased brother's family line by cohabiting with his widowed sister-in-law. In both of these cases the one who refuses to carry out the responsibility of producing offspring is viewed in a negative light, in contrast to Ruth 4, where the nearer relative declines the right to redemption without being publicly rebuked. In neither Genesis 38 nor Deuteronomy 25 is the term גֹּאֵל, "kinsman redeemer," used of a brother-in-law. While there is a concern for carrying on a deceased individual's line in these texts (as in Ruth), the marked differences preclude their being used to impose a legal framework upon the transaction between Boaz and Ruth and upon the plot structure of the book.

LITERARY STRUCTURE

The book of Ruth can be divided into four literary units, corresponding to the chapter divisions. The structure may be outlined as follows:[11]

---

10. The term "levirate," which is often used of these particular laws, is derived from the Latin word *levir*, "brother-in-law."
11. More detailed analyses of the literary structure appear in the commentary below in the introduction to each chapter. For a survey of the various

Prologue: Victims of Famine and Death (1:1–6)

Act One, Scene One: Going Home (1:7–19a)
Act One, Scene Two: Demanding a New Name (1:19b–21)
Epilogue to Act One: Fertility in the Air (1:22)

Prologue to Act Two: Seeking Food (2:1–3c)
Act Two, Scene One: A "Chance" Encounter in the Barley Field
(2:3d–17)
Act Two, Scene Two: Ruth Returns Home (2:18–22)
Epilogue to Act Two: Finishing Up the Harvest (2:23)

Act Three, Scene One: Matchmaker! Matchmaker! (3:1–5)
Act Three, Scene Two: Planned Encounter at the Barley Threshing
Floor (3:6–15e)
Act Three, Scene Three: Debriefing Ruth (3:15f–18)

Act Four, Scene One: A Potential Wrong Ending Averted (4:1–12)
Act Four, Scene Two: A Marriage, a Birth, and a Doting Grandmother
(4:13–17)
Epilogue: What's in a Genealogy? An Official Record of God's Blessing
(4:18–22)

Chapter one consists of a prologue (vv. 1–6), the first act of the story in two scenes (vv. 7–21), and an epilogue (v. 22). The first scene takes place on the road from Moab to Bethlehem (vv. 6–19a), the second in Bethlehem itself (vv. 19b–21). The epilogue's reference to the barley harvest (v. 22) has a transitional function, for the barley harvest provides the background for both the second and third acts (Hubbard 1988b, 130–31).

Chapter two consists of a prologue (vv. 1–3c), the story's second act in two scenes (vv. 3d–22), and an epilogue (v. 23). The first scene takes place in the barley field (vv. 3d–17) and the second in town (vv. 18–22). The epilogue's reference to the harvest (v. 23) brings closure to the second act and forms an inclusio with the epilogue to the first act (1:22), which also mentions the harvest and, as noted earlier, has a transitional function in the book's structure.

The third act in the drama unfolds in three scenes. The first scene (3:1–5) takes place presumably at the home of Naomi, the second

---

ways interpreters have understood the book's structure, see Korpel 2001, 5–28.

(3:6–15e) at the threshing floor, and the third (3:15f–18) back at Naomi's home.

Chapter four consists of the story's fourth act in two scenes and an epilogue. The setting of the first scene (4:1–12) shifts to the more public arena of the town, where Naomi's initial encounter with the women of Bethlehem took place (cf. 1:19–21). The second scene (4:13–17) shifts to Boaz's home. The epilogue contains a genealogy that traces the descendants of Perez, mentioned earlier in the blessing of the witnesses (4:11), through Boaz to David.

Several scholars have proposed that the book has a rather elaborate macrostructure that is at least in part chiastic. Bertman suggests the book's structure may be outlined as follows: A B C C' B' A' (1965, 165–68). The family history of 1:1–5 (A) corresponds to the family history provided at the end of the book in 4:18–22 (A'). The B units are 1:6–22 and 4:1–17. In both, he argues, "ties of kinship are at issue" (1:8–18; 4:1–12) and a dialogue between Naomi and the women of Bethlehem occurs (1:19–21; 4:14–17). Within each of the C units (chapters 2 and 3, respectively) there is a paneled structure of five elements, with the sequence in chapter three standing parallel to that of chapter two. However, as Bertman's outline acknowledges, there are certain verses that do not fit within the proposed scheme (cf. 2:11, 15–17; 4:13).

Porten's structural outline is very similar to Bertman's (1978, 23).[12] He divides Bertman's B units into separate major units (B and C), but, unlike Bertman, he sees the structure of chapter one only partially mirroring chapter four: A (1:1–6), B (1:7–19a), C (1:19b–22) // B' (4:1–12), C' (4:13–17), A' (4:18–22).[13] In Porten's outline the B and C elements are reversed in chapter four. Like Bertman, he sees a paneled structure in chapters two and three, but he lists only three elements in each (as opposed to Bertman's five), designating them D, E, and F. Unlike Bertman's outline, Porten's proposed structure encompasses all of the book's verses.[14] However, to do so he must make his unit labels more general than Bertman's. For example, Porten's first E unit covers

---

12. Gow concurs with Porten's analysis (1984, 318).

13. See as well Wendland 1988, 32. Wendland divides the units differently: A (1:1–5), B (1:6–19a), C (1:19b–22) // B' (4:1–10), C' (4:11–17), A' (4:18–22). Wendland also detects concentric structures in each of the book's main segments (1:1–6, 7–22; 2:1–23; 3:1–18; 4:1–11a, 11b–17, with 4:18–22 being an exception) (40–45). But these "segments" do not correspond exactly to his linear chiastic outline of chapters one and four (32).

14. He assigns 2:1 to his first D unit, 2:15–17 to his first E unit, and 4:13 to his second C unit.

2:4–18a and is simply labeled "Boaz favors Ruth." Bertman assigns these verses to two separate units (C 3–4) and offers more detailed descriptions of each.

Luter and Rigsby propose a chiastic structure that differs from Bertman's outline in several respects: A (1:1–5), B (1:6–22), C (2:1–23) // C' (3:1–18), B` (4:1–12), A' (4:13–17) (1996, 16). Within the C units they isolate 2:18–23 and 3:1–5 as D and label it the "central focus." But how can these verses, which already appear within the C units, constitute a separate D unit? Furthermore, the epilogue (4:18–22) lies outside the chiastic structure. Nevertheless, Luter and Rigsby have identified some broad thematic parallels: (1) Naomi's loss in 1:1–5 is balanced by the arrival of Obed in 4:13–17; (2) the departure of Orpah in the first B unit corresponds to the refusal of the nearer kinsman in the second B unit, while the commitment of Ruth is mirrored in the commitment of Boaz; and (3) chapters 2 and 3 deal with the widows' "immediate" and "longer term provision," respectively. However, there are some problems with this arrangement. The women's speech to Naomi in 4:14–15, located in the second A unit, appears to correspond to Naomi's speech to the women in 1:20–21, located in the first B unit. Luter and Rigsby set chapters 2 and 3 in the harvest field, but actually chapter 3 is set primarily at night at the threshing floor, while chapter two is set in the daytime in the field.

Radday proposes a chiastic structure for the book consisting of seven elements (A–G), but the chiasmus breaks down in 4:11b–16, where one expects the order to be D' C' B', but finds instead the order B' C' D', as in chapter one (1981, 71). Hongisto's proposed chiasmus is even more elaborate, consisting of A–J elements (1985, 23). However, several of the proposed correspondences seem contrived and asymmetrical. For example, he labels all of chapter one as A and assigns it the label "Naomi—too old to conceive." Surely this general description is not adequate to cover the entire chapter. He assigns only one verse (4:17) to the corresponding A' element. Similarly D covers only one verse (2:3), while 4:2–12 is assigned to D' and given the rather general label "Ruth and a field."

The variation between these proposals suggests they reflect their authors' creativity more than they do the design of the biblical author. Often labels are too general and correspondences too loose to be convincing. However, it is apparent that there are correspondences and contrasts within the book, and all of these scholars have drawn attention to these. For example, the closing genealogy, with its focus on birth, does contrast with the prologue's description of famine and death. The women's words to Naomi in 4:14–15, in which they affirm

Ruth's superiority to seven sons, stand in sharp contrast to Naomi's lament in 1:20–21, where she regards herself as empty-handed due to the loss of her husband and sons. There are corresponding panels in the macrostructure of chapters two and three, as Porten's outline in particular bears out (1978, 23).[15] Each chapter begins with a plan being formulated (by Ruth in chapter two, by Naomi in chapter three). Boaz then shows favor to Ruth and each chapter concludes with Naomi and Ruth evaluating what has happened.

THE ROLE OF SETTING IN THE STORY

The general temporal setting is the period of the Judges (1:1), but, more specifically, the primary events of the story occur at the time of the barley and wheat harvests (1:22; 2:23). The fact that the bulk of the story occurs in conjunction with renewed agricultural fertility gives it a positive, hopeful mood.

The story's physical setting moves from Bethlehem to Moab and back, with a significant conversation occurring on the road from Moab to Bethlehem. Once Naomi returns to Bethlehem, major events and conversations take place in the town, in the barley field, at the threshing floor, and at the town gate. The changes in setting mark movements within the drama, as an examination of the book's literary structure reveals (see above). There are public events, including Naomi's conversations with the women of the town (1:19–21; 4:14–15), Boaz's initial encounter with Ruth in the field (2:8–16), and Boaz's confrontation with the nearer kinsman and his legal declaration at the city gate (4:1–12). But along the way there are also private conversations, including the various dialogues between Ruth and Naomi, and the secret meeting between Boaz and Ruth at the threshing floor. Public events tend to focus on Naomi's dilemma and its resolution, while private conversations highlight the commitment of the characters to the well-being of others. In these private conversations we see Ruth's devotion to Naomi (1:15–18; 2:2–3; 3:5), Naomi's motherly concern for Ruth (2:19–22; 3:1–5, 16–18), and, of course, Boaz's commitment to the widows (3:9–15).

POINT OF VIEW IN THE STORY

Berlin speaks of "three senses in which the term point of view can be applied" 1983, 47). (1) The "perceptual point of view" is "the perspective through which the events of the narrative are perceived." In a general sense the narrator of Ruth displays the omniscient, reliable perspective that characterizes Hebrew narrative. But on at least two occasions

---

15. See also Wendland 1988, 32, 35–36.

he assumes the more limited perspective of one of the characters—
Ruth in 2:3 and Boaz in 3:8 (Chisholm 2002, 404–05, 409). Of course,
along the way the various perspectives of the characters are revealed
through quotation and dialogue. (2) The "conceptual point of view" is
"the perspective of attitudes, conceptions, world view." The narrator's
attitude is one of sympathy toward Naomi and Ruth. Though some
have interpreted Elimelech's move to Moab and his sons' marriages
as sinful, and their deaths as divine punishment, the narrator refuses
to tip his hand in this regard.[16] These events are merely incidental,
albeit tragic, occurrences that set the stage for the comic plot that follows. This is not a story about human sin and divine judgment, but
about redemption and restoration. God is not depicted as Judge (other
than in Naomi's speech to the women of Bethlehem in chapter 1), but
as a benefactor and ally of the widows.[17] Only twice does God directly
intervene—to bring relief from the famine (1:6) and to grant Ruth the
capacity to conceive a child (4:13). In both cases he brings fertility and
life where there was none, and relief to those who were in a precarious
position. (3) The "interest point of view" is "the perspective of someone's benefit or disadvantage." In the book of Ruth, Naomi is the focus
of the narrator's interest, as the following section explains.

CHARACTERIZATION IN RUTH

To appreciate the message of the book, it is important to understand
how the characters function in the story. Though Ruth lends her name
to the book, Naomi is the story's protagonist or central character. As
noted above, the plot tension revolves around her situation, as God delivers her from the effects of her tragic loss. Her dilemma is introduced
early on (1:3) and resolved by the end of the story (4:17), indicating she
is the narrator's focal point.[18] At the beginning she is deprived of her

---

16. Some have argued that the narrator does not overtly speak of sin and punishment because readers familiar with the Law would not need such interpretive comments to know that the men had sinned and were suffering
the consequences of their deeds. However, in the commentary we address
these points and argue that the Law does not indicate that leaving the
land and marrying Moabite wives were necessarily wrong.
17. In the commentary below we argue that the narrator does not agree with
Naomi's assessment of her situation.
18. Another indication of Naomi's centrality is the fact that Ruth disappears,
as it were, from the story's conclusion. In 4:17 it is the women, not Ruth
the mother, who name the child and Naomi, not Ruth, is viewed as the
child's mother. See van Wolde 1997a, 9 and Parker 1988, 138. Ruth speaks
in the story for the last time at the end of chapter three (see Linafelt 1999,

husband and two sons; at the end she has another son who will be her protector.[19] The story traces God's redemptive work on her behalf as he rescues her from destitution and despair. We see her bitterness gradually change to hope and then contentment as her future is secured.[20] If Naomi is indeed the central character, then the story, at a fundamental level, focuses on God's concern for the needy and his predisposition to

---

61). Naomi does not speak after chapter three either, but she is directly addressed, not just spoken of in the third person.

19. According to Bush, the literary structure of 4:13–17 shows that "the central point of the scene is to describe Naomi's restoration to life and fullness" (1996a, 252). He adds: "Our story has come full circle. Death and emptiness (1:3–5, 21) have given way to life and fullness" (1996a, 264). On Naomi's centrality in the story, see as well Tollers 1990, 252–59, and Lapsley 2005, 90. Tollers points out that Naomi "is offstage only when it would be inappropriate for her to be present, such as in the nocturnal meeting between Ruth and Boaz or at the gathering of men by the city gate; and when she is offstage, the narrator often summarizes events and later presents them through her eyes" (255).

20. Baylis takes an overly negative view of Naomi's character and behavior that is antithetical to her centrality in the story and to the story's comedic plot structure. Evaluating Naomi's actions against the backdrop of the Mosaic covenant, he interprets her behavior from start to finish in a very negative light (2004, 413–31). Baylis argues that the entire Old Testament must be read within the framework of the Mosaic covenant. When one does so, actions that may seem neutral or even commendable in light of "common values," may prove to be wrong. He illustrates his point by appealing to Judges 17:1–4, where the actions of Micah's mother may seem commendable when viewed in isolation. But once one reads the story against the backdrop of the Law, she stands condemned. Of course, Baylis is correct that Micah's mother's actions should be viewed negatively. The narrator sends a clear signal of how the epilogue of the book should be read (cf. 17:6; 21:25 in light of Deut. 17:14–20). But the author of Ruth does not send any such signal that would invite us to measure Naomi's actions against the backdrop of a particular law or set of laws. One could argue that the author simply assumes the audience would be aware of the Law and that no signal is needed. But even if we grant this for the sake of argument, one can challenge Baylis' interpretation of certain laws that he feels illuminate Naomi's actions (see our comments on 1:15 below). The book of Ruth is about God's concern for the needy and the rewards that lie in store for those who share that concern. The intersection of the Law with the book of Ruth is not in the region of covenantal violations, but in the vicinity of Ruth's and Boaz's faithfulness (cf. Deut. 10:18–19).

deliver them from their plight.[21] Naomi's experience may be viewed as a microcosm of the biblical macroplot, which tells how God redeems those victimized by the tragic realities of the fallen world, the chief of which is death.

Though not the story's protagonist, Ruth is a major character whose exemplary behavior naturally makes her the most celebrated of the book's characters. Her role as God's instrument of deliverance is essential to the plot resolution.[22] While Naomi's attitudes are not always exemplary, Ruth's example of love and loyalty is held up by the author as a model for all to follow. Some interpreters have spoken of Boaz, in his role of kinsman-redeemer, as a type of Christ (see, for example, Rossow 1991, 17), but Ruth is just as deserving, if not more so, of such an elevated and honored label. The sacrificial love she displayed, which so impressed Boaz, finds its ultimate expression in Jesus' redemptive work. As others recognize her merits, they pronounce blessings upon her (1:8; 2:12; 3:10). As these are fulfilled in due time, Ruth becomes a model of one who is rewarded for her sacrifice.

Boaz is also a major character in the story. As he arrives on stage for the first time, he is depicted as one who both imparts and receives blessing (2:4). This foreshadows the role he will play in the unfolding drama. Though wealthy and secure, he recognizes and values Ruth's loyalty. This prompts him to be generous and to use his social power to secure the future of two vulnerable widows and to maintain the integrity of his extended family's line. He reminds us that those who are in a place of advantage economically and socially must use that advantage to help the vulnerable. As others recognize his generosity and concern for preserving family stability, they pronounce blessings upon him (2:19–20; 4:11–12). When the Lord responds to these prayers and bestows blessings upon him, he becomes, like Ruth, a paradigm of the faithful individual who receives the divine rewards that inevitably result from faithful behavior.

All three of these major characters contribute to the book's message and readers of the story will certainly be able to relate to at least

---

21. After noting that "Naomi is designated as the legitimate mother" of Obed in the book's final chapter (cf. 4:17), Prinsloo observes: "From the first to the fourth pericope the emphasis thus falls on the fact that the seemingly hopeless situation of Naomi is changed into a promising one" (1977–78, 125).

22. Prinsloo (1977–78, 125) notes that Ruth "has an important function as the faithful mediator between Naomi as the needy and Boaz as the benefactor."

one of them. As Moore states: "Not only does each character bring a different 'voice' to the 'performance,' each listener brings a different ear to the biblical 'score.' One reader hears the melody line as that of a broken woman trying to find her way 'home.' Another resonates to the 'alto part' sung by the loyal daughter-in-law. Another gravitates to the 'bass line' sung by the benevolent patriarch" (2001, 41). Placing the story in its larger canonical-historical context, where it stands in stark contrast to Judges 17–21 in particular, Moore observes: "This trio is soon joined, however, by a much larger orchestra in which the countermelodies of justice and compassion blend and blur into the grander harmonies of a greater canonical symphony. Discerning listeners soon discover that the story of Ruth is a quiet place in this symphony where 'Maras' of all sorts can find the strength to become 'Naomi' again, where 'wanderers' can find a reason to keep looking for 'home'—and where discerning kings can learn the difference between 'political power' and 'servant leadership.'"

MAJOR THEMES AND PURPOSE

At least four major theological themes emerge from the book of Ruth.

(1) First, the book demonstrates that God is concerned about needy people. Psalm 146:9 states: "The Lord protects those residing outside their native land; he lifts up the fatherless and the widow" (cf. also Deut. 10:18–19). The book of Ruth puts flesh on this hymnic affirmation. It shows how the Lord provided for two needy widows, Naomi and Ruth. Naomi had lost her husband and both of her sons while living in Moab. She returned to Bethlehem a bitter and impoverished woman who had little, if any, hope. But the Lord transformed her situation and attitude as he lifted her out of the depths.[23]

(2) The Lord accomplished this through two people, Ruth and Boaz,

---

23. Sakenfeld suggests that Naomi's words in 1:20–21 are not simply a complaint for human ears (2003:141). Rather "they are meant for God to hear" and constitute an indirect lament, which God answers indirectly through human agency. If this is correct, then God's intervention on Naomi's behalf is in response to prayer, and we have another example of a theme that permeates Scripture: prayer, particularly lamentation, is often the catalyst for God's involvement in our experience. Some might object that this cannot be a lament because it is not addressed to God in a formal manner. But Sakenfeld points out that no one addresses God in prayer in this book, yet the indirect prayers of blessing are answered by God, albeit providentially rather than by direct intervention. In the same way, Sakenfeld suggests, Naomi's complaint, though not addressed to God, may be viewed as a prayer.

who were willing to live out God's principles of loyalty and kindness.[24] So, while the book of Ruth shows us God is concerned about needy people, it also reminds us that he often meets their needs through people who are willing to do what is right and to sacrifice for the good of others.[25] Sakenfeld aptly observes: "Here is indeed a model for understanding God's ways with our lives and in our world. God's working is hidden and mysterious, like yeast at work in a loaf of bread till all is transformed. To be sure, from time to time there may be some change in life that we attribute only to the intervention of God, but more often God is at work through the everyday actions of faithful people seeking to manifest divine loyalty in their interactions with those around them,

---

24. Dearman observes that Ruth and Boaz "are the human instruments of redemption who play a role in the blessing provided by the God of Israel" (1998, 121). Ruth and Boaz, of course, operate within the societal framework of their time—one that was clearly patriarchal. In this regard, Dearman writes: "They make their commitments within these family structures and work through the customary roles given them in their culture. Modern readers may be put off by the confining nature and seeming irrelevancy of ancient customs, but it is worth remembering that human need and societal assumptions often conspire to limit options in a given context. A faithful response to human need may not have the luxury of expressing disapproval of the prevailing cultural norms" (121–22). Fewell and Gunn appear annoyed that the book of Ruth seemingly places "faithfulness in the service of patriarchy" (1990, 12). Granted, the book of Ruth does reflect the "patriarchy" of ancient Israelite society, but at the same time it illustrates the important truth that God blesses those who act faithfully, even when that faithfulness is expressed within social structures that they cannot change and in which they may be trapped. Human faithfulness and divine blessing are inevitably contextualized in history, but the various contextualized forms of divine blessing merely foreshadow a purer eschatological form that will be experienced by those who reflect God's faithfulness as they live out their lives in a very less than ideal, sin-ridden world.

25. Korpel states the theme this way: "The Book of Ruth invites human beings to become faithful servants of the LORD, implementing his covenantal love on earth" (2001, 229). See as well Hubbard 1989, 283; and 1997, 209. In the latter, Hubbard observes that the human characters in the book "are neither puppets manipulated by Yahweh's hidden hands nor bystanders gawking at the unfolding plot from the sidelines. Rather, Yahweh oversees and implements dynamism through their actions." He concludes: "In sum, the book of Ruth models the divine-human relationship as a cooperative venture—God working through his people to reward them and to achieve his larger purposes." See as well Atkinson 1983, 62.

seeking to make this world a less precarious place for all its inhabitants" (1999b, 227).

(3) A third major theme of the book may be stated as follows: God rewards those who are faithful to their God-given relationships.[26] Psalm 18:25 states, "You prove to be loyal to one who is faithful." The book of Ruth illustrates this truth. Twice in the book the Hebrew word חֶסֶד, "kindness, loyal love, devotion, commitment, faithfulness," is used of Ruth. In 1:8 Naomi says to her daughters-in-law: "May the Lord show you the same kind of devotion (חֶסֶד) that you have shown to the dead and to me!" Ruth had already been devoted to Naomi and her family during the days in Moab, even before she took the solemn oath recorded in 1:16–17. Later in 3:10 Boaz says to Ruth: "This latter act of devotion (חֶסֶד) is greater than what you did before." Ruth also exhibited love. In 4:15 the women of the town, in response to Obed's birth, say to Naomi: "Your daughter-in-law, who loves you, has given him birth. She is of greater value to you than seven sons." God showed the same kind of commitment and devotion to Ruth that she had shown to others. He gave her a husband, the ability to bear a son, and a famous descendant. Like Ruth, Boaz exhibited חֶסֶד as he showed kindness to the widows and loyalty to their deceased husbands (2:20). As a prominent member of the community, he generously used his substantial means to secure the widows' future and, as a result, experienced God's blessing.

The concluding genealogy (4:18–22) shows that God's blessings sometimes extend beyond the lifetime of the recipients. Through Boaz's and Ruth's descendant David, God rewarded their faithfulness in a way that brought great fame to the family and to his people Israel. Through David and ultimately the Messiah, God's blessings to Boaz and Ruth were extended to Israel and the whole world.

As one looks more closely at the reward theme in the book, a definite pattern emerges. An individual or group asks God to reward others (specifically, Ruth or Boaz) for kind and faithful deeds they have performed. The book then records the fulfillment of the prayer:[27]

---

26. The Jewish midrashic text Ruth Rabbah (II.14) states: "This scroll tells us nothing of cleanliness or of uncleanliness, either of prohibition or permission. For what purpose, then, was it written? To teach how great is the reward of those who do deeds of kindness." See Beattie 1977b, 203.

27. We omit from the following list the brief blessings exchanged by Boaz and his workers (2:4), for these appear to be general, polite greetings. However, Sakenfeld argues that these are more than "perfunctory" greetings: "In this instance, however, the greeting is incorporated into a narrative that is shot through with occasions in which the characters invoke divine

(a) Ruth 1:8–9

Prayer: Naomi asked God to reward her daughters-in-law for their kindness to her and her sons by giving them new husbands.

Answer: We are not certain what happened to Orpah, who disappears from the story (1:14), but the Lord gave Ruth a new husband, Boaz (4:10–13).

(b) Ruth 2:12

Prayer: Boaz asked God to reward Ruth for her kindness to Naomi by providing her with protection and security.

Answer: God answered this prayer through Boaz, who willingly fulfilled the role of family protector by marrying Ruth (cf. 3:9).

(c) Ruth 2:19–20

Prayer: Naomi asked God to reward Boaz for his kindness to Ruth and to her family.

Answer: God answered this prayer by giving Boaz a worthy wife (cf. 3:11) who provided him with a child (4:13).

(d) Ruth 3:10

Prayer: Boaz asked God to reward Ruth for her faithfulness to her deceased husband.

Answer: God answered this prayer through Boaz, who married Ruth and provided her with a child.

(e) Ruth 4:11–12

Prayer: The people asked God to give Boaz offspring and to make him prosperous and famous.

Answer: God answered this prayer by enabling Ruth to bear a son, Obed, who was the ancestor of the great king David (4:13, 17–22).

Apart from two references (1:6; 4:13), the narrator does not describe God as directly intervening in human affairs. However, this pattern

---

blessing upon one another (1:8; 2:12; 2:19, 20; 3:10; 4:11). In such a setting, Boaz's greeting should be read with its full theological meaning. . . . Boaz appears on stage giving and receiving divine blessing" (1999c, 40–41). If she is correct, then the workers' public, albeit formulaic sounding, blessing of Boaz anticipated the more substantive blessings that he subsequently receives in the story (2:19–20; 4:11–12).

of prayer fulfillment demonstrates he was involved providentially in blessing those who exhibited kindness and faithfulness.[28]

(4) When one views the book of Ruth from a canonical, Christian perspective, it takes on a christotelic dimension. Ancient Israelite readers, because of their historical situation, would not have discerned this. But they would have seen, from the concluding genealogy, that the book of Ruth contributes to the theme of David's divine election (see the commentary below on 4:18–22). By tracing David's ancestry back to Perez, a son of Judah, and by mentioning Judah by name (cf. 4:12), the book also links David with the ancient patriarchal blessing that depicted Judah as a leader (Gen. 49:8–12) (cf. Howard 1993, 154). The book thus projects a messianic trajectory.

This trajectory runs parallel to one of the book's major themes, sacrificial love (see above). Sacrificial love, as exemplified by Ruth, is at the heart of the biblical message. Jesus says the whole Law can be summed up in two commands: to love the Lord God with all one's being, and to love one's neighbors as oneself (Matt. 22:37–39). As he commands his disciples to love one another, he reminds them that the greatest expression of love is to give one's life for one's friends (John 15:12–13). His death becomes the ultimate expression of such love.

This theme of sacrificial love and the book's messianic trajectory intersect in Isaiah's fourth servant song, where the royal servant voluntarily submits to the divine will and suffers so that "the many" might be reconciled to God.[29] Once sacrificial love is joined to the messianic image, it comes to fruition in the cross. Again, while all of this extends beyond the boundaries of the book of Ruth, it is foreshadowed there. A distinctly Christian exposition of the book of Ruth, or of the entire Old Testament for that matter, is not complete until it leads to Jesus.

One can summarize the message of the book as follows: God cares for needy people like Naomi and Ruth; he is their ally in a world

---

28. See Hals 1969, 6–8; Bland 1981, 130–31; and Thompson 1993, 203–10. Thompson argues that two prayers of thanksgiving are strategically placed within (cf. 2:19–20) and after (4:14) the series of intercessory prayers to emphasize that divine and human activity work in concert. In my opinion, 2:19–20 is intercessory (Naomi asks that Boaz be rewarded for his faithfulness), but it is significant that the women's praise of the Lord in 4:14 caps off the prayers of the book, reminding us that the Lord has indeed redeemed the bitter widow described in chapter one and that the actions of Ruth and Boaz served his providential purposes.
29. On the servant's royal identity, see Chisholm 2006b.

where death often leaves people helpless and vulnerable. In response to prayer God richly rewards faithful people like Ruth and Boaz who demonstrate love and generosity and in so doing become his instruments in helping the needy. God's rewards for those who sacrificially love others can come in surprising ways. His rewards sometimes exceed their wildest imagination and transcend their lifetime. Those who sacrificially love also foreshadow (if before the cross) or mirror (if after the cross) the ultimate act of sacrificial love, Christ's atoning death for sinners.

Based on the message of the book, we propose that the book had a threefold purpose in its original setting. The book reminded its ancient Israelite audience of the following truths and principles:

(1) Israel's God is concerned for the needy.

(2) Israel's God expects his people to share his concern for the needy and to demonstrate loyalty in their relationships.

(3) Such faithfulness pays off because those who demonstrate loyal love can expect to be richly rewarded by the Lord.

In its canonical setting, a fourth purpose becomes clear:

(4) The sacrificial love displayed in the book foreshadows Christ's supreme act of sacrificial love.

MODERN PROCLAMATION OF RUTH

In developing a proclamation strategy for the book of Ruth, we will utilize the same approach as in Judges. This approach involves three steps: (1) thematic analysis, (2) theological analysis, and (3) contemporary application.

Step one involves moving back into the world of the text and attempting to answer the question: What did this text mean in its ancient Israelite context? This begins with a close exegetical-literary reading of the text that surfaces the thematic emphases of each major literary unit. Such analysis will yield an exegetical idea for each unit that succinctly captures the message of that unit in its cultural-historical context.

In step two we move outside the boundaries of the specific text being studied and attempt to answer the following questions: What theological principles emerge from or are illustrated by a thematic analysis of the text? How, if at all, are these principles nuanced in their larger canonical context? Answers to these questions will enable us to develop a theological idea for each literary unit. These theological ideas express the enduring principles or truths that are rooted in the text and are relevant for a modern audience.

The third step is to return to our modern world, where we develop homiletical trajectories from the theological idea of the passage. These trajectories begin from homiletical vantage points that reflect the overall message of the book of Ruth (see a fuller discussion below). Following the trajectories enables us to produce one or more preaching ideas for each literary unit.

As noted above, the book of Ruth has three major purposes:

(1) The book demonstrates that God is concerned about needy people. It depicts God providentially delivering suffering and bitter Naomi from despair and replacing her pain with joy.

(2) The book also reminds us that God often helps the needy through people who display loyalty and sacrificial love.

(3) The book also shows that God rewards those who are faithful to their God-given relationships. These rewards sometimes extend beyond the lifetime of the recipients.

To be faithful to the message of the book, a homiletical approach should be sensitive to each of these themes as they emerge and are developed in the book. These themes provide us with homiletical angles or vantage points from which we can consider the text's relevance for us. After the commentary on each major literary unit, we will consider what the text teaches and illustrates about (1) God's concern for the needy, (2) his people's responsibility to be his instruments in extending his kindness to the needy, and (3) God's rewards for those who exhibit faithfulness in their relationships. Starting from these vantage points, we can develop homiletical trajectories that begin at the theological idea and lead to one or more preaching ideas for each literary unit. When preaching any given section of the book, one may attempt to integrate the homiletical trajectories into one all-encompassing message, but it may be preferable to focus on one trajectory in any given sermon.

For the convenience of the would-be expositor, we include here a proposed preaching series on the book of Ruth that provides an overview of the exegetical idea, theological idea, homiletical trajectories, and primary preaching idea(s) included below in the commentary section:

Sermon One: Sacrificial Love on Display (Ruth 1)

Exegetical idea: *Naomi experienced tragic loss and felt rejected by God, but Ruth vowed to stay with her, even though such sacrificial love may have seemed risky and been unappreciated.*

Theological idea: *People may experience tragedy and feel rejected by God, but followers of Christ should reach out to them in sacrificial love, even though such love may seem risky and unappreciated.*

Homiletical Trajectories

(1) One trajectory will focus on Naomi's experience and her faulty perception of the Lord. In this chapter we see that personal tragedy and pain can overwhelm those who live in the fallen world. Yet in the midst of such suffering, we should not necessarily attribute our pain directly to God or cast him in the role of an enemy. If we look carefully, we can detect his gracious hand, bringing relief from famine, as it were. We can take comfort in the fact God is the ally of his people, not their enemy. Though he may not insulate us from the tragic realities of the fallen world, he cares for the needy and is predisposed to intervene on their behalf.

(2) A second trajectory will focus on Ruth and her example of self-sacrificial love. When we encounter people who feel as if they are targets of God's anger, we should reach out to them in sacrificial love, as Ruth did to Naomi. Such love demands great moral courage and commitment, for it can be risky and unappreciated.

(3) The book's third theme (see introduction)—that God rewards those who love sacrificially—is only hinted at in chapter one, when Naomi pronounces a blessing upon Ruth (1:8–9). However, Ruth's self-imprecation appears to trump the blessing (1:17) and creates tension in the plot. Given the seemingly risky task Ruth has taken up, one wonders if her loyalty will really pay off, especially when Naomi disregards her allegiance.

Preaching idea: *When people experience tragedy and feel rejected by God, we must reach out to them in Christlike sacrificial love, even though such love may seem risky and unappreciated.*

Sermon Two: Events Take a Turn for the Better (Ruth 2)

Exegetical idea: *As Ruth sought to provide for Naomi's needs, the Lord providentially guided her footsteps to the field of Boaz, a potential benefactor of Elimelech's family. Impressed by her faithfulness, he rewarded her loyalty by providing her with an ample amount of food. This, in turn, began the transformation of Naomi's attitude from bitterness to hope.*

Theological idea: *The Lord often accomplishes his redemptive work through faithful human instruments and providentially guides their footsteps when they decide to love sacrificially, no matter how meager their means appear to be.*

Homiletical Trajectories

(1) Operating through human instruments that mirror his own concern for the needy, God begins to work providentially to deliver Naomi from her despair and bitterness. When we recognize the hand of God at work in our experience, hope can begin to push despair aside.

(2) We see God helping the needy by using the loyal actions of those who love sacrificially and take family commitments seriously. As noted above, though human beings may be limited in what they can do, God honors loyalty and sacrificial love and comes alongside faithful people like Ruth to bless their efforts.

(3) The reward theme begins to blossom in this chapter. Boaz, who recognizes Ruth's faithfulness to Naomi (2:11–12; cf. 3:10), asks God to reward her loyalty and sacrificial love. However, this theme will not reach its consummation until chapter four.

Preaching idea: *Because the Lord often accomplishes his redemptive work through faithful human instruments, we can be confident he will providentially guide our footsteps when we decide to love sacrificially, no matter how meager our means appear to be.*

Sermon Three: A Marriage Proposal at the Threshing Floor (Ruth 3)

Exegetical idea: *God's providential, redemptive work in and through Ruth and Boaz restored Naomi's hope. Boaz recognized Ruth's sacrificial love and promised to reward it by securing her future.*

Theological idea: *God's providential, redemptive work in and through the lives of godly people restores hope and secures the future.*

Homiletical Trajectories

(1) Continuing to operate through human instruments, God once more works providentially to deliver Naomi from her despair and bitterness. When we recognize the hand of God at work in our experience, we can look to the future with hope and even reciprocate the kindness shown by others.

(2) As in chapter two, God continues to help the needy by utilizing the loyal actions of those who love sacrificially and take family commitments seriously.

(3) The reward theme becomes more prominent in this chapter. Boaz, who marvels at Ruth's faithfulness to Naomi (3:10), again blesses her and assures both Ruth and Naomi that their future will be secure.

Preaching idea: *As we show sacrificial love for others, we can be confident that God's providential, redemptive work in and through us will restore hope and secure the future.*

Sermon Four: All's Well that Ends Well (Ruth 4)

Exegetical idea: *As God brought his redemptive work to culmination, he gave security to afflicted Naomi, proving to be her ally, not her enemy. In response to prayers of blessing, he richly rewarded faithful Ruth and Boaz for their loyalty and love in ways that transcended their lifetime.*

Theological idea: *As God brings his redemptive work to culmination, he restores security to the afflicted and richly rewards the faithful for their loyalty and love in ways that transcend their lifetime. He is predisposed to answer the prayers of blessing offered up on behalf of his faithful servants and reward them for their loyalty and love.*

Homiletical Trajectories

(1) The resolution of the story's plot complication yields one trajectory. Naomi's deliverance reminds us that the afflicted find their circumstances reversed when God's redemptive work reaches its culmination and joy replaces despair.

(2) In chapter four Boaz takes center stage as God's instrument of deliverance. As we see in earlier chapters, God's instruments of redemption take the initiative to help others and persist in their work until the mission is accomplished.

(3) The reward theme dominates the final chapter. We see that God does indeed reward the faithful, sometimes in ways that transcend their lifetime and exceed their wildest imagination.

Preaching idea: *As God brings his redemptive work to culmination, we can be confident that he will richly reward the loyalty and love of his faithful followers, sometimes in ways that transcend their lifetime.*

Since these rewards are bestowed in response to prayer, we can develop an additional preaching idea from chapter four: We should ask God to bless those who demonstrate kindness and faithfulness, for our prayers can be the catalyst for God's blessings in their lives and in the lives of the covenant community.

MAJOR CONTEMPORARY COMMENTARIES ON RUTH
This section offers a brief evaluation of several contemporary commentaries on Ruth, dividing them into two categories: (1) technical, semitechnical, and (2) expositional.

Technical, Semitechnical

Highly Recommended
Bush, Frederic. 1996. *Ruth, Esther.* WBC. Nashville: Nelson. 514 pp.
   (The Ruth portion covers 268 pages.)
   Approach: Bush's approach is exegetical and literary. The *WBC* series is aimed at a broad spectrum of readers, including "the fledgling student, the working minister, and colleagues in the guild of professional scholars and teachers." This may be a bit ambitious and misleading. Those untrained in the biblical languages will find this commentary daunting. Depending on the extent of their language training, some may even find the exegetical comments overly technical in places.
   Format: Each major literary unit includes the author's translation accompanied by technical notes, a discussion of "form/structure/ setting," detailed exegetical comments arranged in a verse-by-verse manner, and a concluding section entitled "explanation" that offers a synthetic overview of the unit from a literary perspective. Hebrew is used liberally throughout the notes and comments.
   Usability: The clearly organized format facilitates use of the commentary. The author leaves no stone unturned and provides an admirable model of how biblical exegesis should be conducted. He interacts with alternative viewpoints and defends his own positions with

convincing linguistic and contextual arguments. Those who are serious about the exposition of the book of Ruth will find this work to be an exegetical gold mine.

Hubbard, Robert. 1988. *The Book of Ruth*. NICOT. Grand Rapids: Eerdmans. 331 pp.

Approach: Hubbard's approach is exegetical. *NICOT* is aimed at scholars, pastors, and serious Bible students. Those trained in the biblical languages will find this commentary useful; others will find it cumbersome. Some may find the exegetical comments overly technical in places.

Format: Each major literary unit includes the author's translation and detailed exegetical comments on the text arranged in a verse-by-verse manner. At the end of each chapter the author includes brief comments, unmarked by a heading, on the chapter's main themes. Transliteration is used for the many Hebrew references throughout the footnotes and comments.

Usability: The author provides some help with literary synthesis and theology in the introduction in sections labeled "Themes" and "Theology," but the commentary serves primarily as an exegetical reference work.

Wilch, John. 2006. *Ruth*. CC. St Louis: Concordia. 418 pp.

Approach: The author takes an exegetical and literary approach. The series is designed to "assist pastors, missionaries, and teachers of the Scriptures to convey God's Word with greater clarity, understanding, and faithfulness to the divine intent of the text." The commentary is written from an evangelical and confessional perspective that reflects commitment to the author's Lutheran heritage.

Format: Each major literary unit includes the author's translation accompanied by very extensive, thorough textual notes that deal with morphological, syntactical, lexical, and text-critical issues. Hebrew is used liberally throughout these notes. The commentary proper follows, offering detailed exegetical comments on the text arranged in a verse-by-verse manner.

Usability: Those trained in the biblical languages will find the textual notes useful. The commentary proper is very readable. It serves as an exegetical reference work and also provides insights with respect to literary synthesis and theology. The introduction contains lengthy sections dealing with motifs, theological themes, and contemporary relevance. Consequently, most should find it to be a helpful tool in sermon preparation. The theological approach is christotelic. Such an approach can fall prey to an allegorical hermeneutic that is more eisegetical than exegetical, but Wilch has avoided such excess.

Recommended
Block, Daniel I. 1999. *Judges, Ruth*. NAC. Nashville: Broadman & Holman. 765 pp. (The Ruth portion covers 150 pages.)
    Approach: The author's approach is exegetical, literary, and theological. The *NAC* series is aimed at "the minister or Bible student who wants to understand and expound the Scriptures."
    Format: Each major literary unit includes the *NIV* translation, brief introductory remarks, exegetical comments arranged in verse-by-verse format, and concluding observations on "theological and practical implications." More technical issues are discussed in the footnotes. Hebrew is confined to the footnotes; transliteration is used in the body of the text.
    Usability: The commentary's format is user-friendly and its exegetical insights, presented from an evangelical perspective, helpful in sermon preparation. However, as my commentary on chapter one will reveal, I disagree with Block on some fundamental interpretive issues. Consequently, my endorsement of his work on Ruth is not as enthusiastic as my evaluation of his commentary on Judges.

Campbell, Edward. *Ruth*. 1975. AB. New York: Doubleday. (Now available in paperback in the AYBC series. 2003. New Haven, CN: Yale University Press. 214 pp.)
    Approach: Campbell takes a historical-critical and exegetical approach. The commentary is aimed at "layman and scholar alike," but it leans toward the scholarly side.
    Format: In the commentary proper, each section includes the author's translation, extensive technical notes, and exegetical comments. Transliteration, rather than Hebrew script, is used throughout.
    Usability: Most should find the commentary useful as an exegetical reference work, especially with regard to archaeological backgrounds and literary analysis.

Linafelt, Tod, and Timothy K. Beal. 1999. *Ruth and Esther*. BO. Collegeville, MN: Liturgical Press, 1999. 130 pp. (Linafelt is the author of the commentary on Ruth, while Beal did the work on Esther.)
    Approach: Linafelt's approach is primarily literary. According to the book jacket, the *Berit Olam* commentary series is aimed at "all interested in the Bible, be they lay people, professional biblical scholars, students, or religious educators."

Format: The author provides a running commentary on the text that focuses on literary issues. He divides the text into its main literary units and proceeds for the most part in a verse-by-verse fashion.

Usability: The commentary is readable; Hebrew is transliterated and translated. The author focuses on literary issues, giving particular attention to structure and characterization. Focusing on the book's placement in the Greek and English translations, the author sees the book as "a narrative link between the stories of the judges and the story of David, and the monarchy." His reading of the story cuts against the grain of the typical theological understanding of the book. He downplays divine involvement in the story and highlights the human dimension.

Expositional

Highly Recommended

Sakenfeld, Katharine D. *Ruth.* 1999. Interpretation. Louisville: Westminster John Knox. 91 pp.

Approach: Sakenfeld takes a literary and theological approach. Like other volumes in the Interpretation series, it is aimed at "those who teach, preach, and study the Bible in the community of faith." It falls somewhere between a "historical critical commentary" and "homiletical aids to preaching." It seeks "to provide a third kind of resource, a commentary which presents the integrated result of historical and theological work with the biblical text."

Format: The commentary divides the book up into its major literary units and proceeds in a verse-by verse fashion.

Usability: The style is readable and nontechnical. This volume should be useful for its literary insights, especially with respect to characterization. The author also addresses "feminist and cross-cultural concerns."

Recommended

Atkinson, David. 1974. *The Message of Ruth*. BST. Downers Grove, IL: InterVarsity. 128 pp.

Approach: Atkinson's approach is theological and homiletical. The BST series has a "threefold ideal: to expound the biblical text with accuracy, to relate it to contemporary life, and to be readable." The editors specifically say that the volumes in the series are neither commentaries (which they view as primarily works of reference) nor sermons (which, in their view, may not take Scripture seriously enough), but rather expositions.

Format: The author divides the book into major literary units and focuses on key theological themes that emerge from a reading of the text.

Usablility: As the editors suggest, the volume should not be used as a substitute for an exegetical commentary. The author gives little attention to exegetical issues, but instead focuses on themes that surface in the story and how those themes are developed in a broader canonical context. Some may find the volume helpful as they consider directions to travel in application and exposition.

Luter, A. Boyd, and Barry C. David. 2003. *Ruth & Esther: God Behind the Seen*. Focus on the Bible. Ross-shire, Scotland: Christian Focus. 384 pp. (Luter did the work on Ruth, pp. 13–95.)
Approach: The approach is literary and theological, with pastors as the intended audience.
Format: Luter provides readable and insightful expositions of the book's major literary units that include illustrative material as well.
Usability: This is by no means an exegetical reference and will not substitute for one. Once pastors have done their own exegetical research, they should find it helpful as they seek to build the bridge from text to sermon.

Younger, K. Lawson, Jr. *Judges and Ruth*. 2002. NIVAC. Grand Rapids: Zondervan, 2002. 512 pp. (The portion on Ruth covers 103 pages.)
Approach: Like other commentaries in this category, the approach is literary and theological. The NIVAC series is designed to bring "an ancient message into a modern context" by helping the reader "think through the process of moving from the original meaning of a passage to its contemporary significance." According to the series editors, these volumes are "commentaries" and "works of reference," not "popular expositions" or "devotional literature."
Format: Each major literary unit includes the NIV translation and a discussion of the text's "original meaning" focusing on its paragraphs (the format is not verse-by-verse), followed by sections entitled "bridging contexts" and "contemporary significance." In these last two sections the author brings the text's theological themes to the surface and builds a bridge from text to sermon.
Usability: The well-organized format makes the commentary user-friendly. Its exegetical insights are helpful, especially as regards the text's literary features and cultural background. In fact, this volume could be listed in the technical/semi-technical section above. The

sections on bridging contexts and contemporary significance provide useful insights and homiletical trajectories. However, despite the editors' concern to guide the reader through the process of moving from text to sermon, the third section does not reflect a clear-cut, well-defined homiletical philosophy or method.

DATE OF AUTHORSHIP

The events of the book are set in the Judges period (cf. 1:1), but the date of authorship is uncertain. The closing genealogy, which traces Boaz's genealogy to David, shows that the book, at least in its final form, postdates the birth of David. But this is not decisive for dating the story, since the genealogy could have been added sometime after the story was composed. The explanatory note in 4:7 shows signs of originating at a relatively late date (see below), but this does not prove anything about the date of the story's composition.

On the basis of the concluding genealogy, one could make a case for a preexilic date of authorship. It links the story with David, demonstrating that he came from a godly line and was himself the answer to the prayers of blessing offered up at his ancestors' wedding. However, this desire to put the Davidic dynasty in a positive light was present from the time of David right on through the monarchical period and on into exilic and postexilic times (see, for example, Ezek. 34:23–24; 37:24–25; Hag. 2:20–23; Zech. 12:7–12; 13:1). Therefore, the genealogy does not necessitate a preexilic dating for the book.

Scholars inevitably appeal to linguistic evidence when attempting to date material. However, the linguistic evidence in the book of Ruth is ambiguous. On the one hand, there is evidence for a relatively early date of authorship (or at least of some source material), including the preservation of common dual forms (see 1:8, 19, 22; 4:11) and of the older pattern of the second feminine singular form of the perfect with *yod* ending (see 3:3–4).[30] On the other hand, alleged Aramaisms would seem to point to a relatively late date of authorship, but some do not find the evidence in this regard compelling.[31] Aramaisms, even

---

30. The older pattern of the second feminine singular form of the perfect occurs several times in Jeremiah and Ezekiel, as well as in 1QIsa. See Joüon and Muraoka, 132–33; and Myers 1955, 11. Holmstedt argues that these forms do *not* preserve an archaic pattern (2010, 23–24, 152–53).

31. See Campbell 1975, 24; Holmstedt 2010, 34–39; and Eskhult 2003, 15–16. Eskhult states: "In conclusion, it is clear that the idea of 'the many Aramaisms' in Ruth is ill-founded, and still worse is the conclusion that these alleged Aramaisms point to a late date" (16). Zevit observes that

if present, at best provide evidence for later editing or linguistic up-dating, but they do not necessarily prove a late date for authorship.

Drawing on recent research on the linguistic development of bib-lical Hebrew, Bush argues that the book displays features of both stan-dard biblical Hebrew (SBH; c. 1000–600 B.C.) and late biblical Hebrew (LBH; c. 600–400 B.C.).[32] He cites ten features that appear to be SBH, including (1) the preference for the first person singular pronoun אָנֹכִי, rather than אֲנִי;[33] (2) the widespread use of the *waw*-consecutive; (3) the appearance of the temporal indicators וְהָיָה/וַיְהִי;[34] (4) the use of כִּי with a subordinating function;[35] (5) the word order predicate-subject in a substantival clause introduced by כִּי, "that";[36] (6) the absence of the preposition –לְ, "to, for," as a direct object marker; (7) the defective, as opposed to *plene*, spelling of David's name; (8) the use of בֵּין . . . בֵּין, "between . . . between," to indicate alternatives;[37] (9) the behavior of prefixed מִן, "from"; and (10) the aforementioned use of the common dual form.[38]

Bush also detects eight features of LBH, including (1) the preference

---

assigning a late date to the book on the basis of Aramaisms "is essentially baseless because the Aramaisms are not concentrated." He adds: "Arama-isms, such as there may be, could reflect the peculiarities of a particular Hebrew dialect or even casual speech" (2005, 575).

32. Bush 1996a, 20–30. Bush draws primarily on the research of Hurvitz, Polzin, and Rooker. Their conclusions have not gone unchallenged. Recent works on the subject include Young 2003, as well as Young and Rezetko, 2007.

33. See as well Holmstedt 2010, 32. Revell attempts to show that a speak-er's choice of אָנֹכִי or אֲנִי follows a pattern: "In general, then, the use of אֲנִי by humans shows either that the speaker is status-marked, or that the clause is 'immediate', is central to the interests of the speaker, or the addressee, or both. The use of אָנֹכִי marks the speaker as non-status, or shows that the clause is 'non-immediate', peripheral to the speaker's con-cerns, unimportant" (1995, 211–12).

34. Holmstedt (2010, 25–26) regards this feature as inconclusive for dating.

35. Holmstedt (2010, 26) acknowledges that Ruth does seem to follow the SBH pattern here.

36. Holmstedt (2010, 26) challenges this criterion and argues that it is not determinative for dating.

37. Holmstedt (2010, 26) contends that "the single occurrence in Ruth should not be taken as determinative."

38. Holmstedt (2010, 24) rejects the notion that these forms are common dual and prefers to see "gender neutralization" here, where the more common forms (in this case masculine) replace less common (in this case feminine) forms.

to attach a pronominal object directly to the verb, rather than the object marker; (2) the attaching of the third feminine singular suffix to the second masculine plural verb in 2:11; (3) the preference to use the preposition –לְ, "to, for," rather than אֶל, "to," with the verb אמר, "say"; (4) the use of the verb נשׂא, "lift up," for "taking a wife" in 1:4;[39] (5) the use of the *piel* stem of קוּם, "arise," in 4:7; (6) the use of the *waw* conjunctive with perfect, rather than the *waw* consecutive, in 4:7; (7) the use of שׁלף, "remove," with נַעַל, "sandal," in 4:7; and (8) the use of שׁבר, "wait," in 1:13.[40] The last four of these features appear to be due to Aramaic influence. Features 5–7 appear in 4:7, which is admittedly relatively late. However, it is important to observe that late features

---

39. However, it is important to observe that לקח, which is typical of LBH, is used of taking a wife in 4:13. See Holmstedt 2010, 33. Guenther (2005, 400) argues that נשׂא indicates that Elimelech's sons married "poverty-stricken or low status women who brought no dowry into the marriage."

40. Zevit lists eight "lexical data" that reflect "a transitional phase between Hebrew of the monarchical period and that which evolved during the exilic and post-exilic period" (2005, 592–93). Three of these (Zevit's 1, 6, and 7) appear in Bush's list of LBH features (see 4, 5, and 7 above, respectively). Zevit's additional examples of transitional lexical features include הֲלָהֵן (the interrogative *he* prefixed to a debated form that appears to be either an Aramaic particle meaning "therefore," or a prepositional phrase with suffix, "for them") in 1:13; the verbal root צבט (meaning "to hand over"?) in 2:14; the noun צְבָתִים ("ears of grain"?) in 2:16; the idiom קָנָה אִשָּׁה ("acquire a wife") in 4:5, 10; and the expression נָתַן הֵרָיוֹן ("grant conception") in 4:13. Zevit also argues that the orthography of Ruth with regard to the use of *matres lectionis* suggests a transitional date between 600–500 B.C. for the book's composition. He explains: "On the one hand, Ruth employs *matres lectionis* more generously than do most books dated by scholars on other grounds to the pre-exilic period. On the other, F. I. Andersen and D. N. Freedman demonstrate that Ruth's orthography uses *matres lectionis* more sparingly than do Ecclesiastes, a book commonly assigned to the Persian period on the basis of its contents, and Esther which was certainly written then or early in the Hellenistic period" (594–95). For a summary of orthographic evidence, see Holmstedt (2010, 19, 22. He concludes, "the orthographic profile of the Book of Ruth provides us with no good evidence for its date of composition" (22). Holmstedt (2010, 27–31) proposes an additional intermediate feature. He suggests that the use of the *he* relative in Ruth may indicate "that the book sits on the relative dating cline between books like Gen–Deut, Josh–Kings on the one side, and Ezra-Neh, Chronicles, and Qohelet on the other" (31).

only prove the book has been edited and updated linguistically in some respects; they do not preclude an earlier date of origin/authorship.[41]

To summarize, there are indications the story originated in a relatively early time period, perhaps in oral form. There is ample evidence the book was written in standard preexilic Hebrew, though its late features show it has undergone some degree of linguistic updating in the exilic and postexilic periods.[42]

IS RUTH PROSE OR POETRY?

Most writers assume that the book of Ruth is a narrative in prose form, but not everyone is convinced of this. Myers detected a substantial amount of parallelism in the book, prompting him to suggest there was "a poetic original underlying" it (1955, 42). In a detailed analysis of the book's structure, Korpel concludes the book "is a narrative text in poetic form" (2001, 223). She adds: "The cola are generally shorter than they are in Classical Hebrew prose and parallelism accounts for many of the seemingly superfluous repetitions in the Book of Ruth." However, she qualifies this assertion to some degree: "However, if it is poetry indeed, it is a special kind of poetry. The number of sentences running on through several cola is higher than it is in poetry." She adds: "The negative verdict of many scholars with regard to the poetic nature of the Book of Ruth may well have been influenced by a rather

---

41. In this regard, see the remarks of Young 2003, 312. Citing one of his own articles, he states: "the linguistic profiles of the attested copies of biblical books cannot simply be assumed to represent the form of language used by the 'original author'. Instead, language, as with all other features of the emergent biblical text, was subject to constant revision at the hands of the scribes who passed the material down through the generations."

42. Glanzman, on the basis of the linguistic evidence, suggests the book has gone through three stages of literary development (1959, 201–07). As evidence for an early date, he cites the older second feminine singular form of the perfect, the morphology of the book's proper names, which have an affinity to Ugaritic names, and the use of imperfect forms with the paragogic *nun*. Some explain the linguistic evidence differently. Gordis, for example, dogmatically states: "There is only one adequate explanation for these superficially contradictory phenomena, the occurrence of both early and late Hebrew usages in Ruth: the author was a late writer who was consciously archaizing and using colloquial speech, in order to give an antique flavor to his narrative, which he set in the period of the Judges" (1974, 245). Likewise, Ap-Thomas calls the apparently early linguistic features "obvious gimmicks" designed to create an "'olde-worlde' atmosphere" (1968, 370).

strict definition of poetry which took line parallelism as its main criterion and did not allow for the possibility of different poetic genres."[43]
Unless, with Korpel, one is willing to broaden the definition and traditional understanding of what constitutes Hebrew poetry, it is difficult
to label the book poetic. However, we may be able to call the prose
elevated and recognize that it has a poetic flavor in places, especially
within the quoted material.[44] For example, the following passages, at
least in part, do seem to display a poetic parallelistic structure: 1:8
(see Korpel, 61), 13 (Korpel, 63), 16 (Korpel, 64), 21 (Korpel, 66); 2:8
(Korpel, 105), 12 (Korpel, 107); 4:11 (Korpel, 186), 15 (Korpel, 188).

---

43. Korpel's work expands the research of de Moor 1984, 262–83; 1986, 16–46.
44. Of the book's 85 verses, 59 (69%) contain dialogue. See Lim 2007, 270.

RUTH 1:1–22
Sacrificial Love on Display

TRANSLATION AND NARRATIVE STRUCTURE[1]

1a During the time when the judges ruled, (*introductory*)
1b there was a famine in the land. (*introductory*)
1c A man from Bethlehem in Judah went to live as a resident alien in the region of Moab, along with his wife and two sons.[2] (*initiatory*)

---

1. The translation of Ruth appearing in this commentary is a revised version of a translation the author originally prepared for *The NET Bible*. As in the commentary on Judges, we combine a translation of the text with an analysis of its narrative structure. The outline distinguishes between the three main elements of a narrative: (1) mainline (*wayyiqtol*) clauses, (2) offline clauses (indicated in bold), and (3) quotations (placed in *italics*). All mainline and offline clauses in the narrative framework are classified (within parentheses and with *italics*). Clauses within quotations are not analyzed. For the categories utilized, see the section "Narrative Structure of Judges" in the introduction to the commentary on Judges.
2. The phrase should be translated "his two sons" here, rather than "two of his sons" (as if there were more). When the construct of שְׁנֵי, "two," is followed by a suffixed noun, it can occasionally refer to two out of a larger number (see Gen. 22:3; 40:2; Num. 22:22; 2 Kings 5:23), but it can also refer to two items which comprise exclusively a given category (see Gen.

2a   **The man's name was Elimelech,** (*supplemental*),

2b   **his wife's name was Naomi,** (*supplemental*)

2c   **and his two sons were Mahlon and Kilion.** (*supplemental*)

2d   **They were Ephrathites from Bethlehem in Judah.**[3] (*supplemental*)

2e   They entered the region of Moab (*resumptive-sequential*)

2f   and settled there. (*sequential*)

3a   Now Elimelech, Naomi's husband, died; (*sequential*)

3b   she was left alone, along with her two sons. (*consequential*)

4a   Her sons married Moabite women. (*sequential*)

4b   **(One was named Orpah** (*supplemental*)[4]

4c   **and the other Ruth.)** (*supplemental*)

4d   They lived there about ten years. (*resumptive-sequential*)

5a   Then Naomi's two sons, Mahlon and Kilion, also died. (*sequential*)

9:22; 48:1, 5; Exod. 18:3, 6; 32:15; 1 Sam. 2:34; Ezek. 15:4; Song 4:5; 7:3 [Hebrew 7:4]). The context in Ruth 1 leads us to believe that Mahlon and Kilion were Elimelech's only sons. One gets the impression their deaths robbed Naomi of all the men in her life (see v. 21).

3. Most commentators discuss the meaning of these names and their possible symbolic significance. However, with the exception of Naomi (v. 21), the narrator attaches no significance to them. The names appear to be purely referential. See Bush 1996a, 63. It is, of course, possible that an ancient Israelite audience would have picked up on the connotations of certain names with no explanation being needed. The name Mahlon might suggest the idea of "sickly person" (*HALOT*, 569), if one derives or associates it with the root חלה, "grow weak, tired; fall sick, be ill; feel pain" (*HALOT*, 316). The name Kilion might suggest the idea "frailty, mortal" (*HALOT*, 479), if one derives or associates it with כלה, "stop, come to an end; be finished, completed; vanish, fade; perish; fail" (*HALOT*, 476–77). It seems unlikely that Naomi would have intended such connotations in naming her sons, so the association with these roots would most likely be retrospective popular etymologizing. Another option is that they are literary names, provided by the author to characterize the unfortunate destiny of these individuals. It is not certain what connotative value the name Elimelech, meaning, "My God is king," might have. As for the names Boaz and Ruth that subsequently appear in the story, scholars are not certain of their derivation and meaning, so we should not speculate about such matters. Of course, the original readers, who were more attuned to their native language, may have detected some connotation that we do not recognize.

4. The disjunctive clause in verse 4b is asyndic (the initial conjunction is omitted).

5b and she was left alone, without her two boys[5] and her husband. (*consequential*)

6a Then she, along with her daughters-in-law, decided to leave (*sequential*)

6b and she returned from Moab because she had heard in Moab that the LORD had intervened by providing[6] food for his people. (*sequential*)[7]

7a She left the place where she had been living, (*focusing*)

7b **accompanied by her two daughters-in-law,** (*supplemental*)

7c and they began the trip back to the land of Judah. (*resumptive-sequential*)

8a Naomi said to her two daughters-in-law, (*sequential*)

8b *"Go back, each of you, to your mother's home.*

---

5. Naomi's sons are called יְלָדִים, "boys, youths," here (rather than בָּנִים, "sons"). This is the only place where יֶלֶד, "boy," is used of married men. Since the word connotes youthfulness, perhaps this reflects Naomi's motherly perspective. Most commentators, following Campbell, suggest the word choice is designed to establish an intertextual connection with 4:16, where the infant Obed is called a יֶלֶד. See Campbell 1975, 56. The repetition might suggest the theme of restoration; God eventually replaced the social security that Naomi had lost when her sons died.

6. The infinitive construct indicates either manner (cf. the translation) or purpose, "in order to provide."

7. The *wayyiqtol* clause in verse 6b is difficult to analyze. It may summarize the story that follows (Naomi returned; cf. v. 22). See Holmstedt 2010, 68. If so, then the *wayyiqtol* clause in verse 7a begins a more focused, detailed account of Naomi's return. Another option is to understand the verbal collocation (literally, "she arose . . . and she returned") as having an ingressive force, "she arose in order to return," or "she set out to return." (See Dorn 1978, 318.) In this case verse 7a is simply sequential. For a fuller discussion of this issue, see the commentary below.

8c *May the LORD show*[8] *you*[9] *the same kind of devotion that you have shown*[10] *to the dead and to me!*

9a *May the LORD give each of you security in the home of a new husband!"*

9b Then she kissed them goodbye (*sequential*)

9c and they wept loudly. (*sequential*)[11]

10a They said to her, (*sequential*)

10b *"No! We will return with you to your people."*

11a But Naomi replied, (*sequential*)

11b *"Go back, my daughters! Why would you want to come with me? Am I still capable of having sons and supplying you with husbands?*

12 *Go back, my daughters! Go, for I am too old to get married again. Suppose I were to say, 'I have hope!' Suppose I got married this very night and had sons.*

13 *Would you wait until they grew up? Would you remain unmarried all that time? No, my daughters! You should not have to experience my intense suffering. After all, the LORD has attacked me!"*

14a They wept loudly again. (*sequential*)

14b Then Orpah kissed her mother-in-law goodbye,[12] (*sequential*)

---

8. The translation follows the *Qere* here, which reads a jussive form (cf. 2 Sam. 2:6) instead of the imperfect in the *Kethib*. The latter may have arisen by virtual dittography (cf. the following יהוה).

9. The apparent second masculine plural suffix is probably an early feminine or common dual form. See Campbell 1975, 65; and Bush 1996a, 75–76. Holmstedt (2010, 24) rejects the notion that these forms are common dual and prefers to see "gender neutralization" here, where more common forms (in this case masculine) replace less common (in this case feminine) forms.

10. The apparent second masculine plural ending is probably an early dual verbal ending. See the previous note.

11. Verse 9c reads literally, "and they lifted their voice(s) and wept." There are two *wayyiqtol* clauses here, but the collocation is treated as a single clause in the outline above. (See also v. 14a.)

12. After לַחֲמוֹתָהּ, "to her mother-in-law," the Septuagint adds, "and she returned to her people," which, when retroverted to Hebrew, would read וַתָּשָׁב אֶל־עַמָּהּ (see *BHS* note a). (The verb form is a *qal wayyiqtol*, 3fs, from שׁוּב, "return.") This may be an interpretive addition in the Septuagint. In this case the translator (or his source) made the implicit explicit and harmonized the text of verse 14 with verse 15. However, it is also possible that the extra clause was accidentally omitted. A scribe's eye could

14c **but Ruth hugged her tightly**. (*contrastive*)[13]

15a Then Naomi said, (*sequential*)

15b *"Look, your sister-in-law has returned to her people and to her god.*[14] *Follow your sister-in-law back home!"*

16a But Ruth replied, (*sequential*)

16b *"Stop urging me to abandon you and to leave you. For wherever you go I will go. Wherever you stay, I will stay. Your people will be my people, and your God will be my God.*

17 *Wherever you die I will die and I will be buried there. The LORD will punish me severely if I do not keep my promise. Nothing but death will separate you and me."*

18a When Naomi saw that she was determined to go with her, (*sequential*)

18b she said no more about it. (*sequential*)

19a The two of them[15] went on their way until they entered Bethlehem. (*sequential*)

19b When they entered Bethlehem, (*introductory*)[16]

19c the whole town was excited about their arrival. (*initiatory*)

19d The women of the town[17] said, (*sequential*)

19e *"Can this be Naomi?"*

20a Naomi replied to them, (*sequential*)

---

have jumped from the initial *waw* on וַתָּשָׁב, "and she returned," to the initial *waw* on וְרוּת, "but Ruth," in the following clause, leaving out the intervening words: וַתֵּשֶׁב אֶל עַמָּהּ וְרוּת, "*and she returned to her people,* but Ruth." Or his eye could have jumped from the final *he* on לַחֲמוֹתָהּ, "[to] her mother-in-law," to the final *he* on עַמָּהּ, "her people," leaving out the intervening words: לחמותה ותשב אל עמה, "[to] her mother-in-law, *and she returned to her people.*"

13. The disjunctive clause in verse 14c contrasts Ruth's action with Orpah's goodbye kiss.

14. The form may be translated as singular or as plural, depending on how one understands the Hebrew plural. Our translation assumes the Hebrew form is here a concretized abstract plural referring to Chemosh, the Moabite patron deity. See the discussion in the commentary below.

15. Many medieval Hebrew manuscripts have a feminine suffix (see *BHS* textual note 19a), but it is more likely that the suffix is an archaic dual form. See 1:8.

16. The *wayyehi* (וַיְהִי, literally, "and it was") clause in verse 19b marks the beginning of a new scene (see Wendland 1988, 33), with the *wayyiqtol* (וַתֵּהֹם, "was excited") in verse 19c initiating the action of this scene.

17. Literally, "they said," but the use of the feminine plural verb form indicates the women of the town are in view.

20b   *"Don't call me Naomi. Call me Mara, because the Sovereign One
has treated me very harshly.*
21   *I left here full, but the LORD has caused me to return empty-
handed. Why do you call me Naomi, seeing that the LORD has
opposed me and the Sovereign One has made me suffer?"*
22a   So Naomi returned, (*summarizing*)[18]
22b   **accompanied by her daughter-in-law Ruth, the Moabite
woman who returned**[19] **with her from the region of Moab.**
(*supplemental*)
22c   **They**[20] **arrived in Bethlehem at the beginning of the
barley harvest.** (*supplemental-concluding*)[21]

OUTLINE

Prologue: Victims of Famine and Death (1:1–6)
   Leaving home (1:1–2)
   A husband dies (1:3)
   Two sons die (1:4–5)
   Hopeful news from home (1:6)

Act One, Scene One: Going Home (1:7–19a)
   Heading for home (1:7)
   An adamant mother-in-law (1:8–13)
   A persistent daughter-in-law (1:14–19a)

---

18. The *wayyiqtol* clause in verse 22a has a summarizing function (cf. v. 6b).
   See Holmstedt 2010, 100.
19. This form is difficult to analyze (see also 2:6; 4:3). Based on the placement of the accent (under the *shin*), it appears to be a *qal* perfect, third
   feminine singular form, from שׁוּב, "return," with a prefixed article. For
   a defense of this see Holmstedt 2010, 28, 100. However, it is rare for a
   perfect verbal form to appear with an article. For examples, see GKC, 447
   (para. 138. k); *IBHS*, 339. According to GKC (447), Joüon-Muraoka (538
   [para. 146. e]), and *IBHS* (339–40), apparent examples with hollow verbs
   should probably be read as participles. The article on the form functions
   like a relative pronoun (*IBHS*, 338–39). Actually the form is substantival
   and appositional to "Ruth . . . her daughter-in-law," and can be translated
   "the one who returned."
20. An apparent masculine plural form of the independent pronoun is used of
   the women. Once again it is probably an archaic common or feminine dual
   form. See 1:8, as well as Bush 1996a, 94–95.
21. The disjunctive clause in verse 22c signals closure for the first act of
   the story, while at the same time setting the stage for the next act. See
   Younger 2002, 425.

Act One, Scene Two: Demanding a New Name (1:19b–21)
    Creating a stir in Bethlehem (1:19b)
    "Pleasant" renames herself "Bitter" (1:20–21)

Epilogue: Fertility in the air (1:22)

LITERARY STRUCTURE

The first chapter consists of a prologue (vv. 1–6), the story's first act in two scenes (vv. 7–21), and an epilogue (v. 22). The first scene takes place on the road from Moab to Bethlehem (vv. 7–19a), the second in Bethlehem itself (vv. 19b–21). The chapter begins with a reference to a famine (v. 1) and ends with a reference to the barley harvest (v. 22). This thematic contrast forms an inclusio for the first act and hints that this story will have a comic plot structure, despite its tragic beginning. While the reference to the barley harvest lends closure to the first act, it also has a transitional function, for the barley harvest provides the background for both the second and third acts (Hubbard 1988b, 130–31).

The prologue can be divided into four parts.[22] Dual *wayyehi* (וַיְהִי, literally, "and it was") clauses introduce the story, setting its temporal background (v. 1a) and describing the circumstances giving rise to it (v. 1b).[23] The narrator initiates the story proper by telling us that a certain man from Bethlehem took his family to Moab to escape the famine (v. 1c). We are introduced to the man and his family via a series

---

22. We treat 1:1–6 as a prologue (perhaps to both the first act and the entire book), rather than a scene, because it summarizes in a few short sentences events that transpired over a period of at least ten years. Furthermore, 6 of its 17 independent clauses are disjunctive and supply background information. Verse 6, if understood as a summary statement, previews what will transpire in the scenes to follow. If staged as a drama, one doubts the events described so tersely in these verses could even be portrayed effectively. It would be more appropriate to supply the information in the program before the list of scenes. The drama *per se* begins in verse 7.

23. The syntactical structure of verse 1 is rare (וַיְהִי + -בְּ, literally, "and it was in," followed by another וַיְהִי). In the only other example (2 Sam. 7:4 = 1 Chron. 17:3) the prepositional phrase is temporal, as in Ruth 1:1. Similar constructions occur in Exodus 19:16 (where a temporal clause introduced by an infinitive construct appears between the prepositional phrase and the second וַיְהִי) and in Judges 19:1 (where a disjunctive clause appears between the prepositional phrase and the second וַיְהִי). In both cases the initial וַיְהִי and prepositional phrase provide temporal orientation, as in Ruth 1:1.

of disjunctive clauses (v. 2a–d), and then informed that they arrived in Moab and settled there (v. 2ef). The references to traveling (v. 1c) and settling down (v. 2f) form an inclusio for this brief introductory subunit.

With the reference to a famine, the story begins with tension. A serious complication occurs, as we are told of Elimelech's death, which left his wife, Naomi, and her sons without their primary breadwinner (v. 3). The sons took Moabite wives, but then the sons died as well, leaving Naomi in a vulnerable position, without male support in a foreign land (vv. 4–5). These two subunits end with a similar refrain, in both cases introduced by the verb וַתִּשָּׁאֵר, "she was left alone" (vv. 3b, 5b).[24]

The prologue (v. 6) concludes with a summary statement that Naomi returned from Moab. It also provides the reason why she did this (God's intervention) and signals that this story may have a happy ending after all.

The first scene begins with Naomi's departure from Moab (v. 7). The scene is rounded off by the reference to Naomi's arrival in Bethlehem (v. 19a). Throughout the scene discourse and narrative are interwoven in the following pattern: Naomi's exhortation (vv. 8–9a), the girls' response in actions and words (vv. 9b–10), Naomi's second exhortation (vv. 11–13), the girls' response in contrasting actions (v. 14), Naomi's third exhortation (v. 15), Ruth's verbal response (vv. 16–17), Naomi's response in action (v. 18).

The transition between the two scenes is marked by the *wayyehi* (וַיְהִי) clause in verse 19b and by the repeated reference to the women's arrival in Bethlehem (cf. עַד־בֹּאָנָה בֵּית לֶחֶם, "until they entered Bethlehem," in v. 19a with כְּבֹאָנָה בֵּית לֶחֶם, "when they entered Bethlehem," in v. 19b). After a brief reference to the town's response to the news of their arrival (v. 19c), the scene consists of a dialogue between the women of the town and Naomi (vv. 19d–21).

The epilogue contains a summary statement (v. 22a) that repeats the summary statement of the prologue (v. 6b) (cf. וַתָּשָׁב, "returned," in both) (Hubbard 1988b, 99).[25] These summary statements bracket the scenes. The repeated reference to their arrival in Bethlehem (v. 22c)

---

24. Bovell proposes a chiastic structure for verses 3–5 (as part of a larger chiastic arrangement he detects in vv. 1–6) (2003, 179). Verses 3 and 5 clearly correspond (the C elements in Bovell's outline), but the proposed link between the first and last clauses in verse 4 (his D elements) is forced. There are no verbal links between the two clauses.

25. Verse 22 is best viewed as an epilogue because it does not further the action of the story. It includes a summary statement that links with the

links the epilogue with the preceding scene (cf. כְּבֹאָנָה בֵּית לֶחֶם, "when they entered Bethlehem," in v. 19b with the statement וְהֵמָּה בָּאוּ בֵּית לֶחֶם, "they arrived in Bethlehem," in v. 22c).

The connection between verses 6b and 22a warrants further discussion. Verse 6 begins with a statement that Naomi arose, along with her daughters-in-law, to leave the land. However, verse 6b uses a singular verb (וַתָּשָׁב, "and she returned"), not the expected plural form. There is only one other case where a *wayyiqtol* form of שׁוּב, "return," follows a *wayyiqtol* form of קוּם, "arise," with no intervening verb; it is instructive for our understanding of the syntax of verse 6 and of the discourse structure of this first act. In Genesis 21:32 we read: "And they made a treaty in Beersheba and Abimelech arose (וַיָּקָם), along with Phicol the captain of his army, and they returned (וַיָּשֻׁבוּ) to the land of the Philistines" (author's literal translation). Based on this parallel, one might expect to read in Ruth 1:6: "And she arose, along with her daughters-in-law, and *they* (plural) returned from the region of Moab." But instead the singular "she returned" is used. Perhaps there is already a hint here that both women will not accompany Naomi back to Bethlehem.[26] Verse 22a repeats the summary statement, but then qualifies it with a disjunctive clause informing us that Ruth accompanied Naomi on her trip home.

EXPOSITION

Victims of Famine and Death (1:1–6)
1:1–5. The story takes place during the period of the Judges (v. 1a). Normally the expression "in the days of" is merely a temporal indicator, orienting the reader to the time period when the narrated events occurred (see, e.g., Judg. 5:6; 8:28; 15:1, 20; 1 Sam. 17:12; 2 Sam. 21:1, 9). However, in this case the temporal setting of the story probably has greater literary significance. This was a dark period in Israel's history,

---

prologue (v. 6b) and two disjunctive clauses that provide supplemental information.

26. One might think that the singular is used because the girls could not technically "return" to Bethlehem since they had not come from there. See Block 1999, 632. However, this problem is actually one of English idiom. Twice Ruth is called the one "who returned" from Moab with Naomi (see 1:22; 2:6). In 1:7 the girls travel with Naomi "in order to return" (literal translation) to Judah, and in 1:10 both declare their intention to "return" with Naomi. The Hebrew verb need not imply that the subject is completing a round trip.

when most people followed their own moral and ethical code, rather than the Lord's standards (Judg. 17:6; 21:25). The heading provides a dark backdrop for the inspiring story that follows. During a time when people were selfish and refused to follow the moral compass God had provided them, this story tells of a woman (a non-Israelite at that!) who demonstrated genuine love for her mother-in-law and her deceased husband. Her actions stand in sharp contrast to the moral chaos that characterized this period. In fact, one could subtitle the story, "A Light in the Darkness."[27]

The reference to a famine (v. 1) might suggest an act of divine discipline or judgment (cf. Deut. 28:48; 2 Sam. 21:1; 24:13; 1 Kings 18:2) (Block 1999, 624; Younger 2002, 414; and Baylis 2004, 420). However, the narrator does not attribute this famine to God.[28] Furthermore, the Old Testament sometimes presents famines in a neutral light, not necessarily as punishment from God (cf. Gen. 12:10; 26:1; 41:27). It is also noteworthy that there are no references in Judges to a famine; it is not one of the forms of divine judgment depicted in that book (Nielsen 1997, 40).

To escape the famine, Elimelech moved his family from Bethlehem

---

27. Nielsen sees the introductory clause in 1:1 as stimulating the "reader's curiosity" (1997, 40). She asks: "Are we about to hear a tale of injustice and lawlessness or about God's intervention on behalf of his people through the creation of something new?" It is highly unlikely that the author of Ruth is attempting to counter the Deuteronomistic portrayal of the Judges period as a time of turmoil, as Curtis contends (1996, 143–44). In his view, the narrator of Ruth is asserting, contrary to Judges, that "Judah was a prosperous thriving settled agricultural society completely free of the barbarity of the North." Rather than pitting Ruth against Judges, it is preferable to see the author using the Judges period as a foil for his story in order to highlight the qualities of Ruth and Boaz and to highlight the monarchical theme in both books. In this way one is able to preserve the integrity of both books. On the many contrasts between Ruth and Judges 17–21 in particular, see Moore 2001, 30, 36–40. He points to three thematic contrasts: wandering-restoration, religion-ethics, chaos-kindness.

28. Oddly enough, Baylis states: "That this famine was due to God's intentional action is seen in verse 6, which refers to Yahweh as the provider of food" (2004, 420). Verse 6 states that Yahweh brought relief from the famine; nowhere does the text say he brought the famine! To assume the latter from the former is unwarranted logically, contextually, and theologically. Baylis assumes God brought the famine because he assumes the famine was a covenant curse, but the book of Judges never mentions famine as being a divine judgment during the Judges period.

to Moab (v. 1).[29] Should we interpret this in a negative light as a failure to trust God (Block 1999, 626–27; Baylis 2004, 420–21; Berman 2007, 28; and Berger 2009a, 270–71)? Not necessarily. In Genesis the patriarchs Abraham and Jacob left the land because of a famine and were subsequently richly blessed by God (Nielsen 1997, 40–41). In Jacob's case the move to Egypt was even engineered by divine providence (Gen. 45:6–8; cf. 2 Kings 8:1–6).[30] On the other hand, when Isaac started to leave the land during a famine, the Lord told him to remain there and assured him of his blessing (Gen. 26:1–6). In light of this ambiguous testimony, we should probably not view Elimelech's move in a negative light. Both the famine and the family's move appear to be incidental

---

29. Many point out the irony of famine overtaking Bethlehem, which means, at least by popular etymology, "house of bread." Linafelt finds further irony in the fact that Elimelech seeks food in Moab, "the place associated in Israel's memory with the withholding of food" (cf. Deut. 23:3–4) (1999, 4). One might think that a famine would impact Moab, as well as Judah. However, Amos 4:7–8 indicates that rain and drought could sometimes be quite localized. Furthermore, modern analysis of the climatology of the region supports this. See Bush 1996a, 62; and Wilch 2006, 119–20. For a discussion of the geography, terrain, and economy of Moab, see Mattingly 1994, 318–21.

30. Baylis, though admitting, "there were no warnings in the Mosaic Covenant about leaving the land," nevertheless affirms, "departure from the land was so unthinkable it was only mentioned as a judgment" (2004, 421). One wonders, then, why the prophet Elisha instructed the Shunammite woman to sojourn outside the land (2 Kings 8:1). Though his words to her lack specificity (literally, "sojourn where you can sojourn"), it is clear he means for her to leave the land, because he warns that the famine will overtake "the land." She goes to Philistine territory "in accordance with" the prophet's word (v. 2). It is difficult to believe the prophet Elisha would advocate an action that was "unthinkable" and that would bring a "curse" down upon the woman. In response, an advocate of Baylis' position might object that Philistine territory was technically within the boundaries of the promised land, while Moab was not (cf. Gen. 26:1–5, where Isaac settles in Philistine territory after being instructed by God not to leave the land during the famine). However, by the time of Elisha, the "land of the Philistines" was viewed as foreign territory outside the boundary of "the land" occupied by the covenant community (cf. 2 Kings 8:1–2). In addition, it was a place where other gods were worshiped (cf. 2 Kings 1). Given Baylis' line of reasoning, one would not expect Elisha, the Lord's prophet, to give the woman the freedom to go to this or some other foreign place, yet *in the face of the famine* he does so. Apparently desperate times called for desperate measures!

details that provide the background for the story and set the stage for its comic plot structure.[31]

If the story is read against the backdrop of Judges (as the heading suggests it should be), then the move from Bethlehem may have a foreboding quality to it, literarily speaking. As noted above, both of the stories in the epilogue to Judges mention Bethlehem. Both are also tragic accounts. When the Levite moved from Bethlehem (Judg. 17:7) and settled down with Micah of Ephraim, nothing but trouble ensued (Judges 17–18). When another Levite left Bethlehem with his concubine (Judg. 19:1–2) and stopped for the night in Gibeah, a chain of horrible events was set in motion (Judges 19–21). As Grant observes, in these two stories "everyone suffered and everyone lost" (1991, 426). He adds: "By now the idea is fixed in the reader's mind that departure from Bethlehem will probably lead to trouble" (426). And, of course, it does. However, there is, as Grant points out, "an important difference." He explains: "In the previous two narratives, the structure that tied the tragic events to their long-term consequences received the focus. In the Ruth narrative, the tragic events and the consequences that followed on Elimelech's departure from Bethlehem are at their worst by 1:5. Following verse 5, the return motif (based on the good news that 'the Lord had visited His people in giving them food' [v. 6]) and Ruth's faithfulness to Naomi (vv. 16–17) combine to suggest at least the remote possibility of comic resolution. The focus shifts subtly then from the tragic to the (potentially) comic with the introduction of this news" (426). So the move from Bethlehem, while foreboding and initially followed by tragedy, as one might expect, does not lead to unmitigated disaster. The narrator, as it were, turns the story on its head.

How should we interpret the death of Elimelech and his sons (vv. 3, 5)? Were their deaths an act of divine judgment for leaving the land and, in the case of the sons, for marrying foreign wives? After all, the Law might be interpreted to prohibit marriage to foreigners (Deut. 7:1–6) and Naomi later speaks of God as taking an adversarial role against her by depriving her of the men in her life (vv. 20–21). Jewish exegesis has traditionally interpreted the text along these lines (Campbell 1975, 58).[32]

---

31. See Bush who states: "There is not the faintest suggestion . . . that there is any opprobrium to be attached to the move to Moab or that the famine is Israel's punishment for her sin" (1996a, 67).

32. The Targum to Ruth reads in 1:4–5a: "And they transgressed the ordinance of the Memra of the Lord, and they took for themselves foreign

Recently Block has argued that the narrator views the marriages of Naomi's sons (v. 4) negatively. While acknowledging, "the narrator does not declare his own opinion," he then adds, "but several features of the account may be telling" (Block 1999, 628). According to Block, there are five of these features: (1) The idiom נָשָׂא אִשָּׁה, literally, "lift up a wife," has negative connotations; (2) the Mosaic Law prohibits "marriage with pagans" (cf. Deut. 7:3–4); (3) the Deuteronomic covenant curse list views marriage to foreigners as a divine judgment (cf. Deut. 28:32); (4) "Naomi's sons lived in their married state for ten years but without fathering children. The barrenness of Ruth and Orpah (vv. 4b–5) too must be interpreted as evidence of the punitive though hidden hand of God" (cf. Deut. 28:18) (see also Baylis 2004, 422); (5) Mahlon and Chilion died without leaving Naomi a "male remnant" (Block 1999, 628–29). Earlier in his discussion Block also suggests that Naomi's being "left alone" (v. 5) may imply judgment, since the *niphal* of שׁאר, "be left," is sometimes used of "those who have survived the wrath and judgment of God" (Block 1999, 627–28).

Block's case is unconvincing, however, for the following reasons:

(1) According to Block, the relatively rare idiom נָשָׂא אִשָּׁה, literally, "lift up a wife" (v. 4), is used nine times in the Old Testament, always with a negative connotation. It refers to marriage by abduction (Judg. 21:23) or to "illegitimate marriages, especially with non-Israelites, whether by kings or laymen" (Block 1999, 629). For examples involving "laymen," he cites Ezra 9:2, 12; 10:44, and Nehemiah 13:25. However, these texts do not use the precise idiom employed in Ruth 1:4. Ezra 9:2 uses נָשָׂא, "lift up," with the preposition מִן, "from," followed by "their daughters" and then the reflexive "for themselves" (literally, "and they lifted up from [i.e., some of] their daughters for themselves"). The syntax in Nehemiah 13:25 is almost identical to that of Ezra 9:2 (literally, "or lift up from [i.e., some of] their daughters for your sons or for yourselves"). In Ezra 9:12 "their daughters" is the object of the verb, while in Ezra 10:44 the phrase *"foreign* women" appears as the object.

---

wives. . . . And because they had transgressed the ordinance of the Memra of the Lord by marrying into foreign nations, their days were cut short." See Levine 1973, 48–49. For an analysis of how the Targum converts the story of Ruth "into a manifesto for ethnoreligious extremism," see Moore 1998, 213–15. Jewish scholar Hayyim Angel is not convinced that the death of Elimelech and his sons should be explained in terms of sin and punishment: "Does the text itself yield a sin/punishment conclusion? It remains possible, but no more compelling than a non-sin/punishment reading" (2005, 93).

One wonders if these relatively late texts, which do not use the precise idiom in question, are even relevant to the discussion. Even if one allows Ezra 10:44 as a parallel (since נָשִׁים, "women," does appear as an object here), the practice described in this text must not be viewed as determinative for all times and places. Hubbard states: "Though Ezra and Nehemiah later totally forbade such marriages [with foreigners] (Ezra 9:1—10:44; Neh. 13:23–27)—indeed, they sought to expel all foreigners (Neh. 13:1–3)—Esther shows that their prohibition was apparently not considered valid in a foreign land" (Hubbard 1988b, 93, note 10). The use of the idiom in Judges 21:23 is unique, while texts from 2 Chronicles use the expression of polygamous royal marriages (cf. 2 Chron. 11:21 [used of Rehoboam taking 18 wives], 13:21 [of Abijah taking multiple wives], 24:3 [of Jehoiada securing two wives for Josiah]). True, the idiom does seem to have a negative connotation in at least some of these texts, but the specific connotations (abduction or royal polygamy) obviously do not apply in the case of Mahlon and Kilion. Where usage is so limited, one should not make general assumptions about an idiom and then impose a supposed negative connotation on a text where the contextual circumstances that suggest the alleged connotative value elsewhere are absent.

(2) As Block admits, Deuteronomy 7:1–6 concerns the Canaanite peoples who were to be exterminated. This list does not include the Moabites, yet Block argues that the "spirit of the law" would have included them (see also Baylis 2004, 421, note 28). However, Moses viewed the Moabites in a different light and did not permit Israel to commit genocide against them (see Deut. 2:8–9, 28–29) (Campbell 1975, 59). Ezra 9:1–2 and Nehemiah 13:23–27 specifically mention Moabite women in their denunciation of marriages to foreign women, seemingly broadening the principle stated in Deuteronomy 7:1–6. However, this denunciation appears to be contextualized. It relates to the postexilic situation where Israelite men were divorcing their Israelite wives in order to take foreign (including Moabite) wives. Mahlon's and Kilion's marriages occurred long before this under entirely different circumstances. The Deuteronomic legislation has a particular group of people in view; it is doubtful if one should broaden its applicability by appealing to its "spirit." If we understand Ruth as an off-limits, contaminated foreigner, it is odd that she becomes the heroine of the book and a shining example of a genuine Yahweh worshiper. Rather than implicitly placing her in a negative light, it is more likely the narrator challenges or at least qualifies common opinion.

(3) Block's use of Deuteronomy 28:32 is puzzling. If marriage to foreigners is to be viewed as a judgment, then are we to assume that

God brought about the marriages of Mahlon and Kilion for punitive purposes?[33] If so, is it not strange that one of these foreign women ends up being the heroine of the book? This Deuteronomic text is in a list of covenant curses describing the consequences of disobedience for those swept away into exile. It depicts the covenant community's disintegration and loss of identity. The discourse is predictive (descriptive), not hortatory (prescriptive), and is of no relevance in evaluating the legitimacy of the marriage of two resident aliens.

(4) Deuteronomy 28:18 is also in a list of covenant curses. Barrenness can sometimes be a form of divine judgment, but this is not always the case, as Sarah, Rebekah, Rachel, and Hannah could attest.

(5) The failure of Mahlon and Kilion to provide a "male remnant" is certainly tragic, but not proof they were guilty of some particular sin that brought such a fate upon them. In Numbers 27:1–4 the daughters of Zelophehad explain that their father died without a male heir, simply due to the fact that he shared the sinful condition of all humanity. The following verses (5–11) anticipate further instances where men might die without a male heir. No mention is made of this being due to divine judgment.

(6) As Block points out, the *niphal* of שׁאר, "be left" (v. 5), can be used of those who have survived divine judgment, but it can also refer to survivors in general (Gen. 32:8; 42:38) and does not carry a technical sense or have an inherently negative connotation.[34]

Though not mentioned by Block, one might also appeal to Deuteronomy 23:3–8, which prohibits a Moabite from participating in Israel's cultic worship. However, this text does not refer to marriage *per se*. If one wants to interpret it to mean that a Moabite is excluded from the covenant community, then the book of Ruth demonstrates there could be exceptions! In this regard Fischer draws out the contrast between Ruth and the Deuteronomic passage. She explains that the Deuteronomic "prohibition is based on the fact that Moab did not support Israel on its way to the promised land." She adds: "Yet in the book of Ruth a starving family of Judah is accommodated in Moab. Yes, the Moabite woman provides for bread even in Bethlehem. In gleaning, Ruth provides for bread for her mother-in-law and herself."

---

33. Baylis (whom Block cites here, in an earlier unpublished version) perhaps sheds light on Block's reasoning: "marriage to non-Israelites . . . was also considered so unthinkable that it, like the move to Moab, was a judgment of God" (2004, 421).
34. As for Naomi's claim that the Lord had opposed her by taking away her husband and sons, we will reserve discussion for later (see vv. 20–21).

She concludes: "Therefore the book of Ruth pleads for differentiated judging of the criterion for admission to the congregation, which also includes a differentiated view of integrating alien women by marriage" (1999, 36).

To support his argument that the deaths of Elimelech and his sons were due to divine punishment, Berman makes four points: (1) The statement "and they remained there" (1:2) means they intended to stay in Moab indefinitely. This "act of remaining out of the land of Israel . . . warranted Elimelech his death" because he "left 'the presence of the Lord' . . . out of his own volition" (cf. 1 Sam. 26:19); (2) the use of "also" in verse 5 implicates the sons in Elimelech's crime; (3) Naomi attributes the death of her husband and sons to God; (4) God is the ultimate cause behind all that happens in the book (2007, 27–29).

Each of these points can be countered.

(1) The collocation שָׁם הָיָה (v. 2), literally "to be there," but often with the nuance "remain, wait there," is used over forty times in the Hebrew Bible. It need not mean that the subject intended to remain in a location permanently; the context must determine how long the "stay" is intended to be. Certainly the statement in Ruth 1:2 must be understood within the framework of the statement in verse 1, "and he went . . . to sojourn." The collocation of חלך, "go," and גור, "sojourn," occurs in two other passages, neither of which suggests the sojourning is intended to be permanent (cf. Judg. 17:9 in light of the Levite's subsequent actions, and 2 Kings 8:1–2). In 2 Kings 8:1 Elisha advises the Shunammite woman to go and sojourn in another place because a seven-year famine is about to descend on the land. She does so (v. 2) and then returns to the land (v. 3). Since famines are rarely if ever permanent, it is unlikely Elimelech went to Moab thinking he would never return. The most natural way to understand the language of Ruth 1:1 is that he moved there to live until the famine was over. We have every reason to suspect that he, like Naomi (cf. 1:6), would have returned home when he heard of God's renewed favor to the land. As noted above, departure from the land due to famine must not be viewed as inherently wrong. The famine is best understood as an incidental detail that provides the background for the story and sets the stage for its comic plot structure.

(2) "Also" in verse 5 simply modifies the preceding verb, indicating that the sons, like their father, died. The subsequent clauses in both verses 3 and 5 indicate this. In verse 3, after being told of Elimelech's death, we read that Naomi was left with just her two sons. In verse 5, after being told of the sons' death, we read that Naomi was now left without her sons and her husband. The focus in both verses is on the simple fact of their physical death and nothing more.

(3) Naomi's view that God has judged her will be discussed below (see my comments on 1:20–21).

(4) God's providence is certainly an important theme in the book. But it is incorrect to say he is directly responsible for all that happens in the story. The narrator attributes only two actions to God—bringing relief from the famine (1:6) and giving Ruth fertility (4:13). In both cases the verb נָתַן, "give," appears (note לָתֵת, literally, "to give," in 1:6 and וַיִּתֵּן, literally, "and he gave," in 4:13). God is depicted as one who "gives," that is, as the one who imparts blessing. God intervenes in the story to bring life and fertility where there has been death and sterility. Apart from these two references, the narrator does not describe God as directly intervening in human affairs. However, as noted above, a pattern of prayer-fulfillment emerges in the book. An individual or group asks God to reward others (specifically, Ruth or Boaz) for kind and faithful deeds they have performed. God is invited to intervene in blessing (cf. 1:8–9; 2:12, 20; 3:10; 4:11–12, 14–15), and by the end of the book we see that he has done so. (In two of these blessings, the verb נָתַן, "give," refers to anticipated divine gifts. See 1:9 and 4:12.) God is working behind the scenes in this story, but to a particular end— the deliverance of Naomi from her tragic despair and the blessing of faithful Ruth and Boaz, his instruments of deliverance.

To summarize, the tragic deaths of Elimelech and his sons should not be interpreted as acts of divine judgment because there is not enough evidence in the immediate context or in the broader context of the Old Testament to sustain such a theory. On the contrary, it would seem that their deaths, like the famine and their move to Moab, are incidental details that set the stage for the story to follow, rather than main themes that should drive one's interpretation of the story (Bush 1996a, 67–68).[35] While these details may fulfill our initial fear that the story will have a tragic conclusion, the narrator exploits this and

---

35. See as well Wilch, who states regarding 1:5: "Again, no judgment is expressed, so it would be presumptuous to claim that their early deaths were punishment from God" (2006, 127). Sakenfeld, after acknowledging that the judgment theory of the deaths of Elimelech and his sons is "certainly a possible interpretation," observes that "the narrator's lack of attention to any reason" for their deaths suggests that the reason for their deaths is "not central to the meaning of the story." She adds: "The deaths of the three men serve to draw our attention to Naomi, whose life up to this point in her culture would have revolved around her husband and sons. What is to become of this Hebrew widow with no male support in a foreign land?" (1999c, 21)

instead turns the story on its head. This is not a story about sin and judgment, but about divine compassion and deliverance.

1:6. The tension in the plot eases momentarily when we read that Naomi decided to return to Judah because she had received the news that the Lord had brought relief from the famine. The verb פָּקַד has the primary meaning "pay attention to, observe with care, interest." Here it refers by metonymy to the consequence of the Lord's attention and has the connotation "visit graciously" (see Gen. 21:1; 50:24–25; Exod. 13:19; 1 Sam. 2:21; Ps. 65:9 [Hebrew v. 10]). The next clause explains more specifically that he brought relief from the famine and restored Israel's crops. One wonders if Naomi may also find some relief from her plight (Bush 1996a, 69).

Going Home (1:7–19a)

1:7–13. Naomi's daughters-in-law set out for Judah with her.[36] But an element of tension reappears, as Naomi suddenly urges them to go back to Moab, where they belong. Commentators puzzle over Naomi's exhortation: "Go back, each of you, to your mother's home" (v. 8, literally, "Go back each to her mother's house"), pointing out that a widow usually returns to her father's house (cf. Gen. 38:11; Lev. 22:13). Various explanations, some of which are overly complex, have been offered. It appears that Naomi was not speaking in technical, legal terms. Rather, she was suggesting the girls' first responsibility was to their own mothers, not their mother-in-law (Bush 1996a, 75).[37]

---

36. We cannot be certain how long a trip it was back to Bethlehem because we do not know the precise location of Naomi's home in Moab. Nor can we be sure of the route that they took. Hubbard (1988b, 102, note 34) gives two options—one around the northern end of the Dead Sea and the other across the Lishon, the peninsula that extends into the Dead Sea from Moab toward the southern end of the sea. Due to difficult terrain on both sides of the sea, the women would have followed trade routes and roads. For maps of the major routes, see Aharoni and Avi-Yonah 1977, 17 (map 10), and Aharoni 1979, 44. If they came around the northern end of the sea, they may have taken the King's Highway north to the Way to Beth-jeshimoth, traveled west on the Way to the Arabah, and then south on the Way to Ephrath. For a description of these various routes, see Aharoni 1979, 54–62.

37. For the phrase "house of her/my mother," see Genesis 24:28; Song of Songs 3:4; 8:2. Campbell suggests that the "mother's house" may have been "the locus for matters pertinent to marriage, especially for discussion and planning for marriage" (1975, 64). If so, then Naomi's exhortation is a subtle

Naomi pronounced a blessing on the girls (v. 8) for the kindness (חֶסֶד) they had shown her and their deceased husbands. The primary meaning of the word חֶסֶד is "loyalty, devotion, commitment." Clark writes that חֶסֶד "is not merely an attitude or emotion; it is an emotion that leads to an activity beneficial to the recipient" (1993, 267). He states that an act of חֶסֶד "is a beneficent action performed, in the context of a deep and enduring commitment between two persons or parties, by one who is able to render assistance to the needy party who in the circumstances is unable to help him- or herself."[38] When collocated with עָשָׂה, "do," it normally refers to fair or benevolent treatment as a reward for good deeds rendered, usually as an act of allegiance. (See Gen. 40:14; 47:29; Josh. 2:12, 14; Judg. 1:24; 8:35; 1 Sam. 20:14; 2 Sam. 2:6; 9:1, 3, 7.) The remainder of the prayer (see v. 9) suggests Naomi had the security of marriage in mind. She asked God to reward the girls' past devotion by giving them new husbands.

In the context of Naomi's hortatory discourse (note the two imperatives in v. 8a), the formal blessing has a performative and dynamic (motivational) function.[39] It was intended to activate divine blessing and

---

way of suggesting they need to find new husbands; it sets up nicely her subsequent argument (v. 9). For a contrary opinion see Linafelt 1999, 11–12. The use of the expression may simply reflect the female perspective of the characters. Bronner shows that the phrase is "linked to love, wisdom, women's agency and marriage" (1999, 188). In Song of Songs the mother's house is "a place where love can and does reside" (187). As Bronner points out, we cannot be certain "what associations Naomi has with the mother's house—whether she thinks of it as a place that will take in these bereft daughters-in-law in [sic] grudgingly or as a place where they will be welcomed." Yet, as Bronner, adds: "Given the tone of the rest of this scroll, surely Naomi hopes that she is sending them to a place like the mother's house in the Song of Songs" (188).

38. For another major study of the word, see Sakenfeld 1978. For a convenient summary of her conclusion regarding the meaning of the term, see 1999c, 24. She states that the term "refers to an action by one person on behalf of another under circumstances that meet three main criteria," namely, (a) "the action is essential to the survival or basic well-being of the recipient," (b) "the needed action is one that only the person doing the act of *ḥesed* is in a position to provide," and (c) "an act of *ḥesed* takes place or is requested within the context of an existing, established, and positive relationship between the persons involved."

39. According to Macky, performative language is a speech-act in which the statement "performs some non-linguistic act, such as a judge decreeing, 'The defendant is acquitted'" (1990, 16). Macky explains that dynamic speech is "intended to change hearers personally." It can be affective

to assure the girls they had been loyal and were deserving of a reward. Convinced they had fulfilled their duty, they should have been willing to act in accordance with common sense and go home (Sakenfeld 1999c, 24). Supporting her appeal with action, Naomi kissed her daughters-in-law goodbye, prompting them to weep loudly.

The daughters refused to accept Naomi's words; they affirmed their intention to accompany her back to Judah. This brief but powerful response has an expressive and dynamic function.[40] The girls expressed their strong loyalty to Naomi and hoped to convince her to permit them to remain with her.

After again urging them to go back (v. 11, cf. v. 8), Naomi mounted an even more compelling argument for why they should do so. She asked rhetorically why they would want to come with her.[41] Certainly their primary concern should have been finding new husbands, but Naomi was in no position to provide for their need because she was too old to bear any more sons. She repeated her earlier exhortation (cf. שֹׁבְנָה ... לֵכְנָה, literally, "return ... go," in v. 11 with לֵכְנָה שֹׁבְנָה, literally, "go, return," in v. 8), and then developed her argument even further. Naomi was too old to get remarried, but even if she were to do so and were to bear more sons, Ruth and Orpah would not want to wait around until these sons reached marriageable age.[42] If this was not

---

("aimed at arousing emotions"), pedagogical ("intended to illuminate darkness"), or transforming ("intended to change hearers' attitudes, values and commitments, often by first arousing emotion and illuminating the darkness"). It often presents a case or argument designed to convince the listener(s) of the truth of a statement.

40. In expressive speech the speaker verbalizes "feelings without any concern to affect others" (Macky 1990, 16). However, as Macky points out, "Very often such expressive speech is integrated with other kinds when we know others hear us."

41. On Naomi's use of rhetorical questions in verses 11–13, see Hyman 1984, 190–91. Hyman shows the questions are "critical/corrective." They "constitute a short, tactical argument to convince Orpah and Ruth to alter their plans and return home to find Moabite husbands" (191). Naomi's interrogative discourse has a persuasive-dynamic speech function designed to convince the girls to return to Moab.

42. We are not told Naomi's age. Sakenfeld makes a reasonable case for Naomi being in her early forties: "The reader is not told the ages of any of the story's characters, but if we begin with the common assumption that marriages in that culture usually took place during the mid-teen years, Naomi's perspective makes narrative sense. If she herself married at the age of fifteen, she would have been about thirty-two by the time her sons

convincing enough, she capped off her speech with a particularly powerful, double-barreled argument. The girls should not have to bear her
burden, which had been placed upon her by the Lord himself. In other
words, Naomi was convinced she was a special object of the Lord's displeasure and it would be too burdensome and even dangerous for the
girls to remain with her (Hubbard 1988b, 113).

This final element in Naomi's argument requires closer attention.
If אַל בְּנֹתַי, "no, my daughters" (v. 13), is the answer to the preceding
question(s) (v. 11) (Hubbard 1988b, 112; Block 1999, 637), then Naomi
reasoned they would not be willing to wait around for her to provide
new husbands for them because her suffering would be too much for
the girls to bear and they would be unwilling to stay with her that long.
A better option is that the words אַל בְּנֹתַי are Naomi's response to their
stated intention of returning with her (cf. v. 10).[43] In this case, she told
them they must not stay with her because her suffering was too much
for her to ask them to bear. Her use of the comparative מִן, "from,"
seems to suggest Naomi's pain exceeded that of Orpah and Ruth; after
all, she had lost a husband and two sons, while each of them had lost
just a husband. However, as noted above, her point may be that her
suffering was too great a burden for them to have to bear (Bush 1996a,

---

were fifteen and ready to enter into their marriages with Ruth and Orpah.
If some or all of the ten years' time mentioned in verse 4 elapsed during
the time of those marriages, Naomi could be as old as her early forties,
with Ruth and Orpah in their mid-twenties. In a world where life expec-
tancy was forty years or less, Naomi's insistence that she is not marriageable and that her daughters-in-law cannot wait another fifteen years or so
for re-marriage is common sense, powerfully stated" (1999c, 27).

43. Elsewhere when כִּי, "for," follows אַל, "no," there is almost always an intervening verb. In 2 Kings 3:13 כִּי directly follows אַל. In this case the speaker
is rejecting a command and then giving his reasons for doing so. Apart
from Ruth 1:13, the only other example of כִּי following אַל with an intervening vocative is in 1 Samuel 2:24 (literally, "no, my sons, for..."). Eli has
just asked a rhetorical question (v. 23), but אַל does not provide an answer
to it. Rather it expresses his rejection of the report he had heard (cf. v. 22;
note how *NET* translates אַל in v. 24: "this ought not to be"). Though the
precise discourse sequence in Ruth 1:11–13 differs from that of 1 Samuel
2:22–24, it is possible (on the basis of the parallel use of אַל + vocative +
כִּי) to argue that אַל in Ruth 1:13 expresses Naomi's rejection of the girls'
stated intention (v. 10), rather than supplying an answer to her rhetorical
questions. Furthermore, there is no other example in the Old Testament
of a rhetorical question introduced by an interrogative *he* that is answered
with אַל.

80–81). In this case the comparative preposition has the force of "too much for."[44]

Naomi described her condition as "bitter" (v. 13). This verb (מַר, from the root מרר) is used here of Naomi's emotional distress (cf. 1 Sam. 30:6; 2 Kings 4:27; Isa. 38:17; Lam. 1:4; 3:15; Zech. 12:10), though there may be a connotation of economic destitution as well (cf. the use of the related adjective in 1 Sam. 22:2). The reason for this bitterness, according to Naomi, was divine opposition (cf. v. 20 as well). She lamented, "the hand of the Lord has gone out against me" (literal translation). The language is unique. יָד, "hand," and יצא, "go out," are collocated only here, and יצא is used with adversative -בְּ, "against," only here (Sasson 1979, 26). The phrase "hand of the Lord" is often used of God's power, typically in contexts of war and/or judgment (cf. Exod. 9:3; 16:3; Deut. 2:15; Josh. 4:24; 22:31; Judg. 2:15; 1 Sam. 5:6, 9; 7:13; 12:15; 2 Sam. 24:14).

1:14–19a. Naomi's argument had the intended effect on Orpah, who kissed her mother-in-law goodbye and returned to Moab. But Ruth hugged Naomi, communicating her reluctance to leave (v. 14c). Elsewhere the idiom -בְּ דבק means (1) cling to, stay close to, stick to (Gen. 2:24; Num. 36:7, 9; Deut. 13:17; 28:60; Ruth 2:23; 2 Kings 5:27; Job 19:20; 31:7; Ps. 101:3; Ezek. 29:4), (2) be bound to emotionally (Gen. 34:3), (3) be loyal to (Deut. 4:4; 10:20; 11:22; 13:4; 30:20; Josh. 22:5; 23:8; 2 Sam. 20:2; 1 Kings 11:2; 2 Kings 18:6; Pss. 63:8; 119:31), (4) form alliances with (Josh. 23:12). In verse 14 Ruth's action contrasts with Orpah's goodbye kiss, so a hug is apparently in view (hence our translation "hugged her tightly"). Of course, this hug was an expression of her deep emotional attachment and loyalty to Naomi.[45]

---

44. This is the so-called comparison of capability. See *IBHS*, 266–67. *IBHS* cites Ruth 1:13, but states that it is "difficult to distinguish" in this case "between a positive comparison and a comparison of capability" (p. 267). Joüon-Muraoka (pp. 523–24) lists our passage under the category of an "elliptical comparison," understood in the sense of "too much for."

45. Berquist points out that the verb דבק, "cling," when used of human relations outside of the book of Ruth, refers to a man's attachment to a woman, including "the male role in initiating marriage" (1993, 27). Consequently, "when Ruth clings to Naomi, Ruth takes the male role in initiating a relationship of formal commitment, similar to marriage." While retaining her role as daughter-in-law, Ruth "adds the male role of 'clinging' to Naomi as a husband." Berquist (24–25) calls such a shift in roles "dedifferentiation" and contends that crisis is what "catalyzes role shifts."

Orpah, as a mere agent in the story, serves as a foil for Ruth.[46] Orpah did what one expects. In the face of Naomi's logic, she said goodbye and went home. But Ruth's love for Naomi caused her to stay with her mother-in-law, even when such devotion seemed illogical and downright foolish. Orpah was not a bad person; on the contrary she was a good daughter-in-law who had treated Naomi well. She deserved and received Naomi's blessing (v. 8). But Ruth was beyond good; her love for Naomi transcended the norm. The contrast between the two girls should not be expressed as a polarity (bad versus good) but in terms of degree (good versus great). The narrator's purpose in mentioning and describing Orpah is not to criticize her, but to highlight Ruth (Hubbard 1988b, 115–16; Berlin 1983, 85; Sakenfeld 1999c, 11, 30).

Ruth's persistence prompted another exhortation from Naomi (v. 15). She urged Ruth to follow Orpah's example and return to her own people and her own god(s). Naomi strengthened her argument here by appealing to common sense, as exemplified by Orpah, and to cold reality. Ruth really had no place in Judah. Like Orpah, she was a Moabite and she would do well to go back to her native land and its god(s).[47]

The form אֱלֹהֶיהָ may be translated "her gods" (since Orpah was probably a polytheist) or "her god," since the Moabites worshiped

---

46. An agent is a minor, flat character that has a limited role to fulfill in a story; a foil is a character that stands in contrast to another character, thereby highlighting one or more of the latter's characteristics or traits.

47. Baylis accuses Naomi of committing a serious sin by urging Ruth to return to Moab and to her god(s) (2004, 428). He regards her action as a violation of Deuteronomy 13:6–10, which warns the covenant community not to listen to anyone who encourages members of the community to worship other gods. Baylis suggests Naomi should have been executed: "To influence anyone to follow other gods was a deed so severe it was punishable by death." But is it not odd that the story, rather than condemning Naomi, focuses on God's deliverance of Naomi from her distress and pain? The Deuteronomic law was not addressing a situation like the one described in Ruth 1. Ruth was not a member of the covenant community when Naomi spoke the words of 1:15 (throughout the story her *Moabite* ethnicity is stressed), but once she committed herself by oath to enter the Israelite community (1:16), Naomi no longer urged her to return. Perhaps we could criticize Naomi (albeit somewhat anachronistically) for not being "evangelistic" enough, but she was not violating the Deuteronomic code. In fact her statement, implying Moab was not directly under Yahweh's rule, is consistent with Deuteronomy, which speaks of God allotting the nations to delegated heavenly ruling authorities (cf. Deut. 4:19–20; 32:8 [cf. Qumran, LXX]).

Chemosh as their national patron deity (Block 1999, 639; Mattingly 1994, 329).[48] The suffixed form of אֱלֹהִים can be used as a plural of respect for foreign gods (see, for example, Judg. 9:27; 1 Sam. 5:7; 1 Kings 18:24), including Chemosh (Judg. 11:24; cf also 1 Kings 11:33). In a recent study of אֱלֹהִים Burnett argues that the plural form should be understood as a "concretized abstract plural, according to which the nominal plural form expresses an abstraction in reference to an individual or thing that holds a particular status named by the abstract category in question. Thus the plural of the noun 'god' occurs with the meaning 'deity'" (2001, 53). He states: "In connection with the concept of the patron deity, *'ĕlōhîm* designates the god who stands in special relationship to a particular individual, group, territory, or nation" 2001, 66).[49]

Four times Naomi urged Ruth to "return" to her native land (vv. 8, 11–12, 15). Ruth countered by telling her mother-in-law, "Do not urge me to abandon you by returning from after you" (v. 16, literal translation). The collocation of the verb עֲזֹב, "abandon," with the verb שׁוּב, "return," was a powerful rhetorical move on Ruth's part. Its inclusion reflects Ruth's perspective. As far as she was concerned, to return to Moab would mean abandoning Naomi and leaving her even more vulnerable than she already was. Ruth declared in no uncertain terms that she intended to stay with Naomi. She announced she would follow Naomi and live with her. For Naomi's sake, Ruth was willing to renounce her native land and god(s) and to identify with Naomi's people and God.[50] She promised she would stay with Naomi for the rest of her life and even be buried in the same place as her mother-in-law.

Ruth capped off her promise with a self-imprecation (v. 17) in which she used Yahweh's name, as if to show that she was indeed serious about identifying with Naomi's God (Prinsloo 1977–78, 115;

---

48. For a defense of the singular reading in verse 15, see Hunter 1981, 433.

49. On the use of אֱלֹהִים as a concretized abstract plural for national patron deities, see Burnett, 65–66.

50. The significance of Ruth's words has been understood in various ways—as expressing conversion, as cementing bonds, and as establishing or affirming covenantal loyalty. See Smith 2007, 243–47. Smith (247–58) argues that family relationships are the basis for covenantal language and concepts. Ruth's words, then, establish "a family relationship with Naomi that transcends the death of the male who had connected them, and in fact this relationship represents a family tie closer than that expressed by the formal status of former in-laws" (247). In the end, "theirs is nothing less than the love of a mother and her daughter. For, from the beginning to the end of the story, Naomi calls Ruth 'my daughter'" (258).

Bush 1996a, 87; and Ziegler 2007, 78–80). Ruth's oath transformed her hortatory-predictive discourse into a performative declaration. This silenced Naomi, for she understood the implications of such a radical promise.[51] Within chapter one there is an interesting interplay between speech-acts. Naomi's blessing (vv. 8–9) seemingly released Ruth and assured her of God's blessing, but Ruth's self-imposed curse (v. 17) counterbalanced and trumped the blessing. Ironically, Ruth's oath validated Naomi's blessing, for it provided proof of her loyal love and worthiness of divine favor.

The structure of Ruth's oath requires closer examination to appreciate its meaning. The first part of the oath consists of two clauses, each introduced by כֹּה, "thus," and describes the punishment for breaking the promise. The second part of the oath, introduced by כִּי, "indeed, certainly," gives the condition of the oath. This structure is formulaic, appearing with slight variations in 1 Samuel 14:44; 20:13; 2 Samuel 3:9; 1 Kings 2:23; 19:2. The description of the punishment is vague and stereotypical. It reads literally, "Thus will the Lord do to me, and thus will he add." The presence of כֹּה seems to assume the presence of a more specific form of punishment, but this element is implied, rather than stated.[52] One may paraphrase the formula as follows: "The Lord will punish me severely." Based on the usage of כִּי in the other examples of this oath formula, it appears that the final clause, introduced by כִּי, affirms what will or must happen for the punishment to be averted. Consequently כִּי may be understood as an emphasizer and translated "indeed, certainly" (Bush 1996a, 83; Block 1999, 642–43).[53]

The NRSV, "if even death," understands כִּי in the sense of "certainly not, if even," but this would require כִּי־אִם, as 2 Samuel 3:35 indicates. Nevertheless, some commentators support this position. Hubbard argues that the preceding statement ("Wherever you die I will die and I

---

51. The text simply informs us that Naomi ceased the debate. There is a gap in the narrative; we are not told what she was thinking (Linafelt 1999, 17). However, it does become apparent in verse 21 that she does not yet appreciate Ruth's sacrifice or value.

52. Ziegler (2008, 57) observes, "the word כֹּה may suggest that this oath formula was accompanied by an act, speech or gesture which suggested the manner of punishment in case of violation of this oath." She adds: "In the Bible, the word כֹּה can introduce speech (Gen. 32:4; Num. 6:23). Perhaps, then, the word כֹּה indicates that this oath originally included a verbal enumeration of punishments which would occur in case of its violation."

53. One may paraphrase Ruth 1:17b as follows: "Indeed death alone will separate me and you." (Note NIV [cf. also NASB, NLT], "anything but death," KJV, "if ought but death," and our translation, "nothing but death.")

will be buried there") indicates that death would *not* separate Naomi and Ruth, for Ruth was determined to live with Naomi's people and to be buried in the same place as her mother-in-law (1988b, 119–20).[54] Campbell argues the same point, appealing for additional support to archaeological evidence for the practice of common burial (1975, 74–75). The noun מָוֶת, "death," is collocated with the verb פָּרַד, "separate," in only one other text, 2 Samuel 1:23. Regarding Saul and Jonathan, David stated, "not even in their deaths [literally, death] were they separated." Saul and Jonathan died together on the battlefield; so it could be said that they were not separated in death. However, in Ruth's case, she undoubtedly anticipated Naomi's death preceding her own. Though Ruth would stay as close as possible to Naomi's grave and eventually be buried with her, death would, at least for a time, separate them, for it cuts the deceased off from the land of the living (Ps. 52:5 [Hebrew, v. 7]; Isa. 38:11; 53:8; Jer. 11:19; Ezek. 26:20, cf. 1 Sam. 12:25; Job 7:21).

Demanding a New Name (1:19b–21)

1:19b. The women's arrival in Bethlehem created a stir. The women of the town expressed surprise when they saw Naomi, asking, "Is this Naomi?" The emotional tone of the question is not readily apparent. Were they shocked by Naomi's appearance? Or were they delighted with joy at the sight of her? An examination of usage elsewhere does not clear up the ambiguity. The collocation interrogative *he* + demonstrative pronoun + noun occurs in only three other texts. In Genesis 43:29 ("Is this your youngest brother?") the question expresses Joseph's excitement and delight at seeing Benjamin, but in Isaiah 14:16 ("Is this the man who shook the earth?") and Lamentations 2:15 (literally, "Is this the city that said?") it expresses sarcastic disdain.

Several commentators argue that the question expresses the women's joy at seeing Naomi (Hubbard 1988b, 123–24; Bush 1996a, 91–92; Nielsen 1997, 51; Campbell 1975, 75). For support they appeal to the use of the verb הוּם, "shake," elsewhere (cf. וַתֵּהֹם, "was excited"). The *niphal* of הוּם appears in two other texts; in both it is associated with excitement and joy, not shock (cf. 1 Sam. 4:5; 1 Kings 1:45). Furthermore, Bush contends that Naomi's response (cf. v. 20) "challenges the tone of their exclamation" and "makes much better sense if she is reacting to glad and joyous recognition rather than shocked and amazed consternation and concern" (Bush 1996a, 92).

---

54. Hubbard argues that the syntax in the other examples of the formula is ambiguous (119, note 33). However, see Bush's response to this (1996a, 83).

However, not everyone is convinced of this position (see, for example, Block 1999, 645). The *niphal* of הום does not describe joy *per se*, but rather the effect of joyous shouts upon the environment (the ground in 1 Sam. 4:5; the town in 1 Kings 1:45). Furthermore, in other stems the verb refers to a negative emotional response (Deut. 7:23; Ps. 55:2 [Hebrew v. 2]; Mic. 2:12 is ambiguous), and the derived noun מְהוּמָה consistently refers to panic, tumult, trouble, and shock (Deut. 7:23; 28:20; 1 Sam. 5:9, 11; 14:20; 2 Chron. 15:5; Prov. 15:16; Isa. 22:5; Ezek. 7:7 [contrasted with joyous shouting]; 22:5; Amos 3:9; Zech. 14:13). As for Naomi's response, it could be corrective in nature, as Bush suggests, but it could also be explanatory and clarifying. In other words, as Naomi heard the shocked women ask, "Is this Naomi," she demanded a new name, Mara (= "Bitter"), that reflected more accurately what they sensed and explained why she looked like such "a haggard and destitute old woman" (Block 1999, 645). In the final analysis, we cannot be certain of the women's tone, for the lexical and contextual evidence is ambiguous.[55]

1:20–21. In response to the women's question, Naomi lashed out in bitterness, demanding they call her by a new name, Mara. Her response is both hortatory (she demanded they call her by a different name) and expository (she gave a convincing case for the name change). Her words carry an expressive function—she vented her emotions, expressing her disappointment and her feeling that she was an enemy of God.[56]

The name נָעֳמִי is derived from a verbal root meaning "be lovely, pleasant." Naomi felt this name was inappropriate, given the hardship

---

55. Linafelt suggests that the ambiguity is intentional: "The undecidability between shock and joy, between a negative evaluation of Naomi's circumstance and a positive one, may be taken as a cipher for the reader's response to the narrative thus far, a narrative that is negotiating a delicate balance between the poles of blessing and curse" (1999, 18).

56. Rauber shows that Naomi had come to the point where she felt empty and was hopeless (1970, 29–30). Freedman observes that in an ancient Israelite context Naomi had ample reason to feel this way, for she was a childless widow who could no longer have children, living in a culture where women, for good reason, put a premium on bearing children (2003, 30–34). In modern western culture widows, if protected through a husband's life insurance or savings, are not in a vulnerable position economically. But in the ancient Israelite world, they were left without a breadwinner and legal status and, consequently, were often viewed as part of a group that was especially vulnerable and dependent on the kindness of others. See Cornelis van Leeuwen, "אַלְמָנָה," in *NIDOTTE* 1:413–15.

she was enduring. She wanted a new name, מָרָא, meaning "bitter," because she was convinced God had brought bitterness (הֵמַר) into her life. The verb used here reflects her deep emotional pain. The *hiphil* of מרר, "be bitter," also appears in Job 27:2, where Job accuses God of making his soul bitter by denying him justice, and in Zechariah 12:10, where it describes the bitter grief one feels over the loss of an only child.

In attributing her pain to God, Naomi referred to him as Shaddai. This divine name or title emphasizes God's sovereign position. The derivation of the name is debated, but it may be derived from a root meaning "mountain," in which case it may designate God as the "one of the mountain" and depict him as ruling from a mountain (cf. Ps. 48:2), like Canaanite deities are sometimes pictured doing (cf. Isa. 14:13; Ezek. 28:14, 16) (Block 1999, 645–46). This divine title depicts God as the judge of the world who both gives and takes away life. The patriarchs knew God primarily as El (meaning "God") Shaddai (Exod. 6:3). When the title is used in Genesis, God appears as the source of fertility and life (see Gen. 17:1–8; 28:3; 35:11; 48:3–4).[57] The name is especially prominent in the book of Job, where it occurs thirty-one times. Job and his friends regard Shaddai as the sovereign king of the world (11:7; 37:23a) who is the source of life (33:4b) and promotes justice (8:3; 34:10–12; 37:23b). He provides blessings, including children (22:17–18; 29:4–6), but he also disciplines and judges (5:17; 6:4; 21:20; 23:16). Psalm 91:1 pictures Shaddai as his people's protector, while Psalm 68:14; Isaiah 13:6; and Joel 1:15 portray him as a warrior.[58] To summarize, Shaddai is the sovereign judge who dispenses both life and death in accordance with his just decisions (see Campbell 1975, 77; Hubbard 1988b, 125). For this reason, we have chosen to translate the divine title "Sovereign One" in verses 20–21, rather than simply transliterate the word.

In developing her argument, Naomi accused God of causing her

---

57. Sakenfeld points out the irony of Naomi's use of Shaddai in light of its usage in Genesis: *"First,* the name appears in Genesis in the context of *promise of numerous offspring;* by contrast, Naomi's cry is called forth by *the loss of her offspring,* as well as of her husband and the possibility of bearing more children. . . . *Second,* in Genesis both Abraham and Israel *receive their new names* in the context of promise from El Shaddai. Naomi in her pain *asks that her name be changed* because of what Shaddai has done" (emphasis hers, 2003, 133).

58. A comparison of Naomi's words with Psalm 91 also yields irony. The psalmist was confident Shaddai (v. 1) would protect him from harm (רָעָה, v. 10), but Naomi lamented that Shaddai had harmed her (הֵרַע, v. 21). See Sakenfeld 2003, 137–38.

grief by taking away the men in her life (see v. 21). She even added the adverb מְאֹד, "very," to emphasize the depth of her pain. She went away "full" in the sense that she left with a husband and two sons. She returned "empty" in the sense that all three were taken from her by death. Apparently, from Naomi's perspective, ever-loyal Ruth, who stood silently at her side, did not really count.[59]

According to Naomi, the Lord had opposed her, as if in a court of law. Collocated with the preposition -בְּ, the *qal* verbal form עָנָה, "to answer," has a legal connotation, "testify against" (see BDB, 772–73, 3.a; *HALOT*, 852). Some translations, following the Greek Septuagint, have "afflicted me" (see NIV; cf. NRSV, NLT). This reading assumes an emendation of the Hebrew text to עִנָּה, a *piel* form of a homonymic root meaning "afflict" (see BDB, 776; *HALOT*, 853). However, this *piel* form never introduces its object with the preposition -בְּ When this preposition is used with this verb, it is always adverbial ("in, with, through").[60]

Naomi also lamented that Shaddai had made her suffer (הֵרַע). When collocated with -לְ + object, the *hiphil* of the verb רעע has the basic idea "do harm to" (Gen. 19:9; Num. 11:11). In some contexts, especially with God as subject, it carries the nuance "judge, punish" (Josh. 24:20; Jer. 25:6; Zech. 8:14). In other cases it means, "treat unfairly" (Gen. 43:6; Exod. 5:22–23; Num. 20:15; 1 Sam. 26:21; Ps. 105:15). It is not clear if Naomi had one of these connotations in mind, but it is apparent she regarded God as directly responsible for the death of her husband and sons and for her subsequent misery.[61]

---

59. Sakenfeld aptly observes: "The presence of Ruth goes completely unremarked as she explains the absence of her husband and sons as God's calamity" (1999c, 36). Yet we should not be too hard on Naomi. After all, with the death of her husband and sons, she had been deprived of her two major roles in this patriarchal culture—wife and mother. Berquist states: "The beginning crisis, then, is three-fold: a famine of national or international scale, the death of three men and virtual role death for Naomi" (1993, 26).

60. For a defense of the *qal* reading, see Campbell 1975, 77; Hubbard 1988b, 126–27; and Sasson 1979, 35. Moore argues that the reading is intentionally ambiguous, expressing "the multidimensional depth of Naomi's pain." He adds, "We feel not only her sense of legal impotence but also her sense of emotional betrayal" (1997, 237–38).

61. The basic sense of the *hiphil* is causative; cf. the *qal* meaning "be injured." Sakenfeld argues that Naomi's words do not necessarily mean that she considered herself "guilty of some wrongdoing or offense against God (or that the narrator assumed such guilt on her part). Naomi gives no indication that she considers herself deserving of the bitter dealing, emptiness,

Was she correct? When interpreting narrative literature, one cannot assume that quotations from characters reflect the viewpoint of the narrator. The interpreter must assess quotations in light of the surrounding context and the overall theme(s) of the story or book. When one examines the book of Ruth, one notices the narrator does not attribute the deaths of the men to God, nor does God appear in an antagonistic role. On the contrary, the narrator depicts God as Naomi's ally and as her source of blessing. In this regard it is noteworthy that the famine is not attributed to the Lord (cf. 1:1), but the Lord is identified as the one who brings relief from it (1:6). While Naomi claimed that God had singled her out for punishment (1:20–21), in the end objective observers viewed her as an object of divine blessing (4:14) (see Hongisto 1985, 26).

Freedman mounts a convincing case that the narrator does not share Naomi's adversarial view of God (2003, 34–35). First, she points out there are twenty-one direct references to God in the book, only five of which are negative. All five of these "come from Naomi and Naomi alone." She adds: "In terms of sheer numbers, the book's positive and neutral references to God outweigh the negative references. Thus, Naomi's is the lone voice in the story criticizing God, and her voice is effectively drowned out by all the other voices that praise God." Second, "the book of Ruth explicitly counters Naomi's negative remarks about God several times." Naomi tells others to call her Mara, but no one ever does. Thirteen times after this she is called Naomi by the narrator, Boaz's foreman, and Boaz himself. When Naomi complains she has returned empty-handed, the narrator reminds us of Ruth's presence, and in the final chapter the women counter her claim, by affirming Ruth's great value. Third, the book concludes with a "positive evaluation of God" as the women praise him for providing Naomi with a redeemer. Freedman notes: "This final and lingering emphasis on God as a generous deity also serves to discredit Naomi's negative understanding of

---

and calamity that has befallen her. It can equally well be argued that rather than implicitly accepting blame, she makes here a defiant, if frustrated and deeply hurt, expression of her innocence. Like the action of God in the life of Job, divine action in the life of Naomi is bitter and yields bitterness precisely because it is so utterly inexplicable" (2003, 136). Linafelt goes a bit further and suggests that Naomi "is flat out attributing evil or wicked actions to God—that is, unmotivated or wrongly motivated affliction" (1999, 20). Lapsley suggests that Naomi accused God of making her a widow and of acting contrary to the hymnic affirmation that he cares for widows (cf. Ps. 146:9) (2005, 96–98).

God and God's behavior toward her." She concludes: "Taken together, these narrative strategies make Naomi's negative understanding of God appear invalid when viewed in the context of God's characterization in the book of Ruth as a whole. The text of Ruth suggests that God is benevolent to God's people and the source of all the assistance that Naomi and Ruth experience. Thus, the text implies that Naomi is wrong when she attributes her suffering to God. . . . Naomi's criticism of a tormenting God, a criticism that comes from her experience as a woman, is invalidated by the text's otherwise glowing picture of a benevolent God" (2003, 35).

We cannot assume that God struck down Elimelech and his sons. The context suggests he did not.[62] One should respect the silence of the narrator and not assume that he agrees with Naomi's assessment of her situation. As Freedman and others have shown, the narrator actually seems to counteract Naomi; he pictures God as one who blesses people and restores fertility and life. Perhaps he even exploits the potential for reading the earlier events in terms of sin and judgment. While one may suspect initially that this is a story of sin and judgment, this proves not to be the case as the narrator turns the tale on its head. Ironically a foreign woman becomes the heroine of the story and God proves to be Naomi's ally, not her enemy![63]

While all that happens in the world ultimately falls under the umbrella of God's sovereign dominion, this hardly means the death of loved ones is an act of divine judgment! The Scriptures depict God's relationship to death as quite complex.[64] On the one hand, he is sovereign over death and sometimes uses it as an instrument of judgment (1 Sam.

---

62. Some argue that God was responsible for the death of Elimelech and his sons, but stop short of attributing their deaths to some sin on their part. Hubbard, for example, prefers to attribute their deaths to "the mystery of God" (1988b, 127). In light of what we see in some of the lament psalms (see especially Ps. 44) and in Job (cf. Campbell 1975, 83), this middle ground position is certainly possible. However, the fact remains that the narrator stops short of attributing their deaths to God, at least directly.

63. Grant points out that after chapter one "the narrative builds on the difference between Naomi's perception of 'things as they are' and actual truth" (1991, 432). He adds: "In the first two scenes of the first act Naomi interpreted God in light of her circumstances. She looked at her situation and said in effect, 'This bitterness is the only reality I know or that can be known. This is 'truth,' and by it I will redefine my concept of God. In other words Naomi interpreted God in light of the phenomena rather than interpreting the phenomena in light of what she knew to be true of God."

64. Chisholm 2004, 117.

2:6; Isa. 5:14). On the other hand, death is God's archenemy, which he must defeat in a final battle (Ps. 18:9–14; Isa. 25:6–8). According to the New Testament, death entered the world through sin (Rom. 5:12–21). Satan holds the power of death and uses it to terrorize the human race (Heb. 2:14–15). For Paul death is the "last enemy" and will be "swallowed up in victory" as a result of Christ's resurrection (1 Cor. 15:26, 54–55). When one views Naomi's experience within the framework of biblical theology as a whole, her determinism is simplistic.[65] Within this broader context, it is apparent she was a victim of God's enemy, who ravages the fallen race. As the narrative unfolds, she discovers God is her advocate, not her adversary.[66]

Fertility in the Air (1:22)

Having recorded Naomi's bitter tirade, the narrator now gives the reader an emotional break. The summary statement concerning Naomi's return combines with verse 6b to form a bracket around the scenes of this first act in the story. It also plays an important role literarily, for it catapults the return motif above the themes of death and barrenness that have occupied so much of the chapter.[67] The reference to Ruth having returned with Naomi is a subtle reminder that Naomi's statement about returning "empty-handed" (v. 21) was shortsighted.[68] As noted earlier, the reference to the barley harvest lends closure to

---

65. Many Old Testament theologians argue that ancient Israel had a monistic understanding of God that presupposed divine omni-causality. See, for example, C. Dohmen "רעע," in *TDOT* 13:575–78. Some advocates of this view espouse the so-called "demonic-in-Yahweh" viewpoint, according to which God is morally neutral and the source of both good and evil. See, for example, Penchansky 1999. Lindström has challenged and refuted the monistic view. He demonstrates that Job 2:10, Isaiah 45:7, Lamentations 3, and the many other texts used to defend the theory are inappropriately universalized and do not support a monistic reading when examined within their contexts (1983).

66. Korpel argues that theodicy is at the heart of the book of Ruth as its "superficially veiled central theme" (2003, 334). She contends, "the justification of God was the main concern of the author" (347). By the end of the story, one realizes "Naomi had been wrong to question God's righteousness" (346). While it is unlikely that theodicy is the book's *central* theme, the book's author does indeed correct Naomi's faulty and limited perspective.

67. In this regard, see the insightful comments of Grant 1991, 427–28, 430.

68. On the syntactical prominence of the reference to Ruth, see Bush 1996a, 94. On the foreshadowing function of the reference, see Bush 1996a, 96.

the first act, while also providing the background for what follows.[69] The chapter begins with a famine (v. 1); it ends with a barley harvest, driving home the point that the Lord had indeed intervened on behalf of his people (v. 6). One wonders if Naomi, who by now has become the focal point of the story, may be the beneficiary of such a reversal, perhaps through the instrumentality of the one just mentioned in the preceding disjunctive clause.[70] Fertility is in the air as the people harvest their barley. Perhaps fertility will be restored to Naomi as well, in spite of her despair (cf. vv. 11–13).[71]

MESSAGE AND APPLICATION

Thematic Emphases

Naomi's husband and sons died, leaving her in a vulnerable position as a widow living in a foreign land. Naomi attempted to convince Ruth to return to her Moabite family, arguing that God had made her a target of his judgment and that her suffering was too much for Ruth to have to endure. She even pronounced a blessing upon Ruth for her kindness. But Ruth refused to take her blessing and return to the relative security of her own people and family. She sealed her commitment to Naomi with an oath. Sensing Ruth's resolve, Naomi finally gave in, but, upon returning to Bethlehem, she lamented that she had returned empty-handed, even though ever-loyal Ruth stood by her side.

---

69. According to the Gezer Calendar, the barley harvest occurred during the fifth period (eighth month) of the annual agricultural cycle, i.e., between late March and late April. See Borowski 1987, 91.

70. In this regard, see Hubbard 1988b, 130–31, as well as Campbell 1975, 84. Rauber observes that the reference to the harvest "convinces us beyond any doubt that all is well, that this is indeed a divine comedy" (1970, 30).

71. According to Green, "the story's main intent is to relate the restoration of seed: food in the land, food for Naomi and Ruth, a husband for Ruth, a redeemer for Naomi and an heir (leading to a king) for the whole people" (1982, 56). While this theme may not be the story's "main intent," it surely is an important theme that is signaled by the reference to the restoration of crops in 1:22. More recently, Sutskover has demonstrated the importance of the fertility theme in the book. Examining the book's use of the lexical fields of land and fertility, she concludes, "the unique patterns connected with terms from these fields highlight a thematic development focusing on the fertility of the land and of Ruth" (2010, 293).

Exegetical idea: *Naomi experienced tragic loss and felt rejected by God, but Ruth vowed to stay with her, even though such sacrificial love may have seemed risky and been unappreciated.*

Theological Principles

The only action attributed to God by the narrator is a gracious one— God came to the aid of his people and reversed the effects of the famine (1:6). Naomi viewed God as the one who rewards those who are worthy (1:8–9), yet she also depicted him as her adversary who had afflicted her by killing her husband and sons (1:13, 20–21). However, neither this chapter nor the story as a whole suggests Naomi's perspective is correct. Contrary to Naomi, the narrator portrays God as one who is predisposed to intervene on behalf of the afflicted.

Sacrificial love, as exemplified by Ruth, is at the heart of the biblical message. Jesus says the whole Law can be summed up in two commands: to love the Lord God with all one's being, and to love one's neighbors as oneself (Matt. 22:37–39). As he commands his disciples to love one another, he reminds them that the greatest expression of love is to give one's life for one's friends (John 15:12–13). The implication is that genuine love may have its risks and even demand the ultimate sacrifice.

Theological idea: *People may experience tragedy and feel rejected by God, but followers of Christ should reach out to them in sacrificial love, even though such love may seem risky and unappreciated.*

Homiletical Trajectories

(1) One trajectory will focus on Naomi's experience and her faulty perception of the Lord. In this chapter we see that personal tragedy and pain can overwhelm those who live in the fallen world. Yet in the midst of such suffering, we should not necessarily attribute our pain directly to God or cast him in the role of an enemy. If we look carefully we can detect his gracious hand, bringing relief from famine, as it were. We can take comfort in the fact that God is the ally of his people, not their enemy. Though he may not insulate us from the tragic realities of the fallen world, he cares for the needy and is predisposed to intervene on their behalf.

(2) A second trajectory will focus on Ruth and her example of self-sacrificial love. When we encounter people who feel as if they are targets of God's anger, we should reach out to them in sacrificial love, as Ruth did

to Naomi. Such love demands great moral courage and commitment, for it can be risky and unappreciated.

(3) The book's third theme (see introduction)—that God rewards those who love sacrificially—is only hinted at in chapter one, when Naomi pronounces a blessing upon Ruth (1:8–9). However, Ruth's self-imprecation appears to trump the blessing (1:17) and creates tension in the plot. Given the seemingly risky task Ruth has taken up, one wonders if her loyalty will really pay off, especially when Naomi disregards her allegiance.

Preaching idea: *When people experience tragedy and feel rejected by God, we must reach out to them in Christlike sacrificial love, even though such love may seem risky and unappreciated.*

RUTH 2:1–23

Events Take a Turn for the Better

TRANSLATION AND NARRATIVE STRUCTURE

1a **Now Naomi had a relative on her husband's side, a wealthy, prominent man from the clan of Elimelech.** (*introductory-backgrounding*)

1b **His name was Boaz.** (*introductory-backgrounding*)[1]

2a Ruth, the Moabite woman, said to Naomi, (*initiatory*)[2]

2b *"Let me go[3] to the field so I can gather[4] grain behind someone who permits me to do so."*

2c She replied, (*sequential*)

2d *"You may go, my daughter."*

3a So she went, (*consequential*)

---

1. The disjunctive clauses in verse 1 introduce a new character who plays an important role in the story to follow and provide background information for the narrative.
2. This clause initiates the action in this second act.
3. The cohortative expresses Ruth's request. Note Naomi's response later in verse 2 ("you may go"). See Bush 1996a, 102.
4. Following the preceding cohortative, this cohortative with *waw*-conjunctive indicates purpose/result.

3b arrived at a field,[5] (*sequential*)

3c and gathered grain in the field behind the harvesters. (*sequential*)

3d She just happened to come to the portion of the field belonging to Boaz, who was from the clan of Elimelech. (*focusing-specifying*)[6]

4a Now Boaz arrived from Bethlehem, (*dramatic*)[7]

4b and said to the harvesters, (*sequential*)

4c *"May the LORD be with you!"*

4d They replied, (*sequential*)

4e *"May the LORD bless you!"*

5a Boaz said to his servant, the one in charge of the harvesters, (*sequential*)

5b *"To whom does this young woman belong?"*[8]

6a The servant in charge of the harvesters replied, (*sequential*)

6b *"She's a Moabite woman, the one who returned with Naomi from the region of Moab.*

7 *She asked, 'May I go behind the harvesters and gather*[9] *grain in bundles?'*[10] *She has stayed here since she arrived. From this morning until right now, she has taken only a brief rest."*[11]

---

5. The words "at a field" are not in the Hebrew text; they are added for the sake of English style.

6. Rather than furthering the action, this clause specifies where she gathered grain (cf. v. 3c) and begins a more focused and detailed account of what happened when she arrived there.

7. This disjunctive clause, introduced by וְהִנֵּה, "and look," has a dramatic function; it invites the reader to enter into the world of the story and observe Boaz's arrival firsthand.

8. The question reflects the patriarchal social structure of ancient Israel, in which women and children were viewed as being under the authority of a male. See Bush 1996a, 112–13.

9. On the use of the perfect with *waw*-consecutive after the cohortative, see *IBHS*, 530.

10. Another option is to translate, "May I glean and gather (grain) among the bundles?" But see Bush 1996a, 114, 117, and Block 1999, 656.

11. The Hebrew text reads literally, "and she came and she stood, from then, the morning, and until now, this, her sitting (in) the house a little." Bush takes עמד, "to stand," in the sense "to stay, remain," connects זֶה, "this," with the preceding עַתָּה, "now," as an emphasizing adverb of time ("just now," see BDB, 261), and emends שִׁבְתָּהּ הַבַּיִת, "her sitting (in) the house," to שָׁבְתָה, "she rested" (omitting הַבַּיִת, "the house," as virtually dittographic) 1996a, 118–19). He translates (107): "So she came and remained here. From morning until just now she has stopped only a moment." Another option is to translate: "She came and has stood here from this morning

8a   Boaz said to Ruth, (*sequential*)

8b   *"Listen carefully,*[12] *my daughter. Do not leave to gather grain in another field. You need not*[13] *go beyond the limits of this field. You may go along close to*[14] *my female workers.*

9   *Take note of the field where the men*[15] *are harvesting and follow along after the female workers.*[16] *I will tell the servants*[17] *to leave you alone.*[18] *When you get thirsty, you may go to*[19] *the water jars and drink some of the water the servants draw."*[20]

10a She knelt before him, (*sequential*)

10b bowed low to the ground, (*sequential*)

10c and said to him, (*sequential*)

---

until now. She's been sitting in the house for a short time." In this view the servant has made Ruth wait to get permission from Boaz. It is difficult to envision, however, a "house" being in the barley field. For summaries of various interpretations of verse 7b, see Campbell 1975, 94–96, and more recently Moore 1997, 239–40.

12. The Hebrew text reads literally, "Have you not heard?" The idiomatic, negated rhetorical question is equivalent to an affirmation. See Bush 1996a, 119; and GKC, 474, para. 150e.

13. The switch from the negative particle אַל (see the preceding statement, "do not leave") to לֹא may make this statement more emphatic. Perhaps it indicates that the statement is a policy applicable for the rest of the harvest (see v. 21).

14. The imperfect here has a permissive force.

15. The Hebrew verb is masculine plural, indicating that the male workers are in view.

16. The Hebrew text reads, "and go after them." The pronominal suffix is feminine plural, indicating that the female workers are in view.

17. Male servants are in view, as the masculine plural form of the noun indicates.

18. The Hebrew text reads literally, "Have I not commanded the servants not to touch (i.e., "harm") you?" The negated rhetorical question is equivalent to an affirmation (see v. 8). The perfect indicates a speech-act (see Bush 1996a, 107, 121–22, who translates, "I am herewith ordering") and/or is emphatic/rhetorical, indicating the action is as good as done. Holmstedt (2010, 123) labels this a performative use.

19. The juxtaposition of two perfects, each with *waw* consecutive, here indicates a conditional sentence (see GKC, 337, para. 112kk).

20. The imperfect probably indicates characteristic or typical activity, or is anterior future, referring to a future action (drawing water) which logically precedes another future action (drinking).

10d *"Why are you so kind to me and so attentive, even though I am a foreigner?"*[21]

11a Boaz replied to her, *(sequential)*

11b *"I have been given a full report of*[22] *all that you have done for your mother-in-law following the death of your husband—how you left*[23] *your father, your mother and your homeland and came to live among people you did not know before.*

12 *May the LORD reward your efforts! May your wages be paid in full*[24] *by the LORD God of Israel, under whose wings you have come to find shelter!"*

13a She said, *(sequential)*

13b *"You really are being kind to me,*[25] *my master, for you have*

---

21. The Hebrew text reads literally, "Why do I find favor in your eyes by recognizing me, though I am a foreigner?" The infinitive construct with prefixed -לְ indicates manner. The final, subject-fronted clause (note the pattern *waw* + subject + predicate nominative) has a circumstantial-concessive function. On the grammatical point (our passage not cited), see Williams 1976, 83, para. 494; 88, para. 528.

22. The Hebrew text reads literally, "it has been fully reported to me." The infinitive absolute emphasizes the following finite verb, referring to either the clarity or completeness of the report. See Hubbard 1988b, 153, note 6.

23. The *waw*-consecutive within the quotation has a specifying function. This and the following clause explain specifically what she did for her mother-in-law.

24. The verbal form וּתְהִי, literally, "and let it be," is a distinct jussive form, indicating this is a prayer for blessing. This strongly suggests that the preceding verb יְשַׁלֵּם, literally, "let him reward," be understood as a jussive as well.

25. The Hebrew text reads literally, "I am finding favor in your eyes." In verse 10, where Ruth uses the perfect, she simply states the fact that he is kind. Here she switches to the imperfect and emphasizes the ongoing attitude of kindness displayed by Boaz. It is possible to take the form as a cohortative (Hubbard 1988b, 168), since III-*aleph* verbs only rarely have the distinctive cohortative ending. See Joüon-Muraoka, 202, para. 78h; 374. However, a cohortative sense does not fit well with the following causal clauses. See Bush 1996a, 124. Holmstedt's conclusion that a present progressive nuance does not make good sense in this context is inexplicable (2010, 130).

reassured me and encouraged your servant, though I could never be[26] *equal to one of your servants.*"[27]

14a At mealtime Boaz said to her, (*sequential*)

14b *"Come here and have some food! Dip your bread in the vinegar!"*

14c So she sat down beside the harvesters. (*consequential*)

14d Then he handed[28] her some roasted grain. (*sequential*)

14e She ate her fill (*sequential*)[29]

14f and saved the rest. (*sequential*)

15a When she got up to gather grain, (*sequential*)

15b Boaz commanded his servants, (*sequential*)

15c *"Let her gather grain among the bundles! Don't chase her off!*

16 *Make sure you pull out*[30] *ears of grain for her and drop them so she can gather them up. Don't yell at her!"*

17a She gathered grain in the field until evening. (*sequential*)

17b When she beat out what she had gathered, (*sequential*)

17c there were about thirty pounds[31] of barley! (*consequential*)

18a She carried it back to town, (*sequential*)

18b and her mother-in-law saw[32] how much grain she had gathered. (*sequential*)

---

26. The imperfect verbal form of היה, "to be," is used here. Bush argues that usage elsewhere indicates the form should be taken as future (1996a, 124–25).

27. The subject-fronted clause (note the pattern *waw* + subject + verb) is circumstantial-concessive here.

28. The verb צבט, "hand over," occurs only here in the Old Testament. For discussion of its meaning, see BDB, 840; Hubbard 1988b, 174; and Bush 1996a, 125–26.

29. There are actually two *wayyiqtol* verb forms in the Hebrew text, which reads literally, "and she ate and she was full." For English stylistic reasons we have combined these verbs in our translation.

30. The infinitive absolute precedes the finite verb for emphasis.

31. The Hebrew text reads literally, "an ephah."

32. The Hebrew text has the *qal* form of the verb with "her mother-in-law" as subject. A few medieval Hebrew manuscripts (supported by the Syriac and Latin Vulgate) read the *hiphil* form of the verb, "and she showed her mother-in-law what she had gathered." This reading has the advantage of making Ruth the subject of all the verbs in the verse, but one expects the accusative sign to appear before "her mother-in-law" if it were the object of the *hiphil* verb. (Note Deut. 3:24, where the accusative sign appears before the accusatives after a *hiphil* form of ראה, "to show [accusative sign] your servant [accusative sign] your greatness and [accusative sign] your mighty hand.")

18c Then she gave her the roasted grain she had saved from mealtime. (*sequential*)

19a Her mother-in-law asked her, (*sequential*)

19b *"Where did you gather grain today? Where did you work? May the one who took notice of you be rewarded!"*

19c Then she told her mother-in-law with whom she had worked. (*consequential*)

19d She said, (*specifying*)

19e *"The name of the man with whom I worked today is Boaz."*

20a Naomi said to her daughter-in-law, (*sequential*)

20b *"May he be rewarded by the* LORD *because he has not abandoned his loyalty to the living*[33] *or to the dead!"*

20c Then Naomi said to her, (*sequential*)

20d *"This man is a close relative of ours; he is one of our benefactors."*[34]

21a Ruth, the Moabite woman, replied, (*sequential*)

21b *"He even*[35] *told me, 'You may go along beside my male servants*[36] *until they have finished gathering all my harvest.'"*

22a Naomi then said to Ruth, her daughter-in-law, (*sequential*)

22b *"It is good, my daughter, that you should go out to work with his female servants. That way you will not be harmed,*[37] *which could happen in another field."*

23a So she worked beside Boaz's female servants, gathering grain until the end of the barley and wheat harvests. (*summarizing*)

---

33. The translation understands חַסְדּוֹ, "his loyalty," as the object of the preceding verb and takes אֵת as the preposition "with." For other examples of the collocation חֶסֶד + אֵת, "loyalty with," see Genesis 24:49; 2 Samuel 16:17; Zechariah 7:9.

34. The term גֹּאֵל is traditionally understood to mean "redeemer" or "kinsman-redeemer." Since the term is not used in a technical, soteriological sense (as in "Christ our Redeemer") in the Old Testament, we prefer "benefactor" to avoid a misleading notion. For fuller discussion, see the commentary below on 2:20.

35. On the force of the phrase גַּם כִּי, literally, "also even," here, see Bush 1996a, 138–39.

36. The imperfect has a permissive nuance here. The word "servants" in this case is masculine plural.

37. The idiom used here (פָּגַע בְּ-) refers to a hostile encounter. See Shepherd 2001, 452–53.

23b After that she stayed home with her mother-in-law.[38]
      (*concluding*)

OUTLINE:
Prologue to Act Two: Seeking Food (2:1–3c)
    Introducing a new player in the drama (2:1)
    Ruth goes gleaning (2:2–3c)

Act Two, Scene One: A "Chance" Encounter in the Barley Field
(2:3d–17)
    Boaz arrives (2:3d–7)
    Kindness and gratitude (2:8–13)
    More kindness (2:14)
    Still more kindness (2:15–17)

Act Two, Scene Two: Going Home (2:18–22)

Epilogue to Act Two: Finishing Up the Harvest (2:23)

LITERARY STRUCTURE:
Chapter two consists of a prologue (vv. 1–3c), the story's second act in
two scenes (vv. 3d–22), and an epilogue (v. 23).[39] The first scene takes
place in the barley field (vv. 3d–17), the second in town (vv. 18–22).
The epilogue's reference to the harvest (v. 23) brings closure to the
second act and forms an inclusio with 1:22, which also mentions the

---

38. A few Hebrew manuscripts (as well as the Latin Vulgate) read וַתָּשָׁב אֶל,
      "and she returned [from שׁוּב] to (her mother-in-law)," as opposed to MT's
      וַתֵּשֶׁב אֶת, "and she lived [from יָשַׁב] with (her mother-in-law)." If one were
      to follow this alternative reading, the idea would be that she returned
      to her mother-in-law at the end of each workday. Surely she did not live
      away from home during the harvest period!
39. We treat 2:1–3c as a prologue, rather than a scene, because it includes
      background information (v. 1) and ends with a summary statement of
      what will transpire in the scenes to follow. Granted, there is a brief inter-
      change between Naomi and Ruth that could constitute a scene, but its pri-
      mary purpose is to set the stage for what follows, as indicated by the fact
      that it is quickly terminated by the summary statement. We treat verse
      23 as an epilogue because it describes tersely actions that occurred over
      a period of time and has the tone of a summary statement. As in 1:1–6, it
      would be difficult to stage the actions described in this verse.

harvest and, as noted earlier, has a transitional function in the book's structure.[40]

The prologue begins by introducing Boaz, a character who plays an important role in the act to follow and the story as a whole (v. 1). The action is initiated when Ruth asks Naomi if she may go out gleaning (v. 2a–b). Naomi grants her permission (v. 2c–d) and the narrator reports that she went and gleaned behind the harvesters (v. 3a–c).

The stage is set for the first scene, which takes place in the barley field. The scene is initiated with a specifying *wayyiqtol* clause (v. 3d) that flashes back to the beginning of Ruth's day in the field. The narrator informs us she just happened to go to the portion of the field belonging to the aforementioned Boaz, who, the text reminds us (cf. v. 1), was a relative of Elimelech. This specifying clause begins a more focused, detailed account of Ruth's experience. As in chapter one, a brief summary (v. 3a–c; cf. 1:6) is expanded upon (vv. 3d–17; cf. 1:7–22) (Campbell 1975, 92). Boaz becomes the focal point of this first movement in the scene (note וְהִנֵּה־בֹעַז, "and look, Boaz," in v. 4a) as he arrives at the field, greets his workers, and consults with his foreman (vv. 4–7).

The second movement in the scene consists of a dialogue between Boaz and Ruth (vv. 8–13). Again Boaz is the focal point as he initiates the conversation (v. 8a). The scene has four parts: (1) Boaz gives Ruth permission to join his workers (vv. 8–9), (2) Ruth expresses her surprise at his kindness (v. 10), (3) Boaz commends her for her loyalty to Naomi and pronounces a blessing upon her (vv. 11–12), and (4) Ruth expresses her gratitude (v. 13).

A reference to mealtime marks a shift to the scene's third movement in which Boaz extends further kindness to Ruth by inviting her to share their food (v. 14). Again Boaz is the focal point as he initiates the conversation.

The fourth and final movement in the scene occurs when Ruth returns to work and Boaz instructs his workers to make sure Ruth is able to glean a large amount of barley (vv. 15–16). Once more Boaz is the focal point as he initiates the conversation with the workers. The narrator informs us that Ruth gleaned until evening and then threshed what she had gathered (v. 17ab). A *wayyehi* (וַיְהִי) clause concludes the scene by telling us how much she gathered (v. 17c). The reference to Ruth gleaning in the field (וַתְּלַקֵּט בַּשָּׂדֶה) rounds off the scene nicely and forms a link with the summary statement that concludes the prologue (cf. v. 3c) (Wendland 1988, 34). Both the prologue and the first scene

---

40. See Gow 1984, 313.

begin with references to Boaz (cf. v. 1 with v. 3d) and conclude with references to Ruth gleaning.

A change in setting from the field to the town (v. 18) marks the shift to the second scene, which consists primarily of a dialogue between Ruth and Naomi. For the first time in the second act the narrator does not focus attention on Boaz at the very beginning of a literary unit or subunit (cf. 2:1, 3d–4, 8, 14, 15), but nevertheless he quickly becomes the main topic of conversation (v. 19) as Naomi pronounces a blessing upon him (v. 20).

EXPOSITION

Seeking Food (2:1–3c)

Before beginning the next act in the drama, the narrator introduces a new character, Boaz, who was a relative of Elimelech.[41] As is typical in Hebrew narrative, the introduction of a new character via a disjunctive clause is a signal the individual will play an important role in the story.

Boaz is characterized as a גִּבּוֹר חַיִל. This phrase frequently refers to a warrior ("mighty man of strength"), but this does not seem to be the point here. In Boaz's case the expression carries the nuance "prominent man of substance" (cf. 1 Sam. 9:1) (Sasson 1979, 39–40). In addition to referring to physical strength, the noun חַיִל can refer to wealth and property (*HALOT*, 311; BDB, 298–99).

The two widows needed food to survive, so Ruth, the younger and more able of the two, asked for permission to go to the field with the hope she might be allowed to glean there. The narrator refers to her as

---

41. The Hebrew text has a *Qere* reading in verse 2. The consonantal text (*Kethib*) is מידע, which should be vocalized as a *pual* participle. Understood substantivally, it refers to an "acquaintance" or "confidant" (*HALOT*, 392; BDB, 394), not necessarily a relative. The *Qere* substitutes a *waw* for the *yod* and reads מוֹדַע, a noun that apparently refers to a relative. The term appears elsewhere only in Proverbs 7:4, where it is defectively written and stands parallel to אֲחֹתִי, "my sister," in the poetic structure. This suggests that it refers to a close relative. The feminine form of the noun occurs in Ruth 3:2 (מֹדַעְתָּנוּ, "our close relative"). The textual variant appears to be due to *waw/yod* confusion. Even if we choose the *Kethib* reading here, it becomes obvious later in the verse that Boaz is a relative of Elimelech, for the narrator tells us Boaz was from the same "clan" (מִשְׁפָּחָה) as Elimelech. In ancient Israelite social structure, the מִשְׁפָּחָה, "clan," was the next level down from the "tribe" and the next level above the בֵּית אָב, "father's house" (cf. Josh. 7:16–18). See King and Stager 2001, 36–40; and McNutt 1999, 87–94.

"the Moabite woman" (cf. 1:22), perhaps to emphasize her vulnerability and to heighten the drama (Hubbard 1988b, 137; Nielsen 1997, 54).[42] The Law of Moses legislated that the poor, widows, and resident foreigners be permitted to glean the corners of fields and pick up what the harvesters failed to gather (Lev. 19:9–10; 23:22; Deut. 24:19). Ruth's request may reflect this, though she did not assume a right to glean. She hoped someone would treat her with favor.[43] When she arrived at the field, she did not claim any legal right, but instead asked for and received permission to glean (vv. 7–8).[44]

A "Chance" Encounter in the Barley Field (2:3d–17)

2:3d–7. After the summary statement in verse 3c, the story flashes back to Ruth's arrival at the field. According to the narrator, she "just happened" to come to Boaz's portion of the field. The expression translated "just happened" (וַיִּקֶר מִקְרֶהָ) occurs only here and in Ecclesiastes 2:14–15. It appears to refer to that which occurs without intent or design, perhaps comparable to our idea of chance or "luck."[45] Does this really

---

42. Ruth is also subsequently called "the Moabite woman" by both the narrator (2:2, 21) and the story's characters (2:6; 4:5, 10). However, by story's end, she is the one who enters Boaz's home (4:11), indicating "her final shift into full membership into the Bethlehem/Israelite community. She leaves behind previous social labels and officially joins the discourse community of Bethlehem." See Matthews 2006, 53, as well as our comments on 4:13 below.

43. For a discussion of the idiom "find favor in the eyes" see the commentary on 2:10.

44. LaCocque contends that Ruth, as a Moabite, was "outside the law" and consequently had to ask for permission to glean (2004, 62–63). However, having returned with Naomi, she would have come under the stipulation relating to resident foreigners (cf. Lev. 19:10; 23:22; Deut. 24:19). See H. Matthews 2004, 225; Siquans 2009, 450. Ruth's refusal to press her legal right is better explained as being due to ignorance or to a protocol of politeness. On the latter, see Hubbard 1988b, 139. Another option is that Israel was simply not observing the letter of the Law at this point in its history. In this regard see Bush 1996a, 104. Lim takes a different approach to the problem, focusing on the nature of Ruth's request, rather than her status. He argues that Ruth asked to do more than the Law allowed: "She asks special permission to glean . . . *and* gather among the sheaves . . . behind the harvesters (v. 7). She has to do so, because she was asking more than what she was entitled by law; she wanted to gather among the sheaves and not just pick up the grains that had fallen on the ground" (2007, 276).

45. Bush argues that the idea of chance or luck "is foreign to OT thought" (1996a, 104), but 1 Samuel 6:9 suggests that the Philistines had room in

reflect the narrator's perspective? In the previous chapter Naomi prayed that the Lord would reward faithful Ruth by providing her with another husband (1:8–9). As the book unfolds, we see the Lord answer this prayer through a set of providential twists and turns. In fact, throughout the book the narrator develops a theology of divine providence in which the Lord answers the prayers of worthy characters. Therefore, it is unlikely the narrator viewed Ruth's arrival in Boaz's field as a chance occurrence. The narrator here uses a clever rhetorical device. Rather than writing from his own omniscient perspective, he briefly assumes the limited perspective of Ruth. As I have written elsewhere: "One can imagine the narrator winking at the reader as he wrote this. Rather than promoting a theology of chance, the narrator was highlighting God's sovereign control of human affairs. And by reflecting Ruth's perspective he showed this encounter with Boaz was not something Ruth or Naomi engineered. From Ruth's perspective she randomly picked a field, but God was steering her to the right one."[46]

When Boaz arrived at the field, he spotted Ruth and asked about her identity. The foreman explained that she was the young Moabite woman who had accompanied Naomi back from Moab. He also informed Boaz of Ruth's request to glean behind the reapers. Our translation (see above) assumes the foreman had given Ruth permission to glean and that she was taking a brief break from her work at the time Boaz arrived. However, the textual difficulties presented by the second half of verse 7 make it impossible to know if this is a correct understanding of what transpired. Others understand verse 7 as indicating

---

their world view for such a concept. Perhaps the same was true in Israel. See Linafelt 1999, 28.

46. Chisholm 2002, 409. See as well Block 1999, 653–54, Hubbard 1988b, 141, and Hals 1969, 11–12. The narrator uses this technique again in 3:8 (see the commentary below). For a hermeneutical analysis of the technique employed here, see Chisholm 2002, 404–14. For a rather strong objection to this line of interpretation, see Linafelt 1999, 28. Linafelt is correct in objecting to the determinism that may underlie some theological readings of the story and in pointing out that God's direct involvement in the story is limited to two passages (1:6 and 4:13 [he incorrectly gives the reference as 4:3]). However, he fails to discuss the pattern of prayer-fulfillment and thus neglects the dimension of providential involvement in the story. He is concerned that the book's theme of human responsibility not be swallowed up by divine sovereignty (see as well pp. xvi–xvii). This is a legitimate concern, but prayer brings both together in a delicate balance. Prayer is the catalyst for divine involvement, an invitation to God to act in human experience and to bring to pass what only he can accomplish.

the foreman did not grant Ruth permission to work in the field, but instead made her wait until Boaz's arrival.[47]

2:8–13. In granting Ruth permission to glean, Boaz emphasized she should stay in his field (note the repetition in v. 8b) and then instructed her to stick close to his female workers. She was to watch the reapers' movements and then follow closely behind the female workers as they gathered the grain. The phrase עִם דָּבַק, "go along close to" (literally, "stay close with"), is unique to Ruth 2 (cf. v. 21; the usual expression is בְּ– דָּבַק [cf. 1:14; 2:23]), but it undoubtedly expresses close proximity.

Apparently, the procedure for harvesting grain was as follows: (1) The reapers (קוֹצְרִים) cut down the stalks of grain with their sickles and left them lying on the ground. (2) Another group of workers gathered the stalks into bundles, which were then bound into sheaves (Borowski 1987, 59–61). It would appear that in Boaz's work force the female workers (נְעָרֹת) did this bundling and binding, at least in part. By allowing Ruth to stay close to them, Boaz was giving her an opportunity to gather more grain than the typical gleaner who came to the field.

Boaz also informed Ruth he would order his male workers (נְעָרִים) not to interfere with her. In this context the verb נגע, "touch," probably has the connotation "remove" (from the field). Perhaps the workers typically "roughed up" anyone who tried to mix in with the bundlers without being granted permission to do so.[48] Apparently, Boaz's male workers served as a security force, making sure only authorized personnel were in the field (cf. also vv. 15–16), and as a support staff, making sure water was available for the harvesters.

---

47. See, for example, Sasson 1979, 48; Hubbard 1988b, 152; Campbell 1975, 96. For a concise summary of the interpretive options, see Sakenfeld 1999c, 42. The latter half of verse 7 has generated a great deal of discussion. See the articles by Beattie 1977a, Carasik 1995, Hurvitz 1983, Loader 1992, Min 1989, and Moore 1997, listed in the bibliography. Hurvitz argues that the overseer's "apologetic and confused" speech was intentional because he was unsure if Boaz would approve of his decision to allow Ruth to sit in the house reserved for the workers (122; see as well Rendsburg 1998–99, 3–4, section 2).

48. See Hubbard 1988b, 159. Nielsen's suggestion that a "sexual attack" is in view seems far-fetched in this context 1997, 58, note 90; see also Block 1999, 659–60. It is highly unlikely that Boaz's workers were so prone to attack women that he had to prohibit such an action! While the verb נגע can refer to sexual contact (Gen. 20:6; Prov. 6:29), such a notion must be clearly indicated from the context. Furthermore, in neither of these texts is rape or sexual assault in view.

As a further act of kindness, Boaz gave Ruth permission to drink from the water supply that had been drawn for the workers (v. 9). In other words, she had the same status and privileges as one of his workers.

In light of Boaz's kindness, Ruth's response comes as no surprise. She fell before him and asked him why he was being so kind to her (v. 10). After all, as a foreigner she had not expected such kind treatment. "To find favor in the eyes of" (cf. מָצָאתִי חֵן בְּעֵינֶיךָ) means "to be the recipient or object of one's kindness." The kindness extended is offered freely and without obligation (Ruth 2:2; cf. Gen. 19:19; 47:25), but it can be prompted by the recipient's character or actions (Gen. 6:8 [cf. v. 9]; 39:4 [cf. v. 3]; 1 Sam. 16:22 [cf. v. 21]). This was certainly true in Ruth's case, as Boaz explained. He had a full report of Ruth's devotion to Naomi. She had left the security of her native land and taken a significant risk in moving to a new land. When she crossed the border into Israel, she placed herself under the protective care of Israel's God (cf. Ruth 1:17), whom Boaz compared to a mother bird (cf. Ps. 91:4). Boaz pronounced a blessing upon her, asking the Lord to repay her for her kindness to Naomi.[49]

In his prayer (v. 12) Boaz used the idiom of a monetary transaction. The *piel* of שׁלם, "be complete, whole," can refer to making compensation (e.g., Exod. 21:36) or paying back a debt (2 Kings 4:7). When used metaphorically it can be used of both judgment (cf. Jer. 25:14; 50:29, the only other texts where the verb is collocated with פֹּעַל, "work") and reward (1 Sam. 24:19) because in either case one receives just compensation for one's deeds. Boaz's prayer depicts Ruth as one who has worked (cf. פֹּעַל) and deserves to be compensated (cf. מַשְׂכֻּרְתֵּךְ, "your wage") in full for her effort. Ironically, through Boaz's kindness the Lord had already begun to answer his prayer.

Ruth affirmed Boaz's continuing kindness to her, expressed through

---

49. It is perhaps noteworthy that the narrator refers to Ruth simply by name in verse 8, whereas he included a reference to her ethnicity in 1:22 and 2:2. Glover is convinced that this stylistic technique, which is utilized again in 2:22 and 4:13, is rhetorically significant. He proposes "that Ruth's name is used without the Moabite tag whenever her re-situation within Israel has been recognized." He adds: "The first of these moments occurs with Boaz (2.8): the man who recognizes that she has left her father, mother, birthplace, and is now re-situated under the wings of Yhwh" (2009, 302). Of course, the name Ruth is used without an accompanying description of ethnicity in 1:14, 16, but Glover is focusing on references to her once she arrives in Bethlehem (p. 301).

his encouraging words (v. 13). The *piel* of נחם has the nuance "to console, comfort." It is often used of consoling one who is suffering or has experienced a painful loss (cf. Gen. 37:35; 2 Sam. 10:2; 12:24). Ruth had lost her husband, but Boaz's words focus on her sacrificial love for Naomi, not her loss. Consequently, it is more likely in this context that the verb has the nuance "encourage, reassure" (someone who is in a vulnerable position) (cf. Gen. 50:21; Ps. 23:4). The parallel clause (note וְכִי דִבַּרְתָּ עַל־לֵב שִׁפְחָתֶךָ, literally, "and because you have spoken to the heart of your servant") suggests this as well. The idiom "speak to the heart" can have a romantic connotation (Gen. 34:3; Hos. 2:14 [Hebrew v. 16]), but that seems premature at this point in the story. In this context the expression carries the meaning, "encourage, reassure" (cf. Gen. 50:21; 2 Sam. 19:7; 2 Chron. 30:22; Isa. 40:2) (Bush 1996a, 124).

Because Boaz had essentially given her the status of a servant by permitting her to work alongside his female workers, Ruth inadvertently referred to herself as his שִׁפְחָה, "female servant." Perhaps realizing this might sound presumptuous, she quickly acknowledged she could never really occupy such a position. This sets the reader up for the irony that will follow. In 3:9 Ruth approaches Boaz and confidently refers to herself as אֲמָתֶךָ, "your female servant," using a term (אָמָה) that is a synonym of the word used here (שִׁפְחָה). Unlike שִׁפְחָה, which casts her merely in the role of a female worker, אָמָה highlights her gender and therefore the fact that she is marriageable. (For further discussion of this point and its relevance to the story, see the commentary on 3:9.)

2:14–17. Later in the day, when mealtime arrived, Boaz again demonstrated kindness to Ruth by inviting her to share a meal with him and his reapers. Lunch consisted of bread dipped in vinegar and parched grain.[50] When Ruth finished her meal, Boaz extended even further kindness to her. He told his workers to let her gather grain among the bundles, which was more advantageous than walking closely behind the workers (cf. vv. 8–9) because it allowed her to gather up grain before it was bundled and bound into sheaves. In fact, he even ordered his male workers to remove some of the grain from the bundles for

---

50. The term חֹמֶץ, "vinegar," refers to acetic acid, a product of the fermentation process (Num. 6:3). During fermentation, when the carbon dioxide is allowed to escape, if the grape juice is exposed to the air for too long and not stirred adequately, vinegar will be the result. See Walsh 2000, 189. Apparently vinegar was not discarded, but used as a condiment.

Ruth to pick up.[51] Boaz also emphasized that the workers should not humiliate her or speak harshly to her, as they probably typically did to any unauthorized intruders (cf. v. 9).

Boaz's generosity paid off, for Ruth had an entire ephah of barley to show for her labor after she threshed what she had gathered.[52] An ephah was apparently equivalent to a "bath," a liquid measure (Ezek. 45:11, 14). Jars labeled "bath" found at archeological sites in Israel could contain approximately 5.8 U.S. gallons, or one-half to two-thirds of a bushel. Thus an ephah of barley would have weighed about twenty-nine to thirty pounds.[53] Younger concludes that an ephah was one-tenth of a homer (cf. Exod. 16:36; Ezek. 45:11). Using evidence from Mesopotamia, he estimates that the homer (or "assload") was 150 liters of barley. An ephah, then would have been 10–20 liters (a bushel is approximately 35 liters) (Younger 1998, 123–24). This was enough grain to provide for Naomi and Ruth for a considerable period of time.[54] Younger states that "the ancient norm for a daily food ration seems to have been widely regarded as ≈ 1 liter, usually of barley." Thus, Ruth gleaned enough barley to last the women "for a little more than a week." He adds: "If Ruth averaged roughly the same total each day (i.e., one *ephah*), and worked the entire two months [the time between the beginning of the barley harvest and the end of the wheat harvest], she would have gleaned a considerable amount of barley and wheat that would have fed the two women, at the minimum pre-exilic rate, approximately two-thirds of a year, or at the maximum pre-exilic rate, more than an entire year." As Younger observes, the ancient hearers of the story "would have perceived the import of this gleaning detail [in Ruth 2:17] as heightening the generosity of Boaz towards the two widows on a scale greater than modern readers of the story have even begun to perceive" (Younger 1998, 125; and 2002, 448).

---

51. Porten sees in Boaz's instructions the beginnings of the fulfillment of his prayer for Ruth. Pointing out the repetition of the verb עזב, "leave," in verses 11 and 16, he states: "Boaz is beginning to fulfill his own prayer for payment to Ruth. Because she took the extraordinary step of 'leaving' her home (2:11) he is 'leaving' her extra gleanings" (1978, 36).
52. On the threshing technique used by Ruth, see Borowski 1987, 63.
53. Hubbard 1988b, 179. Using another basis for calculation, some conclude that an ephah would have been equivalent to 45–50 pounds. For a discussion of the options, see Campbell 1975, 104, and Russell Fuller, "אֵיפָה," in *NIDOTTE*, 1:384–85.
54. See 1 Samuel 17:17, where Jesse sends an ephah of roasted grain and ten loaves of bread to his sons to supply their needs during a military campaign. See Sasson 1979, 57.

Going Home (2:18–22)

When Naomi saw all that Ruth had gathered, as well as the leftovers from her meal, she realized someone must have shown Ruth favor. She asked Ruth the name of her benefactor, but before Ruth had a chance to answer, Naomi pronounced a blessing upon him. A blessing was a formal prayer in which a petitioner appealed to the Lord as the righteous judge to reward another for kind deeds rendered. (Conversely, a "curse" was a formal prayer in which a petitioner appealed to the divine judge to punish another for unjust actions.) Ruth identified her benefactor as Boaz, prompting Naomi to repeat her blessing, but with more specificity. This time she identified the Lord as the agent of blessing and included the reason why Boaz was worthy of a reward. She went on to explain that Boaz was a near relative and one of the family's potential benefactors. In that capacity he had taken his family commitments seriously and demonstrated kindness to the living (Ruth and Naomi) by providing them with food, and to the dead (their deceased husbands) by caring for the vulnerable widows they had left behind. This portrait of Boaz as one who demonstrated חֶסֶד, "loyalty, devotion," makes him a suitable match for Ruth, who exhibited this quality as well (cf. 1:8; 3:10). The narrator is laying the ground for what will transpire in the following chapters.

The syntax of Naomi's blessing in Ruth 2:20 requires analysis. Literally, she prayed: "May he be blessed by the Lord,[55] who has not

---

55. When collocated with the passive participle of בָּרַךְ, "bless," the phrase לַיהוָה, "for/to Yahweh," appears to indicate the agent of blessing. See Judges 17:2; 1 Samuel 15:13; 23:21; 2 Samuel 2:5; Psalms 115:15; Ruth 3:10. Basing their analysis on Pardee's study of blessing formulas in Ugaritic, Waltke and O'Connor (*IBHS*, 207) translate the formula in Ruth 2:20, "May he be pronounced blessed to Yhwh." According to Bush, if this view is correct, then it is "virtually certain that the following אֲשֶׁר clause gives the grounds for which the person is commended to Yahweh for blessing rather than being a relative clause modifying Yahweh" (1996a, 136). Yet Bush questions the validity of this analysis for biblical Hebrew because the corresponding "active construction" (בָּרַךְ + personal name + לְ + divine name, "commend PN for blessing to DN"), which is attested in cognate languages and extra-biblical Hebrew, does not occur in the Old Testament. For examples from cognate literature, see *DNWSI*, 1:201. The latter source understands the active construction in the sense of "mention in blessing formulae in (the name of) DN," and the passive construction (cf. Ruth 2:20) in the sense of "blessed in the name of," that is, "blessed by."

abandoned[56] his kindness to the living and dead." The referent of the relative pronoun אֲשֶׁר, "who," is not readily apparent in an English translation. Is it Boaz or the Lord? One might think the Lord is the antecedent since the pronoun immediately follows his name. However, analysis of the collocation used by Naomi reveals the antecedent is Boaz, not the Lord.[57] Elsewhere when אֲשֶׁר, "who," follows the blessing formula "blessed" (*qal* passive participle) + proper name/pronoun, it always introduces the reason the recipient of the blessing deserves a reward.[58] If the pronoun refers to the Lord here, then this verse, contrary to usage elsewhere, does not give a reason for the recipient being blessed. 2 Samuel 2:5 provides the closest syntactical parallel to Ruth 2:20 and validates our conclusion. It reads literally: "May you (plural) be blessed by the Lord (לַיהוָה), you who (אֲשֶׁר) have extended (plural) such kindness to your master Saul." The relative pronoun אֲשֶׁר refers back to the plural independent pronoun אַתֶּם, "you," as the second plural verb עֲשִׂיתֶם, "you have done," after אֲשֶׁר, "who," indicates. By caring for the impoverished widows' physical needs, Boaz had demonstrated loyalty

---

56. Though Naomi does not yet know the name of Ruth's benefactor, there may be a subtle play on the name Boaz here (cf. Porten 1978, 36). Boaz (בֹּעַז) had not abandoned (עָזַב) his kindness.

57. See Rebera 1985, 317–27; Bush 1996a, 134–36; and Hubbard 1988b, 186. In light of the compelling linguistic evidence presented by Rebera and others, Cohen's view that the syntax is intentionally ambiguous cannot be sustained (1997, 32–33). See as well Holmstedt 2010, 141–42; Younger 2002, 396; Linafelt 1999, 41–42; Sakenfeld 1999c, 47; and Collins 1993, 100. Collins has "no doubt that Naomi herself meant either the Lord or Boaz as the referent," but he concludes, "in the haste of ordinary conversation (as opposed to the careful language of literary craft), she framed the clause ambiguously. The narrator found this useful in conveying his message." On the contrary, the ambiguity exists only for the modern reader. Naomi, though clearly excited, formulated her blessing according to the pattern we see elsewhere.

58. Genesis 14:20; 24:27; Exodus 18:10; Ruth 4:14; 1 Samuel 25:32–33, 39; 2 Samuel 2:5; 18:28; 1 Kings 1:48; 5:7 (Hebrew v. 21); 8:15, 56; 2 Chronicles 2:12 (Hebrew v. 11); 6:4; Ezra 7:27; Psalms 66:20; Jeremiah 17:7. The structure in 2 Chronicles 2:12 is unique in that two relative clauses follow the subject of the blessing (Yahweh). The first (literally, "who made the heavens and the earth") is purely descriptive, while the second (literally, "who has given to David the king a wise son...") gives the basis for the blessing and fits the pattern seen elsewhere. In Jeremiah 17:7 a causal translation of אֲשֶׁר is awkward in English, but the relative clause does give the basis for the blessing.

to both the living (the impoverished widows) and the dead (their late husbands).

Contrary to the demands of the syntax, several commentators have understood the Lord as the antecedent of אֲשֶׁר, "who," in Ruth 2:20.[59] They present two primary arguments for this view: (1) an alleged parallel in Genesis 24:27, where the antecedent of אֲשֶׁר is the Lord and the relative pronoun is then followed by לֹא־עָזַב חַסְדּוֹ, "(who) has not abandoned his faithful love," as in Ruth 2:20, and (2) the appearance of the masculine form of the adjective הַחַיִּים, "the living," which supposedly refers in a general way to the recipients of divine favor, rather than being a specific reference to Naomi and Ruth. However, both of these arguments can be countered:

(1) The alleged parallel in Genesis 24:27 is not syntactically identical to Ruth 2:20, as the following demonstrates:

Genesis 24:27: בָּרוּךְ יְהוָה . . . אֲשֶׁר לֹא־עָזַב חַסְדּוֹ
"Blessed be Yahweh... who has (i.e., because he has) not forsaken his faithful love"

Ruth 2:20: בָּרוּךְ הוּא לַיהוָה אֲשֶׁר לֹא־עָזַב חַסְדּוֹ
"May he be blessed by (or "commended to") Yahweh because
he has not forsaken his faithful love."

The phrase לַיהוָה, "for/to Yahweh," indicating the agent of blessing, does not appear in Genesis 24:27. In the blessing formulae the corresponding subjects are Yahweh in Genesis 24:27 and הוּא, "he" (i.e., Boaz) in Ruth 2:20. In both cases אֲשֶׁר, "who," refers back to the subject and introduces the reason why the subject is deserving of blessing. The structure of Genesis 24:27 actually supports the view that Boaz is the antecedent of אֲשֶׁר in Ruth 2:20.

(2) At first glance it does seem odd that the substantival adjective הַחַיִּים, "the living," if referring to the widows, is masculine in form. However, the feminine plural form of the adjective (חַיּוֹת) is exceedingly rare (used only in Lev. 14:4, where it is attributive, not substantival) and the feminine plural noun חַיּוֹת is used exclusively of animals (BDB, 312; *HALOT*, 310). The masculine plural adjectival form is frequently used substantivally, usually as a genitival modifier of אֶרֶץ, "land of," or in collocation or juxtaposition with מֵתִים, "the dead" (Num. 17:13;

59. See Campbell 1975, 106; Block 1999, 672–74; Nielsen 1997, 63; Wilch 2006, 235, 240–41, as well as Sakenfeld 1978, 104–07, and Clark 1993, 200–01.

Isa. 8:19; Eccl. 4:2; 9:5). The masculine plural form appears to be used idiomatically for human beings, regardless of gender.[60]

In addition to these grammatical points, Sakenfeld argues that divine faithfulness must be in view here, for, she reasons, "it is scarcely obvious that allowing the girl to glean and to glean a few extra stalks of grain can be regarded as *ḥesed* to the dead husbands, or even to Ruth herself." She adds, "Boaz's actions thus far cannot readily be described as *ḥesed* in terms of the characteristics established . . . for the meaning of the term in secular usage. He has only the most generalized responsibility for Ruth as a poor person, . . . Furthermore, his action, even in arranging for the generous extra leavings, cannot really be described as supplying an essential need which Ruth could not have fulfilled otherwise. And there would be recourse—presumably legal action could be taken if he refused to permit her to glean (cf. Lev. 19:9–10)." She then proceeds to argue that God's actions, in contrast to those of Boaz, do fit the pattern and requirements of חֶסֶד, "loyalty, devotion" (1978, 106–07).

Bush correctly observes that Sakenfeld's argument "rather badly misjudges the significance of Boaz's actions." He points out that Boaz's

---

60. Block offers another syntactical argument in favor of his view that Yahweh is the antecedent of אֲשֶׁר (1999, 673). He contends that the appearance of הָאִישׁ, "the man," later in Ruth 2:20 "is difficult to explain" if Boaz is the antecedent of אֲשֶׁר. He reasons, "one would have expected the simple pronoun" here, "as at the end of the verse." He adds, "On the other hand, if Yahweh is the one who has faithfully demonstrated *ḥesed*, then the reference to 'the man' is necessary to distinguish the subject of the last two clauses of the verse from the subject of the preceding clause." However, the inclusion of הָאִישׁ is hardly necessary to "distinguish the subject of the last two clauses of the verse from the subject of the preceding clause," since it is unlikely in this context that Ruth would view Yahweh as the near relative or family guardian to whom Naomi refers. It is more likely that Naomi's use of הָאִישׁ simply mirrors Ruth's use of the phrase to refer to Boaz in her earlier answer to Naomi's question (v. 19). If so, one wonders why הָאִישׁ was not used in the blessing formula. But it is exceedingly rare for a noun with a definite article to follow בָּרוּךְ, "blessed," in a blessing formula (only in Jer. 17:7); it is far more common for a pronoun to appear as the subject, though apart from this passage the pronoun is invariably second person. (Num. 22:12 is not a true exception, for בָּרוּךְ הוּא, "he is blessed," is in an explanatory clause, not a blessing formula.) The appearance of the pronoun הוּא as the subject of בָּרוּךְ in a blessing formula is unique to this passage, but the use of the pronoun may be an adaptation of the typical pattern (with a second person pronoun) due to the fact that Boaz was not present.

actions can be viewed as demonstrating חֶסֶד, "loyalty, devotion," even if one follows Sakenfeld's definition. He explains: "(1) Naomi knows they spring from an existing relationship: Boaz is a relative . . . ; (2) it involves an urgent need on the part of the recipient: the two women are destitute and without means; (3) it is a free act on Boaz's part: he has responsibility as a relative, but no legal obligation; and (4) it involves 'going beyond the call of duty': from the moment he knew who Ruth was, he treated her in an extraordinarily generous manner" (1996a, 135).

In response to Sakenfeld, several other observations are in order: (1) Any husband worth his salt would be concerned about the needs of those left behind when he dies. (This is why so many men today buy life insurance!) Certainly Boaz's kindness to the widows can and should be viewed as kindness to their departed husbands, who, after all, were his family members.[61] (2) Boaz's actions, in addition to meeting the widows' immediate need for food, also assured them of his concern and intention to provide for them in the future. (3) If one downplays the significance of Boaz's actions as an expression of חֶסֶד, "loyalty, devo-tion," it becomes difficult to understand how God's leading the widows to Boaz can be viewed as an act of divine חֶסֶד! (4) If, for the sake of ar-gument, one insists on diminishing the significance of Boaz's kindness, perhaps it would be useful to consider the language function of Naomi's statement. Naomi's reaction may be exaggerated and her words more expressive of her emotions than technically correct in some legal sense. If so, perhaps she can be forgiven for such hyperbole in light of the fact she was probably close to starving and had no clear idea as to where her sustenance would come from in the days ahead!

It is noteworthy that more recently Sakenfeld has revised her as-sessment of Boaz's actions. She suggests that the syntax of verse 20 refers to "both God and Boaz as doers of acts of loyal kindness" (1999c, 47). She then shows how Boaz's actions fit her definition of חֶסֶד. She acknowledges that Boaz acted within the framework of the extended family and provided food "beyond the ordinary" (48). She observes: "To be sure, his action so far is limited, but already he has done more than was expected of him" (48). She then points out that Boaz is the

---

61. Perhaps the reader will indulge the author at this point as he shares a personal anecdote. When my wife's brother Mark passed away in 1995 at the age of 37, leaving behind a wife and five young daughters, ages 3–11, my wife and I, as well as other members of the family, decided to provide regular financial support for his widow and children. We did this due to their need, but also as an act of love and respect for Mark.

instrument whereby God extended his kindness to Naomi and Ruth and concludes, "Divine loyalty takes shape in the community and in individual lives through human actions" (48). We have argued against the viewpoint that the syntax of verse 20 is ambiguous and in favor of the view that Boaz is the sole grammatical referent. At the syntactical level of the text, Naomi refers specifically to Boaz's loyalty, not God's. However, Sakenfeld's point about Boaz's loyalty being an expression of God's loyalty is valid, when Boaz's actions are placed in the broader literary context. Boaz's kindness to Ruth may be viewed as an out-working and initial fulfillment of the prayers offered earlier by both Naomi (1:8) and Boaz himself (2:12). Through Boaz's kindness to Ruth, God's positive response to those prayers of blessing was beginning to materialize.

Naomi informed Ruth that Boaz was their "close relative" and a "benefactor" of their family. Naomi's use of the plural pronoun ("our") in both instances indicates this relationship applied to Ruth, as well as Naomi, undoubtedly because Ruth, though a foreigner, was the widow of Elimelech's son.

When used of human relationships, קָרוֹב, "close relative," covers a broad range of relationships, including those who are from the same tribe (2 Sam. 19:42 [Hebrew v. 43]), members of one's extended family (Lev. 25:25; Num. 27:11), and immediate family members (Lev. 21:2–3). In any given case, the immediate context must determine the precise nature of the relationship.

As described in legal literature, a גֹּאֵל, traditionally "kinsman-redeemer," was, broadly speaking, a guardian of the extended family's interests. He could recover property the family had sold (Lev. 25:25–34), including family members who had been sold as slaves to pay off a debt (Lev. 25:48–49). A family guardian could also avenge a murdered family member (Num. 35:19). Apart from the book of Ruth, there is no reference in the Old Testament to a גֹּאֵל producing offspring for a deceased family member by cohabiting with his widow.[62]

Perhaps the Israelite community expanded the role of the גֹּאֵל to include other responsibilities than those outlined in the legal literature, such as producing offspring for a deceased relative. Another option is that the verb גָּאַל, traditionally "redeem," is used in Ruth in a more general sense, rather than in a technical legal sense. Bush, who proposes this interpretation, defines the term, when used in this more general

---

62. For a summary of the Old Testament evidence pertaining to the responsibilities of a family guardian (גֹּאֵל), see Robert L. Hubbard, Jr., "גָּאַל," in *NIDOTTE*, 1:790–92; and Younger 2002, 400–01.

sense, as follows: "to deliver a member of one's kinship group (family, clan, tribe, or people) from evil of any kind" (1996a, 137). According to Bush, this more general sense applies when God is the subject of the verb and in Ruth 4:14, where Ruth's child is said to be Naomi's גֹּאֵל, in the sense that he would care for her when she was old and vulnerable (v. 15). Following Bush's lead, we translate Naomi's statement in 2:20, "he is one of our benefactors."

Apparently sensing Naomi's excitement, Ruth eagerly explained that Boaz had even given her permission to glean in his field for the rest of the harvest. Though Boaz did not say this in so many words, his statement in 2:8 implies as much. Furthermore, it is possible the text does not record everything Boaz said to Ruth (Wilch 2006, 245). In reporting Boaz's words, Ruth also said Boaz had instructed her to stay close to his male workers (הַנְּעָרִים, v. 21). Of course, Boaz had actually told her to stay close to his female workers (cf. נַעֲרֹתָי, v. 8) as they followed the harvesters. As if she had heard Boaz's actual words, Naomi remarked it was good that Ruth was allowed to work with Boaz's *female* workers (cf. נַעֲרוֹתָיו, v. 22). In light of the fact that she was concerned for Ruth's safety (see the next sentence), she may have been subtly warning Ruth not to get too close to the men (Block 1999, 677). If so, this is a heart-warming touch to the story that reflects the bond between the two women and their mutual concern. However, there may be more to Naomi's advice than meets the eye. Perhaps her subtle alteration of Ruth's words hints at what will transpire in chapter 3, where Naomi encourages Ruth to confront Boaz with the possibility of marriage, and Boaz remarks that Ruth has chosen him over one of the younger, apparently more likely candidates. We cannot be certain, but Naomi may have already decided to pursue Boaz as a husband for Ruth. If so, this would explain why she qualified Ruth's statement in this way.[63]

---

63. See Wilch 2006, 246, but note also the caution of Hubbard 1988b, 191–92. For Glover, the narrator's description of Ruth as "her daughter-in-law" in verse 22 (as opposed to "Ruth the Moabite" in v. 21) is significant, for it shows that Ruth has become a full-fledged member of the community. He writes: "Only when her mother-in-law recognizes that she has an invitation to join Boaz's harvesters can reference to Ruth's Moabite origins be abandoned. Naomi has at last responded to the pledge of 1.16–17. Since Ruth is now situated in the field of Boaz, she is now 'Ruth her daughter-in-law' (2.22)" (2009, 302). In other words, Naomi has now recognized what Boaz understood earlier (see our earlier remarks on 2:8 and our interaction with Glover).

Finishing Up the Harvest (2:23)

Ruth did indeed stay close to Boaz's *female* workers. When the barley harvest, which occurred from late March to late April, was finished, Ruth even continued working through the wheat harvest, which took place from late April through late May (Borowski 1987, 88, 91).

The meaning of the final statement in verse 23 is uncertain. The Hebrew text reads literally, "and she lived with her mother-in-law." This may mean she lived with her mother-in-law while working during the harvest. In other words, she worked by day and then came home to Naomi each evening, just as chapter two describes her doing at the end of her first day of gleaning. Others understand the statement to mean that, once the harvest ended, she stayed at home each day with Naomi and no longer went out looking for work (see, for example, Bush 1996a, 140). Either way, it is clear Ruth remained devoted to Naomi.

MESSAGE AND APPLICATION

Thematic Emphases

The author continues to focus on Ruth's devotion to Naomi. Ruth was a widow and a resident alien (though never specifically called either one) in a foreign land; there did not appear to be much she could do to help Naomi. Yet she took the initiative and went out to glean, hoping someone would show her compassion. Ruth arrived in Boaz's field and experienced his favor. From Boaz's perspective, he rewarded Ruth for her devotion to Naomi. He also appealed to the Lord to bless Ruth for her loyalty and kindness. When Naomi saw and heard what had happened, she prayed that the Lord would bless Boaz for his kindness to the widows and for his loyalty to his deceased family members. Naomi's response to Boaz's kindness hints at a changing perspective—she focused on God as provider and the one who blesses. Even in her distress she recognized God as the source of blessing (cf. 1:8–9), but this portrait of God was swallowed up by her sense that she was a target of divine judgment (cf. 1:13, 20–21). By the end of chapter two, her bitterness seemed to be receding as she began to view herself as a recipient of blessing, rather than a victim of divine disfavor.

Exegetical idea: *As Ruth sought to provide for Naomi's needs, the Lord providentially guided her footsteps to the field of Boaz, a potential benefactor of Elimelech's family. Impressed by her faithfulness, he rewarded her loyalty by providing her with an ample amount of food. This in turn began the transformation of Naomi's attitude from bitterness to hope.*

Theological Principles

The narrator portrays God as one who works providentially to deliver the afflicted, using human instrumentality to accomplish his purposes. Though the narrator uses a veiled style that reflects Ruth's limited perspective, the reader detects the providence of God when Ruth "just happens" to land in Boaz's field. As Ruth continued to display sacrificial love, the Lord began to reward her efforts, using Boaz's kindness as his instrument. Though Ruth's social position seemed to limit what she could do to help Naomi, God honored her loyalty to Naomi and providentially guided her steps in a direction that eventually led to great blessing.

Theological idea: *The Lord often accomplishes his redemptive work through faithful human instruments and providentially guides their footsteps when they decide to love sacrificially, no matter how meager their means appear to be.*

Homiletical Trajectories

(1) Operating through human instruments that mirror his own concern for the needy, God begins to work providentially to deliver Naomi from her despair and bitterness. When we recognize the hand of God at work in our experience, hope can begin to push despair aside.

(2) We see God helping the needy by using the loyal actions of those who love sacrificially and take family commitments seriously. As noted above, though human beings may be limited in what they can do, God honors loyalty and sacrificial love and comes alongside faithful people like Ruth to bless their efforts.

(3) The reward theme begins to blossom in this chapter. Boaz, who recognizes Ruth's faithfulness to Naomi (2:11–12; cf. 3:10), asks God to reward her loyalty and sacrificial love. However, this theme will not reach its consummation until chapter four.

Preaching idea: *Because the Lord often accomplishes his redemptive work through faithful human instruments, we can be confident he will providentially guide our footsteps when we decide to love sacrificially, no matter how meager our means appear to be.*

A Marriage Proposal at the Threshing Floor

TRANSLATION AND NARRATIVE STRUCTURE

1a   Her mother-in-law Naomi said to her, (*initiatory*)

1b   *"My daughter, I must find a home for you so you will be secure.*[1]

2   *Now Boaz, with whose female servants you worked, is our relative.*[2] *Look, tonight he is winnowing*[3] *barley at the threshing floor.*[4]

---

1. The Hebrew text has a negated rhetorical question here, which is equivalent to an affirmation (see 2:8–9).

2. Again the negated rhetorical question is equivalent to an affirmation (see 2:8–9; 3:1). Boaz is the referent of מֹדַעַת, "relative," a term that is feminine in form (the masculine form is used of Boaz in the *Qere* of 2:1). It occurs only here in the Old Testament. On the use of the feminine form see Joüon and Muraoka, 266–67, para. 89b.

3. We cannot be sure if nighttime had already arrived or if Naomi is anticipating its arrival. If the former, then we could paraphrase, "this very night (even as we speak) he is winnowing." If the latter, then we should translate, "tonight he will winnow," assuming that she is speaking during the daytime prior to the arrival of "tonight." The participle is only rarely used with הַלַּיְלָה, "tonight." In 1 Samuel 19:11 Michal urged David to escape during the night because Saul's men were outside waiting to kill him when morning arrived. Though David's escape took place at night, it is not clear if Michal warned him at night or earlier in the day.

4. The text reads literally, "he is winnowing the barley threshing floor." The accusative sign may introduce the direct object, in which case גֹּרֶן,

3   *So bathe,[5] rub on some perfumed oil,[6] and get dressed up.[7] Then go down[8] to the threshing floor. But don't let the man know you're there until he finishes his meal.*

4   *When he gets ready to go to sleep, take careful notice of the place where he lies down. Then go, uncover his legs, and lie down beside him. He will tell you what you should do."*

5a   Ruth replied, (*sequential*)

5b   *"I will do everything you tell[9] me to do."[10]*

"threshing floor," stands by metonymy for the contents of the floor, namely the barley gathered there. Another option is to take גֹּרֶן as an adverbial accusative (see our translation). The accusative sign occasionally appears before adverbial accusatives (*IBHS*, p. 181).

5. The perfect with prefixed *waw*-consecutive here introduces a series of instructions. See GKC, 335, para. 112aa, for other examples of this construction functioning in this way. One might expect the sequence of instructions to begin with an imperative or imperfect, but occasionally such sequences commence with a *weqatal* form. The next three verbs in the sequence are also *weqatal* forms. This is typical in procedural discourse, where a routine is rehearsed. See Longacre 1994, 52–54.

6. For the meaning of the verb, see *HALOT*, 745–46, and Bush 1996a, 150. The construction is elliptical, with the object (oil) implied (cf. 2 Sam. 12:20 with 14:2).

7. The noun may refer to clothes in general (see Hubbard 1988b, 197, note 7) or to a long outer garment (see Bush 1996a, 150–51).

8. The *Kethib* is וְיָרַדְתִּי; the *Qere* is the more common second feminine singular form וְיָרַדְתְּ. The *Kethib* form appears to be first person singular, but this would make no sense here. It is actually an archaic second feminine singular form. See GKC, 121, para. 44h. See as well verse 4, where the *Kethib* is וְשָׁכַבְתִּי (archaic 2fs perfect) and the *Qere* is the modernized וְשָׁכַבְתְּ. For a different explanation of the apparent first person forms, see Irwin 2008, 331–38. He argues that the forms are indeed first person and "are an intentional emendation of the text" designed to "remove Ruth from any possible intimate encounter with Boaz and replace her with Naomi" (331). Holmstedt also argues that these forms do *not* preserve an archaic pattern (2010, 23–24, 152–53).

9. The Hebrew imperfect is used, even though Naomi's instructions appear to be finished. According to GKC (316, para. 107h), the imperfect can sometimes "express actions, &c, which although, strictly speaking, they are already finished, are regarded as still lasting on into the present time, or continuing to operate in it." Perhaps Ruth was not certain if Naomi was finished, yet she wanted to assure her mother-in-law that she was ready and willing to follow all of her instructions, including any that Naomi might add to those just given.

10. The *Qere* adds "to me" after "you are saying."

6a   She went down to the threshing floor (*sequential*)

6b   and did everything her mother-in-law had instructed her to do. (*sequential*)

7a   When Boaz had finished his meal[11] (*specifying / focusing*) [12]

7b   and was feeling satisfied, (*sequential*)

7c   he lay down to sleep at the far end of the grain heap. (*sequential*)

7d   Then Ruth sneaked up quietly, (*sequential*)

7e   uncovered his legs (*sequential*) [13]

7f   and lay down beside him. (*sequential*)

8a   In the middle of the night (*introductory*)

8b   he was startled (*initiatory*)

8c   and rolled over.[14] (*sequential*)

8d   **Then[15] he saw a woman lying beside him.** (*dramatic*)

9a   He said, (*sequential*)

9b   "Who are you?"[16]

9c   She replied, (*sequential*)

9d   "I am Ruth, your servant. Marry your servant, for[17] you are a benefactor of the family."

10a   He said, (*sequential*)

10b   "May you be rewarded by the LORD, my daughter! This latter act of devotion is greater than what you did before. You have not pursued one of the young men, whether poor or rich.

---

11. In the Hebrew text there are actually two clauses, "and Boaz ate and drank." The second *wayyiqtol* clause ("and drank") complements the first.

12. Verse 6 is a summary statement for the following narrative. Verses 7–15 give the particulars. For this same stylistic technique, see 1:6–7 and 2:3.

13. Though the text gives no indication of a time lapse, she must have given him enough time to fall asleep, for he did not notice when she uncovered his legs and took her position beside him.

14. The verb occurs only here, and in Job 6:18 and Judges 16:29, where it seems to mean "grab hold of." Here the verb seems to carry the meaning "bend, twist, turn," like its Arabic cognate (see *HALOT*, 533, and Bush 1996a, 163).

15. With a dramatic flair, the narrator invites the reader to view the situation through Boaz's eyes.

16. Boaz uses the feminine form of the pronoun; he knows a woman is present, but he does not know her identity.

17. Sasson argues that כִּי is emphatic here (1979, 81–82), but Bush shows that in this syntactical environment it has a causal force (1996a, 165–66).

11 *Now, my daughter, don't worry! I intend to do for you everything you propose,*[18] *for everyone in town*[19] *knows that you are a worthy woman.*[20]

12 *Now yes, it is true that*[21] *I am a benefactor, but there is another benefactor who is a closer relative than I.*

13 *Remain here tonight. Then in the morning, if he agrees to marry you, fine, let him do so. But if he does not want to marry you, I promise, as surely as the LORD lives, to marry you.*[22] *Sleep here until morning."*

14a So she slept beside him until morning. (*consequential*)

---

18. Literally, "everything which you are saying I will do for you." As in verse 5, the Hebrew imperfect is used (note "you are saying"), even though Ruth's request appears to be finished. See the note there. The imperfect אֶעֱשֶׂה could be translated "I will do," but since there are legal complications which must first be resolved, it is better to take the form as indicating Boaz's desire or intention (if the legal matters can be worked out).

19. Literally, "all the gate of the town." This could refer to everyone in town or to the leaders and prominent citizens of the community (Boaz's peers) who transacted business and made legal decisions at the town gate.

20. Or "woman of strong character." The same phrase is used in Proverbs 31:10 to describe the ideal wife.

21. The *Kethib* has כִּי אִם, while the *Qere* omits אִם. The entire sequence עַתָּה כִּי אָמְנָם כִּי אִם (literally, "now, surely, truly, surely"), with or without אִם, occurs only here in the Hebrew Bible. The various collocations within the construction are either rare or unattested. כִּי עַתָּה occurs four other places, but in each case כִּי functions differently than in Ruth 3:12. Elsewhere it introduces the object of the verb "to see" (Deut. 32:39; 1 Chron. 28:10), has a temporal function (Job 35:15), or is explanatory (1 Sam. 9:12). כִּי אָמְנָם appears only here and in Job 36:4, where כִּי, unlike the use in Ruth 3:12, is explanatory. אָמְנָם כִּי occurs only here and in Job 12:2, where, as in Ruth 3:12, it seems to have an emphatic function. The text seems to be overloaded with emphatic particles. Unless Boaz is stammering in his effort to respond appropriately to Ruth's offer and to soften the impact of what he must say next (see Berlin 1983, 90), it would appear the text is suffering from dittography, as the repetition of the consonantal sequence כי אמ/ם suggests. The most likely scenario is that the text originally read כִּי אָמְנָם, "indeed it is true," or אָמְנָם כִּי, "it is true, indeed."

22. Boaz uses the verb גאל, traditionally, "redeem," three times; in each case we have translated, "marry." In their capacity of a גֹּאֵל, "benefactor" (traditionally, "kinsman-redeemer"), Boaz and the other individual were protectors of the extended family's interests and possessions. In this case, the family benefactor would protect the family's stability by marrying Mahlon's widow and raising up offspring to continue Elimelech's family

14b She woke up while it was still dark. (*sequential*)

14c Boaz told her, (*sequential*)

14d *"No one must know that a woman visited the threshing floor."*[23]

15a Then he said, (*sequential*)

15b *"Hold out*[24] *the shawl you are wearing and grip it tightly."*

15c As she gripped it tightly, (*consequential*)

15d he measured out about eighty pounds of barley into the shawl (*sequential*)

15e and put it on her shoulders. (*sequential*)

15f Then she[25] went into town. (*sequential*)

16a When she approached her mother-in-law, (*sequential*)

16b Naomi asked, (*sequential*)

16c *"Is that you,*[26] *my daughter?"*

---

line. For further discussion see the commentary on 2:20 above and on 3:10–13 below.

23. The article on הָאִשָּׁה, "the woman," is probably dittographic (note the final *he* on the preceding verb בָאָה, "she came"). *NIV* takes the article as generic ("a woman"), but in none of the other 107 occurrences of הָאִשָּׁה in the Hebrew Bible is this the case. Since it would be odd for Boaz to refer to Ruth as "the woman" when speaking to her, some understand וַיֹּאמֶר as indicating self-reflection, "and he thought." See Hubbard 1988b, 220; and Bush 1996a, 177–78.

24. The form הָבִי has been traditionally derived from יהב, "give," though the vocalization is problematic (one expects הָבִי; cf. GKC, 190, par. 69o). Appealing to rabbinical and masoretic evidence, Martín-Contreras (2009) argues that the form is actually a defectively written *hiphil* imperative, second masculine singular, from בוא and should be translated "bring." The gender is problematic in this case (Ruth is addressed), but, according to Martín-Contreras, "that was not a problem for the rabbis" (264). One rabbinic proposal is that "he addressed her in the masculine, that none should notice her" (263). Of course, this explanation is hardly satisfying, since two distinct feminine singular forms are used right after this in his address to her!

25. The Hebrew text reads "he went," but many medieval Hebrew manuscripts, the Syriac, and the Vulgate understand Ruth as the subject. See *NASB, NKJV, RSV,* and *Tanakh.*

26. Literally, "Who are you?" Rebera points out that questions structured in this way invariably seek the identity of the addressee (1987a, 234–37). He suggests that Naomi's question be understood in the sense of "Is that you, daughter?" It draws attention to the fact that it was still quite dark, too dark in fact for anyone to recognize Ruth. In this way it assures us that secrecy has been achieved (cf. Boaz's concern in 3:14). Some, doubting that Naomi would need to ask about Ruth's identity, understand the question

16d Ruth told her all the man had done for her. (*sequential*)
17a She said, (*specifying*)
17b *"He gave me these eighty pounds of barley, for he said to me, 'Do not go to your mother-in-law empty-handed.'"*
18a Then Naomi said, (*sequential*)
18b *"Stay put, my daughter, until you know how the matter[27] turns out. For the man will not rest until he has taken care of the matter today."*

OUTLINE:

Act Three, Scene One: Matchmaker! Matchmaker! (3:1–5)
    Naomi's proposal (3:1–4)
    Ruth's obedience (3:5)

Act Three, Scene Two: A Planned Encounter at the Barley Threshing Floor (3:6–15e)
    Ruth sneaks into position (3:6–7)
    Boaz's surprise (3:8–9b)
    Ruth's proposal (3:9cd)
    Boaz's reply (3:10–13)
    Boaz's kindness (3:14–15e)

Act Three, Scene Three: Debriefing Ruth (3:15f–18)

LITERARY STRUCTURE:

The third chapter contains the third act in the drama, which unfolds in three scenes. The first scene (3:1–5) takes place presumably at the dwelling place of Naomi and Ruth, wherever that was. It consists of a dialogue in which Naomi proposes that Ruth meet Boaz at the threshing floor and Ruth agrees to follow her instructions to the letter.

Ruth's descent to the threshing floor marks the shift to the second

---

to pertain to Ruth's status after the encounter at the threshing floor, "Are you his wife?" See Hubbard 1988b, 223–24, and Bush 1996a, 184–85. But Rebera (235) argues that there was a more natural way of asking for such information, namely, "Is everything all right?" (הֲשָׁלוֹם; cf. 2 Kings 9:11).

27. It is not certain why the article is omitted. Perhaps the expression was idiomatic or proverbial. Elsewhere the collocation of the verb נפל, "fall," with the subject דָּבָר, "word, matter," occurs only in Joshua 21:45; 23:14; and 1 Kings 8:56. In each case the perfect form of the verb (נָפַל) is negated and the expression has the nuance, "a promise did not fail." The collocation does not carry this meaning in Ruth 3:18.

scene (3:6–15e). The initial focus is on Ruth's movements, which are in obedience to Naomi's instructions and culminate with her positioning herself next to the sleeping Boaz (vv. 6–7). The next movement within the scene is formally marked by *wayyehi* (וַיְהִי) and a temporal clause, indicating the passing of time (v. 8a). After a description of how Boaz happened to wake up, the scene consists of a dialogue including Ruth's marriage proposal and Boaz's reply (vv. 8b–13). Once again Ruth is depicted as obedient (v. 14a). The scene's final movement is marked by a temporal shift (from the middle of the night to early morning, v. 14b) and consists of Boaz's instructions to Ruth as well as another act of kindness (vv. 14c–15e).

Ruth's return to the city marks the shift to the third scene (v. 15f), in which a dialogue is again central (vv. 16–18). As in scene one, Naomi initiates the dialogue with a question. Her assuring words that Boaz will take care of the matter without delay pave the way for the next act, which takes place at the city gate.

EXPOSITION

Matchmaker! Matchmaker! (3:1–5)

Unlike the first two acts in the drama, this third act has no prologue. It begins abruptly with Naomi's proposal that Ruth offer herself in marriage to Boaz. She began by making it clear she had Ruth's best interests in mind. More specifically, she felt she must seek security (מָנוֹחַ, "rest") for Ruth. מָנוֹחַ is the masculine form of the word Naomi used in her earlier prayer of blessing for Orpah and Ruth (cf. 1:9).[28] She had asked that the Lord would provide מְנוּחָה, "security," for each of them in the home of a new husband. In her depressed condition, Naomi thought God could provide this security only in Moab, but now she realized that divine providence had been at work and her prayer could be answered in an unexpected manner. Earlier she asked God to bless the girls and then told them she was incapable of being God's instrument in making the prayer a reality (1:11–13). But now she realized she could play a part in the outworking of God's providence.[29] She

---

28. Hubbard sees the variation in gender as a stylistic device that facilitates a thematic connection between the two passages (1989, 288–89).

29. Hubbard states: "Naomi's role is both as responder to divine initiative and as advancer of its plans. Along with the actions of Ruth and Boaz (2:2–17; 3:9; 4:1–6), her shrewdness is the link which connects Yahweh's earlier direct intervention, the gift of food (1:6), with its sequel, the gift of conception (4:13)" (1989, 291).

spoke of *seeking* (note אֲבַקֶּשׁ) Ruth's security, whereas earlier she spoke simply of the girls *finding* (מָצָא) security (cf. 1:9).

Naomi indicated she had Boaz in mind as a potential husband for Ruth (v. 2). She identified him as a relative (מֹדַעַת), perhaps implying this made him a likely candidate for marriage. Earlier Naomi referred to Boaz as a גֹּאֵל, "benefactor" (2:20). This is the term Ruth uses later when she confronts Boaz at the threshing floor (3:9). Apparently, in the ancient Israelite view of family solidarity, being a relative made one a potential benefactor for needy family members.

After informing Ruth that Boaz would be winnowing grain at the threshing floor, Naomi gave her a series of instructions (vv. 3–4).[30] Ruth should bathe, rub on some perfumed oil, and put on her garments (v. 3). Since mourners would sometimes wear mourning clothes and refrain from washing or using cosmetics (Gen. 38:14, 19; 2 Sam. 12:20; 14:2), Ruth's attire and appearance would communicate that her period of mourning was over and that she was now available for remarriage (Bush 1996a, 152).[31] Following these preparations, Ruth was to go down to the threshing floor.[32] However, she was not to confront Boaz immediately. Rather, she was to wait until he finished his meal and settled down for the night. Only then was Ruth to approach him, uncover his legs, and lie down beside him (v. 4). Then Boaz would tell

---

30. It is likely that Boaz waited until the wheat harvest was completed before winnowing his barley. On the chronology of the story, see Wilch 2006, 255–56. On the technique of winnowing in ancient Israel, see Borowski 1987, 65–69.

31. Sakenfeld responds that Bush's proposal "is not compelling" (1999c, 54). She suggests that Naomi simply "wants Ruth to be attractive in every way" as she encounters Boaz. She explains: "Bathing was probably not an everyday or even weekly practice in ancient Israel and the use of oil (implied by the choice of the Hebrew verb 'anoint') in such a non-utilitarian way as bodily anointing would surely have been even less frequent."

32. One might expect the threshing floor to be on a hill so that Ruth would have to "go up" to reach it, not "go down." However, this need not be the case. As Hubbard explains, winnowing occurred at sites where there was "a steady breeze—but not one too strong or gusty" (1988b, 201). Apparently in Bethlehem the threshing floor, which was probably used by the entire community (Matthews 2004, 231–32), was located in a suitable place below the city gate, perhaps on "a neighboring hill lower than the town" (Hubbard 1988b, 201, note 21). Such a proposal is consistent with the statement that Boaz ascended (note "had gone up") from the threshing floor to the city (4:1). See Campbell 1975, 141.

Ruth what to do next. Ruth assured Naomi she would follow her instructions (v. 5).

There is some debate over the meaning of מַרְגְּלֹתָיו, which we have translated, "his legs" (v. 4). Some define the noun as "the place for the feet" (see *HALOT*, 631), but in Daniel 10:6 the word appears to refer to the legs, or "region of the legs." For this reason "legs" or "lower body" is the preferred translation.[33] The significance of this action is not entirely clear, but it is likely that uncovering Boaz's legs was a symbolic gesture inviting Boaz to take her as a wife (see our discussion of v. 9 below).[34]

Van Wolde suggests that the *piel* form of גלה, "uncover, expose," has a reflexive nuance here and that מַרְגְּלֹתָיו is an adverbial accusative of place. This would yield the following translation: "and uncover yourself (at) the place of his feet." She contends that מַרְגְּלֹתָיו is a "spatial marker," not an object. The absence of the accusative sign before the suffixed (and therefore definite) noun appears to favor this. In this case Ruth was to disrobe in front of Boaz, inviting him to take her sexually (van Wolde 1997a, 19–21; Nielsen 1997, 69–70). Van Wolde describes Ruth's action as "striptease by night."

However, this interpretation is problematic for at least two reasons: (1) One would expect the *niphal* or *hithpael* form of the verb גלה in this case. In 2 Samuel 6:20 the *niphal* form (נִגְלָה) is used of David exposing himself in public as he celebrated the return of the ark to Jerusalem. In Genesis 9:21 the *hithpael* form (וַיִּתְגַּל) is used of drunken Noah exposing himself.[35] (2) In fifty-one of its fifty-four uses outside

---

33. Bush 1996a, 152. Because "foot" is sometimes used euphemistically for the genitals (cf. Isa. 7:20), some feel that Ruth uncovered Boaz's genitals. For a critique of this view, see Bush 1996a, 153.

34. It is possible that Ruth is setting the stage for her invitation to Boaz to spread his "wing" (i.e., skirt) over her (cf. v. 9). By pulling the cover back, so to speak, she gives Boaz the opportunity to spread it out, not only over his lower legs, but also over her. In this way she makes it possible for Boaz to act out the idiom. See Mundhenk and de Waard 1975, 428–29. Based on ancient Near Eastern parallels, Kruger suggests the action is "a symbolic declaration of the husband to provide for the sustenance of his future wife" (1984, 86).

35. The *piel* form of גלה is sometimes understood as reflexive in Isaiah 57:8. For a discussion of the issue, see Oswalt 1998, 479. Interpretive options include: (1) pointing the form as a *qal* (see *BHS*, note a), (2) taking "bed" as the accusative for all three of the preceding verbs (but, as Oswalt points out, the absence of the conjunction on the third verb makes this problematic), (3) assuming an ellipsis or accidental omission of the object.

of Ruth 3, the *piel* form of גִּלָּה is collocated with a direct object.[36] This makes it very likely that מַרְגְּלֹתָיו is the direct object in Ruth 3:4, 7. The fact that it indicates a place does not preclude its function as an object, if it is metonymic for what resides in the place, namely Boaz's "feet."[37] Furthermore, this is not the only instance of a noun of place (prefixed with *mem*) serving as the object of the *piel* of גלה (see Jer. 49:10). As for the accusative sign, it is not consistently used before the object of the *piel* of גלה when the object is a suffixed noun (see Lev. 18:7, 9–11, 15, 17–19), though examples in narrative texts are rare. In the book of Ruth, the accusative sign does not consistently appear before suffixed nouns functioning as objects. (See Ruth 1:9, 14; 2:11–12, 14, 20; 3:3, 9–10; 4:4, 7–8, 17.)[38] In summary, when the evidence is examined, it is apparent that the Hebrew collocation used in Ruth 3:4, 7 does not behave as van Wolde suggests, nor did Ruth.

Yet one does find in this passage a clustering of terms that sometimes have a sexual connotation. This is striking and may be intended for literary effect (cf. שָׁכַב, "lie down," יָדַע, "know," and בוא, "enter"). Moshe Bernstein explains that the words do not refer to actual sexual activity in Ruth 3: "Taken alone, out of the context of the chapter, these ambiguous words could point to the occurrence of sexual activity, but the configuration of the words, the sense of the sentences which they form, points in the opposite direction" (1991, 19). Yet, according to Bernstein, the appearance of these words here is not coincidental. He explains:

None of these is compelling. At this point we probably need to admit that the meaning of the collocation of the *piel* with מֵאִתִּי, "from (with) me," attested only here, escapes our understanding. Though a reflexive nuance seems possible here (perhaps analogous to the reflexive use of the *piel* of כסה, "cover," in Gen. 38:14; Deut. 22:12; Jon. 3:6), this text does not support van Wolde's reading of the *piel* in Ruth 3:4, 7, for an object is readily available in Ruth 3:4, 7, unlike Isaiah 57:8, where the verb is collocated with a prepositional phrase with no object in sight.

36. In Lamentations 2:14 and 4:22 the verb is collocated with the preposition עַל, which introduces the object of the verb. Twenty-seven times עֶרְוָה, "nakedness," appears as the object of the verb (cf. Lev. 18:6–19; 20:11, 17–21; Ezek. 16:37; 22:10; 23:10, 18).

37. See Ruth 3:2 for a possible parallel, where "threshing floor" (a place) is preceded by the accusative sign and may stand by metonymy for the floor's contents, the barley.

38. For a fuller discussion of this issue, see Bush 1996a, 153.

The artistic function of the conflicting connotations of words versus sentences must be to furnish, on a level beyond the literal, the sense of the sexual and emotional tension felt by the characters in the vignette. The narrative tells us straightforwardly that no sexual intercourse has taken place on the threshing floor, that final resolutions await the scene at the city gate. All the while, however, the vocabulary of the scene indicates it might have, that the atmosphere was sexually charged. Thus the ambivalence. The words point, beneath the surface, to the might-have-been which the characters felt might be, while the combinations of the words emphasize the opposing reality (19–20).[39]

By creating an "atmosphere" that is "sexually charged," the narrator may be foreshadowing the consummation of Boaz's and Ruth's budding relationship described in the next chapter. Perhaps it also contributes to the theme of Boaz and Ruth being impeccable in their character. At the barley threshing floor, under the veil of night, with the smell of fertility in the air, some might have capitulated to physical desire, but not Boaz and Ruth, who moved toward the consummation of their relationship in a proper, morally upright manner.

A Planned Encounter at the Barley Threshing Floor (3:6–15e)

Ruth went down to the threshing floor and followed Naomi's instructions (v. 6). She waited until Boaz had finished his meal and had settled down for the night. Then she crept up beside him and uncovered his legs (v. 7).[40] As far as we can tell, Naomi had not mentioned anything

---

39. See as well Harm 1995, 19–27. Van Wolde (1997a, 21–22) cites Bernstein favorably and seems to agree that Boaz and Ruth did not actually have intercourse at the threshing floor.

40. Kruger points out that this invasion of Boaz's *"intimate space"* is the culmination of a progression that began in chapter two, when Boaz and Ruth saw each other for the first time. That initial encounter took place "on the level of *public distance.*" When Boaz addresses her in 2:8 as "my daughter," Ruth "is promoted to his *social space.*" Later, when he invites her to participate in the meal (2:14), "she is drawn into his *personal zone* of involvement" (2009, 12–13, emphasis his). Of course, one could take this one step further and argue that the symbolic act of 3:7 achieves its climax and fulfillment when Boaz reciprocates Ruth's earlier action by invading her intimate space and having marital relations with her. As Kruger states, "by accepting" Ruth's invitation Boaz "extends his intimate sphere to enfold hers" (14).

about creeping up on Boaz, but Ruth had to employ this tactic to be able to uncover his legs. Otherwise he would have sensed her approaching and sat or stood up, making it difficult for her to perform the symbolic action (Mundhenk and de Waard 1975, 429).

Ruth patiently lay at Boaz's side until finally, in the middle of the night, he was startled and woke up (v. 8). Lying there at his legs was "a woman"! The narrator's use of הִנֵּה, "look, behold," invites the audience to experience the scene through Boaz's eyes. The audience knows the woman is Ruth because the narrator has informed us of that fact (vv. 6–7). But he heightens the drama by assuming Boaz's limited perspective (Berlin 1983, 91–92).

When Boaz asked her to identify herself, she gave her name and then described herself as his אָמָה (*'amah*), "female servant" (v. 9). This is a different term than the word she employed in 2:13. In that earlier scene in the field, Ruth had just arrived from Moab and was very much aware of her position as a foreigner (2:10). She acknowledged Boaz's kindness and emphasized her own humility by using the term שִׁפְחָה (*shiphchah*), "female servant," though she admitted she did not even occupy that lowly position on the social scale.[41] However, here in chapter three, where Naomi sends her to Boaz to propose marriage, she uses a more elevated term to describe herself because she is now aware of Boaz's position as a close relative of her deceased husband. The term שִׁפְחָה views a female servant as a laborer, while אָמָה focuses on gender. Consequently שִׁפְחָה can be used to emphasize subservience, while אָמָה can be used to draw attention to a servant's vulnerability and need for protection. Since אָמָה focuses on gender, it is also the preferred term when one wants to make the point that a female servant is marriageable or married.[42] Ruth's use of the term is appropriate for she was about to propose marriage to Boaz.

---

41. For a study of the rhetorical use of the terms in speeches by women in 1–2 Samuel, see Chisholm 1998, 42–43.

42. Richard Schultz, "אָמָה," in *NIDOTTE*, 1:418–21; and "שִׁפְחָה," in *NIDOTTE*, 4:211–13. See also Hamlin, who suggests using the labels "female slave" for שִׁפְחָה and "household servant" for אָמָה (1995, 139). By using the latter, Ruth was implying "her eligibility to become his wife." Reuter takes a different view, arguing that "the choice of terms appears instead to be determined by the nature of the relationship." אָמָה is the term of choice when the focus is "the total family and the woman's relationship to the husband," while שִׁפְחָה is preferred "when the relationship to the mistress is expressed." See his "שִׁפְחָה," *TDOT*, 15:408. This distinction appears to be valid when one views the usage of the terms in Genesis. See Chisholm 1998, 43–44.

Ruth's next statement to Boaz seems a bit cryptic, "and spread your wing over your servant" (v. 9). In the metaphorical account in Ezekiel 16:8, God spreads his skirt (literally, "wing") over naked Jerusalem as an act of protection and as a precursor to marriage. So Ruth's words can be taken as an idiomatic marriage proposal.[43] Ruth's use of the term כָּנָף, "wing," may provide an intertextual link with Boaz's prayer in 2:12. On that occasion he asked the Lord to reward Ruth for her devotion to Naomi, noting that Ruth had sought protection under the "wings" of Israel's God. By referring here to Boaz's "wing," Ruth was suggesting that Boaz had the opportunity to be God's instrument in fulfilling his earlier prayer of blessing by providing security for her.[44]

By proposing marriage, Ruth appears to go beyond Naomi's instructions. Naomi told her to uncover Boaz's legs, lie beside him, and then wait for instructions from Boaz (cf. 3:4). However, when Boaz asked, "Who are you," she identified herself and then proposed marriage without waiting for him to tell her what to do. Actually Ruth's behavior was true to form. Just as she had done previously (1:16–18; 2:2), she actively pursued Naomi's welfare. She may have carried out Naomi's instructions more aggressively than her mother-in-law intended, but her proposal was certainly consistent with the symbolic action of uncovering Boaz's legs. For this reason the narrator can say she carried out Naomi's instructions to the letter (3:6), even though she did add her own signature to the event (Chisholm 2002, 412–13).[45]

---

43. Bush refutes the faulty notion that Ruth's invitation had a sexual connotation and was an attempt to seduce Boaz (1996a, 164–65).
44. See Rauber 1970, 33, as well as Hubbard, 1988b, 212; Korpel 2001, 171; and LaCocque 2004, 96.
45. Berger suggests that Naomi intended "to prompt a sexual encounter" (2009b, 442, note 16), but this seems unlikely. The text states that Ruth did as Naomi told her, so she cannot have intentionally altered Naomi's plan in such a radical way. To make his theory work, Berger must argue that the statements about Ruth's doing all that Naomi said "do not extend to one crucial, implied component of the plan: seductively prompting Boaz to 'tell [Ruth] what . . . to do'" (443). Granted, Ruth carried out Naomi's wishes more aggressively than Naomi intended (see the discussion below), but she still acted in accordance with the essential plan (to propose marriage to Boaz). Berger's proposal flies in the face of what the text specifically says. The same criticism applies to Glover's proposal that Naomi intended Ruth to seduce the older Boaz, just as Lot's daughters had seduced their father (2009, 304). On the contrary, in following Naomi's instructions, Ruth acts in contrast to Lot's daughter. Fischer explains: "The atmosphere on the threshing floor described by the book of Ruth is highly

As a basis for her proposal (note כִּי, "for"), Ruth appealed to Boaz's status as a גֹּאֵל, "benefactor" (v. 9). We should probably assume the term has the same sense as in 2:20 (see our discussion above). If the term is used in a general sense of "deliverer, helper," then Naomi simply identified Boaz as a relative and potential benefactor (cf. 2:20), and Ruth appealed to Boaz on the basis of this relationship (3:9). However, this does not fully explain Boaz's response. He regarded Ruth's proposal as a faithful act (חַסְדֵּךְ הָאַחֲרוֹן, "your latter act of loyalty," v. 10) that surpassed her earlier expression of loyalty. This prior act of loyalty must have been Ruth's decision to leave her homeland and return with Naomi (cf. 2:11–12, though חֶסֶד, "loyalty, devotion," is not used there). But how was a marriage proposal an act of loyalty (חֶסֶד)? Ruth was not obligated to marry Boaz (3:10), but her decision to marry a גֹּאֵל, "benefactor," was apparently motivated by her desire to carry on her deceased husband's line (cf. 4:5, 9) and thereby provide for Naomi's future well-being (cf. 4:14–15). It seems Ruth understood that Boaz, if willing to marry her, would assume these responsibilities. Of course, one could argue that Boaz *thought* she was appealing to him on this basis (his subsequent words and actions are consistent with this) or that he was in essence saying, "Whether you realize it or not, your proposal is an act of חֶסֶד, because it has implications for your deceased husband and for Naomi." In this scenario neither Naomi nor Ruth understood fully the implications of the proposed marriage.[46] But such an interpretation diminishes the magnitude of Ruth's decision. It is more likely both she and Naomi understood that certain responsibilities attended to the position of a family benefactor once he married the widow of a family member. By proposing marriage to Boaz, Ruth was demonstrating concern for Naomi and for her deceased husband. But how would Ruth know about the customs related to a גֹּאֵל, "benefactor"? The story leaves a gap in this regard, but it is reasonable to assume that Naomi told her.

If this is the case, why did Naomi omit the term גֹּאֵל, "benefactor," when broaching the subject of marriage to Ruth (cf. 3:1–2), even though she had used it earlier to describe Boaz's relationship to both her and Ruth (2:20)? Knowing that Boaz was perhaps not the most natural

---

erotic, but is interrupted abruptly through Ruth's request, which appeals to ethics. In doing so, the Moabite woman redeems the incestuous deed of her ancestress. She does it for Naomi's sake and because Naomi advises her to do so" (1999, 45).

46. See Bush 1996a, 171, 174, 181. Berlin states, "Boaz now pretends that she was intentionally and heroicly placing Naomi's interests above her own" 1983, 90).

choice (cf. Boaz's response in 3:10), she may have avoided using the term in order to give Ruth an "easy out" and allow her to save face.[47] By identifying Boaz as a *relative* (מוֹדַעַת, v. 2), not a *benefactor* (גֹּאֵל), Naomi made it sound as if she was simply suggesting that Ruth seek a husband for the sake of her own security. This gave Ruth the opportunity to reject her suggestion without making it so obvious she was unwilling to subordinate her own preferences to the good of Naomi and the deceased.[48]

Even if we assume that the role of גֹּאֵל, "benefactor," carried with it certain responsibilities, it is important to note that prior to assuming such a role Boaz was not obligated to marry Ruth. According to 3:11, he was willing to accept Ruth's request, not because he was under legal

---

47. Her use of questions in verses 1–2 may support our proposal. Hyman states: "By the very way she structures her two questions, Naomi involves Ruth in her plan while at the same time allowing her to dissent and assert her freedom if she so desires" (1984, 195–96).
48. Hubbard explains Ruth's use of גֹּאֵל, "benefactor," differently (1988b, 213). He suggests that Ruth's proposal was a "surprising departure from Naomi's instructions," which were "intended simply to obtain a husband for Ruth—a concern of the older widow throughout the book (1:8–9, 11–13; 3:1)." Ruth appealed to the גֹּאֵל custom "on her own initiative" and thereby "subordinated her own happiness to the family duty of providing Naomi an heir." Does Hubbard mean to suggest that Boaz would be free of such a duty if Ruth simply appealed to him as a relative and that he could have married her without being obligated to Naomi or Mahlon? Did her use of גֹּאֵל really place her request in a different category? Furthermore, how is this interpretation to be harmonized with the narrator's statement (cf. 3:6) that Ruth did exactly as Naomi instructed? (In this regard, see Hubbard 1988b, 206.)

Berlin also argues that Ruth went beyond Naomi's instructions, turning a purely "romantic mission" into a "quest for a redeemer" (1983, 90). To make this interpretation work, however, she must understand 3:6, which indicates that Ruth carried out Naomi's instructions to the letter, as reflecting Ruth's perspective. She states that the narrator "is adopting Ruth's point of view here—Ruth really thought that she was following instructions" (90–91). To support her argument, Berlin appeals to (1) Ruth's use of גֹּאֵל, "benefactor," rather than מוֹדַעַת, "relative," the term used by Naomi in verse 2, and to (2) the fact that Ruth crept up to Boaz and uncovered his legs only after he fell asleep. But, as we have noted above, (1) Naomi's failure to use גֹּאֵל may be explained as an attempt to be polite, and (2) it would have been difficult and awkward for Ruth to uncover Boaz's legs before he fell asleep. For further discussion, see Chisholm 2002, 411–12.

obligation to do so, but because she was a woman of worthy character and good reputation.

Furthermore, Ruth's invitation and Boaz's response have no formal connection with the so-called levirate (i.e., related to the widow's brother-in-law) practice and law mentioned elsewhere in the Old Testament (cf. Genesis 38; Deuteronomy 25). Boaz was not the brother of Mahlon (Wilch 2006, 287). As noted above, neither Ruth nor Boaz acted under legal obligation, in contrast to what we see in the episode recorded in Genesis 38, where Judah's sons were obligated to raise up offspring for their deceased brother, and in the Mosaic Law (Deut. 25:5–10), where a brother-in-law was likewise obligated to carry on a deceased brother's family line by cohabiting with his widowed sister-in-law (Leggett 1974, 206). In both cases anyone who refused to carry out the responsibility of producing offspring was viewed in a negative light, in contrast to Ruth 4, where the nearer relative declined the right to redemption without being publicly rebuked. In neither Genesis 38 nor Deuteronomy 25 is the term גֹּאֵל, "benefactor," used of a brother-in-law. While there is a concern for carrying on a deceased individual's line in these texts (as in Ruth), the marked differences preclude their being used to impose a legal framework upon the transaction between Boaz and Ruth.[49]

Boaz's response to Ruth (vv. 10–13) requires a closer examination.[50]

---

49. See Bush 1996a, 221–25, as well as Gordis 1974, 246–52; Anderson 1978, 171–83; and Beattie 1974, 264–65. I find it unnecessary and unwarranted to suggest that the book of Ruth is seeking to counter and challenge Deuteronomy's view of the levirate, as Curtis argues (1996, 144–45). Nor is it necessary to propose, as Davies does, a historical development from Genesis 38 (where the levirate is an "unavoidable obligation") to Deuteronomy 25 (where it is "possible to evade the duty," albeit with a "certain stigma" attached to the refusal) to Ruth 4 (where "the duty is no longer regarded as obligatory, and refusal carried no shame") (1981, 267). See as well Zevit 2005, 581. For a survey of opinion on the debated issue of whether or not the levirate law provides the background for Boaz's marriage to Ruth, see Loader 1994, 127–37.

50. In addition to its simple informative elements, Boaz's speech to Ruth displays elements of hortatory and predictive discourse. (For a brief summary of discourse types, see Chisholm 2006a, 58–59.) The function of the speech is at once performative (note the blessing in v. 10 and the oath formula in v. 13), evaluative (vv. 10–11, note especially "you are a worthy woman"), dynamic (vv. 11–13, note especially "do not fear"), and relational (v. 13, note "I will redeem you"). Performative speech, like Boaz's formal blessing and oath, performs an action; evaluative speech expresses the

He began by pronouncing a blessing upon her, asking that the Lord would reward her because of her faithful act, which surpassed her prior act of loyalty to her mother-in-law (v. 10). As noted above, her marriage proposal is viewed as an act of חֶסֶד, "loyalty, devotion," apparently because Ruth's marriage to Boaz would secure Naomi's future as well as carry on the family line of the deceased Mahlon (Sakenfeld 1999c, 61). One gets the impression Boaz was not the most likely candidate, perhaps because of an age disparity. The narrator does not tell us how old either Boaz or Ruth was at this time, but Boaz seemed to think one of the younger men would have been a more likely choice, suggesting Ruth was significantly younger than he was. The term הַבַּחוּרִים refers to "the young men" of the town who were in the prime of life and of marriageable age (cf. Judg. 14:10; Ps. 78:31; Eccl. 11:9; Isa. 40:30; 62:5). The word בָּחוּר, "young man," is often paired with בְּתוּלָה, "young woman" (see, e.g., Amos 8:13) and is the polar opposite of זָקֵן, "old man" (Prov. 20:29; Jer. 31:13; 51:22; Joel 2:28 [Hebrew 3:1]).

The language of Boaz's response suggests that he and Ruth were well-suited for each other. Just as Boaz pronounced a blessing upon Ruth (cf. בְּרוּכָה, "blessed," in 3:10), so Naomi had blessed Boaz when she heard of his kindness to her and Ruth (cf. בָּרוּךְ, "blessed," in 2:19–20). Both Boaz and Ruth were worthy individuals who deserved to be rewarded by the Lord because both had performed significant acts of loyalty (חֶסֶד).

Boaz assured Ruth of his intention to marry her (vv. 11–12). As noted earlier, he was apparently under no obligation to accept her invitation, but he was willing to do so for Ruth had proven her worthy character before the entire town. The phrase אֵשֶׁת חַיִל, "woman of strength," refers to Ruth as a woman of noble character. The primary meaning of חַיִל is "strength," but it can be used of ability and character as well as physical strength. The phrase אֵשֶׁת חַיִל appears in Proverbs 12:4, where

---

speaker's evaluation of, or judgment about, a person or situation; dynamic speech seeks to impact the hearer's perspective and motivate a particular response; and relational language is designed to facilitate or enhance a relationship between the speaker and hearer. (On the types of language function see Macky 1990, 16; and Chisholm 2006a, 60–61.) Having Boaz extol Ruth's value is more effective than if the narrator did so directly. Berlin explains, "the narrator does not tell us how wonderful Ruth's loyalty to Naomi is; he has Boaz tell us in 2:11. And later at the threshing-floor Boaz tells Ruth that her second kindness is better than her first, and that everyone knows she is an אשת חיל ('worthy woman'—3:10–11). . . . This internal or embedded evaluation is more authentic and more dramatic than a narrator's comment" (1983, 105).

such a woman brings honor to her husband, and in Proverbs 31:10 at the beginning of a passage that extols the value of such a wife and gives a lengthy character profile of this kind of woman. The character profile highlights her devotion to her family and others within her social circle, as well as her capacity to work hard. Ruth demonstrated these same character qualities (see Sakenfeld 1999c, 62). She swore to never leave Naomi's side and worked hard in the fields to provide food for her destitute mother-in-law. The use of this phrase may suggest Ruth would make a suitable wife for Boaz, whom the narrator earlier described as *a man of substance* (cf. אִישׁ גִּבּוֹר חַיִל in 2:1) (Prinsloo 1977–78, 120).[51]

Despite Boaz's willingness to marry Ruth and their obvious suitability, there was a snag in the plan that creates a twist in the developing plot (v. 12). Boaz was indeed a family benefactor, but he was not the closest such relative. Another potential benefactor was more closely related to Elimelech and therefore had the first option to fulfill the role of גֹּאֵל, "benefactor." But if he was not willing to exercise his option, Boaz vowed to Ruth that he would serve as her גֹּאֵל (v. 13). Having assured her he would follow the matter through to its end, he instructed her to sleep beside him until morning, probably out of concern for her safety (cf. Song 5:7).

In compliance with Boaz's instructions, Ruth spent the night beside him (v. 14). She awakened at early dawn, before anyone would be able to identify her from a distance. Boaz told her not to let anyone know she had been to the threshing floor. Apparently it was not considered appropriate for a woman to visit the threshing floor, though, if so, this did not inhibit Naomi from sending Ruth there!

As a further act of kindness and a guarantee that he would seek her best interests, Boaz loaded Ruth down with barley (v. 15). The Hebrew text gives the amount as simply שֵׁשׁ־שְׂעֹרִים, "six of barley," without providing the unit of measure (v. 15, cf. v. 17 as well). There are three options: the ephah, seah, and omer. As Bush explains, six ephahs would have weighed between 180–300 pounds, too large an amount for Ruth to carry home in her shawl. Six omers (an omer was one-tenth of an ephah) would have weighed 18–30 pounds, which seems too small in

---

51. Sakenfeld observes that the characterization of Boaz as a man of substance (חַיִל) in 2:1 "places Boaz at great social distance from the poverty-stricken returnee Naomi and her foreign daughter-in-law." But then the text uses the same word (חַיִל) to characterize Ruth as a woman of noble character, "thus collapsing literarily the socio-cultural distance between" Boaz and Ruth (1999c, 38).

light of the amount Ruth was able to glean in a day (cf. 2:17). So the most likely option is that Boaz gave her six seahs (a seah was about one-third of an ephah), which would have weighed between 60–100 pounds.[52]

Debriefing Ruth (3:15f–18)

When Ruth returned from her quest, she related what had happened and showed Naomi the barley (vv. 15f–16). At this point we also learn a detail the narrator omitted in the earlier account (v. 17). When Boaz sent Ruth back with the barley, he said, "Do not go to your mother-in-law empty-handed."[53] Naomi apparently took this as a guarantee that Boaz had their best interests in view. She told Ruth to sit tight and assured her that Boaz would pursue the matter immediately (v. 18).

Boaz's expressed concern for Naomi reveals that he understood the implications of Ruth's request. Ruth had not simply proposed marriage; she had proposed marriage to a גֹּאֵל, "benefactor," with the intention of securing Naomi's future, as well as her own (Wilch 2006, 300). Boaz's use of רֵיקָם, "empty-handed," provides an intertextual link with Naomi's speech to the women of the town when she returned to Bethlehem (1:21). On that occasion she lamented the Lord had brought her back "empty-handed." It is not certain if Boaz knew what she had said and was intentionally playing off her earlier use of the word. From

---

52. Bush 1996a, 178. See as well Campbell 1975, 127–28, and Hubbard 1988b, 222.

53. Berlin takes a different approach to this appearance of previously unreported speech (1983, 98). Writing of Ruth's statement in verse 15, she states: "We can understand it better if we remember that not all direct discourse represents actual speech spoken aloud; some represents thought (or interior monologue)... We would then render Ruth's speech as 'He gave me these six measures of barley because he thought that I should not come empty-handed to my mother-in-law.' This is Ruth's perception, psychologically and ideologically, of Boaz's action, made more scenic through quoted direct discourse as she conveys it to Naomi. We don't know why Boaz gave Ruth the barley. We only know why Ruth thought Boaz gave it to her. The absence of the narrator's viewpoint here, which could either confirm or contradict Ruth's, is in keeping with the tendency in the Book of Ruth for the narrator to limit his own point of view and have the evaluations made by characters." Berlin's proposal complicates the story. As Sakenfeld states, "the thread of the story is more powerful. . . if Ruth's report is taken at face value as Boaz's actual words." She adds: "Boaz's explanation of his gift of grain provides a sure clue that he joins Ruth in her concern for Naomi; he is not focused on Ruth alone" (1999c, 66).

the perspective of the narrator, who includes both quotations, Boaz's response to Ruth's request assured the "empty-handed" one that her circumstances were about to change.[54] The barley represented the fruit of the harvest and signaled that the time of famine, for both Bethlehem and Naomi, was over. It may even foreshadow Obed, who was the fruit of Boaz's union with Ruth and the one who would provide for Naomi's security (cf. 4:14–16).[55]

MESSAGE AND APPLICATION

Thematic Emphases

God's providence, working through Boaz's kindness, transformed Naomi's attitude and restored her hope. Earlier she saw no way she could provide the security Ruth needed (cf. 1:11–13), but now she actively pursued Ruth's well-being as she reciprocated Ruth's kindness to her (3:1). Ruth continued to be an obedient, devoted daughter. By proposing marriage to Boaz, she exhibited faithfulness to both Naomi and her deceased husband. Boaz recognized her sacrificial love for what it was, asked God to reward her for it, and assured her that her future would be secure, though a plot twist occurs when he informed Ruth that a nearer relative had the first option to marry her.

Exegetical idea: *God's providential, redemptive work in and through Ruth and Boaz restored Naomi's hope. Boaz recognized Ruth's sacrificial love and promised to reward it by securing her future.*

Theological Principles

The narrator continues to depict God's providential work, which uses the initiative of faithful human instruments. As Ruth continued to display sacrificial love, the Lord continued to reward her efforts, using Boaz's kindness as his instrument.

Theological idea: *God's providential, redemptive work in and through the lives of godly people restores hope and secures the future.*

---

54. See Hubbard 1988b, 225–26. Rauber suggests that Naomi's receiving grain from Boaz previews the birth of Obed, whom Naomi holds in her lap in the story's final scene (4:16) (1970, 35).

55. Porten observes, "The seed to fill the stomach was promise of the seed to fill the womb" (1978, 40).

Homiletical Trajectories

(1) Continuing to operate through human instruments, God once more works providentially to deliver Naomi from her despair and bitterness. When we recognize the hand of God at work in our experience, we can look to the future with hope and even reciprocate the kindness shown by others.

(2) As in chapter two, God continues to help the needy by utilizing the loyal actions of those who love sacrificially and take family commitments seriously.

(3) The reward theme becomes more prominent in this chapter. Boaz, who marvels at Ruth's faithfulness to Naomi (3:10), again blesses her and assures both Ruth and Naomi that their future will be secure.

Preaching idea: *As we show sacrificial love for others, we can be confident that God's providential, redemptive work in and through us will restore hope and secure the future.*

RUTH 4:1–22
All's Well that Ends Well

TRANSLATION AND NARRATIVE STRUCTURE

1a Now Boaz had gone up[1] to the town gate (*introductory*)

1b and sat there. (*sequential*)

1c **Along came the potential benefactor whom Boaz had mentioned to Ruth.[2]** (*dramatic*)

1d Boaz said, (*sequential*)

1e *"Come over here and sit down, Mr. John Doe!"*

1f So he came over (*consequential*)

1g and sat down. (*sequential*)

2a Boaz chose ten of the town's elders (*sequential*)

2b and said, (*sequential*)

2c *"Sit down here!"*

2d So they sat down. (*consequential*)

---

1. The disjunctive clause structure with fronted subject followed by predicate (a perfect verbal form) signals the beginning of this new episode. There is actually a chronological flashback to where 3:15 left off. For fuller discussion, see Holmstedt 2010, 181.

2. With וְהִנֵּה, literally, "and look," the narrator invites us into the drama as eyewitnesses.

3a Then Boaz said to the benefactor, (*sequential*)

3b *"Naomi, who has returned from the region of Moab, is selling*[3] *the portion of land that belongs to our relative*[4] *Elimelech.*

4a *So I am officially informing you:*[5] *Purchase it before those sitting here and before the elders of my people!*[6] *If you want to exercise your right to redeem it, then do so. But if not, then tell me*[7] *so I will know.*[8] *For you possess the first option to redeem it; I am next in line after you."*

---

3. Some treat this as a perfect of resolve (*IBHS*, 489), but clear examples of this category are difficult to find. It is best to regard it as a simple present use; the perfect focuses on the simple fact of the matter. Another option is to take it as performative, "Naomi is hereby selling," reflecting the legal context. See Holmstedt 2010, 185. On this category, see Arnold and Choi 2003, 56; and van der Merwe, Naudé, and Kroeze 1999, 146. The form cannot be taken as a simple past or present perfect here, because the purchase is said to be from Naomi (vv. 5, 9), not some third party to whom she has already sold the land. See Hubbard 1988b, 239; Leggett 1974, 221; and Ap-Thomas 1968, 372. It is possible, however, that Elimelech had sold the land prior to leaving for Moab. In this case Naomi is "selling" the right to redeem and use the land. See the commentary below for further discussion.

4. Hebrew אָח, "brother," does not refer here to a literal blood-brother, but rather to a relative. See 2:1, 20; 3:2.

5. Literally, "and I said (or perhaps "thought to myself"), 'I will (or 'must') uncover your ear, saying.'"

6. This appears to refer to the leaders who were specially chosen as witnesses (v. 2) and the larger group of community leaders standing by. It is possible that the phrases "before those sitting here" and "before the elders of my people" are appositional and that both refer to the ten leaders mentioned in verse 2. However, it seems more likely that "those sitting here" in verse 2 are to be equated with "all the people" in verses 9, 11. See Bush 1996a, 207.

7. Literally, "but if he will not redeem, tell me." Most prefer to emend the third person verb form to the second person, because Boaz is addressing the benefactor. However, it is possible that he briefly addresses the witnesses and thus refers to the benefactor in the third person. See Sasson 1979, 118, and Linafelt 1999, 66. According to Bush, Sasson's interpretation is "forced and unlikely" (1996a, 210). Korpel sees the use of the third person pronoun as a polite attempt to avoid embarrassing the closer relative (2001, 202). She states that he uses the third person "as an expression of an undefined subject instead of directly addressing his opponent while raising the possibility of a refusal."

8. Following the imperative, the prefixed verb form with *waw* indicates purpose or result.

4b He replied, (*sequential*)

4c *"I will redeem it."*

5a Then Boaz said, (*sequential*)

5b *"When you purchase the field from Naomi, you also purchase Ruth the Moabite woman,*[9] *the wife of our deceased relative, in order to produce a descendant who will inherit his property."*

6a The benefactor said, (*sequential*)

6b *"I am unable to redeem it then, for I would ruin my own inheritance in that case. You may exercise my redemption option for I am unable to redeem it."*

7a (Now this used to be the customary way to finalize a transaction involving redemption in Israel: [*supplemental*]

7b A man removed his sandal [*characterizing / customary-procedural*]

7c and gave it to the other party. [*characterizing / customary-procedural*]

7d This was a legally binding act in Israel.) (*supplemental*)[10]

---

9. The Hebrew text (*Kethib*) reads, "and from Ruth the Moabitess, the wife of the deceased, I acquire." The *Qere* has "you acquire." A comparison with verses 9–10 shows that verse 5 should read, "and also (emending וּמֵאֵת, "and from," to וְגַם אֶת, "and also") Ruth the Moabitess, the wife of the deceased, you acquire." See Leggett 1974, 224–25. For a defense of MT see Gow 1990, 302–11. He reads: "On the day you acquire the field from the hand of Naomi and from Ruth the Moabitess, the widow of the deceased, you acquire **her** in order to raise up the name of the deceased upon his inheritance" (emphasis his, 311). This requires vocalizing the verb קָנִיתִי (*Kethib*)/קָנִיתָ (*Qere*) as קְנִיתָהּ, "you purchase her," a *qal* perfect second masculine singular form with a third feminine singular suffix. Gow argues that the LXX supports his proposal. Another option is that וּמֵאֵת consists of the conjunction, an enclitic *mem*, and the accusative sign, with the enclitic *mem* being misunderstood as a preposition. See *IBHS*, 648, note 2. If one follows the *Kethib*, then it sounds as if Boaz is asserting that he will purchase Ruth at the same time the nearer relative redeems the land. But the context (3:11–13; 4:9–10) indicates that the land and Ruth are purchased together. Furthermore, in 3:13 Boaz makes it clear that the nearer relative has the first option on *Ruth*, not just the land. See Bush 1996a, 227. This favors the *Qere* reading. Boaz informs the relative that if he redeems the land, he also purchases Ruth with it. The *qatal* verb form is either future perfect, "you will have purchased," or performative, "you thereby purchase." For the latter translation, see Hubbard 1988b, 243.

10. This supplemental section begins and ends with subject-fronted clauses (v. 7a, 7d). Verse 7b begins with an asyndetic perfect that has a characteristic function, describing a custom of Boaz's day. Holmstedt (2010, 196)

8a So the benefactor said to Boaz, (*sequential*)

8b *"You may purchase it,"*

8c and he removed his sandal.[11] (*sequential*)

9a Then Boaz said to the elders and all the people, (*sequential*) *"You are witnesses today that I hereby purchase[12] from Naomi all that belonged to Elimelech and to Kilion and Mahlon.*

10 *I also hereby purchase Ruth the Moabite woman, the wife of Mahlon, as my wife in order produce a descendant who will inherit his property so that the name of the deceased might not disappear from among his relatives and from his town. You are witnesses today."*

11a All the people who were at the gate and the elders replied, (*consequential*)

11b *"We are witnesses. May the LORD make the woman who is entering your home like Rachel and Leah, both of whom[13] built up the house of Israel! Then you will[14] accomplish great things[15] in Ephrathah and be famous[16] in Bethlehem.*

---

calls this a "modal *qatal*," used "to express habitual activity in the past." The next clause (v. 7c) begins with a *weqatal* form that has a customary-procedural function.

11. The Septuagint adds "and gave it to him," which presupposes the reading וַיִּתֶּן לוֹ. This appears to be a clarifying addition (see v. 7), though it is possible these words were accidentally omitted, the scribe's eye jumping from the final לוֹ on נַעֲלוֹ, "his sandal," to לוֹ, "to him," and accidentally omitting the intervening letters.

12. The translation assumes that the perfect verbal forms in verses 9–10 are performative in function, indicating the accomplishment of the purchase through the very declaration made here.

13. The apparent third masculine pronominal suffix is probably a common dual form (see 1:8 and the note there).

14. Following the jussive, the imperative with prefixed *waw* indicates purpose or result.

15. This probably means "acquire wealth" (i.e., through the offspring of the union). Noting that חַיִל can refer to sexual strength (cf. Prov. 31:3), Parker suggests the expression here may mean, "have a large family" 1976, 23, note 2). Labuschagne understands the expression in the sense of "engender procreative power." He argues that it is a wish for Boaz to be "virile and potent enough to bear a child" (1967, 366).

16. Literally, "and call a name." This statement appears to be elliptical. Labuschagne understands the expression in the sense "act as a name-giver" (i.e., by fathering a child) (1967, 366). Usually the person named and the name given follow this expression. Perhaps וּקְרָא־שֵׁם, "and call a name," should be emended to וְיִקָּרֵא־שִׁמְךָ, "and your name will be called

12   *May your family, the offspring the* LORD *gives you through this young woman, be like the family of Perez, whom Tamar bore to Judah!"*

13a   So Boaz married Ruth (*sequential*)

13b   and had marital relations with her. (*sequential*)

13c   The LORD allowed her to conceive (*sequential*)

13d   and she gave birth to a son. (*consequential*)

14a   The women said to Naomi, (*sequential*)

14b   *"May the* LORD *be praised because he has not left you without a benefactor today! May his name be perpetuated in Israel!*

15   *He will sustain your life and provide for you when you are old, because your daughter-in-law, who loves you, has given him birth. She is of greater value to you than seven sons."*

16a   Naomi took the child (*sequential*)

16b   and placed him on her lap; (*sequential*)

16c   she became his nurse. (*consequential*)[17]

17a   The neighbor women named him, saying, (*sequential, to 16b*)[18]

17b   *"A son has been born for Naomi."*

17c   They named him Obed. (*specifying*)

17d   He was the father of Jesse, David's father. (*concluding*)

18a   These are the descendants of Perez: (*supplemental / concluding*)

18b   Perez was the father of Hezron;[19]

19a   Hezron was the father of Ram;

---

out," that is, "perpetuated" (see Gen. 48:16; cf. Ruth 4:14b). The omission of the suffix with "name" could be explained as virtual haplography (note the letter *bet*, which is similar to *kaf*, at the beginning of the next word). The same explanation could account for the omission of the prefixed *yod* on the verb "call" (*yod* and *waw* are similar in earlier script phases). Whether one reads the imperative (the form in the Hebrew text) or the jussive (the emended form), the construction indicates purpose or result following the earlier jussive "may he make" (v. 11).

17.   This does not mean that Naomi, who was beyond childbearing age, breast-fed the child! While the participial form of the verb can refer to one who breast-feeds a baby (Num. 11:12), it can also refer more generally to one who cares for a child, as its use in 2 Samuel 4:4 (which speaks of five-year-old Mephibosheth's nurse) and Esther 2:7 (where the masculine form is used of Mordechai as the one who cares for Esther) indicate. See Sakenfeld 1999c, 83.

18.   Verse 17a is sequential in relation to verse 16b, making verse 16c consequential in relation to 16b, but parenthetical in the structure as a whole.

19.   The syntactical form throughout the list is *waw* + subject (name of father) + verb + accusative sign + direct object (name of son).

19b Ram was the father of Amminadab;

20a Amminadab was the father of Nachshon;

20b Nachshon was the father of Salmah;

21a Salmon[20] was the father of Boaz;

21b Boaz was the father of Obed;

22a Obed was the father of Jesse;

22b Jesse was the father of David.

OUTLINE:

Act Four, Scene One: A Potential Wrong Ending Averted (4:1–12)
    Court in session (4:1–2)
    Mr. John Doe surrenders his option (4:3–8)
    Boaz formalizes the agreement (4:9–10)
    The witnesses pronounce a blessing (4:11–12)

Act Four, Scene Two: A Marriage, a Birth, and a Doting Grandmother (4:13–17)
    Ruth has a baby (4:13)
    The women pronounce blessings (4:14–15)
    A picture of contentment (4:16)
    The women name the baby (4:17)

Act Four, Epilogue: What's in a Genealogy? An Official Record of God's Blessing (4:18–22)

LITERARY STRUCTURE:

Chapter four contains the fourth and final act in the drama in two scenes, followed by an epilogue. The setting of the second and third acts was outside the town (in the field and at the threshing floor) or in the privacy of Naomi's home. In this final episode the setting shifts back to the more public arena of the town, where Naomi's initial encounter with the women of Bethlehem took place (cf. 1:19–21). The first scene is formally introduced by a disjunctive clause, shifting the focus from the women (3:16–18) to Boaz. There are four movements within the scene: Boaz gathers the nearer relative and the witnesses for the legal proceedings (vv. 1–2), interacts with the nearer relative (vv. 3–8), and formalizes the agreement by appealing to the witnesses (vv. 9–10). The scene concludes with the witnesses pronouncing a blessing upon Ruth so that Boaz will achieve fame in Bethlehem (vv. 11–12)

The second scene shifts from the town gate, where the legal

---

20. Salmon appears to be an alternate spelling of the preceding Salmah.

transaction took place, to Boaz's home, where Boaz consummated the transaction, as it were. The scene begins with Boaz "taking" (לָקַח) Ruth as his wife. He has marital relations with her, she conceives, and gives birth to a son. The women of the town then pronounce blessings upon the giver (the Lord) and the gift (the son), making the point that the latter will care for Naomi in her old age. The story line continues with Naomi "taking" (לָקַח) the child, placing him on her lap, and becoming his guardian. The women of the town speak again and give the child a name (Obed, "one who serves") that describes his future relationship to Naomi. The paneled structure may be outlined as follows (Bush 1996a, 250–51):

a (13)
    b (14–15)
a' (16),
    b' (17).

The scene concludes with an asyndetic clause that extends the genealogical line from Obed to David, showing that the blessings of the women and of the witnesses (vv. 11–12) were realized.

The act and the book conclude with a genealogy that traces the descendants of Perez, mentioned earlier in the blessing of the witnesses (v. 11), through Boaz to David. At first this seems like an anticlimactic way for the story to end, but it illustrates the extent of the blessing that came to Ruth and Boaz as a reward for their worthy deeds and contributes in a powerful way to the story's overall message.

EXPOSITION

A Potential Wrong Ending Averted (4:1–12)
4:1–2. Naomi's confidence in Boaz was well-placed (cf. 3:18). Boaz wasted no time in resolving the legal complications surrounding Ruth's marriage proposal. He waited at the city gate until the closer relative (הַגֹּאֵל, "the benefactor") passed by. Boaz summoned him to join him and also enlisted ten men to serve as witnesses to the legal proceedings.

In addressing the closer relative, Boaz used the words פְּלֹנִי אַלְמֹנִי, the meaning of which is not entirely clear.[21] In its two other uses, the expression has a locative sense, "in such and such (a place)" (cf. 1

---

21. The words rhyme and form a type of wordplay that is also present in English expressions such as "hodge-podge," "helter-skelter," "heebie-jeebies," and "hocus-pocus." See Sasson 1979, 106; and Block 1999, 705–06.

Sam. 21:3; 2 Kings 6:8). If taken that way here, one could translate, "Turn aside, sit here in such and such a place." However, in this context the referent may be the closer relative, in which case the expression means, "a certain one, so-and-so," the equivalent of the English "John Doe." One would expect Boaz to use the man's name, but the narrator's presence is detected here (Berlin 1983, 99). The narrator seems to have altered Boaz's words in order to suppress the nearer relative's name. If the narrator did not know the man's name or felt it too unimportant to include, one might expect him to simply omit a vocative altogether. By including these words, he draws attention to the man's anonymity in the story (Bush 1996a, 197). This is appropriate, because he serves as a literary foil for Boaz. In contrast to Boaz, he refuses to fulfill the role of family protector. Because he does nothing memorable, he remains anonymous in a chapter that is otherwise filled with names.[22] His anonymity contrasts sharply with Boaz's prominence in the story and the fame he attains through the child born to Ruth.[23]

---

22. See Hubbard, who rather tentatively suggests this (1988b, 234–35). Wilch (2006, 324) and Block (1999, 707) seem more confident of this interpretation.

23. Campbell (1975, 141–42) lists four possible reasons for the omission of the relative's name, all of which he rejects: (1) Boaz did not know the relative's name. As Campbell notes, this seems unlikely in such a small town. (2) The narrator did not know his name. In this case, one would expect him to simply omit a vocative. (3) The narrator wanted to avoid embarrassing the relative's descendants. According to Campbell, this explanation makes sense only if the relative's action is viewed as "deplorable," a view with which Campbell disagrees. Furthermore, he argues there is no indication in the context that his rejection of his option is viewed in a negative light. Campbell rejects this suggestion too hastily. The relative's action is certainly not "deplorable," but in contrast to Boaz he appears to be motivated strictly by self-interest. One should also not underestimate the importance of "saving face" in such an Oriental community. (4) The narrator wanted to dismiss the relative as being "an unimportant character." Campbell argues that this could have been achieved "by using no designation at all." Campbell offers a final suggestion, which he labels speculative. He suggests that the expression may have a connotation of secrecy, perhaps indicating that Boaz initially spoke "in an undertone to the near redeemer, in order to get him seated" (143). Unfortunately, Campbell does not really address the suggestion offered in the text above—that the narrator draws attention to the relative's anonymity to facilitate his function as a foil for Boaz.

4:3–8. One expects Boaz to confront the nearer relative with the matter of Ruth's marriage proposal. However, he delayed mention of Ruth and instead informed the relative that Naomi was "selling" (מָכְרָה) the "portion of the field" belonging to Elimelech. The relative agreed to purchase, or "redeem" the land. (The verb גָּאַל, "redeem," is used, probably because the purchaser of the land would be protecting the family interests by keeping the land in the extended family's possession.) This plot twist, with its threat of a potentially wrong ending, gets resolved quickly. Boaz confronted the relative with his obligation to purchase Ruth along with the land in order to produce offspring for Elimelech's line so that Elimelech's land would stay within his family.[24] The relative announced that he was unable to do so, because such a purchase would seriously jeopardize his own family's inheritance. The relative agreed to transfer his option to Boaz and sealed the deal by handing one of his sandals to Boaz in the presence of the witnesses seated at the gate (see further discussion below).

Apparently Ruth's marriage proposal entailed legal complications involving the property of the deceased Elimelech and his sons. As the scene unfolds, it becomes apparent that Ruth, if taken in marriage by a family protector (גֹּאֵל, "benefactor"), would be part of a package deal along with the land owned by Elimelech. Furthermore, by marrying Ruth, the relative would assume the responsibility to produce offspring for the deceased Elimelech and Mahlon so as to perpetuate their family line and keep their family inheritance intact (vv. 5, 10). The son born to this union would be responsible for Naomi's well being (vv. 14–17), suggesting the relative must care for her in the meantime. In fact, it seems likely that Naomi, though mentioned as the agent in the transfer of Elimelech's land (vv. 3, 9), was also included among the property of Elimelech, all of which would transfer to the buyer of the land (v. 9). It is not certain how much of this Ruth understood when she proposed marriage to Boaz, but, as noted earlier, Boaz's initial response to her proposal (cf. 3:10) suggests she knew her request carried important implications for her mother-in-law and her deceased husband. Only if this were the case could her proposal truly be what Boaz labels it—an act of loyalty (חֶסֶד).

We are not told how or by whom Elimelech's land was used after his departure for Moab. What is clear is that Naomi, having returned, had the right to dispose of it. It is uncertain if she actually owned the property rights to the land, but this seems unlikely in light of what is

---

24. On the meaning of the expression, "raise up the name of the deceased over his property," see Bush 1996a, 219–21.

known about ancient Israelite property laws.[25] It is more likely that Naomi held only the right to use the land until the time of her remarriage or death (Bush 1996a, 202–04; Gordis 1974, 255–59). Elimelech may have sold the land when he left for Moab. Naomi, as Elimelech's widow, had the right, but not the means, to redeem and work the land. It is this right of redemption and subsequent use that she offered here to the closer relative. In this case, as Bush explains, the verb מָכַר means, "to dispose of (the rights to)," and the verb קָנָה means, "to acquire (the rights to) (Bush 1996a, 214–15)." Prior to this scene, Naomi had made no statement of her intention to dispose of the land, but apparently Boaz understood that Ruth's marriage proposal implied as much and reflected Naomi's decision in this regard (Block 1999, 710–11).

As noted earlier, one should not impose the framework of the so-called levirate law (Genesis 38; Deut. 25:5–10) upon the story so that a closer relative, simply by being related to Mahlon, is legally obligated to produce offspring for Mahlon through Ruth. Nevertheless, the similarities between these texts and Ruth 4 are undeniable, especially in light of the reference to Judah's producing a child (Perez) through Tamar, the widow of his deceased son (cf. v. 12). While the levirate law *per se* does not provide the background for the story (since Boaz was not Mahlon's brother or Ruth's brother-in-law), Bush argues that "a communally recognized *moral* obligation" existed (Bush 1996a, 225 [emphasis his]). He explains: "The threefold purpose of this marriage [Boaz's marriage to Ruth] is identical to that of levirate marriage: to provide descendants for the deceased, to prevent the alienation of the family estate, and, concomitantly, to provide for the protection and security of the widow" (Bush 1996a, 225–26). Bush concludes, "the name 'levirate law' should be restricted to the legally required social custom prescribed in Deut 25:5–10 and evidenced in the narrative of Gen 38. However, the book of Ruth does assume a family responsibility, moral not legal in nature." He prefers to call this a "levirate-type responsibility."[26]

---

25. See Bush 1996a, 203; Block 1999, 709; and Levine 1983, 103. For a contrary opinion see Campbell 1975, 157–58. Zevit, who dates the composition of the book of Ruth to the seventh century B.C., argues, based on his dating of Pentateuchal legal materials, that by this time women in Judah "could own land and they could inherit and alienate land permanently or temporarily" (2005, 591–93). Pertinent texts in the debate include Numbers 27:1–11; 36:6–9; Deuteronomy 21:15–17; and 2 Kings 8:1–6.

26. Bush 1996a, 227. For a similar assessment, see Leggett 1974, 246; and Weisberg 2004, 418. Loader (1994, 134) suggests that the author of Ruth

We are assuming that *once a relative agreed to buy the land,* he was then obligated legally to purchase Ruth and the rest of Elimelech's property as well (vv. 5, 9–10). The wording of verse 5 favors this view, for Boaz seems to indicate that purchasing the right to the land entails purchasing Ruth. In fact, he uses a *qatal* verbal form (קָנִיתָה, *Qere*) with either a future perfect ("you will have purchased") or performative ("you thereby purchase") sense.

If this is indeed the case, why did Boaz mention only the land initially? Perhaps, by making the transaction appear to be a mere land deal, Boaz gave the nearer relative a chance to surrender his option in a way that would save face. But, if this is the case, how do we explain the closer relative's initial willingness to purchase the land? Did he not know about Ruth or the customs related to redemption? One would think that he did (see 3:11) (Bush 1996a, 229). Bush argues that acquiring Ruth was a moral obligation, but nevertheless a voluntary act. According to Bush, "the nearer redeemer could doubtless plan on quietly ignoring the voluntary family responsibility to marry Ruth" (Bush 1996a, 244). However, by conducting the transaction in a public forum and confronting the relative with his moral obligation and his need to save face, Boaz forced him either to reject the offer entirely or to include Ruth in the deal. Either way, Ruth would be cared for and Elimelech's inheritance maintained intact.

Davies argues that the closer relative accepted the proposal initially because he erroneously assumed that Naomi, not Ruth, was the widow in question: "The kinsman, therefore, initially accepted the responsibility of redeeming the land and marrying the widow, since he would have reasoned that Naomi, owing to her advanced age, would not conceive another child, and the land would ultimately have been his own." He adds, "Thus the new information which Boaz imparts to the kinsman and which occasions his change of mind (Ruth iv 5) is not that a widow would have to be acquired along with the property (since this would already have been understood) but that the widow in question was in fact Ruth and not Naomi. This would then account for the

---

"created a story in which a natural and thoroughly credible legal situation is posited," but one that differs in its particulars from the laws of Deuteronomy 25 and Leviticus 25, which give "the basic and normal situation for which the law is intended." The story of Ruth "prompts the reader to consider that the spirit of the law ... and the practical application of the law ought to operate in this way." The story "can be read as a constructive representation of how the law should be applied." Furthermore, "in the process" he "shows what the spirit of the law should be: *hesed*" (138).

kinsman's change of mind, for it would be more likely that Ruth would conceive a son, and the kinsman's refusal was based on the assumption that this son would eventually inherit not only the property which he had redeemed but also, in all probability, a share of his own personal estate" (Davies 1983, 234; cf. Atkinson 1983, 113).

It is unclear exactly how acquiring Ruth and producing an heir for Elimelech would "ruin" the nearer relative's inheritance. Granted, the child would eventually inherit Elimelech's land, but before that happened the relative would be able to enjoy the produce of the land, in exchange for taking care of Naomi, Ruth, and the child. It seems likely that his concern pertained to his own land, not the redeemed land. Apparently the child, in addition to carrying on the line of Elimelech and Mahlon, would become an heir of the relative's line. The people's subsequent blessing upon Boaz (4:11–12) and the concluding genealogy (4:18–22) suggest as much (Campbell 1975, 160–61). Adding an heir to his family line was unacceptable to the relative, perhaps because it would diminish the inheritance of his other children (assuming he had some).[27] This explanation may not satisfy fully the strong language used by the relative (note the *hiphil* of שחת, meaning "ruin, destroy"), but one must make allowances for hyperbole here, since it is likely the relative was concerned about saving face.

Because Boaz, in contrast to the relative, was willing to produce offspring for Elimelech's line, one might assume his circumstances were different. Perhaps he was widowed or had no heirs alive. However, one could just as easily assume he had heirs, but, unlike the relative, gave greater priority to his wider family responsibilities, no matter what the ramifications might be for his own estate. We simply do not know Boaz's status and must respect the silence of the text in this regard.

Apart from the fact that it finalized the transaction, the significance of the sandal ritual is unclear.[28] At some point the practice

---

27. See Thompson 1968, 98, as well as Hubbard (1988b, 245–46), who also surveys the various ways in which the relative's words in verse 6 have been interpreted (246, note 52).

28. Niehaus proposes that the sandal symbolized ownership of the land; he offers ancient Egyptian evidence in support of this. He states: "The sandal stood for the owner's right to tread upon his land. The transfer of the sandal from owner to purchaser symbolized the transfer of that right. In the case of Boaz and Ruth, the man who had first option to buy the land from Naomi and Ruth gave up that right in favor of Boaz. He symbolized his decision by giving Boaz his sandal, which would have trodden on the land had he acquired it" (2008, 68).

ceased, for the author (or an editor) felt it necessary to explain the import of the ritual (v. 7) before reporting it (v. 8). Though this ritual bears some resemblance to the one described in Deuteronomy 25:9, a close comparison reveals that the marked differences between the two outweigh any superficial similarities that may exist. As noted earlier, Deuteronomy 25:5–10 pertains to a surviving brother producing offspring for his deceased brother through cohabitation with his sister-in-law, a scenario that is not in view in Ruth 4. If the brother refused to marry his sister-in-law, she was to remove the brother's sandal and spit in his face. Nothing of this sort takes place in Ruth 4, where one male relative removes his own sandal and hands it to another, symbolizing the transfer of the right to redemption.[29]

4:9–12. After the nearer relative surrendered his right to redeem the land, Boaz formalized the agreement by appealing to the witnesses. He affirmed that he was acquiring from Naomi all that belonged to Elimelech and his sons, including Ruth. His stated purpose in marrying Ruth was to produce a descendant for Mahlon so that Elimelech's family line might continue and his inheritance remain intact.[30]

The witnesses responded positively and then pronounced a blessing upon Ruth.[31] They asked the Lord to give her the capacity to bear children. In formulating their blessing, they compared Ruth to Rachel and Leah, who "built up" Israel's "house" by giving him eight sons (not counting the four born to surrogate mothers).[32]

Ruth's fruitfulness would result in prosperity and prestige for

---

29. See Wilch 2006, 342–43; Matthews 2004, 240; Sakenfeld 1999c, 74–75; and Leggett 1974, 253. It is surprising that Zevit would say: "The sandal ceremony in Deuteronomy is exactly the same as in Ruth" (2005, 580).
30. Boaz's legal oath in verses 9–10 expands his earlier words to the nearer relative (vv. 3–5) by (1) identifying all of Elimelech's property (not just the field) as the object of purchase, (2) naming Ruth's deceased husband, and (3) adding a fuller explanation of his purpose in making the purchase. See the chart in Younger 2002, 478.
31. Pronouncing a marriage blessing such as this was probably customary in this cultural context, where human fertility was greatly valued. For a similar blessing, focusing on the bride's fertility, in the Ugaritic texts (dating prior to 1200 B.C.), see Parker 1976, 23–30.
32. The idiom "build a house" is used of producing children in Deuteronomy 25:9, but there the subject of the verb "build" is the man who refuses to carry out his levirate duty for his deceased brother, in contrast to Ruth 4:11, where Israel's wives are the subject of "build." Usage shows that the idiom was applicable to either a man or woman and was not a technical

Boaz. Elsewhere the collocation עָשָׂה חַיִל, literally, "act (in) strength," is used of (a) rescuing needy people (with God as subject, Ps. 118:15–16), (b) achieving military success (Num. 24:18; 1 Sam. 14:48; Pss. 60:12 [Hebrew v. 14]; 108:13 [Hebrew v. 14]), (c) accomplishing a variety of beneficial tasks for one's family (the deeds of the ideal wife are in view, Prov. 31:29), and (d) acquiring wealth (Deut. 8:17–18 [cf. vv. 12–13]; Ezek. 28:4). The fourth nuance is closest to the idea expressed in the people's blessing, which envisioned Boaz, through the children produced by Ruth, attaining wealth and the prestige and security that came with it.[33] In this culture children were viewed as an economic asset and a source of security (cf. Ps. 127:3–5).

The witnesses also prayed that Boaz's "house" (or family) would be like that of Perez, whom Tamar bore to Judah (cf. Gen. 38:29). The comparison to Perez is especially appropriate here, because (1) he was an ancestor of Boaz (cf. vv. 18–22), (2) he was born to Tamar by a surrogate father (Judah) after the death of her husband, and (3) he had an unbroken line of male descendants extending over several generations (see again vv. 18–22).

A Marriage, a Birth, and a Doting Grandmother (4:13–17)

Ruth's marriage to Boaz makes her a full-fledged member of the covenant community. For only the third time since Ruth's arrival in Bethlehem, the narrator refers to her simply by name in 4:13; no reference to her Moabite ethnicity is included. As in the earlier instances (see 2:8, 22, and the footnotes in this regard), Glover sees this as a signal of her new status. He writes: "Boaz has twice referred to 'Ruth the Moabite' (4.5, 10), possibly a gesture towards the viewpoint of the assembly. After the marriage takes place the assembly can celebrate Ruth's re-situation within the house of Boaz (4.12–13) and by reference

---

expression for producing children for a deceased brother. In 2 Samuel 7:11 the Lord promises to "build a house" for David by giving him offspring.

33. Labuschagne contends, "references to his wealth and good reputation do not fit the context of the wish for a fruitful marriage" 1967, 365). He regards such an idea as "totally irrelevant" and sees the blessing as pertaining to the aging Boaz's virility (366–67). But if the imperative וַעֲשֵׂה (literally, "and do") is logically subordinate (note the *waw*) to the preceding jussive (cf. יִתֵּן, "may he give"), then the blessing must pertain to a *consequence* of Ruth's bearing many children (such as the economic and social benefits of a large family), not to a cause for her doing so (viz., being impregnated by a virile man). Thus, it is more likely that this portion of the blessing alludes to the wealth and security that many children will bring to Boaz's family line.

to Rachel and Leah, within the house of Israel. At last, they too refer to her as 'Ruth'." He adds: "Thus the naming of Ruth represents her threefold re-situation: first, in the eyes of Boaz [cf. 2:8], then Naomi [cf. 2:22], and finally the entire assembly of the people. These actors have recognized that something has happened to Ruth, she has been socially re-situated. It is not that Ruth remains a Moabite despite this no longer being mentioned; rather, her ethnic status has actually changed. The removal of the 'Moabite' designation indicates that Ruth has entered the Israelite *ethnie*. As such, she will be named as all other members of the *ethnie*: Boaz is not named 'Boaz the Israelite', he is simply 'Boaz'; 'Naomi' is not called 'Naomi the Israelite', she is Naomi. Likewise Ruth is not to be called 'Ruth the Israelite', she is simply 'Ruth'" (2009, 302; brackets added).

When Boaz married Ruth, Naomi's prayer that Ruth would find marital security in the home of a new husband was answered (cf. 1:8–9), as were Boaz's more general blessings upon her (cf. 2:12; 3:10) and Naomi's blessing upon Boaz (cf. 2:20). In response to the witnesses' blessing (cf. 4:11), the Lord enabled Ruth to have a baby—something she had apparently been unable to do while married to Mahlon. As elsewhere in the Old Testament, the Lord is the one who grants a woman the capacity to conceive a child (see Gen. 18:10; 20:18; 21:1–2; 25:21; 29:31; 30:22; 49:25; 1 Sam. 2:5; cf. Hos. 9:11).

Verse 13 is one of only two texts in the narrative framework of Ruth (excluding quotations) where the Lord appears as the subject of a verb (Hals 1969, 3; Howard 1993, 152). In 1:6 the narrator informs us that the Lord visited (פָּקַד) his people in order to give (cf. לָתֵת, "to give," from the verbal root נתן) them food. Here he grants (נתַן, literally, "gives") conception to Ruth. In the first instance the Lord intervened in the experience of his people to restore the staples of life where there had been famine (cf. 1:1), while in the second case he intervened to produce life-giving capacity where there had been none. As the only two texts in the story's narrative framework that depict the Lord acting, these passages are thematically central to this book, which first and foremost presents the Lord as the one who gives life to those who have experienced its antithesis.

In a book that highlights human initiative, this reference to divine intervention is especially important.[34] Prinsloo explains: "Until this stage, the book strongly emphasizes the collaboration between human initiative and divine blessing. Human action sometimes even replaces divine action. *Nevertheless, the word wayyitten which is strategically*

---

34. On the theme of human initiative in Ruth, see Younger 2002, 398–99.

placed shows that there is a limit to human initiative and that human initiative is futile without the divine blessing or action. It is in the last instance Yahweh who resolves the problem by causing Ruth to conceive" (Prinsloo 1980, 339 [emphasis his]).

The women of the town praised the Lord and pronounced a blessing upon the child. Literarily, their words stand in contrast to Naomi's speech when she returned to Bethlehem (cf. 1:20–21) (see van Wolde 1997b, 109–11). In response to the women's question (1:19), Naomi had demanded to be called by a new name, Mara ("Bitter"), explaining that the Lord had actively opposed her and left her empty-handed by taking away her husband and sons. Here at the end of the story, the women refuted her claim, pointing out that the Lord had proven to be her benefactor, not her enemy, by providing someone to care for her in her old age. Furthermore, Naomi did not return to Bethlehem empty-handed, for ever-loyal Ruth, who was superior to seven sons, accompanied her.

One might think that the benefactor (גֹּאֵל) mentioned in verse 14 is Boaz, but the presence of הַיּוֹם, "today," suggests otherwise, and verse 15 clearly shows this is not the case, for it speaks of Ruth giving birth to the protector. The antecedent of the third masculine singular suffix on the verbal form יְלָדַתּוּ, "has given him birth," is גֹּאֵל (Bush 1996a, 253–55; Leggett 1974, 255–58).

The *niphal* prefixed form יִקָּרֵא is best understood as a jussive expressing a prayer or wish, literally, "may his name be called." It is coordinate with the preceding בָּרוּךְ, "blessed, praised" (cf. Gen. 9:26; 2 Sam. 22:47; Ps. 72:19). When collocated with שֵׁם, "name," the *niphal* of קָרָא, "call," can refer to someone being called by a specific name (cf. Gen. 35:10; Deut. 25:10), but no name is given in this sentence. The text simply says, "May his name be called in Israel." The expression probably refers here to the name being perpetuated among one's offspring (cf. Gen. 48:16).

The antecedent of the third masculine singular suffix on שְׁמוֹ, "his name," could theoretically be the Lord, who is being praised (cf. בָּרוּךְ יְהוָה, "blessed be the Lord"), or the benefactor (גֹּאֵל), who is the subject of the next verb in the sequence (וְהָיָה, "and he will be/and may he be," cf. v. 15). If the latter, the subject shifts within the blessing. For another example of such a switch, see Genesis 9:26, where the Lord is praised (cf. בָּרוּךְ), but then Canaan becomes the subject of the following coordinated jussive (cf. וִיהִי כְנַעַן, "may Canaan be").

The women characterized the child, in his capacity as protector, as one who would sustain Naomi's life in her advancing years. The expression הֵשִׁיב נֶפֶשׁ, literally, "restore life," usually refers elsewhere to delivering (Job 33:30; Ps. 35:17), preserving (Lam. 1:11, 16, 19), or safeguarding (Ps. 19:7 [English v. 8]) one's physical life, though it can also describe emotional encouragement (Prov. 25:13).[35] Perhaps both nuances apply here. When Naomi grew old, vulnerable, and too weak to take care of her own basic needs, the child would provide her with shelter and food, as well as bring her joy and satisfaction.

The women referred to Ruth's love for Naomi. The verb אָהֵב, "to love," has a broad spectrum of usage, ranging all the way from romantic love to loyal devotion. The latter sense is in view here. Ruth loved Naomi in the sense that she subordinated her own welfare and preferences to Naomi's well-being. From the time she left Moab, Ruth's decisions and actions had Naomi's welfare as their ultimate goal.

The hyperbolic reference to seven sons would have had great rhetorical impact, for sons were especially valued in ancient Israel and the number seven was used throughout ancient Near Eastern literature as a symbol for completeness. Naomi had lost two sons and considered herself empty-handed (cf. 1:21), but Ruth, a seemingly insignificant Moabite widow and resident alien, had proven to be of greater value than the ideal number of sons (cf. 1 Sam. 2:5; Job 1:2; 42:13).[36] She had done everything one would expect from sons.[37] Through her sacrificial love she had made provision for Naomi's security.[38]

When Naomi's female neighbors saw her holding the child, they named him Obed, meaning "one who serves."[39] They recognized the

---

35. The women's use of the *hiphil* of שׁוּב, "return," may echo Naomi's use of the *hiphil* of this same verb in 1:21. She lamented that the Lord had "brought her back empty" (literal translation); now the women anticipate the child (literally) "bringing back life." See Younger 2002, 482.

36. The Ugaritic legend of Kirtu uses numerical parallelism in referring to the house of the king as containing "seven brothers" and "eight mothers' sons" (14:8–9). See Gibson 1978, 82. Later the god El announces that Kirtu's wife will bear him "seven sons . . . indeed eight" (15 ii 24; Gibson 1978, 91).

37. On the role of Ruth as Naomi's "son," see Saxegaard 2001, 257–75.

38. Fischer draws a correlation between the women's statement in 4:15 and the short genealogy of verse 17, which mentions Obed, Jesse, and David. In contrast to the full genealogy in the epilogue, which contains ten names, including Obed, Jesse, and David, the short genealogy has only the three names. What happened to the other seven? According to Fischer, "they are replaced by Ruth!" (1999, 45).

39. Ruth 1:5 speaks of Naomi losing *her children* (יְלָדֶיהָ), but 4:16 describes her holding a *child* (יֶלֶד). The repetition might suggest the theme of restoration; God eventually replaced the social security that Naomi had lost when her sons died. See Campbell 1975, 56. For a linguistic analysis of

birth of the child was advantageous to Naomi, for once the child grew he would "serve" Naomi.[40] The statement יֻלַּד־בֵּן לְנָעֳמִי, literally, "a son has been born for Naomi," reflects this. When the preposition -לְ, "to, for," follows a passive form of ילד, "to bear" (whether *qal* passive, as here, or *niphal*), it almost always introduces the father of the one who is born. But Naomi's name follows here, where the preposition indicates advantage, "for the benefit of Naomi" (cf. Isa. 9:6 [Hebrew v. 5]).

Naomi is silent in this final scene; we can only guess what she was thinking. Sakenfeld's observation is insightful in this regard: "Because Naomi does not speak in the final scenes of the book, we do not know what she thought as she took the child in her arms. We must not imagine that Boaz, Ruth, and Obed could just replace Elimelech, Chilion, and Mahlon. Those who grieve do not 'just get over it.' Yet the narrative suggests that through the actions of faithful people around her who embody divine faithfulness Naomi is not left in a condition of unrelieved calamity and bitterness. She is offered anew the affection of others, the security of economic survival and of family relationships, and the assurance of care for her time of old age, and she is able to experience these basics of human experience as real and meaningful" (Sakenfeld 2003, 143).

Epilogue: What's in a Genealogy? An Official Record of God's Blessing (4:18–22)

The concluding genealogy demonstrates that the prayers of blessing made at the time of the marriage were fulfilled (Hubbard 1988b, 22). Boaz's line did become like the line of Perez, and both Boaz and Obed became famous (vv. 11–12).[41] The theological message of the book of Ruth may be summarized as follows: God cares for needy people like Naomi and Ruth; he is their ally in this chaotic world. He richly rewards people like Ruth and Boaz who demonstrate sacrificial love and

---

how the repetition serves to link 4:13–17 with the book's prologue, see Rebera 1987b, 144–48.

40. For a sociological analysis of "informal women's networks" in ancient Israel, see Meyers 1999. Regarding the naming of Obed, she observes: "Coming together for this important occasion, this group of women—uniquely in the Hebrew Bible—names the infant; in so doing the women signify solidarity with the new mother" (120).

41. Because of the special circumstances involved, Obed was viewed as both Naomi's (i.e., Elimelech's and Mahlon's) (4:5, 14–17) and Boaz's child (4:11–12). See Leggett 1974, 265–67. To resolve this alleged tension, it is unnecessary to propose that the book is composed of two sources (a Naomi story and a Ruth story), as Brenner does (1983, 385–97).

in so doing become his instruments in helping the needy. The genealogy contributes to this message in a significant way for it shows that God's rewards for those who sacrificially love others sometimes exceed their wildest imagination and transcend their lifetime. God's blessing upon Ruth and Boaz extended beyond their lifetime and immediate family, for their descendant, David, became the greatest of Israel's kings, and his descendant, Jesus the Messiah, will rule over the entire earth in the kingdom to come.[42]

One might think that the mention of Obed and his descendant David in verse 17 would be adequate to develop the reward theme without adding a full genealogy. But, as noted above, the genealogy, which begins with Perez and traces David's lineage through Boaz (not Elimelech), shows that the prayer of verse 12 was indeed fulfilled (Sakenfeld 2004, 413–14). Verse 17 focuses on Obed and David as descendants of Elimelech (implied by the reference to Obed as *Naomi's* child). In the genealogy the author reminds us that Obed and David were also descendants of Boaz. The genealogy contains ten names, beginning with Perez and ending with David.[43] The limits make sense in light of the appearance of both names in the preceding verses (cf. vv. 12 and 17, respectively) (Block 1999, 735). Boaz's name appears in the symbolically significant seventh position, highlighting his prominence in his family's line and in the nation's history. Through this use of numerical symbolism, the author suggests that those who follow Boaz's worthy example can expect to receive similar honor and fame.

If, with the Septuagint (and English versions), we place Ruth after Judges as a bridge to 1 Samuel, the genealogy contributes in an important way to the monarchical theme of the larger literary context

---

42. Prinsloo observes: "This genealogy, which leads up to David, is a visible proof of the abundant and continued blessing of Yahweh" (1980, 340). He adds: "Through the addition of this genealogy the book acquires an additional level of meaning in that the blessings of Yahweh are shown not to be confined to a single family but to extend much further" (341). Loretz states: "How fully this blessing was fulfilled is evident from the family genealogy, leading to David" (1960, 394). Berlin observes: "The connection with David tends to elevate the status of the story as much as the story tends to elevate David" (1983, 110). McCarthy speaks of "God's providence" being "at work in the lives of these very ordinary folk to reward them for steadfastness and upright living by giving them a most illustrious descendant, and in the fuller Christian perspective, an even more illustrious descendant" (1985, 59).

43. The length of the genealogy mirrors the pattern seen in Genesis 5:1–29 and 11:10–26 (Wilch 2006, 375–76).

(Howard 1993, 158). The epilogue of Judges anticipates an ideal king (cf. Judg. 17:6; 18:1; 19:1; 21:25 in light of Deut. 17:14–20); this king eventually arrives in the person of David of Judah (after a false start with Saul of Benjamin). In the Septuagint's arrangement, David's name thus appears before he actually enters the story. By highlighting God's providential work in the lives of his ancestors, as well as God's intervention to enable his ancestress Ruth to give birth to a son (cf. 4:13), the book of Ruth contributes to the theme of David's divine election. In this regard Loretz observes: "His [God's] choice is not made in a moment; it has a long prehistory, and took place before the chosen one was formed in the womb of his mother (cf. Jer 1,5). That this election was the act of God alone is thus made more evident; the mysterious workings of God in behalf of David began during the lives of his ancestors" (1960, 398). McCarthy (who views the genealogy as a later addition to the original story) notes that one of the purposes of a genealogy is to suggest "the reappearance in the descendant of some of the ancestor's characteristics." If so, "it is understandable that davidic [sic] circles would be happy to graft Ruth's virtues of loyalty and generosity into the davidic family tree" (1985, 61).[44] By tracing David's ancestry back to Perez, a son of Judah, and by mentioning Judah by name (cf. 4:12), the book of Ruth also links David with the ancient patriarchal blessing that depicted Judah as a leader (Gen. 49:8–12), a role assumed by the tribe of Judah during the Judges period (cf. Judg. 1:2; 20:18) (cf. Howard 1993, 154).

Since Perez was the son of Judah by Tamar, it is hardly possible that the genealogy is complete. There would have been more than ten generations from Judah to David (Sakenfeld 2004, 411–12). Indeed, the genealogy in Luke 3 adds two names (Admin and Arni) between Hezron and Amminadab (v. 33), though it also omits Ram. If Nachshon, who appears fifth in the list in Ruth 4, was a contemporary of Moses (as Exod. 6:23 and Num. 1:7 suggest), and there are no gaps between Boaz and David, then there must be gaps between Nachshon and Boaz. However, the New Testament suggests that Boaz may have lived earlier. The genealogy in Matthew 1 identifies Rahab (certainly the well-known Rahab who lived in Jericho at the time of the conquest) as Boaz's mother, just as it identifies Tamar

---

44. Sutskover observes that the theme of Ruth's fertility would also contribute to a positive view of David: "The book of Ruth, then, intends to present Ruth as an appropriate ancestress of David. This is achieved by closely associating her with the Land of Beit-leḥem, David's birthplace, and the fertile state now associated with its women" (2010, 294).

as the mother of Perez and Zerah (v. 3), Ruth as Obed's mother (v. 5) and Uriah's wife (i.e., Bathsheba) as Solomon's mother (v. 6). If Salmon, Nachshon's son (v. 4), were indeed the husband of Rahab, this would harmonize well with Nachshon being a contemporary of Moses. However, placing Boaz this early in Israel's history would mean there are several generations omitted between Obed and Jesse, for we know that Obed was Boaz's son and that Jesse was David's father. In this case, the events recorded in the book date to a time early in the Judges period.

The genealogy in 1 Chronicles 2, which gives the same order of Perez's descendants as does Ruth 4:18–22 (that is, Perez-Hezron-Ram-Amminadab-Nachshon-Salmah-Boaz-Obed-Jesse-David; cf. vv. 5, 9–15), indicates that Nachshon could have been a contemporary of Moses. Nachshon is listed as the grandson of Ram (v. 10). The genealogy of Ram's brother, Caleb (v. 9), lists Hur as Caleb's son, Uri as Hur's son, and Bezalel as Uri's son (vv. 19–20). Hur and Bezalel were both contemporaries of Moses (cf. Exod. 17:10, 12; 24:14; 31:2; 35:30; 38:22).

MESSAGE AND APPLICATION

Thematic Emphases

God's providential work on behalf of Naomi culminates in this chapter. As Naomi held her grandson Obed, it should have been apparent to all that God was her ally and deliverer, not her enemy. Though Naomi believed she had returned to Bethlehem empty-handed (cf. 1:21), her faithful daughter-in-law proved to be of inestimable value, as the women of the town reminded Naomi (4:14–15).

Ruth and Boaz, the instruments used by God to deliver Naomi from despair, experienced the rewards of faithfulness. When Boaz married Ruth, Naomi's prayer that Ruth would find security in the home of a new husband (1:8–9) was answered, as was Boaz's prayer that Ruth would find security under the Lord's protective hand (2:12). When Ruth produced a son, the prayers of Naomi, who had asked the Lord to reward Boaz (2:20), of Boaz, who had asked the Lord to reward Ruth (3:10), and of the people, who had asked that Ruth be fertile (4:11a), were fulfilled. When David eventually appeared in Boaz's family line, the people's prayers that Boaz would achieve fame (4:11b) were fulfilled.

Exegetical idea: *As God brought his redemptive work to culmination, he gave security to afflicted Naomi, proving to be her ally, not her enemy.*

In response to prayers of blessing, he richly rewarded faithful Ruth and Boaz for their loyalty and love in ways that transcended their lifetime.

Theological Principles
When God's providential work reaches its full fruition, the attitudes of the afflicted are transformed. His faithful human instruments experience God's blessings as he rewards them for their kindness and sacrificial love. These rewards are often imparted in response to prayers of blessing that God, in his capacity as the just king of the world, is predisposed to answer.

Theological idea: *As God brings his redemptive work to culmination, he restores security to the afflicted and richly rewards the faithful for their loyalty and love in ways that transcend their lifetime. He is predisposed to answer the prayers of blessing offered up on behalf of his faithful servants and to reward them for their loyalty and love.*

Homiletical Trajectories
(1) The resolution of the story's plot complication yields one trajectory. Naomi's deliverance reminds us that the afflicted find their circumstances reversed when God's redemptive work reaches its culmination and joy replaces despair.

(2) In chapter four Boaz takes center stage as God's instrument of deliverance. As we see in earlier chapters, God's instruments of redemption take the initiative to help others and persist in their work until the mission is accomplished.

(3) The reward theme dominates the final chapter. We see that God does indeed reward the faithful, sometimes in ways that transcend their lifetime and exceed their wildest imagination.

Preaching idea: *As God brings his redemptive work to culmination, we can be confident that he will richly reward the loyalty and love of his faithful followers, sometimes in ways that transcend their lifetime.*

Since these rewards are bestowed in response to prayer, an additional *preaching idea* would be: *We should ask God to bless those who demonstrate kindness and faithfulness, for our prayers can be the catalyst for God's blessings in their lives and in the lives of the covenant community.*

REFERENCES
FOR RUTH

Aharoni, Yohanan. 1979. *The Land of the Bible*. rev. ed. Translated and edited by Anson F. Rainey. Philadelphia: Westminster.

Aharoni, Yohanan, and Michael Avi-Yonah. 1977. *The Macmillan Bible Atlas*. rev. ed. New York: Macmillan.

Anderson, A. A. 1978. "The Marriage of Ruth." *JSS* 23:171–83.

Angel, Hayyim. 2005. "A Midrashic View of Ruth: Amidst a Sea of Ambiguity." *JBQ* 33, 91–99.

Ap-Thomas, Dafydd R. 1968. "The Book of Ruth." *ExpTim* 79:369–73.

Arnold, Bill T., and John H. Choi. 2003. *A Guide to Biblical Hebrew Syntax*. Cambridge: Cambridge University Press.

Atkinson, David. 1983. *The Message of Ruth: The Wings of Refuge*. BST. Downers Grove: InterVarsity.

Baylis, Charles P. 2004. "Naomi in the Book of Ruth in Light of the Mosaic Covenant." *BSac* 161:413–31.

Beattie, Derek R. G. 1971. "*Kethibh* and *Qere* in Ruth IV 5." *VT* 21:490–94.

_____. 1974. "The Book of Ruth as Evidence for Israelite Legal Practice." *VT* 24:251–67.

_____. 1977a. "A Midrashic Gloss in Ruth 2:7." *ZAW* 89:122–24.

_____. 1977b. *Jewish Exegesis of the Book of Ruth*. JSOTSup 2. Sheffield: JSOT.

_____. 1978. "Redemption in Ruth, and Related Matters: A Response to Jack M. Sasson." *JSOT* 5:65–68.

Berger, Yitzhak. 2009a. "Ruth and Inner-Biblical Allusion: The Case of 1 Samuel 25." *JBL* 128:253–72.

_____. 2009b. "Ruth and the David-Bathsheba Story: Allusions and Contrasts." *JSOT* 33:433–52.

Berlin, Adele. 1983. *Poetics and Interpretation of Biblical Narrative.* Sheffield: Almond.

Berman, Joshua. 2007. "Ancient Hermeneutics and the Legal Structure of the Book of Ruth." *ZAW* 119, 22–38.

Bernstein, Moshe J. 1991. "Two Multivalent Readings in the Ruth Narrative." *JSOT* 50:15–26.

Berquist, Jon L. 1993. "Role Dedifferentiation in the Book of Ruth." *JSOT* 57:23–37.

Bertman, Stephen. 1965. "Symmetrical Design in the Book of Ruth." *JBL* 84:165–68.

Bland, Dave. 1981. "God's Activity as Reflected in the Books of Ruth and Esther." *ResQ* 24:129–47.

Block, Daniel I. 1999. *Judges, Ruth.* NAC. Nashville: Broadman & Holman.

Borowski, Obed. 1987. *Agriculture in Iron Age Israel.* Winona Lake: Eisenbrauns.

Bos, Johanna W. H. 1988. "Out of the Shadows: Genesis 38; Judges 4:17–22; Ruth 3." *Semeia* 42, 37–67.

Bovell, Carlos. 2003. "Symmetry, Ruth and Canon." *JSOT* 28 (2):175–91.

Brenner, Athalya. 1983. "Naomi and Ruth." *VT* 33:385–97.

_____, ed. 1999. *Ruth and Esther.* FCBSS. Sheffield: Sheffield Academic.

Bronner, Leila Leah. 1999. "The Invisible Relationship Made Visible: Biblical Mothers and Daughters." In *Ruth and Esther,* edited by Athalya Brenner, 172–91. FCBSS. Sheffield: Sheffield Academic.

Burnett, Joel S. 2001. *A Reassessment of Biblical Elohim.* SBLDS 183. Atlanta: Society of Biblical Literature.

Bush, Frederic W. 1996a. *Ruth, Esther.* WBC. Dallas: Word.

_____. 1996b. "Ruth 4:17: A Semantic Wordplay." In *"Go to the Land I Will Show You": Studies in Honor of Dwight W. Young,* edited by Joseph E. Coleson and Victor H. Matthews, 3–14. Winona Lake: Eisenbrauns.

Campbell, Edward F., Jr. 1974. "The Hebrew Short Story: A Study of Ruth." In *A Light Unto My Path: Old Testament Studies in Honor of Jacob M. Myers,* edited by Howard N. Bream, Ralph D. Heim, and Carey A. Moore, 83–110. Philadelphia: Temple University Press.

_____. 1975. *Ruth*, AB. Garden City, NY: Doubleday.

_____. 1999. "Ruth Revisited." In *On the Way to Nineveh: Studies in Honor of George M. Landes*, edited by Stephen L. Cook and S. C. Winter, 54–76. Atlanta: Scholars Press.

Carasik, Michael. 1995. "Ruth 2,7: Why the Overseer was Embarrassed." *ZAW* 107:493–94.

Carmichael, Calum M. 1977. "A Ceremonial Crux: Removing a Man's Sandal as a Female Gesture of Contempt." *JBL* 96:321–36.

_____. 1980. "'Treading' in the Book of Ruth." *ZAW* 92:248–66.

Chisholm, Robert B., Jr. 1998. *From Exegesis to Exposition*. Grand Rapids: Baker.

_____. 2002. "A Rhetorical Use of Point of View in the Old Testament." *BSac* 159:404–14.

_____. 2004. "Ruth." In *The Bible Knowledge Word Study: Joshua–2 Chronicles*, edited by E. H. Merrill, 113–22. Colorado Springs: Cook Communications Ministries.

_____. 2006a. *Interpreting the Historical Books: An Exegetical Handbook*. Handbooks for Old Testament Exegesis. Grand Rapids: Kregel.

_____. 2006b. "The Christological Fulfillment of Isaiah's Servant Songs." *BSac* 163:387–404.

Clark, Gordon R. 1993. *The Word hesed in the Hebrew Bible*. JSOTSup 157. Sheffield: Sheffield Academic Press.

Cohen, Mordechai. 1997. "Hesed: Divine or Human? The Syntactic Ambiguity of Ruth 2:20." In *Hazon Nahum: Studies in Jewish Law, Thought, and History Presented to Dr. Norman Lamm,* edited by Yaakov Elman and Jeffrey S. Gurock, 11–38. Hoboken: Ktav.

Coleson, Joseph E. 1996. "The Peasant Woman and the Fugitive Prophet: A Study in Biblical Narrative Settings." In *"Go to the Land I Will Show You": Studies in Honor of Dwight W. Young*, edited by Joseph E. Coleson and Victor H. Matthews, 27–44. Winona Lake: Eisenbrauns.

Collins, C. John. 1993. "Ambiguity and Theology in Ruth: Ruth 1:21 and 2:20." *Presbyterion* 19:97–102.

Coxon, Peter W. 1989. "Was Naomi a Scold? A Response to Fewell and Gunn." *JSOT* 45:25–37.

Curtis, John B. 1996. "Second Thoughts on the Book of Ruth." *PEGLMBS* 16, 141–49.

Davies, Eryl W. 1981. "Inheritance Rights and the Hebrew Levirate Marriage." *VT* 31:138–44, 257–68.

_____. 1983. "Ruth IV 5 and the Duties of the *Gō'ēl*." *VT* 33:231–34.

de Moor, Johanne C. 1984. "The Poetry of the Book of Ruth (Part 1)." *Or* 53:262–83.

_____. 1986. "The Poetry of the Book of Ruth (Part 2)." *Or* 55:16–46.

Dearman, J. Andrew. 1998. "The Family in the Old Testament." *Int* 52:117–29.

Dearman, J. Andrew, and Sabelyn A. Pussman. 2005. "Putting Ruth in Her Place: Some Observations on Canonical Ordering and the History of the Book's Interpretation." *HBT* 27:59–86.

Derby, Josiah. 1994. "A Problem in the Book of Ruth." *JBQ* 22:178–85, 172.

Dorn, Louis. 1978. "Chronological Sequence in Two Hebrew Narratives." *BT* 29:316–22.

Eskhult, Mats. 2003. "The Importance of Loanwords for Dating Biblical Hebrew Texts." In *Biblical Hebrew: Studies in Chronology and Typology*, edited by Ian Young, 8–23. JSOTSup 369. London: T & T Clark.

Fewell, Danna N. and David M. Gunn. 1988. "'A Son is Born to Naomi!': Literary Allusions and Interpretation in the Book of Ruth." *JSOT* 40:99–108.

_____. 1989a. "Boaz, Pillar of Society: Measures of Worth in the Book of Ruth." *JSOT* 45:45–59.

_____. 1989b. "Is Coxon a Scold? On Responding to the Book of Ruth." *JSOT* 45:39–43.

_____. 1990. *Compromising Redemption: Relating Characters in the Book of Ruth*. Louisville: Westminster John Knox.

Fisch, Harold. 1982. "Ruth and the Structure of Covenant History." *VT* 32:425–37.

Fischer, Irmtraud. 1999. "The Book of Ruth: A Feminist Commentary to the Torah?" In *Ruth and Esther,* edited by Athalya Brenner, 24–49. FCBSS. Sheffield: Sheffield Academic.

Freedman, Amela D. 2003. "Naomi's Experience of God and its Treatment in the Book of Ruth." PEGLMBS 23:29–38.

Gage, Warren A. 1989. "Ruth Upon the Threshing Floor and the Sin of Gibeah: A Biblical-Theological Study." *WTJ* 51:369–75.

Gibson, John C. L. 1978. *Canaanite Myths and Legends*. 2nd ed. Edinburgh: T & T Clark.

Glanzman, George S. 1959. "The Origin and Date of the Book of Ruth." *CBQ* 21:201–07.

Glover, Neil. 2009. "Your People, My People: An Exploration of Ethnicity in Ruth." *JSOT* 33:293–313.

Gordis, Robert. 1974. "Love, Marriage, and Business in the Book of Ruth." In *A Light Unto My Path: Old Testament Studies in Honor of Jacob M. Myers*, edited by Howard N. Bream, Ralph D. Heim, and Carey A. Moore, 241–64. Philadelphia: Temple University Press.

Goswell, Greg. 2009. "The Order of the Books in the Greek Old Testament." *JETS* 52:449–66.

Goulder, Michael. 1993. "Ruth: A Homily on Deuteronomy 22–25?" In *Of Prophets' Visions and the Wisdom of the Sages: Essays in Honour of R. Norman Whybray on his Seventieth Birthday,* edited by Heather A. McKay and David J. Clines, 307–19. Sheffield: Sheffield Academic.

Gow, Murray D. 1984. "The Significance of Literary Structure for the Translation of the Book of Ruth." *BT* 35:309–20.

_____. 1990. *"Ruth Quoque*—a Coquette? (Ruth 4:5)." *TynBul* 41:302–11.

Grant, Reg. 1991. "Literary Structure in the Book of Ruth." *BSac* 148:424–41.

Green, Barbara. 1982. "The Plot of the Biblical Story of Ruth." *JSOT* 23:55–68.

Guenther, Allen R. 2005. "A Typology of Israelite Marriage: Kinship, Socio-Economic, and Religious Factors." *JSOT* 29.4:387–407.

Hals, Ronald M. 1969. *The Theology of the Book of Ruth*. Philadelphia: Fortress.

Hamlin, E. John. 1995. "Terms for Gender and Status in the Book of Ruth." PEGLMBS 15:133–43.

Harm, Harry J. 1995. "The Function of Double Entendre in Ruth Three." *JOTT* 7:19–27.

Holmstedt, Robert D. 2010. *Ruth: A Handbook on the Hebrew Text*. Waco: Baylor University Press.

Hongisto, Leif. 1985. "Literary Structure and Theology in the Book of Ruth." *AUSS* 23:19–28.

Howard, David M., Jr. 1993. *An Introduction to the Old Testament Historical Books*. Chicago: Moody.

Hubbard, Robert L., Jr. 1988a. "Ruth IV 7: A New Solution." *VT* 38:293–301.

_____. 1988b. *The Book of Ruth*. NICOT. Grand Rapids: Eerdmans.

_____. 1989. "Theological Reflections on Naomi's Shrewdness." *TynBul* 40:283–92.

_____. 1991. "The Go'el in Ancient Israel: Theological Reflections on an Israelite Institution." *BBR* 1:3–19.

_____. 1997. *"Ganzheitsdenken* in the Book of Ruth." In *Problems in Biblical Theology: Essays in Honor of Rolf Knierim*, edited by Henry T. C. Sun and Keith L. Eades with James M. Robinson and Garth I. Moller, 192–209. Grand Rapids: Eerdmans.

Hunter, Alistair. 1981. "How Many Gods Had Ruth?" *SJT* 34:427–36.

Hurvitz, Avi. 1983. "Ruth 2:7—A Midrashic Gloss?" *ZAW* 95:121–23.

Hyman, Ronald T. 1983. "Questions and the Book of Ruth." *HS* 24:17–25.

_____. 1984. "Questions and Changing Identity in the Book of Ruth." *USQR* 39:189–202.

Irwin, Brian P. 2008. "Removing Ruth: *Tiqqune Sopherim* in Ruth 3.3–4?" *JSOT* 32:331–38.

Jobling, David. 1993. "Ruth Finds a Home: Canon, Politics, Method." In *The New Literary Criticism and the Hebrew Bible*, edited by J. Cheryl Exum and David J. A. Clines, 125–39. JSOTSup 143. Sheffield: JSOT.

Jongeling, Bastiaan. 1978. "*Hzt N'my* (Ruth i 19)." *VT* 28:474–77.

Joüon, Paul. 1993. *A Grammar of Biblical Hebrew*. Translated and revised by T. Muraoka. 2 vols. Rome: Editrice Pontificio Istituto Biblio.

Keita, Schadrac, and Janet W. Dyk. 2006. "The Scene at the Threshing Floor: Suggestive Readings and Intercultural Considerations." *BT* 57:17–32.

King, Greg A. 1998. "Ruth 2:1–13." *Int* 52:182–84.

King, Philip J., and Lawrence E. Stager. 2001. *Life in Biblical Israel*. Louisville: Westminster John Knox.

Korpel, Marjo C. A. 2001. *The Structure of the Book of Ruth*. Assen: Koninklijke Van Gorcum.

_____. 2003. "Theodicy in the Book of Ruth." In *Theodicy in the World of the Bible*, edited by Antti Laato and Johannes C. de Moor, 334–50. Leiden: Brill.

Kruger, Paul. 1984. "The Hem of the Garment in Marriage: The Meaning of the Symbolic Gesture in Ruth 3:9 and Ezek 16:8." *JNSL* 12:79–86.

_____. 2009. "Nonverbal Communication and Narrative Literature: Genesis 39 and the Ruth Novella." *BN* NF 141: 5–17.

Labuschagne, Casper J. 1967. "The Crux in Ruth 4:11." *ZAW* 79:364–67.

LaCocque, André. 2004. *Ruth*. Continental Commentary. Translated by K. C. Hanson. Minneapolis: Fortress.

Landy, Francis. 1994. "Ruth and the Romance of Realism, or Deconstructing History." *JAAR* 62:285–317.

Lapsley, Jacqueline E. 2005. *Whispering the Word: Hearing Women's Stories in the Old Testament*. Louisville: Westminster John Knox.

Leder, Arie C. 2002. "Paradise Lost: Reading the Former Prophets by the Rivers of Babylon." *CTJ* 37:9–27.

Leggett, Donald A. 1974. *The Levirate and Goel Institutions in the Old Testament with Special Attention to the Book of Ruth*. Cherry Hill: Mack Publishing.

Levine, Baruch A. 1983. "In Praise of the Israelite *Mispaha*: Legal Themes in the Book of Ruth." In *The Quest for the Kingdom of God: Studies in Honor of George E. Mendenhall*, edited by Hebert B. Huffmon, Frank A. Spina, and Alberto R. W. Green, 95–106. Winona Lake: Eisenbrauns.

Levine, Étan. 1973. *The Aramaic Version of Ruth*. AnBib 58. Rome: Biblical Institute Press.

Lim, Timothy H. 2007. "The Book of Ruth and its Literary Voice." In *Reflection and Refraction: Studies in Biblical Historiography in Honour of A. Graeme Auld*, edited by Robert Rezetko, Timothy H. Lim, and W. Brian Aucker, 261–82. VTSup 113. Leiden: Brill.

Linafelt, Tod, and Timothy K. Beal. 1999. *Ruth and Esther*. BO. Collegeville: Liturgical.

Lindström, Fredrik. 1983. *God and the Origin of Evil: A Contextual Analysis of Alleged Monistic Evidence in the Old Testament*. Lund: CWK Gleerup.

Loader, J. A. 1992. "Ruth 2:7—an Old Crux." *JSem* 4:151–59.

_____. 1994. "Of Barley, Bulls, Land and Levirate." In *Studies in Deuteronomy in Honour of C. J. Labuschagne on the Occasion of his 65th Birthday*, edited by F. Garcia Martínez, Anthony Hilhorst, Jacques T. A. G. M. van Ruiten, and Adam S. van der Woude, 123–38. Leiden: E. J. Brill.

Longacre, Robert E. 1994. "Weqatal Forms in Biblical Hebrew Prose." In *Biblical Hebrew and Discourse Linguistics*, edited by Robert D. Bergen, 50–98. Winona Lake: Eisenbrauns.

Loretz, Oswald. 1960. "The Theme of the Ruth Story." *CBQ* 22:391–99.

Luter, A. Boyd, and Richard O. Rigsby. 1996. "An Adjusted Symmetrical Structuring of Ruth." *JETS* 39:15–28.

Macky, Peter W. 1990. *The Centrality of Metaphors to Biblical Thought*. Lewiston, NY: Edwin Mellen.

Martín-Contreras, Elvira. 2009. "Masoretic and Rabbinic Lights on the Word הְבִי, Ruth 3:15—יהב or בוא?" *VT* 59:257–65.

Matthews, Victor H. 2004. *Judges and Ruth*. NCBC. Cambridge: Cambridge University Press.

_____. 2006. "The Determination of Social Identity in the Story of Ruth." *BTB* 36:49–54.

Mattingly, Gerald L. 1994. "Moabites." In *Peoples of the Old Testament World*, edited by Alfred J. Hoerth, Gerald L. Mattingly, and Edwin Yamauchi, 317–33. Grand Rapids: Baker.

McCarthy, Carmel. 1985. "The Davidic Genealogy in the Book of Ruth." PIBA 9:53–62.

693

McNutt, Paula M. 1999. *Reconstructing the Society of Ancient Israel.* Louisville: Westminster John Knox.

Merrill, Eugene H. 1985. "The Book of Ruth: Narration and Shared Themes." *BSac* 142:130–41.

Meyers, Carol. 1999. "'Women of the Neighborhood' (Ruth 4.17): Informal Female Networks in Ancient Israel." In *Ruth and Esther,* edited by Athalya Brenner, 100–27. FCBSS. Sheffield: Sheffield Academic.

Min, Young-Jin. 1989. "Problems in Ruth 2.7." *BT* 40:438–41.

Moore, Michael S. 1997. "Two Textual Anomalies in Ruth." *CBQ* 59:234–43.

_____. 1998. "Ruth the Moabite and the Blessing of Foreigners." *CBQ* 60:203–17.

_____. 2001. "To King or Not to King: A Canonical-Historical Approach to Ruth." *BBR* 11:27–41.

Mundhenk, Norman, and Jan de Waard. 1975. "Missing the Whole Point and What to Do About It—With Special Reference to the Book of Ruth." *BT* 26:420–33.

Myers, Jacob M. 1955. *The Linguistic and Literary Form of the Book of Ruth.* Leiden: E. J. Brill.

Nash, Peter T. 1995. "Ruth: An Exercise in Israelite Political Correctness or a Call to Proper Conversion?" In *The Pitcher is Broken: Memorial Essays for Gösta W. Ahlström,* edited by Steven W. Holloway and Lowell K. Handy, 347–54. JSOTSup 190. Sheffield: JSOT.

Niehaus, Jeffrey J. 2008. *Ancient Near Eastern Themes in Biblical Theology.* Grand Rapids: Kregel.

Nielsen, Kirsten. 1997. *Ruth,* OTL. Translated by Edward Broadbridge. Louisville: Westminster John Knox.

Ostriker, Alicia. 2002. "The Book of Ruth and the Love of the Land." *BibInt* 10:343–59.

Oswalt, John N. 1998. *The Book of Isaiah, Chapters 40–66.* Grand Rapids: Eerdmans.

Parker, Simon B. 1976. "The Marriage Blessing in Israelite and Ugaritic Literature." *JBL* 95:23–30.

_____. 1988. "The Birth Announcement." In *Ascribe to the Lord: Biblical and Other Studies in Memory of Peter C. Craigie,* edited by Lyle Eslinger and Glen Taylor, 133–49. JSOTSup 67. Sheffield: Sheffield Academic.

Penchansky, David. 1999. *What Rough Beast? Images of God in the Hebrew Bible.* Louisville: John Knox.

Phillips, Anthony. 1986. "The Book of Ruth—Deception and Shame." *JJS* 37:1–17.

Porten, Bezalel. 1978. "The Scroll of Ruth: A Rhetorical Study." *GCAJS* 7:23–49.

Prinsloo, Willem S. 1977–78. "The Function of Ruth in the Book of Ruth." *OTWSA* 20/21:110–29.

_____. 1980. "The Theology of the Book of Ruth." *VT* 30:330–41.

Radday, Yehuda. 1981. "Ruth." In *Chiasmus in Antiquity*, edited by John W. Welch, 71–76. Hildesheim: Gerstenberg.

Rauber, D. F. 1970. "Literary Values in the Bible: The Book of Ruth." *JBL* 89:27–37.

Rebera, Basil. 1985. "Yahweh or Boaz? Ruth 2.20 Reconsidered." *BT* 36:317–27.

_____. 1987a. "Translating Ruth 3.16." *BT* 38:234–37.

_____. 1987b. "Lexical Cohesion in Ruth: A Sample." In *Perspectives on Language and Text: Essays and Poems in Honor of Francis I. Andersen's Sixtieth Birthday, July 28, 1985,* edited by Edgar W. Conrad and Edward G. Newing, 123–49. Winona Lake: Eisenbrauns.

Rendsburg, Gary A. 1998–99. "Confused Language as a Deliberate Literary Device in Biblical Hebrew Narrative." *The Journal of Hebrew Scriptures* 2:6. doi:10.5508/jhs.1999.v2.a6.

Revell, Ernest J. 1995. "The Two Forms of First Person Singular Pronoun in Biblical Hebrew: Redundancy or Expressive Contrast?" *JSS* 40:199–217.

Rossow, Francis C. 1991. "Literary Artistry in the Book of Ruth and its Theological Significance." *ConJ* 17, 12–19.

Sakenfeld, Katherine. D. 1978. *The Meaning of* Hesed *in the Hebrew Bible.* HSM 17. Missoula, MT: Scholars Press.

_____. 1999a. "Ruth 4, An Image of Eschatological Hope." In *Liberating Eschatology: Essays in Honor of Letty M. Russell*, edited by Margaret A. Farley and Serene Jones, 55–67. Louisville: Westminster John Knox.

_____. 1999b. "The Story of Ruth: Economic Survival." In *Realia Dei: Essays in Archaeology and Biblical Interpretation in Honor of Edward F. Campbell Jr. at his Retirement*, edited by Prescott H. Williams Jr. and Theodore Hiebert, 215–27. Atlanta: Scholars Press.

_____. 1999c. *Ruth.* Interpretation. Louisville: John Knox.

_____. 2003. "Naomi's cry: Reflections on Ruth 1:20–21." In *A God So Near: Essays on Old Testament Theology in Honor of Patrick D. Miller,* edited by Brent A. Strawn and Nancy R. Bowen, 129–43. Winona Lake: Eisenbrauns.

_____. 2004. "Why Perez? Reflections on David's Genealogy in Biblical Tradition." In *David and Zion: Biblical Studies in Honor of J. J.*

M. Roberts, edited by Bernard F. Batto and Kathryn L. Roberts, 405–16. Winona Lake: Eisenbrauns.

Sasson, Jack M. 1978. "Ruth III: A Response." *JSOT* 5:49–51.

_____. 1979. *Ruth*. Baltimore: The Johns Hopkins University Press.

Saxegaard, Kristin M. 2001. "'More Than Seven Sons': Ruth as Example of the Good Son." *SJOT* 15:257–75.

Shepherd, David. 2001. "Violence in the Fields? Translating, Reading, and Revising in Ruth 2." *CBQ* 63:444–63.

Siquans, Agnethe. 2009. "Foreignness and Poverty in the Book of Ruth: A legal Way for a Poor Foreign Woman to Be Integrated into Israel." *JBL* 128:443–52.

Smith, Mark S. 2007. "'Your People Shall Be My People': Family and Covenant in Ruth 1:16–17." *CBQ* 69:242–58.

Sutskover, Talia. 2010. "The Themes of Land and Fertility in the Book of Ruth." *JSOT* 34.3:283–94.

Thompson, Michael E. W. 1993. "New Life Amid the Alien Corn: The Book of Ruth." *EQ* 65:197–210.

Thompson, Thomas and Dorothy. 1968. "Some Legal Problems in the Book of Ruth." *VT* 18:79–99.

Tollers, Vincent L. 1990. "Narrative Control in the Book of Ruth." In *Mappings of the Biblical Terrain: The Bible as Text*, edited by Vincent L. Tollers and John Maier, 52–59. Lewisburg: Bucknell University Press.

van der Merwe, Christo H. J., Jackie A. Naudé, and Jan H. Kroeze. 1999. *A Biblical Hebrew Reference Grammar*. Sheffield: Sheffield Academic Press.

van Wolde, Ellen. 1997a. "Texts in Dialogue with Texts: Intertextuality in the Ruth and Tamar Narratives." *BibInt* 5:1–28.

_____. 1997b. *Ruth and Naomi*. Translated by John Bowden. London: SCM.

Walsh, Carey E. *The Fruit of the Vine: Viticulture in Ancient Israel*. HSM 60. Winona Lake: Eisenbrauns.

Weisberg, Dvora E. 2004. "The Widow of Our Discontent: Levirate Marriage in the Bible and Ancient Israel." *JSOT* 28 (4):403–29.

Wendland, Ernst R. 1988. "Structural Symmetry and its Significance in the Book of Ruth." In *Issues in Bible Translation*, edited by Philip C. Stine, 30–63. London: United Bible Societies.

Wilch, John R. 2006. *Ruth*. CC. St. Louis: Concordia.

Williams, Ronald J. 1976. *Hebrew Syntax: An Outline*. 2nd edition. Toronto: University of Toronto Press.

Young, Ian, ed. 2003. *Biblical Hebrew: Studies in Chronology and Typology*. JSOTSup 369. London: T & T Clark.

Young, Ian, and Robert Rezetk, eds. *Linguistic Dating of Biblical Texts: An Introduction to Approaches and Problems*. London: Equinox.

Younger, K. Lawson, Jr. 1998. "Two Comparative Notes on the Book of Ruth." *JANES* 26:121–32.

_____. 2002. *Judges and Ruth*. NIVAC. Grand Rapids: Zondervan.

Zevit, Ziony. 2005. "Dating Ruth: Legal, Linguistic and Historical Observations." *ZAW* 117:574–600.

Ziegler, Yael. 2007. "'So Shall God Do ...': Variations of an Oath Formula and its Literary Meaning." *JBL* 126, 59–81.

_____. 2008. *Promises to Keep: The Oath in Biblical Narrative*. VTSup 118. Leiden: Brill.